About the Author

Ward Churchill (Creek and enrolled Keetoowah Band Cherokee) is a longtime native rights activist, writer, and public speaker. A member of the Governing Council of the Colorado chapter of the American Indian Movement, he also serves as Coordinator of American Indian Studies for the University of Colorado. He is a past national spokesperson for the Leonard Peltier Defense Committee, has served as a delegate to the United Nations Working Group on Indigenous Populations, and as a jurist with the International People's Tribunal, Hawai'i. He currently serves as an advocate/prosecutor with the First Nation's International Tribunal for the Chiefs of Ontario in Canada.

Cover design by Katherine Berney
Text design and production in Bernhard Modern and Palatino typeface by the South End Press collective.

Printed in the U.S.A.

Library of Congress Cataloging-in-Publication Data

Churchill, Ward.
From a native son: selected essays in indigenism, 1985-1995/Ward Churchill; introduction by Howard Zinn.
p. cm.
Includes bibliographical references and index.
ISBN 0-89608-553-8 (alk. paper). —ISBN 0-89608-554-6 (alk. cloth)
1. Indians of North America—Social conditions. 2. Indians of North America—Politics and government. 3. Indians of North America—land tenure. I. Title.
E98.S67C58   1996
970.004'97—dc20

96-26168

CIP

® GCIU 745-C

South End Press, 116 Saint Botolph Street, Boston, MA 02115
02 01 00 99 98 97 96   1 2 3 4 5 6 7

From a Native Son

From a
Native Son

SOUTH END PRESS
Boston, Massachusetts

Ward Churchill

Selected Essays in Indigenism, 1985–1995

with an introduction by

HOWARD ZINN

for Aunt Bonnie, who inspired me more than she knew…

Books by Ward Churchill

Authored: *Fantasies of the Master Race: Literature, Cinema and the Colonization of American Indians* (1992)

Struggle for the Land: Indigenous Resistance to Genocide, Ecocide and Expropriation in North America (1993)

Indians Are Us? Culture and Genocide in Native North America (1994)

Since Predator Came: Notes from the Struggle for American Indian Liberation (1995)

Draconian Measures: A History of FBI Political Repression (1997)

Co-authored: *Culture versus Economism: Essays on Marxism in the Multicultural Arena* (1984) with Elisabeth R. Lloyd

Agents of Repression: The FBI's Secret Wars Against the Black Panther Party and the American Indian Movement (1988) with Jim Vander Wall

The COINTELPRO Papers: Documents from the FBI's Secret Wars Against Dissent in the United States (1990) with Jim Vander Wall

Pacifism as Pathology: Reflections on the Role of Armed Struggle in North America (1996) with Ed Mead and Mike Ryan

Edited: *Marxism and Native Americans (1983): Critical Issues in Native North America* (2 Vols., 1989-1990)

Co-edited: *Cages of Steel: The Politics of Imprisonment in the United States* (1992) with J.J. Vander Wall

Islands in Captivity: The Record of the International Tribunal on the Rights of Indigenous Hawaiians (3 Vols., 1997) with Sharon H. Venne

Interviews: *Acts of Rebellion*: Interviews with Ward Churchill (1996) with Mike Ryan and J.J. Vander Wall

Acknowledgments

All of the material included in this book has previously appeared elsewhere. "Deconstructing the Columbus Myth" was originally published in *Indigenous Thought*, Vol. 1, Nos. 1-2 (March-June, 1991). "Since Predator Came" first appeared in *Covert Action Information Quarterly*, No. 40 (Spring 1992). "Perversions of Justice" has seen print in several places, most recently in David S. Caudill and Stephen Jay Gould, eds., *Radical Philosophy of Law: Contemporary Challenges to Mainstream Legal Theory and Practice* (Atlantic Highlands, NJ: Humanities Press, 1995). The latest iteration of "The Earth is Our Mother" was in my own *Since Predator Came: Notes on the Struggle for American Indian Liberation* (Littleton, CO: Aigis Press, 1995). "Genocide in Arizona?" first appeared in my *Critical Issues in Native North America*, Vol. II (Copenhagen: IWGIA Doc. 63, 1990). Over a dozen versions of "Native North America: The Political Economy of Radioactive Colonialism" have been published over the years. "Like Sand in the Wind" made its initial appearance in *Since Predator Came*. "A Little Matter of Genocide" and "Another Dry White Season" were published in *Bloomsbury Review* (in September 1988 and April 1992, respectively).

The present versions of "Literature and the Colonization of American Indians" and "Fantasies of the Master Race" were first published in my *Fantasies of the Master Race: Literature, Cinema and the Colonization of American Indians* (Monroe, ME: Common Courage Press, 1992). "Spiritual Hucksterism" and "Semantic Masturbation on the Left" came out originally in *Z Magazine* (December 1990 and November 1989, respectively). "Lawrence of South Dakota" made its debut in *Alternative Index*, Vol. 95, No. 20 (May 25, 1991). "Indians 'R' Us" was written for my *Indians Are Us? Culture and Genocide in Native North America* (Monroe, ME: Common Courage Press, 1994), as was "And They Did It Like Dogs in the Dirt..." "Death Squads in the United States" first appeared in the *Yale Journal of Law and Liberation*, No. 3 (Fall 1992). "White Studies" has appeared in several forms; the current version will be found in *Since Predator Came*, as well as Sandra Jackson and José Solís, eds., *Beyond Comfort Zones in Multiculturalism: Confronting the Politics of Privilege* (Westport, CT: Bergin & Garvey, 1995).

"Let's Spread The 'Fun' Around" and "In the Matter of Julius Streicher" were initially prepared on behalf of the American Indian Anti-Defamation Council as op-ed pieces for the *Rocky Mountain News* in Denver. After that exalted publication rejected them—they were not "up to the standards" of the paper, according to editorial page editor Vincent "If I only had a brain" Carroll—they have been published and republished some 20 times internationally, most recently as part of a "Best American Essays Series" (Robert Atwan and Jon Roberts, eds., *Left, Right and Center: Voices from Across the Political Spectrum* [New York: Bedford Books/St. Martin's Press, 1996]). "Way to go, Vinnie. " You are at least consistent in the extent of your "unbiased professionalism."

"Nobody's Pet Poodle" was first published in *The Spirit of Crazy Horse*, newsletter of the Leonard Peltier Defense Committee, during the summer of 1992. "False Promises" was originally prepared as a Phyllis Burger Memorial Lecture at Montana State University in 1987; its initial publication was in *Society and Nature*, Vol. 1, No. 2 (1992); it is included in the German language version of my *Marxism and Native Americans*, entitled *Die indigenen Nationen Nordamerikas und die Marxistische Tradition: Debatte über eine revolutionäre Theorie der Kultur* (Bremen: AGIPA Press, 1993). "Another Vision of America" came out in *New Studies on the Left* (Spring-Summer, 1988). "I Am Indigenist" was written for *Z Papers*, Vol. 1, No. 3 (July-September,1992). It was subsequently used as the capstone piece of my *Struggle for the Land: Indigenous Resistance to Genocide, Ecocide and Expropriation in Contemporary North America* (Monroe, ME: Common Courage Press, 1993).

Among those who, each in their own way, have made the most positive and constructive contributions to the work contained in this volume are Faith Townsend Attiguile, Bobby Castillo, Noam Chomsky, Chrystos, Angela Davis, Shelly Davis, Dan Debo, Vine Deloria, Bill Dunne, Larry Giddings, Don Grinde, Jr., bell hooks, Dennis Jones, Lilikala Kame'eleihiwa, Winona LaDuke, Russ Means, Dian Million, John Mohawk, Glenn Morris, Bob Robideau, Mike Ryan, Kirk Sale, Paul Schultz, David Stannard, George Tinker, Haunani-Kay and Mililani Trask, Jim and Jenny Vander Wall, Sharon Venne and Howard Zinn. Thanks are also due to the South End Press collective, especially Dionne, for enabling me to put this sort of collection together; to Howard Zinn for his fine introduction; and to Katherine Berney for the cover.

Finally, I owe a real debt of gratitude to those who have been most important in supporting, nurturing, and sustaining me personally while this collection was being completed. These include, in no particular order, my United Keetoowah Band of Cherokees, the membership of Colorado AIM (especially Auntie Vivian and Uncle Joe Locust), the faculty of the Department of Ethnic Studies at the University of Colorado at Boulder, as well as my family, both Allens and Kellys. And, of course, there is Leah, love of my life...

Contents

Maps

INTRODUCTION

by Howard Zinn

One of the remarkable developments of the past two decades has been the emergence of a new generation of Native-American scholars who, by their deliberate self-thrust into the struggles of their people, must be characterized as scholar-activists. Among these is Ward Churchill, a Keetoowah Cherokee, whose writing—powerful, eloquent, unsparing of cant and deception—has inspired so many others of his people to join the fray, to take a stand. He has been a prolific writer—books, essays, reviews—and what we have here is a collection, bold and biting in his usual style, of some of his best work of the past 10 years, material which is, as the title indicates, truly "from a native son."

The long attempt to annihilate physically the native people of this continent was carried on by a succession of profit-seeking, expansionist European powers, and finally by the English colonies of North America. Great Britain, having expelled France from the continent, and wanting to avoid endless war with the indigenous nations that lay just beyond the colonies, proclaimed in 1763 that the colonists could not settle beyond the Appalachian Mountains.

When the War for Independence was won (a more apt title than "Revolutionary War" because separation from England did not bring about a true social revolution), the colonists were free to move westward, a matter they considered their "Manifest Destiny." There followed a century of warfare in which the superior military power of the United States prevailed. Piece by piece, the land on which Indians had lived for millennia was gobbled up until they were confined to reservations comprising, in total, something less than 5 percent of their original holdings.

The physical attack on and decimation of the native population, as well as their expulsion from their lands, was accompanied by a cultural assault. Under late 19th- and early 20th-century "assimilation" policies, the vanquished were coerced by various means into emulating their conquerors, the idea being that identifiable remnants of Indian societies would disappear. Another part of the process was to keep secret from generations of Americans the cruelties that lay behind the euphemism "Westward Expansion." The secrets were buried, never to appear in textbooks, popular entertainment, or general histories of the country.

In the struggle of Native Americans to reclaim both their land and their heritage, the unearthing of these secrets plays a crucial role. This is the task Ward Churchill has set for himself, and which he fulfills with overwhelming evidence and meticulous argument. His opening essay, "Deconstructing the Columbus Myth," exemplifies his combination of passion and substance, all with impressive documentation. He meets head-on the complaint that it is wrong to compare the actions of Columbus and his fellow Spaniards to the Holocaust under Hitler, and patiently sifts through the evidence which justifies such comparisons.

For those in danger of getting lost in the complex history of indigenous people in North America, Churchill provides, in his second essay, "Since Predator Came," a guide in the form of a brief survey of what has happened to the native populations of the continent from 1492 to the present.

Ward Churchill moves easily from colonial history to the present: the current struggles of American Indians to regain control over their land ("The Earth is Our Mother"), and to prevent the theft of valuable mineral deposits under these lands ("Genocide in Arizona?" and "Native North America: The Political Economy of Radioactive Colonialism," the latter written with Winona LaDuke). He also gives us a chilling picture, in "Death Squads in the United States: Confessions of a Government Terrorist," of the manner in which federal agencies like the FBI have sought to block such efforts: "death squads" set loose on activists and supporters of the American Indian Movement.

Churchill's critique takes us through what he calls the "intellectual imperialism" of higher education in the United States, the "false promises" he discerns in Marxian contributions to theories of indigenous liberation, the meaning of using Indian imagery in sports team names and logos, as well as current "New Age" attempts to expropriate native spiritual traditions for purposes of turning them into marketable commodities. His criticisms of the role of literature in the colonization of American Indians are useful and incisive. A bonus for me in this collection is the devastating analysis of films, like *Dances With Wolves* and *Black Robe*, purporting to "do right" by native people.

There are many other surprises in these pages, each of them testifying to the breadth of the author's interests and knowledge, an overall outlook he calls "indigenism." What Ward Churchill gives us here is an unusual gift: a rich education, in one volume, in the history of the European/Native encounter in North America. I am grateful to him for this accomplishment, and I expect other readers will share my feeling.

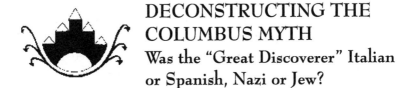

DECONSTRUCTING THE COLUMBUS MYTH
Was the "Great Discoverer" Italian or Spanish, Nazi or Jew?

Christopher Columbus was a genuine titan, a hero of history and of the human spirit...To denigrate Columbus is to denigrate what is worthy in human history and in us all.

—Jeffrey Hart, *National Review*, October 15, 1990

It is perhaps fair to say that our story opens at Alfred University, where, during the fall of 1990, I served as distinguished scholar of American Indian Studies for a program funded by the National Endowment for the Humanities. Insofar as I was something of a curiosity in that primarily Euroamerican staffed and attended institution, situated as it is within an area populated primarily by white folk, it followed naturally that I quickly became a magnet for local journalists seeking to inject a bit of color into their otherwise uniformly blanched columns and commentaries. Given our temporal proximity to the much-heralded quincentennial celebration of Christopher Columbus' late 15th-century "discovery" of a "New World" and its inhabitants, and that I am construed as being in some part a direct descendant of those inhabitants, they were wont to query me as to my sentiments concerning the accomplishments of the Admiral of the Ocean Sea.

My response, at least in its short version, was (and remains) that celebration of Columbus and the European conquest of the Western hemisphere he set off is greatly analogous to celebration of the glories of nazism and Heinrich Himmler. Publication of this remark in local newspapers around Rochester, New York, caused me to receive, among other things, a deluge of lengthy and vociferously framed letters of protest, two of which I found worthy of remark.

The first of these was sent by a colleague at the university, an exchange faculty member from Germany, who informed me that while the human costs begat by Columbus' navigational experiment were "tragic and quite regrettable," comparisons between him and the

1

Reichsführer SS were nonetheless unfounded. The distinction between Himmler and Columbus, his argument went, resided not only
in differences in "the magnitude of the genocidal events in which each
was involved," but in the *ways* in which they were involved. Himmler,
he said, was enmeshed as "a high-ranking and responsible official in
the liquidation of entire human groups" as "a matter of formal state
policy" guided by an explicitly "racialist" ideology. Furthermore, he
said, the enterprise Himmler created as the instrument of his genocidal ambitions incorporated, deliberately and intentionally, considerable economic benefit to the state in whose service he acted. None
of this pertained to Columbus, the good professor concluded, because
the "Great Discoverer" was ultimately "little more than a gifted
seaman," an individual who unwittingly set in motion processes over
which he had little or no control, in which he played no direct part,
and which might well have been beyond his imagination. My juxtaposition of the two men, he contended, therefore tended to "diminish
understanding of the unique degree of evil" which should be associated with Himmler, and ultimately precluded "proper historical understanding of the Nazi phenomenon."

The second letter came from a member of the Jewish Defense League
in Rochester. His argument ran that, unlike Columbus (whom he described as "little more than a bit player, without genuine authority or
even much of a role, in the actual process of European civilization in the
New World which his discovery made possible"), Himmler was a "responsible official in a formal state policy of exterminating an entire
human group for both racial and economic reasons," and on a scale
"unparalleled in all history." My analogy between the two, he said,
served to "diminish public respect for the singular nature of the Jewish
experience at the hands of the Nazis," as well as popular understanding
of "the unique historical significance of the Holocaust." Finally he added,
undoubtedly as a crushing capstone to his position, "It is a measure of
your anti-semitism that you compare Himmler to Columbus" because
"Columbus was, of course, himself a Jew."

I must confess the last assertion struck me first, and only partly
because I'd never before heard claims that Christopher Columbus was
of Jewish ethnicity. "What possible difference could this make?" I

asked in my letter of reply. "If Himmler himself were shown to have been of Jewish extraction, would it then suddenly become anti-semitic to condemn him for the genocide he perpetrated against Jews, Gypsies, Slavs, and others? Would his historical crimes then suddenly be unmentionable or even 'okay'?" "To put it another way," I continued, "simply because Meyer Lansky, Dutch Schultz, Bugsy Siegel, and Louis Buchlter Lepke were all Jewish 'by blood,' is it a gesture of anti-semitism to refer to them as gangsters? Is it your contention that an individual's Jewish ethnicity somehow confers exemption from negative classification or criticism of his/her conduct? What *are* you saying?" The question of Columbus' possible Jewishness nonetheless remained intriguing, not because I held it to be especially important in its own right, but because I was (and am still) mystified as to why any ethnic group, especially one which has suffered genocide, might be avid to lay claim either to the man or to his legacy. I promised myself to investigate the matter further.

A Mythic Symbiosis

Meanwhile, I was captivated by certain commonalities of argument inherent to the positions advanced by my correspondents. Both men exhibited a near-total ignorance of the actualities of Columbus' career; nor did they demonstrate any particular desire to correct the situation. Indeed, in their mutual need to separate the topic of their preoccupation from rational scrutiny, they appeared to have conceptually joined hands in a function composed more of faith than fact. The whole notion of the "uniqueness of the Holocaust" serves both psychic and political purposes for Jew and German alike, or so it seems. The two groups are bound to one another in a truly symbiotic relationship foundationed in the mythic exclusivity of their experience: one half of the equation simply completes the other in a perverse sort of collaboration, with the result that each enjoys a tangible benefit.

For Jews, at least those who have adopted the zionist perspective, a "unique historical suffering" under nazism translates into fulfillment of a biblical prophecy that they are "the chosen," entitled by virtue of the destiny of a special persecution to assume a rarified status among—and to consequently enjoy preferential treatment from—the remainder of humanity. In essence, this translates into a demand that the Jewish segment of the Holocaust's victims must now be allowed to participate equally in the very system which once victimized them, and to receive an equitable share of the spoils accruing therefrom. To this end, zionist scholars such as Irving Louis Horowitz and Elie Wiesel have labored long and mightily, defining genocide in terms exclusively related to the forms it assumed under nazism. In their version of "truth," one must literally see smoke pouring from the chimneys of Auschwitz in order to apprehend that a genocide, *per se*, is occurring.[1] Conversely, they have coined terms such as "ethnocide" to encompass the fates inflicted upon other peoples throughout history.[2] Such semantics have served, not as tools of understanding, but as an expedient means of arbitrarily differentiating the experience of their people—both qualitatively and quantitatively—from that of any other. To approach things in any other fashion would, it must be admitted, tend to undercut ideas like the "moral right" of the Israeli settler state to impose itself directly atop the Palestinian Arab homeland.

For Germans to embrace a corresponding "unique historical guilt" because of what was done to the Jews during the 1940s is to permanently absolve themselves of guilt concerning what they may be doing *now*. No matter how ugly things may become in contemporary German society, or so the reasoning goes, it can *always* be (and is) argued that there has been a marked improvement over the "singular evil which was nazism." Anything other than outright nazification is, by definition, "different," "better, " and therefore "acceptable" ("Bad as they are, things could always be worse."). Business as usual— which is to say assertions of racial supremacy, domination and exploitation of "inferior" groups, and most of the rest of the nazi agenda—is thereby freed to continue in a manner essentially unhampered by serious stirrings of guilt among the German public *so long as it does not adopt the literal trappings of nazism*. Participating for profit and with gusto in the deliberate starvation of much of the Third World is no particular problem if one is careful not to goose step while one does it.

By extension, insofar as Germany is often seen (and usually sees itself) as exemplifying the crowning achievements of "Western Civilization," the same principle covers all European and Euro-derived societies. No matter what they do, it is never "really" what it seems unless it was done in precisely the fashion the nazis did it. Consequently, the nazi master plan of displacing or reducing by extermination the population of the western USSR and replacing it with settlers of "biologically superior German breeding stock" is roundly (and rightly) condemned as ghastly and inhuman. Meanwhile, people holding this view of nazi ambitions tend overwhelmingly to see consolidation and maintenance of Euro-dominated settler states in places like Australia, New Zealand, South Africa, Argentina, the United States, and Canada as "basically okay," or even as "progress." The "distinction" allowing this psychological phenomenon is that each of these states went about the intentional displacement and extermination of native populations, and their replacement, in a manner slightly different in its particulars from that employed by nazis attempting to accomplish exactly the same thing. Such technical differentiation is then magnified and used as a sort of all purpose veil, behind which almost anything can be hidden, so long as it is not openly adorned with a swastika.

Given the psychological, sociocultural, and political imperatives involved, neither correspondent, whether German or Jew, felt constrained to examine the factual basis of my analogy between Himmler and Columbus before denying the plausibility or appropriateness of the comparison. To the contrary, since the paradigm of their mutual understanding embodies the *a priori* presumption that there *must be no such analogy*, factual investigation is precluded from their posturing. It follows that any dissent on the "methods" involved in their arriving at their conclusions, never mind introduction of countervailing evidence, must be denied out of hand with accusations of "overstatement," "shoddy scholarship," "stridency," and/or "anti-semitism." To this litany have lately been added such new variations as "white bashing," "ethnic McCarthyism," "purveyor of political correctitude," and any other epithet deemed helpful in keeping a "canon of knowledge" fraught with distortion, deception, and outright fraud from being "diluted."[3]

Columbus as Protonazi

It is time to delve into the substance of my remark that Columbus and Himmler, nazi *lebensraumpolitik* and the "settlement of the New World," bear more than a casual resemblance to one another. It is not, as my two correspondents wished to believe, because of his "discovery." This does not mean that if this were "all" he had done he would be somehow innocent of what resulted from his find, no more than is the scientist who makes a career of accepting military funding to develop weapons in any way "blameless" when they are subsequently used against human targets. Columbus did not sally forth upon the Atlantic for reasons of "neutral science" or altruism. He went, as his own diaries, reports, and letters make clear, fully expecting to encounter wealth belonging to others. It was his stated purpose to seize this wealth, by whatever means necessary and available, in order to enrich both his sponsors and himself.[4] Plainly, he prefigured, both in design and by intent, what came next. To this extent, he not only symbolizes the process of conquest and genocide which eventually consumed the indigenous peoples of America, but also bears the personal responsibility of having participated in it. Still, if this were all there was to it, I might be inclined to dismiss him as a mere thug rather than branding him a counterpart to Himmler.

The 1492 "voyage of discovery" is, however, hardly all that is at issue. In 1493 Columbus returned with an invasion force of 17 ships, appointed at his own request by the Spanish Crown to install himself as "viceroy and governor of [the Caribbean islands] and the mainland" of America, a position he held until 1500.[5] Setting up shop on the large island he called Española (today Haiti and the Dominican Republic), he promptly instituted policies of slavery (*encomiendo*) and systematic extermination against the native Taino population.[6] Columbus' programs reduced Taino numbers from as many as eight million at the outset of his regime to about three million in 1496.[7] Perhaps 100,000 were left by the time of the governor's departure. His policies, however, remained, with the result that by 1514 the Spanish census of the island showed barely 22,000 Indians remaining alive. In 1542, only 200 were recorded.[8] Thereafter, they were considered extinct, as were Indians throughout the Caribbean Basin, an aggregate population which totalled more than 15 million at the point of first contact with the Admiral of the Ocean Sea, as Columbus was known.[9]

This, to be sure, constitutes an attrition of population *in real numbers every bit as great as the toll of 12 to 15 million—about half of them Jewish—most commonly attributed to Himmler's slaughter mills. Moreover, the proportion of indigenous Caribbean population destroyed by the Spanish in a single generation is, no matter how the figures are twisted, far greater than the 75 percent of European Jews usually said to have been exterminated by the nazis.*[10] Worst of all, these data apply *only* to the Caribbean Basin; the process of genocide in the Americas was only just beginning at the point such statistics become operant, not ending, as they did upon the fall of the Third Reich. All told, it is probable that more than 100 million native people were "eliminated" in the course of Europe's ongoing "civilization" of the Western hemisphere.[11]

It has long been asserted by "responsible scholars" that this decimation of American Indians which accompanied the European invasion resulted primarily from disease rather than direct killing or conscious policy.[12] There is a certain truth to this, although starvation may have proven just as lethal in the end. It must be borne in mind when considering such facts that a considerable portion of those who perished in the nazi death camps died, not as the victims of bullets and gas, but from starvation, as well as epidemics of typhus, dysentery, and the like. Their keepers, who could not be said to have killed these people directly, were nonetheless found to have been culpable in their deaths by way of deliberately imposing the conditions which led to the proliferation of starvation and disease among them.[13] Certainly, the same can be said of Columbus' regime, under which the original residents were, as a first order of business, permanently dispossessed of their abundant cultivated fields while being converted into chattel, ultimately to be worked to death for the wealth and "glory" of Spain.[14]

Nor should more direct means of extermination be relegated to incidental status. As the matter is framed by Kirkpatrick Sale in his book *The Conquest of Paradise*:

> The tribute system, instituted by the Governor sometime in 1495, was a simple and brutal way of fulfilling the Spanish lust for gold while acknowledging the Spanish distaste for labor. Every Taino over the age

of fourteen had to supply the rulers with a hawk's bill of gold every three months (or, in gold-deficient areas, twenty-five pounds of spun cotton); those who did were given a token to wear around their necks as proof that they had made their payment; those who did not were, as [Columbus' brother, Fernando] says discreetly, "punished"—by having their hands cut off, as [the priest, Bartolomé de] Las Casas says less discreetly, and left to bleed to death.[15]

It is entirely likely that upwards of 10,000 Indians were killed in this fashion , on Española alone, as a matter of policy, during Columbus' tenure as governor. Las Casas' *Brevísima relación*, among other contemporaneous sources, is also replete with accounts of Spanish colonists (*hidalgos*) hanging Tainos *en masse*, roasting them on spits or burning them at the stake (often a dozen or more at a time), hacking their children into pieces to be used as dog feed and so forth, all of it to instill in the natives a "proper attitude of respect" toward their Spanish "superiors."

[The Spaniards] made bets as to who would slit a man in two, or cut off his head at one blow; or they opened up his bowels. They tore the babes from their mother's breast by their feet and dashed their heads against the rocks...They spitted the bodies of other babes, together with their mothers and all who were before them, on their swords.[16]

No SS trooper could be expected to comport himself with a more unrelenting viciousness. And there is more. All of this was coupled to wholesale and persistent massacres:

A Spaniard...suddenly drew his sword. Then the whole hundred drew theirs and began to rip open the bellies, to cut and kill [a group of Tainos assembled for this purpose]–men, women, children and old folk, all of whom were seated, off guard and frightened...And within two credos, not a man of them there remains alive. The Spaniards enter the large house nearby, for this was happening at its door, and in the same way, with cuts and stabs, began to kill as many as were found there, so that a stream of blood was running, as if a great number of cows had perished.[17]

Elsewhere, Las Casas went on to recount how:

In this time, the greatest outrages and slaughterings of people were perpetrated, whole villages being depopulated...The Indians saw that without any offense on their part they were despoiled of their kingdoms, their lands and liberties and of their lives, their wives, and homes. As they saw themselves each day perishing by the cruel and inhuman treatment of the Spaniards, crushed to earth by the horses, cut in pieces by swords, eaten and torn by dogs, many buried alive and suffering all kinds of exquisite tortures...[many surrendered to their fate, while the survivors] fled to the mountains [to starve].[18]

The butchery continued until there were no Tainos left to butcher. One might well ask how a group of human beings, even those like the Spaniards of Columbus' day, maddened in a collective lust for wealth and prestige, might come to treat another with such unrestrained ferocity over a sustained period. The answer, or some substantial portion of it, must lie in the fact that the Indians were considered by the Spanish to be *untermenschen*, subhumans. That this was the conventional view is borne out beyond all question in the recorded debates between Las Casas and the nobleman Francisco de Sepulveda, who argued for the majority of Spaniards that American Indians, like African Blacks and other "lower animals," lacked "souls." The Spaniards, consequently, bore in Sepulveda's estimation a holy obligation to enslave and destroy them wherever they might be encountered.[19] The eugenics theories of nazi "philosopher" Alfred Rosenberg, to which Heinrich Himmler more or less subscribed, elaborated the mission of the SS in very much the same terms.[20] It was upon such profoundly racist ideas that Christopher Columbus grounded his policies as initial governor of the new Spanish empire in America.[21]

In the end, all practical distinctions between Columbus and Himmler—at least those not accounted for by differences in available technology and extent of sociomilitary organization—evaporate upon close inspection. They are cut of the same cloth, fulfilling precisely the same function and for exactly the same reasons, each in his own time and place. If there is one differentiation which may be valid, it is that while the specific enterprise Himmler represented ultimately failed and is now universally condemned, that represented by Columbus did not and is not. Instead, as Sale has observed, the model for colonialism and concomitant genocide Columbus pioneered during his reign as governor of Española was to prove his "most enduring legacy," carried as it was "by the conquistadors on their invasions of Mexico, Peru, and La Florida."[22] The Columbian process is ongoing, as is witnessed by the fact that, today, his legacy is celebrated far and wide.

The Emblematic European

This leaves open the question as to whom, exactly, the horror which was Columbus rightly "belongs." There is, as it turns out, no shortage of contenders for the mantle of the man and his "accomplishments." It would be well to examine the nature of at least the major claims in order to appreciate the extent of the mad scramble which has been undertaken by various peoples to associate themselves with what was delineated in the preceding section. One cannot avoid the suspicion that the spectacle bespeaks much of the Eurocentric character.

Was Columbus Italian?

The popular wisdom has always maintained that Christopher Columbus was born in Genoa, a city state which is incorporated into what is now called Italy. Were this simply an historical truth, it might be accepted as just one more uncomfortable fact of life for the Italian people, who are—or should be—still trying to live down what their country did to the Libyans and Ethiopians during the prelude to World War II. There is much evidence, however, militating against Columbus' supposed Genoese origin. For instance, although such records were kept at the time, there is no record of his birth in that locale. Nor is there reference to his having been born or raised there in any of his own written work, including his personal correspondence. For that matter, there is no indication that he either wrote or spoke any dialect which might be associated with Genoa, nor even the Tuscan language which forms the basis of modern Italian. His own writings—not excluding letters penned to Genoese friends and the Banco di San Grigorio, one of his financiers in that city—were uniformly articulated in Castilian, with a bit of Portuguese and Latin mixed in.[23] Moreover, while several variations of his name were popularly applied to him during his lifetime, none of them was drawn from a dialect which might be considered Italian. He himself, in the only known instance in which he rendered his own full name, utilized the Greek *Xρõual de Colón*.[24] Still, Genoa, Italy, and those of Italian descent elsewhere in the world (Italoamericans, most loudly of all) have mounted an unceasing clamor during the 20th century, insisting he *must* be theirs. Genoa itself invested considerable resources into "resolving" the question during the 1920s, ultimately printing a 288-page book assembling an array of depositions and other documents—all of them authenticated—attesting that Columbus was indeed Genoese. Published in 1931, the volume, entitled *Christopher Columbus: Documents and Proofs of His Genoese Origin*, presents what is still the best circumstantial case as to Columbus' ethnic identity.[25]

Spanish?

Counterclaims concerning Columbus' supposed Iberian origin are also long-standing and have at times been pressed rather vociferously. These center primarily in the established facts that he spent the bulk of his adult life in service to Spain, was fluent in both written and spoken Castilian, and that his mistress, Beatriz Enríquez de Arana, was Spanish.[26] During the 1920s, these elements of the case were bolstered by an assortment of "archival documents" allegedly proving conclusively that Columbus was a Spaniard from cradle to grave. In 1928, however, the Spanish Academy determined that these documents had been forged by parties overly eager to establish Spain's exclusive claim to the Columbian legacy. Since then, Spanish chauvinists have had to content themselves with arguments that The Discoverer is theirs by virtue of employment and nationality, if not by birth. An excellent summary of the various Spanish contentions may be found in Enrique de Gandia's *Historia de Cristóbal Colón: analisis crítico*, first published in 1942.[27]

Portuguese?

Portuguese participation in the fray has been less pronounced, but follows basically the same course—*sans* forged documents—as that of the Spanish. Columbus, the argument goes, was plainly conversant in the language, and his wife, Felipa Moniz Perestrello, is known to have been Portuguese. Further, the first point at which his whereabouts can be accurately determined, was in service to Portugal, plying that country's slave trade along Africa's west coast for a period of four years. Reputedly, he was also co-proprietor of a book and map shop in Lisbon and/or Madeira for a time, and once sailed to Iceland on a voyage commissioned by the Portuguese Crown. Portugal's desire to extend a serious claim to Spain's Admiral of the Ocean Sea seems to be gathering at least some momentum, as is witnessed by Manuel Luciano de Silva's 1989 book *Columbus Was 100% Portuguese*.[28]

Jewish?

The idea that Columbus might have been a Spanish Jew is perhaps best known for having appeared in Simon Weisenthal's *Sails of Hope* in 1973.[29] Therein, it is contended that the future governor of Española hid his ethnicity because of the mass expulsion of Jews from Spain ordered by King Ferdinand of Aragon on March 30, 1492 (the decree was executed on August 2 of the same year). Because of this rampant anti-semitism, the Great Navigator's true identity has remained shrouded in mystery, lost to the historical record. Interestingly, given the tenacity with which at least some sectors of the Jewish community have latched on to it, this notion is not at all Jewish in origin. Rather, it was initially developed as a speculation in a 1913 article, "Columbus a Spaniard and a Jew?," published by Henry Vignaud in the *American History Review*.[30] It was then advanced by Salvador de Madariaga in his unsympathetic 1939 biography, *Christopher Columbus*. Madariaga's most persuasive argument, at least to himself, seems to have been that Columbus' "great love of gold" proved his "Jewishness." [31] This theme was resuscitated in Brother Nectario Maria's *Juan Colón Was A Spanish Jew* in 1971.[32] Next, we will probably be told that *The Merchant of Venice* was an accurate depiction of medieval Jewish life, after all. And, from there, that the International Jewish Bolshevik Banking Conspiracy really exists, and has since the days of the Illuminati takeover of the Masonic Orders. One hopes the JDL doesn't rally to the defense of these "interpretations" of history as readily as it jumped aboard the "Columbus as Jew" bandwagon.[33]

Other Contenders

By conservative count, there are presently 253 books and articles devoted specifically to the question of Columbus' origin and na-tional/ethnic identity. Another 300-odd essays or full volumes address the same questions to some extent while pursuing other matters.[34] Claims to his character, and some imagined luster therefrom, have been extended not only by the four peoples already discussed, but also by Corsica, Greece, Chios, Majorca, Aragon, Galicia, France, and Poland.[35] One can only wait with bated breath to see whether or not the English might not weigh in with a quincentennial assertion that he was actually a Briton born and bred, sent to spy on behalf of Their Royal British Majesties. Perhaps the Swedes, Danes, and Norwegians will advance the case that Columbus was actually the descendant of a refugee Viking king, or the Irish that he was a pure Gaelic adherent of the teachings of Saint Brendan. And then there are, of course, the Germans.

In the final analysis, it is patently clear that we really have no idea who Columbus was, where he came from, or where he spent his formative years. It may be that he was indeed born in Genoa, perhaps of some "degree of Jewish blood," brought up in Portugal, and ultimately nationalized as a citizen of Spain, Province of Aragon. Perhaps he also spent portions of his childhood being educated in Greek and Latin while residing in Corsica, Majorca, Chios, or all three. Maybe he had grandparents who had immigrated from what is now Poland and France. It *is* possible that each of the parties now vying for a "piece of the action" in his regard are to some extent correct in their claims. And, to the same extent, it is true that he was actually *of* none of them in the sense that they mean it. He stands, by this definition, not as an Italian, Spaniard, Portuguese, or Jew, but as the quintessential European of his age, the emblematic personality of all that Europe was, had been, and would become in the course of its subsequent expansion across the face of the earth.

As a symbol, then, Christopher Columbus vastly transcends himself. He stands before the bar of history and humanity, culpable not only for his literal deeds on Española, but, in spirit at least, for the carnage and cultural obliteration which attended the conquests of Mexico and Peru during the 1500s. He stands as exemplar of the massacre of Pequots at Mystic in 1637, and of Lord Jeffrey Amherst's calculated distribution of smallpox-laden blankets to the members of Pontiac's confederacy a century and a half later. His spirit informed the policies of John Evans and John Chivington as they set out to exterminate the Cheyennes in Colorado during 1864, and it rode with the 7th U.S. Cavalry to Wounded Knee in December of 1890. It guided Alfredo Stroessner's machete-wielding butchers as they strove to eradicate the Aché people of Paraguay during the 1970s, and applauds the policies of Brazil toward the Jivaro, Yanomami, and other Amazon Basin peoples at the present moment.

Also, the ghost of Columbus stood with the British in their wars against the Zulus and various Arab nations, with the U.S. against the "Moros" of the Philippines, the French against the peoples of Algeria and Indochina, the Belgians in the Congo, the Dutch in Indonesia. He was there for the Opium Wars and the "secret" bombing of Cambodia, for the systematic slaughter of the indigenous peoples of California during the 19th century and of the Mayans in Guatemala during the 1980s. And, yes, he was very much present in the corridors of nazi power, present among the guards and commandants at Sobibor and Treblinka, and within the ranks of the *einsatzgruppen* on the Eastern Front. The Third Reich was, after all, never so much a deviation from as it was a crystallization of the dominant themes—racial suprema-cism, conquest, and genocide—of the European culture Columbus so ably exemplifies. Nazism was never unique: it was instead only one of an endless succession of "New World Orders" set in motion by "The Discovery." It was neither more nor less detestable than the order imposed by Christopher Columbus upon Española; 1493 or 1943, they are part of the same irreducible whole.

The Specter of Hannibal Lecter

At this juncture, the entire planet is locked, figuratively, in a room with the sociocultural equivalent of Hannibal Lecter. An individual of consummate taste and refinement, imbued with indelible grace and charm, he distracts his victims with the brilliance of his intellect, even while honing his blade. He is thus able to dine alone upon their livers, his feast invariably candlelit, accompanied by lofty music and a fine wine. Over and over the ritual is repeated, always hidden, always denied in order that it may be continued. So perfect is Lecter's pathology that, from the depths of his scorn for the inferiors upon whom he feeds, he advances himself as their sage and therapist, he who is in comparably endowed with the ability to explain their innermost meanings, who professes to be their savior. His success depends upon being embraced and exalted by those upon whom he preys. Ultimately, so long as Lecter is able to retain his mask of omnipotent gentility, he can never be stopped. The sociocultural equivalent of Hannibal Lecter is the core of an expansionist European "civilization" which has reached out to engulf the planet.

In coming to grips with Lecter, it is of no useful purpose to engage in sympathetic biography, to chronicle the nuances of his childhood and catalogue his many and varied achievements, whether real or imagined. The recounting of such information is at best diversionary, allowing him to remain at large just that much longer. More often, it inadvertently serves to perfect his mask, enabling him not only to maintain his enterprise, but also to pursue it with ever more arrogance and efficiency. At worst, the biographer is aware of the intrinsic evil lurking beneath the subject's veneer of civility, but—because of morbid fascination and a desire to participate vicariously—deliberately obfuscates the truth in order that his homicidal activities may continue unchecked. The biographer thus reveals not only a willing complicity in the subject's crimes, but also a virulent pathology of his or her own. Such is and has always been the relationship of "responsible scholarship" to expansionist Europe and its derivative societies.

The sole legitimate function of information compiled about Lecter is that which will serve to unmask him and thereby lead to his apprehension. The purpose of apprehension is not to visit retribution upon the psychopath—he is, after all, by definition mentally ill and consequently not in control of his more lethal impulses—but to put an end to his activities. It is even theoretically possible that, once he is disempowered, he can be cured. The point, however, is to understand what he is and what he does well enough to stop him from doing it. This is the role which must be assumed by scholarship *vis-à-vis* Eurosupremacy, if scholarship itself is to have any positive and constructive meaning. Scholarship is *never* "neutral" or "objective"; it *always* works either for the psychopath or against him, to mystify sociocultural reality or to decode it, to make corrective action possible or to prevent it.

It may well be that there are better points of departure for intellectual endeavors to capture the real form and meaning of Eurocentrism than the life, times, and legacy of Christopher Columbus. Still, since Eurocentrists the world over have so evidently clasped hands in utilizing him as a (perhaps *the*) preeminent signifier of their collective heritage, and are doing so with such an apparent sense of collective jubilation, the point has been rendered effectively moot. Those who seek to devote their scholarship to apprehending the psychopath who sits in our room thus have no alternative but to use him as a primary vehicle of articulation. In order to do so, we must approach him through deployment of the analytical tools which allow him to be utilized as a medium of explanation, a lens by which to shed light upon phenomena such as the mass psychologies of fascism and racism, a means by which to shear Eurocentrism of its camouflage, exposing its true contours, revealing the enduring coherence of the dynamics which forged its evolution.

Perhaps through such efforts we can begin to genuinely comprehend the seemingly incomprehensible fact that so many groups are presently queuing up to associate themselves with a man from whose very memory wafts the cloying stench of tyranny and genocide. From there, it may be possible at last to crack the real codes of meaning underlying the sentiments of the Nuremberg rallies, those spectacles on the plazas of Rome during which fealty was pledged to Mussolini, and that amazing red-white-and-blue, tie-a-yellow-ribbon frenzy gripping the U.S. public much more lately. If we force ourselves to see things clearly, we can understand. If we can understand, we can apprehend. If we can apprehend, perhaps we can stop the psychopath before he kills again. We are obligated to try, from a sense of sheer self-preservation, if nothing else. Who knows, we may even succeed. But first we must stop lying to ourselves, or allowing others to do the lying for us, about who it is with whom we now share our room.

Notes

1. See, for example, Horowitz, Irving Louis, *Genocide: State Power and Mass Murder* (New Brunswick, NJ: Transaction Books, 1976) and Wiesel, Elie, *Legends of Our Time* (New York: Holt, Rinehart and Winston Publishers, 1968). The theme is crystalized

in Manvell, Roger, and Heinrich Fraenkel, *Incomparable Crime; Mass Extermination in the 20th Century: The Legacy of Guilt* (London: Hinemann Publishers, 1967).

2. See, as examples, Richard Falk, "Ethnocide, Genocide, and the Nuremberg Tradition of Moral Responsibility," in *Philosophy, Morality, and International Affairs*, ed. Virginia Held, Sidney Morganbesser, and Thomas Nagel (New York: Oxford University Press, 1974), pp. 123-37; Beardsley, Monroe C., "Reflections on Genocide and Ethnocide," in *Genocide in Paraguay*, ed. Richard Arens (Philadelphia, PA: Temple University Press, 1976), pp. 85-101; and Jaulin, Robert, *L'Ethnocide à travers Les Amériques* (Paris: Gallimard Publishers, 1972) and *La décivilisation, politique et pratique de l'ethnocide* (Brussels: Presses Universitaires de France, 1974).

3. Assaults upon thinking deviating from Eurocentric mythology have been published with increasing frequency in U.S. mass circulation publications such as *Time, Newsweek, U.S. News and World Report, Forbes, Commentary, Scientific American* and the *Wall Street Journal* throughout 1990-91. A perfect illustration for our purposes here is Hart, Jeffrey, "Discovering Columbus," *National Review* (October 15, 1990): pp. 56-57.

4. See Morison, Samuel Eliot, ed. and trans., *Journals and Other Documents on the Life and Voyages of Christopher Columbus* (New York: Heritage Publishers, 1963).

5. The letter of appointment to these positions, signed by Ferdinand and Isabella, and dated May 28, 1493, is quoted in full in Keen, Benjamin, trans., *The Life of the Admiral Christopher Columbus by His Son Ferdinand* (New Brunswick, NJ: Rutgers University Press, 1959), pp. 105-6.

6. The best sources on Columbus' policies are Floyd, Troy, *The Columbus Dynasty in the Caribbean, 1492-1526* (Albuquerque: University of New Mexico Press, 1973) and Schwartz, Stuart B., *The Iberian Mediterranean and Atlantic Traditions in the Formation of Columbus as a Colonizer* (Minneapolis: University of Minnesota Press, 1986).

7. Regarding the eight million figure, see Cook, Sherburne F., and Woodrow Borah, *Essays in Population History*, vol. I (Berkeley: University of California Press, 1971), especially chap. VI. The three million figure pertaining to the year 1496 derives from a survey conducted by Bartolomé de Las Casas in that year, covered in Thatcher, J. B., *Christopher Columbus*, vol. 2 (New York: Putnam's Sons Publishers, 1903-1904), p. 348ff.

8. For summaries of the Spanish census records, see Hanke, Lewis, *The Spanish Struggle for Justice in the Conquest of America* (Philadelphia: University of Pennsylvania Press, 1947), p. 200ff. Also see Madariaga, Salvador de, *The Rise of the Spanish American Empire* (London: Hollis and Carter Publishers, 1947).

9. For aggregate estimates of the precontact indigenous population of the Caribbean Basin, see Denevan, William, ed., *The Native Population of the Americas in 1492* (Madison: University of Wisconsin Press, 1976); Dobyns, Henry, *Their Numbers Become Thinned: Native American Population Dynamics in Eastern North America* (Knoxville: University of Tennessee Press, 1983); and Thornton, Russell, *American Indian Holocaust and Survival: A Population History Since 1492* (Norman: University of Oklahoma Press, 1987). For additional information, see Dobyns' bibliographic *Native American Historical Demography* (Bloomington: University of Indiana Press, 1976).

10. These figures are utilized in numerous studies. One of the more immediately accessible is Kuper, Leo, *Genocide: Its Political Use in the Twentieth Century* (New Haven, CT: Yale University Press, 1981).

11. See Dobyns, Henry F., "Estimating American Aboriginal Population: An Appraisal of Techniques with a New Hemispheric Estimate," *Current Anthropology*, no. 7: pp. 395-416.

12. An overall pursuit of this theme will be found in Ashburn, P. M., *The Ranks of Death* (New York: Coward Publishers, 1947). Also see Duffy, John, *Epidemics in Colonial America* (Baton Rouge: Louisiana State University Press, 1953). Broader and more sophisticated articulations of the same idea are embodied in Crosby, Alfred W., Jr., *The Columbia Exchange: Biological and Cultural Consequences of 1492* (Westport, CT: Greenwood Press, 1972) and *Ecological Imperialism: The Biological Expansion of Europe, 900-1900* (Melbourne, Australia: Cambridge University Press, 1986).

13. One of the more thoughtful elaborations on this theme may be found in Smith, Bradley F., *Reaching Judgement at Nuremberg* (New York: Basic Books, 1977).

14. See Todorov, Tzvetan, *The Conquest of America* (New York: Harper & Row Publishers, 1984).

15. Sale, Kirkpatrick, *The Conquest of Paradise: Christopher Columbus and the Columbian Legacy* (New York: Alfred A. Knopf Publishers, 1990), p. 155.

16. Las Casas, Bartolomé de, *The Spanish Colonie (Brevísima revacíon)* (University Microfilms reprint, 1966).

17. Las Casas, Bartolomé de, *Historia de las Indias*, ed. Augustin Millares Carlo and Lewis Hanke, vol. 3 (Mexico City: Fondo de Cultura Económica, 1951), especially chap. 29.

18. Las Casas, quoted in Thatcher, *op. cit.*, pp. 348ff.

19. See Hanke, Lewis, *Aristotle and the American Indians: A Study in Race Prejudice in the Modern World* (Chicago, IL: Henry Regnery Company, 1959). Also see Williams, Rob, *The American Indian in Western Legal Thought* (London: Oxford University Press, 1989).

20. The most succinctly competent overview of this subject matter is probably Cecil, Robert, *The Myth of the Master Race: Alfred Rosenberg and Nazi Ideology* (New York: Dodd and Mead Company, 1972).

21. The polemics of Columbus' strongest supporters among his contemporaries amplify this point. See, for example, Oviedo, *Historia general y natural de las Indias*, Seville, 1535; Salamanca, 1547, 1549; Valladoid, 1557; Academia Historica, Madrid, 1851-55, especially chaps. 29, 30, 37.

22. Sale, *op. cit.*, p. 156.

23. On Columbus' written expression, see Milani, V. I., "The Written Language of Christopher Columbus," *Forum italicum* (1973). Also see Jane, Cecil, "The Question of Literacy of Christopher Columbus," *Hispanic American Historical Review*, vol. 10 (1930).

24. On Columbus' signature, see Thatcher, *op. cit.*, p. 454.

25. City of Genoa, *Christopher Columbus: Documents and Proofs of His Genoese Origin*, Instituto d'Arti Grafiche (Genoa: 1931; English language edition, 1932).

26. de la Torre, José, *Beatriz Enríquez de Harana* (Madrid: Iberoamericana Publishers, 1933).

27. Gandia, Enrique de, *Historia de Cristóbal Colón: analisis crítico* (Buenos Aires: 1942).

28. Silva, Manuel Luciano de, *Columbus Was 100% Portuguese* (Bristol, RI: self published, 1989).

29. Weisenthal, Simon, *Sails of Hope* (New York: Macmillan Publishers, 1973).

30. Vignaud, Henry, "Columbus a Spaniard and a Jew?", *American History Review*, vol. 18 (1913). This initial excursion into the idea was followed in more depth by Martínez, Francisco Martínez in his *El descubrimiento de América y las joyas de doña Isabel* (Seville, 1916) and Jacob Wasserman in *Christopher Columbus* (Berlin: S. Fisher Publishers, 1929).

31. Madariaga, Salvador de, *Christopher Columbus* (London: Oxford University Press, 1939). His lead was followed by Armando Alvarez Pedroso in an essay, "Cristóbal Colón no fue hebero," *Revista de Historica de América* (1942) and Antonio Ballesteros y Beretta in *Cristóbal Colón y el descubrimiento de América* (Barcelona/Buenos Aires: Savat Publishers, 1945).

32. Maria, Brother Nectario, *Juan Colón Was A Spanish Jew* (New York: Cedney Publishers, 1971).

33. A much sounder handling of the probabilities of early Jewish migration to the Americas may be found in Keyserling, Meyer, *Christopher Columbus and the Participation of the Jews in the Spanish and Portuguese Discoveries* (London: Longmans, Green Publishers, 1893; reprinted, 1963).

34. For a complete count, see Conti, Simonetta, *Un secolo di bibliografia colombiana 1880-1985* (Genoa: Cassa di Risparmio di Genova e Imperia, 1986).

35. These claims are delineated and debunked in Heers, Jacques, *Christophe Columb* (Paris: Hachette Publishers, 1981).

SINCE PREDATOR CAME
A Survey of Native North America
Since 1492

History, history! We fools, what do we know or care? History begins for us with murder and enslavement, not with discovery. No, we are not Indians, but we are men of their world. The blood means nothing; the spirit, the ghost of the land moves in the blood, moves the blood. It is we who ran to the shore naked, we who cried "Heavenly Man!" These are the inhabitants of our souls, our murdered souls that lie...agh.

—William Carlos Williams

On October 12, 1492, the day Christopher Columbus first washed up on a Caribbean beach, North America was long-since endowed with an abundant and exceedingly complex cluster of civilizations. Having continuously occupied the continent for at least 50,000 years, the native inhabitants evidenced a total population of perhaps 15 million, cities as large as the 40,000-resident urban center at Cahokia (in present-day Illinois), highly advanced conceptions of architecture and engineering, spiritual traditions embodying equivalents to modern ecoscience, refined knowledge of pharmacology and holistic medicine, and highly sophisticated systems of governance, trade, and diplomacy.[1] The traditional economies of the continent were primarily agricultural, based in environmentally sound farming procedures which originated well over half the vegetal foodstuffs now consumed by peoples the world over.[2] By and large, the indigenous societies demonstrating such attainments were organized along extremely egalitarian lines, with real property held collectively, and matrifocality a normative standard.[3] War, at least in the Euro-derived sense in which the term is understood today, was virtually unknown.[4]

The "Columbian Encounter," of course, unleashed a predatory, five-century-long cycle of European conquest, genocide, and colonization in the "New World," a process which changed the face of Native America beyond all recognition. Indeed, over the first decade of Spanish presence in the Caribbean, the period in which Columbus himself served as governor, the mold was set for all that would follow. By 1496, the policies of slavery (*encomiendo*) and wanton slaughter implemented by the "Great Discoverer" had, in combination with the introduction of Old World pathogens against which they had no immunity, reduced the native Taino population of just one island, Española (presently the Dominican Republic and Haiti), from as many as eight million to fewer than three million. Six years later, the Tainos had been diminished to fewer than 100,000, and, in 1542, only 200 could be found by Spanish census-takers.[5] Thereafter, the "Indians" of Española were declared extinct, along with the remainder of the indigenous peoples of the Caribbean Basin, an overall body which had numbered upwards of 14 million only a generation before.[6]

In North America, a similar dynamic was set in motion by the 1513 expedition of Ponce de Léon into Florida. The resulting smallpox pandemic spanned the continent, and before it had run its course in 1524, it had destroyed about three-quarters of all indigenous people north of the Río Grande. This was only the beginning. Between 1520 and 1890, no fewer than 41 smallpox epidemics and pandemics were induced among North American Indians. To this must be added dozens of lethal outbreaks of measles, whooping cough, tuberculosis, bubonic plague, typhus, cholera, typhoid, diphtheria, scarlet fever, pleurisy, mumps, venereal disease, and the common cold.[7] The corresponding attrition of native population by disease has usually been treated as a tragic but wholly inadvertent and unintended by-product of contact between Indians and Europeans. Such was certainly not the case in all instances, however, as is attested to by the fact that the so-called "King Philip's War" of 1675-76, fought between the Wampanoag and Narragansett nations and English colonists, resulted largely from the Indians' belief that the latter had deliberately inculcated smallpox among them.[8]

> That such perceptions of British tactics and intentions were hardly far-fetched is amply borne out by written orders issuing from Lord Jeffrey Amherst in 1763, instructing a subordinate, Colonel Henry Bouquet, to infect the members of Pontiac's Algonquain confederacy "by means of [smallpox contaminated] blankets as well as...every other means to extirpate this execrable race." A few days later, it was reported to Amherst that, "[W]e gave them two blankets and a handkerchief out of the smallpox hospital. I hope it will have the desired effect." It did. At

a minimum, 100,000 Indians died in the epidemic brought on by Amherst's resort to biological warfare.[9] In a similar instance, occurring in 1836, the U.S. Army knowingly distributed smallpox-laden blankets among the Missouri River Mandans; the resulting pandemic claimed as many as a quarter-million native lives.[10]

Beginning in the early 17th century, with establishment of England's Plymouth and Virginia colonies, and the Dutch toehold at New Amsterdam, the eradication of North America's indigenous population also assumed much cruder forms. A classic example occurred on the night of May 26, 1637, when the British surrounded the Pequot town of Mystic (Connecticut), set it ablaze, and then slaughtered some 800 fleeing men, women, and children, hacking them to pieces with axes and swords.[11] Such "incidents" occurred with ever-greater frequency throughout most of the 18th century, a period which found Britain and France engaged in the "French and Indian Wars," a protracted series of struggles in North America to determine which country would wield ultimate hegemony over the continent. While the outcome of these contests eventually proved all but irrelevant to the European colonial powers, given the subsequent revolt and decolonization of the initial 13 U.S. states, the nature of the fighting created a context in which indigenous nations were increasingly compelled to battle one another to the death. The reduction of indigenous population was thereby accelerated dramatically.[12]

Enter The United States

For its part, the fledgling United States embarked almost immediately upon a course of territorial acquisition far more ambitious than any exhibited by its Euro-colonial precursors. Although it renounced rights of conquest and pledged to conduct its affairs with Indians in "utmost good faith" via the 1789 Northwest Ordinance, the United States comported itself otherwise from the outset.[13] From 1810-1814, a sequence of extremely brutal military campaigns was conducted against the followers of the Shawnee leader Tecumseh in the Ohio River Valley, and against the Creek Confederacy further south.[14] With native military capacity east of the Mississippi thus eliminated, the government launched, during the 1820s and '30s, a policy of forced relocation of entire indigenous nations to points west of that river, "clearing" the eastern United States more or less *in toto* for repopulation by white "settlers."[15] Attrition among the affected populations was quite severe; more than half of all Cherokees, for example, died along the 1,500-mile "Trail of Tears" over which they were marched at bayonet-point.[16] This federal "removal policy" was to find echoes, of course, in the articulation of *"lebensraumpolitik"* by Adolf Hitler a century later.[17]

To cast a veneer of legality over his government's conduct, Chief Justice of the Supreme Court John Marshall penned a series of high court opinions during the 1820s and '30s, based in large part upon the medieval Doctrine of Discovery. He remained on firm juridical ground long enough to contend that the doctrine imparted a right to the United States to acquire Indian territory by treaty, a matter which led to ratification of at least 371 such nation-to-nation agreements over the next four decades. In a bizarre departure from established principles of international law, however, Marshall also argued that the United States possessed an inherently "higher" sovereignty than the nations with which it was treating: Indians held no right *not* to sell their land to the United States, in his view, at whatever price the United States cared to offer. Within this formulation, *any* resistance by "the savages" to the taking of their territories could thus be cast as an "act of war" theoretically "justifying" a U.S. "response" predicated in armed force.[18] By 1903 the "Marshall Doctrine" had evolved—and the indigenous ability to offer physical resistance had been sufficiently crushed—to the point that the Supreme Court was confident in asserting an "intrinsic" federal "plenary" (full) power over all Indians within its borders, releasing the United States from any treaty obligations it found inconvenient while leaving the land title it purported to have gained through the various treaty instruments intact. In conjunction with this novel notion of international jurisprudence, the high court simultaneously expressed the view that the government enjoyed "natural" and permanent "trust" prerogatives over all residual native property.[19]

Meanwhile, having consolidated its grip on the eastern portion of its claimed territoriality during the 1840s—and having militarily seized "rights" to the northern half of Mexico as well—the United

States proclaimed itself to be imbued with a "Manifest Destiny" to expand westward to the Pacific.[20] There being essentially no land available within this conception for Indian use and occupancy, a rhetoric of outright extermination was quickly adopted both by federal policymakers and by a sizable segment of the public at large.[21] These sentiments led unerringly to a lengthy chain of large-scale massacres of Indians in the Great Plains and Basin regions by U.S. troops. Among the worst were the slaughters perpetrated at the Blue River (Nebraska, 1854), Bear River (Idaho, 1863), Sand Creek (Colorado, 1864), Washita River (Oklahoma, 1868), Sappa Creek (Kansas, 1875), Camp Robinson (Nebraska, 1878), and Wounded Knee (South Dakota, 1890).[22] In 1894, the U.S. Census Bureau observed that the United States had waged "more than 40" separate wars against native people in barely a century, inflicting some number of fatalities "very much greater" than its minimum estimate of 30,000 in the process.[23]

The indigenous death toll generated by "private actions" during U.S. continental expansion was also, the Census Bureau admitted, "quite substantial." In all probability, it was far higher than that stemming from formal military involvement, given that the native population of the state of California alone was reduced from approximately 300,000 in 1800 to fewer than 20,000 in 1890, "chiefly [because of] the cruelties and wholesale massacres perpetrated by...miners and the early settlers."[24] In Texas, to take another prominent example, a bounty was placed upon the scalp of any Indian brought to a government office, no questions asked: "The facts of history are plain. Most Texas Indians [once the most diverse population in North America] were exterminated or brought to the brink of extinction by [Euroamerican civilians] who often had no more regard for the life of an Indian than they had for that of a dog, sometimes less." [25] The story in other sectors of the western United States, while sometimes less spectacular, reveals very much the same pattern. As the indigenous population was liquidated—along with the buffalo and other animal species consciously exterminated in order to deny Indians a "commissary" once their agricultural economies had been obliterated by the invaders—white settlers replaced them on the vast bulk of their land.[26]

By 1890, fewer than 250,000 Indians remained alive within the United States, a degree of decimation extending into the upper ninetieth percentile.[27] The survivors were lodged on a patchwork of "reservations" even then being dismantled through application of what was called the "General Allotment Act."[28] Under provision of this statute, effected in 1887, a formal eugenics code was utilized to define who was (and who was not) "Indian" by U.S. "standards."[29] Those who could, or were willing to, prove to federal satisfaction that they were "of one-half or more degree of Indian blood," and to accept U.S. citizenship into the bargain, received a deed to an individual land parcel, typically of 160 acres or less.[30] Once each person with sufficient "blood quantum" had received his or her allotment of land, the remaining reservation land was declared "surplus" and opened up to non-Indian homesteading, corporate acquisition, or conversion into national parks and forests. Through this mechanism, the best 100 million acres of the reserved native land base were stripped away by 1930, the Indians ever more concentrated within the 50 million arid or semi-arid acres—about 2.5 percent of their original holdings—left to them.[31] The model was later borrowed by the apartheid government of South Africa in developing its "racial homeland" system of territorial apportionment.[32]

The Contemporary Era

Culmination of this trajectory in U.S. colonial administration of Indian Country occurred during the mid-1950s, with the enactment of a series of "termination" statutes by which the federal government unilaterally dissolved more than a hundred indigenous nations and their reservation areas.[33] Concomitantly, legislation was effected to "encourage" the relocation of large numbers of Indians from the remaining reservations to selected urban centers, a strategy designed to preclude reemergence of social cohesion within most land-based native communities.[34] Although it was suspended in the late 1970s, the federal relocation program had by 1990 fostered a native diaspora which found more than half of all indigenous people in the United States, a total of about 880,000 persons, scattered in the ghettos of cities.[35]

The government's termination and relocation policies coupled quite well with other techniques employed by the Bureau of Indian Affairs (BIA) to undermine the sociocultural integrity of native existence. Salient in this regard is a generations-long program of "blind adoptions" in which Indian babies are placed for adoption with non-Indian families, their birth records permanently sealed so they can never know their true heritage.[36] Similarly, beginning in the 1870s and continuing into the present moment, the BIA administered a system of boarding schools to which indigenous children were sent, often for a decade or more without being allowed to return home, speak their native languages, practice their religions, or otherwise manifest their identity as Indians.[37] Encompassed under the benign-sounding rubric of "assimilation," both youth-oriented undertakings are blatant violations of the provision of the 1948 Convention on Punishment and Prevention of the Crime of Genocide which makes it a crime against humanity for a government to engage in the systematic forced transfer of the children of a targeted racial or ethnic group to another group.[38] Contemporary violation of another provision of the Genocide Convention may be found in a program of involuntary sterilization imposed by the BIA's "Indian Health Service" upon approximately 40 percent of the female population of childbearing age during the 1970s.[39]

Ironically, the final and complete dissolution of Native North America seems to have been averted mainly by the fact that the barren areas left to native habitation after allotment turned out to be inordinately rich in mineral resources. Current estimates suggest that about two-thirds of all U.S. domestic uranium deposits, a quarter of the readily accessible low sulphur coal, a fifth of the oil and natural gas, and substantial deposits of copper and other ores lie within reservation boundaries.[40] By 1920 government planners discovered certain advantages in terms of their ability to control the pace and nature of resource extraction, royalty rates, and the like, through exercise of federal "trust responsibilities" over indigenous assets.[41] The same principle was seen to pertain to manipulations of water policy throughout the arid West.[42] Such options being unavailable to them should Indian Country as a whole be converted into private property under state and local jurisdiction, it was found to be in the United States's interest that the majority of reservations be maintained as discrete internal colonies.

To this end, the Indian Reorganization Act (IRA) was passed in 1934 to create a federally designed regulatory or "governing" body on most reservations.[43] Although the IRA boards were and are composed exclusively of native people, their authority stems from—and thus their primary allegiance adheres to—the United States rather than their ostensible indigenous constituents; their major function during the half-century of their existence has been to sow confusion, providing an illusion of Indian consent to the systematic Euroamerican expropriation of native resources, and to vociferously denounce any Indian audacious enough to object to the theft. They serve, in effect, as American Indian Movement (AIM) leader Russell Means once put it, as "Vichy Indians."[44] For this reason, their position in Indian Country has been steadily reinforced over the years by passage of additional federal statutes, among them the Indian Civil Rights Act of 1968 and the Indian "Self-Determination" and Educational Assistance Act of 1975.[45]

The results have embodied themselves in situations like the "Hopi-Navajo Land Dispute" in northeastern Arizona, a scenario in which the United States has been able to utilize the carefully tailored pronouncements of two of its puppet governments to create the impression of an inter-Indian conflict requiring federal intervention/resolution as a means of "avoiding bloodshed." Behind this humanitarian facade resides a U.S. governmental/corporate desire to bring about the compulsory relocation of more than 10,000 traditional Navajos from the contested area, a matter which will serve to clear the way to the real objective: the strip mining of more than 20 billion tons of high-quality coal.[46] Comparable circumstances have prevailed with regard to the conversion of the Western Shoshone homeland (Newe Segobia) in Nevada into a U.S. nuclear weapons testing area, removal of more than 90 percent of the 1868 Fort Laramie Treaty Territory from Lakota control, upcoming implementation of the "Alaska Native Claims Settlement Act," and elsewhere.[47]

Coherent efforts by native people to oppose such manipulations—AIM's resistance during the mid-70s to IRA/government collaboration in a plan to transfer title over one-eighth of the Pine Ridge Reservation to the National Forest Service, for example—have been put down by application of outright counterinsurgency warfare techniques (such as the use of death squads) similar in many respects to the methods employed by U.S. agencies in Asia, Africa, and Latin America.[48] During the Pine Ridge "reign of terror" alone, the body count came to about 70 fatalities and nearly 350 serious physical assaults of AIM members and supporters over a bare three-year period.[49] This was correlated to an outright military-style occupation of the reservation by federal forces, a comprehensive government propaganda campaign directed against the "insurgents," and an extensive series of show trials, such as those of the so-called "Wounded Knee Leadership" during 1974-75, and of the "RESMURS Defendants" (including AIM security leader Leonard Peltier) in 1976-77.[50]

For grassroots Indian people, the broader human costs of ongoing U.S. domination are abundantly clear. The 1.6 million American Indians within the United States remain, nominally at least, the largest per capita land owners in North America.[51] Given the extent of resources within their land base, Indians should by logical extension comprise the wealthiest "ethnic group" in North American society. Instead, according to the federal government's own statistics, they are the poorest, demonstrating far and away the lowest annual and lifetime incomes, the highest rate of unemployment, lowest rate of pay when employed, and lowest level of educational attainment of any North American population aggregate. Correspondingly, they suffer, by decisive margins, the greatest incidence of malnutrition and diabetes, death by exposure, tuberculosis, infant mortality, plague disease, and similar maladies.[52] These conditions, in combination with the general disempowerment which spawns them, breed an unremitting sense of rage, frustration, and despair, which is reflected by spiraling rates of domestic and other forms of intragroup violence, alcoholism and resulting death by accident or fetal alcohol syndrome.[53] Consequently, the average life expectancy of a reservation-based Native American male in 1980 was a mere 44.6 years, that of his female counterpart fewer than three years longer.[54] Such a statistical portrait is obviously more indicative of a Third World environment than that expected of people living within one of the world's most advanced industrial states.

Moving Forward

Plainly, all official polemics to the contrary notwithstanding, the agony induced by 500 years of European/Euroamerican predation in North America is anything but abated at this juncture. For the indigenous people of the continent it has become obvious that there are no real alternatives but either to renew their commitment to struggle for survival or to finally pass into the realm of extinction which has been relentlessly projected for them since the predator's arrival on their shores. For everyone else, the situation is rapidly becoming—or in some cases has already become—much the same. The time has arrived when a choice *must* be made: non-Indians, in both the New World and the Old, must decide whether they wish to be a willing part of the final gnawing on the bones of their native victims, or whether they are at last prepared to join hands with Native North America, ending the wanton consumption of indigenous lands and lives which has marked the nature of our relationship to date.

The sort of alliance at issue no longer represents, as it did in the past, an exercise in altruism for non-Indians. Anti-imperialism, opposition to racism, colonialism, and genocide, while worthy enough stances in and of themselves, are no longer the fundamental issues at hand. Ultimately, the same system of predatory goals and values which has so busily and mercilessly consumed the people of the land these past five centuries has increasingly set about consuming the land itself. Not only indigenous peoples, but also the land to which they are irrevocably linked, is now dying. When the land itself dies, it is a certainty that *no* humans can survive. The struggle which confronts us—*all* of us—is thus a struggle to save our collective habitat, to maintain it as a "survivable" environment, not only for ourselves, but also for the generations to come. Self-evidently, this cannot be approached either from the posture of the predator or from any other position which allows the predator to continue with business as usual.

At long last, we have arrived at the point where there is a tangible, even overriding, confluence of interests between natives and non-natives.

The crux of the matter rests, not merely in resistance to the predatory nature of the present Eurocentric status quo, but in conceiving viable sociocultural alternatives. Here, the bodies of indigenous knowledge evidenced in the context of Native North America at the point of the European invasion—large-scale societies which had perfected ways of organizing themselves into psychologically fulfilling wholes, experiencing very high standards of material life, and *still* maintaining environmental harmony—shine like a beacon in the night. The information required to recreate this reality is still in place in many indigenous cultures. The liberation of significant sectors of Native America stands to allow this knowledge to once again be actualized in the "real world," not to recreate indigenous societies as they once were, but to recreate themselves as they *can be* in the future. Therein lies the model—the laboratory, if you will—from which a genuinely liberatory and sustainable alternative can be cast for all humanity. In a very real sense, then, the fate of Native North America signifies the fate of the planet. It follows that it is incumbent upon every conscious human—red, white, black, brown, or yellow, old or young, male or female—to do whatever is within their power to ensure that the next half-millennium heralds an antithesis to the last.

Notes

1. For a good survey of the data indicating native occupancy in North America for fifty millennia or more, see Goodman, Jeffrey, *American Genesis: The American Indian and the Origins of Modern Man* (New York: Summit Books, 1981). On population size, see Dobyns, Henry F., *Their Numbers Become Thinned: Native American Population Dynamics in Eastern North America* (Knoxville: University of Tennessee Press, 1983). On Cahokia, see Fowler, Melin T., "A Pre-Columbian Urban Center on the Mississippi," *Scientific American*, no. 233 (1975): pp. 92-101. On architecture and engineering, see Nabokov, Peter, and Robert Easton, *Native American Architecture* (London/New York: Oxford University Press, 1988). On medicine and pharmacology, see Vogel, Virgil, *American Indian Medicine* (Norman: University of Oklahoma Press, 1975). On governance and diplomacy, see, for example, Brandon, William, *Old Worlds for New: Reports from the New World and their Effect on the Development of Social Thought in Europe, 1500-1800* (Athens: Ohio University Press, 1986).

2. According to even a hostile source like Hurt, R. Douglas, *Indian Agriculture in America: Prehistory to the Present* (Lawrence: University Press of Kansas, 1987),

about two-thirds of the dietary requirements of Native North Americans were met by "horticultural" rather than "hunting and gathering" means. As to the variety of vegetal foodstuffs developed by precontact indigenous people in this hemisphere and then adopted elsewhere, see Weatherford, Jack, *Indian Givers: How the Indians of the Americas Transformed the World* (New York: Crown Publishers, 1988).

3. A good, if somewhat overstated, examination of Native North American sexuality and gender relations may be found in Gunn Allen, Paula, *The Sacred Hoop: Recovering the Feminine in American Indian Traditions* (Boston, MA: Beacon Press, 1986).

4. See Holm, Tom, "Patriots and Pawns: State Use of American Indians in the Military and the Process of Nativization in the United States," in *The State of Native America: Colonization, Genocide and Resistance*, ed. M. Annette Jaimes (Boston, MA: South End Press, 1992).

5. See Sale, Kirkpatrick, *The Conquest of Paradise: Christopher Columbus and the Columbian Legacy* (New York: Alfred A. Knopf Publishers, 1990).

6. *Ibid.*, citing Borah, Woodrow W., and F. Cook Sherburne.

7. Dobyns, *op. cit.*, pp. 15-23.

8. See Leach, Douglas Edward, *Flintlocks and Tomahawks: New England in King Philip's War* (New York: W.W. Norton Publishers, 1958).

9. Stearn, E. Wagner, and Allen E. Stearn, *The Effects of Smallpox on the Destiny of the Amerindian* (Boston, MA: Bruce Humphries, 1945), pp. 44-45; Ashburn, P. M., *The Ranks of Death* (New York: Coward, 1947).

10. The dispensing of smallpox-infected blankets at Fort Clark is covered in Thornton, Russell, *American Indian Holocaust and Survival: A Population History Since 1492* (Norman: University of Oklahoma Press, 1987), pp. 94-96.

11. The estimate of Pequot casualties derives from an extremely conservative source. See Utley, Robert M., and Wilcomb E. Washburn, *Indian Wars* (Boston, MA: Houghton-Mifflin Co., 1977), p. 42.

12. An excellent analysis of these dynamics can be found in Jennings, Francis, *The Invasion of America: Indians, Colonialism, and the Cant of Conquest* (New York: W.W. Norton and Co., 1976).

13. 1 Stat. 50; for background, see Abernathy, Thomas Perkins, *Western Lands and the American Revolution* (New York: Russell and Russell, 1959).

14. On Tecumseh, see Sugden, John, *Tecumseh's Last Stand* (Norman: University of Oklahoma Press, 1985). On the Red Sticks, see Martin, Joel W., *Sacred Revolt: The Muskogees' Struggle for a New World* (Boston, MA: Beacon Press, 1991).

15. The policy was implemented under provision of the Indian Removal Act (ch. 148, 4 *Stat.* 411), passed on May 28, 1830. For details, see Foreman, Grant, *Indian Removal: The Immigration of the Five Civilized Tribes* (Norman: University of Oklahoma Press, 1953).

16. See Thornton, Russell, "Cherokee Population Losses During the Trail of Tears: A New Perspective and a New Estimate," *Ethnohistory*, no. 31 (1984): pp. 289-300.

17. The *lebensraum* concept is laid out in Hitler, Adolf, *Mein Kampf* (Verlag FRZ, Eher Nachf, G.M.B.H., 1925). Also see Cecil, Robert, *The Myth of the Master Race: Alfred Rosenberg and Nazi Ideology* (New York: Dodd, Mead & Co., 1972).

18. The sequences of cases consists of *Johnson v. McIntosh* (21 U.S. 98 [Wheat.] 543 [1823]); *Cherokee Nation v. Georgia* (30 U.S. [5 Pet.] 1 [1831]); and *Worcester v. Georgia* (31 U.S. [6 Pet.] 551 [1832]).

19. *Lonewolf v. Hitchcock* (187 U.S. 553 [1903]). A prelude to articulation of this juridical absurdity may be found in *U.S. v. Kagama* (118 U.S. 375 [1886]).

20. For a brilliant elaboration of this theme, see Horsman, Reginald, *Race and Manifest Destiny: The Origins of Racial Anglo-Saxonism* (Cambridge, MA: Harvard University Press, 1981).

21. See, for example, Svaldi, David, *Sand Creek and the Rhetoric of Extermination: A Case-Study in Indian-White Relations* (Washington, D.C.: University Press of America, 1989).

22. On Bear River, see Madsen, Brigham D., *The Shoshone Frontier and the Bear River Massacre* (Salt Lake City: University of Utah Press, 1985). On Sand Creek and the Washita, see Hoig, Stan, *The Sand Creek Massacre* (Norman: University of Oklahoma Press, 1961) and *The Battle of the Washita: The Sheridan-Custer Indian Campaign of 1867-69* (Lincoln: University of Nebraska Press, 1976). On Blue River, see Sandoz, Mari, *Crazy Horse: The Strange Man of the Oglalas* (Lincoln: University of Nebraska Press, 1961), pp. 63-85; on Sappa Creek and Camp Robinson, see her *Cheyenne Autumn* (New York: Avon Books, 1964). For an excellent overview of the sort of warfare waged against the indigenous people of the plains region, see Andrist, Ralph, *The Long Death: The Last Days of the Plains Indians* (New York: Collier Books, 1964).

23. U.S. Bureau of the Census, *Report on Indians Taxed and Indians Not Taxed in the United States (except Alaska) at the Eleventh U.S. Census: 1890* (Washington, D.C.: U.S. Government Printing Office, 1894), pp. 637-38.

24. Mooney, James M., "Population," in *Handbook of the Indians North of Mexico*, ed. Frederick W. Dodge, Bureau of American Ethnology, vol. 2, bulletin no. 30 (Washington, D.C.: Smithsonian Institution, 1910), pp. 286-87.

25. Newcome, W. W., Jr., *The Indians of Texas* (Austin: University of Texas Press, 1961), p. 334.

26. On "eradication" of the North American bison, see Haines, Francis, *The Buffalo* (New York: Thomas Y. Crowell, 1970).

27. U.S. Bureau of the Census, *Abstract of the Eleventh Census: 1890* (Washington, D.C.: U.S. Government Printing Office, 1896).

28. Ch. 119, 24 *Stat.* 388, now codified as amended at 25 U.S.C. § 331 *et seq.* The General Allotment Act is also known as the "Dawes Act" or "Dawes Severalty Act" after its sponsor, Massachusetts Senator Henry M. Dawes.

29. On this aspect, see Churchill, Ward, "Nobody's Pet Poodle: Jimmie Durham, An Artist for Native America," in this book.

30. As of 1924, all Native Americans who had not been made U.S. citizens through the allotment process were unilaterally declared to be such—*en mass, and whether they wanted to be or not*—through provision of the Indian Citizenship Act (ch. 233, 43 *Stat.* 25).

31. See McDonnell, Janet A., *The Dispossession of the American Indian, 1887-1934* (Bloomington/Indianapolis: Indiana University Press, 1991).

32. On these linkages, see Frederickson, George M., *White Supremacy: A Comparative Study in American and South African History* (London/New York: Oxford University Press, 1981).

33. The "Act" is actually House Concurrent Resolution 108, pronounced on August 1, 1953, which articulated a federal policy of unilaterally dissolving specific native nations. What followed was the "termination"—suspension of federal services to and recognition of the existence of—the Menominee on June 17, 1954 (ch. 303, 68 *Stat.* 250); the Klamath on August 13, 1954 (ch. 732, 68 *Stat.* 718, codified at 25 U.S.C. § 564 *et seq.*); the "Tribes of Western Oregon" on August 13, 1954 (ch. 733, 68 *Stat.* 724, codified at 25 U.S.C. § 691 *et seq.*); and so on. In all, 109 native nations, or elements of native nations, were terminated by congressional action during the late 1950s. A handful were "restored" to federal recognition during the 1970s.

34. The "Relocation Act" (PL 959) was passed in 1956 to provide funding to establish "job training centers" for American Indians in various urban centers, and to finance the relocation of individual Indians and Indian families to these locales. It was coupled to a denial of funds for similar programs and economic development on the reservations themselves. Those who availed themselves of the "opportunity" for jobs, etc. represented by the federal relocation programs were usually required to sign agreements that they would not return to their respective reservations to live. For further information, see Fixico, Donald L., *Termination and Relocation: Federal Indian Policy, 1945-1960* (Albuquerque: University of New Mexico Press, 1986).

35. U.S. Bureau of the Census, *1990 Census of the Population, Preliminary Report* (Washington, D.C.: U.S. Government Printing Office, 1991).

36. See Walker, Tillie Blackbear, "American Indian Children: Foster Care and Adoptions," in *Conference on Educational and Occupational Needs of American Indian Women, October 1976*, U.S. Department of Education, Office of Educational Research and Development, National Institute of Education (Washington, D.C.: U.S. Government Printing Office, 1980), pp. 185-210.

37. For a comprehensive overview of this process, see Noriega, Jorgé, "American Indian Education in the U.S.: Indoctrination for Subordination to Colonialism," in *The State of Native America, op. cit.*

38. For the complete text of the 1948 Genocide Convention, see Brownlie, Ian, ed., *Basic Documents on Human Rights* (London/New York: Oxford University Press, 1971).

39. See Dillingham, Brint, "Indian Women and IHS Sterilization Practices," *American Indian Journal*, vol. 3, no. 1 (January 1977): pp. 27-28. Also see Larson, Janet, "And Then There Were None: IHS Sterilization Practice," *Christian Century*, no. 94 (January 26, 1976). Also see Wagner, Bill, "Lo, the Poor and Sterilized Indian," *America*, no. 136 (January 29, 1977).

40. On resource distribution, see generally, Garrity, Michael, "The U.S. Colonial Empire is as Close as the Nearest Reservation," in *Trilateralism: The Trilateral Commission and Elite Planning for World Government*, ed. Holly Sklar (Boston, MA: South End Press, 1980), pp. 238-68. Also see Jorgenson, Joseph, ed., *Native Americans and Energy Development II* (Cambridge, MA: Anthropology Resource Center/Seventh Generation Fund, 1984).

41. The prototype for this policy emerged with the BIA's formation of the "Navajo Grand Council" to approve drilling leases at the behest of Standard Oil in 1923. See Kelly, Laurence C., *The Navajo Indians and Federal Indian Policy, 1900-1935* (Tucson: University of Arizona Press, 1968).

42. See Guerrero, Marianna, "American Indian Water Rights: The Blood of Life in Native North America," in *The State of Native America, op. cit.* Also see McCool, Daniel, *Command of the Waters: Iron Triangles, Federal Water Development, and Indian Water* (Berkeley: University of California Press, 1987).

43. The IRA (ch. 576, 48 *Stat.* 948, now codified at 25 U.S.C. §§ 461-279) is also known as the "Wheeler-Howard Act" after its Senate and House sponsors.

44. Quoted in Robbins, Rebecca, "Self-Determination and Subordination: The Past, Present and Future of American Indian Governance," in *The State of Native America, op. cit.* On propaganda functions, see Churchill, Ward, "'Renegades, Terrorists and Revolutionaries': The U.S. Government's Propaganda War Against the American Indian Movement," *Propaganda Review,* no. 4 (spring 1989).

45. The Indian Civil Rights Act, PL 90-284 (82 *Stat.* 77, codified in part at 25 U.S.C. § 1301 *et seq.*) locked indigenous governments—as a "third level" of the federal government—into U.S.constitutional requirements. The "self-determination" aspect of the 1975 Act (PL 93-638; 88 *Stat.* 2203, codified at 25 U.S.C. § 450a and elsewhere in titles 25, 42 and 50, U.S.C.A.)—dubbed the "Self-Administration Act" by Russell Means—provides for a greater degree of Indian employment within the various federal programs used to subordinate native people.

46. On the supposed dispute between the Hopis and Navajos, and the federal-corporate role in fostering it, see Kammer, Jerry, *The Second Long Walk: The Navajo-Hopi Land Dispute* (Albuquerque: University of New Mexico Press, 1980). Also see Parlow, Anita, *Cry, Sacred Ground: Big Mountain, USA* (Washington, D.C.: Christic Institute, 1988).

47. On Western Shoshone, see Morris, Glenn T., "The Battle for Newe Segobia: The Western Shoshone Land Rights Struggle," in *Critical Issues in Native North America, Vol. II,* ed. Ward Churchill (Copenhagen: IWGIA Document 68, 1991), pp. 86-98. On the Black Hills, see the special issue of *Wicazo Sa Review,* vol. IV, no. 1 (spring 1988). On Alaska, see Berry, M.C., *The Alaska Pipeline: The Politics of Oil and Native Land Claims* (Bloomington/Indianapolis: Indiana University Press, 1975).

48. The best overview—including the uranium connection—may be found in Matthiessen, Peter, *In the Spirit of Crazy Horse* (New York: Viking Press, [second edition] 1991). Also see Weyler, Rex, *Blood of the Land: The U.S. Government and Corporate War Against the American Indian Movement* (Philadelphia: New Society, [second edition] 1992).

49. The term "reign of terror" accrues from an official finding by the U.S. Commission on Civil Rights, *Report of an Investigation: Oglala Sioux Tribe, General Election, 1974* (Denver, CO: Rocky Mountain Regional Office, 1974). For statistical comparison to Third World contexts, see Johansen, Bruce, and Roberto Maestas, *Wasi'chu: The Continuing Indian Wars* (New York: Monthly Review Press, 1978).

50. For detailed analysis, see Churchill, Ward, and Jim Vander Wall, *Agents of Repression: The FBI's Secret Wars Against the Black Panther Party and the American Indian Movement* (Boston, MA: South End Press, 1988). Official use of the term "insurgents"—as opposed to "extremists," or even "terrorists"—vis-à-vis AIM is documented via FBI memoranda in Churchill, Ward, and Jim Vander Wall, *The COINTELPRO Papers: Documents from the FBI's Secret Wars Against Dissent in the United States* (Boston, MA: South End Press, 1990). On the RESMURS (Reservation

Murders) trials, see Messerschmidt, Jim, *The Trial of Leonard Peltier* (Boston, MA: South End Press, 1983).

51. This is based against the approximately 50 million acres still designated as reservation land. It should be noted that the United States never acquired even a pretense of legal title via treaties and other "instruments of cession" to fully one-third of the area (about 750 million acres) encompassed by the 48 contiguous states. The larger acreage should be balanced against the fact that, while federal census data recognizes only about one and a half million Indians residing within the United States, the actual number may well be 10 times that; see Forbes, Jack D., "Undercounting Native Americans: The 1980 Census and the Manipulation of Racial Identity in the United States," *Wicazo Sa Review*, vol. VI, no. 1 (spring 1990).

52. U.S. Department of Health and Human Services, *Chart Series Book* (Washington, D.C.: Public Health Service, 1988 [HE20.9409.988]).

53. See Wood, Rosemary, "Health Problems Facing American Indian Women," in *Conference on Educational and Occupational Needs of American Indian Women, op. cit.* Also see Asetoyer, Charon, "Fetal Alcohol Syndrome—'Chemical Genocide'," in *Indigenous Women on the Move* (Copenhagen: IWGIA Document 66, 1990), pp. 87-92.

54. *Chart Series Book, op. cit.*

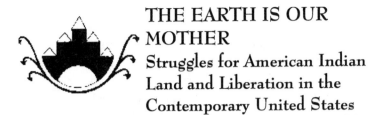

THE EARTH IS OUR MOTHER
Struggles for American Indian Land and Liberation in the Contemporary United States

The inhabitants of your country districts regard—wrongfully, it is true—Indians and forests as natural enemies which must be exterminated by fire and sword and brandy, in order that they may seize their territory. They regard themselves, and their posterity, as collateral heirs to all the magnificent portion of land which God has created from Cumberland and Ohio to the Pacific Ocean.

—Pierre Samuel Du Pont de Nemours,
letter to Thomas Jefferson, December 17, 1801

Of course our whole national history has been one of expansion...That the barbarians recede or are conquered, with the attendant fact that peace follows their retrogression or conquest, is due solely to the power of the mighty civilized races which have not lost their fighting instinct, and which by their expansion are gradually bringing peace into the red wastes where the barbarian peoples of the world hold sway.

—Theodore Roosevelt, *The Strenuous Life,* 1901

Since the inception of the American republic, and before, control of land and the resources within it has been the essential source of conflict between the Euroamerican settler population and indigenous nations. In effect, contentions over land usage and ownership have served to define the totality of U.S./Indian relationships from the first moment onward to the present day, shaping not only the historical flow of interactions between invader and invaded, but also the nature of ongoing domination of native people in areas such as governance and jurisdiction, identification, recognition, and education. The issue of a proprietary interest of non-Indians in the American Indian land base has also been and remains the fundament of popular (mis)conceptions of who and what Indians were and are, whether they continue to exist, and even whether they ever "really" existed. All indications are that these circumstances will continue to prevail over the foreseeable future.

The situation prefigured from the period of planning which went into Columbus' first voyage, which—according to the "Great Discoverer's" own journals—was never about discovery or scientific inquisitiveness as such, but always about seizing wealth belonging to others for his sponsors and himself.[1] But this is not to imply that Columbus enjoyed an entirely free hand. Contrary to contemporary orthodoxy, there were even then laws concerning how such wealth, especially land, might be legitimately acquired by mercenary adventurers like Columbus, and the various European Crowns which fielded them. Primary among these were the so-called "Doctrine of Discovery," and pursuant "Rights of Conquest." Such elements of the "Laws of Nations" are much misunderstood in North America today, largely as a result of their systematic misinterpretation over the past century by Eurocentric academics and the U.S. Supreme Court. In its actual formulation, however, the Discovery Doctrine never conveyed title to discoverers over any lands already occupied at the time of the discovery.[2]

> [The doctrine's] basic tenet—that the European nation which first "discovered" and settled lands previously unknown to Europeans thereby gained the right to acquire those lands from their inhabitants—became part of the early body of international law dealing with aboriginal peoples…[B]y the time Europeans settled in North America, it was well-established international law that natives had property rights which could not be lawfully denied by the discovering European nation…The right of discovery served mainly to regulate the relations between European nations. It did not limit the powers or rights of Indian nations in their homelands; its major limitation was to prohibit Indians from diplomatic dealings with all but the "discovering" European nation…Moreover, the right of discovery gave a European nation the right to extinguish Indian land title only when the Indians consented to it by treaty.[3]

Conquest rights were also quite restrictive, pertaining only to the results of "Just Wars," conflicts fought as the result of unprovoked Indian aggression against their supposed discoverers.[4] Hence, although the Laws of Nations were—as was certainly the case with Columbus—plainly broken from time to time:[5]

> As a matter of both legal principle and practicality, European nations dealt with Indian nations as they did other nations in the world. In

general, Indian lands were acquired by agreement, through the use of international diplomacy—specifically, through formal treaties of cession. Indian lands were seldom acquired by military conquest or fiat, and the practices of Spain, France, [England, Portugal] and the Netherlands did not differ in this regard.[6]

The reality of colonial North America was that indigenous nations tended to be militarily superior to their would be colonizers, or at least held the balance of military power between European states such as England and France.[7] The matter was of such concern in London that, in 1763, King George III—specifically to retain the allegiance of the powerful Haudenosaunee (Iroquois) and Muskogee (Creek) Confederacies *vis-à-vis* England's French rivals—issued a proclamation prohibiting acquisition of lands west of a line drawn along the Allegheny and Appalachian mountain chains (see Map I).[8] This, probably more than "taxation without representation," was a major contributing factor in sparking the extended decolonization struggle which resulted in the independence of the original 13 U.S. states.[9] George Washington, Thomas Jefferson, John Adams, James Madison, Anthony Wayne, and numerous others among the "Founding Fathers" all had considerable speculative investments in westerly Indian lands at the time the 1763 edict was handed down. The rank and file soldiers who fought in their "revolutionary" army arguably did so, not for abstract ideals of "freedom" and "equality," but because of promises made by their leaders that their services would be rewarded with grants of Indian land "in the West" after victory had been secured.[10]

U.S. Theory and Practice

As Vine Deloria, Jr., has observed, the United States emerged from its successful war against the British Crown (perhaps the most serious offense imaginable under prevailing law) as a pariah, an outlaw state which was considered utterly illegitimate by almost all other countries and therefore shunned by them, both politically and economically. Survival of the new nation was entirely dependent upon the ability of its initial government to change such perceptions and thereby end its isolation. Desperate to establish itself as a respectable entity, and lacking other alternatives with which to demonstrate its sense of international legality, the government was virtually com-

pelled to present the appearance of adhering to the strictest of protocols in its dealings with Indians.[11] Indeed, what the Continental
Congress needed more than anything at the time was for indigenous
nations—many of whose formal national integrity and legitimacy had
already been recognized by the European powers through treaties—to
convey a comparable recognition upon the fledgling United States by
entering into treaty relationships with *it*.

Consequently, both the Articles of Confederation and the Constitution of the United States contain clauses reserving interactions with
Indian peoples, as recognized "foreign powers," to the federal government. The United States also officially renounced, in the 1789
Northwest Ordinance and elsewhere, any aggressive intent *vis-à-vis*
these nations, especially with regard to their land base. As it was put
in the Ordinance:

> The utmost good faith shall always be observed towards the Indian; their
> land property shall never be taken from them without their consent; and
> in their property, rights, and liberty, they shall never be invaded or
> disturbed...but laws founded in justice and humanity shall from time
> to time be made, for wrongs being done to them, and for preserving
> peace and friendship with them.

Such lofty-sounding (and legally correct) rhetoric was, of course,
belied by the actualities of U.S. performance. As the first Chief Justice
of the Supreme Court, John Marshall, pointed out rather early on,
almost every white-held land title in "our whole country"—New
England, New York, New Jersey, Pennsylvania, Maryland, and parts
of the Carolinas—would have been clouded had the standards of
international law truly been applied.[12] More, title to the pre-revolu-
tionary acquisitions made west of the 1763 demarcation line by the
new North American politico-economic elite would have been negated, along with all the thousands of grants of land in that region
bestowed by Congress upon those who'd fought against the Crown.
Not coincidental to Marshall's concern in the matter was the fact that
he and his father had each received 10,000-acre grants of such land in
what is now West Virginia.[13] Obviously, a country which had been
founded largely on the basis of a lust to possess native lands was not
about to relinquish its pretensions to "ownership" of them, no matter
what the law said. Moreover, the balance of military power between

Indians and whites east of the Mississippi River began to change rapidly in favor of the latter during the post-revolutionary period. It was becoming technically possible for the United States to simply seize native lands at will.[14]

Still, the requirements of international diplomacy dictated that things *seem* otherwise. Marshall's singular task, then, was to forge a juridical doctrine which preserved the image of enlightened U.S. furtherance of accepted international legality in its relations with Indians, on the one hand, while accommodating a pattern of illegally aggressive federal expropriations of Indian land on the other. This he did in opinions rendered in a series of cases, beginning with *Fletcher v. Peck* (1810) and extending through *Johnson v. McIntosh* (1822) to *Cherokee Nation v. Georgia* (1831) and *Worcester v. Georgia* (1832).[15] By the end of this sequence of decisions, Marshall had completely inverted international law, custom, and convention, finding that the Doctrine of Discovery imparted "preeminent title" over North America to Europeans, the mantle of which implicitly passed to the United States when England quit-claimed its 13 dissident Atlantic colonies, mainly because Indian-held lands were effectively "vacant" when Europeans "found" them. The Chief Justice was forced to coin a whole new politico-legal expression—that of "domestic, dependent nations"—to encompass the unprecedented status, neither fish nor fowl, he needed native people to occupy.[16]

Within this convoluted and falsely premised reasoning, Indian nations were entitled to keep their land, but only so long as the intrinsically superior U.S. sovereignty agreed to their doing so. Given this, Indians could legally be construed as committing "aggression" whenever they resisted invasion by the United States, a matter which rendered literally any military action the United States chose to pursue against native people, no matter how unprovoked, a "Just War." With all this worked out, Marshall argued that the United States should nonetheless follow accepted European practice wherever possible, obtaining by formal treaty negotiations involving purchase and other considerations native "consent" to land cessions. This, he felt, would complete the veneer of "reason and moderation" attending international perceptions of federal expropriations of Indian land.

Ultimately, Marshall's position reduces to the notion that indigenous nations inherently possess sufficient sovereign rights "for purposes of treating" to hand over legal title to their territories, but never enough to retain any tract of land the United States wants as its own.

The carefully balanced logical contradictions imbedded in the "Marshall Doctrine," which allowed the United States to pursue one course of action with regard to Indian land while purporting to do the exact opposite, formed the theoretical basis for the entire statutory body of what is now called "Indian Law" in this country. Through a lengthy series of subsequent "interpretive" decisions—especially *Ex Parte Crow Dog* (1883), *U.S. v. Kagama* (1886), *Lonewolf v. Hitchcock* (1903), *Tee-Hit-Ton v. United States* (1955), and *Dann v. United States* (1985)—the Supreme Court extended Marshall's unfounded concept of native nations occupying a status of subordinate or "limited" sovereignty to include the idea that the United States enjoyed an inherent "plenary" (full and absolute) power over them in such crucial domains as governance and jurisdiction.[17] An aspect of this self-assigned power, articulated most clearly in *Lonewolf*, is that Congress has the prerogative to unilaterally abrogate aspects of U.S. treaties with Indian nations which it finds inconvenient or burdensome while continuing to hold the Indians to those provisions of the treaties by which they agreed to cede land.[18]

In these decisions, the high court also extended Marshall's baseless notion that self-sufficient indigenous nations were somehow "dependent" upon the United States to include the idea that the federal government thereby inherited a "trust responsibility" to Indians—actually *control* over their remaining property—in the "management of their affairs." While the "Trust Doctrine" has been used as a device to offset and soften the impressions created by exercise of the "Rights of Plenary Power" over indigenous people, it has in reality served as an instrument through which that power is administered:

> [U]nder United States law, the government has no legal trusteeship duties toward Indians except those it imposes upon itself. Stripped of its legal trappings, the Indian trust relationship becomes simply an assertion of unrestrained political power over Indians, power that may be exercised without Indian consent and without substantial legal restraint. An early twentieth century critic of the European colonial "trusteeship

for civilization" [in Africa and Asia], which is closely related to the American model, summed it up as "an impudent act of self assertion."[19]

While the U.S. judiciary was thus busily collaborating with the federal legislature in creating a body of "settled law" to serve as "the perfect instrument of empire," the federal government was also consistently engaged in creating the physical fact of that empire, all the while declaring itself in the most vociferous possible terms to be devoutly *anti*-imperial.[20] This was done by the conducting of at least 40 "Indian Wars"[21]—each of which was packaged as a campaign to defend U.S. citizens against the "depredations" of "savage natives" resisting the invasion of their homelands or comparable abuse—and negotiation of several hundred treaties and agreements with native nations.[22] Together with an assortment of unilateral executive and congressional actions, these wars and negotiated arrangements resulted by the early 20th century in Native America being constricted to about 2.5 percent of its original two-billion-acre land base within the 48 contiguous states of the union (see Map I).[23] And federal control over even this residue was virtually complete. Under such circumstances it is not difficult to see why Indians were viewed, often hopefully, as a "vanishing race" during this period.[24]

The Indian Claims Commission

At the turn of the century, Indian efforts to maintain what little real property was left to them, or to receive compensation for lands which were still being arbitrarily seized by the government, were ridiculed and largely dismissed out of hand.[25] Although native people were supposedly entitled to due process through U.S. law after a District Court in Nebraska recognized them as "persons" during the 1879 *Standing Bear v. Crook* case, the import was largely meaningless.[26] From 1881 to 1918, only 31 claims involving the illegal taking of native land were accepted by federal courts; 14 resulted in recoveries of land adding up to fewer than 10,000 acres.[27] In 1928, a government commission termed even this degree of judicial recourse to be "burdensome and unfair" to non-Indians.[28] Meanwhile, some 100 million acres—about two-thirds of all land native people had left at the conclusion of the period of their military resistance—were stripped

Map I

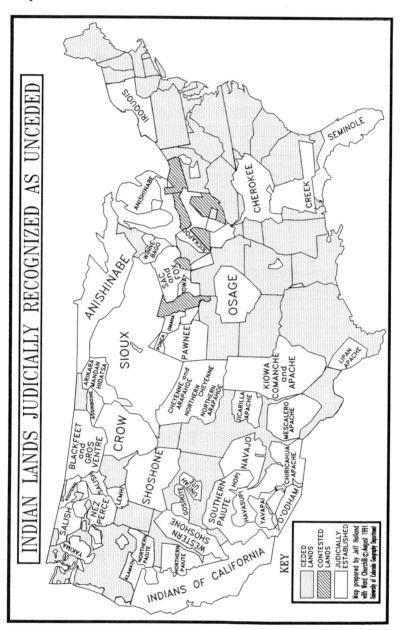

INDIAN LANDS JUDICIALLY RECOGNIZED AS UNCEDED

KEY

CEDED LANDS

CONTESTED LANDS

JUDICIALLY ESTABLISHED

Map prepared by Jeff Holland
with Ward Churchill © August 1991
University of Colorado Geography Department

away under provision of the 1887 General Allotment Act.[29] Power and possession, the rule of thugs, as it were, constituted all of the law in North America where Indian land rights were concerned.

Throughout most of the first half of the 20th century, the United States devoted itself to perfecting the mechanisms through which it would administer the tiny residual fragments of Indian Country for its own purposes. Nothing beyond the most *pro forma* gesture was made to address the fact that a considerable proportion of the land which was said to have passed from native ownership during the previous 150 years had been transferred in direct contravention of every known form of legality, including even the patently self-serving theories of U.S./Indian property relations developed by the United States itself. In 1924, federal courts accepted a mere five native land claims cases; in 1925, there were seven; in 1926, there were ten; in 1927, the total was fifteen. Most of these were dismissed in the early stages; none resulted in land recovery or payment of significant compensation.[30] Things might have remained locked firmly in this mode, were it not for geopolitical considerations emerging in the context of World War II.

As part of an overall strategy to advance U.S. interests in its planned postwar role as a hegemonic global power, the United States set out to project an enhanced image of itself as a "white knight" to the world's oppressed peoples. At least temporarily, until its own preferred style of neocolonialism could become entrenched as the dominant force in international affairs, the United States needed to be widely perceived as a beneficent and staunchly democratic alternative, not only to the "totalitarian impulse" represented by fascism and communism, but also to the classic colonial orders maintained in Third World locales by France, Great Britain, and other American allies. A part of this ploy resided within President Franklin D. Roosevelt's wartime opposition to reconstitution of the old European empires of the French and Dutch in Africa and Asia after the conclusion of hostilities (this trend was shortly reversed by Roosevelt's successor, Harry Truman, as part of his Cold War policy of prioritizing "containment of communism" above all else).[31]

The centerpiece of the entire international public relations gambit, however, rested in the U.S. assumption of the decisive role in formulating and implementing the "Nuremberg Doctrine" under which the surviving leadership of nazi Germany was accused, tried, convicted, and in most cases executed or imprisoned, for having engaged in "Crimes Against the Peace," "Aggressive War," and "Crimes Against Humanity."[32] The primary messages intended for popular consumption in the United States performance against the nazi defendants were that behavior such as that displayed by the nazis was considered criminal and intolerable by all "civilized peoples," and that the United States—first and foremost—would stand as guarantor that all governments would be held accountable to the standards of comportment established at Nuremberg. The nazi leaders were to stand forever as the symbol of the principle that international aggression would be punished, not rewarded (this is, of course, precisely the same line trotted out by George Bush in explaining the rather interesting U.S. behavior against Iraq during 1990-91).[33]

A primary flaw in this otherwise noble-seeming U.S. posture on international human rights law was (and is) that no less prominent a nazi than Adolf Hitler had long since made it quite clear he had based many of his more repugnant policies directly on earlier U.S. conduct against Native America. Hitler's conception of *lebensraumpolitik*—the idea that Germans were innately entitled by virtue of their racial and cultural superiority to land belonging to others, and that they were thus morally free to take it by aggressive military action—obviously had much in common with the 19th-century American sense of "Manifest Destiny."[34] Further, his notion of how to attain this "living room"—the "clearing of inferior racial stock" from its land base in order that vacated areas might be "settled by ethnic Germans"—followed closely from such U.S. precedents as the 1830 Indian Removal Act and subsequent military campaigns against the indigenous nations of the Great Plains, Great Basin, and Sonora Desert regions. Even the nazi tactic of concentrating "undesirables" prior to their forced "relocation or reduction" was drawn from actual U.S. examples, including internment of the Cherokees and other "Civilized Tribes" during the 1830s, before the devastatingly lethal Trail of Tears was forced upon them, and the comparable experience of the Navajo people at the Bosque Redondo during the period 1864-68.[35]

This potential embarrassment to U.S. pretensions abroad precipitated something of a sea of change in the country's approach to indigenous issues. Seeking to distance its own history from comparison to that of the Germans it was even then prosecuting—and thus to stand accused of conducting an exercise in mere "victor's justice" at Nuremberg—the federal government was for the first time prepared to admit openly that "unfortunate and sometimes tragic errors" had been made in the process of its continental expansion. Unlike nazi Germany, federal spokespersons intoned, the United States had never held aggressive territorial intentions, against Indians or anyone else; the Indian Wars notwithstanding, the United States had always bought, rather than conquered, the land it occupied. As proof of this thesis, it was announced that a formal mechanism was being created for purposes of "resolving any lingering issues" among Native Americans concerning the legitimacy of U.S. title to its territory.[36] The book, which had been closed on Indian land claims for a full generation and more, was suddenly opened again.

What was ultimately established, on August 13, 1946, was a quasi-judicial entity, dubbed the "Indian Claims Commission," of the sort long desired by those who had followed the wisdom of Chief Justice Marshall's enjoinder that appearances demanded that a veneer of legality, even one applied *post hoc*, be affixed to all U.S. expropriations of native territory. As early as 1910, Indian Commissioner Francis E. Leupp had suggested "a special court, or the addition of a branch to the present United States Court of Claims, to be charged with the adjudication of Indian claims exclusively."[37] He was followed by Assistant Commissioner Edgar B. Merritt, who recommended in 1913 that a special commission be empaneled to investigate the extent to which native land had been taken without legal justification/rationalization, and what would be necessary to attain retroactive legitimation in such instances.[38] In 1928, the Merriam Commission had recommended a similar expedient.[39] Congress had persistently balked at the ideas of acknowledging that the United States had effectively stolen much of its territoriality, and/or of belatedly making even token payments for what had been taken.[40]

The new commission was charged with investigating *all* native claims contesting U.S. title, to define precisely the territory involved in each case, and to determine whether legal procedures not devolving on outright conquest had ever been applied to its transfer out of Indian hands. In instances where it was concluded that there was no existing legal basis for non-Indian ownership of contested lands, or where the price originally paid for such lands was deemed "unconscionably low," the commission was responsible for fixing what might have been a "fair market price" (according to the buyers, not the sellers) *at the time the land was taken*. Corresponding sums were then paid by Congress—$29.1 million (about 47 cents per acre) for the entire state of California in the 1964 "Pit River Land Claim Settlement," for example—as "just compensation" to indigenous nations for their loss of property.[41] At the point such payment was accepted by an Indian people, the title at issue in its land claim was said to be "quieted" and "justice served."

In reality, as Jack Forbes and others have pointed out, non-Indian titles were being *created* where none had existed before.[42] As even the Chair of the Senate Subcommittee on Indian Affairs, Henry M. Jackson, put it at the time: "[Any other course of action would] perpetuate clouds upon white men's title that interfere with development of our public domain."[43] The stated presumptions underlying the commission's mandate were simply a continuation of the Marshall Doctrine that preeminent rights over Indian Country were inherently vested in the United States, and that native nations had in any event always wished to sell their land to the federal government. The unstated premise, of course, was that Indians had no choice in the matter anyway. Even if they *had* desired to convert their property into cash by the late 1940s, the commission was not authorized other than in a very narrow range of circumstances to award payment interest in retroactive land "sales," although the "bills" owed by the government were in many instances more than a century overdue.[44] In *no* event was the commission authorized to return land to native claimants, no matter *how* it had been taken from them.[45] Hence, during the 1950s, the commission served as a perfect "liberal" counterpart to the more extremist ("conservative") federal termination policies.

Nonetheless, the existence of the Claims Commission afforded native people a forum in which they might clarify the factual nature of their grievances for the first time. Consequently, by the end of 1951, more than 600 cases (only 26 of which were adjudicated at that point) had been docketed.[46] Things continued to move grudgingly, a matter which caused the process to be extended.[47] During the first 15 years of its operations, the commission completed only 80 cases, dismissing 30 outright, and finding "validity" to only 15. Its awards of monetary compensation totalled only $17.1 million by 1959. The "civil rights era" of the early '60s saw something of a surge in performance, with 250 cases completed (another $111 million in awards) and 347 pending (of which 42 have still seen no action at all).[48] During the early '70s, Indians began increasingly to appeal the commission's rulings to federal courts; of 206 such appeals filed by 1975, the commission was affirmed in 96, partially affirmed on 31, and overruled on 79.[49] At the end of its life on September 30, 1978, the Claims Commission still had 68 docketed cases (plus an indeterminate number of emerging appeals) still pending. These were turned over to the U.S. Court of Claims.[50]

Cracks in the Empire

While it is clear that the Indian Claims Commission functioned mainly as a subterfuge designed and intended to cast an undeserved mantle of humanitarianism and legitimacy over U.S. internal territorial integrity,[51] it inadvertently served indigenous interests as well. As a result of its lengthy exploration of the factual record, necessary to its mission of nailing down federal land title in every area of the country, the commission revealed the full extent to which the United States had occupied areas to which it had no lawful title (even under its own rules of the game). Indeed, one cumulative result of the commission's endeavor was to catalogue the fact that, according to the last known U.S. judicial rulings and legislative actions in each respective instance, legal title to more than 35 percent of the continental United States remained in the hands of native nations (see Map I).

> The fact is that about half the land area of the country was purchased by treaty or agreement at an average price of less than a dollar an acre; another third of a [billion] acres, mainly in the West, were confiscated without compensation; another two-thirds of a [billion] acres were

Map II

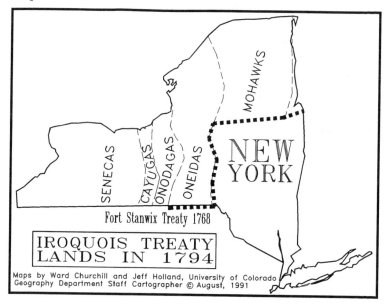

Fort Stanwix Treaty 1768

IROQUOIS TREATY
LANDS IN 1794

Maps by Ward Churchill and Jeff Holland, University of Colorado
Geography Department Staff Cartographer © August, 1991

claimed by the United States without pretense or a unilateral action extinguishing native title.[52]

Indians were quick to seize upon the implications of this, arguing that the commission process had no bearing at all on land title other than to resolve questions concerning who held title to precisely which parts of the United States, and providing a means by which the government could provide native owners with "back rent" on lands which had been "borrowed" by the United States for generations. The "underbrush of confusion as to who owns what" having been finally cleared away, it is appropriate in this view for Indians inside the United States to begin reasserting their national property rights over the approximately 750 million acres of North America which remain theirs by accepted legal definition.[53] Such knowledge has fueled a resurgent indigenous national "militancy" which, beginning in the early 1970s with the emergence of the American Indian Movement (AIM), has led to a series of spectacular extralegal confrontations over land and liberty (several of them covered elsewhere in this volume) with federal authorities. These, in turn, have commanded the very sort of international attention to U.S. territorial claims, and Indian policy more generally, that the Claims Commission was supposed to avert.

Beginning in the late '70s, the Native North Americans—spearheaded by AIM's "diplomatic arm," the International Indian Treaty Council—were able to escalate this trend by establishing a place for themselves within the United Nations structure, and entering annual reports concerning the conduct of both the U.S. and Canadian governments *vis-à-vis* native peoples and their lands. In this changing context, the federal government has once again begun to engage in "damage control," allowing a calculated range of concessions in order to preserve what it seeks to project as its image abroad. Notably, in 1974, the U.S. Supreme Court announced for the first time that Indians had a right to pursue actual recovery of stolen land through the federal judiciary.[54] Although resort to the courts of the conqueror is hardly an ideal solution to the issues raised by Indian nations, it does place another tool in the inventory of means by which they can now pursue their rights. And it has resulted in measurable gains for some of them over the past 15 years.

Probably the best example of this is that of the suit, first entered in 1972 under auspices of a sponsoring organization, of the basically landless Passamaquoddy and Penobscot Nations in present-day Maine regarding some 12 million acres acknowledged as being theirs in a series of letters dating from the 1790s and signed by George Washington.[55] Since it was demonstrated that no ratified treaty existed by which the Indians had ceded their land, U.S. District Judge Edward T. Gignoux ordered a settlement acceptable to the majority of the native people involved.[56] This resulted in the recovery, in 1980, of some 300,000 acres of land, and payment of $27 million in compensatory damages by the federal government.[57] In a similarly argued case, the Narragansetts of Rhode Island—who were not previously recognized by the government as still existing—were in 1978 able not only to win recognition of themselves, but also to recover 1,800 acres of the remaining 3,200 stripped from them in 1880 by unilateral action of the state.[58] In another example, the Mashantucket Pequot people of Connecticut filed suit in 1976 to recover 800 of the 2,000 acres comprising their original reservation, created by the Connecticut colony in 1686 but reduced to 184 acres by the state of Connecticut after the American Revolution.[59] Pursuant to a settlement agreement arrived at with the state in 1982, Congress passed an act providing funds to acquire the desired acreage. It was promptly vetoed by Ronald Reagan on April 11, 1983.[60] Only after the Senate Select Committee on Indian Affairs convened hearings on the matter did Reagan agree to a slight revision of the statute, finally affixing his signature on October 18 of the same year.[61]

Other nations, however, have not fared as well, even in an atmosphere in which the United States has sometimes proven more than usually willing to compromise as a means to contain questions of native land rights. The Wampanoags of the Mashpee area of Cape Cod, for instance, filed suit in 1974 in an attempt to recover about 17,000—later reduced to 11,000—of the 23,000 acres which were historically acknowledged as being theirs (the Commonwealth of Massachusetts having unilaterally declared their reservation a "township" in 1870). At trial, the all-white jury, all of whom had property interests in the Mashpee area, were asked to determine whether the Wampanoag plaintiffs were "a tribe within the meaning of the law." After deliberating for 21 hours, the jury returned with the absurd finding that they were *not* such an entity in 1790, 1869, and 1870 (the years which were key to the Indians' case), but that they *were* in 1834 and 1832 (years which it was important for them to have been "a tribe" for purposes of alienating land to the government). Their claim was then denied by District Judge Walter J. Skinner.[62] An appeal to the U.S. First Circuit Court failed, and the U.S. Supreme Court refused to review the case.[63]

Still pending land claims cases include those of the presently landless Schaghticoke and Mohegan peoples of Connecticut, each of which is attempting to recover approximately 1,000 acres lost to unilateral state actions during the 19th century.[64] Another case is that of the Catawbas of South Carolina, who filed suit in 1980 for recovery of their original 144,000-acre reservation, created by George III in 1760 and 1763, and acknowledged by the fledgling United States before being dissolved in a fraudulent treaty negotiated by the state and ratified by the Senate.[65] In 1981, the state, arguing that federal termination of the Catawbas in 1959 invalidated their right to sue, asked for and received a dismissal of the case. On appeal in 1983, however, the Fourth Circuit reinstated the case.[66]

Given such mixed results, it is plain that justice in native land claims cases in the United States cannot really be expected to accrue through the federal court system. Eventual resolution must inevitably reside within bodies such as the United Nations Working Group on Indigenous Populations (a subpart of the Commission on Human Rights), which is even now engaged in drafting a new element of international law entitled "The Universal Declaration of the Rights of Indigenous Peoples," and the World Court, which must interpret and render opinions based in such law.[67] From there, it can be expected that international scrutiny and pressure, as well as changed sentiments in a growing portion of the U.S. body politic, will serve to force the United States to edge ever closer to a fair and equitable handling of indigenous rights.

In the meantime, nearly every litigation of land claims within the federal system adds to the weight of evidence supporting the international case presented by native people: when they win, it proves they were entitled to the land all along; when they lose, it proves that the "due process rights" the United States insists protect their interests are, at best, inconsistently available to them. Either way, these legalistic endeavors force cracks in the ideological matrix of the American empire. In combination with extralegal efforts such as refusal to leave their homes by Indian traditionals and physical occupations of contested areas by groups such as AIM, as well as the increasing extent of international work by indigenous delegations, they comprise the core of the ongoing land struggles which represent the future survival of Native North America.

Current Land Struggles

Aside from those already mentioned, there is no shortage of ongoing struggles for their land rights undertaken by native people within the United States today, any or all of which are admirably suited to illustrate various aspects of the phenomenon. In Florida, the descendants of a group of Seminole (Miccosukee) "recalcitrants," who had managed to avoid forced relocation to Oklahoma during the 1830s by taking refuge in the Everglades, simply "squatted" in their homeland for more than 130 years, never agreeing to a "peace accord" with the United States until the mid-'60s. Because of their unswerving resistance to moving, the state finally agreed to create a small reservation for these people in 1982, and the Congress concurred by statute in 1982.[68] In Minnesota, there is the struggle of Anishinabe Akeeng (People's Land Organization) to reassert indigenous control over the remaining 20 percent—250,000 acres—of the White Earth Chippewa reservation, and to recover some portion of the additional million acres reserved as part of White Earth under an 1854 treaty with the United States but declared "surplus" through the General Allotment Act in 1906.[69]

In southern Arizona, the Tohono O'Odam (Papago) Nation continues its efforts to secure the entirety of its sacred Baboquivari Mountain Range, acknowledged by the government to be part of the Papago reservation in 1916, but opened to non-Indian "mineral development interests"—especially those concerned with mining copper—both before and since.[70] In the northern portion of the same state, there are ongoing struggles by both the Hopis and Diné (Navajos) to block the U.S. Forest Service's scheme to convert San Francisco Peaks, a site sacred to both peoples, into a ski resort complex.[71] And, of course, there is the grueling and government-instigated land struggle occurring between the tribal councils of these same two peoples within what was called the "Navajo-Hopi Joint Use Area." The matter is bound up in energy development issues—primarily the strip mining of an estimated 24 billion tons of readily accessible low sulphur coal—and entails a program to forcibly relocate as many as 13,500 traditional Diné who have refused to leave their land.[72]

In Massachusetts, the Gay Head Wampanoags, proceeding slowly and carefully so as to avoid the pitfalls encountered by their cousins at Mashpee, are preparing litigation to regain control over ancestral lands.[73] In Alaska, struggles to preserve some measure of sovereign indigenous (Indian, Aleut, and Inuit) control over some 40 million oil-rich acres corporatized by the 1971 Alaska Native Claims Settlement Act are sharpening steadily.[74] In Hawai'i, the native owners of the islands, having rejected a proffered cash settlement for relinquishment of their historic land rights in 1974,[75] are pursuing a legislative remedy which would both pay monetary compensation for loss of use of their territory while restoring a portion of it.[76] The fact of the matter is that, wherever there are indigenous people within the United States, land claims struggles are occurring with increasing frequency and intensity.

In order to convey a sense of the texture of these ongoing battles over land, it will be useful to consider a small selection of examples in a depth not possible, given constraints upon essay length, in every case which has been cited. For this purpose, the claims of the Iroquois Confederacy in upstate New York, the Lakota Black Hills Land Claim in South Dakota, and the Western Shoshone claims, primarily in Nevada, should serve quite well. Although they are hardly unique in many of their characteristics—and are thus able to represent the generalities of a broad range of comparable struggles—they are among the most sustained and intensively pursued of such efforts.

The Iroquois Land Claims

One of the longest fought and more complicated land claims struggles in the United States is that of the Haudenosaunee, or Iroquois Six Nations Confederacy. While the 1782 Treaty of Paris ended hostilities between the British Crown and its secessionist subjects in the 13 colonies, it had no direct effect upon the state of war existing between those subjects and indigenous nations allied with the Crown. Similarly, while by the treaty George III quitclaimed his property rights under the Doctrine of Discovery to the affected portion of North America, it was the opinion of Thomas Jefferson and others that this had done nothing to vest title to these lands in the newly born United States.[77] On both counts, the Continental Congress found it imperative to enter into treaty arrangements with Indian nations as expeditiously as possible. A very high priority in this regard was accorded the Iroquois Confederacy, four members of which—the Mohawks, Senecas, Cayugas, and Onondagas—had fought with the British (the remaining two, the Oneidas and Tuscaroras, having remained largely neutral but occasionally providing assistance to the colonists).[78]

During October 1784, the government conducted extensive negotiations with representatives of the Six Nations at Fort Stanwix, the result being a treaty by which the Indians relinquished claim to all lands lying west of a north-south line running from Niagara to the border of Pennsylvania—territory within the Ohio Valley (this was a provision reinforced in the 1789 Treaty of Fort Harmar)—and the land on which Fort Oswego had been built. In exchange, the United States guaranteed three of the four hostile nations the bulk of their traditional homelands. The Oneida and Tuscarora were also "secured in the possession of the lands on which they are now settled." Altogether, the area in question came to about six million acres, or half of the present state of New York (see Map II). The agreement, while meeting most of the Indians' needs, was quite useful to the U.S. central government:

> First...in order to sell [land in the Ohio River area] and settle it, the Continental Congress needed to extinguish Indian title, including any claims by the Iroquois [nations] of New York. Second, the commissioners wanted to punish the...Senecas. Thus they forced the Senecas to surrender most of their land in New York [and Pennsylvania] to the United States...Third, the United States...wanted to secure peace by confirming to the [nations] their remaining lands. Fourth, the United States was anxious to protect its frontier from the British in Canada by securing land for forts and roads along lakes Erie and Ontario.[79]

New York state, needless to say, was rather less enthusiastic about the terms of the treaty, and had already attempted, unsuccessfully, to obtain additional land cessions from the Iroquois during meetings conducted prior to arrival of the federal delegation at Fort Stanwix.[80] Further, such efforts by the state were barred by Article IX of the Articles of Confederation—and subsequently by Article I (Section 10) and the commerce clause of the Constitution—all of which combined to render treaty-making and outright purchases of Indian land by states illegal. New York then resorted to subterfuge, securing a series of 26 "leases," many of them for 999 years, on almost all native territory within its boundaries. The Haudenosaunee initially agreed to these transactions because of Governor Robert N. Clinton's duplicitous assurances that leases represented a way for them to *keep* their land, and for his government to "extend its protection over their property against the dealings of unscrupulous white land specula-

Map III

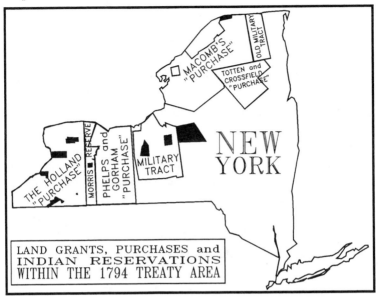

LAND GRANTS, PURCHASES and
INDIAN RESERVATIONS
WITHIN THE 1794 TREATY AREA

tors" in the private sector. The first such arrangement was forged with
the Oneidas. In a meeting begun at Fort Schuyler on August 28, 1788:

> The New York commissioners...led them to believe that they had [al-
> ready] lost all their land to the New York Genesee Company, and that
> the commissioners were there to restore title. The Oneidas expressed
> confusion over this since they had never signed any instruments to that
> effect, but Governor Clinton just waved that aside...Thus the Oneidas
> agreed to the lease arrangement with the state because it seemed the only
> way they could get back their land. The state received some five million
> acres for $2,000 in cash, $2,000 in clothing, $1,000 in provisions, and $600
> in annual rental. So complete was the deception that Good Peter [an
> Oneida leader] thanked the governor for his efforts.[81]

Leasing of the Tuscaroras' land occurred the same day, by a
parallel instrument.[82] On September 12, the Onondagas leased almost
all their land to New York under virtually identical conditions.[83] The
Cayugas followed suit on February 25, 1789, in exchange for payment
of $500 in silver, plus an additional $1,625 the next June and a $500
annuity.[84] New York's flagrant circumvention of constitutional restric-
tions on non-federal acquisitions of Indian land was a major factor in

congressional tightening of its mechanisms of control over such activities in the first of the so-called Indian Trade and Intercourse Acts
of 1790 (1 *Stat*. 37).[85] Clinton, however, simply shifted to a different
ruse, back-dating his maneuvers by announcing in 1791 that the state
would honor a 999-year lease negotiated in 1787 by a private speculator named John Livingston. The lease covered 800,000 acres of
mainly Mohawk land, but had been declared null and void by the state
legislature in 1788.[86]

Concerned that such dealings by New York might push the
Iroquois, the largely landless Senecas in particular, into joining the
Shawnee leader Tecumseh's alliance resisting further U.S. expansion
into the Ohio Valley, the federal government sent a new commission
to meet with the Haudenosaunee leadership at the principal Seneca
town of Canandaigua in 1794. In exchange for the Indians' pledge not
to bear arms against the United States, their ownership of the lands
guaranteed them at Fort Stanwix was reaffirmed, the state's leases
notwithstanding, and the bulk of the Seneca territory in Pennsylvania
was restored.[87] New York nonetheless began parceling out sections of
the leased lands in subleases to the very "unscrupulous whites" it had
pledged to guard against. On September 15, 1797, the Holland Land
Company—in which many members of the state government had
invested—assumed control over all but 10 tracts of land, totalling 397
square miles, of the Fort Stanwix Treaty area. The leasing instrument
purportedly "extinguished" native title to the land.[88] (See Map III)

Given the diminishing military importance of the Six Nations
after Tecumseh's 1794 defeat at Fallen Timbers, Washington did nothing to correct the situation despite Iroquois protests. New York was
thus emboldened to proceed with its appropriations of native land. In
1810, the Holland Company sold some 200,000 acres of its holdings in
Seneca and Tuscarora land to its accountant, David A. Ogden, at a
price of 50 cents per acre. Ogden then issued shares against development of this land, many of them to Albany politicians. Thus capital-
ized, he was able to push through a deal in 1826 to buy a further 81,000
acres of previously unleased reservation land at 53 cents per acre. A
federal investigation into the affair was quashed by Secretary of War
Peter B. Porter, himself a major stockholder in the Ogden Land Com-

Map IV

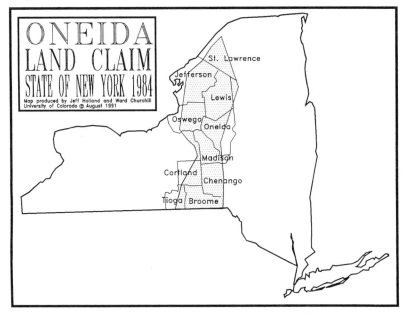

pany, in 1828.[89] Under such circumstances, most of the Oneidas requested in 1831 that what was left of their New York holdings, which they were sure they would lose anyway, be exchanged for a 500,000-acre parcel purchased from the Menominees in Wisconsin. President Andrew Jackson, at the time pursuing his policy of general Indian removal to points west of the Mississippi, readily agreed.[90]

In the climate of removal, Washington officials actively colluded with the speculators. On January 15, 1838, federal commissioners oversaw the signing of the Treaty of Buffalo Creek, wherein 102,069 acres of Seneca land were "ceded" directly to the Ogden Company. The $202,000 purchase price was divided almost evenly between the government (to be held "in trust" for the Indians) and individual non-Indians seeking to buy and "improve" plots in the former reservation area. At the same time, what was left of the Cayuga, Oneida, Onondaga, and Tuscarora holdings were wiped out, at an aggregate cost of $400,000 to Ogden.[91] The Iroquois were told they should relocate *en masse* to Missouri. Although the Six Nations never consented to the treaty, and it was never properly ratified by the Senate, President Martin Van Buren proclaimed it to be the law of the land on April 4, 1840.[92]

By 1841, Iroquois complaints about the Buffalo Creek Treaty were being joined by increasing numbers of non-Indians outraged not so much by the loss of land to Indians as by the obvious corruption involved in its terms.[93] Consequently, in 1842, a second Treaty of Buffalo Creek was negotiated. Under its provisions, the United States again acknowledged the Haudenosaunee right to reside in New York and restored small areas as the Allegheny and Cattaraugus Seneca reservations. The Onondaga reservation was also reconstituted on a 7,300-acre land base, and the Tuscarora reservation on about 2,500 acres. The Ogden Company was allowed to keep the rest.[94] The Tonawanda Seneca Band immediately filed a formal protest of these terms with the Senate, and, in 1857, received a $256,000 "award" of their own money with which to "buy back" a minor portion of their former territory from Ogden.[96]

Beginning in 1855, the Erie Railway Company entered the picture, setting out to lease significant portions of both Cattaraugus and Allegheny. Sensing the depth of then-prevailing federal support for railroad construction, the state judiciary seized the opportunity to cast an aura of legitimacy upon all of New York's other illicit leasing arrangements:

> Though the leases were ratified by New York, the state's supreme court in 1875 invalidated them. In recognition of this action, the New York legislature passed a concurrent resolution [a century after the fact] that state action was not sufficient to ratify leases because "Congress alone possesses the power to deal with and for the Indians." Instead of setting aside the leases, Congress in 1875 passed an act authorizing [them]. The state now made leases renewable for twelve years, and by an amendment in 1890 the years were extended to ninety-nine. Later the Supreme Court of New York deemed them perpetual.[97]

As a result, by 1889, 80 percent of all Iroquois reservation land in New York was under lease to non-Indian interests and individuals. The same year, a commission was appointed by Albany to examine the state's "Indian Problem." Rather than "suggesting that the leasing of four-fifths of their land had deterred Indian welfare, the commission criticized the Indians for not growing enough to feed themselves," thereby placing an "undue burden" on those profiting from their land. Chancellor C.N. Sims of Syracuse University, a commission member, argued strongly that only "obliteration of the tribes, conferral of citizenship, and allotment of lands" would set things right.[98] Washington duly set out to undertake allotment, but was stunned to discover it was stymied by the "underlying title" to much of the reserved Iroquois land it had allowed the Ogden Company to obtain over the years. In 1895, Congress passed a bill authorizing a buy-out of the Ogden interest (again at taxpayer expense), but the company upped its asking price for the desired acreage from $50,000 to $270,000. Negotiations thereupon collapsed, and the Six Nations were spared the trauma (and further land loss) of the allotment process.[99]

Not that the state didn't keep trying. In 1900, Governor Theodore Roosevelt created a commission to reexamine the matter. This led to the introduction of another bill (HR 12270) in 1902 aimed at allotting the Seneca reservations (with 50,000 in all, they were by far the largest remaining Iroquois land areas) by paying Ogden $200,000 of the *Indians'* "trust funds" to abandon his claims on Allegheny and Cattaraugus.[100] The Senecas retained attorney John Van Voorhis to argue that the Ogden claim was invalid because, for more than 100 years, the company had not been compelled to pay so much as a nickel of tax on the acreage it professed to "own." By this, VanVoorhis contended, both Ogden and the government had all along admitted—for purposes of federal law—that the land was really still the property of "Indians not taxed." The new bill was withdrawn in some confusion at this point, and allotment was again averted.[101] In 1905, the Senecas carried the tax issue into court in an attempt to clear their land title, but the case was dismissed under the premise that they had "no legal standing to sue" non-Indians.[102]

A third attempt to allot the Six Nations reservations (HR 18735) foundered in 1914, as did a New York state constitutional amendment, proposed in 1915, to effectively abolish the reservations. Even worse, from New York's viewpoint, in 1919 the U.S. Justice Department for the first time acted in behalf of the Iroquois, filing a suit which (re)established a 32-acre "reservation" in the state for the Oneidas.[103]

The state legislature responded by creating yet another commission, this one headed by attorney Edward A. Everett, to conduct a comprehensive study of land title questions in New York and to make recommendations as to how they might be cleared up across the board, once and for all.[104] After more than two years of hearings and intensive research, Everett handed in a totally unanticipated conclusion. The Six Nations still possessed legal title to all six million acres of the Fort Stanwix treaty area:

> He cited international law to the effect that there are only two ways to take a country away from a people possessing it—purchase or conquest. The Europeans who came here did recognize that the Indians were in possession and so, in his opinion, thus recognized their status as nations...If then, the Indians did hold fee to the land, how did they lose it?...[T]he Indians were [again] recognized by George Washington as a nation at the Treaty of 1784. Hence, they were as of 1922 owners of all the land [reserved by] them in that treaty unless they had ceded it by a treaty equally valid and binding.[105]

Everett reinforced his basic finding with reference to the Treaties of Fort Harmar and Canandaigua, discounted both Buffalo Creek Treaties as fraudulent, and rejected both the leases of the state and those taken by entities such as the Holland and Ogden Companies as having no legal validity at all.[106] The Albany government quickly shelved the report rather than publishing it, but it couldn't prevent its implications from being discussed throughout the Six Nations. On August 21, 1922, a council meeting was held at Onondaga for purposes of retaining Mrs. Lulu G. Stillman, Everett's secretary, to do research on the exact boundaries of the Fort Stanwix treaty area.[107] The Iroquois land claim struggle had shifted from dogged resistance to dispossession, to the offensive strategy of land recovery, and the first test case, *James Deere v. St. Lawrence River Power Company* (32 F.2d 550), was filed on June 26, 1925, in an attempt to regain a portion of the St. Regis Mohawk reservation taken by New York. The federal government declined to intervene in the Mohawks' behalf—as it was its "trust responsibility" to do—and the suit was dismissed by a district court judge on October 10, 1927. The dismissal was upheld on appeal in April 1929.[108]

Things remained quiet on the land claims front during the 1930s, as the Haudenosaunee were mainly preoccupied with preventing the supplanting of their traditional Longhouse form of government by "tribal councils" sponsored by the Bureau of Indian Affairs via the Indian Reorganization Act of 1934. Probably as a means of coaxing them into a more favorable view of federal intentions under the IRA, Indian Commissioner John Collier agreed towards the end of the decade that his agency would finally provide at least limited support to Iroquois claims litigation. This resulted, in 1941, in the Justice Department's filing of *U.S. v. Forness* (125 F.2d 928) in behalf of the Allegheny Senecas. The suit—ostensibly aimed at eviction of an individual who had refused to pay his $4 per year rent to the Indians for eight years—actually sought to enforce a resolution of the Seneca Nation cancelling hundreds of low cost 99-year leases taken in the City of Salamanca, on the reservation, in 1892. Intervening for the defendants was the Salamanca Trust Corporation, a mortgage institution holding much of the paper at issue. Although the case was ultimately unsuccessful in its primary objective, it did clarify that New York law had no bearing on Indian leasing arrangements.[109]

This was partly "corrected," in the state view, on July 2, 1948, and September 13, 1950, when Congress passed bills placing the Six Nations under New York jurisdiction in first criminal and then civil matters.[110] Federal responsibility to assist Indians in pursuing treaty-based land claims was nonetheless explicitly preserved.[111] Washington, of course, elected to treat this obligation in its usual cavalier fashion, plunging ahead during the 1950s—while the Indians were mired in efforts to prevent termination of their federal recognition altogether—with the flooding of 130 acres of the St. Regis reservation near Messena (and about 1,300 acres of the Caughnawaga [Kahnawake] Mohawk reserve in Canada) as part of the St. Lawrence Seaway Project.[112] The government also proceeded with plans to flood more than 9,000 acres of the Allegheny reservation as a by-product of constructing the Kinzua Dam. Although studies revealed an alternative siting of the dam would not only spare the Seneca land from flooding but also better serve "the greater public good" for which it was supposedly intended, Congress pushed ahead.[113] The Senecas protested the project as a clear violation of the Fort Stanwix guarantees, a position with which lower federal courts agreed, but the Supreme Court declined to review the question and the Army Corps of Engineers completed the dam in 1967.[114]

Meanwhile, the New York State Power Authority was attempting to seize more than half (1,383 acres) of the Tuscarora reservation, near Buffalo, as a reservoir for the Niagara Power Project. In April 1958, the Tuscaroras physically blocked access by construction workers to the site and several were arrested (charges were later dropped). A federal district judge entered a temporary restraining order against the state, but the appellate court ruled that congressional issuance of a license to the Federal Power Commission constituted sufficient grounds for the state to "exercise eminent domain" over native property.[115] The Supreme Court again refused to hear the resulting Haudenosaunee appeal. A "compromise" was then implemented in which the state flooded "only" 560 acres, or about one-eighth of the remaining Tuscarora land.[116]

By the early 1960s, it had become apparent that the Iroquois, because their territory fell "within the boundaries of one of the original thirteen states," would be disallowed from seeking redress through the Indian Claims Commission.[117] The decade was largely devoted to a protracted series of discussions between state officials and various sectors of the Iroquois leadership. Agreements were reached in areas related to education, housing, and revenue sharing, but on the issues of land claims and jurisdiction, the position of Longhouse traditionals was unflinching. In their view, the state holds *no* rights over the Iroquois in either sphere.[118] Their point was punctuated on May 13, 1974, when Mohawks from St. Regis and Caughnawaga [Kahnawake] occupied an area at Ganiekeh (Moss Lake), in the Adirondack Mountains. They proclaimed the site to be sovereign Mohawk territory under the Fort Stanwix Treaty—"[We] represent a cloud of title not only to [this] 612.7 acres in Herkimer County but to all of northeastern N.Y."—and set out to defend it (and themselves) by force of arms.[119]

After a pair of local vigilantes engaged in harassing the Indians were wounded by return gunfire in October, the state filed for eviction in federal court. The matter was bounced back on the premise that it was not a federal issue, and the New York attorney general—undoubtedly discomfited at the publicity prospects entailed in an armed confrontation on the scale of the 1973 Wounded Knee siege—let the case die.[120] Alternatively, the state dispatched a negotiating team headed by future governor Mario Cuomo. In May 1977, the "Moss Lake Agreement" was reached, and the Mohawks assumed permanent possession of a land parcel at Miner Lake, in the town of Altona, and another in the McComb Reforestation Area.[121] Mohawk possession of the sites remains ongoing in 1991, a circumstance which has prompted others among the Six Nations to pursue land recovery through a broader range of tactics and, perhaps, with greater vigor than they might have otherwise (e.g., Mohawk actions taken in Canada, concerning a land dispute at the Kanesatake territory bordering on the town of Oka, near Montreal, during 1990).

As all this was going on, the Oneidas had, in 1970, filed the first of the really significant Iroquois land claims suits. The case, *Oneida Indian Nation of New York v. County of Oneida* (70-CV-35 (N.D.N.Y.)), charged that the transfer of 100,000 acres of Oneida land to New York via a 1795 lease engineered by Governor Clinton was fraudulent and invalid on both constitutional grounds and because it violated the 1790 Trade and Intercourse Act. It was dismissed because of the usual "Indians lack legal standing" argument, but reinstated by the Supreme Court in 1974.[122] Compelled to actually examine the merits of the case for the first time, the U.S. District Court agreed with the Indians (and the Everett Report) that title still rested with the Oneidas.

> The plaintiffs have established a claim for violation of the Nonintercourse Act. Unless the Act is to be considered nugatory, it must be concluded that the plaintiffs' right of occupancy and possession of the land in question was not alienated. By the deed of 1795, the State acquired no rights against the plaintiffs; consequently, its successors, the defendant counties, are in no better position.[123]

Terming the Oneidas a "legal fiction," and the lower courts' rulings "racist," attorney Allan Van Gestel appealed to the Supreme Court. On October 1, 1984, the high court ruled against Van Gestel and ordered his clients to work out an accommodation, indemnified by the state, including land restoration, compensation, and rent on unrecovered areas.[125] Van Gestel continued to howl that "the common people" of Oneida and Madison Counties were being "held hostage," but as the Oneidas' attorney, Arlinda Locklear, put it in 1986:

> One final word about responsibility for the Oneida claims. It is true that the original sin here was committed by the United States and the state of New York. It is also no doubt true that there are a number of innocent landowners in the area, i.e., individuals who acquired their land with no knowledge of the Oneida claim to it. But those facts alone do not end the inquiry respecting ultimate responsibility. Whatever the knowledge of the claims before then, the landowners have certainly been aware of the Oneida claims since 1970 when the first suit was filed. Since that time, the landowners have done nothing to seek a speedy and just resolution of the claims. Instead, they have as a point of principle denied the validity of the claims and pursued the litigation, determined to prove the claims to be frivolous. Now that the landowners have failed in that effort, they loudly protest their innocence in the entire matter. The Oneidas, on the other hand, have since 1970 repeatedly expressed their preference for an out-of-court resolution of their claims. Had the landowners joined with the Oneidas sixteen years ago in seeking a just resolution, the claims would no doubt be resolved today. For that reason, the landowners share in the responsibility for the situation in which they find themselves today.[126]

Others would do well to heed these words because, as Locklear pointed out, the Oneida case "paved the legal way for other Indian land claims." [127] Not least of these are other suits by the Oneidas themselves. In 1978, the New York Oneidas filed for adjudication of title to the entirety of their Fort Stanwix claim—about 4.5 million acres—a case affecting not only Oneida and Madison counties, but Broome, Chenango, Cortland, Herkimer, Jefferson, Lewis, Onondaga, Oswego, St. Lawrence, and Tiago counties as well (this matter was shelved, pending final resolution of the first Oneida claims litigation).[128] In December 1979, the Oneida Nation of Wisconsin and the Thames Band of Southgold, Ontario, joined in an action pursuing rights in the same claim area, but naming the state rather than individual counties as defendant.[129] The Cayuga Nation, landless throughout the twentieth century, have also filed suit against Cayuga and Seneca counties for recovery of 64,015 acres taken during Clinton's leasing foray of 1789 (the Cayuga claim may develop into an action overlapping with those of the Oneida; see Map IV).[130]

The latter case, filed on November 19, 1980, resulted from attempts by the Cayugas to negotiate some sort of land base and compensation for themselves with federal, state, and county officials from the mid-'70s onward. By August 1979, they had worked out a tentative agreement that would have provided them with the 1,852-acre Sampson Park area in southern Seneca County, the 3,629-acre Hector Land Use Area in the same county, and an $8 million trust account established by the Secretary of Interior (up to $2.5 million of which would be used to buy additional land).[131] Although not one square inch of their holdings was threatened by the arrangement, the response of the local non-Indian population was rabid. To quote Paul D. Moonan, Sr., president of the local Monroe Title and Abstract Company: "The Cayugas have no moral or legal justification for their claim." Wisner Kinne, a farmer near the town of Ovid, immediately founded the Seneca County Liberation Organization, premised on a virulent anti-Indianism. SCLO attracted several hundred highly vocal members from the sparsely populated county.

A bill to authorize the settlement subsequently failed due to this "white backlash," and so the Cayugas went to court to obtain a much larger area, eviction of 7,000 county residents, and $350 million in trespass damages. Attempts by attorneys for SCLO to have the suit dismissed failed in 1982, as did a 1984 compromise offer initiated by Representative Frank Horton. The latter, which might well have been accepted by the Cayugas, would have provided them the 3,200-acre Howland Game Management Reserve along the Seneca River, a 2,850-acre parcel on Lake Ontario (owned by the Rochester Gas and Electric Company), and a 2,000-acre parcel adjoining Sampson State Park. Additionally, the Cayugas would have received "well in excess" of the $8 million they'd originally sought. While SCLO appears to have decided acquiescence was by this point the better part of valor, the proposal came under heavy attack from non-Indian environmentalists "concerned about the animals in the Howland Reserve." Ultimately, it was nixed by Ronald Reagan in 1987, not because he was concerned with area fauna, but because he was angry with Horton for voting against Contra aid. The suit is therefore ongoing.[132]

At the town of Salamanca, the leases to which expire at the end of 1991, the Allegheny Senecas also undertook decisive action during the second half of the 1980s. Beginning as early as 1986, they stipulated the intent not to renew, and to begin eviction proceedings against non-Indian lease and mortgage holders in the area, unless the terms of any new arrangement were considerably recast in their favor (i.e., clarification of Seneca title, shorter leasing period, fair rates for property rental, and "preeminent jurisdiction" over both the land and cash income derived from it).[133] A further precondition to lease renewal was that compensation be made for all non-payment and under-payment of fair rental values of Seneca property accruing from the last lease. Although these demands unleashed a storm of protest from local whites—who, as usual, argued vociferously that the Indian owners of the land held no rights to it—they were unsuccessful in both court and Congress.[134] At this juncture, all essential Seneca terms have been met, and Congress has passed the Seneca Nation Settlement Act of 1990, including a settlement award of $60 million (the cost of which is to be shared by federal, state, and local non-Indian governments) for rental monies they should have received over the past 99 years, but didn't.[135]

The Black Hills Land Claim

A much more harshly fought struggle, at least in terms of physical combat, has been the battle waged by the Lakota Nation ("Western Sioux") to retain their spiritual heartland, the Black Hills. In 1851, in exchange for right-of-away to California and Oregon along what was called the Platte River Road, the government entered into the first Fort Laramie Treaty with the Lakota. The treaty recognized Lakota ownership of and sovereignty within a vast area amounting to approximately five percent of the continental United States (see Map V).[136] By 1864, however, silver had been discovered in Montana, and the United States, seeking the shortest route to the mines, violated the treaty by attempting to establish the "Bozeman Trail" directly through Lakota territory. This led to the so-called Red Cloud War of 1866-68, in which the Lakota formed a politico-military alliance with the Cheyenne and Arapaho Nations, laid siege to U.S. military posts along the trail, and

Map V

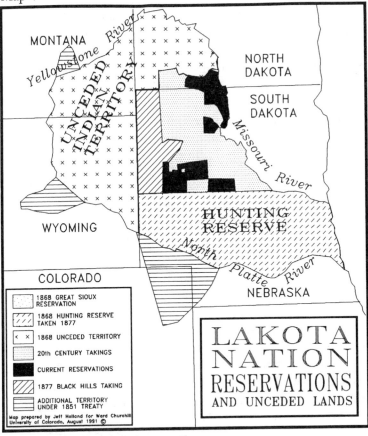

MONTANA

Yellowstone River

UNCEDED INDIAN TERRITORY

NORTH DAKOTA

SOUTH DAKOTA

Missouri River

WYOMING

HUNTING RESERVE

North Platte River

COLORADO

NEBRASKA

1868 GREAT SIOUX RESERVATION

1868 HUNTING RESERVE TAKEN 1877

1868 UNCEDED TERRITORY

20th CENTURY TAKINGS

CURRENT RESERVATIONS

1877 BLACK HILLS TAKING

ADDITIONAL TERRITORY UNDER 1851 TREATY

Map prepared by Jeff Holland for Ward Churchill University of Colorado, August 1991 ©

LAKOTA NATION RESERVATIONS AND UNCEDED LANDS

defeated the Army several times in the field. For the first time in its history, the government sued for peace. All Lakota terms were agreed to in a second Fort Laramie Treaty, signed during the spring of 1868, in exchange for the United States being allowed to withdraw its remaining soldiers without further damage.[137]

The provisions of the 1868 Fort Laramie Treaty were clear and unequivocal. All land from the east bank of the Missouri River westward within the present boundaries of the state of South Dakota was recognized by the United States as a "Great Sioux reservation," exclusively for Indian use and occupancy. Contiguous portions of North Dakota and Montana and about a third of Wyoming were also recognized as being "Unceded Indian Territory" belonging to the "Greater Sioux Nation," and all of Nebraska north of the North Platte River was perpetually reserved as hunting territory. A stipulation in the 1868 treaty acknowledged that its terms would not impair any Lakota land rights reserved under any earlier treaties, and the United States pledged to use its military to prevent its citizens from trespassing again in Lakota territory.[138] Finally, the way in which any future transfer of Lakota title might occur was spelled out:

> No [subsequent] treaty for cession of any portion of the reservation herein described which may be held in common shall be of any validity or force as against said Indians, unless executed and signed by at least three-fourths of all adult male Indians, occupying or interested in the same.[139]

In 1863, a Catholic priest named Jean de Smet, after sojourning illegally in the Black Hills, reported the presence of gold there. In short order, this incentive proved sufficient to cause Washington to violate the new treaty, sending Lt. Colonel George Armstrong Custer and his elite 7th Cavalry Regiment (heavily reinforced) to explore the Hills. When Custer, during the summer of 1874, reported that he too had found gold, the government dispatched a commission to purchase the region from the Lakotas, while developing contingency plans for a military seizure in the event negotiations were unsuccessful.[140] During the fall of 1875, the commission reported failure, and "Sioux Affairs" were shifted to the War Department.[141] The latter announced that all Lakotas who failed to congregate by mid-January at Army posts—where they could be taken under military command—would be henceforth considered "hostile" and subject to "punishment" the following summer. In Washington, the refusal of most Lakotas to comply with this presumption was publicized as an "Act of War" against the United States.[142]

Seeking to compensate for its earlier humiliation at the hands of these same Indians, the Army launched a huge three-pronged invasion, involving several thousand troops, of the Powder River sector of Unceded Indian Territory during the spring of 1876. The idea was to catch all the "Sioux recalcitrants" in a giant vise, overwhelm them, and then—with the Lakota military capacity destroyed—simply take whatever land area the United States desired. Things did not work

Map VI

TRADITIONAL SHOSHONE TERRITORY

IDAHO

WYOMING

Wind River

Duck Valley

Fort Hall

NEVADA

UTAH

COLORADO

ARIZONA

Map from Ward Churchill and Glenn Morris
prepared by Jeff Holland © August 1991

CALIFORNIA

Newe Segobia

Other Traditional Territory

Contemporary Reservations

out so quickly or so easily. First, on June 17, the southern command (a force of about 1,500 under General George Crook) was met and decisively defeated along the Rosebud Creek by several hundred warriors led by the Oglala Lakota Crazy Horse.[143] Then, on June 25, Custer and a portion of his 7th Cavalry (part of the eastern command) were annihilated in the valley of the Little Big Horn River by a combined force of perhaps 1,000 led by Crazy Horse and Gall, a Hunkpapa Lakota.[144] The balance of the U.S. troops spent the rest of the summer and fall chasing Indians they could never quite catch.[145]

In the end, the Army was forced to resort to "total war" expedients, pursuing a winter campaign of the type developed on the southern plains with the 1864 Sand Creek Massacre and Custer's massacre at the Washita River in 1868. An expert in such operations, Colonel Ranald McKenzie, was imported for this purpose and spent the snowy months of 1876-77 tracking down one village after another, killing women, children, and ponies as he went.[146] By the spring of 1877, all Lakota groups other than a portion of the Hunkpapas led by Sitting Bull and Gall, and a segment of the Oglalas led by Crazy Horse, had surrendered. The Hunkpapas sought asylum in Canada, while U.S. negotiators tricked Crazy Horse into standing down in May.[147] The great Oglala leader was assassinated on September 5, 1877.[148]

With the Lakotas increasingly disarmed, dismounted, and under guard, Congress felt confident in taking possession of the western-most portion of the Great Sioux reservation, in which the Black Hills were located. On August 15, 1876, it had passed an act (Ch. 289, 19 *Stat*. 176, 192) announcing the Lakota Nation had given up its claim to the desired geography. Concerned that this appear to be a legitimate transfer of title rather than outright conquest, however, the act was written so as not to take effect until such time as Lakota "consent" was obtained. Another commission, this one headed by George Manypenny, was dispatched for this purpose. When even noncombatant Lakota men refused to cooperate, rations for the captive people as a whole were suspended. Ultimately, some 10 percent of all "adult Lakota males" signed the cession instrument in order to feed their families. Although this was a far cry from the 75 percent express written consent required by the 1868 treaty to make the matter legal, Congress decided the gesture was sufficient. Meanwhile, on February 28, 1877, the legislators followed up with another law (19 *Stat*. 254) stripping away the Unceded Indian Territory. Since the 1851 treaty boundaries were simply ignored, the Great Sioux Nation had shrunk, almost overnight, from approximately 134 million acres to fewer than 15 million.[149]

Beginning in 1882, the United States began to impose an "Assimilation Policy" upon the Lakota Nation, outlawing key spiritual practices such as the Sun Dance, extending its jurisdiction over Lakota territory through the 1885 Major Crimes Act, and systematically removing children to remote boarding schools at which their language and cultural practices were not only prohibited, but replaced with those of their conquerors.[150] As part of this concerted drive to destroy the socio-cultural integrity of the Lakotas, allotment of the Great Sioux reservation was undertaken, starting in 1889, with the consequence that some 80 percent of the remaining Lakota land base was declared surplus by unilateral action of the federal government over the next 20 years. Resulting land losses—about seven million acres—caused separation of the various Lakota bands from one another for the first time, through emergence of a "complex" of much smaller reservations (i.e., Pine Ridge for the Oglala, Rosebud for the Sicangu [Brûlé], Standing Rock for the Hunkpapa and Minneconjou, and Cheyenne River for the Itazipco [Sans Arcs], Sihasapa [Blackfeet], and Oohinunpa [Two Kettles]; see Map V).[151]

By 1890, despair at such circumstances was so great among the Indians that there was widespread adoption of the Ghost Dance religion, a phenomenon entailing belief among its adherents that performance of specified rituals would cause a return of the buffalo and people killed by the Army, as well as disappearance of the invaders themselves. Deliberately misconstruing the Ghost Dance as evidence of "an incipient uprising," local Indian agents seized the opportunity to rid themselves of those most resistant to the new order they were seeking to install. A special police unit was used to murder Sitting Bull—who had returned from Canada in 1881—at his home on December 15. On December 28, four companies of the reconstituted 7th Cavalry were used to massacre some 350 followers of Big Foot, a Minneconjou leader, along Wounded Knee Creek. In Washington, it was generally believed "the recalcitrant Sioux" and other "Indian troublemakers" had finally "gotten the message" concerning the permanent and unconditional nature of their subordination.[152] The government felt free to consolidate its grip over even the last residue of land left nominally in native hands:

> In 1891 an amendment was made to the General Allotment Act (26 *Stat.* 794) that allowed the secretary of interior to lease the lands of any allottee who, in the secretary's opinion, "by reason of age or other disability," could not "personally and with benefit to himself occupy or improve his allotment or any part thereof." In effect this amendment gave almost dictatorial powers over the use of allotments since, if the local agent disagreed with the use to which lands were being put, he could intervene and lease the land to anyone he pleased.[153]

During the early part of the 20th century, virtually every useful parcel of land on the Lakota lands had been let in this fashion on longterm, extremely lowcost leases ($1 per acre, per year for 99 years being the typical arrangement).[154] At the same time, however, Sioux resistance surfaced in another form. A young Santee Dakota named Charles Eastman began to publish books including, among other things, accounts of the means by which the Black Hills had been expropriated and his own experiences as part of a burial detail at Wounded Knee. These were widely read in Europe.[155] Hence, questions on such topics were posed to U.S. observers at the Geneva convention of the newly founded League of Nations in 1919. (There is a school of thought holding that Congress refused to allow formal U.S. participation in the League because, at least in part, it was aware that federal Indian policy would never stand up to international scrutiny.) Always inclined to paste a patina of fairness and legality over even its most murderous misdeeds, the United States responded to this embarrassment with an act (41 *Stat.* 738) authorizing the Lakota to file suit in federal court if they felt they'd been dealt with "less than honorably." The thinking was apparently that an "equitable settlement"—consisting of a relatively minor amount of cash—would end the matter.

No consideration at all seems to have been given to the possibility that the Lakotas might have other ideas as to what "equity" might look like. In 1923, they pitched a curve, entering the first Black Hills case with the U.S. Court of Claims, premised on land restoration rather than monetary compensation. Bewildered by this unexpected turn of events, the claims court simply stalled for 19 years, endlessly entertaining motions and counter-motions while professing to "study" the matter. Finally, in 1942, when it became absolutely clear the Lakota Nation would not accept cash in lieu of land, the court simply dismissed the case, asserting that the situation was a "moral issue" rather than a constitutional question over which it held jurisdiction.[156] In 1943, the U.S. Supreme Court refused to review the claims court decision.[157]

Although the litigational route appeared stalemated at this point, passage of the Indian Claims Commission Act in 1946 revived the

Lakotas' judicial strategy. A case was filed with the commission in 1950, but was deemed by the commissioners to have been "retired" by the earlier claims court dismissal and Supreme Court denial of *certiorari*. Thus, the commission also dismissed the case in 1954.[158] Undeterred, the Lakota entered an appeal, which was denied and refiled. In 1958, the Black Hills claim was reinstated on the basis of a ruling that the Lakota had been represented by "inadequate counsel" during the 1920s and '30s. The Justice Department then attempted to have the whole issue simply set aside, submitting a *writ of mandamus* in 1961, which requested "extraordinary relief" from continued Lakota litigation. The government's argument was rejected by the court of claims later in the same year.[159] Hence, the claims commission was compelled to actually consider the case.[160]

After another long hiatus, the commission entered an opinion in 1974 that Congress had been merely exercising its "power of eminent domain" in taking the Lakota land, and that such action was therefore "justified." On the other hand, the commission held, it was constitutionally required that the Indians be "justly compensated" for their loss.[161] The Justice Department responded immediately by filing an appeal to minimize any cash award. This resulted, in 1975, in the government's securing of a *res judicata* prohibition against payment of public funds "in excess of the value of said property at the time it was taken."[162] By official estimation, this came to exactly $17.1 million, against which the Department of Interior levied an "offset" of $3,484 for rations issued to its captives in 1877.[163] The Lakota attempted an appeal to the Supreme Court, but once again the justices declined to review the matter.[164]

As all this was going on, the frustrations of grassroots Lakotas finally boiled over in such a way as to radically alter the extralegal context in which their Black Hills claim was situated. Early in 1973, traditionals on the Pine Ridge reservation requested assistance from AIM in confronting the corrupt (and federally installed) tribal government, in part to block another illegal land transfer. At issue was the uranium-rich northwestern one-eighth of Pine Ridge—known as the Sheep Mountain Gunnery Range—which the Department of Interior wished to incorporate into the adjoining Badlands National Monument. AIM's physical intervention resulted in its being besieged for 71 days in the symbolic hamlet of Wounded Knee by massive federal forces. By the time the spectacular armed confrontation had ended, international attention was riveted on U.S. Indian affairs as never before. In an attempt to contain the situation, the government fought a veritable counterinsurgency war against AIM and the traditional Oglalas of Pine Ridge during the three years following the Pine Ridge siege.[165]

By the time the gunnery range was finally transferred in 1976, the Oglalas—who had sustained at least 69 fatalities and nearly 350 serious physical assaults on their reservation during the period of federal repression—were in no mood to accept further abuse.[166] They not only mounted a storm of protest which caused a partial reversal of the transfer instrument, but also rallied the rest of their nation to demand that the three-fourths express consent clause of the 1868 treaty (now including adult women as well as men) be applied to the claims commission award. Organizing a referendum on the matter under the slogan "The Black Hills Are Not For Sale," the United Sioux Tribes of South Dakota voted overwhelmingly in 1977 to refuse the settlement.[167] Meanwhile, AIM had created the International Indian Treaty Council (IITC) and managed to have Lakota treaty issues (as well as other indigenous rights questions) docketed with the United Nations Commission on Human Rights.[168]

Under these circumstances, Congress once again backpedaled, passing an act in 1978 which set aside all judicial decisions leading up to the 1977 award amount, and ordering *pro novo* review by the claims court on the question of how much the Lakota compensation package should add up to.[169] The following year, the court determined that 5 percent simple annual interest should pertain to the claims commission's award of principal, a factor which upped the amount offered the Lakota to $122.5 million.[170] The Justice Department appealed this outcome to the Supreme Court, a circumstance which prompted the high court—after denying Indian requests to do the same thing for nearly 40 years—to finally examine the Black Hills case.

> In 1980, the Supreme Court, on *writ of certiorari* from the Court of Claims, held that the 1877 act did not effect a "mere change of form in investment in Indian tribal property," but, rather, effected a taking of tribal property

which had been set aside by the treaty of Fort Laramie for the Sioux's exclusive occupation, which taking implied an obligation on the government's part to make just compensation, including an award of interest, to the Sioux. Justice Rehnquist filed a blistering dissenting opinion in which he charged the majority had been led astray by "revisionist historians." [171]

The Lakota remained entirely unsatisfied. Opponents to monetary settlement pointed out that Homestake Corporation alone had removed about $18 *billion* in gold from one site near the Black Hills towns of Lead and Deadwood since 1877. They also noted that a 1979 poll of the reservations showed that the great bulk of residents, although being among the most impoverished people in North America, were no more willing to accept the new offer than they had been the old one.[172] In July 1980—while a week-long "Survival Gathering" attended by 10,000 people was occurring just across the fence from the Strategic Air Command's Ellsworth Air Force Base, 10 miles from the Hills—the Oglalas filed a new suit demanding return of significant acreage and $11 billion in damages.[173] Although the case was dismissed by a federal district judge in September of the same year on the premise that "the matter has already been resolved," and was subsequently denied on appeal, the point had been made.[174]

It was punctuated in April 1981 when AIM leader Russell Means led a group to an 880-acre site in the Black Hills about 13 miles outside Rapid City, named it "Yellow Thunder Camp,"and announced it was the first step in the physical reoccupation of "Paha Sapa," as the Hills are known in the Lakota language. The U.S. Forest Service, which claimed the land on which Yellow Thunder Camp was situated, filed suit for eviction, and requested that the federal marshals' service carry it out. When it became apparent that AIM was prepared to offer physical resistance *à la* Wounded Knee, a federal judge in the state capital of Pierre issued a restraining order on federal authorities.[175] During the following summer, several other occupation camps sprang up, some of them sponsored by usually more timid tribal council governments.[176] Although they were mostly short-lived, the AIM occupation was continuous for nearly five years.

While it was going on, the Forest Service eviction suit was litigated before U.S. District Judge Robert O'Brien, with AIM countersuing on the basis that the federal government was in violation of the 1868 treaty, the 1978 American Indian Religious Freedom Act (AIRFA), and several of its own anti-discrimination statutes. In 1985, the government was stunned when O'Brien upheld AIM's contentions, entering a potential landmark opinion that whole geographical areas rather than specific locations might be considered "sacred lands" within the meaning of AIRFA, and enjoining the Forest Service from further harassing Yellow Thunder occupants.[177] The decision was reversed by the Eighth Circuit Court in 1988, however, in the wake of the Supreme Court's decision in the *Lyng* case. By that time, the government had deposited the Lakota settlement monies in an escrow account at an Albuquerque bank, where it continues to draw interest (reportedly, it now totals slightly more than $200 million, no Lakota having accepted a disbursement check).[178]

Throughout the first half of the 1980s, IITC reported developments in the Black Hills struggle annually to the UN Working Group on Indigenous Populations, formed by the Human Rights Commission in 1982.[179] The U.S. United Nations delegation was forced to file formal responses to information provided through this medium, a circumstance causing greater international exposure of the inner workings of federal Indian policy than ever before. This, in combination with the persistence of Lakota litigation efforts and physical confrontations, precipitated an unprecedented governmental initiative to resolve the Black Hills issue during the late '80s. It took the form of a bill, S.1453, first introduced by New Jersey Senator Bill Bradley in 1987, to "reconvey title"—including water and mineral rights—over 750,000 acres of forest land within the Paha Sapa to the Lakota Nation. Additionally, specified sacred sites adding up to several thousand acres, and a 50,000-acre "Sioux Park," would be retitled without mineral rights. A "Sioux National Council," drawn from all Lakota reservations, would share jurisdictional and policymaking prerogatives—as well as revenues from leasing, royalties, etc.—over the balance of the original Great Sioux reservation with federal and state authorities. Finally, the 1980 claims court award, plus subsequently accrued interest, would be converted into compensation for damages rather than payment for land *per se*.[180]

Although the Bradley Bill hardly afforded a full measure of Lakota rights to land and sovereignty, it was the sort of substantive compromise arrangement which the bulk of Lakotas might have accepted as workable. Certainly, Lakota support for the bill had become pronounced by 1988, even as a local white backlash—whipped up in part by South Dakota Senator Larry Pressler and former governor William Janklow—mounted steadily. If enacted in some form, it might have created a viable model for eventual indigenous land rights resolutions throughout North America. Unfortunately, the bill was withdrawn by its sponsor in 1990, after a two-year period of highly publicized anti-Bradley agitation by an individual named Phil Stevens, previously unknown to the Indians but purporting to be "Great Chief of all the Sioux." (At present, Lakota land claim efforts are primarily devoted to resuscitating the bill, or developing a reasonable variant of it).[181]

The Western Shoshone Land Claim

A differently waged, and lesser known, struggle for land has been waged by the Western Shoshone, mainly in the Nevada desert region. In 1863, the United States entered into the Treaty of Ruby Valley (13 *Stat.* 663) with the Newe (Western Shoshone) Nation, agreeing—in exchange for Indian commitments of peace and friendship, willingness to provide right-of-way through their lands, and the granting of assorted trade licenses—to recognize the boundaries encompassing the approximately 24.5 million acres of the traditional Western Shoshone homeland, known in their language as Newe Segobia (see Map VI).[182] The United States also agreed to pay the Newes $100,000 in restitution for environmental disruptions anticipated as a result of Euroamerican "commerce" in the area. As researcher Rudolph C. Ryser has observed:

> Nothing in the Treaty of Ruby Valley ever sold, traded or gave away any part of the New Country to the United States of America. Nothing in this treaty said that the United States could establish counties or smaller states within New Country. Nothing in this treaty said the United States could establish settlements of U.S. citizens who would be engaged in any activity other than mining, agriculture, milling and ranching.[183]

From the signing of the treaty until the mid-20th century, no action was taken by either Congress or federal courts to extinguish native title to Newe Segobia.[184] Essentially, the land was an area in which the United States was not much interested. Still, relatively small but steadily growing numbers of non-Indians did move into Newe territory, a situation which was generally accommodated by the Indians so long as the newcomers did not become overly presumptuous. By the late 1920s, however, conflicts over land use had begun to sharpen. Things worsened after 1934, when the federal government installed a tribal council form of government—desired by Washington but rejected by traditional Newes—under a provision of the Indian Reorganization Act (IRA).[185] It was to the IRA council heading one of the Western Shoshone bands, the Temoak, that attorney Ernest Wilkinson went with a proposal in early 1946.

Wilkinson was a senior partner in the Washington-based law firm Wilkinson, Cragun, and Barker, commissioned by Congress toward the end of World War II to draft legislation creating the Indian Claims Commission. The idea he presented to the Temoak council was that his firm be retained to "represent their interests" before the claims commission.[186] Ostensibly, his objective was to secure the band's title to its portion of the 1863 treaty area. Much more likely, given subsequent events, his purpose was to secure title for non-Indian interests in Nevada, and to collect the 10 percent attorney's fee he and his colleagues had written into the Claims Commission Act as pertaining to any compensation awarded to native clients.[187] In any event, the Temoaks agreed, and a contract between Wilkinson and the council was approved by the Bureau of Indian Affairs in 1947.[188] Wilkinson followed up, in 1951, with a petition to the claims commission that his representation of the Temoaks be construed as representing the interests of the entire Newe Nation. The commission concurred, despite protests from the bulk of the people involved.[189]

From the outset, Wilkinson's pleadings led directly away from Newe rights over the Ruby Valley Treaty Territory. As Glenn T. Morris has framed the matter in what is probably the best article on the Western Shoshone land struggle to date:

In 1962, the commission conceded that it "was unable to discover any formal extinguishment" of Western Shoshone title to lands in Nevada, and could not establish a date of taking, but nonetheless ruled that the lands were taken at some point in the past. It did rule that approximately two million acres of Newe land in California was taken on March 3, 1853 [contrary to the Treaty of Ruby Valley, which would have supplanted any such taking], but without documenting what specific Act of Congress extinguished the title. Without the consent of the Western Shoshone Nation, on February 11, 1966, Wilkinson and the U.S. lawyers arbitrarily stipulated that the date of valuation for government extinguishment of Western Shoshone title to over 22 million acres of land in Nevada occurred on July 1, 1872. This lawyers' agreement, entered without the knowledge or consent of the Shoshone people, served as the ultimate loophole through which the U.S. would allege that the Newe had lost their land.[190]

By 1872 prices, the award of compensation to the Newe for the "historic loss" of their territory was calculated, in 1972, at $21,350,000, an amount revised upwards to $26,154,600 (against which the government levied an offset of $9,410.11 for "goods" delivered in the 1870s) and certified on December 19, 1979.[191] In the interim, by 1976, even the Temoaks had joined the other Newe bands in maintaining that Wilkinson did not represent their interests; they fired him, but the BIA continued to renew his contract "in their behalf" until the claims commission itself was concluded in 1980.[192] Meanwhile, the Newes had retained other counsel and filed a motion to suspend commission proceedings with regard to their case. This was denied on August 15, 1977, appealed, but upheld by the U.S. Court of Claims. The basis was that if the Newe desired "to avert extinguishment of their land claims, they should go to Congress" rather than the courts for redress; $26,145,189.89 was then placed in a trust account with the U.S. Treasury Department in order to absolve the United States of further responsibility in the matter.[193]

One analyst of the case suggests that if the United States were honest in its valuation date of the taking of Newe land, the date would be December 19, 1979—the date of the ICC award—since the commission could point to no other extinguishment date. The United States should thus compensate the Shoshone in 1979 land values and not those of 1872. Consequently, the value of the land that would be more realistic, assuming the Western Shoshone were prepared to ignore violations of the Ruby Valley Treaty, would be in the neighborhood of $40 billion. On a per capita basis of distribution, the United States would be paying each Shoshone roughly $20 million...The [U.S.] has already received billions of dollars in resources and use from Newe territory in the past 125 years. Despite this obvious benefit, the U.S. government is only prepared to pay the Shoshone less than a penny of actual value for each acre of Newe territory.[194]

The Newes as a whole have refused to accept payment for their land, under the premise articulated by Raymond Yowell, Chair of the Western Shoshone Sacred Lands Association, that: "We entered into the Treaty of Ruby Valley as co-equal sovereign nations...The land to the traditional Shoshone is sacred. It is the basis of our lives. To take away the land is to take away the lives of the people."[195] Giving form to this sentiment, two sisters—Mary and Carrie Dann—refused eviction from their homes by the U.S. Bureau of Land Management, which claimed by that point to own property that had been in their family for generations—and challenged *all* U.S. title contentions within the Newe treaty area when the Bureau attempted to enforce its position in court. The litigation has caused federal courts to flounder about in disarray ever since.

In 1977, the federal district court for Nevada ruled that the Dann sisters were "trespassers" because the claims commission had resolved all title questions. This decision was reversed on appeal to the Ninth Circuit Court in 1978 because, in its view, the question of land title "had not been litigated, and has not been decided."[196] On remand, the district court waited until the claims commission award had been paid into the Treasury, and then ruled against the Danns in 1980. The court, however, in attempting to rationalize both its present decision and its past reversal, observed that, "Western Shoshone Indians retained unextinguished title to their aboriginal lands *until December of 1979*, when the Indian Claims Commission judgement became final (emphasis added)."[197] This, of course, demolished the basis for the commission's award amount. It also pointed to the fact that the commission had comported itself illegally in the Western Shoshone case insofar as the Indian Claims Commission Act explicitly disallowed the commissioners (never mind attorneys representing the Indians) from extinguishing previously unextinguished land titles.

Thus armed, the Danns went back to the Ninth Circuit Court and obtained another reversal.[198]

The government appealed the circuit court's ruling to the Supreme Court and, entering yet *another* official (and exceedingly ambiguous) estimation of when Newe title was supposed to have been extinguished, the justices reversed the circuit court's reversal of the district court's last ruling. Having thus served the government's interest on appeal, the high court declined in 1990 to hear an appeal from the Danns concerning the question of whether they might retain individual aboriginal property rights based on continuous occupancy even if the collective rights of the Newe were denied.[199] As of this writing, despite their adverse experiences with the federal judiciary, the Dann sisters remain on their land in defiance of federal authority. Their physical resistance, directly supported by most Newes, forms the core of whatever will come next.

One route open to them—and undoubtedly the locus of much of the intensity with which the government has rejected their land claims—rests in the fact that U.S. nuclear weapons testing facilities lie squarely in the heart of Newe territory. According to geographer Bernard Nietschmann, the U.S. detonation of 651 atomic weapons there since 1963 makes Newe Segobia "the most bombed country in the world." [200] The Newe portion of Nevada was also the area specified for siting of the MX missile system, and, currently, the government is planning to store a variety of nuclear wastes in repositories bored into Yucca Mountain, in the southwestern sector of Newe treaty land. For obvious reasons, the Newes oppose both testing and the dumping of such wastes in their homeland. Given this opposition, it may be possible that their land rights may be fruitfully pursued through emergence of a broad coalition with non-Indian environmental, anti-war, and anti-nuclear organizations. That such a potential is not furthest from the minds of Newe strategists is witnessed by the wording of a permit issued to all protestors arriving to oppose nuclear experiments at military bases in the area: "The Western Shoshone Nation is calling upon citizens of the United States, as well as the world community of nations, to demand that the United States terminate its invasion of our lands for the evil purpose of testing nuclear bombs and other weapons of war."[201]

Where Do We Go From Here?

The question which inevitably arises with regard to indigenous land claims, especially in the United States, is whether they are "realistic." The answer, of course, is, "No, they aren't." Further, *no* form of decolonization has *ever* been realistic when viewed within the construct of a colonialist paradigm. It wasn't realistic at the time to expect George Washington's rag-tag militia to defeat the British military during the American Revolution. Just ask the British. It wasn't realistic, as the French could tell you, that the Vietnamese should be able to defeat U.S.-backed France in 1954, or that the Algerians would shortly be able to follow in their footsteps. Surely, it wasn't reasonable to predict that Fidel Castro's pitiful handful of guerrillas would overcome Batista's regime in Cuba, another U.S. client, after only a few years in the mountains. And the Sandinistas, to be sure, had no prayer of attaining victory over Somoza 20 years later. Henry Kissinger, among others, knew that for a fact.

The point is that in each case, in order to begin their struggles at all, anti-colonial fighters around the world have had to abandon orthodox realism in favor of what they knew (and their opponents knew) to be right. To paraphrase Daniel Cohn-Bendit, they accepted as their agenda—the goals, objectives, and demands which guided them—a redefinition of reality in terms deemed quite impossible within the conventional wisdom of their oppressors. And, in each case, they succeeded in their immediate quest for liberation.[202] The fact that all but one (Cuba) of the examples used subsequently turned out to hold colonizing pretensions of its own does not alter the truth of this—or alter the appropriateness of their efforts to decolonize themselves—in the least. It simply means that decolonization has yet to run its course, that much remains to be done.

The battles waged by native nations in North America to free themselves, and the lands upon which they depend for ongoing existence as discernible peoples, from the grip of U.S. (and Canadian) internal colonialism are plainly part of this process of liberation. Given that their very survival depends upon their perseverance in the face of all apparent odds, American Indians have no real alternative but to carry on. They must struggle, and where there is struggle there is always hope. Moreover, the unrealistic or "romantic" dimensions of our aspiration to quite literally dismantle the territorial corpus of the U.S. state begin to erode when one considers that federal domination of Native North America is utterly contingent upon maintenance of a perceived confluence of interests between prevailing governmental/corporate elites and common non-Indian citizens. Herein lies the prospect of long-term success. It is entirely possible that the consensus of opinion concerning non-Indian "rights" to exploit the land and resources of indigenous nations can be eroded, and that large numbers of non-Indians will join in the struggle to decolonize Native North America.

Few non-Indians wish to identify with or defend the naziesque characteristics of U.S. history. To the contrary, most seek to deny it in rather vociferous fashion. All things being equal, they are uncomfortable with many of the resulting attributes of federal posture and—in substantial numbers—actively oppose one or more of these, so long as such politics do not intrude into a certain range of closely guarded self-interests.

This is where the crunch comes in the realm of Indian rights issues. Most non-Indians (of all races and ethnicities, and both genders) have been indoctrinated to believe the officially contrived notion that, in the event "the Indians get their land back," or even if the extent of present federal domination is relaxed, native people will do unto their occupiers exactly as has been done to them; mass dispossession and eviction of non-Indians, especially Euroamericans, is expected to ensue.

Hence, even those progressives who are most eloquently inclined to condemn U.S. imperialism abroad and/or the functions of racism and sexism at home tend to deliver a blank stare or profess open "disinterest" when indigenous land rights are mentioned. Instead of attempting to come to grips with this most fundamental of all issues on the continent upon which they reside, the more sophisticated among them seek to divert discussion into "higher priority" or "more important" topics like "issues of class and gender equity" in which "justice" becomes synonymous with a redistribution of power and loot deriving from the occupation of Native North America even while the occupation continues (presumably permanently). Sometimes, Indians are even slated to receive "their fair share" in the division of spoils accruing from expropriation of their resources. Always, such things are couched—and typically seen—in terms of some "greater good" than decolonizing the .6 percent of the U.S. population which is indigenous.[203] Some marxist and environmentalist groups have taken the argument so far as to deny that Indians possess *any* rights distinguishable from those of their conquerors.[204] AIM leader Russell Means snapped the picture into sharp focus when he observed in 1987 that:

> So-called progressives in the United States claiming that Indians are obligated to give up their rights because a much larger group of non-Indians "need" their resources is exactly the same as Ronald Reagan and Elliot Abrams asserting that the rights of 250 million North Americans outweigh the rights of a couple million Nicaraguans. Colonialist attitudes are colonialist attitudes, and it doesn't make one damn bit of difference whether they come from the left or the right.[205]

Leaving aside the pronounced and pervasive hypocrisy permeating these positions, which add up to a phenomenon elsewhere described as "settler state colonialism,"[206] the fact is that the specter driving even most radical non-Indians into lockstep with the federal government on questions of native land rights is largely illusory. The alternative *reality* posed by native liberation struggles is actually much different:

- While government propagandists are wont to trumpet—as they did during the Maine and Black Hills land disputes of the 1970s—that an Indian win would mean individual non-Indian property owners losing everything, the native position has always been the exact opposite. Overwhelmingly, the lands sought for actual recovery have been governmentally and corporately held. Eviction of small land owners has been pursued only in instances where they have banded together—as they have during certain of the Iroquois claims cases— to prevent Indians from recovering any land at all, and to otherwise deny native rights.

- Official sources contend this is inconsistent with the fact that all non-Indian title to any portion of North America *could* be called into question. Once "the dike is breached," they argue, it's just a matter of time before "everybody has to start swimming back to Europe, or

Africa, or wherever." [207] Although there is considerable technical accuracy to admissions that all non-Indian title to North America is illegitimate, Indians have by and large indicated they would be content to honor the cession agreements entered into by their ancestors, even though the United States has long since defaulted. This would leave somewhere close to two-thirds of the continental United States in non-Indian hands, with the real rather than pretended consent of native people. The remaining one-third, the areas delineated in Map II to which the United States never acquired title at all, would be recovered by its rightful owners.

- The government holds that, even at that, there is no longer sufficient land available for unceded lands, or their equivalent, to be returned. In fact, the government itself still directly controls more than one-third of the total U.S. land area, about 770 million acres. Each of the states also "owns" large tracts, totalling about 78 million acres. It is thus quite possible—and always has been—for *all* native claims to be met in full without the loss to non-Indians of a single acre of privately held land. When it is considered that 250 million-odd acres of the "privately" held total are now in the hands of major corporate entities, the *real* dimension of the "threat" to small land holders (or, more accurately, lack of it) stands revealed. [208]

- Government spokespersons have pointed out that the disposition of public lands does not always conform to treaty areas. While this is true, it in no way precludes some process of negotiated land exchange wherein the boundaries of indigenous nations are redrawn by mutual consent to an exact, or at least a much closer conformity. All that is needed is an honest, open, and binding forum—such as a new bilateral treaty process—with which to proceed. In fact, numerous native peoples have, for a long time, repeatedly and in a variety of ways, expressed a desire to participate in just such a process.

- Nonetheless, it is argued, there will still be at least some non-Indians "trapped" within such restored areas. Actually, they would not be trapped at all. The federally imposed genetic criteria of "Indian-ness" discussed elsewhere in this book notwithstanding, indigenous nations have the same rights as any other to define citizenry by allegiance (naturalization) rather than by race. Non-Indians could apply for citizenship, or for some form of landed alien status which would allow them to retain their property until they die. In the event they could not reconcile themselves to living under any jurisdiction other than that of the United States, they would obviously have the right to leave, and they *should* have the right to compensation from their own government (which got them into the mess in the first place).[209]

- Finally, and one suspects this is the real crux of things from the government/corporate perspective, any such restoration of land and attendant sovereign prerogatives to native nations would result in a truly massive loss of "domestic" resources to the United States, thereby impairing the country's economic and military capacities (see "Radioactive Colonialism" essay for details). For everyone who queued up to wave flags and tie on yellow ribbons during the United States' recent imperial adventure in the Persian Gulf, this prospect may induce a certain psychic trauma. But, for progressives at least, it should be precisely the point.

When you think about these issues in this way, the great mass of non-Indians in North America *really* have much to gain, and almost nothing to lose, from the success of native people in struggles to reclaim the land which is rightfully ours. The tangible diminishment of U.S. material power which is integral to our victories in this sphere stands to pave the way for realization of most other agendas—from anti-imperialism to environmentalism, from African-American liberation to feminism, from gay rights to the ending of class privilege—pursued by progressives on this continent. Conversely, succeeding with any or even *all* these other agendas would still represent an inherently oppressive situation if their realization is contingent upon an ongoing occupation of Native North America without the consent of Indian people. Any North American revolution which failed to free indigenous territory from non-Indian domination would be simply a continuation of colonialism in another form.

Regardless of the angle from which you view the matter, the liberation of Native North America, liberation of the land first and foremost, is *the* key to fundamental and positive social changes of many other sorts. One thing, as they say, leads to another. The question has always been, of course, which "thing" is to be first in the sequence. A preliminary formulation for those serious about achieving (rather than merely theorizing and endlessly debating) radical change in the United States might be "First Priority to First Americans." Put another way, this would mean, "U.S. Out of Indian Country." Inevitably, the logic leads to what we've all been so desperately seeking: the United States—at least as we've come to know it—out of North America altogether. From there, it can be permanently banished from the planet. In its stead, surely we can join hands to create something new and infinitely better. That's *our* vision of "impossible realism." Isn't it time we *all* went to work on attaining it?

Notes

1. See Morison, Samuel Eliot, ed. and trans., *Journals and Other Documents on the Life and Voyages of Christopher Columbus* (New York: Heritage Publishers, 1963). For context, see Parry, John Horace, *The Establishment of European Hegemony, 1415-1713* (New York: Harper & Row Publishers, [revised edition] 1966).

2. See Vattel, M. D., *The Laws of Nations* (Philadelphia: T. & J. W. Johnson Publishers, 1855), pp. 160-61. Vattel is drawing on the mid-16th century discourses of Spanish legal theorist Franciscus de Victoria, published as *De Indis et De Jure Belli Reflectiones* by the Carnegie Institution in 1917. Also see Scott, James Brown, *The Spanish Origin of International Law* (Oxford: Clarendon Press, 1934) and Nussbaum, Alfred, *A Concise History of the Laws of Nations* (New York: Macmillan Publishers, [revised edition] 1954).

3. Coulter, Robert T., and Steven M. Tullberg, "Indian Land Rights," in *The Aggressions of Civilization: Federal Indian Policy Since the 1880s*, ed. Sandra L. Cadwalader and Vine Deloria, Jr. (Philadelphia: Temple University Press, 1984), pp. 185-213, quote at pp. 190-91. Additional information may be obtained from Parry, John Horace, *The Spanish Theory of Empire in the Sixteenth Century* (Cambridge, MA: Cambridge University Press, 1940).

4. Victoria, following Saint Augustine, framed the conditions for "Just Wars" by Europeans against Indians in 1577. For articulation and analysis, see Williams, Robert A., Jr., *The American Indian in Western Legal Thought: The Discourses of Conquest* (New York: Oxford University Press, 1990), pp. 96-108. With regard to England *per se*, see Knorr, K., *British Colonial Theories, 1570-1850* (Toronto: University of Toronto Press, 1944). On the Augustinian formulation, see Deane, Herbert Andrew, *The Political and Social Ideas of St. Augustine* (New York: Columbia University Press, 1963).

5. On Columbus' violation of prevailing laws, both international and Spanish, see Floyd, Trof, *The Columbus Dynasty in the Caribbean, 1492-1526* (Albuquerque: University of New Mexico Press, 1973). Also see Sale, Kirkpatrick, *The Conquest of Paradise: Christopher Columbus and the Columbian Legacy* (New York: Alfred A. Knopf Publishers, 1990).

6. Coulter and Tullberg, *op. cit.*, p. 191. The authors are drawing on Oppenheim, L., *International Law*, vol. I (London: Longmans, Green and Co., Publishers, 1955), pp. 588-89. For a comprehensive overview, see Peckman, Howard, and Charles Gibson, ed., *Attitudes of the Colonial Powers Towards American Indians* (Salt Lake City: University of Utah Press, 1969). On evolution of the British tradition in this respect, see Quinn, David Beers, *England and the Discovery of America, 1481-1620* (New York: Alfred A. Knopf Publishers, 1974). Excellent collections of the actual treaty texts

at issue may be found in Davenport, Francis Gardiner, ed., *European Treaties Bearing on the History of the United States and Its Dependencies*, 2 vols. (Washington, D.C.: Carnegie Institution of Washington, 1917) and Vaughan, Alden T., *Early American Indian Documents: Treaties and Laws, 1607-1789* (Washington, D.C.: University Publications of America, 1979).

7. For an examination of the military balance, see Peckman, Howard Henry, *Pontiac and the Indian Uprising* (New York: Russell and Russell Publishers, 1970). For deeper background, see Porter, Harry Culverwell, *The Inconstant Savage: England and the American Indian, 1500-1600* (London: Duckworth Publishers, 1979).

8. On the British military alliance with the Iroquois Confederacy, see Flexner, James Thomas, *Lord of the Mohawks: A Biography of Sir William Johnson* (Boston, MA: Little, Brown Publishers, 1979). On the Muscogee, see Robinson, Walter Stilt, *The Southern Colonial Frontier, 1607-1763* (Albuquerque: University of New Mexico Press, 1979). Overall, see Jacobs, Wilbur, *Dispossessing the American Indian: Indians and Whites on the Colonial Frontier* (New York: Charles Scribner, Publisher, 1972).

9. This thesis is brought forward quite forcefully in Jensen, Merrill, *Founding of a Nation: A History of the American Revolution, 1763-1776* (London/New York: Oxford University Press, 1968), pp. 3-35. Also see Abernathy, Thomas Perkins, *Western Lands and the American Revolution* (New York: Russell and Russell, Publishers, 1959) and Bailyn, Bernard, *The Ideological Origins of the American Revolution* (Cambridge, Ma.: Harvard University Press, 1967).

10. In general, see Jensen, Merrill, *The Articles of Confederation: An Interpretation of the Socio-Constitutional History of the American Revolution, 1774-1778* (Madison: University of Wisconsin Press, 1940), especially pp. 154-62, 190-232. Also see Wood, Gordon, *The Creation of the American Republic, 1776-1787* (Chapel Hill: University of North Carolina Press, 1969) and Lewis, Gordon, *The Indiana Company, 1763-1798* (Glendale, CA: Clark Publishers, 1941).

11. Deloria, Vine, Jr., "Sovereignty," in *Economic Development in American Indian Reservations*, ed. Roxanne Dunbar Ortiz and Larry Emerson, Native American Studies Center (Albuquerque: University of New Mexico, 1979). For context, see Mohr, Walter Harrison, *Federal Indian Relations, 1774-1788* (Philadelphia: University of Pennsylvania Press, 1933).

12. The case at issue is *Johnson v. McIntosh* (1822); see legal table in this volume.

13. Baker, L., *John Marshall: A Life in Law* (New York: Macmillan Publishers, 1974), p. 80.

14. See Horsman, Reginald, *Expansion and American Indian Policy, 1783-1812* (East Lansing: Michigan State University Press, 1967).

15. For further discussion of Marshall's and others' thinking during this period, see Berman, Howard R., "The Concept of Aboriginal Rights in the Early Legal History of the United States," *Buffalo Law Review*, no. 28 (1978): pp. 637-67. Also see Cohen, Felix S., "Original Indian Title," *Minnesota Law Review*, no. 32 (1947): pp. 28-59.

16. Interesting analysis of Marshall's emerging doctrine may be found in Barsh, Russel, and James Youngblood Henderson, *The Road: Indian Tribes and Political Liberty* (Berkeley: University of California Press, 1980).

17. See Harvey, C., "Constitutional Law: Congressional Plenary Power Over Indian Affairs—A Doctrine Rooted in Prejudice," *American Indian Law Review*, no. 10 (1982): pp. 117-50.

18. See Estin, Ann Laquer, *Lonewolf v. Hitchcock: The Long Shadow,* in Cadwalader and Deloria, *op. cit.,* pp. 215-45. Also see Wilkinson, Charles F., and John M. Volkman, "Judicial Review of Treaty Abrogation: 'As Long as the Water Flows, or Grass Grows upon the Earth'—How Long a Time is That?" *California Law Review,* no. 63 (May 1975): pp. 601-61.

19. Coulter and Tullberg, *op. cit.,* p. 203. The authors are quoting from Hobson, J. A., *Imperialism: A Study* (Ann Arbor: University of Michigan Press, 1965), p. 240. Also see Coulter, Robert T., "The Denial of Legal Remedies to Indian Nations Under U.S. Law," *American Indian Law Journal,* vol. 9, no. 3 (1977), pp. 5-9.

20. Professions of formal U.S. anti-imperialism began to be put forward in serious fashion by government propagandists in 1823, the year in which the Monroe Doctrine was articulated (that is, within one year of the *Johnson v. McIntosh* opinion in which John Marshall began his project of legitimating wholesale conquest and colonization of Native America). It was always used as a cover for North American economic and political domination. See Pearce, Jenny, *Under the Eagle: U.S. Intervention in Central America and the Caribbean* (Boston, MA: South End Press, 1982).

21. The count of 40 Indian Wars is the conservative official view. See U.S. Bureau of the Census, *Report on Indians Taxed and Indians Not Taxed in the United States (except Alaska) at the Eleventh Census: 1890* (Washington, D.C.: U.S. Government Printing Office, 1894), p. 637.

22. The standard count has been that the U.S. Senate ratified 371 treaties with various indigenous nations between 1778 and 1868. The texts of these are reproduced verbatim in Kappler, Charles J., *Indian Treaties, 1778-1883* (New York: Interland Publishing Co., 1973). In addition, the Sioux scholar Vine Deloria, Jr., has collected the texts of an additional nine ratified treaty texts not contained in Kappler, as well as the texts of some 300 additional treaty instruments negotiated by the federal executive, and upon which the U.S. now professes to anchor title to assorted chunks of territory, although they were never ratified. For further background, see Jones, Dorothy V., *License for Empire: Colonialism by Treaty in Early America* (Chicago: University of Chicago Press, 1982). Also see Worcester, Donald, ed., *Forked Tongues and Broken Treaties* (Caldwell, ID: Caxton Publishers, 1975).

23. The official record of the cumulative reductions in native land base leading to this result may be found in Royce, Charles C., *Indian Land Cessions in the United States: 18th Annual Report, 1896-97,* Bureau of American Ethnography, 2 vols. (Washington, D.C.: Smithsonian Institution, 1899). The 2.5 percent figure derives from computing 50 million acres against the total acreage.

24. For use of the term during the period at issue, see Wanamaker, Rodman, *The Vanishing Race: A Record in Picture and Story of the Last Great Indian Council, Including the Indians' Story of the Custer Fight* (New York: Crown Publishers, MCMXIII).

25. In 1903, the U.S. Supreme Court opined in the *Lonewolf v. Hitchcock* case that Indians had no right either to block the wholesale transfer of their reserved and treaty-guaranteed lands to non-Indians under the 1887 General Allotment Act, or to receive compensation for the loss of such lands. The high court held that federal plenary power over native property was absolute, and that Indians had no right to sue the government for breach of its concomitant trust responsibility in such matters. See Cohen, Felix S., *Handbook on Federal Indian Law* (Albuquerque: Uni-

versity of New Mexico Press, [reprint of 1942 U.S. Government Printing Office Edition] n.d.), p. 96.

26. See Jackson, Helen Hunt, *A Century of Dishonor* (New York: Harper Torchbooks, [reprint of the 1881 edition by A. F. Rolfe Publishers] 1965), p. 204.

27. U.S. House of Representatives, Committee on Interior and Insular Affairs, *Indirect Services and Expenditures by the Federal Government for the American Indian*, 86th Cong., 1st Sess. (Washington, D.C.: U.S. Government Printing Office, 1959), pp. 11-14.

28. Merriam, Lewis, *et al.*, *Problems of Indian Administration* (Baltimore: Johns Hopkins University Press, 1928), pp. 805-11.

29. On the effects of the General Allotment Act, or "Dawes Act" as it is often known, see McDonnell, Janet A., *The Dispossession of the American Indian, 1887-1934* (Bloomington/Indianapolis: Indiana University Press, 1991). Also see Otis, D. S., *The Dawes Act and the Allotment of Indian Land* (Norman: University of Oklahoma Press, 1973).

30. Ehrenfeld, Alice, and Robert W. Barker, comps., *Legislative Material on the Indian Claims Commission Act of 1946* (Washington, D.C.: unpublished study, n.d.)

31. An interesting handling of the geopolitical dynamics involved during the Roosevelt era may be found in Varg, Paul A., *America: From Client State to World Power* (Norman: University of Oklahoma Press, 1990), especially pp. 167-207. Also see Isaacson, Walter, and Evan Thomas, *The Wise Men: Six Friends and the World They Made* (New York: Simon and Schuster Publishers, 1986). On Truman's shift, see Chomsky, Noam, *Towards a New Cold War: Essays on the Current Crisis and How We Got There* (New York: Pantheon Books, 1982).

32. On the formulation of Nuremberg Doctrine, and the primacy of the U.S. role in that regard, see Smith, Bradley F., *The Road to Nuremberg* (New York: Basic Books, 1981).

33. On the handling of the Nuremberg Trials, and the messages embodied in it, see Smith, Bradley F., *Reaching Judgement at Nuremberg: The Untold Story of How the Nazi War Criminals Were Judged* (New York: Basic Books, 1977). Also see Davidson, Eugene, *The Trial of the Germans: Nuremberg, 1945-1946* (New York: Macmillan Publishers, 1966). Concerning George Bush's recent use of Nuremberg rhetoric, see Cheney, George, "'Talking War': Symbols, Strategies, and Images," *New Studies on the Left*, vol. XIV, no, 3 (Winter 1990-91): pp. 8-16.

34. For detailed analysis of the American concept, see Merk, Frederick, *Manifest Destiny and Mission in American Life* (New York: Vintage Books, 1966) and Horsman, Reginald, *Race and Manifest Destiny* (Cambridge, MA: Harvard University Press, 1981). To sample the philosophy at issue from the proverbial horse's mouth, see Fiske, John, "Manifest Destiny," in *American Political Ideas Viewed from the Standpoint of Universal History* (New York: Houghton-Mifflin Publishers, 1885). For purposes of comparison to nazi ideology, see Koehl, Robert L., *German Resettlement and Population Policy, 1939-1945* (Cambridge, MA: Harvard University Press, 1957).

35. See Hitler, Adolf, *Hitler's Secret Conversations* (New York: Signet Books, 1961) and *Hitler's Secret Book* (New York: Grove Press, 1961). The nazi leader's attributions to U.S. policy are also remarked in Hoffman, Heinrich, *Hitler Was My Friend* (London: Burke Publishers, 1955); Toland, John, *Adolf Hitler*, 2 vols. (Garden City, NJ: Doubleday Publishers, 1976); and elsewhere. For detail on nazi policy appli-

cations, see Dallin, Alexander, *German Rule in Russia, 1941-1944* (London: Macmillan Publishers, 1957).

36. Discussion of such measures began in Congress in the fall of 1944, at the same time that planning for Nuremberg was entering its final stages. See Smith, Bradley F., *The American Road to Nuremberg: The Documentary Record* (Palo Alto, CA: Stanford University Press, 1981). For summative discussion of the mechanism to be used in retiring Indian claims and motives for creating it, see U.S. House of Representatives, Committee on Indian Affairs, *Hearings on H.R. 1198 and H.R. 1341*, 79th Cong., 1st Sess. (Washington, D.C.: U.S. Government Printing Office, 1945).

37. Leupp, Francis E., *The Indian and His Problem* (New York: Charles Scribner's Sons Publishers, 1910), pp. 194-96. For an overview of such sentiments, see Vance, John T., "The Congressional Mandate and the Indian Claims Commission," *North Dakota Law Review*, no. 45 (1969): pp. 325-36.

38. U.S. House of Representatives, Committee on Indian Affairs, *Hearing on the Appropriation Bill of 1914*, 64th Cong., 2d Sess. (Washington, D.C.: U.S. Government Printing Office, 1913), p. 99.

39. Merriam, *et al., op. cit.*, pp. 805-11.

40. See, as examples, U.S. Senate, Committee on Interior and Insular Affairs, Subcommittee on Indian Affairs, *Hearings on S. 2731*, 74th Cong., 1st Sess. (Washington, D.C.: U.S. Government Printing Office, 1935) and U.S. House of Representatives, Committee on Indian Affairs, *Hearings on H.R. 7837*, 74th Cong., 1st Sess. (Washington, D.C.: U.S. Government Printing Office, 1935).

41. The case involved was *Thompson v. United States*, 13 Ind. Cl. Comm. 369 (1964). For further information, see Jaimes, M. Annette, "The Pit River Indian Land Claim Dispute in Northern California," *Journal of Ethnic Studies*, vol. 4, no. 4 (winter 1987).

42. Forbes, Jack, "The 'Public Domain' of Nevada and Its Relationship to Indian Property Rights," *Nevada State Bar Journal*, no. 30 (1965): pp. 16-47.

43. *Congressional Record* (May 20, 1946): p. 5312.

44. The exception here involved claims entered under provision of the Fifth Amendment, of which there were almost none. Interest was denied as a matter of course in other types of claim, based on the outcome of the *Loyal Creek Case* (1 Ind. Cl. Comm. 22). See LaDuc, Thomas, "The Work of the Indian Claims Commission Under the Act of 1946," *Pacific Historical Review*, no. 26 (1957): pp. 1-16.

45. Actually, there is one exception. In 1965, the Claims Commission recommended (15 Ind. Cl. Comm. 666) restoration of 130,000 acres of the Blue Lake area to Taos Pueblo (see Gordon-McCutchan, R. C., *The Taos Indians and the Battle for Blue Lake* [Santa Fe, NM: Red Crane Books, 1991]). In 1970, Congress followed up by restoring a total of 48,000 acres (85 *Stat.* 1437). For further information, see Nielson, Richard A., "American Indian Land Claims: Land versus Money as a Remedy," *University of Florida Law Review*, vol. 19, no. 3 (1973): pp. 308-26.

46. U.S. House of Representatives, Committee on Indian Affairs, *Providing a One-Year Extension of the Five-Year Limitation on the Time for Presenting Indian Claims to the Indian Claims Commission*, H. Rep. 692, 82d Cong., 1st Sess. (Washington, D.C.: U.S. Government Printing Office, 1951), pp. 593-601.

47. The Claims Commission was initially authorized for 10 years longevity. In 1956, it was extended for a further five years. The process was repeated in 1961, 1967, 1972, and 1976. See U.S. House and Senate, Joint Committee on Appropriations,

Hearings on Appropriations for the Department of Interior, 94th Cong., 1st Sess. (Washington, D.C.: U.S. Government Printing Office, 1976).

48. U.S. Senate, Committee on Interior and Insular Affairs, Subcommmittee on Indian Affairs, *Hearings on S. 307*, 90th Cong., 1st Sess. (Washington, D.C.: U.S. Government Printing Office, 1967).

49. U.S. Senate, Committee on Interior and Insular Affairs, Subcommittee on Indian Affairs, *Hearings on S. 876*, 94th Cong., 1st Sess. (Washington, D.C.: U.S. Government Printing Office, 1975).

50. Indian Claims Commission, *Final Report* (Washington, D.C.: U.S. Government Printing Office, 1978).

51. For a prime example of the sort of academic apologetics for U.S. conduct engendered by the Claims Commission process, see Sutton, Imre, ed., *Irredeemable America: The Indians' Estate and Land Tenure* (Albuquerque: University of New Mexico Press, 1985).

52. Barsh, Russel, "Indian Land Claims Policy in the United States," *North Dakota Law Review*, no. 58 (1982): pp. 1-82.

53. See, for instance, Deloria, Vine, Jr., *A Better Day for Indians* (New York: Field Foundation, 1977). For official quantification of the acreage involved, see Public Land Law Review Commission, *One Third of the Nation's Land* (Washington, D.C.: U.S. Department of Interior, 1970).

54. *Oneida Indian Nation v. County of Oneida*, 414 U.S. 661 (1974). For background on the strategy involved in such litigation, see Kellogg, Mark, "Indian Rights: Fighting Back With White Man's Weapons," *Saturday Review* (November 1978): pp. 24-30.

55. The letters were found in an old trunk by an elderly Passamaquoddy woman in 1957, and turned over to Township Governor John Stevens. It took the Indians 15 years to bring the matter to court, largely because it was denied they had "legal standing" to do so. See Brodeur, Paul, *Restitution: The Land Claims of the Mashpee, Passamaquoddy, and Penobscot Indians of New England* (Boston, MA: Northeastern University Press, 1985).

56. *Passamaquoddy Tribe v. Morton*, 528 F.2d, 370 (1975). For additional background, see O'Toole, Francis J., and Thomas N. Tureen, "State Power and the Passamaquoddy Tribe: A Gross National Hypocrisy?" *Maine Law Review*, vol. 23, no. 1 (1971): pp. 1-39.

57. Maine Indian Land Claims Settlement Act of 1980, 94 *Stat.* 1785.

58. The case is *Narragansett Tribe of Indians v. S.R.I. Land Development Corporation*, 418 F. Supp. 803 (1978). The decision was followed by the Rhode Island Indian Claims Settlement Act of 1978, 94 *Stat.* 3498.

59. *Western Pequot Tribe of Indians v. Holdridge Enterprises, Inc.*, Civ. No. 76-193 (1976).

60. The Mashantucket Pequot Indian Claims Settlement Act (S.366) was passed by Congress in December 1982. Reagan's veto is covered in the *Congressional Quarterly*, vol 41, no. 14: pp. 710-11.

61. The revised version of the Mashantucket Pequot Indian Claims Settlement Act (S.1499) was signed on October 18, 1983.

62. *Mashpee Tribe v. Town of Mashpee*, 447 F. Supp. 940 (1978).

63. *Mashpee Tribe v. New Seabury Corporation*, 592 F.2d (1st Cir.) 575 (1979), *cert. denied* (1980). For further information, see Wallace, Harry B., "Indian Sovereignty and the

Eastern Indian Land Claims," *New York University Law School Law Review*, no. 27 (1982): pp. 921-50. Also see Brodeur, *op. cit.*

64. *Mohegan Tribe v. Connecticut*, 483 F. Supp. 597 (D. Conn. 1980) and *Schaghticoke Tribe v. Kent School Corporation*, 423 F. Supp. 780 (D. Conn. 1983).

65. By the 1840 Treaty of Nation Ford, the Catawbas agreed to relinquish the reservation in exchange for a $5,000 acquisition of replacement lands. The state defaulted on the agreement, and the Catawbas were left entirely homeless for two years. Finally, in 1842, South Carolina spent $2,000 to buy 630 acres (apparently from itself) *of the former reservation* for "Catawba use and occupancy." See Hudson, Charles M., "The Catawba Indians of South Carolina: A Question of Ethnic Survival," in *Southeastern Indians Since the Removal Era*, ed. Walter L. William (Athens: University of Georgia Press, 1979), pp. 110-20.

66. *Catawba Indian Tribe of South Carolina v. State of South Carolina* (October 11, 1983).

67. For an assessment of the progress made in this arena, see Anaya, S. James, "The Rights of Indigenous Peoples and International Law in Historical and Contemporary Perspective," in *American Indian Law: Cases and Materials*, ed. Robert N. Clinton, Nell Jessup Newton, and Monroe E. Price (Charlottesville, VA: The Michie Co., Law Publishers, 1991), pp. 1257-76. For the principles involved in resolving issues of this sort through such means, see Lillich, Richard B., *International Claims: Their Adjudication by National Commission* (Syracuse, NY: Syracuse University Press, 1962).

68. Florida Indian Land Claim Settlement Act, 96 *Stat.* 2012 (1982). For background, see Coulter, Robert T., *et al.*, "Seminole Land Rights in Florida and the Award of the Indian Claims Commission," *American Indian Journal*, vol 4, no. 3 (August 1978): pp. 2-27.

69. See LaDuke, Winona, "The White Earth Land Struggle," in *Critical Issues in Native North America*, ed. Ward Churchill (Copenhagen: Doc. 63, International Work Group on Indigenous Affairs, 1989), pp. 55-71, and "White Earth: The Struggle Continues," in *Critical Issues in Native North America, Vol. II*, ed. Ward Churchill (Copenhagen: Doc. 68, International Work Group on Indigenous Affairs, 1991), pp. 99-103. Also see Peterson, E. M., Jr., "The So-Called Warranty Deed: Clouded Land Titles on the White Earth Reservation in Minnesota," *North Dakota Law Review*, no. 59 (1983): pp. 159-81.

70. See McCool, Daniel, "Federal Indian Policy and the Sacred Mountains of the Papago Indians," *Journal of Ethnic Studies*, vol 9, no. 3 (1981): pp. 57-69.

71. See Lovett, Richard A., "The Role of the Forest Service in Ski Resort Development: An Economic Approach to Public Lands Management," *Ecology Law Review*, no. 10 (1983): pp. 507-78. Also see Lubick, George, "Sacred Mountains, Kachinas, and Skiers: The Controversy Over the San Francisco Peaks," in *The American West: Essays in Honor of W. Eugene Hollan*, ed. R. Lora (Toledo, OH: University of Toledo Press, 1980), pp. 133-53.

72. See Churchill, Ward, "Genocide in Arizona? The Navajo-Hopi Land Dispute in Perspective," in *Critical Issues in Native North America, Vol. II, op. cit.*, pp. 104-46.

73. See Campisi, Jack, "The Trade and Intercourse Acts: Indian Land Claims on the Eastern Seaboard," in Sutton, *op. cit.*, pp. 337-62.

74. For the basis of this struggle, see Berry, M. C., *The Alaska Pipeline: The Politics of Oil and Native Land Claims* (Bloomington/Indianapolis: Indiana University Press,

1975). Also see Berger, John, *Report from the Frontier: The State of the World's Indigenous Peoples* (London: Zed Press, 1987).

75. On the rejection, see U.S. House of Representatives, *House Report 15066*, 94th Cong., 1st Sess. (Washington, D.C.: U.S. Government Printing Office, 1974). In 1980, the Congress passed an act (94 *Stat.* 3321) mandating formation of a Native Hawaiians Study Commission (six federal officials and three Hawaiians) to find out "what the natives really want." The answer, predictably, was *land*.

76. For the basis of the native argument here, see Cannelora, L., *The Origin of Hawaiian Land Titles and the Rights of Native Tenants* (Honolulu: Security Title Corporation, 1974).

77. Jefferson and other "radicals" held U.S. sovereignty accrued from the country itself and did not "devolve" from the British Crown. Hence, U.S. land title could not devolve from the Crown. Put another way, Jefferson—in contrast to John Marshall—held that the British's asserted discovery rights in North America had no bearing on U.S. rights to occupancy on the continent. See Wood, Gordon, *op. cit.*, pp. 162-96.

78. See generally, Graymont, Barbara, *The Iroquois in the American Revolution* (Syracuse, NY: Syracuse University Press, 1975). The concern felt by Congress with regard to the Iroquois as a military threat, and the consequent need to reach an accommodation with them, is expressed often in early official correspondence. See Ford, Washington C., *et al.*, ed. and comps., *Journals of the Continental Congress, 1774-1789*, 34 vols. (Washington, D.C.: U.S. Government Printing Office, 1904-1937).

79. Campisi, Jack, "From Fort Stanwix to Canandaigua: National Policy, States' Rights and Indian Land," in *Iroquois Land Claims*, ed. Christopher Vescey and William A. Starna (Syracuse, NY: Syracuse University Press, 1988), pp. 49-65; quote from p. 55. Also see Manley, Henry M., *The Treaty of Fort Stanwix, 1784*, (Rome, NY: Rome Sentinel Publications, 1932).

80. For an account of these meetings, conducted by New York's Governor Clinton during August and September 1784, see Hough, Franklin B., ed., *Proceedings of the Commissioners of Indian Affairs, Appointed by Law for Extinguishment of Indian Titles in the State of New York*, 2 vols. (Albany, NY: John Munsell Publishers, 1861), pp. 41-63.

81. Campisi, *op. cit.*, p. 59. Clinton lied, bold faced. New York's references to the Genesee Company concerned a bid by that group of land speculators to lease Oneida land which the Indians had not only rejected, but which the state legislature had refused to approve. In effect, the Oneida's had lost *no* land, were unlikely to, and the governor knew it.

82. See Clinton, George, *Public Papers of George Clinton: First Governor of New York*, vol. 8 (Albany, NY: 1904).

83. The price paid by New York for the Onondaga lease was "1,000 French Crowns, 200 pounds in clothing, plus a $500 annuity." See Upton, Helen M., *The Everett Report in Historical Perspective: The Indians of New York* (Albany: New York State Bicentennial Commission, 1980), p. 35.

84. *Ibid.*, p. 38.

85. The relevant portion of the statute's text reads: "[N]o sale of lands made by any Indians, or any nation or tribe of Indians within the United States, shall be valid

to any person or persons, or to any state, whether having the right of pre-emption to such lands or not, unless the same shall be made and duly executed at some public treaty, held under the authority of the United States."

86. Upton, *op. cit.*, p. 40.

87. For ratification discussion on the meaning of the Treaty of Canandaigua, see *American State Papers: Documents, Legislative and Executive of the Congress of the United States, from the First Session to the Third Session of the Thirteenth Congress, Inclusive*, vol. 4 (Washington, D.C.: Gales and Seaton Publishers, 1832), pp. 545-70. On Tecumseh's alliance, see Edmunds, R. David, *Tecumseh and the Quest for Indian Leadership* (Boston, MA: Little, Brown and Company, Publishers, 1984).

88. See Edwards, Paul D., *The Holland Company* (Buffalo, NY: Buffalo Historical Society, 1924).

89. See Nammack, Georgiana C., *Fraud, Politics, and the Dispossession of the Indians: The Iroquois Frontier and the Colonial Period* (Norman: University of Oklahoma Press, 1969). Also see Manley, Henry S., "Red Jacket's Last Campaign," *New York History*, no. 21 (April 1950).

90. See Manley, Henry S., "Buying Buffalo from the Indians," *New York History*, no. 28 (July 1947).

91. Kappler, *op. cit.*, pp. 374-78. Also see Society of Friend (Hicksite), *The Case of the Seneca Indians in the State of New York* (Stanfordville, NY: Earl E. Coleman Publisher, [reprint of 1840 edition] 1979).

92. Most principle leaders of the Six Nations never signed the Buffalo Creek Treaty. Each of the three consecutive votes taken in the Senate on ratification (requiring two-thirds affirmation to be lawful) resulted in a tie, broken only by the "aye" vote of Vice President Richard Johnson. See Manley, "Buying Buffalo from the Indians," *op. cit.*

93. U.S. House of Representatives, H. Doc. 66, 26th Cong., 2d Sess. (January 6, 1841).

94. Kappler, *op. cit.*, p. 397.

95. The Tonawanda protest appears as U.S. Senate, S. Doc. 273, 29th Cong., 2d Sess. (April 2, 1842).

96. On the award, made on November 5, 1857, see *Documents of the Assembly of the State of New York*, 112th Sess., Doc. 51 (Albany: 1889), pp. 167-70.

97. Upton, op. cit., p. 53. The New York Supreme Court's invalidation of the leases is covered in *U.S. v. Forness*, 125 F.2d 928 (1942). On the court's deeming of the leases to be perpetual, see U.S. House of Representatives, Committee on Indian Affairs, *Hearings in Favor of House Bill No. 12270*, 57th Cong., 2d Sess. (Washington, D.C.: U.S. Government Printing Office, 1902).

98. Assembly Doc. 51, *op. cit.*, pp. 43, 408.

99. 28 *Stat.* 887 (March 2, 1895).

100. *Hearings in Favor of House Bill No. 12270, op. cit.* p. 23.

101. *Ibid.*, p. 66.

102. The original case is *Seneca Nation v. Appleby*, 127 AD 770 (1905). It was appealed as *Seneca Nation v, Appleby*, 196 NY 318 (1906).

103. The case, *United States v. Boylan*, 265 Fed. 165 (2d Cir. 1920), is important not because of the paltry quantity of land restored, but because it was the first time the federal judiciary formally acknowledged New York had never acquired legal

title to Iroquois land. It was also one of the very few times in American history when non-Indians were actually evicted in order that Indians might recover illegally-taken property.

104. New York State Indian Commission Act, Chapter 590, Laws of New York (May 12, 1919).

105. Upton, *op. cit.*, p. 99.

106. The document is Everett, Edward A., *Report of the New York State Indian Commission* (Albany, NY: unpublished, March 17, 1922), pp. 308-9, 322-30.

107. Stenographic record of August 21, 1922 meeting, Stillman files.

108. Upton, *op. cit.*, pp. 124-29.

109. The total amount to be paid the Senecas for rental of their Salamanca property was $6,000 per year, much of which had gone unpaid since the mid-'30s. The judges found the federal government to have defaulted on its obligation to regulate state and private leases of Seneca land, and instructed it to take an active role in the future. See Hauptman, Laurence M., "The Historical Background to the Present-Day Seneca Nation-Salamanca Lease Controversy," in *Iroquois Land Claims, op. cit.*, pp. 101-22. Also see Merrill, Arch, "The Salamanca Lease Settlement," *American Indian*, no. 1 (1944).

110. These laws, which were replicated in Kansas and Iowa during 1952, predate the more general application of state jurisdiction to Indians embodied in Public Law 280, passed in August 1953. U.S. Congress, Joint Legislative Committee, *Report* (Leg. Doc. 74), 83rd Cong., 1st Sess. (Washington, D.C.: U.S. Government Printing Office, 1953).

111. This was based on a finding in *United States v. Minnesota* (270 U.S. 181 [1926], s.c. 271 U.S. 648) that state statutes of limitations do not apply to federal action in Indian rights cases.

112. See Campisi, Jack, "National Policy, States' Rights, and Indian Sovereignty: The Case of the New York Iroquois," in *Extending the Rafters: Interdisciplinary Approaches to Iroquoian Studies*, ed. Michael K. Foster, Jack Campisi, and Marianne Mithun (Albany: State University of New York Press, 1984).

113. For the congressional position, and commentary on the independent study of alternative sites undertaken by Dr. Arthur Morgan, see U.S. Senate, Committee on Interior and Insular Affairs, *Hearings Before the Committee on Interior and Insular Affairs: Kinzua Dam Project, Pennsylvania*, 88th Cong., 1st Sess. (Washington, D.C.: U.S. Government Printing Office, May-December 1963).

114. For further detail on the struggle around Kinzua Dam, see Hauptman, Lawrence M., *The Iroquois Struggle for Survival: World War II to Red Power* (Syracuse, NY: Syracuse University Press, 1986).

115. *Tuscarora Indians v. New York State Power Authority*, 257 F.2d 885 (1958).

116. On the compromise acreage, see Hauptman, Laurence M., "Iroquois Land Claims Issues: At Odds with the 'Family of New York'," in *Iroquois Land Claims, op. cit.*, pp. 67-86.

117. It took another 10 years for this to be spelled out definitively; *Oneida Indian Nation v. United States*, 37 Ind. Cl. Comm. 522 (1971).

118. For a detailed account of the discussions, agreements, and various factions within the process, see Upton, *op. cit.*, pp. 139-61.

119. See Treur, Margaret, "Ganiekeh: An Alternative to the Reservation System and Public Trust," *American Indian Journal*, vol. 5, no. 5 (1979), pp. 22-26.

120. *State of New York v. Danny White, et al.*, Civ. No. 74-CV-370 (N.D.N.Y., April 1976); *State of New York v. Danny White, et al.*, Civ. No. 74-CV-370, Memorandum Decision and Order (March 23, 1977).

121. On the Moss Lake Agreement, see Kwartler, Richard, "'This Is Our Land': *Mohawk Indians v. The State of New York*," in *Roundtable Justice: Case Studies in Conflict Resolution*, ed. Robert B. Goldman (Boulder, CO: Westview Press, 1980).

122. *Oneida Indian Nation of New York v. County of Oneida*, 14 U.S. 661 (1974).

123. *Oneida Indian Nation of New York v. County of Oneida*, 434 F. Supp. 527, 548 (N.D.N.Y., 1979).

124. Van Gestel, Allan, "New York Indian Land Claims: The Modern Landowner as Hostage," in *Iroquois Land Claims*, op. cit., pp. 123-39. Also see the revision published as "When Fictions Take Hostages," in *The Invented Indian: Cultural Fictions and Government Policies*, ed. James E. Clifton (New Brunswick, NJ: Transaction Books, 1990), pp. 291-312, and "The New York Indian Land Claims: An Overview and a Warning," *New York State Bar Journal* (April 1981).

125. *County of Oneida v. Oneida Indian Nation of New York*, 84 L.Ed.2d 169, 191 (1984).

126. Locklear, Arlinda, "The Oneida Land Claims: A Legal Overview," in *Iroquois Land Claims, op. cit.*, pp. 141-53.

127. *Ibid.*, p. 148.

128. This suit was later recast to name the state rather than the counties as primary defendant, and enlarged to encompass six million acres. It challenged, but upheld on appeal; *Oneida Indian Nation of New York v. State of New York*, 691 F.2d 1070 (1982). Dismissed by a district judge four years later (Brennan, Claire, "Oneida Claim to 6 Million Acres Voided," *Syracuse Post-Standard* [November 22, 1986]), it was reinstated by the Second Circuit Court in 1988 (*Oneida Indian Nation of New York v. State of New York*, 860 F.2d 1145), and is ongoing as of this writing.

129. *Oneida Nation of Indians of Wisconsin v. State of New York*, 85 F.D.R. 701, 703 (N.Y.D.C., 1980).

130. New York has attempted various arguments to obtain dismissal of the Cayuga suit. In 1990, the state's contention that it had obtained bona fide land title to the disputed area in leases obtained in 1795 and 1801 was overruled at the district court level (*Cayuga Indian Nation of New York v. Cuomo*, 730 F. Supp. 485). In 1991, an "interpretation" by the state attorney general that reservation of land by the Six Nations in the Fort Stanwix Treaty "did not really" invest recognizable title in them was similarly overruled (*Cayuga Indian Nation of New York v. Cuomo*, 758 F. Supp. 107). Finally, in 1991, a state contention that only a special railroad reorganization would have jurisdiction to litigate claims involving areas leased to railroads was overruled (*Cayuga Indian Nation of New York v. Cuomo*, 762 F. Supp. 30). The suit is ongoing.

131. The terms of the agreement were published in *Finger Lakes Times* (August 18, 1979).

132. For further details, see Lavin, Chris, "The Cayuga Land Claims," in *Iroquois Land Claims, op. cit.*, pp. 87-100.

133. The one jurisdictional exception is that the Second Circuit ruled in 1988 that a federal statute passed in 1875 empowers the City of Salamanca, rather than the

Senecas, to regulate zoning within the leased area so long as the leases exist (*John v. City of Salamanca*, 845 F.2d 37).

134. The non-Indian city government of Salamanca, a sub-part of which is the Salamanca Lease Authority, filed suit in 1990 to block settlement of the Seneca claim as "unconstitutional," and to compel a new 99 year lease on its own terms (*Salamanca Indian Lease Authority v. Seneca Indian Nation*, Civ. No. 1300, Docket 91-7086). They lost and appealed. The lower court decision was affirmed by the Second Circuit Court on March 15, 1991, on the basis that the Senecas enjoy "sovereign immunity" from any further such suits.

135. Public Law 101-503, 104 *Stat.* 1179.

136. For the treaty text, see Kappler, *op. cit.*, pp. 594-96. For background, see Nadeau, Remi, *Fort Laramie and the Sioux* (Lincoln: University of Nebraska Press, 1967) and Hafen, LeRoy R., and Francis Marion Young, *Fort Laramie and the Pageant of the West, 1834-1890* (Lincoln: University of Nebraska Press, 1938).

137. See Brown, Dee, *Fort Phil Kearny: An American Saga* (Lincoln: University of Nebraska Press, 1971). Also see Hebard, Grace, and E. A. Brindenstool, *The Bozeman Trail*, 2 vols. (Cleveland, OH: Arthur H. Clark Publishers, 1922).

138. The treaty text will be found in Kappler, *op. cit.*. Lakota territorality is spelled out in Articles 2 and 16, non-abrogation of 1851 treaty land provisions in Article 17.

139. *Ibid.*, Article 12. The gender provision is of United States rather than Lakota origin.

140. See Jackson, Donald, *Custer's Gold: The United States Cavalry Expedition of 1874* (Lincoln: University of Nebraska Press, 1966). Also see U.S. Department of Interior (William Ludlow), *Report of a Reconnaissance of the Black Hills of Dakota* (Washington, D.C.: U.S. Government Printing Office, 1875). It should also be noted that, prior to the outbreak of hostilities in 1876, a second U.S. invasion of Lakota territory—the 1875 "Jenny Expedition"—was sent into the Black Hills to corroborate Custer's findings; see U.S. Department of Interior, Walter P. Jenny, *Report to Congress on the Mineral Wealth, Climate and Rainfall, and Natural Resources of the Black Hills of South Dakota*, Exec. Doc. 51, 44th Cong., 1st Sess. (Washington, D.C.: U.S. Government Printing Office, 1876). The Lakota responded militarily to neither violation of the treaty.

141. U.S. Department of Interior, Bureau of Indian Affairs, *Annual Report of the Commissioner of Indian Affairs, 1875* (Washington, D.C.: U.S. Government Printing Office, 1875).

142. U.S. Department of War, *Annual Report of the Secretary of War*, 43rd Cong., 2d Sess. (Washington, D.C.: U.S. Government Printing Office, 1876), p. 441. Also see Olsen, James C., *Red Cloud and the Sioux Problem* (Lincoln: University of Nebraska Press, 1965).

143. With Vaughn, J. W., *With Crook at the Rosebud* (Lincoln: University of Nebraska Press, 1956).

145. On the Custer fight, see Sandoz, Mari, *The Battle of the Little Big Horn* (New York: Curtis Books, 1966). For further contextualization, see Gray, John E., *Centennial Campaign: The Sioux War of 1876* (Norman: University of Oklahoma Press, 1988). Another excellent reading is Ambrose, Stephen E., *Crazy Horse and Custer: The Parallel Lives of Two American Warriors* (Garden City, NJ: Doubleday Publishers, 1975).

146. For a detailed account of one of these slaughters, see Greene, Jerome, *Slim Buttes, 1877: An Episode in the Great Sioux War* (Norman: University of Oklahoma Press, 1982). For more on McKenzie, who had made his reputation in a winter attack upon a Comanche village in Palo Duro Canyon (Texas) in 1874, see Fehrenbach, T. R., *Comanches: The Destruction of a People* (New York: Alfred A. Knopf Publishers, 1975), pp. 516-21.

147. On the Hunkpapa evasion to Canada, see Vestal, Stanley, *Sitting Bull: Champion of the Sioux* (Norman: University of Oklahoma Press, 1932). On the false promises made to Crazy Horse (through Red Cloud), see Brown, Dee, *Bury My Heart at Wounded Knee: An Indian History of the American West* (New York: Holt, Rinehart and Winston Publishers, 1970), pp. 308-10.

148. For first-hand accounts, see Clark, Robert A., ed., *The Killing of Chief Crazy Horse* (Lincoln: University of Nebraska Press, 1976).

149. This legislative history is covered quite well in a contribution entitled "1986 Black Hills Hearing on S.1453, Introduction," prepared by the staff of Senator Daniel Inouye, Chair of the Senate Select Committee on Indian Affairs, for *Wicazo Sa Review*, vol. IV, no. 1 (spring 1988). Total "Sioux" treaty territory—including that of the Nakota ("Prairie Sioux") and Dakota ("Woodland Sioux") east of the Missouri River—added up to 160 to 175 million acres according to the Indian Claims Commission *Final Report, op. cit.*

150. See Fritz, Henry E., *The Movement for Indian Assimilation, 1860-1890* (Philadelphia: University of Pennsylvania Press, 1963).

151. See *Sioux Tribe v. United States* (2 Ind. Cl. Comm. 671) for computation of acreage.

152. For a good dose of the propaganda prevailing at the time, see Welsh, Herbert, "The Meaning of the Dakota Outbreak," *Scribner's Magazine* (April 1891): pp. 439-52. A more comprehensive and considered topical view, albeit one generally conforming to ideological requirements, is Mooney, James M., *The Ghost-Dance Religion and the Sioux Outbreak of 1890*, Bureau of American Ethnology, Smithsonian Institution (Washington, D.C.: U.S. Government Printing Office, 1896). The most balanced and accurate account may probably be found in *Bury My Heart at Wounded Knee, op. cit.*

153. Deloria, Vine, Jr., and Clifford M. Lytle, *American Indians, American Justice* (Austin: University of Texas Press, 1983), p. 10.

154. For an official assessment of this situation, see the memorandum of Indian Commissioner John Collier, U.S. House of Representatives, Committee on Indian Affairs, *Hearings on HR 7902 before the House Committee on Indian Affairs*, 73rd Cong., 2d Sess. (Washington, D.C.: U.S. Government Printing Office, 1934), pp. 16-18.

155. Eastman's books include *Old Indian Days* (New York: McClure Publishers, 1907), *The Soul of the Indian: An Interpretation* (New York: Johnson Reprint Corp., 1971; originally published in 1911), *From Deep Woods to Civilization: Chapters in an Autobiography of an Indian* (Boston, MA: Little, Brown Publishers, 1916), and *Indian Heroes and Great Chieftains* (Boston, MA: Little, Brown Publishers, 1918).

156. *Sioux Tribe v. United States*, 97 Ct. Cl. 613 (1942).

157. *Sioux Tribe v. United States*, 318 U.S. 789, *cert. denied* (1943).

158. *Sioux Tribe v. United States*, 2 Ind. Cl. Comm. (1956).

159. *Wicazo Sa Review, op. cit.*, pp. 10-11.

160. *United States v. Sioux Nation of Indians*, 448 U.S. 371, 385 (1968). The grounds, however, were exceedingly narrow. The commission was charged only with discovering 1) What, if any, land rights *vis-à-vis* the Black Hills had been acquired in 1877, 2) What consideration had been given by the United States in exchange for these lands, and 3) If no consideration had been given, had the United States made *any* payments that might offset its obligation to provide consideration.

161. *Sioux Nation v. United States*, 33 Ind. Cl. Comm. 151 (1974); the decision was, of course, legally absurd. The United States holds "eminent domain" powers over the property of *no* foreign nation, such as the Lakota *had* to be in order for the 1868 treaty to be consummated. Fifth Amendment compensation hardly provides redress to an invaded country. See Meinhart, Nick, and Diane Payne, "Reviewing U.S. Commitments to the Lakota Nation," *American Indian Journal,* no. 13 (November-December 1975), pp. 15-17.

162. *United States v. Sioux Nation of Indians*, 207 Ct. Cl. 234, 518 F.2d 1293 (1975).

163. *Wicazo Sa Review, op. cit.*, p. 12. On the concept of government "offsets," see White, John R., "Barmecide Revisited: The Gratuitous Offset in Indian Claims Cases," *Ethnohistory*, no. 25 (1978), pp. 179-92.

164. *Sioux Nation of Indians v. United States*, 423 U.S. 1016, *cert. denied* (1975).

165. For additional information, see Matthiessen, Peter, *In the Spirit of Crazy Horse* (New York: Viking Press, [2d edition] 1991). Also see Churchill, Ward, and Jim Vander Wall, *Agents of Repression: The FBI's Secret Wars Against the Black Panther Party and the American Indian Movement* (Boston, MA: South End Press, 1988).

166. The transfer instrument, entitled *Memorandum of Agreement Between the Oglala Sioux Tribe of South Dakota and the National Park Service of the Department of Interior to Facilitate Establishment, Development, Administration and Public Use of the Oglala Sioux Tribal Lands, Badlands National Monument*, was signed secretly by Tribal President Richard Wilson on January 2, 1976. Although the arrangement hardly conformed to the provisions for Lakota land cessions in the still-binding 1868 treaty, Congress acted as it had in 1877, quickly passing Public Law 90-468 to take possession of the property. When Lakota protest became too great, the act was amended to provide that the Indians could recover the *surface* rights at any time they elected to do so by referendum (thus inverting the treaty requirements), but not the *mineral* rights (thus removing any question as to whether the whole thing hadn't been about taking the Lakota uranium rather than enlarging a national park). See Huber, Jacqueline, *et al.*, *The Gunnery Range Report*, Oglala Sioux Tribe, Office of the Tribal President (Pine Ridge, SD, 1981).

167. "The Black Hills Are *Not* For Sale," *Native American Support Committee (NASC) Newsletter*, vol. V, no. 10 (October 1977).

168. On the building of IITC, see Weyler, Rex, *Blood of the Land: The U.S. Government and Corporate War Against the American Indian Movement* (New York: Everest House Publishers, 1982), pp. 213-16.

169. Public Law 95-243, 25 U.S.C. #70s (Supp. II, 1978).

170. *Sioux Nation of Indians v. United States*, 220 Ct. Cl. 442, 601 F.2d 1157 (1979).

171. Washburn, Wilcomb E., "Land Claims in the Mainstream," in Sutton, *op. cit.*, pp. 21-33; quote from p. 26. The opinion is *Sioux Nation of Indians v. United States*, 448 U.S. 371 (1980). For a sample of Rehnquist's own extremely inaccurate and highly politicized historical revisionism, see his opinion in the 1978 *Oliphant* case.

172. Means, Russell, "The Black Hills: They're Still Not For Sale!" *Oyate Wicaho* (May 1980). Also see Hanson, Steven C., "*United States v. Sioux Nation*: Political Questions, Moral Imperative and National Honor," *American Indian Law Review*, vol. 8, no. 2 (1980): pp. 459-84.

173. On the 1980 Black Hills Survival Gathering, see Anonymous, *Keystone for Survival* (Rapid City, SD: Black Hills Alliance, 1981). Also see Tabb, Bill, "Marx versus Marxism," in *Marxism and Native Americans*, ed. Ward Churchill (Boston, MA: South End Press, 1983), pp. 159-74.

174. *Oglala Sioux Tribe v. United States*, Cir. No. 85-062 (W.D.N.D., 1980); 448 U.S. 371, *cert. denied* (1980).

175. For analysis of the AIM strategy in the Yellow Thunder occupation, see Churchill, Ward, "Yellow Thunder *Tiyospaye*: Misadventure or Watershed Action?" *Policy Perspectives*, vol. 2, no. 2 (spring 1982). Also see Weyler, *op. cit.*; especially Chapter 8, "Yellow Thunder," pp. 251-64.

176. The Oglala Sioux Tribal Council, for example, sponsored what was called Crazy Horse Camp, in Wind Cave State Park, from July through September, 1981. The Cheyenne River Sioux established a camp at Craven Canyon, deep in the Black Hills, during the same period.

177. *United States v. Means, et al.*, Civ. No. 81-5131 (D.S.D., December 9, 1985).

178. The deposit was made pursuant to a claims court ruling; *Sioux Tribe v. United States*, 7 Cl. Ct. 80 (1985).

179. On establishment of the Working Group, and its mandate, see Anaya, *op. cit.*

180. Further delineation of the Bradley Bill, and comprehensive analysis of its implications will be found in *Wicazo Sa Review, op. cit.*

181. Stevens was a successful Defense Department contractor in the Los Angeles area, who retired and sold off his company at a reputed $60 million profit during the early '80s. He then allegedly discovered he was in some part Lakota, traveled to South Dakota, and announced "his people" were entitled to much more than was being offered in the Bradley Bill (which, of course, was true). He then stipulated that, if he were named "Great Chief of all the Sioux" (a position that has never existed), he would be able—based on his executive expertise—to negotiate a multi-billion dollar settlement and recover the whole 1868 reservation area. Some Lakotas endorsed this strategy. Tellingly, once S.1453 was withdrawn, Stevens also withdrew, and has not been heard from since. It is widely suspected he was an operative for anti-Indian interests. For details, see *Lakota Times* (1988-89, inclusive).

182. The full treaty text may be found in Kappler, *op. cit.*

183. Ryser, Rudolph C., *Newe Segobia and the United States of America* (Kenmore, WA: Occasional Paper, Center for World Indigenous Studies, 1985). Also see Matthiessen, Peter, *Indian Country* (New York: Viking Press, 1984), pp. 261-89.

184. Actually, under U.S. law, a specific Act of Congress is required to extinguish aboriginal title; *United States ex rel. Hualapi Indians v. Santa Fe Railroad*, 314, U.S. 339, 354 (1941). On Newe use of the land during this period, see Clemmer, Richard O., "Land Use Patterns and Aboriginal Rights: Northern and Eastern Nevada, 1858-1971," *The Indian Historian*, vol. 7, no. 1 (1974): pp. 24-41, 47-49.

185. Ryser, *op. cit.*, pp. 15-16.

186. Wilkinson had already entered into negotiations to represent the Temoak before the Claims Commission Act was passed; *Ibid.*, p. 13, n. 1.

187. The Temoaks have said consistently that Wilkinson always represented the claim to them as being for land rather than money. The firm is known to have run the same scam on other Indian clients; *Ibid.*, pp. 16-17.

188. *Ibid.*, p. 16. Also see Coulter, *op. cit.*, and Coulter and Tullberg, *op. cit.*

189. See Morris, Glenn T., "The Battle for Newe Segobia: The Western Shoshone Land Rights Struggle," in *Critical Issues in Native North America, vol. II, op. cit.*, pp. 86-98.

190. *Ibid.*, p. 90. The case is *Western Shoshone Identifiable Group v. United States,* 11 Ind. Cl. Comm. 387, 416 (1962). The whole issue is well covered in Forbes, Jack D., "The 'Public Domain' in Nevada and Its Relationship to Indian Property Rights," *Nevada State Bar Journal*, no. 30 (1965): pp. 16-47.

191. The first award amount appears in *Western Shoshone Identifiable Group v. United States,* 29 Ind. Cl. Comm. 5 (1972), p. 124. The second award appears in *Western Shoshone Identifiable Group v. United States,* 40 Ind. Cl. Comm. 305 (1977).

192. The final Court of Claims order for Wilkinson's retention in *Western Shoshone Identifiable Group v. United States,* 593 F.2d 994 (1979). Also see "Excerpts from a Memorandum from the Duckwater Shoshone Tribe, Battle Mountain Indian Community, and the Western Shoshone Sacred Lands Association in Opposition to the Motion and Petition for Attorney Fees and Expenses, July 15, 1980," in *Rethinking Indian Law, op. cit.*, pp. 68-69.

193. *Western Shoshone Identifiable Group v. United States,* 40 Ind. Cl. Comm. 311 (1977).

194. Morris, quoting Ryser, *op. cit.*, p. 8, n. 4.

195. Quoted in Ryser, *op. cit.*, p. 20.

196. *United States v. Dann,* 572 F.2d 222 (1978). For background, see Foot, Kristine L., "*United States v. Dann*: What It Portends for Ownership of Millions of Acres in the Western United States," *Public Land Law Review*, no. 5 (1984): pp. 183-91.

197. *United States v. Dann,* Civ. No. R-74-60 (April 25, 1980).

198. *United States v. Dann,* 706 F.2d 919, 926 (1983).

199. Morris, *op. cit.*, p. 94.

200. Nietschmann, Bernard, and William Le Bon, "Nuclear States and Fourth World Nations," *Cultural Survival Quarterly*, vol. 11, no. 4 (1988): pp. 4-7. Also see Knack, Martha C., "MX Issues for Native American Communities," in *MX in Nevada: A Humanistic Perspective*, ed. Francis Hartigan (Reno: Nevada Humanities Press, 1980), pp. 59-66.

201. Nietschmann and Le Bon, *op. cit.*, p. 7.

202. The actual quote, used as a slogan during the French student rebellion of 1968, is "Be realistic, demand the impossible." For details, see Cohn-Bendit, Daniel, *Obsolete Communism: The Left-Wing Alternative* (New York: McGraw-Hill Books, 1968).

203. See, for example, Sutton, Imre, "Indian Land Rights and the Sagebrush Rebellion," *Geographical Review*, no. 72 (1982): pp. 357-59. Also see Lyons, David, "The New Indian Claims and Original Rights to Land," *Social Theory and Practice*, no. 4 (1977): pp. 249-72, and Clayton, Richard D., "The Sagebrush Rebellion: Who Would Control Public Lands?" *Utah Law Review*, no 68 (1980): pp. 505-33.

204. For a sample of environmentalist arguments, see Watkins, T. H., "Ancient Wrongs and Public Rights," *Sierra Club Bulletin*, vol. 59, no. 8 (1974): pp. 15-16, 37-39; Blumm, M. C., "Fulfilling the Parity Promise: A Perspective on Scientific

Proof, Economic Cost and Indian Treaty Rights in the Approval of the Columbia Fish and Wildlife Program," *Environmental Law*, vol. 13, no. 1 (1982): pp. 103-59; and every issue of *Earth First!* from 1986-89. For exemplary marxist articulations, see Revolutionary Communist Party, U.S.A., "Searching for the Second Harvest," in *Marxism and Native Americans, op. cit.*, pp. 35-58, and Muga, David, "Native Americans and the Nationalities Question: Premises for a Marxist Approach to Ethnicity and Self-Determination," *Nature, Society, Thought*, vol. 1, no. 1 (1987).

205. Means, Russell, speech at the University of Colorado at Denver, tape on file (April 1986).

206. For use of the term, and explanation, see Stock, David, "The Settler State and the U.S. Left," *Forward Motion*, vol. 9, no. 4 (January 1991): pp. 53-61.

207. The quote can be attributed to paleo-conservative pundit Patrick J. Buchanan, delivered on the CNN talk show *Crossfire* (1987).

208. See Ensworth, Laurie, "Native American Free Exercise Rights to the Use of Public Lands," *Boston University Law Review*, no. 63 (1983): pp. 141-79. Also see Hooker, Barbara, "Surplus Lands for Indians: One Road to Self-Determination," *Vital Issues*, vol. 22, no. 1 (1972), and Hodge, R. A., "Getting Back the Land: How Native Americans Can Acquire Excess and Surplus Federal Property," *North Dakota Law Review*, vol. 49, no. 2 (1973): pp. 333-42.

209. This is taken up in some detail in Means, Russell, and Ward Churchill, *TREATY: A Program for the Liberation of Native North America*, forthcoming from the Fourth World Center for Indigenous Law and Politics, University of Colorado at Denver, Fall 1991.

GENOCIDE IN ARIZONA?
The "Navajo-Hopi Land Dispute" in Perspective

Genocide is always and everywhere a political occurrence.

— Irving Louis Horowitz, *Genocide*

There are an estimated 20 billion tons of high grade, low-sulfur coal underlying a stretch of Arizona desert known as Black Mesa. Rich veins of the mineral rest so near the surface that erosion has exposed them to sunlight in many places. A veritable strip-miner's delight, the situation presents obviously lucrative potentials to the corporate interests presently profiting from America's spiraling energy consumption. The only fly in the oil of commerce at this point is the fact that the land which would be destroyed in extracting the "black gold" is inhabited by a sizable number of people who will not—indeed, from their perspective, cannot—leave. This problem has caused the federal government to engage in one of the more cynical and convoluted processes of legalized expropriation in its long and sordid history of Indian affairs.

Historical Background

It all began in the 1860s when the army fought "The Kit Carson Campaign," a vicious war designed to eliminate the Diné (Navajo) people of the Southwest as a threat to ranching and mining concerns. The war featured a scorched earth policy directed against such targets as the Diné sheep herds and the peach orchards which had been carefully established over several generations at the bottom of Cañon de Chelly, in northeastern Arizona. The plan was to starve the Indians into submission, and it worked very well. The whole thing culminated in the forced march of virtually the entire Diné people to a concentration camp at Bosque Redondo, in eastern New Mexico, a desolate place where about a third of them died of disease and exposure in barely two years.[1] In 1868, hoping to avoid a scandal concerning its own treatment of a vanquished foe after having tried and convicted officers of the Confederate Army for engaging in comparable atrocities against U.S. troops at such prison camps as Andersonville, the government entered into a treaty with the Diné. It acknowledged, among other things, their right to a huge piece of barren land, mostly in western New Mexico.[2]

Over the next decade, however, it was discovered that much of the new reservation was usable as rangeland. Consequently, the government continually "adjusted" the boundaries westward, into Arizona, until the territory of the Diné completely engulfed that of another people, the Hopi. Still, there was no particular problem in many ways. The Diné, whose economy was based on sheep herding, lived dispersed upon the land, while the Hopi, agriculturalists, lived clustered in permanent villages. Conflict was minimal; the Indians coexisted in a sort of natural balance, intermarrying frequently enough to create an interethnic entity called the Tobacco Clan.[3]

This began to change in 1882, when President Chester A. Arthur, in order to provide jurisdiction to J.H. Fleming, an Indian agent assisting Mormon missionaries in kidnapping Hopi children ("to educate them"), created a Hopi reservation within the area already reserved for the Diné. Arbitrarily designated as being a rectangle of one degree longitude by one degree latitude, the new reservation left Moenkopi, a major Hopi village, outside the boundary. Conversely, much Diné pasturage—and at least 300 Diné—was contained within the area, a matter supposedly accommodated by stating that it would be the territory of the Hopi and "such other Indians as the President may select."[4]

For nearly a generation equilibrium was maintained. Then, in 1919, a group of mining companies attempted to negotiate mineral leases on Diné land. In 1920, the traditional Diné council of elders ("chiefs"), a mechanism of governance drawn in equal proportions from each of the clans comprising the nation, and which still held undisputed power in such matters, unanimously rejected the idea. The companies lobbied, and, in 1923, the federal government unilaterally replaced the traditional Diné government with a "Grand Council" composed of individuals of its own choosing. Being made up of men compulsorily educated off-reservation rather than traditionals, and owing their status to Washington rather than to the people they ostensibly represented, the new council promptly signed the leasing instruments. Thereafter, the council was the only entity recognized by the federal government as "legitimately" representing Diné interests.[5]

This experiment was such a success that an idea was shortly hatched to replace *all* traditional Indian governments with modern "democratic" forms, based on models of corporate management. In 1934, with passage of the so-called "Indian Reorganization Act" (IRA; 25 U.S.C.A. § 461), this concept became law. Indian resistance to the IRA varied from place to place, a "rule of thumb" being that the more "acculturated" the people, the greater the ease with which it was accepted.[6] At Hopi, where the traditional *Kikmongwe* form of government was/is still very much alive, 90 percent of all people eligible to vote for or against reorganization simply refused to participate, boycotting entirely a referendum required to garner at least the illusion they had accepted reorganization. As BIA employee Oliver LaFarge observed at the time:

> [T]here were only 13 people in the [Hopi village of Hotevilla] willing to go to the polls out of a potential voting population of 250, [a spiritual leader] having announced he would have nothing to do with so un-Hopi a thing as a referendum. Here we also see the Hopi method of opposition …abstention of almost the whole village should be interpreted as a heavy opposition vote.[7]

The same situation prevailed in each of the Hopi villages. Indian Commissioner John Collier overcame this "difficulty" by declaring all abstentions as being "yes" votes, providing the appearance (to outsiders, such as the American public) that the Hopis had all but unanimously approved implementation of the IRA. Despite its clear rejection of Washington's governmental formula, Hopi was then quickly reorganized, opening a deep schism within that society which has not only never healed, but which is in some ways more acute today than it was fifty years ago.[8]

Effects of Reorganization

As is usually the case where patently imposed forms of governance are utilized by a colonial power to administer a subject people,

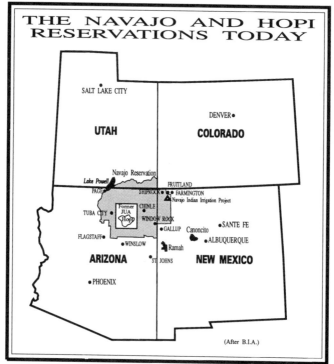

THE NAVAJO AND HOPI RESERVATIONS TODAY

(After B.I.A.)

the new Hopi tribal council rapidly learned to convert service to the oppressor into personal profit. Leadership of the 10-15 percent segment of Hopi society which had been assimilated into non-Hopi values via compulsory education and Mormon indoctrination—this group represented the literal totality of Hopi voter turnout during reorganization, and in all subsequent Hopi "elections"—had long been the station of the Sekaquaptewa family.[9] The men of the family—Abbott and Emory; later Emory, Jr. and Wayne—rapidly captured political ascendancy within the council. Correspondingly, they garnered a virtual monopoly on incoming U.S. government contracts and concessions, business starts, and the like. The new wealth and position were duly invested in a system of patronage among the Mormon Hopis, and this most un-Hopi sector of Hopi society became far and away its richest and most powerful strata. In short order, what had by and large remained a remarkably homogeneous and egalitarian culture was thus saddled with the sorts of ideological polarization, class structure, and elitism marking Euroamerican "civilization."[10]

Indian Commissioner Collier was meanwhile quite concerned that the concept of reorganization—upon which he had staked his political future and personal credibility—would work in terms of making IRA governments functional "successful" reflections of mainstream corporate society. The Mormon Hopis were only too happy to oblige in moving Collier's grand scheme along, serving as something of a showpiece in exchange for a *quid pro quo* arrangement by which they became the only Hopi entity with which the U.S. would deal directly. The ability of the *Kikmongwe* to fulfill its traditional role of conducting Hopi affairs was correspondingly undermined drastically. By 1940, the Sekaquaptewas and their followers had converted their alignment with the federal government into control, not only of all Hopi political offices, appointed positions, and the budgets that went with them, but also of the sole Hopi newspaper (*Qua Toqti*), grazing interests, and externally generated cash flow as well. However, they had still bigger plans.

These had emerged clearly by 1943, when the council, in collaboration with the Bureau of Indian Affairs (BIA) and over the strenuous objections of the *Kikmongwe*, successfully consummated a lobbying effort for the creation of "Grazing District 6," a 650,013-acre area surrounding the main Hopi villages and marked off for "exclusive Hopi use and occupancy." Insofar as nothing within the traditional Hopi lifeways had changed to cause them to disperse across the land, the only beneficiaries were the Sekaquaptewa clique. Their grazing activities and revenues were considerably expanded as a result of the establishment of the district. Meanwhile, some 100 Diné families who had lived on the newly defined District 6 land for generations were forced to relocate beyond its boundaries into the remainder of the 1882 Executive Order Area.[11]

Enter John Boyden

By the early 1950s, with their gains of the '40s consolidated and digested, the Sekaquaptewas were once again casting about for ways to expand their clout and income. Following the consolidation of Grazing District 6, they had allowed their council activities to lapse for several years while they pursued personal business enterprises. In

1951, however, they appear to have determined that reconstitution of the IRA government would be an expedient means through which to advance their interests. Devout Mormons, it was perhaps natural that they should retain the services of a well-connected Salt Lake City Mormon lawyer named John Boyden to pursue this end in the name of Hopi self-governance.[12] Undoubtedly sensing a potential for immense profitability both for himself and for his church in the move, Boyden accepted the position of Hopi Tribal Attorney. At the top of his list of priorities in doing so, by agreement with the Sekaquaptewas, was an initiative to claim *all* of the 1882 Executive Order Area in the name of the Hopi IRA government. This he pursued through a strategy of first authoring legislation allowing him to do so, and then pursuing lawsuits such as the *Healing v. Jones* cases.[13]

What was at issue was no longer merely the land, concomitant grazing rights, and the like. By 1955, the mineral assets of the Four Corners region were being realized by the U.S. government and corporations.[14] Anaconda, Kerr-McGee, and other energy conglomerates were buying leases and opening mining/milling operations feeding the guaranteed market established by the ore-buying program of the Atomic Energy Commission. Standard, Phillips, Gulf, and Mobil (among others) were moving in on oil and natural gas properties.[15] The "worthless desert" into which the U.S. had shoved the Indians was suddenly appearing to be a resource mecca, and it was felt that the 1882 Executive Order Area might be a particularly rich locale.

Indications are that Boyden and the Sekaquaptewas originally hoped that what might be argued in court as constituting Hopi territory would overlie a portion of the Grants Uranium Belt. This did not pan out, however, and royalties (and contamination) from the uranium boom continued to accrue only to neighboring peoples such as the Navajo and Laguna Pueblo (see "Native North America: The Political Economy of Radioactive Colonialism," in this volume). Still, oil exploration proved a more lucrative proposition, and Boyden opened sealed bidding for leasing rights with District 6 during the fall of 1964. The proceeds came to $2.2 million, of which a flat one million in fees and bonuses was paid to Boyden's Salt Lake City law firm.[16]

With his own coffers brimming, the attorney turned to the service of his church as well as his Hopi and corporate clientele. Enlisting the assistance of a pair of regional politicos—Secretary of Interior Stewart Udall (a fellow Mormon) and Colorado Representative Wayne Aspinall—both of whom professed that energy development would be "good for the West," he was able to negotiate a triangular coal leasing arrangement between the federally approved Navajo and Hopi councils, on the one hand, and the Peabody Coal Company (which he represented, along with the Hopi council), on the other. Kayenta, location of the Peabody mine, on Black Mesa in the northern extreme of the 1882 Executive Order Area, sits astride what has turned out to be perhaps the richest low-sulfur coal vein ever discovered in North America. Not coincidentally, a controlling interest in Peabody was held at that time by the Mormon Church, for which Boyden was also serving as legal counsel during the lease negotiations. Overall, the attorney's take on the deal is said to have again run into seven figures.[17] For him, things were moving right along.

The Nature of the "Land Dispute"

With a long-term moneymaker functioning at Black Mesa, Boyden returned his attentions to his real agenda: securing the entirety of the Executive Order Area, and the fossil fuels underlying it, on behalf of the Sekaquaptewa faction. While opening moves in this gambit had been made during the 1950s, the serious campaign really got off the ground during the early 1970s. In a major suit, *Hamilton v. Nakai*, Boyden argued that an earlier judicial determination—advanced in the second *Healing v. Jones* case—that both the Hopi and Diné were entitled to "equal use and benefit" from the 1882 Executive Order Area outside of Grazing District 6 meant that the Diné had no right to keep livestock in numbers exceeding "their half" of the federally established "carrying capacity" of the land. This held true, he said, even if no Hopis were keeping livestock there. Boyden was thereby able to obtain court orders requiring a 90 percent reduction in the number of Diné livestock within the Joint Use Area (JUA).[18] Any such reduction being tantamount to starvation for a people like the traditional Diné, dependent for subsistence upon a sheep economy, Boyden and the

Sekaquaptewas anticipated this courtroom victory would literally drive their opponents out of the JUA, into the Navajo Nation proper. With virtually no Diné living in the contested territory, arguments concerning the exclusivity of Hopi interests and prerogatives therein would be much more plausible than had previously been the case.

On the judicial front, however, the Boyden/Sekaquaptewa combine had apparently not calculated on the fact that the targeted Diné really had no place to go (the land base of the Navajo Nation already being saturated with sheep). The Diné had no alternative but to refuse to comply, a situation which forced Boyden into a whole series of related suits, each of which generated additional judicial decrees against them—a freeze was placed upon their ability to build new homes, corrals, or other structures within the JUA, for example—but none of which in themselves translated into the desired result of forcing the Diné out of the 1882 area. [19] Federal authorities could find no interest of sufficient magnitude in the JUA issue to motivate them to deploy the level of force necessary to implement their courts' various decisions.

The situation changed again with the arrival of the "energy crisis" of the 1970s. Overnight, "energy self-sufficiency" became a national obsession. Shale oil, coal gasification, and other esoteric terminology became household matters of discussion. Congress sat down to do a quick inventory of its known energy assets, and suddenly the Black Mesa coal, which had barely elicited a "ho-hum" response from legislators a few months before, became a focus of attention. Arizona superhawks such as Barry Goldwater and Representative Sam Steiger in particular saw a way to put their state on the energy map of "national interest" by consummating plans already laid by powerful economic entities such as Western Energy Supply and Transmission (WEST) Associates.[20]

There was only one hitch to the program: it was/is impossible to strip-mine the land so long as Diné people were/are living on it. The solution, of course, for the federal government as well as the Hopi council and the energy corporations, was to remove the people. Hence, as early as 1971, Boyden offered his services in drafting a bill to be introduced in the U.S. House of Representatives calling for the formal division of the JUA into halves. The draft called for all Hopis living on the Diné side of the partition line to be compulsorily relocated into Hopi territory and vice versa. Given that virtually no Hopis actually lived in the JUA, the law would serve the purpose of emptying half of the desired acreage of population and thereby open it up for mining.[21] Several scientific studies already suggested that once strip-mining and slurry operations commenced in so substantial a portion of Black Mesa, the adjoining areas would be rendered uninhabitable in short order, forcing the Diné off even their remaining portion of the 1882 area.[22] The Boyden/Steiger plan was thus clearly to use the appearance of an "equitable resolution" to a property rights question as a means to totally dispossess the JUA Diné, accomplishing what the Mormon Hopis had been trying to do all along.

Steiger dutifully introduced his draft legislation in 1972, but it met with certain PR problems. After all, the mass forced relocation of indigenous people was something which had not been done in North America since the nineteenth century. While it squeaked through the House by a narrow margin, it stalled in the Senate.[23] The congressional fear seems to have been that, energy crisis notwithstanding, the American public might balk at such a policy; this seemed especially true in the immediate context of the civil rights, anti-war, and Black Power movements. Democratic Party presidential nominee George McGovern came out against the idea of partition and relocation in the JUA, and even Goldwater, the arch-conservative, expressed doubts about the wisdom of the plan under such circumstances.[24] A plausible "humanitarian cover" was needed, under which to effect the legislation necessary to clear the population from much of the JUA.

Here, Boyden once again proved his mettle. Retaining David Evans & Associates—yet another Mormon-controlled Salt Lake City firm—to handle the "public image of the Hopi Tribe," he oversaw the creation of something called "the Navajo-Hopi range dispute." Within this scenario, which the Evans PR people packaged rather sensationally and then fed to the press in massive doses, the Hopis and Diné occupying the JUA were at irreconcilable odds over ownership of the land. The result of this was a virtual "shooting war" between the two indigenous peoples, fueled not only by the property rights dispute but also by "deep historical and intercultural animosities." No mention was made of mineral interests, or that Evans was simultaneously representing WEST Associates, voracious as that consortium was in its desire to mine and burn JUA coal. As *Washington Post* reporter Mark Panitch recounted in 1974:

> The relationship between the Hopi council and the power companies became almost symbiotic. On the one hand, [Hopi Tribal Chair Clarence] Hamilton speeches written by Evans would be distributed through the public relations machinery of 23 major Western utilities [comprising the WEST group]. On the other hand, these utilities would tell their customers, often through local media contacts, that the Hopis were "good Indians" who wouldn't shut off the juice which ran their air conditioners...Because of the efforts by representatives of the Hopi to present the [IRA government's] viewpoint, the Hopi rapidly took on the aura of the underdog who just wanted to help his white brother. Some of the Navajo, on the other hand, were saying threatening things about closing down polluting power plants and requiring expensive reclamation of strip-mined land.[25]

The image of "range war type violence" was reinforced by Evans photographers' snapshots of out-buildings and junk vehicles abandoned at various locations in the JUA. These were subsequently used for target practice by teenaged "plinkers" (a common enough practice throughout rural America), and were therefore often riddled with bullet holes. The Evans group presented their photos to the media as evidence of periodic "firefights" between Hopis and Dinés. As Panitch put it:

> During 1971-72, few newspapers escaped a Sunday feature on the "range war" about to break out between two hostile tribes. Photos of burned corrals and shot up stock tanks and wells were printed ...By calling Evans and Associates, a TV crew could arrange a roundup of trespassing Navajo stock. Occasionally, when a roundup was in progress, Southwestern newsmen would be telephoned and notified of the event.[26]

What real violence there was came mainly from a group of thugs, such as a non-Indian named Elmer Randolph, put on the payroll and designated as "Hopi Tribal Rangers" by the Mormon faction. Their specialty was beating to a pulp and arresting for trespass any Diné who had come to retrieve sheep that had strayed into Grazing District 6.[27] When a group of Diné attempted to erect a fence to keep their livestock off the Hopi land, the Sekaquaptewas first called a television crew to the spot and then personally tore the fence down, demanding before the cameras that the Arizona National Guard be dispatched to "restore order" within the JUA. This, too, was straight-facedly passed off by news commentators as indication of "the level of violence existing among the Indians."[28] The federal government was morally obligated, so the argument went, to physically separate the two "warring groups" before there were fatalities. Predictably, Representative Steiger gave this theme official voice:

> There is nothing funny about the violence which has already transpired—livestock mutilations, corral burnings, fence destruction, water tank burnings, and at least one shooting incident. If we permit ourselves to be seduced into some kind of legal procrastination and someone is killed, I am sure we would assume the responsibility that is patently ours. Let us not wait for that kind of catalyst.[29]

At this juncture, Arizona Senator Barry Goldwater, one of the more powerful political figures in the country, decided the time was ripe to weigh in along the Boyden/Sekaquaptewa/Steiger axis. "I have not supported the Steiger approach mostly because it involved money [to relocate the impacted Diné]," Goldwater announced, "[but now] I do not think we have to pay money to relocate Indians, when in the case of the Navajo they have sixteen million acres [outside the JUA]." He went on to assert with bold-faced falsity that the Diné had "literally tens of thousands of acres that are not being used" and which were therefore available to absorb those displaced by the partition and relocation proposal, ostensibly without significantly altering their way of life.[30] John Boyden seized this opportunity to draft a new bill, this one to be introduced by Goldwater and Arizona's other senator, Pat Fannin. It called for partition and the rapid, uncompensated, and compulsory relocation of all Diné residing within the Hopi portion of the JUA. By comparison, the Steiger draft bill, which had called for the federal government to underwrite all costs associated with relocation, including the acquisition of additional lands as needed to resettle those affected, seemed benign.[31] This, of course, did much to attract support to the latter.

Relocation Becomes Law

The Goldwater/Fannin initiative was a ruse designed to drive liberal Democrats into countering the draft bill's harsh proposals with a "gentler" plan of their own. This assumed the form of House Resolution 10337, yet another draft bill in which Boyden took a hand, this one introduced by liberal Utah Representative Wayne Owens. It called not only for compensation to the victims of the partition, as the Steiger draft had already done, but also for a decade-long time period during which the relocation was to be "phased in," so that those to be moved would not be overly traumatized. Tellingly, when Owens placed his proposition on the table, Steiger promptly abandoned his own draft and became an endorser of the Owens Bill. This newly hatched liberal/conservative coalition was destined to finally produce Boyden's desired result.

Despite a letter sent by Arizona Representative Manuel Lujan that passage of H.R. 10337 might result in "a bloodbath in northern Arizona that would make the My Lai Massacre look like a Sunday School picnic," and that it would in any event be "the most shameful act this government has perpetrated on its citizens since Colonial days," the Owens/Boyden concept was approved by the House Interior Committee by voice vote in February 1974.[32] It was then forwarded to the full House for passage. This was accomplished on May 29, 1974, by a vote of 290 to 38.[33] On the same day, Judge Walsh issued a contempt of court decree against Chair Peter McDonald and the Navajo tribal government for having failed to comply with his order to reduce Diné livestock in the JUA.[34]

The bill was passed by the Senate shortly thereafter, by a vote of 72 to 0 and in a somewhat different form from that which had been approved by the House. Although this usually precipitates an *ad hoc* committee meeting involving representatives of both chambers in order to hammer out a mutually acceptable joint version of the legislation, in this instance the House took the extraordinary step of simply approving the Senate version without further discussion.[35] The statute was then routed on an urgent basis to President Gerald R. Ford, who signed it without reading it, while enjoying a ski vacation in Vail, Colorado.[36]

Enacted as Public Law 93-531, the bill required a fifty-fifty division of the JUA, with the actual partition boundary to be established by the federal district court in Arizona.[37] It established a three-member Navajo-Hopi Relocation Commission, to be appointed by the

Secretary of Interior. Within two years of the date the court's partition line was defined, the commission was charged with submitting a plan to Congress detailing how relocation was to be accomplished. Thirty days after Congress approved the relocation plan, a five-year period would begin during which relocation would be carried out.

A total of $37 million was initially budgeted, both to underwrite the relocation commission's functioning and to pay "incentive bonuses" of $5,000 to the head of each Diné family which "voluntarily" agreed to relocate during the first operational year of the program. Bonuses of $4,000 were slated to be paid to those who agreed to go during the second year, $3,000 during the third, and $2,000 during the fourth. In addition, each family of three or fewer individuals was deemed eligible to receive up to $17,000 with which to acquire "replacement housing." Families of four or more could receive up to $25,000 for this purpose.

PL 93-531 also contained several other important provisions. It directed the Secretary of Interior to implement Judge Walsh's order for Diné livestock reduction by outright impoundment. It authorized the secretary to sell to the Navajo Nation up to 250,000 acres of land under jurisdiction of the Bureau of Land Management at "fair market value," and provided Navajo authority to acquire up to 150,000 additional acres of privately held land (this is as opposed to 911,000 acres from which the Diné were ordered removed in the JUA).[38] The law also authorized litigation to resolve Hopi claims to land surrounding the village of Moenkopi, left out of the original Executive Order Area.[39]

Problems with Public Law 93-531

The first grit in PL 93-931's gears appeared almost immediately, when it was discovered that virtually none of the targeted people were likely to relocate on anything resembling a voluntary basis. The second followed shortly thereafter, when it was found that the size of the Diné population to be affected had been dramatically underestimated. This was due to language in the act which stipulated that the partition would "include the higher density population areas of each tribe within the portion of the lands partitioned to each tribe to minimize and avoid undue social, economic, and cultural disruption

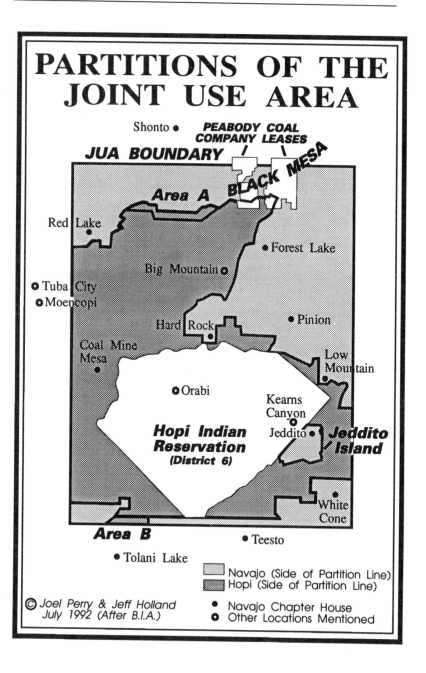

PARTITIONS OF THE JOINT USE AREA

Shonto • **PEABODY COAL COMPANY LEASES**

JUA BOUNDARY

BLACK MESA

Area A

Red Lake

• Forest Lake

Big Mountain ○

• Tuba City
○ Moencopi

Hard Rock

• Pinion

Coal Mine Mesa

Low Mountain

○ Orabi

Kearns Canyon

Hopi Indian Reservation
(District 6)

Jeddito •
○

Jeddito Island

White Cone

Area B

• Teesto

• Tolani Lake

☐ Navajo (Side of Partition Line)
▨ Hopi (Side of Partition Line)

© Joel Perry & Jeff Holland
July 1992 (After B.I.A.)

• Navajo Chapter House
○ Other Locations Mentioned

insofar as possible." Congress had apparently accepted without question an assertion made by John Boyden through Evans & Associates that if this principle were adhered to, the number of impacted Diné would be "about 3,500."[40] There was no reason to assume this information was accurate.

More to the point, when the court's partition line was ultimately finalized on February 10, 1977, it conformed much more closely to coal deposits than to demography.[41] Those areas Peabody preferred to mine first, including areas of the northern JUA furthest from the Hopi mesas but adjoining the Kayenta mining sites, were included within the Hopi territory (see map). Consequently, estimates of the number of Diné to be relocated were quickly raised to 9,525 by 1980,[42] and are now calculated to have involved 17,500 people overall.[43] Only 109 Hopis were affected, and their relocation was completed in 1976.[44]

Correspondingly, the costs associated with the relocation program escalated wildly. While in 1974 the Congress estimated the entire effort could be underwritten through allocation of $28 million in direct costs and another $9 million in "administrative overhead," by 1985 the relocation alone was consuming $4 million per year (having by then expended nearly $21 million in all). With a Diné population vastly larger (and more resistant) than originally projected, direct costs were by 1985 being estimated at a level of "at least $500 million."[45] Inflation and other factors have, since then, driven even this enormous amount considerably higher. Similarly, the original timespan conceived as being required for relocation to be fully implemented—which placed the completion of the program in 1982—quickly proved impractical. Revised several times, the completion date was by 1985 being projected into 1993.[46]

Predictably, Barry Goldwater's assertion that the Navajo Nation had "tens of thousands" of idle acres outside the JUA onto which relocatees could move and continue their traditional lifeways proved absolutely false. Leaving aside the spiritual significance of specific JUA geography to its Diné residents, it was well known that the entirety of the reservation, consisting of arid and semi-arid terrain, had been saturated with sheep (and thus with traditional people) since at least as early as the mid-'30s.[47] Meanwhile, the 400,000 acres of "replacement lands" authorized under PL 93-531 for acquisition by the Navajo Nation as a means of absorbing "surplus" relocatees were blocked by a combination of conflicting congressional interests, a requirement in the law that such land be within 18 miles of the reservation's boundaries, non-Indian lobbying, and avarice on the part of the Navajo tribal government itself.[48] The result was that the relocatees were left with no place to go other than to urban areas which represented the very antithesis of their way of life.

Belatedly, Congress also began to "discover" the falsity of the "range war" thesis, and that the Hopis were hardly unified in their desire to see the Diné pushed from half the JUA. There was no excuse for this. As early as the beginning of 1972, *Kikmongwe* Mina Lansa had come before the House Interior Committee, while the Steiger Bill was being considered, and made it clear that the traditional Hopi majority wished to see the Diné remain on the land, insofar as this represented a barrier to strip-mining in the JUA. She further informed the legislators that:

> The [IRA] council of people, Clarence Hamilton and others, say all Hopis are supporting this bill through the newspapers and publicizing to the world that both Hopi and Navajo are going to fight each other. These things are not true, and it makes us very ashamed to see that some of our young people who claim to represent us created much publicity in this way while in this capital lately.[49]

In 1975, Lansa took the unprecedented step (for a *Kikmongwe*) of openly participating in a largely non-Indian coalition seeking to repeal PL 93-531. "We should all work together against Washington to revoke this bill," she said. "The Hopi council favors this bill. But as a Hopi chief, I say no. The Hopis and Navajos can live right where they are."[50] She withdrew her support of the non-Indian group when one of its leaders, Bill Morrall, called for the abolition of both the Hopi and Navajo reservations, *per se*.[51] However, her opposition to the Hopi IRA government and the relocation law, and her support of the JUA Diné, remained outspoken and unswerving. In 1975 and 1976, she and other Hopi spiritual leaders such as David Monongye and Thomas Banyacya supported suits intended to challenge federal authority to implement policy on the say-so of the Hopi IRA government.[52]

The double standard of determining "equity" inherent to U.S. legal treatment of indigenous peoples also became increasingly apparent within the rationalizations through which the relocation act had been passed. The issue goes to the fact that, where the federal government or its non-Indian citizenry has been shown to have illegally acquired Indian land, the victims have never been allowed to recover their property. U.S. judicial doctrine has instead held that they are entitled only to "just compensation," in the form of money, and in an amount determined to be "fair" by those who stole the property in the first place.[53] No white population in North America has ever been relocated in order to satisfy an indigenous land right. Attorney Richard Schifter framed the question plainly and succinctly before the Senate Interior Committee in September 1972:

> Could it be, may I ask, that where the settlers are white, we pay the original owners off in cash; but where the settlers are Indian, we find expulsion and removal an acceptable alternative? Can such a racially discriminatory approach be considered as meeting the constitutional requirement for due process?[54]

Representative Sam Steiger made what appears to be the *de facto* governmental response when he said, "I would simply tell the gentleman that the distinction between that situation and this one is that in those instances we were dealing with non-Indians occupying and believing they have a right in the lands. Here we are dealing with two Indian tribes. That is the distinction."[55]

Under the circumstances, it had become obvious by 1977 that the sort of minimal negative social, economic, and cultural impact upon relocatees so blithely called for under PL 93-531 was simply impossible. Again, there was no excuse for the tardy realization. Aside from an abundance of Diné testimony to the likely consequences of relocation which was entered during the congressional deliberation process, anthropologist David Aberle had reported on May 15, 1973, to the House Subcommittee on Indian Affairs that the outcome would be sociocultural disintegration among the target population:

> Remove the sheepherder to a place where he cannot raise stock, remove the herd, and you have removed the foundation on which the family is vested. Demoralization and social disorganization are the inevitable consequences, and the younger people, no longer beneficiaries of a stable

home life, become just another addition to the problems of maladjustment and alienation in our society.[56]

Yet the relocation program moved forward.

Impact Upon the Diné

Aberle was hardly the only expert warning that the consequences of PL 93-531 would be dire. As early as 1963, sociologists such as Marc Fried had been articulating the high costs of imposed relocation upon various populations.[57] By 1973, anthropologists like Thayer Scudder had also published in-depth studies specifically focusing upon the consequences of forcibly relocating land-based indigenous peoples from rural to urban environments.[58] And, of course, there were the predictions of the Diné themselves. Such information was coming, not only from the traditionals out on the land, but also from younger, college-educated Navajos.[59] As for the traditionals, they had never been less than unequivocal in their assessment. For instance, Katherine Smith, an elder from the Big Mountain area of the northern JUA, told Senate investigators in 1972 that:

> I will never leave the land, this sacred place. The land is part of me, and I will one day be part of the land. I could never leave. My people are here, and have been here forever. My sheep are here. All that has meaning is here. I live here and I will die here. That is the way it is, and the way it must be. Otherwise, the people will die, the sheep will die, the land will die. There would be no meaning to life if this happened.[60]

As the relocation program began to come alive, such warnings began to be borne out. The impact was exacerbated by the tactics used to convince the Diné to "voluntarily" sign up for relocation. High on the list of these was the impoundment of sheep. The day after Judge Walsh signed the order declaring the Simkin partition line official, Hopi Tribal Chairman Abbott Sekaquaptewa (who replaced Clarence Hamilton in that position during 1976) ordered a group of his rangers into the Hopi portion of the JUA to begin seizing every head of Diné livestock they could lay hands on. Sekaquaptewa had no legal authority to undertake such action,[61] but a special force of forty SWAT-trained and equipped BIA police were immediately sent in to back him up.[62] This precipitated a crisis in which Walsh formally enjoined the Hopis from going ahead with their stock impoundment program.[63] Sekaquaptewa, seeming "almost eager for a shootout," defied the order, and demanded the government "get the army and some machine guns out here, because that's all the Navajos understand."[64]

Rather than arresting Sekaquaptewa for inciting violence and blatant contempt of court, BIA's operational director in the JUA, Bill Benjamin (Chippewa), attempted to placate him with a plan whereby the Bureau would buy up Diné sheep within the Hopi partition area at 150 percent of market rate. This, he argued, would remove many of the offending animals peacefully, while—in theory, at least—providing the Diné with funds to underwrite their move to "their own side of the line." Under provisions of the law, Benjamin had five years in which to complete his stock reduction program; using the buy-out scheme, he was able to secure 67,000 of the estimated 120,000 sheep being herded by Diné on Hopi-partitioned land. At the end of the year, however, the BIA refused to allocate the monies promised to make good on Benjamin's "purchases." The people whose stock was at issue were, of course, left destitute, while Benjamin was made to appear a liar, destroying the element of trust which the Diné had extended to him. As he himself put it at the time:

> Those people [the Diné] are under tremendous strain. They are facing the unknown of relocation, and as their stock is taken away they are losing a bank account and a way of life. Traditionally, their day was planned around the needs of the flock, and if they needed money they could sell a sheep or two. But as things are now, we can expect a lot of personal and family problems…All I know is that I can't deliver on a promise I made to people in a very difficult situation.[65]

The stock impoundment effort slowed after this, but has been continued at a steady, deliberate, and—for the Diné—socially, economically, and psychologically debilitating pace ever since. It has not, however, been the only coercive measure used. Judge Walsh's order making the Simkin line official also included an instruction renewing his earlier freeze on Diné construction within the Hopi partition area, other than with "a permit from the Hopi Tribe."[66] The Hopis, of course, have issued no such permits and have used their rangers to destroy any new structures which have appeared (as well as more than a few older ones). Even repair of existing structures has been attacked as a violation of the building freeze. This has caused a steady deterioration in the living conditions of the targeted Diné, as well as a chronic anxiety about whether the very roofs of their hogans might not be simply ripped off from over their heads.[67] The situation has now lasted 13 years.

At the same time, those who bowed to the unrelenting pressure and accepted relocation were meeting a fate at least as harsh as that being visited upon those who refused. As of March 1984, not a single acre of rural land had been prepared to receive relocatees. For those approximately 30 percent of all targeted families who had allowed themselves to be moved into cities or towns,

> even the Relocation Commission's statistics revealed a problem of tremendous proportions: almost forty percent of those relocated to off-reservation communities no longer owned their government-provided house. In Flagstaff, Arizona, the community which received the largest number of relocatees, nearly half the 120 families who had moved there no longer owned their homes. When county and tribal legal services offices discovered that a disproportionate [number] of the houses had ended up in the hands of a few realtors, allegations of fraud began to surface. Lawsuits were filed by local attorneys; investigations were begun by the United States Attorney's Office, the Federal Bureau of Investigation, the Arizona Department of Real Estate, and the Relocation Commission; and the most in-depth review of the Relocation program which has ever been undertaken by a body of Congress was prepared."[68]

A classic case of what was/is happening is that of Hosteen Nez.

> In 1978, Nez, an 82-year-old relocatee, moved to Flagstaff from Sand Springs. Within a year, Nez suffered a heart attack, could not pay his property taxes or utility bills, lost his $60,000 ranch-style home, and moved back to the reservation [where he also had no home, having relocated from his old one].[69]

By the mid-'80s, relocatee reports of increased physical illness, stress and alcoholism, and family breakup were endemic.[70] At least one member of the relocation commission itself had publicly denounced the program as being "as bad as...the concentration camps in World War II," and then resigned his position.[71] Area editorial writers had begun to denounce the human consequences of PL 93-531 in the most severe terms imaginable:

> [I]f the federal government proceeds with its genocidal relocation of traditional Navajos to alien societies, [the problem] will grow a thousandfold and more...The fact that it is a problem manufactured in

Washington does not ease the pain and suffering—nor does it still the anger that fills too many hearts.[72]

Use of the term "genocide" in this connection was by then not uncommon. And such language was neither rhetorical nor inaccurate. Thayer Scudder and others had already scientifically documented the reality of what was being called "the deliberate, systematic, willful destruction of a people."[73] At least two careful studies had concluded unequivocally that U.S. policy *vis-à-vis* the JUA Diné violated a broad range of international laws, including the United Nations' 1948 Convention on Punishment and Prevention of the Crime of Genocide.[74] But still the government moved forward.

Diné Resistance

Resistance to extermination—whether physical or cultural—is a natural and predictable human response. In the case of the JUA Diné, it was foreshadowed in a statement to Indian Commissioner Philleo Nash by Navajo tribal council member Carl Todacheenie. The statement was made in 1963, shortly after the *Healing v. Jones* (II) decision:

> The only way the Navajo people are going to move, we know, is they have to have another Bataan Death March. The United States government will have to do that…We're settled out there [in the JUA], and we're not going to advise our people to move, no matter who says. They probably got to chop off our heads. That's the only way we're going to move out of there.[75]

More than a decade later, on March 3, 1977, when Arizona Representative Dennis DeConcini (who had replaced Sam Steiger in 1976) attended a meeting of Diné at White Cone, in the southeastern Diné partition area, he heard exactly the same thing. "Livestock reduction means starvation to us," DeConcini was told by 84-year-old Emma Nelson. "Washington has taken our livestock without replacing it with any other way of making a living." Another area Diné, Chester Morris, was more graphic: "The enforcement of PL 93-531 means starvation, homelessness, mentally disturbed [*sic*], alcoholism, family dislocation, crime and even death for many." "This is very emotional," Miller Nez, a local resident, went on, "and at some point I think we're going to resist any further attempt by Washington to take away our only source of support. I think sooner or later there will be killing of individuals."[76]

The Diné were, to be sure, already resisting, and had been for twenty-three years, simply by their refusal to comply with the terms of *Healing v. Jones*. Resistance of the sort under discussion, however, may be said to have really begun on October 2, 1977, when a Diné elder named Pauline Whitesinger faced down a crew hired by the BIA to erect a barbed wire fence. When the crew began to construct a section of fence bisecting Whitesinger's sheep graze, she told them to stop. When they didn't, she drove her pickup truck straight at them. They left, but returned the next day and resumed work. This time, she chased them away by throwing handfuls of dirt into their faces. Whitesinger was shortly arrested on assorted charges, but later acquitted.[77]

Often during the following year and a half, fencing crews showed up for work in the morning only to find the wire and posts they'd laboriously installed the day before had been torn down during the night. During mid-summer 1979, a crew appeared on the line of elder Katherine Smith, only to find themselves staring into the muzzle of her .22-caliber rifle. She fired over their heads and, when they scattered, she began dismantling the fence before their eyes. Smith was arrested on serious charges, only to receive a directed verdict of acquittal from a judge responsive to her argument that she had been beside herself with rage in confronting a law she knew to be not only wrong, but immoral.[78]

At about the same time Smith was firing her rifle, the American Indian Movement (AIM) was conducting its Fifth International Indian Treaty Council (IITC) at the sacred site of Big Mountain in the Hopi-partitioned portion of the northern JUA. Convened in that location at the request of the Diné elders, the council was intended as a means of garnering outside support for what the targeted population expected to be a bitter battle for survival. During the council, the elders prepared a statement which read in part:

> We do hereby declare total resistance to any effort or influence to be removed from our homes and ancestral lands. We further declare our right to live in peace with our Hopi neighbors.[79]

Traditional Hopi leaders David Monongye and Thomas Banyacya attended the council, extending unity and support from the *Kikmongwe* to the Big Mountain resistance. IITC pledged itself to take the situation of the JUA Diné before the United Nations.[80] Diné AIM leader Larry Anderson then announced his organization was establishing a permanent survival camp at the council site, located on the property of AIM member Bahe Kadenahe. Anderson also promised to establish a legal defense apparatus to support the Big Mountain effort as rapidly as possible. This was accomplished by securing the services of Boston attorney Lew Gurwitz to head up what became known as the Big Mountain Legal Defense/Offense Committee (BMLD/OC). By 1982, BMLDOC, utilizing funds provided by the National Lawyers Guild (NLG), had opened a headquarters in Flagstaff, the most proximate town of any size to the JUA.[81]

Over the next two years, Gurwitz entered several suits in behalf of individual Diné people suffering under the impact of stock reduction, and began to assemble a legal staff composed primarily of student interns underwritten by the NLG.[82] He also began to organize an external support network for the Big Mountain resistance which at its peak evidenced active chapters in 26 states and several foreign countries.[83] On a related front, BMLD/OC put together an independent commission to study the international legal implications of federal relocation policy in the JUA, and collaborated with organizations such as the Washington, D.C.-based Indian Law Resource Center in making presentations to the UN Working Group on Indigenous Populations.[84]

As this was going on, more direct forms of physical resistance were also continuing. For instance, in 1980, Bahe Kadenahe was arrested along with twenty others (dubbed the "Window Rock 21") during a confrontation with BIA police. Charged with several offenses, he was later acquitted on all counts. At about the same time, elder Alice Benally and three of her daughters confronted a fencing crew, were maced, arrested, and each charged with eight federal crimes. They too were eventually acquitted on all counts. The spring of 1981 saw a large demonstration at the Keams Canyon BIA facility which caused Acting Commissioner of Indian Affairs Kenneth Payton to temporarily suspend livestock impoundment operations. In 1983, after livestock reduction had been resumed, Big Mountain elder Mae Tso was severely beaten while physically resisting impoundment of her horses. Arrested and jailed, she suffered two heart attacks while incarcerated. She was ultimately acquitted of having engaged in any criminal offense.[85]

Matters reached their peak in this regard during June 1986, in preparation for a federally established date (July 7 of that year) when outright forced relocation was to be implemented. The scenario called for large units of heavily armed BIA police and U.S. marshals to move into the Hopi partition area, physically removing all Diné who had refused to relocate in response to less drastic and immediate forms of coercion. In the event, BMLD/OC managed to bring some 2,000 outside supporters into the contested zone, AIM made it known that its contribution to defense of the area would likely be "other than pacifistic," and the government backed down from the specter of what Gurwitz described as "70-year-old Diné grandmothers publicly engaged in armed combat with the forces of the United States of America."[86]

Rather than suffer the international public relations debacle which would undoubtedly have accompanied a resort to open warfare with the Diné resistance, federal authorities opted to engage in a waiting game, utilizing the relentless pressure of stock reduction, fencing, and the like to simply wear down the opposition. Their strategy also seems to have encompassed the likelihood that, absent the sort of head-on government/Indian collision implicit in the imposition of an absolute deadline, the attention of non-Indian supporters would be difficult or impossible to hold. The defense coalition BMLD/OC had so carefully nurtured was thus virtually guaranteed to atrophy over a relatively short term of apparent government inactivity, affording authorities a much greater latitude of operational secrecy in which to proceed than they possessed in mid-1986.[87]

In 1988, Big Mountain defense attorney Lee Brooke Phillips, in collaboration with attorneys Roger Finzel and Bruce Ellison, filed a lawsuit—*Manybeads v. United States*—in an attempt to take the pressure off the Diné by blocking relocation on the basis of the policy's abridgement of first amendment guarantees of religious freedom.[88] Although it initially seemed promising, the suit was dismissed by U.S.

District Judge Earl Carroll on October 20, 1989, because of the Supreme Court's adverse decision in the so-called "G-O Road Case" concerning the rights of indigenous people in northern California to specific geographic areas for spiritual reasons. At present, Phillips is engaged in appeals to have the *Manybeads* suit reinstated, but the outlook is not favorable.[89]

Resistance under these conditions adds up more than anything to a continuing refusal to leave the land. And so it is that by the summer of 1990, approximately 75 percent of the Diné originally targeted for relocation under PL 93-531 remain where they were at the outset, stubbornly replenishing their flocks despite ongoing impoundments, repairing hogans and corrals in defiance of the building freeze, and conducting periodic forays to dismantle sections of the hated partition line fence.[90] Although suffering the full range of predictable effects stemming from the government's fifteen-year sustained effort to push them quietly off their land, there is currently no indication they will alter their position or course of action.

Liberal Obfuscation

Almost from the moment that it became evident Diné resistance would be a serious reality, the government began a campaign to mask the implications of PL 93-531 behind a more liberal and "humanitarian" facade. The first overt attempt along this line occurred in July 1978 when Arizona's conservative senator, Barry Goldwater—a prime mover in the law's passage—responded to a challenge presented by Diné elders Roberta Blackgoat and Violet Ashke during the culmination of AIM's "Longest Walk" in Washington, D.C. the same month. At their invitation, he traveled to Big Mountain to meet with the resisters. Goldwater used the occasion to try and confuse the issue, asserting that the relocation act entailed no governmental policy "that says that [the Diné] have to move or what [they] have to do."[91] Even the establishment press responded negatively to such clumsy distortion.[92]

Finding bold-faced lying an ineffectual tactic, Goldwater quietly made it known that he would not oppose token gestures proposed by congressional liberals to create the public appearance that relocation was less harsh in its implications than was actually the case. The main weight of this effort fell upon Dennis DeConcini, who had replaced Wayne Owens as an Arizona senator in 1976, and Representative Morris Udall, who had already publicly sided with the Sekaquaptewas.[93] Both lawmakers tendered proposals to amend PL 93-531 which would provide for "life estates" allowing limited numbers of Diné elders to remain on 90-acre parcels within the Hopi partition area until they died. No provisions were made to allow these selected elders to retain the familial/community context which lent meaning to their lives, have access to sufficient grazing land to maintain their flocks, or to pass along their holdings to their heirs. In effect, they were simply granted the "right" to live out their lives in impoverished isolation. Not unreasonably, the Diné began in short order to refer to the scheme as an offering of "death estates."

Nonetheless, a combination of the DeConcini and Udall initiatives was passed as PL 96-305 in 1980.[94] Touted as having "corrected the worst of the problems inherent to PL 93-531," the new law immediately became a focus for resistance in its own right. It was generally viewed, as Diné activist Danny Blackgoat put it in 1985, as "a way to divide the unity of the people, setting up struggles between relatives and neighbors over who should receive an 'estate,' and causing those who were offered estates to abandon those who weren't. That way, the resistance would fall apart, and the government would be able to do whatever it wanted." But, as Blackgoat went on to observe, "It didn't work. The people rejected the whole idea, and our struggle actually increased after the 1980 law was passed."[95]

As Diné resistance and outside support mounted with the approach of the government's relocation deadline, the liberals adopted a different strategy. Udall first engineered a February 25, 1986, memorandum of understanding whereby the relocation commission— which was by that point openly admitting it could not meet its goals—would essentially dissolve itself and pass over responsibility for relocation to the BIA. He then secured an agreement from both Ivan Sidney (who had replaced Abbott Sekaquaptewa as Hopi tribal chair) and Indian Commissioner Ross Swimmer to forego forcible relocation, pending "further legislative remedy of the situation." He then teamed up with then Arizona Representative (now senator) John

McCain to introduce "compromise legislation," House Resolution 4281, which would have allowed an exchange of land between Diné and Hopi within the partitioned areas without disturbing the basic premises of PL 93-531 in any way at all.[96]

The Udall-McCain bill was already in the process of being rejected by the resistance—on the grounds that it accomplished nothing of substance—when Barry Goldwater began entering his own objections to the effect that it was time to stop "coddling" the resisters. HR 4281 thus died without being put to a vote. This provoked New Mexico Representative Bill Richardson to propose a bill (HR 4872) requiring a formal moratorium on forced relocation until the matter might be sorted out. Udall killed this initiative in his capacity as chair of the House Interior and Insular Affairs Committee.[97] An informal stasis was maintained until 1987, when California Senator Alan Cranston introduced an initiative (S. 2452) calling for an 18-month moratorium on relocation, pending "further study" and the devising of a new resolution, "to which all parties might agree." This effort continues in altered form as of mid-1990—officially designated as S. 481—and is now cosponsored by Illinois Senator Paul Simon and Colorado Senator Tim Wirth. A lower chamber version of the bill, HR 1235, is presently cosponsored by twenty members of Congress.[98]

Meanwhile, with the help of Udall, McCain was able to push through a draft bill (S. 1236) which became PL 100-666 in 1989. The statute contains elements of the earlier, ineffectual, Udall-McCain draft land exchange legislation while requiring that the relocation commission be reactivated and that relocation go forward, to be completed by the end of 1993. At present, no new relocation commissioner has been named, although the search seems to be centering upon a former executive of the Peabody Coal Company.[99]

The Present Situation

As this manuscript goes to press, the government of the United States has done absolutely nothing to end the process of Diné cultural destruction it began with the passage of PL 93-531 in 1974. There has been no discussion of repealing the offending statute. To the contrary, the federal government has steadfastly maintained the basic legitimacy of its policy in this regard, offering mere variations on the theme of relocation as "alternatives." The options offered amount, in the words of Colorado AIM leader Glenn Morris, to "sugar coated genocide."[100] The fact that the actual physical eviction of the Diné resistance has not been attempted seems to have been little more than a tactical decision, pursuit of a war of attrition rather than a blitzkrieg.

In early 1989, the Peabody Coal Company requested that the federal Office of Surface Mining (OSM) approve expansion of its mining activities on Black Mesa. Although Peabody had never obtained permits, required by law since 1985, to operate at its already existing mine sites, the OSM raised no issue with this new application. Instead, it referred the matter for "review" within the framework of an officially commissioned and supposedly objective environmental impact study released on June 2, 1989. The study is suspect on a number of grounds, not least of which is an assertion that post-extraction reclamation of the area to be strip-mined can be 100 percent effective. Such a claim is not supported by any known body of scientific literature, although it is customarily advanced by representatives of Peabody Coal. Other defects in the study include apparently inadequate assessments of the effects of water drawdown for purposes of increased slurry operations, selenium accumulation, atmospheric pollution, and local social and cultural impacts. "Lack of available information" is typically cited as a reason for these deficiencies, despite the facts that the missing data are known to exist, and that a number of regional experts were never contacted for their opinions.[101]

Although the study reputedly took four years to complete, public response time was limited by the OSM to 60 days, thus severely limiting the type and quantity of countervailing information which might be submitted.[102] While it is true that expanded mining operations in the northern JUA have not yet commenced, all indications are that an official sanction for such activity has already been orchestrated. This in turn establishes the prospect that the question of Diné resistance in the contested area may ultimately be "resolved" through the expedient of simply digging the very ground from beneath the resisters' feet.

The Diné position remains unchanged. As Roberta Blackgoat, a 75-year-old Diné resistance leader, put it:

If they come and drag us all away from the land, it will destroy our way of life. That is genocide. If they leave me here, but take away my community, it is still genocide. If they wait until I die and then mine the land, the land will still be destroyed. If there is no land and no community, I have nothing to leave my grandchildren. If I accept this, there will be no Diné, there will be no land. That is why I will never accept it...I can never accept it. I will die fighting this law.[103]

Beyond this, there seems nothing left to say.

Notes

1. See Kelly, Lawrence, *Navajo Roundup* (Boulder, CO: Pruett Publishing Co., 1970). Also see Thompson, Gerald, *The Army and the Navajo: The Bosque Redondo Reservation Experiment, 1863-1868* (Tucson: University of Arizona Press, 1982). Also see Roessel, Ruth, ed., *Navajo Stories of the Long Walk* (Tsaile, AZ: Navajo Community College Press, 1973).

2. Treaty of 1868, United States-Navajo Nation, 15 *Stat.* 667. For background on the "negotiations" going into this international agreement, see U.S. House of Representatives, *Executive Document 263*, 49th Cong., 1st Sess. (Washington, D.C.: 1868). For further context on the treaty, see Iverson, Peter, *The Navajo* (Albuquerque: University of New Mexico Press, 1981).

3. For context, see Kluckhohn, Clyde, and Dorothea Leighton, *The Navajo* (Cambridge, MA: Harvard University Press, 1948). Also see Downs, James F., *The Navajo* (New York: Holt, Rinehart and Winston Publishers, 1972), and Waters, Frank, *Book of the Hopi* (New York: Viking Press, 1963). Concerning Diné-Hopi intermarriage, see *The Tobacco Clan*, a pamphlet circulated by the Big Mountain Legal Defense/Offense Committee (Flagstaff, AZ: *circa* 1984).

4. The Executive Order was signed on December 16, 1882, demarcating an area 70 miles long by 55 miles wide, enclosing some 2,472,095 acres. It is estimated that approximately 600 Diné and 1,800 Hopis lived within the demarcated zone at the time the order went into effect. For general history, see Kammer, Jerry, *The Second Long Walk: The Navajo-Hopi Land Dispute* (Albuquerque: University of New Mexico Press, 1980). For legal history, see *Healing v. Jones* (II), 210 F. Supp. 125 (D. Ariz 1962). Also see *Hopi Tribe v. United States*, 31 Ind. Cl. Comm. 16 (1973) (Docket 196).

5. See U.S. Commission on Civil Rights, *The Navajo Nation: An American Colony* (Washington, D.C.: September 1975). Also see Allan, R., "The Navajo Tribal Council: A Study of the American Indian Assimilation Process," unpublished 1983 report available from the *Arizona Law Review*).

6. The Indian Reorganization Act (IRA), 25 U.S.C.A. § 461, is also known as the "Wheeler-Howard Act," after its Senate and House sponsors, Senator Burton K. Wheeler and Representative Edgar Howard. An in-depth analysis of the act may be found in Deloria, Vine, Jr., and Clifford M. Lytle, *The Nations Within: The Past and Future of American Indian Sovereignty* (New York: Pantheon Books, 1984). Also see Haas, Theodore H., "The Indian Reorganization Act in Historical Perspective," in *Indian Affairs and the Indian Reorganization Act: The Twenty Year Record*, ed. Lawrence H. Kelly, (Tucson: University of Arizona Press, 1954).

7. LaFarge, Oliver, *Notes for Hopi Administrators*, U.S. Department of Interior, Bureau of Indian Affairs (Washington, D.C.: 1936); quoted in Indian Law Resource Center, *Report to the Kikmongwe and Other Traditional Hopi Leaders on Docket 196 and Other Threats to Hopi Land and Sovereignty* (Washington, D.C.: 1979), p. 49.

8. See La Farge, Oliver, *Running Narrative of the Organization of the Hopi Tribe of Indians*, an unpublished study in the Oliver La Farge Collection, University of Texas at Austin. Also see Lummis, Charles, *Bullying the Hopi* (Prescott, AZ: Prescott College Press, 1968), and Nash, Jay B., Oliver La Farge, and W. Carson Ryan, *New Day for the Indians: A Survey of the Workings of the Indian Reorganization Act* (New York: Academy Press, 1938).

9. See Thompson, Laura, *A Culture in Crisis: A Study of the Hopi Indians* (New York: Harper and Brothers Publishers, 1950). Also see the relevant chapters in Matthiessen, Peter, *Indian Country* (New York: Viking Press, 1984).

10. See Kammer, *op. cit.*, p. 78. Further context may be obtained from Sekaquaptewa, Helen, and Louise Udall, *Me and Mine* (Tucson: University of Arizona Press, 1969), and Clemmer, Richard O., *Continuities of Hopi Culture Change* (Ramona, CA: Acoma Books, 1978).

11. Grazing District 6 has an interesting history. It was initially established in 1936 at the request of the Mormon segment of Hopi society in exchange for their participation in the federally-desired reorganization of Hopi governance. At the time, it was provisionally constituted at 499,248 acres, pending the results of a U.S. Forest Service study which would fix its "permanent" acreage, based on actual Hopi "need" (210 *F. Supp.* 125 [1962]). In November 1939, the "exclusive Hopi use and occupancy area" was expanded to 520,727 acres, upon the recommendation of Forest Service official C. E. Rachford. This was followed, in 1941, with a plan proposed by Indian Commissioner John Collier, responding to Mormon Hopi demands, to expand the grazing district to 528,823 acres. The Sekaquaptewas rejected the Collier proposal in council, arguing that their continued participation in IRA governance entitled them to more. A second Forest Service study was then commissioned, leading to a recommendation by Forester Willard Centerwall that "final boundaries" be drawn that encompassed what he computed as being 631,194 acres. This was accepted by the Sekaquaptewa faction. A 1965 BIA survey disclosed, however, that Centerwall had noticeably miscalculated; the real acreage encumbered within the final version of Grazing District 6 is actually 650,013. See Kammer, *op. cit.*, pp. 40-41.

12. Boyden was first retained by the Hopi IRA government in 1951, to file a claim for preeminence of Hopi mineral rights over the entirety of the 1882 Executive Order Area. Tellingly, this was done over the direct objections of the traditional *Kikmongwe*, who had delivered a formal proclamation in 1948 opposing any and all mineral development by their nation. The precipitating factor underlying the traditional position was the earlier issuance of a report by BIA Solicitor General Felix S. Cohen ("Ownership of Mineral Estate in Hopi Executive Order Reservation," U.S. Department of Interior, Bureau of Indian Affairs [Washington, D.C.: 1946]). Very interesting is the fact that Boyden had gone before the Navajo Tribal Council almost as soon as the Cohen report was released, attempting to market his services in securing its interests *against* the Hopis. In late 1951, the *Kikmongwe* attempted to enter a suit with the Indian Claims Commission that would have

blocked Boyden's actions "in their behalf" on the minerals front. The ICC dismissed this suit out of hand in 1955, insofar as the *Kikmongwe* were not the "federally recognized government" representing the Hopi Nation. See Parlow, Anita, *Cry, Sacred Land: Big Mountain, U.S.A.* (Washington, D.C.: Christic Institute, 1988), pp. 198-99.

13. The primary initiative towards this end was Boyden's authoring of P.L. 85-547, passed by the U.S. Congress in 1958. The statute authorized litigation to resolve conflicting land claims within the 1882 Executive Order Area, once and for all. This allowed Boyden to file what is called the *Healing v. Jones* (I) suit (174 *F. Supp.* 211 [D. Ariz. 1959]), by which he sought to obtain clear title to the entire 1882 parcel for his Mormon Hopi clients. The results of this foray were inconclusive. Hence, Boyden launched the earlier-cited *Healing v. Jones* (II) suit. This gambit failed in 1962, when a special three-judge panel from the U.S. District Court ruled that equal rights applied to both Hopis and Navajos outside of Grazing District 6; this mutually-held territory was proclaimed a "Navajo-Hopi Joint Use Area" (JUA). On appeal, Circuit Judge Frederick Hamley upheld the lower court, observing that—absent a treaty—Hopi held "no special interest" in the disputed area, and that any land rights it might actually possess were subject entirely to the federal "plenary power authority" accruing from the 1903 *Lonewolf v. Hitchcock decision (187 U.S. 553). Hamley clarified his position as being that both Navajos and Hopis were "no more than tenants" in the Executive Order Area (174 F. Supp. 216).* In 1963, the U.S. Supreme Court upheld Hamley's interpretation of the case. For further information, see Schifter, Richard, and Rick West, "*Healing v. Jones*: Mandate for Another Trail of Tears?" *North Dakota Law Review*, no. 73 (1974), and Whitson, Hollis, "A Policy Review of the Federal Government's Relocation of Navajo Indians Under P.L. 95-531 and P.L. 96-305," *Arizona Law Review*, vol. 27, no. 2 (1985), p. 14. For example, in 1955, the BIA and University of Arizona College of Mines completed a $500,000 joint study of mineral resources on both Diné and Hopi lands, suggesting that extensive coal stripping and concomitant electrical power generation were likely in "the foreseeable future." The three-volume report specifically highlighted Black Mesa, in the northern portion of the JUA, as holding up to 21 billion tons of low sulphur coal beneath an almost nonexistent overburden of soil. In 1956, an independent study undertaken by geologist G. Kiersch for the Arizona Bureau of Mines (*Metalliferous Minerals and Mineral Fuels, Navajo-Hopi Indian Reservations*) estimated the Black Mesa deposits at 19 billion tons. By either assessment, the area was seen to hold a rich potential for strip-mining.

15. There was actually a total of 16 energy corporations involved at this stage; see *Petroleum Today* (winter 1965).

16. Oil exploration leases for Grazing District 6 were let by sealed bid during September and October of 1964, generating $984,256 for the top 56 parcels, $2.2 million overall. John Boyden's bill for setting up the leasing procedure was $780,000. The Sekaquaptewas saw to it that he received even more: a total of $1 million in "fees and bonuses" for "services rendered." Ironically, it turned out there was no oil at all under Grazing District 6. See Kammer, *op. cit.*, pp. 77-78.

17. As a matter of record, John Boyden was a legal representative of Peabody Coal's attempted merger with Kennecott Copper during the very period he was negotiating Peabody's Black Mesa lease on behalf of the Hopi IRA government. The

35-year lease was signed in 1966, giving Peabody access to 58,000 acres sitting atop what the Arizona Bureau of Mines estimated in 1970 was 21 billion tons of readily accessible low sulphur coal. Peabody then opened the Kayenta Mine on the northern edge of the JUA, a location directly impacting only Diné, not Hopis. The agreement allowed the corporation to draw off desert groundwater in order to slurry coal 273 miles, to Southern California Edison's Mohave Generating Station, near Bullhead City, Nevada. The Navajo Nation was persuaded by Representative Aspinall, chair of the House Interior Committee and a personal friend of Boyden, to give up rights to some 31,400 acre feet per year in upper Colorado River water—as "compensation" for water used in the Peabody slurry operation—while simultaneously providing right-of-way for Arizona's Salt River Project to construct a 78-mile rail line from the mine site to its Navajo Power Plant, near the town of Page. Udall, whose job as Interior Secretary it was to protect all Indian interests in the affair, saw to it instead that the complex of agreements were quickly and quietly approved; his motivation may be found in the fact that the Interior Department's Bureau of Reclamation owned a 25 percent interest in the Navajo Power Plant, a matter that figured into the Interior's plan to divert some 178,000 acre feet of the Diné share of Colorado River water to its Central Arizona Project, meeting the needs of the state's non-Indian population. All in all, as an editorial writer in the *Gallup* (New Mexico) *Independent* was to observe on May 14, 1974, the whole thing was "a miserable deal for the Navajo Tribe." The Sekaquaptewas were, of course, delighted with the transaction and reputedly paid Boyden some $3.5 million from the Hopi share of the Peabody royalties over the years, for his skill in "finesing" the situation to their advantage. Meanwhile, the Mormon Church, of which both they and their attorney were members, and for which Boyden was also acting as an attorney, owned an estimated 8 percent of Peabody's stock (and a substantial block of Kennecott stock, as well) in 1965. The value of and revenue from the church's Peabody holding nearly doubled during the three years following Boyden's successful participation in the Black Mesa lease initiative. For further information, see Wiley, Peter, and Robert Gottlieb, *Empires in the Sun: The Rise of the New American West* (New York: G.P. Putnam's Sons, 1982). Also see Josephy, Alvin, "Murder of the Southwest," *Audubon Magazine* (July 1971).

18. The suit was *Hamilton v. Nakai* (453 F.2d 152 [9th Cir. 1972], *cert. denied*, 406 U.S. 945), in which Boyden introduced a 1964 BIA range use study indicating that the maximum carrying capacity of the JUA was 22,036 "sheep units." Under provision of the "equal entitlement" stipulations of *Healing v. Jones* (II), he argued, the Diné were entitled to graze the maximal equivalent of 11,018 sheep units in the JUA. He then introduced a BIA stock enumeration showing that some 1,150 traditional Diné families were grazing approximately 63,000 head of sheep and goats, 8,000 cattle, and 5,000 horses—the equivalent of 120,000 sheep units—a number the court was "compelled" to order reduced by about 90 percent. U.S. District Judge James Walsh concurred and, for reasons which are unclear, established a "cap" on Diné grazing rights even lower than 50 percent of carrying capacity: a maximum of 8,139 sheep units.

19. These suits include *Hamilton v. McDonald* (503 F. 2d 1138 [9th Cir. 1974]), *Sekaquaptewa v. McDonald* (544 F. 2d. 396 [9th Cir. 1976]), and *Sidney v. Zah* (718 F. 2d 1453 [9th Cir. 1983]). For further information, see Lapham, Neil, "Hopi Tribal

Council: Stewardship or Fraud?" *Clear Creek Journal* (n.d.); available as a pamphlet from the Big Mountain Legal Office, Flagstaff, AZ.

20. WEST Associates is a consortium of 23 regional utility companies that banded together with the federal Bureau of Reclamation in 1964 to advance a unified strategy for energy development and profit-making in the Southwest. Members include Arizona Public Service Company, Central Arizona Project, El Paso (TX) Electric, El Paso Natural Gas, Public Service of New Mexico, Southern California Edison, Tucson (AZ) Gas and Electric, the Salt River (AZ) Project, Texas Eastern Transmission Company, Los Angeles (CA) Water and Power, San Diego (CA) Gas and Electric, Nevada Power Company, Utah Power and Light, Public Service Company of Colorado, Pacific Gas & Electric. The WEST group is closely interlocked with the so-called "Six Companies" that have, since the 1930s, dominated dam construction, mining and other major development undertakings in the western U.S.; these include Bechtel, Kaiser, Utah International, Utah Construction and Mining, MacDonald-Kahn, and Morrison-Knudson. And, of course, the ripples go much further. In 1977, for example, Bechtel was a key player in a corporate consortium—including Newmont Mining, Williams Company, Boeing, Fluor, and the Equitable Life Insurance Company—which bought Peabody Coal after John Boyden's 1966 attempt to effect a merger between Peabody and Kennecott Copper was blocked by congress on anti-trust grounds. In any event, by the late 1960s, WEST had developed what it called "The Grand Plan" for rearranging the entirety of the Southwest into a "power grid" involving wholesale coal stripping, dozens of huge slurry-fed coal-fired generating plants, a complex of new dams (including those such as Glen Canyon and Echo Canyon, which have in fact been built) for hydroelectric generation purposes, several nuclear reactors adjoining uranium mining/milling sites, and a fabric of high-voltage transmission lines girdling the entire region. Given the fact that infrastructural development costs were designed to be largely underwritten by tax dollars, the potential profitability of the plan for WEST members and affiliated corporations are absolutely astronomical over the long term. See Wiley and Gottlieb, *op. cit.*

21. For further information on the initial draft bill, see Thompson, Gary L., *The American Indian Law Journal*, no. 397 (1975). Also see Tehan, Kevin, "Of Indians, Land and the Federal Government," *Arizona State Law Journal*, no. 176 (1976).

22. Several such studies are alluded to in Ralph Nader Congress Project, *The Environmental Committees* (New York: Grossman Publishers, 1975). These should be understood in the context of the 1970 Arizona Bureau of Mines Bulletin No. 182 (*Coal, Oil, Natural Gas, Helium and Uranium in Arizona*), which articulated the range of incentives available for massive "energy development" programs in the area. For contextual information, see Churchill, Ward, "Letter From Big Mountain," *Dollars and Sense* (December 1985).

23. The senate did not vote the idea down. Rather, it set out to stall any decision it might make until after the 1972 elections. This was accomplished by the house scheduling hearings on the relocation issue in Winslow, AZ. See U.S. Congress, Senate, Subcommittee on Indian Affairs of the Committee on Interior and Insular Affairs, *Authorizing Partition of Surface Rights of Navajo-Hopi Land: Hearings on H.R. 11128* (hereinafter referred to as *Authorization Hearings*), 92d Cong., 2d Sess. (Washington, D.C.: September 14-15, 1972).

24. McGovern wrote in a letter to Navajo Tribal Chairman Peter McDonald that if "there has been no satisfactory agreement reached [between the Hopis and Diné] before next January [1973], I will propose comprehensive new legislation to resolve the problem in such a way that no family is needlessly removed from its homeland" (quoted in the *Gallup Independent*, August 3, 1972). On Goldwater, see Kammer, *op. cit.*, pp. 97-98.

25. Panitch, Mark, "Whose Home on the Range? Coal Fuels Indian Dispute," *Washington Post* (July 21, 1974). It is worth noting that, before going freelance, Panitch had worked as a reporter for the *Arizona Star* in Tucson, covering the land dispute. In this capacity, he had been repeatedly conned into reporting false or distorted information by the Evans PR effort. His analysis of what happened thus offers a significant degree of firsthand authenticity and credibility.

26. *Ibid.* For additional information, see Conason, Joe, "Homeless on the Range: Greed, Religion and the Hopi-Navajo Land Dispute," *Village Voice* (July 29, 1986).

27. As Kammer (*op. cit.*) observes on p. 92, "A particularly nasty incident began when Randolph ordered a ninety-seven-year-old Navajo named Tsinijinnie Yazzie to get off his horse and submit to arrest for trespassing with his sheep. Yazzie did not understand English and remained mounted, so Randolph jerked him off his horse, injuring him seriously. Randolph [then] jailed Yazzie on charges of trespassing and resisting arrest."

28. See Panitch's article on the incident in the *Arizona Star* (March 26, 1972).

29. *Authorizing Partition of Surface Rights of Navajo-Hopi Land, op. cit.*, p. 23. Perhaps ironically, Navajo Tribal Chairman McDonald played directly into his opponents' script by announcing that unless federal authorities acted to curb the Sekaquaptewas' tactics, the Diné would "get their fill of this and take things into their own hands" (*Arizona Sun*, March 1, 1972).

30. Quoted in Kammer, *op. cit.*, p. 105.

31. Fannin went on record as having cosponsored the draconian idea, not only to "avoid violence," but because Diné overgrazing was "killing" the JUA (*Navajo Times*, September 27, 1973). That this was a rather interesting concern for a lawmaker whose professed objective was to see the entire area strip-mined and depleted of groundwater went unremarked at the time.

32. The Lujan language accrues from a "dear colleagues" letter he disseminated to congress on March 16, 1974. In the alternative, Lujan had cosponsored, with Arizona Representative John Conlan, a 1973 proposal that the Diné should be allowed to purchase JUA land from the Hopi, or that congress might appropriate monies for this purpose. These funds might then be used for whatever purpose the Hopis chose, including acquisition of land south of Grazing District 6, upon which no Diné lived, but under which there was no coal. Mineral rights within the JUA would continue to be shared by both peoples. The idea was that such compensation would serve to satisfy both the "equal interest" provisions of the *Healing v. Jones* (II) decision and elementary justice for the Hopis without committing the U.S. to engage in human rights violations against the Diné. New Mexico Senator Joseph Montoya carried a version of the Lujan/Conlan initiative into the senate. It is a testament to the extent to which the "land dispute" was/is really about mining that the enlightened approach offered by the Lujan/Conlan initiative met with vociferous resistance from the entirety of the Boyden/Sekaquap-

tewa/Goldwater/Steiger group, as well as WEST Associate lobbyists. The only responsive party to the proposition turns out to have been the McDonald administration at Navajo, which had been formally offering to buy out Hopi surface interests in the JUA since 1970.

33. The lopsidedness of the house vote is partially accounted for by the fact that influential Arizona Representative Morris "Moe" Udall, brother of former Interior Secretary Stewart Udall, withdrew his opposition to H.R. 10337. He did so, by his own account, at the specific request of Helen Sekaquaptewa, a family friend and fellow Mormon. Udall's articulated position had previously been quite similar to that of Lujan, Conlan, and Montoya (*Congressional Record*, May 29, 1974, p. H4517).

34. *Sekaquaptewa v. McDonald, supra*; it is noted that McDonald was assessed a penalty of $250 per day for each day "excess" stock remained within the JUA.

35. A good portion of the credit for this atypical situation seems due to the effective and sustained lobbying of the Interior Department's Assistant Secretary for Land Management Harrison Loesch, an ardent advocate of mineral development on "public lands" and early supporter of the Steiger draft legislation. It is instructive that less than a year and a half after P.L. 93-531 was passed, Loesch was named vice president of Peabody Coal.

36. Kammer, *op. cit.*, pp. 128-29.

37. 88 *Stat.* 1714 (1974), otherwise known as the "Navajo-Hopi Settlement Act."

38. On this point, see Whitson, *op. cit.*, pp. 379-80.

39. The litigation provision accrued from an effort by Goldwater, *et al.*, to simply assign ownership of 250,000 acres surrounding Moenkopi to the Hopis. An amendment introduced jointly by South Dakota Senator Abourezk and New Mexico Senator Montoya narrowly averted this outcome, by a vote of 37-35, by authorizing a court determination instead.

40. This Boyden/Evans myth was still being repeated as late as the beginning of 1977 by federal mediator William Simkin, charged with establishing the exact placement of the partition line by Judge Walsh. Simkin fixed the number of Diné to be relocated under his plan at 3,495. See *Navajo Times* (January 24, 1977).

41. The 1977 Simkin partition line is virtually identical to that originally proposed by Sam Steiger in 1971. The Steiger line had been drawn by John Boyden, in consultation with Peabody Coal. See Kammer, *op. cit.*, p. 134.

42. Navajo-Hopi Indian Relocation Commission (NHIRC), *1981 Report and Plan* (Flagstaff, AZ: April 1981).

43. This figure is advanced by Whitson (*op. cit.*, p. 372), using the NHIRC *Statistical Program Report for April 1985* (Flagstaff, AZ: May 3, 1985). The commission found that 774 Diné families had been certified and relocated from the Hopi partition zone by that point, while 1,555 families had been certified but not yet relocated. Another 1,707 Diné families had refused both certification and relocation. Using the conventional commission multiplier of 4.5 persons per "family unit," Whitson projected a "conservative estimate of between 10,480 and 17,478 persons, 3,483 of whom had been relocated by May 1985."

44. NHIRC, *1981 Report and Plan, op. cit.*

45. U.S. Department of Interior Surveys and Investigations Staff, *A Report to the Committee on Appropriations, U.S. House of Representatives, on the Navajo and Hopi*

Relocation Commission (hereinafter referred to as *Surveys and Investigations Report*) (Washington, D.C.: January 22, 1985), p. 12.

46. *Ibid.*; testimony of Relocation Commission Chairman Ralph Watkins, p. 6.

47. See U.S. Congress, *Senate, Relocation of Certain Hopi and Navajo Indians*, 96th Cong., 1st Sess. (Washington, D.C.: May 15, 1979).

48. The problem began in July 1975, when Navajo Chairman McDonald announced his government's intent to purchase the full 250,000 acres in BLM replacement lands in House Rock Valley, an area known as the "Arizona Strip" north of the Colorado River. The idea was met first with furious resistance by non-Indian "environmentalist" and "sporting" organizations, such as the Arizona Wildlife Federation and the Save the Arizona Strip Committee (which advocated abolishing Indian reservations altogether). Next, it was discovered that a dozen Mormon families held ranching interests in the valley, and that brought Arizona's Mormon Representative Moe Udall into the fray. In 1979, Udall introduced legislation, ultimately incorporated into P.L. 96-305, the 1980 amendment to P.L. 93-531, which placed Hard Rock Valley out-of-bounds for purposes of Diné acquisition. The next selection was the 35,000 acre Paragon Ranch in New Mexico, apparently chosen by the administration of Navajo Chairman Peterson Zah for its energy development potential rather than as a viable relocation site. In 1982, Interior Secretary James Watt blocked this initiative by withdrawing the ranch from public domain, thereby making it unavailable for acquisition (47 *Fed. Reg.* 9290); Zah filed what was to prove to be an unsuccessful suit, seeking to compel the land transfer (*Zah v. Clark*, Civ. No. 83-1753 BB [D.N.M., filed November 27, 1983]). Meanwhile, in early 1983, the Navajo government indicated it had selected 317,000 acres of public and private lands in western New Mexico, contiguous with the eastern border of the Navajo Nation. The plan met with such fierce reaction from local ranchers that it was soon abandoned (*Surveys and Investigations Report, op. cit.*, p. 24). On June 24, 1983, Zah announced the selection had been switched to five parcels in Arizona (*Navajo Times*, June 29, 1983). By May of 1985, only the Walker Ranch, a 50,000 acre tract, had actually been acquired. There were/are serious problems with water availability, and the ability of the land to sustain grazing was/is subject to serious question ("Water Rights Become Issue in Acquiring Land for Tribe," *Arizona Daily Sun*, April 7, 1985). Such surface water as is available comes mainly from the Rio Puerco, heavily contaminated by the massive July 1979 United Nuclear Corporation Churchrock uranium spill 51 miles upstream at Sanders, AZ (see "Native North America," in this volume; also see Mann, L. J., and E. A. Nemecek, "Geohydrology and Water Use in Southern Apache County," *Arizona Department of Water Resources Bulletin I* [January 1983]). Nonetheless, the first relocatees were moved onto this land in 1987 (Parlow, *op. cit.*, p. 202). As of 1990, there has been no improvement to the situation.

49. Quoted in the *Arizona Republic* (February 17, 1977).

50. Quoted in the *Arizona Star* (August 13, 1975).

51. Morrall was quoted in the *Arizona Daily Sun* (July 9, 1975) as saying, "[The Indians'] future lies in forgetting their "Separate Nation" status and become [*sic*] dues paying Americans like the rest of us."

52. *Lomayatewa v. Hathaway*, 52 F.2d 1324, 1327 (9th Cir. 1975), *cert. denied*, and *Suskena v. Kleppe*, 425 U.S. 903 (1976).

53. Examples of this principle are legion. As illustration, see the U.S. Supreme Court's "resolution" of the Black Hills Land Claim, 448 U.S. 907 (1982).

54. Schifter's query appears in *Authorization Hearings*, *op. cit.*, p. 208. It is possible the Senate Committee might have been swayed by the question. Such logic was, however, more than offset by the efficient and persistent lobbying of the committee's staff director, Jerry Verkler, who appears to have been, among other things, feeding inside information on the committee deliberations directly to Evans and Associates. Shortly after P.L. 93-531 was safely passed in 1974, Verkler left government service. In January 1975, he was named manager of the Washington, D.C. office of Texas Eastern Transmission Company, one of the WEST Associates consortium. By 1980, he had been promoted to fill a position as the corporation's vice president for government affairs. See Kammer, *op. cit.*, pp. 135-36.

55. Steiger's statement appears in the transcript of a meeting of the House Subcommittee on Indian Affairs, November 2, 1973, lodged in the committee files of the National Archives, Washington, D.C., at p. 127.

56. U.S. Congress, House, Subcommittee on Indian Affairs, Committee on Interior and Insular Affairs, *Relocation of Certain Hopi and Navajo Indians*, 92d Cong., 2d Sess. (Washington, D.C.: April 17-18, 1972), p. 35.

57. See, for example, Fried, Marc, "Grieving for a Lost Home," in *The Urban Condition*, ed. L. J. Dunn (New York: Basic Books, 1963), pp. 151-71.

58. Scudder, Thayer, "The Human Ecology of Big Projects: River Basin Development on Local Populations," *Annual Review of Anthropology*, no. 2 (1973): pp. 45-61.

59. For example, see Gilbert, Betty Beetso, "Navajo-Hopi Land Dispute: Impact of Forced Relocation on Navajo Families," unpublished Master of Social Work thesis, Arizona State University, Tempe, 1977.

60. Smith's statement was made to an aide to Massachusetts Senator Ted Kennedy, Wendy Moskop, during a fact-finding trip to the JUA in 1974. Quoted in a flyer distributed by the Big Mountain Legal Defense/Offense Committee (Flagstaff, AZ: *circa* 1982).

61. Walsh's February 10, 1977 order did provide for both Hopi and Navajo jurisdiction on their respective sides of the partition line. However, it also specifically stated that livestock impoundment might proceed only under supervision of the secretary of the interior, who was charged with assuring "the civil rights of persons within the area are not obstructed" in the process. Sekaquaptewa's approach simply discarded Diné civil rights as an irrelevancy.

62. According to Kammer (*op. cit.*, p. 157), "[BIA Phoenix Area Office Director John] Artichoker had the police supplied with enough arms to repulse a tank assault. Weapons flow in from a special BIA arsenal in Utah included grenade launchers and automatic rifles."

63. Sekaquaptewa is quoted in the *Gallup Independent* (March 9, 1977) as saying, regardless of the judge's view, his rangers couldn't have an ordinance around without enforcing it.

64. The "eager for a shootout" description comes from *Ibid.* Abbot Sekaquaptewa is quoted from the *Gallup Independent* (March 18, 1977).

65. The details of Benjamin's plan, and quotation of his remarks, are taken from Kammer, *op. cit.*, p. 158. For analysis of the impact of the compulsory stock reduction program upon the targeted Diné, see Wood, John J., *Sheep is Life: An*

Assessment of Livestock Reduction in the Former Navajo-Hopi Joint Use Area (Flagstaff: Department of Anthropology Monographs, Northern Arizona University, 1982).

66. The actual order is unpublished. It is quoted in part, however, in *Sekaquaptewa v. McDonald* (II), *op. cit.*, and *Sidney v. Zah*, *op. cit.*

67. See Whitson, *op. cit.*, pp. 404-6, for details on the effects of the building freeze.

68. *Ibid.*, p. 389. Whitson draws upon several sources in advancing her claims: Memorandum, "Relocatees Sale and Nonownership of Their Replacement Homes," David Shaw (NHIRC staff) to Steve Goodrich (NHIRC executive director); NHIRC *Report and Plan*, June 1983; *Surveys and Investigations Report*; Schroeder, James, "U.S. Probing Fraud Claims in Relocation of Navajos," *Arizona Republic* (March 7, 1984); *Monroe v. High Country Homes*, Civ. No. 84-189 PCT CLH (D. Ariz, filed Feb. 9, 1984).

69. *Ibid.*, p. 388.

70. See Scudder, Thayer, "Expected Impacts of Compulsory Relocation of Navajos with Special Emphasis on Relocation from the Former Joint Use Area Required by P.L. 93-531," unpublished report (March 1979).

71. "Federal Commissioner says Relocation is like Nazi Concentration Camps," *Navajo Times* (May 12, 1982).

72. See Scudder, Thayer, with the assistance of David F. Aberle, Kenneth Begishe, Elizabeth Colson, Clark Etsitty, Jennie Joe, Jerry Kammer, Mary E. D. Scudder, Jeffrey Serena, Betty Beetso, Gilbert Tippeconnic, Roy Walters, and John Williamson, *No Place To Go: Effects of Compulsory Relocation on Navajos* (Philadelphia, PA: Institute for the Study of Human Issues, 1982).

74. See Churchill, Ward, "JUA/Big Mountain: Examination and Analysis of U.S. Policy Within the Navajo-Hopi Joint Use Area Under Provisions of International Law," *Akwesasne Notes*, vol. 17, nos. 3-4 (May-August 1985). Also see Hawley, Lucy, Todd Howland, Ved P. Nanda, Judith Rhedin, and Sandra Shwader, *Denver Journal of International Law and Policy*, no. 15 (1987).

75. Todacheenie is quoted in Kammer, *op. cit.*, p. 79.

76. All quotes appear in the *Gallup Independent* (May 5, 1977).

77. See Kammer, *op. cit.*, pp. 1-2; Parlow, *op. cit.*, p. 200.

78. See Kammer, *op. cit.*, pp. 209-10; Parlow, *op. cit.*, p. 201.

79. Quoted in Parlow, *op. cit.*, p. 201. For further information, see Lee, Pelican, *Navajos Resist Forced Relocation: Big Mountain and Joint Use Area Communities Fight Removal*, self-published pamphlet (1985); available through the Big Mountain Legal Office, Flagstaff, AZ.

80. This effort was maintained until 1984, at which point AIM fragmented and IITC virtually collapsed due to the insistence of some elements of the leadership of each organization to support Sandinistas rather than Indians in Nicaragua. Strange as this may seem, IITC mounted what might be called a "flying tribunal," sending it around the country to purge "unreliable individuals" guilty of expressing an "impure political line" by demanding rights of genuine self-determination for the Miskito, Sumu and Rama peoples of Nicaragua's Atlantic Coast region. Among those discarded was Gurwitz (in late 1986), who had served as the hub of the BMLDOC operation. The national and international support networks he had built up eroded very quickly, leaving the Big Mountain resistance with only a small and relatively ineffectual portion of the organized external support base it had once enjoyed. As for IITC, at last count, it was down to a staff of three operating

from an office in San Francisco. While no longer a functional entity, it is, to be sure, "ideologically pure."

81. Anderson contacted Gurwitz during a National Lawyers Guild conference in Santa Fe, New Mexico during the spring of 1982. Gurwitz responded immediately, opening the Flagstaff, Arizona office during the fall of the same year.

82. Perhaps most notable among the interns was Lee Brookee Phillips, who ultimately succeeded Gurwitz as head of the legal defense effort. BMLDOC was redesignated as the "Big Mountain Legal Office" (BMLO) in 1987.

83. Parlow, *op. cit.*, p. 117. The foreign countries at issue included Switzerland, West Germany, Austria, Italy, Canada, Great Britain, and Japan.

84. The Indian Law Resource Center intervention was presented to the Working Group by staff attorney Joe Ryan on August 31, 1981. The independent commission, composed of Joan Price, Loughrienne Nightgoose, Omali Yeshitela and Ward Churchill, was first convened during the annual Big Mountain Survival Gathering, April 19-22, 1984. Its collective findings were presented to the elders over the following year.

85. For further information on these and other aspects of the physical resistance, see Parlow, *op. cit.,* especially pp. 115-51 and 201-2. Also see Matthiessen, Peter, "Forced Relocation at Big Mountain," *Cultural Survival Quarterly,* vol. 12, no. 3 (1988).

86. The quote is taken from a speech made by Gurwitz at the University of Colorado/Colorado Springs, February 17, 1986.

87. The federal judgment seems to have been quite sound in this regard, as should be apparent from the events described in note 80, above. At present, organized support for the Big Mountain resistance has fallen to less than 10 percent of 1986 levels, and continues to decline. As of late 1989, the BMLO facility in Flagstaff, Arizona, established by Gurwitz in 1982, had to be closed for lack of financial support.

88. The *Manybeads* suit was based, in large part, upon initially successful litigation of the Yellowthunder case (*United States v. Means, et al.,* Docket No. Civ. 81-5131, Dist. [S.D., December 9, 1985]), in which attorneys Ellison, Finzel, and Larry Leventhal argued that the entire Black Hills region is of spiritual significance to the Lakota. The same principle was advanced on behalf of the Diné resistance with regard to the Big Mountain area. However, the favorable decision reached by the U.S. District Court in Yellowthunder was overturned by the 8th Circuit Court of Appeals in the wake of the Supreme Court's G-O Road decision. This, in turn, led to the dismissal of *Manybeads.*

89. Shortly after the *Manybeads* suit was entered, a second suit—*Attakai v. United States*—was filed, contending that specific sites within the Hopi partition area of the JUA are of particular spiritual significance to the Diné. This case remains active, although the only positive effect it has generated as of the summer of 1990 has been a ruling by Judge Carroll that the federal government and/or Hopi tribal council are required to provide seven days prior notification to both the Big Mountain Legal Office and Navajo tribal council of the "development" of such designated sites. In principle, this is to allow the Diné an opportunity to present information as to why targeted sites should not be physically altered. Rather obviously, however, the time-period involved is too short to allow for effective response. For further information, see Diamond, Phil, "Big Mountain Update," *Akwesasne Notes,* vol. 21, no. 6 (midwinter 1989-90). Concerning the G-O Road

decision, see the essay on this topic by Glenn T. Morris in the first volume of *Critical Issues in Native North America*.

90. During the spring of 1990, the Big Mountain Legal Office estimated that as many as 9,000 of the "at least 12,000" Diné subject to relocation under P.L. 93-531 remained on the land. Official government estimates were unavailable. For further information, see Lacerenza, Deborah, "An Historical Overview of the Navajo Relocation," *Cultural Survival Quarterly*, vol. 12, no. 3 (1988).

91. Quoted from *Navajo Times* (August 31, 1978). At the time Goldwater made this statement, Judge Walsh's order approving the Simkin partition line and requiring relocation of all Dinés within the Hopi partition area had been in effect for more than a year and a half.

92. For example, on August 31, 1978, the *Arizona Star* editorialized, under the title "Goldwater's Confusion," that the senator, "who either has uniformed or inaccurate sources on Arizona Indian affairs, has not spent enough time gathering firsthand information or he has simply lost interest in the subject. If the latter is true, [he] should refrain from public comment."

93. It is instructive to note that Representative Wayne Owens, who sponsored Boyden's successful draft legislation, went to work for Boyden's Salt Lake City law firm after being voted out of office in Arizona. He now serves as a representative from Utah. Such apparent conflict of interest situations are normal within the context of U.S. Indian Affairs.

94. *Stat.* 932; 25 U.S.C. §§ 640d-28 (1983). Perhaps one reason this superficial deviation from the P.L. 93-531 hard line was passed with relatively little furor was that John Boyden died in mid-1980. He was replaced as attorney for the Hopi IRA government by John Kennedy, a senior partner in Boyden's law firm. By all accounts, the stance and attitudes adopted by Boyden over nearly 30 years of involvement in the "land dispute" have been continued unchanged.

95. Danny Blackgoat, interview on radio station WKOA, Denver, CO, March 13, 1985. For further development of this theme, see Redhouse, John, *Geopolitics of the Navajo-Hopi Land Dispute*, self-published (1985); available through the Big Mountain Legal Office, Flagstaff, AZ.

96. Parlow, *op. cit.*, p. 202.

97. *Ibid.* The author quotes Indian Commissioner Ross Swimmer as applauding Udall's action in at least momentarily opening the door for the BIA to begin forced relocation operations. Although Swimmer himself has been replaced as head of the BIA, the sentiments he represented within the Bureau have not changed appreciably.

98. Diamond, *op. cit.*

99. *Ibid.*

100. The term is taken from a speech by Morris delivered at the Federal Building, Denver, CO, May 19, 1989.

101. Diamond, *op. cit.*

102. *Ibid.*

103. The quote is taken from a talk given by Roberta Blackgoat during International Women's Week at the University of Colorado/Boulder, during March 1984. Mrs. Blackgoat is one of several elder women who emerged as primary spokespersons for the Big Mountain Resistance during the 1980s. Her son, Danny, served for a period as head of the BMLD/OC office in Flagstaff (see note 95).

# NATIVE NORTH AMERICA
The Political Economy of
Radioactive Colonialism
with Winona LaDuke

[O]ur defeat was always implicit in the history of others; our wealth has always generated our poverty by nourishing the prosperity of others, the empires and their native overseers...In the colonial and neocolonial alchemy, gold changes to scrap metal and food into poison...[We] have become painfully aware of the mortality of wealth which nature bestows and imperialism appropriates.

—Eduardo Galeano, *Open Veins of Latin America*

Land has always been the issue central to North American politics and economics. Those who control the land are those who control the resources within and upon it. Whether the resource at issue is oil, natural gas, uranium or other minerals, water, or agriculture, land ownership, social control, and all the other aggregate components of power are fundamentally interrelated. At some levels, such a situation seems universal, but in this hemisphere, given the peculiarities of a contemporary socioeconomic apparatus of power which has been literally imported in its entirety, the equation seems all the more acute.

Within North America, American Indian reservations—or "reserves," as they are called in Canada—constitute a small but crucial "piece of the rock." Approximately one-third of all western U.S. low-sulfur coal, 20 percent of known U.S. reserves of oil and natural gas, and over one-half of all U.S. uranium deposits lie under the reservations.[1] Other important minerals such as bauxite and zeolites are also located there in substantial quantities, and a considerable proportion of western U.S. water resources is subject to American Indian priority use through various treaty stipulations. A comparable, if somewhat less pronounced, situation prevails in Canada.[2] Even these figures are misleadingly small. Past (1890-1920) and more recent (1930-1980) land expropriations undertaken by corporate interests such as railroads, agribusiness, and mining concerns, as well as "land withdrawals" from the indigenous nations orchestrated by the federal government under the provisions of the "Allotment Act," the "Homestead Act," the "Termination Act," and other legislation must be considered in any rational assessment.[3] If the areas stripped away from tribal ownership and control in direct violation of standing international agreements are included, the amount of contemporary American Indian resources is suddenly jolted to a much higher level than is conventionally perceived.[4]

One example of this is the southern Arizona copper belt, a deposit yielding fully two-thirds of all U.S. copper ore. The bulk of the area was a part of the Papago reservation until the copper was discovered during the 1920s. The ore-bearing area was subsequently removed from the Papago domain by unilateral decree ("statute") of the U.S. Congress.[5] Similarly, the bulk of the massive Fort Union coal deposit of Wyoming, Montana, and North Dakota which does not underlie current reservation boundaries *does* underlie the territory reserved by the Lakota, Cheyenne, and Arapaho nations under the terms of the Fort Laramie Treaty of 1868. Although some ninety percent of the original treaty area has now "passed" from Indian control, the treaty in question remains an internationally binding document conferring ownership to the signatory indigenous peoples in perpetuity (see Map I).[6]

Aside from the mining interests which have made huge contemporary inroads into what amounts to unceded Indian territory, another focal point of any examination of Indian resources must concern water rights. In the arid but energy-rich western United States, water is both prerequisite and integral to all forms of corporate development. The preponderance of western water is legally owned (by virtue of treaties) by various Indian nations. Hypothetically, even if a given nation could not retain control over a portion of its territoriality, it could still shape the nature and extent of corporate exploitation of the land through assertion of its water rights. Of course, the federal government has systematically acted to diminish or effectively void most Indian exercise of water rights prerogatives.[7]

A final factor worthy of consideration concerns, not resource distribution and control, but the distribution of production itself. For instance, while Indians technically "own" only about half of U.S.

Map I

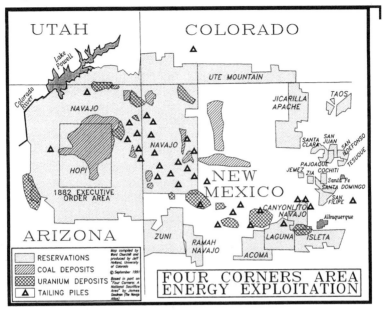

FOUR CORNERS AREA ENERGY EXPLOITATION

uranium resources, production statistics relative to reservation areas are *much* higher. In 1974, 100 percent of all federally controlled uranium production accrued from the contemporary reservation land base.[8] In 1975, there were some 380 leases concerning uranium extraction on reservation lands, as compared to a total of four on *both* public and acquired land. In Canada, the data are quite similar,[9] indicating that while North American Indian resources are perhaps not overwhelmingly large on a global scale, production certainly *is*.

The pattern of colonization prevalent in South America and noted in the quotation from Eduardo Galeano at the outset seems appropriate to conditions currently existing in the North as well. Internal colonialism—the colonization of indigenous peoples—is a malignant, if little discussed, fact of life within both the United States and Canada (and Mexico as well). The centrality of the issue of colonization of such Fourth World peoples to any reasonable strategy of global anti-imperialism seems much more evident in the North than in the South, not for moral reasons, but for pragmatic ones. North America, and the

United States in particular, is the seat of the most comprehensive system of imperialism ever witnessed by humanity. Increasingly, it is a system fueled by nuclear capabilities, fed by uranium. The relationship of the reservations to that uranium is clear. Likewise, the United States and Canada lead the world in "food production"; needless to say, there is a huge stake in maintaining this position of dominance. Again, the relationship of the American Indian treaty lands to primary North American agricultural areas is readily observable. The same can be said relative to a range of crucial resources. Such issues, the internal integrity and hegemony of North American imperialism, and the colonial stranglehold over the resources of internalized sovereignties it implies, are the subject of this essay.

Internal Colonialism

A distinction must be made between property in its economic and legal aspects and property considered as a social institution. The territorial question of American Indian peoples in the United States is fundamentally an economic question, that is, as the source of livelihood, but also involves the survival of human societies, and is, therefore, a question of human rights, and a nationalities question. A people cannot continue as a people without a land base, an economic base, and political independence, as distinguished from a religious group or an ethnic minority of fundamentally the same historical character as the majority society.

—United Nations Subcommittee on Racism, Racial
Discrimination, Apartheid and Decolonization
Final Report (1977)

American Indian nations in North America are today constrained to occupation of approximately 2.5 percent of their original land base.[10] Nonetheless, this land if carefully managed or, in some cases, expanded to reconcile to legally posited treaty boundaries, provides a viable basis for national survival. The Navajo Nation, as one example, holds a territorial base comparable to that of Belgium, the Netherlands, or Denmark. It is considerably larger than such European sovereignties as Luxembourg, Lichtenstein, or Monaco. Its natural resource base is far greater than that of these nations *combined*.[11] The Lakota, or "Great Sioux," reservation of the Dakotas prior to its patently illegal dismemberment under the Allotment and Homestead

Acts (1890-1920), would provide an even more striking example. The Menominees of Wisconsin were almost entirely self-sufficient despite radical reductions of their land base, with a replenishable economy based on timbering, when the nation was unilaterally "dissolved" by congressional fiat under the Termination Act (1955). The peoples of the Pacific Northwest, the "Five Civilized Tribes" (Creek, Cherokee, Chickasaw, Choctaw, and Seminole, relocated from the Southeast to Oklahoma by federal force during the 1830s), the Tohono O'Odam (Papago) of Arizona, the Cheyenne and Crow of Montana—and the list could go on and on—each possesses a treaty-sanctioned and demonstrably viable economic basis for national existence. In Canada, the situation is much the same.

The *foreign* interests represented by the U.S. and Canadian national governments, however, have not been content with past land confiscations. Throughout this century, and into the present moment, each has proceeded with the most insidious and mercenary neocolonial policies imaginable. A primary (and classic) vehicle of neocolonialism was created under the so-called "Indian Reorganization Act" (1934), whereby the United States imposed a system of "tribal council" governments on each reservation, a mechanism designed to replace traditional (and resistant) Indian governmental forms with an apparatus approved by and owing its allegiance to Washington, D.C.

Recognized by the United States after 1934 as the sole governing body of Indian reservations (and peoples), the tribal council system rapidly circumvented or usurped the authority of traditional Indian governmental structures such as the Councils of Chiefs. The U.S. rationale was/is readily apparent. The new "governments" were charged with responsibilities for "economic planning": minerals lease negotiations, contracting with external corporate agencies, long-term agricultural/ranching leasing, water rights negotiations, land transfers, and so on, all of which required direct approval from Bureau of Indian Affairs representatives prior to consummation, and most of which had long been staunchly resisted by the traditional leadership.[12] The "reorganization" brought about a situation through which U.S. "developmental" policies could/can be implemented through a formalized agency *composed of the Indians themselves*. Canada followed suit with a similar ploy during the 1930s.

With the consolidation of political power on this blatantly neo-colonial principle, modern internal colonialism became possible in North America. To inaugurate this fact, federal land management authorities acted immediately (in 1934) to begin the inversion of the extant tribal economies which had been evolved to accommodate both traditional needs and the constrictions of reservation conditions. Stock reduction programs were initiated to alleviate what was termed "overgrazing" of reservation areas by individually and tribally owned cattle. These programs rapidly became permanent—as applied against Indians, *not* against non-Indian ranchers leasing reservation land for grazing purposes—and, since 1935, more than one-half of all Indian livestock resources have been eliminated as a result.

The results of such a policy were predictable and immediate: the economic infrastructure of North American indigenous nations was dramatically undercut. On the Navajo reservation, for instance, 58 percent of the people derived a livelihood from stock raising (mostly sheep) and agriculture (mostly gardening) in 1940. By 1958, fewer than 10 percent were able to do so.[13] Correspondingly, secondary and tertiary aspects of the tribal economy—such as the wool derived from sheep raising, and the blankets derived from wool—were dislocated. Concurrent to this marked and externally imposed reduction in self-sufficiency was the systematic transfer of economic power to the neocolonial structure lodged in the U.S./tribal council relationship: "developmental aid" from the United States implementation of an "educational system" geared to training for the cruder labor needs of industrialism, employment contracts with mining and other resource extraction concerns, "housing programs" to provide appropriate workforce concentrations, and—eventually—actualization of cooptive social control mechanisms such as unemployment and welfare for newly dependent Indian citizens.

On the Navajo reservation in 1978, approximately one-third of the working age population was employed year round. Of those employed, 57.7 percent worked as a result of government subsidies, 29.3 percent received their salaries from private non-Navajo enterprises, and only 13 percent worked in wholly Navajo operations of all types. This, of course, left Navajo *un*employment at approximately 65 percent. Hence, Navajo self-sufficiency may be estimated as accommodating some 4.3 percent of the working-age population, down from 100 percent in 1920.[14] Such a single-generational transition from self-sufficiency to destitution would seem the strongest possible testimony to the negative effects of U.S. internal colonialism on indigenous populations, but it is not: At the Pine Ridge Lakota reservation in South Dakota, to list but one example, unemployment currently hovers over 90 percent and self-sufficiency is unknown.[15]

Overall, reservation unemployment in both the United States and Canada runs at about 65 percent (making the Navajo example somewhat normal).[16] Subsistence is gleaned from a sort of federal per capita payment system which keeps the bulk of the population alive but abjectly dependent. Two Canadian researchers, Mark Zannis and Robert Davis, analyzed the welfare system in Canada and found that:

> The welfare system is a form of pacification. Combined with political and physical repression it keeps people alive at a subsistence level but blunts any attempt at revolt while turning them into captive consumers of industrial products...For the past 2-3 decades, a kind of enclosure movement has taken place, brought on by the very nature of the welfare system and the dictates of corporate profits.[17]

Zannis and Davis go on to note that residential requirements are prerequisite to any form of welfare—nuclear families and individuals receive this sort of income *as opposed* to groups (i.e., "clans" or extended families, the traditional Indian form of social organization). Coupled to the educational system, the result is that "without children, adults are deprived of the essential labor to carry out traditional economic activities. This creates the need for more welfare," and continues the "reorganization" of Indian societies mandated by the Reorganization Act of 1934.

In recent years, it has become obvious that the social and economic disruption inflicted upon many indigenous nations results from needs peculiar to energy corporations. For example, when Peabody Coal requires 400,000 acres of Indian land for a strip-mining operation, not only is the tribal infrastructure (land use, employment, and the like) impacted, but the physical distribution of the people as well. Relocation of people—as is happening at Big Mountain, Hopi, and elsewhere—with accompanying forced transformations of familial integrity, community organization, etc., is very much at issue.[18] The process of phased destruction of tribal entities undertaken as reorganization in the 1930s has greatly accelerated with the advent of the world "energy crisis" in the 1970s.

Compounding this problem in the 1980s and on into the '90s are the budgetary cutbacks in social service spending undertaken by the "supply siders" of the Reagan and Bush administrations. As the federal government defaults on the reservations, native people are driven for bare sustenance into the arms of the very corporations with which they are purportedly to "negotiate" over use of their land and extraction of their resources. Clearly, prostration is a poor bargaining position from which to proceed, but a half-century of neocolonial rule has resulted in little else. Despite the obvious and abundant wealth of land and resources retained by the nations mentioned above, North American Indian populations suffer virtually the full range of conditions observable in the most depressed of Third World areas. Theirs is the highest rate of infant mortality on the continent, the shortest life expectancy, the greatest incidence of malnutrition, the highest rate of death by exposure, the highest unemployment rate, the lowest per capita income, the highest rate of communicable or plague diseases, the lowest level of formal educational attainment, and so on.[19]

Since such data indicate amply that the federal government has failed abjectly in promoting Indian well-being, as promised by the Reorganization Act, there is a strong feeling in many quarters of Indian Country that the turn to the corporations now being necessitated by Reaganite policies is not such a bad idea. Despite the poor bargaining position through which indigenous nations are securing extraction royalty rates in the 2-to-5 percent (of market) range, a pittance in the world market, internal production distribution within North America is such that the sheer quantity of mining and other corporate activities likely to occur over the next 20 years will generate a huge cash flow into the hands of the tribal councils.[20] It is this cash flow, real and potential, which the feds, the tribal governments, and the corporations are all banking on to offset—in the short run, at least—the cumulative effects of internal colonialism on American Indians.

Western energy resource-rich reservations in particular are thus faced with a political and economic turning point at least as vast in its implications as the reorganization of the 1930s or even the 19th-century transitions to reservation status. Should they embrace and participate in the process of industrializing the reservations after the fashion of "developing" Third World nations, or pursue a "Fourth World" strategy of attempting to disengage from dominant processes and procedures altogether?[21] The results of this decision will undoubtedly shape the futures of American Indian peoples irrevocably. At this juncture, even many of the tribal councils are beginning to realize the stakes of the issue, and some are expressing consternation as a result. To date, however, no tribal council member has been able to articulate a clear position favoring the disengagement option *as opposed to* "development." A number have attempted to articulate plans favoring *both* approaches, a stance which has proven so contradictory as to be untenable. Whether some will ultimately break ranks with the federally promulgated vision of "progress" remains to be seen, but will no doubt prove crucial to the number and magnitude of factional splits within the native peoples themselves over the next decade.

The New Colonialism

Simply stated, the difference between the economics of the "old colonialism," with its reliance on territorial conquest and manpower and the "new colonialism," with its reliance on technologically oriented resource extraction and transportation to the metropolitan centers, is the expendable relationship of subject peoples to multinational corporations. This fact has implications for both the new ways in which genocide is committed, and the new kind of dependence created. Under the old colonialism, the economy of subject peoples was more or less incorporated into the colonial system in a fashion which altered the subject people as little as possible. The economic base commodities were extracted and semiprocessed, in part, by the subject people. These people were expected to maintain their own subsistence economy basically intact...Under new style colonialism, the subsistence economy is not a matter of great concern to the corporations. The raw material they wish to process is usually not organic, nor does it require "heavy labor." The multinational corporation today does not see any relationship between what they want (mineral wealth) and the local economy (organic wealth).

—Robert Davis and Mark Zannis,
The Genocide Machine in Canada

Spurred by the advice of the Bureau of Indian Affairs and corporate promises of jobs and royalties, the Navajo Tribal Council approved a mineral extraction agreement with Kerr-McGee in 1952. In return for access to uranium deposits near the New Mexico town of Shiprock on the reservation, and to fulfill risk-free contracts with the U.S. Atomic Energy Commission, Kerr-McGee employed 100 Navajo men in underground mining operations.[22] Wages for these non-union Navajo miners were low, averaging $1.60 per hour, or approximately two-thirds of the then prevailing off-reservation rate.[23] Additionally, the corporation cut operating costs significantly by virtue of lax enforcement of worker safety regulations at its Shiprock site. In 1952, a federal mine inspector found that ventilation units in the mine's primary shaft were not in operation.[24] In 1954, the inspector discovered the ventilation was still not functioning properly, with the fan operating only during the first half of each shift. When the inspector returned in 1955, the ventilation blower ran out of gas during his visit.[25] One report, dating from 1959, noted radiation levels in the Kerr-McGee shaft had been allowed to reach 90 times the "permissible" limit.[26]

For the corporation, low wages and guaranteed labor force, privileged contract status and virtually nonexistent severance taxes, and nonexistent safety regulation provided a great incentive to both maintain and expand operations on the reservation. However, by 1969 Kerr-McGee had exhausted easily recoverable uranium deposits at Shiprock, in both geological and financial terms. Uranium extraction technology at the time was such that further profitable recovery—under any conditions—was rendered unlikely. Further, the Atomic Energy Commission was in the process of phasing out its ore-buying program, the factor which had made the entire mining gambit feasible in the first place. The Shiprock facility was closed, for all practical intents and purposes, in early 1980.

For the Navajo people, Kerr-McGee's abrupt departure shed light upon the "diseconomies" of uranium development. First, the corporation simply abandoned some 71 acres of "raw" uranium tailings at the mining site. These tailings constitute waste by-products of uranium ore refinement, but retain 85 percent of the original radioactivity of the ore.[27] This huge tailing pile begins approximately 60 *feet* from the San Juan River, the only significant surface water source within the Shiprock area.[28] The obvious result has been a considerable dispersal of radioactive contamination to a number of downstream communities which, of necessity, draw upon the river for potable water.[29]

The price of Kerr-McGee's "development" at Shiprock, in terms of life lost in this generation, and in generations yet to come, cannot be calculated by any financial/economic yardstick. Of the 150-odd Navajo miners who worked underground at the Shiprock facility during the 18 years of its operation, by 1975, 18 had died of radiation-induced lung cancer (*not* the "oat cell" variety associated with cigarette smoking) and another 21 were feared dying.[30] By 1980, 20 of this 21 were dead, and another 95 had contracted similar respiratory ailments and cancers.[31] Birth defects such as cleft palate, leukemia, and other diseases commonly linked to increased radiation exposure have increased dramatically both at Shiprock and in the downstream communities of the San Juan watershed.[32] Since 1970, such diseases have come to be the greatest health concerns of the Navajo Nation.

Nonetheless, by 1980, under the leadership of Tribal Chair Peter McDonald—a staunch advocate of energy development and founder of the Council of Energy Resource Tribes (CERT)—the Navajo Nation had allowed 42 uranium mines and seven uranium mills to be located on or immediately adjacent to the reservation.[33] Some 15 new uranium-oriented projects were in the construction stages on Navajo land. Additionally, four coal-stripping operations averaging approximately 30,000 acres each and five coal-fired power plants have been actualized on the reservation. Much more is in the planning stages. As the U.S. uranium industry undergoes a temporary depression in the early '90s, such non-nuclear energy facilities will remain and burgeon, continuing the development of infrastructure upon which "the new colonialism" depends.

The extent of infrastructural development which is to be continued is indicated by the means through which energy corporations are seeking to address the chronic Navajo unemployment spawned by reorganization. In an article entitled "Manpower Gap at the Uranium Mines," *Business Week* observed:

> Currently, 3,200 miners work underground and 900 more are in open pit operations. By 1990, the industry will need 18,400 underground miners and 4,000 above ground...[o]nce on the job, Kerr-McGee estimates that it costs $80,000 per miner in training, salary, and benefits, as well as the costs for the trainees who quit. Kerr-McGee is now operating a training program at its Churchrock mine on the Navajo reservation. The $2 million program is financed by the Labor Department (U.S.), and is expected to turn out 100 miners annually. Labor Department sponsors hope the program will help alleviate the tribe's chronic unemployment.[34]

The training program is still in effect and has been successful in employing a number of Navajos in "practical applications" of their new-found skills. In the case of the Navajo Nation, which now has more trained and educated persons per capita than any reservation in North America, the form of education within financial reach clearly does not question the desirability of reliance on energy resource exploitation as a means to "self-sufficiency," nor the cumulative effects of radioactive contamination. Yet there are lessons to be learned by those who can manage to be de-educated. It seems axiomatic that the "solution" to unemployment being offered by the energy corporations (in direct collusion with the federal government) is—as in the case of the Shiprock miners—lethal. The consequences to the surrounding habitat and inhabitants also hold with the characteristics introduced at Shiprock. Tuba City, Arizona—another location on the Navajo reservation—has been left with raw tailings piles quite comparable to those at Shiprock and with entirely similar effects.[35] The Kerr-McGee mine at Churchrock currently discharges some 80,000 gallons of radioactive water from its primary shaft ("dewatering") per day, contamination which is introduced directly into local and downstream potable water supplies.[36]

In July 1979, the United Nuclear uranium mill, also located at Churchrock, was the site of an enormous accident. The adjacent mill tailings dam broke under pressure and released more than 100 million gallons of highly radioactive water into the Rio Puerco River. Kerr-McGee-style "safety" standards, similar in principle to the ventilation system at Shiprock, were the cause. Although United Nuclear had known of cracks within the dam structure at least two months prior to the break, no repairs were made (or attempted), 1,700 Navajo people were immediately affected, their single water source contaminated beyond any conceivable limit. More than 1,000 sheep and other livestock, which ingested Rio Puerco water in the aftermath, died.[37]

As a token of the "expendability" of the indigenous population under the new colonialism referred to by Davis and Zannis, when the Churchrock community attempted to seek compensation—including emergency water and food supplies for directly affected community members—United Nuclear stonewalled. Through an array of evasions and obfuscations, the corporation was able to avoid any form of redress for *over a year*, finally making a minimal out-of-court settlement when a class action suit was filed in behalf of the town. By then, of course, the immediate life and death situation had passed (long-term effects being, as yet, unknown). The potential outrage of the local citizenry is, however, a bit constrained. Between the aforementioned Kerr-McGee plant and training program, the United Nuclear facility, and several other energy corporations operating in the area, well over half the jobs and nearly 80 percent of income at Churchrock are now derived from uranium production. Dependency, in its most virulent colonial manifestation, has effectively converted Churchrock into an "economic hostage"—and an expendable hostage at that—of the uranium industry.

But Churchrock and Shiprock are only sample cases of the radioactive colonization prevailing across the face of the Navajo Nation (the full extent of the situation is perhaps best revealed by Map I). Nor should the Navajo Nation be considered as unique in its experience of radioactive colonization. To the north, within what, in 1977, the Supreme Court of the United States ruled was rightly the land base of the Lakota people, some 40 energy corporations are currently vying for position within an extremely rich "resource belt."[38] Central to the Lakota territory legally defined by the Fort Laramie Treaty of 1868 is the Black Hills region. As of August, 1979, some 5,163 uranium claims were held in the Black Hills National Forest alone (a claim generally accommodates about 20 acres); 218,747 acres of "private" land in the area are also under mining leases.[39]

In addition to uranium, coal is a major factor within Lakota territory. The huge Fort Union coal deposit underlies approximately half the land, including the whole of both the current Crow and Northern Cheyenne reservations in Montana, the Fort Berthold reservation in North Dakota, and substantial portions of the Standing Rock and Cheyenne River Lakota reservations near the North Dakota/South Dakota state line. According to Harvey Wasserman:

> Overall, the plans for industrializing the Black Hills are staggering. They include a gigantic energy park featuring more than a score of 10,000-megawatt coal-fired plants, a dozen nuclear reactors, huge coal slurry pipelines designed to use millions of gallons of water to move crushed coal thousands of miles, and at least 14 major uranium mines.[40]

Water may be the most immediately crucial issue. The plans for just one mine, Burdock, call for the "depressurization" of aquifers prior to commencement of mining *per se*. This would entail the pumping of some 675 gallons per minute from the area's quite limited ground water resources. As depressurization must be maintained for the duration of mining activities—projected over a full decade in the case of Burdock—the quantity of water at issue is not trivial. Compounded by the number of mines anticipated as being operational during the same period, the quantity becomes truly astronomical. The reason for the ten-year limitation on Burdock projections has little to do with depletion of mineral resources, but with the anticipated *total* exhaustion of regional ground water supplies by the end of the first decade (i.e., by 1995). The pumped-off water is slated to be used in operations such as the Energy Transportation Systems, Inc. (ETSI) pipeline, which is intended to provide a fluid coal transportation system from the Dakotas to the southeastern United States.

Although development and consolidation of the uranium industry within the Lakota territory are not as pronounced as on Navajo reservations, the sorts of environmental phenomena occurring there are similar. On June 11, 1962, 200 tons of radioactive mill tailings washed into the Cheyenne River, an indirect source of potable water for the Pine Ridge reservation.[41] In June 1980, the Indian Health

Service announced that well water at the reservation community of Slim Buttes contained gross alpha levels at least three times the national safety standard.[42] A new well at Slim Buttes, however, tested at 70 picocuries (pCi) per liter. This is *fourteen times* the standard. Similarly, subsurface water on Pine Ridge's Red Shirt Table tested at several times "acceptable" limits of radioactivity, and tests conducted at the towns of Manderson and Oglala revealed comparable results. The distribution of these locations is such as to indicate that the water sources for the entire reservation have been affected.[43]

Stanley Looking Elk, then Tribal President, requested that $175,000 of the $200,000 federal allocation for reservation water management be committed to securing emergency (uncontaminated) water supplies. In a response strikingly similar to that of United Nuclear at Churchrock (in its implications of the "expendability" of the indigenous population), the Bureau of Indian Affairs stipulated that such alternative water supplies could be secured on Pine Ridge, *but only for consumption by cattle.*[44] Perhaps the reason underlying the government's stonewalling on the issue of radioactive contamination on Pine Ridge is that much worse is yet to come. Not the least cause of this could be the circumstance brought out in a situation report carried in *Akwesasne Notes*:

> The Air Force retained an area near which residents have sighted large containers being flown in by helicopter. These reports have raised strong suspicions that the Gunnery Range was being used as a dump for high-level military nuclear waste, which may be leaking radioactivity into the Lakota Aquifer. In the same area, the rate of stillborn or deformed calves has skyrocketed. Northeast of this area are 12 nuclear missile sites whose radioactive effects are unknown.[45]

The "Gunnery Range" is an area within the northwestern quadrant of the Pine Ridge reservation "borrowed" from the Oglala Lakotas in 1942 for use in training Army Air Corps gunners. It was to be returned upon the conclusion of World War II, but never was. In 1975, in "secret negotiations," former Tribal Chair Dick Wilson assigned legal title over the area to the federal government (after 33 years of boldfaced expropriation by the federal government), ostensibly so that it could become a formal part of the Badlands National Monument.[46] Area residents have felt all along that the area was being used as a convenient dumping ground for virulently toxic nuclear waste, away from large concentrations of "mainstream" U.S. citizens.[47]

Whether or not the government is engaged in such a classified operation, it is known that earlier uranium mining and milling activities at the former army ordnance depot at Igloo, South Dakota, left something on the order of 3.5 million tons of exposed tailings lining the banks of the Cheyenne River and Cottonwood Creek, one of the river's tributaries, in the downtown area of nearby Edgemont.[48] While it is known that wind and erosion are carrying significant quantities of this radioactive contaminant into these sources of potable water, it is considered "cost prohibitive" to clear up the wastes.[49] To the contrary, during the period 1987-89, the government purportedly "fixed" the tailings problem at Edgemont by digging up the wastes piled all through the center of Edgemont and redumping them in an open area a few miles outside the village limits. This new "disposal site" is protected by nothing more than signs adorning a chain-link fence, as accompanying maps reveal.

Meanwhile, the same governmental/corporate entities which proclaimed that the commencement of uranium mining at Edgemont, *circa* 1955, carried with it "no public health hazard" are now proclaiming the area so thoroughly contaminated by radiation that there is nothing for it but to use the site as a *national* nuclear waste dump.[50] The cancer death rate among longtime Edgemont residents is currently skyrocketing but government/corporate spokespersons have recently proclaimed that the situation of the dump site in the southern Black Hills area presents "no health danger" to surrounding communities.[51] South Dakota governor William Janklow, who campaigned on a platform plank of not allowing dump sites within the state, has apparently reversed his view, now advocating location of the dump in Edgemont as a boon to the momentarily depressed uranium industry.

What is not stated publicly by either federal or corporate officials is that such a site, and Black Hills uranium production in general, all but inevitably causes radioactive leaching into the Madison Formation, the primary ground water source of the region (and the same water which it is proposed will be transported to the American Southeast via coal slurries). The U.S. Department of the Interior itself quietly summed up this problem in a 1979 report cited in *Akwesasne Notes* and concerning uranium tailing ponds:

> Contamination is well beyond the safe limit for animals. Escape by infiltration into the water table or by breakout to stream drainages could cause contamination by dangerous levels of radioactivity. Stock or humans using water from wells down gradient from tailing ponds would be exposed. Plants and animals encountering contaminated flows or contaminated sediments deposited in drainage channels would be exposed. Increasing the danger is the nondegradable and accumulative nature of this type of contamination.[52]

The same, of course, would pertain, in quantum fashion, to the types of material commonly disposed of in nuclear dumping operations. What the government report does not bring out is that, not only *could* this happen but, in all probability, it already has—as is testified to both by the earlier cited 1962 "spill" at Edgemont, and by reported ground water radiation levels at Pine Ridge. Correspondingly, a tentative study conducted by Women of All Red Nations on Pine Ridge indicates a marked increase in such radiation-associated phenomena as stillbirths, infant deformations such as cleft palate, and cancer deaths among reservation residents since 1970.[53] The relationship between this situation and the disaster at Edgemont seems clear enough, and underscores the cynicism of government/corporate contentions that a continued development of the uranium industry holds no ill effects for area communities. The Greater Sioux Nation, like the Navajo Nation, has become effectively another radioactive colony within the schema of the new colonialism.[54] Again, the data presented are but a narrow sample of the prevailing situation within the aggregate Lakota treaty territory. A fairer portrait is offered by Map II (see next page).

A more candid (and accurate) appraisal of the situation at Navajo and the Sioux Nation, in view both of current circumstances and of developmental projections, came from the Nixon administration in 1972. At that time, in conjunction with studies of U.S. energy development needs and planning undertaken by the Trilateral Commission, the federal government termed and sought to designate both the Four Corners region and the impacted region of the Dakotas, Wyoming, and Montana as "National Sacrifice Areas." That is, areas

Map II

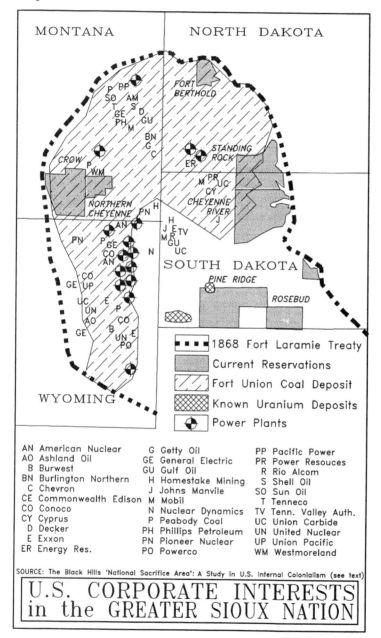

MONTANA   NORTH DAKOTA

P PP
S0 AM   FORT
T   S D   BERTHOLD
GE   GU
PH M

BN
G
CROW P   C   STANDING
      WM   ER   ROCK
NORTHERN   M PR UC
CHEYENNE PN H   CY
              CHEYENNE
PN   AN H   RIVER J
      P GE J E TV
        CO AN M GU
           R UC
GE UP   N   SOUTH DAKOTA
UC E   PINE RIDGE
  UN P   CO   ROSEBUD
AO
GE   B UN E
      PO

WYOMING

● ● ● ● ● 1868 Fort Laramie Treaty
▨ Current Reservations
▧ Fort Union Coal Deposit
▩ Known Uranium Deposits
◕ Power Plants

AN American Nuclear   G Getty Oil   PP Pacific Power
AO Ashland Oil   GE General Electric   PR Power Resouces
 B Burwest   GU Gulf Oil   R Rio Alcom
BN Burlington Northern   H Homestake Mining   S Shell Oil
 C Chevron   J Johns Manvile   SO Sun Oil
CE Commonwealth Edison   M Mobil   T Tenneco
CO Conoco   N Nuclear Dynamics   TV Tenn. Valley Auth.
CY Cyprus   P Peabody Coal   UC Union Carbide
 D Decker   PH Phillips Petroleum   UN United Nuclear
 E Exxon   PN Pioneer Nuclear   UP Union Pacific
ER Energy Res.   PO Powerco   WM Westmoreland

SOURCE: The Black Hills 'National Sacrifice Area': A Study in U.S. Internal Colonialism (see text)

U.S. CORPORATE INTERESTS
in the GREATER SIOUX NATION

rendered literally uninhabitable through the deliberate elimination of the total water supplies for industrial purposes (the aquifers are estimated to take from 5,000 to 50,000 years to effectively replenish themselves) and proliferation of nuclear contamination (much of which carries a lethal half-life of from a quarter to a half-million years). In other words, the destruction anticipated is effectively permanent.[55]

Needless to say, consummation of such plans would immediately eradicate Navajo and the so-called "Sioux Complex" as reservations. The largest block of landholdings remaining to American Indians within the United States would thus be lost utterly and irrevocably. The same situation would of course pertain to smaller reservations such as Hopi and most other Pueblos, Northern Cheyenne, Crow, and possibly Wind River, which lie within the "sacrifice areas." The great likelihood is that the peoples involved, to the extent that they are not physically expended within the immediately projected extraction processes, would cease to function as peoples, once severed from their land base. Like the Klamath people who were "terminated" in the 1950s and never recovered their Oregon homeland, these newly landless nations would in all probability disintegrate rapidly, dissolving into the mists of history. By conventional English definition, such a prospect and such a process can only be termed genocide.[56]

Nor is the situation in Canada appreciably different, in spirit if not in quantity and intensity. The James Bay power project undertaken through conjoint governmental and corporate efforts, for example, threatens to utterly demolish the habitat, lifeways, and self-sufficiency of the Cree people in that area.[57] Comparable sorts of activity in virtually every province of Canada harbor the same results for various indigenous peoples.[58] The native peoples of the entire northern half of the Americas stand in imminent danger of being swallowed up and eliminated entirely by the broader societies which have engulfed their land.

For American Indians to opt toward the very processes sketched as being at work within this section, to embrace transient extractive "industrialism" as a "solution" to the sorts of problems they now confront, problems brought into being and fostered by the representative institutions of industrial control and consolidation itself, seems at best to be a self-defeating strategy. More likely, it promises participation in a route to self-liquidation or, to borrow a phrase from certain analysts of the recent holocaust in Kampuchea and to place it within a rather more accurate framework, to engage in "auto-genocide."[59] Whatever the short-run benefits in terms of diminishing the, by now, all but perpetual cycle of American Indian disease, malnutrition, and despair generated by neocolonialism, the looming longer-term costs vastly outweigh them. In the next section, however, we shall examine whether even the short-term benefits perceived by such agencies of American Indian "progress" as CERT and many tribal councils as roads to prosperity and self-determination are more real or illusory in their immediate potentials.

Radioactive Colonialism

When years before they had first come to the people living on the Ceboleta land grant they had not said what kind of mineral it was. They said they were driving U.S. Government cars, and they paid the land grant association five thousand dollars not to ask questions about the test holes they were drilling...Early in the Spring of 1943, the mine began to flood with water from the subterranean springs. They hauled in big pumps and compressors from Albuquerque...But later in the summer the mine flooded again, and this time no pumps or compressors were sent. They had enough of what they needed, and the mine was closed, but the barbed wire fence and guards remained until August 1945. By then they had other sources of uranium, and it was not top secret anymore...He had been so close to it, caught up in it for so long that its simplicity struck him deep inside his chest; Trinity site, where they had exploded the first atomic bomb, was only three hundred miles to the southeast, at White Sands. And the top-secret laboratories where the bomb had been created were deep in the Jemez mountains on land the Government took from the Cochiti Pueblo: Los Alamos, only a hundred miles Northeast of him now, still surrounded by high electric fences...There was no end to it; it knew no boundaries; and he arrived at the point of convergence where the fate of all living things, and even the earth had been laid. From the jungles of his dreaming he recognized why the Japanese voices merged with the Laguna voices...converging in the middle of witchery's final ceremonial sand painting. From that time on, human beings were one clan again, united by the fate the destroyers had planned for all of them, for all living things; united by a circle of death that devoured people in cities twelve thousand miles away, victims who had never known these mesas, never seen the delicate colors of the rocks that had boiled up their slaughter.

—Leslie Marmon Silko, *Ceremony*

Economic and labor analysts have argued on numerous occasions that improved labor relations and altered mineral development policies could, or would, tip the cost/benefit balance to the favorable side of the scale for American Indians. The careful examination of Lorraine Turner Ruffing in relation to such contentions ("A Mineral Development Policy for the Navajo Nation"), and information available through the Oil, Chemical, and Atomic Workers Union (Denver, Colorado) combine with any fundamental understanding of the general environment in uranium-producing regions to dispute notions that adjusting or "tuning" the production scenario will do much of anything to offset negative factors over either the long or short terms.

The circumstances correlated to the Navajo experience at Shiprock, Churchrock, Tuba City, and elsewhere and, in a slightly different sense, the experiences of the Lakota to the north are not anomalies. There is, and can be, no "safe" uranium mining, processing, or waste disposal, either now or in the foreseeable future. Such facts can be denied, they can be argued upon debater's points or the exclusivity of narrow ranges of technical "expertise," but they cannot be made to go away in the real world where people and environments become contaminated, sicken, and die.

We have already seen how the energy corporations and the government use local Indian workforces at the lowest possible wage, paying little if any heed to community safety, avoiding both severance taxes to cover the community costs incurred by their presence and land reclamation costs to cover even the most lethal of their damages upon departure, and paying the absolute minimum rate in royalties for the milled ore they ship. Equally, we have seen that the nature of the destruction they anticipate creating, and do create, as an integral aspect of their "productive process" is such that there can be *no* further tribal development, post mining. It is unlikely that much beyond the level of amoeba will be able to survive in a National Sacrifice Area, once sacrificed.

In other words, long-term consequences foreclose upon short-term advantages where the uranium production process is concerned. Of course, the "right" Indian negotiator might be able to bargain the royalty rates to a higher, more "acceptable" level; say two, or five, or ten times the going rate in Indian country. But, to what avail? This short-run "gain" is a mirage. No matter what magnitude of cash flow is generated from such resource sales by tribal managerial elites, it can only be "invested" in a homeland which is soon to be uninhabitable, a people soon to be extinguished. Cash can never be sufficient to replace either the homeland or the people. Adjustments to the rate of exchange are thus ultimately irrelevant to the issue at hand, whether over the next two decades, or the next twenty.

The only possibility of even short-term benefits, then, lies in the improbable possibility that a preponderance of tribal members, people who, despite personal confusions of identity and a grinding poverty lasting for generations, have clung steadfastly to overall notions of Indianness and maintained a firm embrace of their homelands, are somehow now prepared to abandon these things for the external reality of the dominant culture. In order for even this dubious prospect to be more than mere illusion, however, the uranium development option (and other energy development options as well) must both be survivable *to participants* (which includes, from an Indian perspective, the ability to bear healthy children, the "unborn generations" leading to familial/tribal survival), and offer them not only a cash reserve, but also the skills and employment situation through which to successfully enter the "mainstream."

The question thus becomes whether in fact there are means available through which such short-run considerations might be met, assuming that Indians desired them. In this connection, it would seem that unionization might provide a key to success. The Oil, Chemical, and Atomic Workers Union (OCAW) is the largest and most influential workers' force within the uranium industry. Although not all miners are unionized within the Grants Uranium Belt of the Southwest, the OCAW has been successful in pressuring the overall uranium industry to a degree. To begin with, the union has essentially achieved standardization of conditions for all miners within the area—union or non-union—brown, red, black, or white.

As a result, conditions such as those prevailing in the Shiprock mine during the 1950s are now uncommon, even exceptional. Yet the industry, by OCAW estimation, remains one of the most dangerous in every phase.[60] Primary union concerns, and actions, have been devoted to increasing worker safety conditions within the mines. In one year, 1967, 525 men were seriously injured in the mines of New Mexico alone; seven of them died. But these are problems which prevail across the mining industry as a whole. The more insidious hazards associated with uranium mining—and the ones which claim the heaviest toll—are those involving chemical and radiation contamination.

In this regard, the OCAW has been active in opposing the "bonus system," the practice by which corporations reward miners financially for operating in "hot spots" and/or working higher grade ore than is normally handled. In essence, the union argues that such sustained exposure as is expected of miners performing under the bonus system virtually guarantees contamination (and an early death), and that the corporations are intentionally down-playing the risks involved. The OCAW has also held that "worker rotation systems" for working hot spots and super-rich ore—often without the benefits of extra pay—fail to solve the contamination problem, serving instead to spread potentially lethal concentrations of radiation—on the order of 6.5 times maximum "safe" dosages—throughout the entire workforce.[61]

In some respects, then, OCAW might be viewed as affording a means by which initial steps have been taken to provide tangible worker safety. In addition, the union has proven quite successful in attaining real wage increases for miners across the board, whether or not they belong to OCAW. But, in fairness, it must be said that the union has ultimately succeeded in eliminating the most extreme forms of abuse routinely conducted by management (such as operating deep shafts without ventilation), while merely exposing rather than correcting the more generic varieties. In this sense, while it is certainly a more humane and progressive entity than the corporations it confronts, it represents no *solution* to the problems with which it deals. Additionally, many of the strategies through which the union has proposed to force wage increases and improved safety standards are much better suited to the usual, highly mobile mine labor force than to "reservation bound" Indian miners.

Similarly, a number of improvements attained by the OCAW in behalf of its miner constituency have, perversely, worked to the detriment of the Indian miners' home communities. Consider the matter of mine ventilation: the uniform installation of proper ventilating blowers within mine shafts is unquestionably a major gain for miners. For transient miners, this is essentially the end of the story: a gain. But, for those whose intention it is to live out their lives within the mining community, and to have their children and their children's children live out *their* lives in the community as well, the question of what becomes of radioactive dust blown from the mine shafts assumes a critical importance.

The answer, of course, is, into the air of the community, from which it settles *upon* the community. Hence, the gain to the Indian miner in terms of increased workplace safety for him/herself is incurred at the direct expense of his/her permanent community. The Gulf-operated Mt. Taylor mine located in San Mateo, New Mexico, is a significant site of such problems. It is but one of many. The town of Questa, New Mexico, has its elementary school built upon a dry tailing pond, at the foot of a tailing pile, situated near shaft ventilators. The OCAW maintains, perhaps rightly, that such matters are beyond its purview. But this leaves the concept of unionization voided in a very important respect for Indian miners and their communities.

Short-run considerations of the ultimate survivability of uranium production would thus seem heavily skewed to the negative, both for participating miners and for participating communities. In view of this fact, concerns with short-term income (wage) benefits seem rather beside the point. There would obviously seem little advantage to be gained from achieving a short-term economic "security" from an occupation which was directly and rapidly killing not only you, but your family and future offspring as well. Given the remote possibility that things are somehow not as they seem, either in the overall or in some particular sense or locale, the short-term economic implications—with an emphasis on individuals—will also be examined.

All uranium-producing American Indian nations, and the individuals who comprise them, are in the position typified by the Navajo's Churchrock community: they are economic hostages of the new colonialism. For example, approximately 7,000 acres of the 418,000-acre Laguna Pueblo landholding is leased to the Anaconda

Corporation. The tribal posture in entering into the leasing agreement was to secure royalty revenues for the group, and jobs/income for individuals within the group. In effect, the land has passed under Anaconda's eminent domain. Anaconda operated uranium stripping operations at Laguna from 1952 until 1981, when, as in the case of Kerr-McGee's Shiprock mine, profitably extractible ore played out. During the operating years, the Laguna Tribal Council negotiated an agreement with the corporation whereby tribal applicants would receive priority hiring to work in the reservation mine. The practice was quite successful, with some 93 percent of the Anaconda labor force ultimately accruing from the pueblo. As the mining operation expanded over the years, so did the workforce, from 350 in 1952 to a peak of 650 in 1979.[62]

Wages to miners, relative to average per capita incomes on reservations, are quite high, and the high concentration of miners within the tiny Laguna population established it as one of the "richer" all-round tribal groups in the country by the early to-mid-1960s.[63] Throughout the 1970s, unemployment within the tribal membership averaged approximately 25 percent, quite high by non-Indian standards, but less than half the prevailing average reservation rate nationally. Further, royalty payments and other mechanisms allowed the Lagunas to symbolically break certain important aspects of the typical reorganization-fostered dependency upon the federal government. By 1979, former Laguna governor Floyd Correa was able to state in an interview that, of the tribal unemployed, only twelve were collecting unemployment benefits (as compared to the estimated 20 percent of the total labor force collecting benefits on most reservations at any given moment). Upon superficial examination, the Lagunas seemed well on the road to recovering the self-sufficiency which had long since passed from the grasp of most North American indigenous nations.

The bubble burst when Anaconda abruptly pulled up stakes and left the husk of their mining operation: a gaping crater and, of course, piles of virulently radioactive slag. Over the years, Laguna's negotiating position had steadily deteriorated as the absolute centrality of the Anaconda operation became apparent to the people—and to the corporation. Consequently very little provision was built into lease renewals which would have accommodated clean-up and land reclamation upon conclusion of mining activities. It will likely cost the pueblo more to repair environmental havoc wrought by the corporation than it earned during the life of the mining contract.[64] And, unlike Anaconda, the Laguna people as a whole cannot simply move away, leaving the mess behind; nor can individual workers. The abrupt departure of Anaconda left the majority of the reservation's income-earners suddenly jobless. Here, a cruel lesson was to be learned. The skills imparted through training and employment in uranium mining are not readily translatable to other forms of employment, nor are they particularly transferable without dissolution of the tribal group itself (i.e., miners and their families moving away from the pueblo in order to secure employment elsewhere). Meanwhile, the steady 30-year gravitation of the Laguna population toward mining as a livelihood caused a correspondingly steady atrophy of the skills and occupations enabling the pueblo to remain essentially self-sufficient for centuries.

Whether or not the former Anaconda employees can "adjust" to their new circumstances and make a sort of reverse transition to more traditional occupations and/or secure adequate alternative employment proximate to the reservation may be in some respects a moot point. While not as pronounced as in the deep shaft mining areas of the Navajo Nation, the pattern of increasing early deaths from respiratory cancer and similar ailments—as well as congenital birth defects—has been becoming steadily more apparent on the reservation.[65] Most of the afflicted no longer retain the health insurance coverage, once a part of the corporate employment package, through which to offset the costs of their illnesses (and those suffered by relatives within the extended family structures by which the pueblo is organized). Thus, the ghost of Anaconda is eating the personal as well as tribal savings accruing from the mining experience.

It seems safe enough to observe that the short-term benefits perceived at Laguna were more illusory than real. Although a temporary sense of economic security was imparted by the presence of a regular payroll, and the "stability" of a "big time" employer, there was never time to consolidate the apparent gains. Costs swiftly overtook gains, although the tribal government was not necessarily immediately privy to the change of circumstances. In the final analysis, the people may well end up much more destitute, and in an infinitely worse environmental position, than was ever the case in the past. As if to underscore the point, water has become a major problem at Laguna, one which may eventually outweigh all the others brought about by its relatively brief relationship with Anaconda. The Rio Paguate River, which once provided the basis for irrigation and a potentially thriving local agriculture, now runs through the unreclaimed ruins of corporate flight. As early as 1973, the federal Environmental Protection Agency (EPA) discovered that the strip-mining operation was contaminating the Laguna water supply.[66]

With agricultural and cattle-raising production withering under the glare of higher paying and more "glamorous" work in the mine, the pueblo converted to ground water in meeting all, rather than a portion, of its potable needs. In 1975, however, the EPA returned to find widespread ground water contamination throughout the Grants Mineral Belt, including that under Laguna.[67] In 1978, the EPA was back again, this time to reassure tribal members that *all* of their available water sources were dangerously contaminated by radioactivity, and that the tribal council building, community center, and newly constructed Jackpile Housing—paid for in substantial proportion by royalty monies—were all radioactive as well.[68] Additionally, Anaconda had used low-grade *uranium ore* to "improve"the road system leading to the mine and village.[69]

Hence, even were the Lagunas able to reclaim the land directly associated with what was once the world's largest open pit uranium mine (preceding Namibia's Rossing Mine for this dubious distinction), no small feat in itself, and even if they were somehow able to avert the seemingly impending carcinogenic and genetic crises, restore an adequate measure of employment and tribal income, and clear up at least the direct sources of contamination to the Rio Paguate, they would *still* be faced with the insurmountable problem of contaminated ground water (which can accrue from quite far-flung locations). And, if they have had enough of such "progress" and wish to attempt a return to the agriculture and animal husbandry which stood them in such good stead for generations? Then they will *still* have to contend with the factor of disrupted ore bodies which persist in leaching out into otherwise reclaimed soil.

When such leaching occurs, radioactive contaminants are drawn into the roots of plants. Animals, whether human or otherwise, consuming contaminated plants likewise become contaminated. This too may well be an insurmountable problem. It seems likely that the damage is done and irreparable, that the way of life the Lagunas have known, and with which they identify and represent themselves as a people, is gone forever. And in exchange? Nothing. At least, nothing of value, unless one wishes to place a value on radioactive community centers and road repairs; or unless one wishes to consider as valuable the bitter legacy and lessons learned as an example from which to base future plans and future actions.

Laguna is not unique in the nature of its experience. The examples drawn earlier from the Navajo Nation and the Lakota territory should be sufficient to demonstrate that. Dozens, scores, even hundreds of additional examples might be cited from Hopi, from Zuni, Acoma, Isleta, Crow, Northern Cheyenne, and elsewhere in the United States, and from the Cree, Métis, Athabasca, and other territories of Canada, through which to illustrate the point. One other example within the United States might be drawn upon to nail things down. This concerns the Department of Energy's nuclear facility at Hanford, on the boundary of the Yakima Nation in central Washington state. Designed on the same pattern as the ill-fated Soviet plant at Chernobyl, Hanford was used for 40 years to produce weapons-grade fissionable material. Finally closed down in 1987, when officials became concerned that a Chernobyl-style disaster might occur there, Hanford was still described by the federal government (in response to growing local concerns about health hazards inherent to the plant) as having functioned in a "safe and essentially accident-free fashion" throughout its operational existence. Finally, in July of 1990, government spokespersons admitted that the weapons facility had been since the early 1950s secretly dumping radioactive wastes into the environment at a level at least 2,000 times greater than those officially deemed "safe."[70]

A year later, in April 1991, this was spelled out as meaning that 444 billion gallons of water laced with plutonium, strontium, tritium, ruthenium, cesium, and assorted "rare earth elements" had been simply poured into a hole in the ground over the years. It was admitted that these materials had long since seeped into local ground water sources, and estimated that the contamination will reach the Columbia River by the end of the decade (the local populace needn't worry about health hazards, however; "progressive" legislators have managed to prohibit cigarette smoking in all the buildings located above the dump site as a means of sparing health-conscious citizens the hazards of breathing such "air pollution").[71] In sum, the residents of Yakima and the surrounding area have been exposed to greater concentrations of radiation—*as a matter of course*—than were those Soviet citizens living in or near Chernobyl during the near meltdown of the reactor there. Further, they, unlike their counterparts in the USSR, had been unknowingly exposed to the contamination for decades.

It should by now be plain that there is neither short- nor long-term advantage to be gained by indigenous nations in entering into energy resource extraction agreements. Advantage accrues only to the corporate and governmental representatives of a colonizing and dominant industrial culture. Occasionally it accrues momentarily, and in limited fashion, to the "Vichy" tribal governments they have reorganized into doing their bidding. For the people, there is only expendability, destruction, and grief under this new colonization. Ironically, the situation was spelled out in the clearest possible terms by Los Alamos Scientific Laboratory, the site of the birth of "controlled" nuclear fission, in its February 1978 *Mini-Report*:

> Perhaps the solution to the radon emission problem is to zone the land into uranium mining and milling districts so as to forbid human habitation.

Viewed in this light, the choices for uranium-rich, land-locked reservation populations are clearly defined. For some, there is cause for immediate retreat from engagement in the uranium extraction process. For others, it is a matter of avoiding a problem not yet begun. In either case, such a choice will necessitate an active resistance to the demands and impositions of the new colonizers.

It seems certain that those who would claim "their" uranium to fuel the engines of empire, both at home and abroad, will be unlikely to accept a polite (if firm) "no" in response to their desires. Strategies must be found through which this "no" may be enforced. Perhaps, in the end, it will be as Leslie Silko put it, that "human beings will be one clan again" united finally by "the circle of death" which ultimately confronts us all, united in putting an end to such insanity. Until that time, however, American Indians, those who have been selected by the dynamics of radioactive colonization to be the first 20th-century national sacrifice peoples, must stand alone, or with their immediate allies, for a common survival. It is a gamble, no doubt, but a gamble which is clearly warranted. The alternative is virtual species suicide. There are bright spots within what has otherwise been painted as a bleak portrait of contemporary Indian Country. It is to these, the representations of the gamble, and what must be hoped are the rudiments of an emerging strategy of resistance, to which we turn in our next and final section.

Conclusion

It is genocide to mine the uranium in our land, no more, no less.

— Russell Means, 1980

Non-Indian America, Euroamerica in particular, has a long and sorry history of blaming the victims of its criminal abuse for the existence of that abuse. Perfectly sincere young professors at Midwestern universities are wont to stand and observe in all seriousness that "the Indians fought each other before the white man came," in a context implying that there is really nothing differentiating traditions of counting coup on the one hand, and wars of annihilation on the other. We are, after all, the same. Others smugly point out that Indians killed the buffalo, often in large numbers, before the advent of professional buffalo hunters. Implication? The extermination of an entire species, in the end as a military tactic, is no different in kind than subsistence hunting. The Indian, it is presumed, will be stifled from complaint by the "fact" of having set an example of butchery for his wanton western brothers.[72]

Again, serious scholars pronounce that dispossession of the Lakota—for example—from their land is little basis for complaint, "given that the Sioux ran the Crows off *their* land, too." Never mind that the Lakota action resulted from the fact that Anishinabes, well-armed with muskets gleaned from the fur trade, had—when being shoved west by encroaching whites—in turn pushed the Lakota, who lacked comparable weaponry, westward into Crow country.[73] Never mind, too, that the Crows, who fought with the U.S. Army rather than against it, and whom no one claims did much dispossessing of anyone, were as readily stripped of their land as were the Lakota. The fate of the Lakota was sealed—through some process of cosmic justice—in the "nature of their own traditions" according to the conventions of liberal Euroamerican academe.[74] Today, the American Indian suffers from the infliction of radioactive colonization. To be sure, it may be rightly contended that Indians have participated, often willingly, in that process. The question which occurs as a result of this obviousness is whether, once again, a form of logical convolution will be applied thereby through which to blame the Indian for his/her fate. And, if such distortive blame is applied, will it be used, as it usually has been, to fabricate a justification for and sanction of the status quo?

In political terms, such an attitude, whether overtly or subtly expressed, has generally led to the assumption that—defects of our own cultures somehow having brought us to our contemporary pass—Indians inherently require, and deserve, non-Indian ideology and leadership. To put it another way, Indians have proven "weak" in a Darwinian sense, have through such weakness been overrun and left prostrate by the "stronger" cultures of Europe, and must now be subsumed as a small but integral component of European conceptions of revolution currently employed against the equally Eurospecific notions of imperialism which generate Indians' (and everyone else's) oppression. For all its "liberatory" veneer, such an outlook is fundamentally similar to that of the current oppressor; it preserves, essentially intact, the prevailing and entirely objectionable status quo of American Indian subordination to an external and dominant cultural reality, both at the conceptual and at the physical levels.[75]

The pattern of victim-blaming mentality underpinning the ideology of most imported "cultures of resistance" within this hemisphere has also led to certain highly distortive strategic assumptions on the part of those purporting to combat North American imperialism from within.[76] Concern with economies of scale has led non-Indian dissidents to ignore or dismiss the Indians of North America as a critical element (real or potential) of anti-imperialist struggle, primarily because of their small numbers. Discounting the fact of Indian existence *necessarily* leads to the missing of their colonial status and the contemporary existence of territorially defined colonies *within* the physical confines of the North American imperial powers.[77] This, to be sure, is no small oversight.

If Indian reality is effectively voided at the intellectual level of avowed anti-imperialists, the result is the view which seems most commonly held among non-Indians: that of the United States and Canada as possessing an essentially seamless (except for class conflicts) internal integrity and hegemony through which their imperialism is uniformly exported to other, usually Third World, nations. Preoccupation with the effects of colonialism, and with indigenous efforts to offset it, thus centers on North America's satellites, seldom upon the continent itself. Such an erroneous view generates a cumbersome method of countering imperial policy, slashing as it does always at the tentacles, never at the heart.[78]

This essay has attempted to show why colonies exist within the countries of North America. Further, it has sought to explain the absolutely crucial nature of the existence of these colonies, by virtue of resource distribution and production, to the maintenance and expansion of North American imperialism. Finally, it has tried to provide a critical insight into the internal colonial methods employed, and the impact of those methods upon the populations most immediately and directly affected by them: the resident populations of the colonies themselves, American Indians. It is to be hoped that within such an articulation lie the seeds of an analysis pointing to an anti-imperialist mode of action which transcends the victim-blaming and misorientation marking past practice.

Within the structural properties and physical characteristics of North American internal colonialism lie the levers with which a properly focused anti-imperialist effort can begin to pry apart the skeletal components of the imperial nations themselves. The application of the broadest possible support to the internationally acceptable (among Third World nations, for example) principle of the sanctity and sovereignty of Indian treaty territories would carry a considerable challenge of and jeopardy to the physical integrity of both the United States and Canada. Perhaps even more crucial is that the specific areas most in question in this regard are such that both nations would find themselves denied ease of access to a major proportion of their strategic reserves of vital raw materials. Similarly, *any* exertion of real tribal sovereignty over the treaty territories would serve to curtail an array of both nations' internal production capabilities, both in terms of denying conveniently "remote" locations, and in denying the water upon which many—if not most—industrial processes depend.

Clearly, such a turn of events would prove crippling to imperialism in ways which confronting its presence within the satellite colonies abroad never has, and in all probability never can. Not that facing the facts of the matter provides a panacea, a magic act through which such conditions can be actualized at a stroke. The treaties and other factors at issue have existed all along, and are well known to both corporate and governmental managers. For what must be obvious reasons, such managers have systematically declined to honor the treaties, to respect American Indian ownership of much of the contemporary basis of North American power. Implementation of treaty terms and provisions, with all that this implies, will necessarily entail a considerable and sustained struggle on the broadest possible popular basis.

The question thus emerges as to who is to lead such a struggle, to provide it form and direction in its day-to-day development. Here, an utter inversion of the principle of blaming the victim and its accompanying orthodoxy of Euro-derived movements is indicated. Currently, representative leaders and movements know little of treaties, their implications and practical potentials in the global arena. Nor is the extent of American Indian territoriality, water rights, resource holdings, and the like—both current and potential (by virtue of treaty rights)—particularly well understood outside the circles of Indian activism. Nor has the background and experience of most non-Indian anti-imperialists especially suited them for direct interaction with and grassroots organization of the internal colonial populations. All of this combines to present a rather poor case for American Indians being led by non-Indians in any struggle to dismantle the North American internal colonial structure. To the contrary, it points very plainly to the prospect that a real and highly visible Indian leadership component of any North American anti-imperialist movement must be accepted as a prerequisite to success.

Native people have, after all, been forced to live in the very front lines of the colonial process, through no choice of their own, for generations. They, among all the people of America, have been imbued with a comprehensive understanding of that process at the most practical level. Inadvertently, this knowledge, and their geographical disposition, has placed them in a position at the very cutting edge of any emergent contestation of North American political economy, regardless of the numerical status of their population and other factors. Hence, the recent actualization of certain American Indian (or Indian led) activist formations and the undertaking of certain actions by these formations should be viewed with hope, as bright spots in what is otherwise a deadening panorama of horror.

The first, and perhaps most obvious, of these has been the founding and continuation of the American Indian Movement (AIM) and, for a time, its subordinate diplomatic component, the International Indian Treaty Council. Another AIM spinoff, and one which should be carefully studied by non-Indian and Indian activists alike, was the Black Hills Alliance. Within this coalition of various regional organizations, native people held a very strong but hardly exclusive leadership position. The formal board of directors was composed not only of AIM members, but also of miners, clergy, area ranchers, and at least one former John Birch Society member (who professes to have shot at AIM people only a few years before). Using treaty rights and the environment as *first* points of contention, this amalgamation was able to successfully articulate a practical program of anti-imperialism within its area which stressed the commonality of issues between

Indians and non-Indians.[79] By adopting such a posture, the Alliance was able to assume a position in the very forefront of local resistance to wholesale mining, uranium production, water diversion, land expropriation (from ranchers and Indians alike), and so forth. It was also able to mount the 1979 and 1980 Black Hills International Survival Gatherings, which formulated a strategy wherein Indian treaty rights were viewed as the key to countering governmental/corporate processes detrimental to the population as a whole, *and* drew unprecedented numbers of non-area activists to the Black Hills region.[80] Having successfully opposed nuclear dumping at Edgemont and the ETSI initiative, the Alliance essentially dissolved, its membership going on to serve as cadre in other local, regional, or national organizations.

While a number of other events and circumstances across the face of Indian Country could be cited to underscore the point being made, the preceding examples should be sufficient to render credible the observation that the rudiments of a serious, seasoned, and effective internal anti-imperialist movement currently exist within AIM and conceptually affiliated organizations. That such a movement must expand tremendously in scale before it can hope to attain its ultimate goals is undeniable. That such expansion can occur within North America only through the attraction of non-Indian allies is equally unquestionable. Here, both the model offered by the Black Hills Alliance, and the earlier mentioned inversion of the usual non-Indian agendas and priorities become crucial.

The struggle currently shouldered by AIM and related native organizations is not merely "for Indians." It is for everyone. To resolve the issue of the colonization of the American Indian would be, at least in part, to resolve matters threatening to the whole of humanity. In altering the relations of internal colonialism in North America, "the AIM idea" would vastly reduce the capability of the major nations there to extend their imperial web into Central and South America, as well as Africa, Asia, and the Pacific Basin. In denying access to the sources of uranium to the industrial powers, American Indians could take a quantum leap toward solving the problem of nuclear proliferation. In denying access to certain other resources, they could do much to force conversion to renewable, nonpolluting alternative energy sources such as solar and wind power. The list could be extended at length.

Ultimately, the Lagunas, the Shiprocks, Churchrocks, Tuba Cities, Edgemonts, and Pine Ridges which litter the American landscape are not primarily a moral concern for non-Indian movements (although they should be that, as well). Rather, they are pragmatic examples, precursors of situations and conditions which, within the not-so-distant future, will engulf other population sectors; which, from place to place, have already begun to actively encroach in a more limited fashion. Circumstance has made the American Indian the first to bear the full brunt of the new colonialism in North America. The only appropriate response is to see to it that they are also the last. The new colonialism knows no limits. Expendable populations will be expended. National sacrifice areas will be sacrificed. New populations and new areas will then be targeted, expended, and sacrificed. There is no sanctuary. The new colonialism is radioactive; what it does can never be undone. Left to its own dynamics, to run its course, it will spread across the planet like the literal cancer it is. It can never be someone else's problem; regardless of its immediate location at the moment, it has become the problem and peril of everyone alive, and who will be alive. The place to end it is where it has now taken root and disclosed its inner nature. The time to end it is now.

Notes

1. See Garrity, Michael, "The U.S. Colonial Empire is as Close as the Nearest Reservation," in *Trilateralism: The Trilateral Commission and Elite Planning for World Management*, ed. Holly Sklar (Boston, MA: South End Press, 1980), pp. 238-68.

2. For an overview on the similarities of the situations prevailing in the U.S. and Canada, see Getty, Ian L., and Donald B. Smith, *One Century Later: Western Canadian Reserve Indians Since Treaty 7* (Vancouver: University of British Columbia Press, 1978). A more specific historical case study is provided in Fisher, Robin, *Contact and Conflict: Indian-European Relations in British Columbia, 1774-1890* (Vancouver: University of British Columbia Press, 1977).

3. See Deloria, Vine, Jr., and Clifford E. Lytle, *American Indians, American Justice* (Austin: University of Texas Press, 1984).

4. See LaDuke, Winona, "Indian Land Claims and Treaty Areas of North America: Succeeding into Native North America," *CoEvolution Quarterly*, no. 32 (winter, 1981): pp. 64-65.

5. Cruz, Roberto, "U.S. Forced Cessions of Papago Land and Resources During the 20th Century," unpublished paper prepared at the Harvard School of Economics, Cambridge, MA (1978), pp. 17-18.

6. See the map of Lakota (forced) cessions of 1868 treaty land contained in Dunbar Ortiz, Roxanne, ed., *The Great Sioux Nation: Sitting in Judgement on America* (New York/San Francisco: International Indian Treaty Council/Moon Books, 1977), p. 94.

7. See Clinton, Robert N., Nell Jessup Newton, and Monroe E. Price, *American Indian Law: Cases and Materials* (Charlottesville, VA: Michie Co., Law Publishers, 1991). Also see Deloria and Lytle, *op. cit.*

8. Internal Council of Energy Resource Tribes memorandum, Smith to McDonald, June 12, 1977.

9. See *One Century Later, op. cit.*

10. See the map of aggregate native land cessions accompanying Ward Churchill's essay on land struggles in this volume.

11. See U.S. Commission on Civil Rights, *The Navajo Nation: An American Colony* (Washington, D.C.: U.S. Government Printing Office, 1976).

12. The way in which the first "modern tribal council," that of the Navajo Nation, was brought into being is instructive. During the 1920s, several emerging U.S. energy corporations (primarily Standard Oil) desired to obtain exploratory leases to seek coal, oil, and natural gas within Navajo territory. These corporate overtures were flatly rejected by the then prevailing traditional Navajo leadership. In 1980, the U.S. Bureau of Indian Affairs—at the behest of corporate lobbyists—created a new "Navajo Grand Council" to represent the nation. This new entity, proclaimed by the Bureau as being the sole "legitimate" instrument of Navajo governance, contained not one of the traditional leaders, accruing their sanction and authority from the Navajo people. Rather, it was composed of a handpicked group of "progressives" trained in white boarding schools and universities. Predictably, the new council shortly delivered the desired leasing agreements to the concerned corporations. This experiment in creating puppet governments to administer tribal politico-economic affairs, harkening as it does back to Washington's long-standing policy of unilaterally designating "chiefs" of various indigenous nations for purposes of treaty signing (e.g., justifying tribal land cessions), was deemed so successful that it was soon adopted by U.S. Indian Commissioner John Collier in his 1934 "reorganization" of American Indian affairs. See Kammer, Jerry, *The Second Long Walk: The Navajo-Hopi Land Dispute* (Albuquerque: University of New Mexico Press, 1978).

13. *The Navajo Nation, op. cit.*

14. *Ibid.*

15. See *TREATY* (True Revolution for Elders, Ancestors, Treaties, and Youth), a campaign document produced by the Dakota American Indian Movement, Porcupine, SD (1983).

16. See *A Statistical Portrait of the American Indian*, DHEW/U.S. Bureau of the Census (Washington, D.C.: U.S. Government Printing Office, 1976), p. 19; data not appreciably changed during intervening seven years, according to statement by U.S. Secretary of the Interior James Watt on May 19, 1982. Circumstances in Canada are brought out in *One Century Later, op. cit.*

17. Davis, Mark, and Robert Zannis, *The Genocide Machine in Canada: The Pacification of the North* (Toronto: Black Rose Books, 1973), p. 93.

18. See *Report of the Ad Hoc Committee Investigating Circumstances Surrounding Forced Relocation of Diné and Hopi People Within the Navajo/Hopi Joint Use Area, Arizona,* Big Mountain Legal Defense/Offense Committee, Flagstaff, AZ (1984). Also see *Report to the Kikmongwe,* American Indian Law Resource Center, Washington, D.C. (1979).

19. See *A Statistical Portrait of the American Indian, op. cit.* For purposes of this essay, "North" America is not considered to include Central American areas. However, the data suggests that direct comparison of the situation of U.S./Canadian/northern Mexican "national" Indian populations to those of Belize, Honduras, and Nicaragua (as examples), or to various South American Indian populations, would not demonstrate that those living in the "developed" north are particularly better off. To the contrary, literature concerning groups such as the Yanomami and the Jivaro of the Amazon Basin region suggest that indigenous populations tend to enjoy a relatively higher standard of living when allowed to enjoy their traditional "primitive" subsistence economies.

20. Durham, Jimmie, "Native Americans and Colonialism," *The Guardian* (March 28, 1979): p. 40.

21. It seems probable that the term "Fourth World" will be confusing to some readers. In essence, the concept derives from the conventional notion that geopolitical reality assumes the configuration of having an industrially developed capitalist order (the First World) counterposed to an industrially developed socialist order (the Second World). Hovering between these two poles is a mass of former colonies now pursuing a course of more or less "independent" industrial development (the Third World). Those who have attempted to place traditional tribal peoples—peoples who have never adopted or who have come to reject the industrial ethos —within this tidy three-part spectrum have been left frustrated. In terms of traditional indigenous populations, the definitions of contemporary convention yield little (if any) explanatory power. This has led to the evolution of the theory that there is a Fourth World or, perhaps more appropriately stated, a Host World of indigenous cultures and societies upon which the various variants of industrialism have been built. These continue to exist, essentially intact, despite the imposition of various industrialized structures upon them. According to the International Work Group for Indigenous Affairs, "The Fourth World is the name given to the indigenous peoples descended from a country's aboriginal population and who today are completely or partly deprived of the right to their territory and riches..." Conceptualization of means to preserve and revitalize the Fourth World/Host World has led lately to a stream of theory and activism loosely termed as "indigenism." Among the better print items available within this context are the final chapter of Weyler, Rex, *Blood of the Land: The FBI and Corporate War Against the American Indian Movement* (New York: Everest House Publishers, 1982), and Diabo, J. R., "The Emergence of Fourth World Politics in the International Arena," unpublished paper presented at the 1984 Western Social Science Association Conference in San Diego, CA. See also Berg, Peter, "Devolving Beyond Global Monoculture," *CoEvolution Quarterly,* no. 38 (winter 1981): pp. 24-30. For a dissenting view on pursuit of a Fourth World ideology, from within the indigenist

movement itself, see Dunbar Ortiz, Roxanne, "The Fourth World and Indigenism: Isolation and Alternatives," *Journal of Ethnic Studies*, vol. 12, no. 1 (spring 1984).

22. In addition to the Navajos employed as underground miners by Kerr-McGee during this period, somewhere between 300 and 500 more were involved in "independent" or Small Business Administration-backed operations going after shallow (50 ft. or less) deposits of rich uranium ore that was sold in small lots to an Atomic Energy Commission buying station located at the Kerr-McGee milling facility. They left behind between 100 and 200 open shafts. See Tso, Harold, and Laura Mangum Shields, "Navajo Mining Operations: Early Hazards and Recent Interventions," *New Mexico Journal of Science*, vol. 20, no. 1 (June 1980): p. 13.

23. See LaDuke, Winona, "The Council of Energy Resource Tribes: An Outsider's View In," in *Native Americans and Energy Development II*, ed. Joseph Joregson (Cambridge, MA: Anthropological Resource Center/Seventh Generation Fund, 1984).

24. Sorenson, J. B., "Radiation Issues: Government Decision Making and Uranium Expansion in Northern New Mexico," *San Juan Basin Regional Uranium Study Working Paper No. 14* (Albuquerque, NM: 1978), p. 39. Also see LaDuke, Winona, "The History of Uranium Mining," *Black Hills/Paha Sapa Report*, vol. 1, no. 1 (1979): p. 2, and McCleod, Christopher, "New Mexico's Nuclear Fiasco," *Minnesota Daily* (August 8, 1979): p. 5.

25. Best, Michael, and William Connally, "An Environmental Paradox," *The Progressive* (October 1976): p. 20. Also see Wagoner, J. K., "Uranium, The U.S. Experience," *Testimony* (April 1980).

26. Barry, Tom, "Bury My Lungs at Red Rock," *The Progressive* (February 1979): pp. 25-27. Also see McCleod, Christopher, *The Four Corners: A National Sacrifice Area?* (San Francisco, CA: Earth Image Films, 1981).

27. "Navajo Uranium Operations: Early Hazards and Recent Interventions," *op. cit.*, pp. 12-13. See also Ford, Bacon, and Davis Utah, Inc., Phase II, Title I, *Engineering Assessment of Inactive Uranium Tailings*, Shiprock Site (Shiprock, MN: March 1977).

28. The measurement accrues from the authors having stepped off the distance. As Tso and Shields note in their 1980 publication ("Navajo Uranium Operations," *op. cit.*), "This tailings site is also within one mile of a day care center, the public schools…the Shiprock business district and cultivated farmlands." See also *Administrator's Guide for Siting and Operation of Uranium Mining and Milling Facilities* (Denver, CO: Stone and Webster Corporation, 1978), and LaDuke, Winona, "How Much Development?" *Akwesasne Notes* (late winter 1979): p. 5.

29. As Michael Garrity has pointed out ("The U.S. Colonial Empire is as Close as the Nearest Reservation," *op. cit.*, p. 258), the Kerr-McGee position on all this was summed up by corporate spokesman Bill Phillips when he told a Washington, D.C. reporter that, "I couldn't tell you what happened at some small mines on an Indian Reservation. We have uranium interests all over the world." For its part, the U.S. government chose to stonewall the matter as well. Amanda Spake of *Mother Jones* found when inquiring about Shiprock in Atomic Energy Commission circles that only one government official was even prepared to acknowledge that he was aware of the issue, and he denied the existence of the mines altogether.

30. As Sorenson points out ("Radiation Issues: Government Decision Making and Uranium Expansion in Northern New Mexico," *op. cit.*), for populations living in

close proximity to mill tailings, the risk of lung cancer doubles; among shaft miners the rate is much higher. V. Archer disclosed (in a presentation titled "Uranium Miners: Clinical Considerations") in a 1980 symposium on uranium conducted in Farmington, NM that, by that year, more than 200 miners had died of lung cancer across the Colorado Plateau as a whole. At the same symposium, L. Gottlieb, an Indian Health Service physician, demonstrated that 40 percent of these miners who had died of the disease were under 40 years of age. See also Samet, J. M., *et al.*, "Uranium Mining and Lung Cancer in Navajo Men," *New England Journal of Medicine*, no. 310 (1984): pp. 1481-84.

31. In his 1980 symposium presentation, L. Gottlieb indicated that "heart defects" had also become a recent leading contender among terminal illnesses prevailing among miners and those otherwise exposed to mining operations in the Shiprock area. See also Nafziger, Rich, "Indian Uranium Profits and Perils," Americans for Indian Opportunity, *Red Paper*, Albuquerque, NM (1976).

32. According to Shields, Laura Mangum, and Alan B. Goodman, "Outcome of 13,300 Navajo Births from 1964-1981 in the Shiprock Uranium Mining Area," an unpublished paper presented at the May 25, 1984 American Association of Atomic Scientists symposium in New York, the rate of birth defects among Navajo newborn near Shiprock during the period 1964-74 was two to eight times as high as the national average. Microcephaly occurred at 15 times the normal rate. They also note that male/female birth ratios may have become somewhat unbalanced during this period in areas associated with uranium mining and milling operations. Shields and Goodman indicate that the rate of birth anomalies seems to have diminished substantially after 1975, although it continues to run well above normal. They tentatively correlate this improvement to four industrially related factors: 1) The covering of a 40-acre, previously exposed tailings pile near Shiprock; 2) The marked decline of uranium mining and milling activities in the area after 1974; 3) Improvement of electrostatic precipitators at the nearby Four Corners Power Plant; and 4) Closure of the Shiprock electronics plant that had chronically exposed Navajo women to a range of organic and inorganic chemicals, including cobalt-60 and krypton-85. This information corresponds well with that of Marjane Ambler, who found in a *High Country News* feature (vol. 12, no. 2 [January 25, 1980]: pp. 3-5) that the rate of infant birth defects, including a pronounced increase in Mongoloidism, at Grand Junction, Colorado (where more than 300,000 tons of raw tailings were utilized in construction projects) had tripled since the commencement of uranium mining/milling activities there.

33. Internal Council of Energy Resource Tribes memorandum, staff report to the director (Peter McDonald), February 9, 1980.

34. "Manpower Gap in the Uranium Mines," *Business Week* (November 1, 1977), cited in Garrity, *op. cit.*, pp. 258-59. It should be noted that the domestic uranium market has since gone "bust" due to the termination of the Atomic Energy Commission's ore buying program in 1979. Both "South African" (i.e., Namibian) and Australian uranium ores are also underselling the U.S. variety by a considerable margin, rendering U.S. production largely unprofitable in commercial markets worldwide. The *Business Week* quotation remains nonetheless instructive concerning what will happen when the uranium "boom" resumes (as surely it must, given present U.S. defense policies and other factors).

35. See Schwagin, Anthony S., and Thomas Hollbacher, "Lung Cancer Among Uranium Miners," *The Nuclear Fuel Cycle* (Cambridge, MA: Union of Concerned Scientists, 1973). Also see Shields and Goodman, *op. cit.*, p. 4, and Rankin, Bob, "Congress Debates Cleanup of Uranium Mill Wastes," *Congressional Quarterly* (August 19, 1978): p. 2180.

36. Churchill, Ward, "Nuclear Contamination Resultant from Extraction Processes in the Southwestern United States," unpublished paper presented at the 1983 International Indian Treaty Council conference, Okema, OK (finding resultant from interviews). The contamination conclusion is largely borne out in a memorandum/news release of the New Mexico Environmental Improvement Agency dated May 21, 1980 made in conjunction with the area office of the Indian Health Service. In these documents, released upon completion of investigations into the so-called "Churchrock Spill" (of water from a United Nuclear Corporation tailings pond), Indian Health Service director William Mohler observed that downstream animals tested for spill-related contamination revealed higher tissue levels of Lead-210 and Polonium-210 (not associated with tailings) than of Thorium-230 and Radium-236 (released in the spill). While this comment was no doubt intended to be reassuring to downstream residents, what it really meant was that animals along the Rio Puerco were already heavily contaminated by nuclear wastes—what Dr. Laura M. Shields has termed "chronic environmental exposures"—prior to the so-called "Churchrock disaster" of 1979.

37. In the memoranda/news releases mentioned in the preceding note, the Indian Health Service actually suggested that Churchrock area residents go ahead and eat their animals—after having delineated the nature and degree of contamination discovered in samples of the same animal tissues—but recommended against consumption (typical among Navajos) of organs such as sheep kidneys and livers as these tissues "tend to concentrate radioactive materials to a greater extent than other parts of the animal." As Christopher McCleod reveals in his "Kerr-McGee's Last Stand" (*Mother Jones*, December 1980), Churchrock sheep herders were still having difficulty finding commercial or governmental agency buyers for their contaminated animals three years after the spill. In other words, the animals were all right for consumption by Navajos, but not by non-Indians in New York, Tokyo, and London.

38. For a full listing of these corporations, see the map accompanying this essay entitled "U.S. Corporate Interest in the Greater Sioux Nation." A glimpse into the implications of this high plains proliferation is offered in the following quotations: "Overall the plans for industrializing the Black Hills are staggering. They include a gigantic energy park featuring more than a score of 10,000 megawatt coal-fired plants, a dozen nuclear reactors, huge coal-slurry pipelines designed to use millions of gallons of water to move crushed coal thousands of miles, and at least 14 major uranium mines" (Wasserman, *op. cit.*); and "Rancher Bud Hollenbach...testified at the Edgemont [South Dakota] TVA Hearing on March 1, 1979 that the production of a flowing well two miles from the (Burdock) mine was cut in half by a two-week pumping test in 1977" (*The Black Hills/Paha Sapa Report*, vol. 1, no. 1 [July 1979]: p. 4). Given the extent of the plans mentioned in the first citation, and the impact of the water consumption of a single mine mentioned in the second, the overall effect of actualizing even a small portion of the entire

governmental "development" concept within a semi-arid region such as the Black Hills can be readily imagined.

39. Irvin, Amelia, "Energy Development and the Effects of Mining on the Lakota Nation," *Journal of Ethnic Studies*, vol. 10, no. 1 (spring 1982).

40. Wasserman, Harvey, "The Sioux's Last Fight for the Black Hills," *Rocky Mountain News* (August 24, 1980).

41. *The Black Hills/Paha Sapa Report, op.cit.*, p. 4.

42. *Indian Health Service Circular,* Aberdeen (SD) Area Office, Pine Ridge District (June 1980).

43. Gilbert, Madonna, "Radioactive Water Contamination on the Red Shirt Table, Pine Ridge Reservation, South Dakota," unpublished report to Women of All Red Nations, Porcupine, SD (March 1980).

44. Women of All Red Nations, "Radiation: Dangerous to Pine Ridge Women," *Akwesasne Notes* (spring 1980).

45. Irvin, *op. cit.*, p. 99.

46. Messerschmidt, Jim, *The Trial of Leonard Peltier* (Boston, MA: South End Press, 1983), p. 4. The area, located around the Sheep Mountain portion of Pine Ridge, also turned out to be rich in uranium in its own right. See U.S. Department of Interior, Bureau of Indian Affairs (J. P. Gries), *Status of Mineral Resource Information on the Pine Ridge Indian Reservation,* South Dakota, BIA Report No. 12, U.S. Department of Interior, Washington, D.C. (1976). Congress formalized illegal—under provision of the Fort Laramie Treaty of 1868—transfer of the Gunnery Range through P.L. 90-468. For further information, see Huber, Jacqueline, *et al., The Gunnery Range Report*, Oglala Sioux Tribe, Office of the President, Pine Ridge, SD (1981).

47. "Radiation: Dangerous to Pine Ridge Women," *op. cit.*

48. *The Black Hills/Paha Sapa Report, op. cit.*, p. 1. Also see Matthiessen, Peter, *Indian Country* (New York: Viking Press, 1984), pp. 203-18.

49. Robert A. Taft Sanitary Engineering Center, *Technical Report W62-12,* published by the U.S. Department of Health, Education and Welfare (Washington, D.C.: U.S. Government Printing Office, 1979), p. 31.

50. "Nuclear Waste Facility Proposed Near Edgemont," *Rapid City Journal* (November 19, 1982).

51. It is a standing area "joke" that an Edgemont resident not killed in a car crash or hunting accident will ultimately die of cancer. Typical of recent governmental/corporate assertions that locating a nuclear waste facility there is "completely safe." See "Edgemont Waste Facility No Health Hazard Says Chem-Nuclear Corp.," *Rapid City Journal* (December 10, 1982): p. 5.

52. "Radiation: Dangerous to Pine Ridge Women," *op. cit.* WARN's contention is well corroborated within "mainstream" scientific literature. See, for example, Lindrop, Patricia J., and J. Rotblat, "Radiation Pollution in the Environment," *Bulletin of Atomic Scientists* (September 1981): especially p. 18. Also see U.S. Department of Interior, Environmental Protection Agency, "National Revised Primary Drinking Water Regulations," *Federal Register*, vol. 48 (October 5, 1983): pp. 45502-21.

53. "Radiation: Dangerous to Pine Ridge Women," *op. cit.* Again, WARN's speculation/concern is hardly "paranoid," as is borne out in surveying reputable

scientific literature on the issue. See, as but two examples, Tamplin, Arthur R., and John W. Gofman, *Population Control Through Nuclear Pollution* (Chicago: Nelson-Hall Publishers, 1971), and Reynolds, Earl E., "Irradiation and Human Evolution," in *The Process of Ongoing Human Evolution* (Detroit, MI: Wayne State University Press, 1960), particularly p. 92. For a more popular non-Indian view of the same general subject matter, see Ibser, H. W., "The Nuclear Energy Game: Nuclear Roulette," *The Progressive* (January 1976).

54. U.S. Department of Energy, Federal Energy Administration, Office of Strategic Analysis, *Project Independence: A Summary* (Washington, D.C.: U.S. Government Printing Office, November 1, 1974).

55. Perhaps the best single study of aquifer contamination and depletion is Bowden, Charles, *Killing the Hidden Waters* (Austin: University of Texas Press, 1977). Also of interest is "Comments on Proposed Cleanup Standards for Inactive Uranium Processing Sites," memorandum to the U.S. Environmental Protection Agency from Dr. E. A. Martell, Docket Number A-79-25 (June 16, 1980).

56. Article II of the 1948 United Nations Convention on Genocide defines the following as acts of genocide when directed against specific, identifiable racial, ethnic, or religious groups: a) Killing members of the group; b) Causing serious bodily or mental harm to members of the group; c) Deliberately inflicting on the group conditions of life calculated to bring about its physical destruction in whole or in part; d) Imposing measures intended to prevent births within the group; and e) Forcibly transferring children of the group to another group. Particularly given points b, c, and d, it is clear to Lorelei Means that there is a firm basis in international law to hold that the U.S. version of industrial development in the Black Hills and Four Corners regions constitutes genocide. Her perspective has been echoed precisely by organizers such as Laura Kadenehe of the Big Mountain Legal Defense/Offense Committee in Arizona. Use of the term "genocide" in such a context is clearly substantive rather than rhetorical. It is no doubt instructive to note that the United States was one of the very few "civilized nations" to refrain from signing this crucial piece of U.N. legislation. See Brownlie, Ian, *Basic Documents on Human Rights* (London/New York: Clarendon Press, Oxford University, 1981).

57. *The Genocide Machine in Canada, op. cit.*, pp. 183-87.

58. *One Century Later, op. cit.* Concerning uranium mining on indigenous land in Canada, see Goldstick, Miles, *Wollaston: People Resisting Genocide* (Montréal: Black Rose Books, 1987). Also see Hardin, Jim, "Indigenous Rights and Uranium Mining in Northern Saskatchewan," in *Critical Issues in Native North America* (IWGIA Doc. 63), ed. Ward Churchill (Copenhagen: International Work Group on Indigenous Affairs, 1989), pp. 116-36.

59. For a full discussion of the use and implications of the term "autogenocide," see Chomsky, Noam, and Edward S. Herman, *The Political Economy of Human Rights, Vol. II: After the Cataclysm: Postwar Indochina and the Reconstruction of Imperial Ideology,* (Boston, MA: South End Press, 1979), pp. 135-300.

60. *Worker Safety and Health Working Papers* (Denver, CO: Oil, Chemical and Atomic Workers Union, 1978).

61. *Ibid.* Also see "Economic Data for Nuclear Industry Bargaining Units," *OCAW Position Paper* (Denver, CO: Oil, Chemical and Atomic Workers Union, 1977).

62. Seib, Gerald F., "Indians Awaken to their Lands' Energy Riches and Seek to Wrest Development from Companies," *Wall Street Journal* (September 20, 1979): p. 40.

63. Owens, Nancy J., "Can Tribes Control Energy Development?" in *Native Americans and Energy Development* (Cambridge, MA: Anthropological Resources Center, 1978), p. 53.

64. *Akwesasne Notes* (late winter 1979): p. 6; (summer 1979): p. 31.

65. *Newsletter of the Native American Solidarity Committee*, Berkeley, CA (spring 1979): pp. 12-13. See also Garrity, *op. cit.*, p. 256.

66. Hoppe, Richard, "A stretch of desert along Route 66—the Grants Belt—is chief locale for U.S. uranium," *Engineering and Mining Journal* (November 1978): pp. 73-93.

67. Environmental Protection Agency, unpublished field report, number deleted, filed with Southwest Information Resource Center, Albuquerque, NM (dated June 1973).

68. Hoppe, *op. cit.* Also see *NASC Newsletter, op. cit.*, and *Akwesasne Notes* (summer 1979), *op. cit.*

69. *Akwesasne Notes* (late winter 1979), *op. cit.*

70. Cable News Network report (July 17, 1990).

71. See Schumacher, Elouise, "440 billion gallons: Hanford wastes would fill 900 King Domes," *Seattle Times* (April 13, 1991).

72. The conversation in question occurred, in all seriousness, between Ward Churchill and a tenured liberal professor of sociology (who shall remain unnamed) at Sangamon State University, Springfield, IL, during the winter of 1978. Variations on the same theme have since been had with a number of academics from other institutions.

73. One need not delve particularly deeply into the literature to discover this pattern. At a reasonably popular level, see Sandoz, Mari, *The Beaver Men* (Lincoln: University of Nebraska Press, 1962), p. 195.

74. A simple review of standard anthropological vernacular, laden as it is with terms such as "primitive," "archaic," "precapitalist," etc. in reference to 19th and 20th century indigenous cultures, should be adequate to prove this point; such vernacular, and the conceptualizations that accompany it, have at this juncture permeated virtually the full range of conventional social sciences and social philosophies.

75. For an in-depth elaboration of the point made in this paragraph, see Churchill, Ward, and Elisabeth R. Lloyd, *Culture versus Economism: Essays on Marxism in the Multicultural Arena* (Denver: Fourth World Center for Study of Indigenous Law and Politics, University of Colorado at Denver, [Second Edition] 1989).

76. A detailed examination of the dynamics involved here is available in the debate lodged under Churchill, Ward, ed., *Marxism and Native Americans* (Boston, MA: South End Press, [second edition] 1990).

77. See Churchill, Ward, "The 'Trial' of Leonard Peltier," preface to Messerschmidt, *op. cit.*, for development of this argument.

78. This argument is made in more depth in the conclusion of *Marxism and Native Americans, op. cit.*

79. See Tabb, Bill, "Marx versus Marxism," in *Marxism and Native Americans, op. cit.*, for a candid assessment of the effectiveness of the Black Hills Alliance effort.

80. *Ibid.*

LIKE SAND IN THE WIND
The Making of an American Indian Diaspora in the United States

They are going away! With a visible reluctance which nothing has overcome but the stern necessity they feel impelling them, they have looked their last upon the graves of their sires—the scenes of their youth, and have taken up the slow toilsome march with their household goods among them to their new homes in a strange land. They leave names to many of our rivers, towns, and counties, and so long as our State remains the Choctaws who once owned most of her soil will be remembered.

—*Vicksburg Daily Sentinel*, February 25, 1832

We told them that we would rather die than leave our lands; but we could not help ourselves. They took us down. Many died on the road. Two of my children died. After we reached the new land, all my horses died. The water was very bad. All our cattle died; not one was left. I stayed till one hundred and fifty-eight of my people had died. Then I ran away.

—Standing Bear, January 1876

Within the arena of Diaspora Studies, the question of whether the field's analytical techniques might be usefully applied to the indigenous population of the United States is seldom raised. In large part, this appears to be due to an unstated presumption on the part of diaspora scholars that because the vast bulk of the native people of the United States remain inside the borders of that nation-state, no population dispersal comparable to that experienced by African Americans, Asian Americans, Latinos—or, for that matter, Euroamericans—is at issue. Upon even minimal reflection, however, the fallacy imbedded at the core of any such premise is quickly revealed.

To say that a Cherokee remains essentially "at home" so long as s/he resides within the continental territoriality claimed by the United States is equivalent to arguing that a Swede displaced to Italy, or a Vietnamese refugee in Korea, would be at home simply because they remain in Europe or Asia. Native Americans, no less than other peoples, can and should be understood as identified with the specific peoples. Mohawks are native to the upstate New York/southern Quebec region, not Florida or California. Chiricahua Apaches are indigenous to southern Arizona and northern Sonora, not Oklahoma or Oregon. The matter is not only cultural, although the dimension of culture is crucially important, but political and economic as well.

Struggles by native peoples to retain use and occupancy rights over their traditional territories, and Euroamerican efforts to supplant them, comprise the virtual entirety of U.S./Indian relations since the inception of the republic. All 40 of the so-called "Indian Wars" recorded by the federal government were fought over land.[1] On more than 370 separate occasions between 1778 and 1871, the Senate of the United States ratified treaties with one or more indigenous peoples by which the latter ceded portions of their land base to the United States. In every instance, a fundamental *quid pro quo* was arrived at: each indigenous nation formally recognized as such through a treaty ratification was simultaneously acknowledged as retaining a clearly demarcated national homeland within which it might maintain its sociopolitical cohesion and from which it could draw perpetual sustenance, both spiritually and materially.[2]

At least five succeeding generations of American Indians fought, suffered, and died to preserve their peoples' residency in the portions of North America which had been theirs since "time immemorial." In this sense, the fundamental importance they attached to continuing their linkages to these areas seems unquestionable. By the same token, the extent to which their descendants have been dislocated from these defined, or definable, land bases is the extent to which it can be observed that the conditions of diaspora have been imposed upon the population of Native North America. In this respect, the situation is so unequivocal that a mere sample of statistics deriving from recent census data will be sufficient to tell the tale:

- By 1980, nearly half of all federally recognized American Indians lived in off-reservation locales, mostly cities. The largest concentration of indigenous people in the country—90,689—was in the Los Angeles Metro Area.[3] By 1990, the proportion of urban-based Indians is estimated to have swelled to approximately 55 percent.[4]

- All federally unrecognized Indians—a figure which may run several times that of the approximately 1.6 million the United States officially admits still exist within its borders—are effectively landless and scattered everywhere across the country.[5]

- Texas, the coast of which was once one of the more populous locales for indigenous people, reported a reservation-based Native American population of 859 in 1980.[6] The total Indian population of Texas was reported as being 39,740.[7] Even if this number included only members of peoples native to the area (which it does not), it would still represent a reduction from about 1.5 million at the point of first contact with Europeans.[8]

- A veritable vacuum in terms of American Indian reservations and population is now evidenced in most of the area east of the Mississippi River, another region once densely populated by indigenous people. Delaware, Illinois, Indiana, Kentucky, Maryland, New Hampshire, New Jersey, Ohio, Pennsylvania, Rhode Island, Tennessee, Vermont, Virginia, West Virginia show no reservations at all.[9] The total Indian population reported in Vermont in 1980 was 968. In New Hampshire, the figure was 1,297. In Delaware, it was 1,307; in West Virginia, 1,555. The reality is that a greater number of persons indigenous to the North American mainland now live in Hawai'i, far out in the Pacific Ocean, than in any of these easterly states.[10]

The ways in which such deformities in the distribution of indigenous population in the United States have come to pass were anything but natural. To the contrary, the major causative factors have consistently derived from a series of official policies implemented over more than two centuries by the federal government of the United States. These have ranged from forced removal during the 1830s, to concentration and compulsory assimilation during the 1880s, to coerced relocation beginning in the late 1940s. Interspersed through it all have been periods of outright liquidation and dissolution, continuing into the present moment. The purpose of this essay is to explore these policies and their effects on the peoples targeted for such exercises in "social engineering."

The Postrevolutionary Period

During the period immediately following the American Revolution, the newly formed United States was in a "desperate financial plight...[and] saw its salvation in the sale to settlers and land companies of western lands" lying outside the original 13 colonies.[11] Indeed, the revolution had been fought in significant part in order to negate George II's Proclamation of 1763, an edict restricting land acquisition by British subjects to the area east of the Appalachian Mountains and thereby voiding certain speculative real estate interests held by the U.S. founding fathers. During the war, loyalty of rank-and-file soldiers, as well as major creditors, had been maintained through warrants advanced by the Continental Congress with the promise that rebel debts would be retired through issuance of deeds to parcels of Indian land, once the revolution had succeeded.[12] A substantial problem for the fledgling republic was that in the immediate aftermath, it possessed neither the legal nor the physical means to carry through on such commitments.

In the Treaty of Paris, signed on September 3, 1783, England quitclaimed its rights to all present U.S. territory east of the Mississippi. Contrary to subsequent Americana, this action conveyed no *bona fide* title to any of the Indian lands lying within the area.[13] Rather, it opened the way for the United States to replace Great Britain as the sole entity entitled under prevailing international law to *acquire* Indian land in the region through negotiation and purchase.[14] The United States—already an outlaw state by virtue of its armed rejection of lawful Crown authority—appears to have been emotionally prepared to seize native property through main force, thereby continuing its initial posture of gross illegality.[15] Confronted by the incipient indigenous alliance espoused by Tecumseh in the Ohio River Valley (known at the time as the "Northwest Territory") and to the south by the powerful Creek and Cherokee confederations, however, the United States found itself militarily stalemated all along its western frontier.[16]

The Indian position was considerably reinforced when England went back on certain provisions of the Treaty of Paris, refusing to abandon a line of military installations along the Ohio until the United States showed itself willing to comply with minimum standards of international legalism, "acknowledging the Indian right in the soil" long since recognized under the Doctrine of Discovery.[17] To the south, Spanish Florida also aligned itself with native nations as a means of holding the rapacious settler population of neighboring Georgia in check.[18] Frustrated, federal authorities had to content themselves with the final dispossession and banishment of such peoples as the Huron (Wyandot) and Delaware (Lenni Lanape)—whose homelands fell within the original colonies, and who had been much weakened by more than a century of warfare—to points beyond the 1763 demarcation line. There, these early elements of a U. S.-precipitated indigenous diaspora were taken in by stronger nations such as the Ottawa and Shawnee.[19]

Meanwhile, George Washington's initial vision of a rapid and wholesale expulsion of all Indians east of the Mississippi, expressed in June 1783,[20] was tempered to reflect a more sophisticated process of gradual encroachment explained by General Philip Schuyler of New York in a letter to Congress the following month:

> As our settlements approach their country, [the Indians] must, from the scarcity of game, which that approach will induce, retire farther back, and dispose of their lands, unless they dwindle to nothing, as all savages have done...when compelled to live in the vicinity of civilized people, and thus leave us the country without the expense of purchase, trifling as that will probably be.[21]

As Washington himself was to put it a short time later, "[P]olicy and economy point very strongly to the expediency of being on good terms with the Indians, and the propriety of purchasing their Lands in preference to attempting to drive them by force of arms out of their Country...The gradual extension of our Settlements will certainly cause the Savage as the Wolf to retire...In a word there is nothing to be gained by an Indian War but the Soil they live on and this can be had by purchase at less expense."[22] By 1787, the strategy had become so well-accepted that the United States was prepared to enact the Northwest Ordinance (1 *Stat.* 50), codifying a formal renunciation of what it had been calling its "Rights of Conquest" with respect to native peoples: "The utmost good faith shall always be observed towards the Indian; their land shall never be taken from them without their consent; and in their property, rights, and liberty, they shall never be invaded or disturbed—but laws founded in justice and humanity shall from time to time be made, for wrongs done to them, and for preserving peace and friendship with them."[23]

The Era of Removal

By the early years of the 19th century, the balance of power in North America had begun to shift. To a certain extent, this was due to a burgeoning of the Angloamerican population, a circumstance actively fostered by government policy. In other respects, it was because of an increasing consolidation of the U.S. state and a generation-long erosion of indigenous strength resulting from the factors delineated in Schuyler's policy of gradual expansion.[24] By 1810, the government was ready to resume what Congress described as the "speedy provision of the extension of the territories of the United States" through means of outright force.[25] Already, in 1803, provision had been made through the Louisiana Purchase for the massive displacement of all eastern Indian nations into what was perceived as the "vast wasteland" west of the Mississippi.[26] The juridical groundwork was laid by the Supreme Court with Chief Justice John Marshall's opinion in *Fletcher v. Peck* (10 U.S. 87), a decision holding that the title of U.S. citizens to parcels of Indian property might be considered valid even though no Indian consent to cede the land had been obtained.[27]

With the defeat of Great Britain in the War of 1812, the subsequent defeat of Tecumseh's confederation in 1813, and General Andrew Jackson's defeat of the Creek Red Sticks in 1814, the "clearing" of the East began in earnest.[28] By 1819, the United States had wrested eastern Florida from Spain, consummating a process begun in 1810 with assaults upon the western ("panhandle") portion of the territory.[29] Simultaneously, the first of a pair of "Seminole Wars" was begun on the Florida peninsula to subdue an amalgamation of resident Miccosukees, "recalcitrant" Creek refugees, and runaway chattel slaves naturalized as free citizens of the indigenous nations.[30] In 1823, John Marshall reinforced the embryonic position articulated in *Peck* with *Johnson v. McIntosh* (21 U.S. 98 Wheat. 543), an opinion inverting conventional understandings of indigenous status in international law by holding that U.S. sovereignty superseded that of native nations, even within their own territories. During the same year, President James Monroe promulgated his doctrine professing a unilateral U.S. "right" to circumscribe the sovereignty of all other nations in the hemisphere.[31]

In this environment, a tentative policy of Indian "removal" was already underway by 1824, although not codified as law until the Indian Removal Act (ch. 148, 4 *Stat.* 411) was passed in 1830. This was followed by John Marshall's opinions, rendered in *Cherokee v. Georgia* (30 U.S. (5 Pet.) 1 (1831)) and *Worcester v. Georgia* (31 U.S. (6 Pet.) 551 (1832)), that Indians comprised "domestic dependent nations," the sovereignty of which was subject to the "higher authority" of the federal government.[32] At that point, the federal program of physically relocating entire nations of people from their eastern homelands to what was then called the "Permanent Indian Territory of Oklahoma" west of the Mississippi became full-fledged and forcible.[33] The primary targets were the prosperous "Five Civilized Tribes" of the Southeast: the Cherokee, Creek, Chickasaw, Choctaw, and Seminole nations. They were rounded up and interned by troops, then concentrated in camps until their numbers were sufficient to make efficient their being force-marched at bayonet-point, typically without adequate food, shelter, or medical attention, often in the dead of winter, as many as 1,500 miles to their new "homelands."[34]

There were, of course, still those who attempted to mount a military resistance to what was happening. Some, like the Sac and Fox nations of Illinois, who fought what has come to be known as the "Black Hawk War" against those dispossessing them in 1832, were simply slaughtered *en masse.*[35] Others, such as the "hard core" of Seminoles who mounted the second war bearing their name in 1835, were forced from the terrain associated with their normal way of life. Once ensconced in forbidding locales like the Everglades, they became for all practical intents and purposes invincible—one group refused to make peace with the United States until the early 1960s—but progressively smaller and more diffuse in their demography.[36] In any event, by 1840, removal had been mostly accomplished (although it lingered as a policy until 1855), with only "the smallest, least offensive, and most thoroughly integrated tribes escaping the pressure to clear the eastern half of the continent from its original inhabitants."[37] The results of the policy were always catastrophic for the victims. For instance, of the approximately 17,000 Cherokees subjected to the removal process, about 8,000 died of disease, exposure, and malnutrition along what they called the "Trail of Tears."[38] In addition:

> The Choctaws are said to have lost fifteen percent of their population, 6,000 out of 40,000; and the Chickasaw...surely suffered severe losses as well. By contrast the Creeks and Seminoles are said to have suffered about 50 percent mortality. For the Creeks, this came primarily in the period immediately after removal: for example, "of the 10,000 or more who were resettled in 1836-37...an incredible 3,500 died of 'bilious fevers.'" [39]

Nor was this the only cost. Like the Seminoles, portions of each of the targeted peoples managed through various means to avoid removal, remaining in their original territories until their existence was once again recognized by the United States during the 20th century. One consequence was a permanent sociocultural and geographic fragmentation of formerly cohesive groups; while the bulk of the identified populations of these nations now live in and around Oklahoma, smaller segments reside on the tiny "Eastern Cherokee" reservation in North Carolina (1980 population 4,844); the "Mississippi Choctaw" reservation in Mississippi (pop. 2,756); the Miccosukee and "Big Cypress," "Hollywood" and "Brighton" Seminole reservations in Florida (pops. 213, 351, 416, and 323, respectively).[40]

An unknown but significant number of Cherokees also went beyond Oklahoma, following their leader, Sequoia, into Mexico in order to escape the reach of the United States altogether.[41] This established something of a precedent for other peoples such as the Kickapoos, a small Mexican "colony" of whom persists to this day.[42] Such dispersal was compounded by the fact that throughout the removal process varying numbers of Indians escaped at various points along the route of march, blending into the surrounding territory and later intermarrying with the incoming settler population. By and large, these people have simply slipped from the historical record, their descendants today inhabiting a long arc of mixed-blood communities extending from northern Georgia and Alabama, through Tennessee and Kentucky, and into the southernmost areas of Illinois and Missouri.[43]

Worse was yet to come. At the outset of the removal era proper, Andrew Jackson—a leading proponent of the policy, who had ridden into the White House on the public acclaim deriving from his role as commander of the 1814 massacre of the Red Sticks at Horseshoe Bend and a subsequent slaughter of noncombatants during the First Seminole War—offered a carrot as well as the stick he used to compel tribal "cooperation."[44] In 1829, he promised the Creeks that:

> Your father has provided a country large enough for all of you, and he advises you to remove to it. There your white brothers will not trouble you; they will have no claim to the land, and you can live upon it, you and all your children, as long as the grass grows or the water runs, in peace and plenty. It will be yours forever.[45]

Jackson was, to put it bluntly, lying through his teeth. Even as he spoke, Jackson was aware that the Mississippi, that ostensible border between the United States and Permanent Indian Territory proclaimed by Thomas Jefferson and others, had already been breached by the rapidly consolidating states of Louisiana, Arkansas, and Missouri in the south, Iowa, Wisconsin, and Minnesota in the north.[46] Nor could Jackson have been unknowing that his close friend, Senator Thomas Hart Benton of Missouri, had stipulated as early as 1825 that the Rocky Mountains rather than the Mississippi should serve as an "everlasting boundary" of the United States.[47] By the time the bulk of removal was completed a decade later, Angloamerican settlement was reaching well into Kansas. Their cousins who had infiltrated the Mexican province of Texas had revolted, proclaimed themselves an independent republic, and were negotiating for statehood. The eyes of empire had also settled on all of Mexico north of the Río Grande, and the British portion of Oregon as well.[48]

Peoples such as the Shawnee and Potawatomi, Lenni Lanape and Wyandot, Peoria, Sac, Fox, and Kickapoo, already removed from their eastern homelands, were again compulsorily relocated as the western Indian Territory was steadily reduced in size.[49] This time, they were mostly shifted southward into an area eventually conforming to the boundaries of the present state of Oklahoma. Ultimately, 67 separate nations (or parts of nations), only six of them truly indigenous to the land at issue, were forced into this relatively small dumping ground.[50] When Oklahoma, too, became a state in 1907, most of the territorial compartments reserved for the various Indian groups were simply dissolved. Today, although Oklahoma continues to report the second largest native population of any state, only the Osage retain a reserved land base which is nominally their own.[51]

Subjugation in the West

The U.S. "Winning of the West" which began around 1850—that is, immediately after the northern half of Mexico was taken in a brief war of conquest—was, if anything, more brutal that the clearing of the East.[52] Most of the U.S. wars against native people were waged during the following 35 years under what has been termed an official "rhetoric of extermination."[53] The means employed in militarily subjugating the indigenous nations of California and southern Oregon, the Great Plains, Great Basin, and northern region of the Sonora Desert devolved upon a lengthy series of wholesale massacres. Representative of these were the slaughter of about 150 Lakotas at Blue River (Nebraska) in 1854, some 500 Shoshones at Bear River (Idaho) in 1863, as many as 250 Cheyennes and Arapahos at Sand Creek (Colorado) in 1864, perhaps 300 Cheyennes on the Washita River (Oklahoma) in 1868, 175 Piegan noncombatants at the Marias River (Montana) in 1870, and at least 100 Cheyennes at Camp Robinson (Nebraska) in 1878. The parade of official atrocities was capped off by the butchery of another 300 unarmed Lakotas at Wounded Knee (South Dakota) in 1890.[54]

Other means employed by the government to reduce its native opponents to a state of what it hoped would be abject subordination included the four-year internment of the entire Navajo (Diné) Nation in a concentration camp at the Bosque Redondo, outside Fort Sumner, New Mexico, beginning in 1864. The Diné, who had been force-marched in what they called the "Long Walk," a 400-mile trek from their Arizona homeland, were then held under abysmal conditions, with neither adequate food nor shelter, and died like flies. Approximately half had perished before their release in 1868.[55] Similarly, if less dramatically, food supplies were cut off to the Lakota Nation in 1877—militarily defeated the year before, the Lakotas were being held under army guard at the time—until starvation compelled its leaders to "cede" the Black Hills area to the United States.[56] The assassination of resistance leaders such as the Lakotas Crazy Horse (1877) and Sitting Bull (1890) was also a commonly used technique.[57] Other recalcitrant figures like Geronimo (Chiricahua) and Satanta (Kiowa) were separated from their people by being imprisoned in remote facilities like Fort Marion, Florida.[58]

In addition to these official actions, which the U.S. Census Bureau acknowledged in an 1894 summary as having caused a minimum of 45,000 native deaths, there was an even greater attrition resulting from what were described as "individual affairs."[59] These took the form of Angloamerican citizens at large killing Indians, often systematically, under a variety of quasi-official circumstances. In Dakota Territory, for example, a $200 bounty for Indian scalps was paid in the territorial capitol of Yankton during the 1860s; the local military commander, General Alfred Sully, is known to have privately contracted for a pair of Lakota skulls with which to adorn the city.[60] In Texas, first as a republic and then as a state, authorities also "placed a bounty upon the scalp of any Indian brought in to a government office—man, woman, or child, no matter what 'tribe'—no questions asked."[61] In California and Oregon, "the enormous decrease [in the native population of 1800] from about a quarter-million to less than 20,000 [in 1870 was] due chiefly to the cruelties and wholesale massacres perpetrated by the miners and early settlers."[62]

Much of the killing in California and southern Oregon Territory resulted, directly and indirectly, from the discovery of gold in 1848 and the subsequent influx of miners and settlers. Newspaper accounts document the atrocities, as do oral histories of the California Indians today. It was not uncommon for small groups or villages to be attacked by immigrants and virtually wiped out overnight.[63]

It has been estimated that Indian deaths resulting from this sort of direct violence may have run as high as a half-million by 1890.[64] All told, the indigenous population of the continental United States, which may still have been as great as two million when the country was founded, had been reduced to well under 250,000 by 1900.[65] As the noted demographer Sherburne F. Cook has observed, "The record speaks for itself. No further commentary is necessary."[66]

Under these conditions, the United States was able to shuffle native peoples around at will. The Northern Cheyennes and closely allied Arapahos, for instance, were shipped from their traditional territory in Montana's Powder River watershed to the reservation of their southern cousins in Oklahoma in 1877. After the Cheyenne remnants, more than a third of whom had died in barely a year of malaria and other diseases endemic to this alien environment, made a desperate attempt to return home in 1878, they were granted a reservation in the north country, but not before the bulk of them had been killed by army troops. Moreover, they were permanently separated from the Arapahos, who were "temporarily" assigned to the Wind River reservation of their hereditary enemies, the Shoshone, in Wyoming.[67]

A faction of the Chiricahua Apaches who showed signs of continued "hostility" to U.S. domination by the 1880s were yanked from their habitat in southern Arizona and "resettled" around Fort Sill, Oklahoma.[68] Hinmaton Yalatkit (Chief Joseph) of the Nez Percé and other leaders of that people's legendary attempt to escape the army and flee to Canada were also deposited in Oklahoma, far from the Idaho valley they'd fought to retain.[69] Most of the Santee Dakotas of Minnesota's woodlands ended up on the wind-swept plains of Nebraska, while a handful of their relatives remained behind on tiny plots which are now called the "Upper" and "Lower Sioux" reservations.[70] A portion of the Oneidas, who had fought on the side of the rebels during the revolution, were moved to a small reservation near Green Bay, Wisconsin.[71] An even smaller reserve was provided in the same area for residual elements of Connecticut's Mahegans, Mohegans, and other peoples, all of them lumped together under the heading "Stockbridge-Munsee Indians."[72] On and on, it went.

Allotment and Assimilation

With the native ability to militarily resist U.S. territorial ambitions finally quelled, the government moved first to structurally negate any meaningful residue of national status on the part of indigenous peoples, and then to dissolve them altogether. The opening round of this drive came in 1871, with the attachment of a rider to the annual congressional appropriations act (ch. 120, 16 *Stat.* 544, 566) suspending any further treaty-making with Indians. This was followed, in 1885, with passage of the Major Crimes Act (ch. 341, 24 *Stat.* 362, 385), extending U.S. jurisdiction directly over reserved Indian territories for the first time. Beginning with seven felonies delineated in the initial statutory language, and combined with the Supreme Court's opinion in *U.S. v. Kagama* (118 U.S. 375 (1886)) that Congress possessed a unilateral and "incontrovertible right" to exercise its authority over Indians as it saw fit, the 1885 act opened the door to subsequent enactment of the more than 5,000 federal laws presently regulating every aspect of reservation life and affairs.[73]

In 1887, Congress passed the General Allotment Act (ch. 119, 24 *Stat.* 388), a measure designed expressly to destroy what was left of the basic indigenous socioeconomic cohesion by eradicating traditional systems of collective land holding. Under provision of the statute, each Indian identified as such by demonstrating "one-half or more degree of Indian blood" was to be issued an individual deed to a specific parcel of land—160 acres per family head, 80 acres per orphan or single person over 18 years of age, and 40 acres per dependent child—within existing reservation boundaries. Each Indian was required to accept U.S. citizenship in order to receive his or her allotment. Those who refused, such as a substantial segment of the Cherokee "full-blood" population, were left landless.[74]

Generally speaking, those of mixed ancestry whose "blood quantum" fell below the required level were summarily excluded from receiving allotments. In many cases, the requirement was construed by officials as meaning that an applicant's "blood" had to have accrued from a single people; persons whose cumulative blood quantum derived from intermarriage between several native peoples were thus often excluded as well. In other instances, arbitrary geographic criteria were also employed; all Cherokees, Creeks, and Choctaws living in Arkansas, for example, were not only excluded from allotment, but permanently denied recognition as members of their respective nations as well.[75] Once all eligible Indians had been assigned their allotments within a given reservation—all of them from the worst land available therein—the remainder of the reserved territory was declared "surplus" and opened to non-Indian homesteaders, corporate acquisition, and conversion into federal or state parks and forests.[76]

Under the various allotment programs, the most valuable land was the first to go. Settlers went after the rich grasslands of Kansas,

Nebraska, and the Dakotas; the dense black-soil forests of Minnesota and Wisconsin; and the wealthy oil and gas lands of Oklahoma. In 1887, for example, the Sisseton Sioux of South Dakota owned 918,000 acres of rich virgin land on their reservation. But since there were only 2,000 of them, allotment left more than 600,000 acres for Euroamerican settlers. The Chippewas of Minnesota lost their rich timber lands; once each member had claimed their land, the government leased the rest to timber corporations. The Colvilles of northeastern Washington lost their lands to cattlemen, who fraudulently claimed mineral rights there. In Montana and Wyoming the Crows lost more than two million acres, and the Nez Percés had to cede communal grazing ranges in Idaho. All 67 of the tribes in Indian Territory underwent allotment. On the Flathead reservation in Montana—which included Flatheads, Pend Oreilles, Kutenais, and Spokanes—the federal government opened 1.1 million acres to settlers. A similar story prevailed throughout the country.[77]

By the time the allotment process had run its course in 1930, the residue of native land holdings in the United States had been reduced from approximately 150 million acres to fewer than 50 million.[78] Of this, more than two-thirds consisted of arid or semi-arid terrain deemed useless for agriculture, grazing, or other productive purposes. The remaining one-third had been leased at extraordinarily low rates to non-Indian farmers and ranchers by local Indian agents exercising "almost dictatorial powers" over remaining reservation property.[79]

Indians across the country were left in a state of extreme destitution as a result of allotment and attendant leasing practices. Worse, the situation was guaranteed to be exacerbated over succeeding generations insofar as what was left of the reservation land base, already insufficient to support its occupants at a level of mere subsistence, could be foreseen to become steadily more so as the native population recovered from the genocide perpetrated against it during the 19th century.[80] A concomitant of allotment was thus an absolute certainty that ever-increasing numbers of Indians would be forced from what remained nominally their own land during the 20th century, dispersed into the vastly more numerous American society-at-large. There, it was predictable (and often predicted) that they would be "digested," disappearing once and for all as anything distinctly Indian in terms of sociocultural, political, or even racial identity. The record shows that such outcomes were anything but unintentional.

The purpose of all this was "assimilation," as federal policymakers described their purpose, or—to put the matter more unabashedly—to bring about the destruction and disappearance of American Indian peoples as such. In the words of Francis E. Leupp, Commissioner of Indian Affairs from 1905 through 1909, the Allotment Act in particular should be viewed as a "mighty pulverizing engine for breaking up the tribal mass" which stood in the way of complete Euroamerican hegemony in North America. Or, to quote Indian Commissioner Charles Burke a decade later, "[I]t is not desirable or consistent with the general welfare to promote tribal characteristics and organization."[81]

The official stance was consecrated in the Supreme Court's determination in the 1903 *Lonewolf v. Hitchcock* decision (187 U.S. 553)—extended from John Marshall's "domestic dependent nation" thesis of the early 1830s—that the United States possessed "plenary" (full) power over all matters involving Indian affairs. In part, this meant the federal government was unilaterally assigning itself perpetual "trust" prerogatives to administer or dispose of native assets, whether these were vested in land, minerals, cash, or any other medium, regardless of Indian needs or desires.[82] Congress then consolidated its position with passage of the 1906 Burke Act (34 *Stat.* 182), designating the Secretary of Interior as permanent trustee over Indian Country. In 1924, a number of loose ends were cleaned up with passage of the Indian Citizenship Act (ch. 233, 43 *Stat.* 25) imposing U.S. citizenship upon all native people who had not otherwise been naturalized. The law was applied across the board to all Indians, whether they desired citizenship or not, and thus included those who had foregone allotments rather than accept it.[83]

Meanwhile, the more physical dimensions of assimilationist policy were coupled to a process of ideological conditioning designed to render native children susceptible to dislocation and absorption by the dominant society. In the main, this assumed the form of a compulsory boarding school system administered by the Interior Department's Bureau of Indian Affairs (BIA), wherein large numbers of indigenous children were taken, often forcibly, to facilities remote from their families and communities. Once there, the youngsters were prevented from speaking their languages, practicing their religions, wearing their customary clothing or wearing their hair in traditional fashion, or in any other way overtly associating themselves with their own cultures and traditions. Instead, they were indoctrinated—typically for a decade or more—in Christian doctrine and European values such as the "work ethic." During the summers, they were frequently "farmed out" to Euroamerican "foster homes" where they were further steeped in the dominant society's views of their peoples and themselves.[83]

> Attendance was made compulsory [for all native children, aged five to eighteen] and the agent was made responsible for keeping the schools filled, by persuasion if possible, by withholding rations and annuities from the parents, and by other means if necessary...[Students] who were guilty of misbehavior might either receive corporal punishment or be imprisoned in the guardhouse [a special "reform school" was established to handle "incorrigible" students who clung to their traditions]...A sincere effort was made to develop the type of school that would destroy tribal ways.[84]

The intention of this was, according to federal policymakers and many of its victims alike, to create generations of American Indian youth who functioned intellectually as "little white people," facilitating the rapid dissolution of traditional native cultures desired by federal policymakers.[85] In combination with a program in which native children were put out for wholesale adoption by Euroamerican families, the effect upon indigenous peoples was devastating.[86] This systematic transfer of children not only served to accelerate the outflow of Indians from reservation and reservation-adjacent settings, but the return of individuals mentally conditioned to conduct themselves as non-Indians escalated the rate at which many native societies unraveled within the reservation contexts themselves.[87]

The effects of the government's allotment and assimilation programs are reflected in the demographic shifts evidenced throughout Indian Country from 1910 through 1950. In the former year, only 0.4 percent of all identified Indians lived in urban locales. By 1930, the total had grown to 9.9 percent. As of 1950, the total had grown to 13.4 percent. Simultaneously, the displacement of native people from reservations to off-reservation rural areas was continuing apace.[88] In 1900, this involved only about 3.5 percent of all Indians. By 1930, the total had swelled to around 12.5 percent, and, by 1950, it had reached nearly 18 percent.[89] Hence, in the latter year, nearly one-third of the federally recognized Indians in the United States had been dispersed to locales other than those the government had defined as being "theirs."

Reorganization and Colonization

It is likely, all things being equal, that the Indian policies with which the United States ushered in the 20th century would have led inexorably to a complete eradication of the reservation system and corresponding disappearance of American Indians as distinct peoples by some point around 1950. There can be no question but that such a final consolidation of its internal land base would have comple-mented the phase of transoceanic expansionism into which the United States entered quite unabashedly during the 1890s.[90] That things did not follow this course seems mainly due to a pair of ironies, one geological and the other unwittingly imbedded in the bizarre status of "quasi-sovereignty" increasingly imposed upon native nations by federal jurists and policymakers over the preceding hundred years.

As regards the first of these twin twists of fate, authorities were becoming increasingly aware by the late 1920s that the "worthless" residue of territory to which indigenous people had been consigned was turning out to be extraordinarily endowed with mineral wealth. Already, in 1921, an exploratory team from Standard Oil had come upon what it took to be substantial fossil fuel deposits on the Navajo reservation.[91] During the next three decades, it would be discovered just how great a proportion of U.S. "domestic" resources lay within American Indian reservations. For example:

> Western reservations in particular...possess vast amounts of coal, oil, shale oil, natural gas, timber, and uranium. More than 40 percent of the national reserves of low sulfur, strippable coal, 80 percent of the nation's uranium reserves, and billions of barrels of shale oil exist on reservation land. On the 15-million-acre Navajo reservation, there are approximately 100 million barrels of oil, 25 trillion cubic feet of natural gas, 80 million pounds of uranium, and 50 billion tons of coal. The 440,000-acre North-ern Cheyenne reservation in Montana sits atop a 60-foot-thick layer of coal. In New Mexico, geologists estimate that the Jicarilla Apache reser-

vation possesses 2 trillion cubic feet of natural gas and as much as 154 million barrels of oil.[92]

This led directly to the second quirk. The more sophisticated federal officials, even then experiencing the results of opening up Oklahoma's lush oil fields to unrestrained corporate competition, realized the extent of the disequilibriums and inefficiencies involved in this line of action when weighed against the longer-term needs of U.S. industrial development.[93] Only by retaining its "trust authority" over reservation assets would the government be in a continuing position to dictate which resources would be exploited, in what quantities, by whom, at what cost, and for what purpose, allowing the North American political economy to evolve in ways preferred by the country's financial elite.[94] Consequently, it was quickly perceived as necessary that both Indians and Indian Country be preserved, at least to some extent, as a facade behind which the "socialistic" process of central economic planning might occur.

For the scenario to work in practice, it was vital that the reservations be made to appear "self-governing" enough to exempt itself from the usual requirements of the U.S. "free market" system whenever this might be convenient to its federal "guardians." On the other hand, the reservations could never become independent or autonomous enough to assume control over their own economic destinies, asserting demands that equitable royalty rates be paid for the extraction of their ores, for example, or that profiting corporations underwrite the expense of environmental clean-up once mining operations had been concluded.[95] In effect, the idea was that many indigenous nations should be maintained as outright internal colonies of the United States rather than being liquidated out-of-hand.[96] All that was needed to accomplish this was the creation of a mechanism through which the illusion of limited Indian self-rule might be extended.

The vehicle for this purpose materialized in 1934, with passage of the Indian Reorganization Act (ch. 576, 48 *Stat.* 948), or "IRA," as it is commonly known. Under provision of this statute, the traditional governing bodies of most indigenous nations were supplanted by "Tribal Councils," the structures of which were devised in Washington, D.C., functioning within parameters of formal constitutions written by BIA officials.[97] A democratic veneer was maintained by staging a referendum on each reservation prior to its being reorganized, but federal authorities simply manipulated the outcomes to achieve the desired results.[98] The newly installed IRA councils were patterned much more closely upon the model of corporate boards than of governments, and possessed little power other than to sign off on business agreements. Even at that, they were completely and "voluntarily" subordinated to U.S. interests: "All decisions of any consequence (in thirty-three separate areas of consideration) rendered by these 'tribal councils' were made 'subject to the approval of the Secretary of Interior or his delegate,' the Commissioner of Indian Affairs."[99]

One entirely predictable result of this arrangement has been that an inordinate amount of mining, particularly that related to "energy development," has occurred on Indian reservations since the mid-to-late 1940s. *All* uranium mining and milling during the life of the U.S. Atomic Energy Commission's (AEC's) ore-buying program (1954-1981) occurred on reservation land; Anaconda's Jackpile Mine, located at the Laguna Pueblo in New Mexico, was the largest open pit uranium extraction operation in the world until it was phased out in 1979.[100] Every year, enough power is generated by Arizona's Four Corners Power Plant alone—every bit of it from coal mined at Black Mesa, on the Navajo reservation—to light the lights of Tucson and Phoenix for two decades, and present plans include a four-fold expansion of Navajo coal production.[101] Throughout the West, the story is the same.

On the face of it, the sheer volume of resource "development" in Indian Country over the past half-century should—even under disadvantageous terms—have translated into *some* sort of "material improvement" in the lot of indigenous people. Yet the mining leases offered to selected corporations by the BIA "in behalf of" their native "wards"—and duly endorsed by the IRA councils—have consistently paid such a meager fraction of prevailing market royalty rates that no such advancement has been discernible. Probably the best terms were those obtained by the Navajo Nation in 1976, a contract paying a royalty of 55 cents per ton for coal; this amounted to 8 percent of market price at a time when Interior Secretary Cecil Andrus admitted the *minimum* rate paid for coal mined in off-reservation settings was

12.5 percent (more typically, it was upwards of 15 percent).[102] Simultaneously, a 17.5 cents per ton royalty was being paid for coal on the Crow reservation in Montana, a figure which was raised to 40 cents—less than half the market rate—only after years of haggling.[103] What are at issue here are not profits, but the sort of "super-profits" usually associated with U.S. domination of economies elsewhere in the world.[104]

Nor has the federally coordinated corporate exploitation of the reservations translated into wage income for Indians. As of 1989, the government's own data indicated that reservation unemployment nationwide still hovered in the mid-60th percentile, with some locales running persistently in the 19th.[105] Most steady jobs involved administering or enforcing the federal order, reservation by reservation. Such "business-related" employment as existed tended to be temporary, menial, and paid the minimum wage, a matter quite reflective of the sort of transient, extractive industry —which brings its cadre of permanent, skilled labor with it—the BIA had encouraged to set up shop in Indian Country.[106] Additionally, the impact of extensive mining and associated activities had done much to disrupt the basis for possible continuation of traditional self-sufficiency occupations, destroying considerable acreage which held potential as grazing or subsistence garden plots.[107] In this sense, U.S. governmental and corporate activities have "underdeveloped" Native North America in classic fashion.[108]

Overall, according to a federal study completed in 1988, reservation-based Indians experienced every index of extreme empoverishment: by far the lowest annual and lifetime incomes of any North American population group, highest rate of infant mortality (7.5 times the national average), highest rates of death from plague disease, malnutrition, and exposure, highest rate of teen suicide, and so on. The average life expectancy of reservation-based Native American males is 44.6 years, that of females fewer than three years longer.[109] The situation is much more indicative of a Third World context than of rural areas in a country that claims to be the world's "most advanced industrial state." Indeed, the poignant observation of many Latinos regarding their relationship to the United States, that "your wealth is our poverty," is as appropriate to the archipelago of Indian reservations in North America itself as it is to the South American continent. By any estimation, the "open veins of Native America" created by the IRA have been an incalculable boon to the maturation of the U.S. economy, while Indians continue to pay the price by living in the most grinding sort of poverty.[110]

And there is worse. One of the means used by the government to maximize corporate profits in Indian Country over the years—again rubber-stamped by the IRA councils—has been to omit clauses requiring corporate reclamation of mined lands from leasing instruments. Similarly, the cost of doing business on reservations has been pared to the bone (and profitability driven up) by simply waiving environmental protection standards in most instances.[111] Such practices have spawned ecological catastrophe in many locales. As the impact of the Four Corners plant, one of a dozen coal-fired electrical generation facilities currently "on-line" on the Navajo reservation, has been described elsewhere:

> The five units of the 2,075 megawatt power plant have been churning out city-bound electricity and local pollution since 1969. The plant burns ten tons of coal per minute—five million tons per year—spewing three hundred tons of fly ash and other waste particulates into the air each day. The black cloud hangs over ten thousand acres of the once-pristine San Juan River Valley. The deadly plume was the only visible evidence of human enterprise as seen from the Gemini-12 satellite which photographed the earth from 150 miles in space. Less visible, but equally devastating is the fact that since 1968 the coal mining operations and power plant requirements have been extracting 2,700 gallons from the Black Mesa water table each minute—60 million gallons per year—causing extreme desertification of the area, and even the sinking of some ground by as much as twelve feet.[112]

Corporations engaged in uranium mining and milling on the Navajo reservation and at Laguna were also absolved by the BIA of responsibility for cleaning-up upon completion of their endeavors, with the result that hundreds of tailings piles were simply abandoned during the 1970s and '80s.[113] A fine sand retaining about 75 percent of the radioactive content of the original ore, the tailings constitute a massive source of wind-blown carcinogenic/mutogenic contaminants affecting all persons and livestock residing within a wide radius of each pile.[114] Both ground and surface water has also been heavily contaminated with radioactive by-products throughout the Four Corners region.[115] In the Black Hills region, the situation is much the same.[116] At its Hanford Nuclear Weapons Facility, located on the Yakima reservation in Washington state, the AEC itself secretly discharged some 440 billion gallons of plutonium, strontium, cesium, tritium, and other high-level radioactive contaminants into the local aquifer between 1955 and 1989.[117]

Given that the half-life of the substances involved is as long as 125,000 years, the magnitude of the disaster inflicted upon Native North America by IRA colonialism should not be underestimated. The Los Alamos National Scientific laboratory observed in its February 1978 *Mini-Report* that the only "solution" its staff could conceive to the problems presented by wind-blown radioactive contaminants would be "to zone the land into uranium mining and milling districts so as to forbid human habitation." Similarly:

> A National Academy of Sciences (NAS) report states bluntly that [reclamation after any sort of mining] cannot be done in areas with less than 10 inches of rainfall a year; the rainfall over most of the Navajo Nation [and many other western reservations] ranges from six to ten inches a year. The NAS suggests that such areas be spared development or honestly labeled "national sacrifice areas."[118]

Tellingly, the two areas considered most appropriate by the NAS for designation as "national sacrifices"—the Four Corners and Black Hills regions—are those containing the Navajo and "Sioux Complex" of reservations, the largest remaining blocks of acknowledged Indian land and concentrations of land-based indigenous population in the United States. For this reason, many American Indian activists have denounced both the NAS scheme, and the process of environmental destruction which led up to it, as involving not only National Sacrifice Areas, but "National Sacrifice Peoples" as well.[119] At the very least, having the last of their territory zoned "so as to forbid human habitation" would precipitate an ultimate dispersal of each impacted people, causing its disappearance as a "human group" *per se*.[120] As American Indian Movement leader Russell Means has put it, "It's genocide...no more, no less."[121]

Regardless of whether a policy of national sacrifice is ever implemented in the manner envisioned by the NAS, it seems fair to observe that the conditions of dire poverty and environmental degradation fostered on Indian reservations by IRA colonialism have contributed heavily to the making of the contemporary native diaspora in the United States. In combination with the constriction of the indigenous land base brought about through earlier policies of removal, concentration, allotment, and assimilation, these conditions have created a strong and ever-increasing pressure upon reservation residents to "cooperate" with other modern federal programs meant to facilitate the outflow and dispersal of Indians from their residual land base. Chief among these have been termination and relocation.

Termination and Relocation

As the IRA method of administering Indian Country took hold, the government returned to such tasks as "trimming the fat" from federal expenditures allocated to support Indians, largely through manipulation of the size and disposition of the recognized indigenous population.

By 1940, the system of colonial governance on American Indian reservations was largely in place. Only the outbreak of World War II slowed the pace of corporate exploitation, a matter that retarded initiation of maximal "development" activities until the early 1950s. By then, the questions concerning federal and corporate planners had become somewhat technical: what to do with those indigenous nations which had refused reorganization? How to remove the portion of Indian population on even the reorganized reservations whose sheer physical presence served as a barrier to wholesale strip-mining and other profitable enterprises anticipated by the U.S. business community?[122]

The first means to this end was found in a partial resumption of 19th-century assimilationist policies, focused this time on specific peoples, or parts of peoples, rather than upon Indians as a whole. On August 1, 1953, Congress approved House Resolution 108, a measure by which the federal legislature empowered itself to enact statutes "terminating" (i.e., withdrawing recognition from, and thus unilaterally dissolving) selected native peoples, typically those which had rejected reorganization, or who lacked the kind of resources necessitating their maintenance under the IRA.[123]

> Among the [nations] involved were the comparatively large and wealthy Menominee of Wisconsin and the Klamath of Oregon—both

owners of extensive timber resources. Also passed were acts to terminate...the Indians of western Oregon, small Paiute bands in Utah, and
the mixed-bloods of the Uintah and Ouray reservations. Approved, too,
was legislation to transfer administrative responsibility for the Alabama
and Coushatta Indians to the state of Texas...Early in the first session of
the Eighty-Fourth Congress, bills were submitted to [terminate the]
Wyandotte, Ottawa, and Peoria [nations] of Oklahoma. These were
enacted early in August of 1956, a month after passage of legislation
directing the Colville Confederated Tribes of Washington to come up
with a termination plan of their own...During the second administration
of President Dwight D. Eisenhower, Congress enacted three termination
bills relating to...the Choctaw of Oklahoma, for whom the termination
process was never completed, the Catawba of South Carolina, and the
Indians of the southern California *rancherias*.[124]

It is instructive that the man chosen to implement the policy was
Dillon S. Myer, an Indian Commissioner whose only apparent "job
qualification" was in having headed up the internment program
targeting Japanese Americans during World War II.[125] In total, 109
indigenous nations encompassing more than 35,000 people were
terminated before the liquidation process had run its course during
the early 1960s.[126] Only a handful, like the Menominee and the Siletz
of Oregon, were ever "reinstated."[127] Suddenly landless, mostly poor,
and largely unemployed, those who were not "reinstated" mostly
scattered like sand in the wind.[128] Even as they went, they were joined
by a rapidly swelling exodus of people from unterminated reservations, a circumstance fostered by yet another federal program.

Passed in 1956, the "Relocation Act" (PL 959) was extended in the
face of a steady diminishment throughout the first half of the decade
in federal allocations to provide assistance to people living on reservations. The statute provided funding to underwrite the expenses of
any Indian agreeing to move to an urban area, establish a residence,
and undergo a brief period of job training. The *quid pro quo* was that
each person applying for such relocation was required to sign an
agreement that s/he would never return to his or her reservation to
live. It was also specified that all federal support would be withdrawn
after relocatees had spent a short period —often no more than six
weeks—"adjusting" to city life.[129] Under the conditions of near-star-
vation on many reservations, there were many takers; nearly 35,000
people signed up to move to places like Los Angeles, Minneapolis,

San Francisco, Chicago, Denver, Phoenix, Seattle, and Boston during the period 1957-1959 alone.[130]

Although there was ample early indication that relocation was bearing disastrous fruit for those who underwent it—all that was happening was that relocatees were exchanging the familiar squalor of reservation life for that of the alien Indian ghettos that shortly emerged in most major cities—the government accelerated the program during the 1960s. Under the impact of termination and relocation during the 1950s, the proportion of native people who had been "urbanized" rose dramatically, from 13.5 percent at the beginning of the decade to 27.9 percent at the end. During the '60s, relocation alone drove the figure upwards to 44.5 percent. During the 1970s, as the program began to be phased out, the rate of Indian urbanization decreased sharply, with the result that the proportion had risen to "only" 49 percent by 1980.[131] Even without a formal federal relocation effort on a national scale, the momentum of what had been set in motion over an entire generation carried the number into the mid-50th percentile by 1990, and there is no firm indication the trend is abating.[132]

Despite much protestation to the contrary, those who "migrated" to the cities under the auspices of termination and relocation have already begun to join the legions of others, no longer recognized as Indians even by other Indians, who were previously discarded and forgotten along the tortuous route from 1776 to the present.[133] Cut off irrevocably from the centers of their sociocultural existence, they have increasingly adopted arbitrary and abstract methods to signify their "Indianness." Federally sanctioned "Certificates of Tribal Enrollment" have come to replace tangible participation in the political life of their nations as emblems of membership. Federally issued "Certificates of Degree of Indian Blood" have replaced discernible commitment to Indian interests as the ultimate determinant of identity.[134] In the end, by embracing such "standards," Indians are left knowing no more of being Indian than do non-Indians. The process is a cultural form of what, in the physical arena, has been termed "autogenocide."[135]

Looking Ahead

The Indian policies undertaken by the United States during the two centuries since its inception appear on the surface to have been varied, even at times contradictory. Openly genocidal at times, they have more often been garbed, however thinly, in the attire of "humanitarianism." In fact, as the matter was put by Alexis de Tocqueville, the great French commentator on the early American experience, it would occasionally have been "impossible to destroy men with more respect to the laws of humanity."[136] Always, however, there was an underlying consistency in the sentiments which begat policy: to bring about the total dispossession and disappearance of North America's indigenous population. It was this fundamental coherence in U.S. aims, invariably denied by responsible scholars and officials alike, which caused Adolf Hitler to ground his own notions of *lebensraumpolitik* ("politics of living space") in the U.S. example.[137]

Neither Spain nor Britain should be the models of German expansion, but the Nordics of North America, who had ruthlessly pushed aside an "inferior" race to win for themselves soil and territory for the future. To undertake this essential task, sometimes difficult, always cruel—this was Hitler's version of the White Man's Burden.[138]

As early as 1784, A British observer remarked that the intent of the fledgling United States with regard to American Indians was that of "extirpating them totally from the face of the earth, men, women, and children."[139] In 1825, Secretary of State Henry Clay opined that U.S. Indian policy should be predicated in a presumption that the "Indian race" was "destined to extinction" in the face of persistent expansion by "superior" Anglo-Saxon "civilization."[140] During the 1870s, General of the Army Phil Sheridan is known to have called repeatedly for the "complete extermination" of targeted native groups as a means of making the West safe for repopulation by Euroamericans.[141] Subsequent assimilationists demanded the disappearance of any survivors through cultural and genetic absorption by their conquerors.[142] Well into the 20th century, Euroamerica as a whole typically referred—often hopefully—to indigenous people as "the vanishing race," decimated and ultimately subsumed by the far greater number of invaders who had moved in upon their land.[143]

Many of the worst U.S. practices associated with these sensibilities have long since been suspended (arguably, because their goals were accomplished). Yet, large-scale and deliberate dislocation of native people from their land is anything but an historical relic. Probably the most prominent current example is that of the Big Mountain Diné, perhaps the largest remaining enclave of traditionally oriented Indians in the United States. Situated astride an estimated 24 billion tons of the most accessible low-sulfur coal in North America, the entire 13,000-person population of the Big Mountain area are even now being forcibly expelled to make way for the Peabody corporation's massive shovels. There being no place left on the remainder of the Navajo reservation in which to accommodate their sheep-herding way of life, the refugees, many of them elderly, are being "resettled" in off-reservation towns like Flagstaff, Arizona.[144] Some have been sent to Phoenix, Denver, and Los Angeles. All suffer extreme trauma and other maladies resulting from the destruction of their community and consequent "transition."[145]

Another salient illustration is that of the Western Shoshone. Mostly resident on a vast expanse of the Nevada desert secured by their ancestors in the 1863 Treaty of Ruby Valley, the Shoshones have suffered the fate of becoming the "most bombed nation on earth" by virtue of the United States' having located the majority of its nuclear weapons testing facilities in the southern portion of their homeland since 1950. During the late '70s, despite its being unable to demonstrate that it had ever acquired valid title to the territory the Shoshones call Newe Segobia, the U.S. government began to move into the northern area as well, stating an intent to construct the MX missile system there. While the MX plan has by now been dropped, the Shoshones are still being pushed off their land, "freeing" it for use in such endeavors as nuclear waste dumps like the one scheduled to be built at Yucca Mountain over the next few years.[146]

In Alaska, where nearly 200 indigenous peoples were instantly converted into "village corporations" by the 1971 Alaska Native Claims Settlement Act (85 *Stat.* 688), there is a distinct possibility that the entire native population of about 22,000 will be displaced by the demands of tourism, North Slope oil development, and other "developmental" enterprises by some point early in the next century. Already, their land base has been constricted to a complex of tiny "townships" and their traditional economy mostly eradicated by the impacts of commercial fishing, whaling, and sealing, as well as the effects of increasing Arctic industrialization on regional caribou herds and other game animals.[147] Moreover, there is a plan—apparently conceived in all seriousness—to divert the waterflow of the Yukon River southward all the way to the Río Grande, an expedient for supporting continued non-Indian population growth in the arid regions of the "lower forty-eight" states and creating the agribusiness complex in the northern Mexican provinces of Sonora and Chihuahua envisioned in a "free trade agreement" recently proposed by the Bush administration.[148] It seems certain that no traditional indigenous society can be expected to stand up against such an environmental onslaught.

Eventually, if such processes are allowed to run their course, the probability is that a "Final Solution of the Indian Question" will be achieved. The key to this will rest, not in an official return to the pattern of 19th-century massacres or the emergence of some Auschwitz-style extermination center, but in the erosion of sociocultural integrity and confusion of identity afflicting any people subjected to conditions of diaspora. Like water flowing from a leaking bucket, the last self-consciously Indian people will pass into oblivion silently, unnoticed and unremarked. The deaths of cultures destroyed by such means usually occur in this fashion, with a faint whimper rather than resistance and screams of agony.

There are, perhaps, glimmers of hope flickering upon the horizon. One of the more promising is the incipient International Convention on the Rights of Indigenous Peoples. Drafted over the past decade by the United Nations Working Group on Indigenous Populations, the instrument is due for submission to the General Assembly during the summer of 1992. When it is ratified by the latter body in October—the 500th anniversary of the Columbian expedition which unleashed the forces discussed herein—the Convention will at last extend to native peoples the essential international legal protections enjoyed by their colonizers the world over.[149] Should it be adhered to by this "nation of laws," the instrument will effectively bar the United States from completing its quietly ongoing drive to obliterate the remains of Native North America. If not—and the United States has historically demonstrated a truly remarkable tendency to simply ignore those elements of international legality it finds inconvenient—the future of American Indians looks exceedingly grim.[150]

Notes

1. U.S. Bureau of the Census, *Report on Indians Taxed and Indians Not Taxed in the United States (except Alaska) at the Eleventh United States Census: 1890* (Washington, D.C.: U.S. Government Printing Office, 1894), pp. 637-38.

2. Texts of 371 ratified treaties may be found in Kappler, Charles J., comp., *Indian Treaties, 1778-1883* (New York: Interland Publishing Co., [second edition] 1973).

3. U.S. Bureau of the Census, "Persons by Race and Sex for Areas and Places: 1980," Table 69, *1980 Census of the Population, Vol. I: Characteristics of the Population* (Washington, D.C.: U.S. Government Printing Office, 1983), pp. 201-12.

4. National Congress of the American Indian (NCAI) Briefing Paper (Washington, D.C.: NCAI, April 1991).

5. See Forbes, Jack D., "Undercounting Native Americans: The 1980 Census and Manipulation of Racial Identity in the United States," *Wicazo Sa Review*, vol. VI, no. 1 (spring 1990): pp. 2-26.

6. U.S. Bureau of the Census, *1980 Census of the Population, Supplementary Report: American Indian Areas and Alaska Native Villages, 1980* (Washington, D.C.: U.S. Government Printing Office, PC80-S1-13, 1984), p. 24.

7. *Ibid.*, Table I, p. 14.

8. Dobyns, Henry F., *Their Numbers Become Thinned: Native American Population Dynamics in Eastern North America* (Knoxville: University of Tennessee Press, 1983), p. 41.

9. Francis Paul Prucha, *Atlas of American Indian Affairs* (Lincoln: University of Nebraska Press, 1990), pp. 151-57.

10. *1980 Census of the Population, Supplementary Report*, Table I, *op. cit.* The American Indian population reported for Hawaii in 1980 was 2,655.

11. Reginald Horseman, *Expansion and American Indian Policy, 1783-1812* (Ann Arbor: University of Michigan Press, 1967), pp. 6-7.

12. See Abernathy, Thomas Perkins, *Western Lands and the American Revolution* (Albuquerque: University of New Mexico Press, 1979).

13. The complete text of the 1783 Treaty of Paris may be found in Miller, Hunter, ed., *Treaties and Other International Acts of the United States of America* (Washington, D.C.: U.S. Government Printing Office, 1931), pp. 151-57.

14. This interpretation corresponds to conventional understandings of contemporaneous international law ("Discovery Doctrine"). See Williams, Robert A., Jr., *The American Indian in Western Legal Thought: The Discourses of Conquest* (London/New York: Oxford University Press, 1990).

15. Reflections on initial U.S. stature as a legal pariah are more fully developed in Deloria, Vine, Jr., "Sovereignty," in *Economic Development in American Indian Reservations*, ed. Roxanne Dunbar Ortiz and Larry Emerson (Albuquerque: Native American Studies Center, University of New Mexico, 1979).

16. On the Northwest Territory, see Downes, Randolph C., *Council Fires on the Upper Ohio: A Narrative of Indian Affairs on the Upper Ohio until 1795* (Pittsburgh, PA: University of Pittsburgh Press, 1940). On the situation further south, see Cotterill, R. S., *The Southern Indians: The Story of the Five Civilized Tribes Before Removal* (Norman: University of Oklahoma Press, 1954).

17. Burt, A. L., *The United States, Great Britain, and British North America, from the Revolution to the Establishment of Peace after the War of 1812* (New Haven, CT: Yale University Press, 1940), pp. 82-105.

18. Whitaker, Arthur P., *The Spanish-American Frontier, 1783-1795* (Gloucester, MA: P. Smith, 1962; *circa* 1927). Also see Caughey, John W., *McGillivray of the Creeks* (Norman: University of Oklahoma Press, 1938).

19. Edmunds, David R., *Tecumseh and the Quest for American Indian Leadership* (Boston, MA: Little Publishers, 1984).

20. Horseman, *op. cit.*, p. 7.

21. Letter from Schuyler to Congress, July 29, 1783, in *Papers of the Continental Congress, 1774-1789* (Washington, D.C.: National Archives, Item 153, III), pp. 601-7.

22. Letter from Washington to James Duane, September 7, 1783, in Fitzpatrick, John C., ed., *The Writings of George Washington from Original Manuscript Sources, 1745-1799,* vol. XXVII (Washington, D.C.: U.S. Government Printing Office, 1931-1944), pp. 133-40.

23. In actuality, legitimate Conquest Rights never had bearing on the U.S. relationship to indigenous nations, exercise of such rights being restricted to the very confined parameters of what was at the time defined as being prosecution of a "Just War." For details, see Williams, *op. cit.*

24. For analysis, see Sheehan, Bernard W., *Seeds of Extinction: Jeffersonian Philanthropy and the American Indian* (Chapel Hill: University of North Carolina Press, 1973).

25. Quoted from "Report and Resolutions of October 15, 1783," *Journals of the Continental Congress, Vol. XXV* (Washington, D.C.: U.S. Government Printing Office, no date), pp. 681-93.

26. The idea accords quite perfectly with George Washington's notion that all eastern Indians should be pushed into the "illimitable regions of the West," meaning what was then Spanish territory beyond the Mississippi (letter from Washington to Congress, June 17, 1783, in Fitzpatrick, *op. cit.*, pp. 17-18). In reality, however, the United States understood that it possessed no lawful right to unilaterally dispose of the territory in question in this or any other fashion. In purchasing the rights of France (which had gained them from Spain in 1800) to "Louisiana" in 1803, the United States plainly acknowledged indigenous land title in its pledge to Napoleon Bonaparte that it would respect native "enjoyment of their liberty, property and religion they profess." Hence, the United States admitted it was not purchasing land from France, but rather a monopolistic French right within the region to acquire title over specific areas through the negotiated consent of individual Indian nations.

27. Further elaboration on the implications of the cases mentioned herein may be found in Churchill, Ward, "Perversions of Justice: Examining the Doctrine of U.S. Rights to Occupancy in North America," in *Struggle for the Land: Indigenous Resistance to Genocide, Ecocide and Expropriation in Contemporary North America* (Monroe, ME: Common Courage Press, 1992). It should be noted here, however,

that Marshall was hardly a disinterested party in the issue he addressed in *Peck*. Both the Chief Justice and his father were holders of the deeds to 10,000-acre parcels in present-day West Virginia, awarded for services rendered during the revolution, but falling within an area never ceded by its aboriginal owners. See Baker, L., *John Marshall: A Life in Law* (New York: Macmillan Publishers, 1974), p. 80.

28. On the War of 1812, see Lens, Sidney, *The Forging of the American Empire* (New York: Thomas Y. Crowell Co., 1971), pp. 40-61. On Tecumseh, see Sugden, John, *Tecumseh's Last Stand* (Norman: University of Oklahoma Press, 1985). On the Red Sticks, see Martin, Joel W., *Sacred Revolt: The Muskogees' Struggle for a New World* (Boston, MA: Beacon Press, 1991).

29. Griffin, C. C., *The United States and the Disruption of the Spanish Empire, 1810-1822* (New York: Columbia University Press, 1937).

30. McReynolds, Edwin C., *The Seminoles* (Norman: University of Oklahoma Press, 1957).

31. Frederick Merk, *The Monroe Doctrine and American Expansionism* (New York: Alfred A. Knopf Publishers, 1967). Also see Weinberg, Albert K., *Manifest Destiny* (New York: Quadrangle Books, 1963), pp. 73-89.

32. This was the ultimate in playing both ends against the judicial middle. Thereafter, Indians could always be construed as sovereign for purposes of alienating their lands to the United States, thus validating U.S. title to territory it desired, but never sovereign enough to refuse federal demands. See generally, Deloria, Vine, Jr., and Clifford M. Lytle, *American Indians, American Justice* (Austin: University of Texas Press, 1983).

33. See generally, Foreman, Grant, *Advancing the Frontier, 1830-1860* (Norman: University of Oklahoma Press, 1933).

34. Jahoda, Gloria, *The Trail of Tears: The Story of the American Indian Removals, 1813-1855* (New York: Holt, Rinehart and Winston Publishers, 1975). Also see Foreman, Grant, *Indian Removal: The Immigration of the Five Civilized Tribes* (Norman: University of Oklahoma Press, 1953).

35. Driven from Illinois, the main body of Sacs were trapped and massacred—men, women, and children alike—at the juncture of the Bad Axe and Mississippi Rivers in Wisconsin. See Eby, Cecil, *"That Disgraceful Affair": The Black Hawk War* (New York: W.W. Norton Publishers, 1973), pp. 243-61.

36. In many ways, the Seminole "hold outs" were the best guerrilla fighters the United States ever faced. The commitment of 30,000 troops for several years was insufficient to subdue them. Ultimately, the United States broke off the conflict, which was stalemated, and in which it was costing several thousand dollars for each Indian killed. See Downey, Fairfax, *Indian Wars of the United States Army, 1776-1865* (New York: Doubleday Publishers, 1963), pp. 116-17.

37. Washburn, Wilcomb E., *The Indian in America* (New York: Harper Torchbooks, 1975), p. 169.

38. Thornton, Russell, "Cherokee Losses During the Trail of Tears: A New Perspective and a New Estimate," *Ethnohistory*, no. 31 (1984): pp. 289-300.

39. *Ibid.*, p. 293.

40. *1980 Census of the Population, Supplementary Report, op. cit.*

41. King, Duane H., *The Cherokee Nation: A Troubled History* (Knoxville: University of Tennessee Press, 1979), pp. 103-9.

42. Debo, Angie, *A History of the Indians of the United States* (Norman: University of Oklahoma Press, 1977), p. 157.

43. Very little work has been done to document this proliferation of communities, although their existence has been increasingly admitted since the 1960s.

44. James, Marquis, *Andrew Jackson: Border Ruffian* (New York: Grossett and Dunlap Publishers, 1933). Jackson's stated goal was not simply to defeat the Red Sticks, but to "exterminate" them. At least 557 Indians, many of them noncombatants, were killed after being surrounded at the Horseshoe Bend of the Tallapoosa River, in northern Alabama.

45. The text of Jackson's talk of March 23, 1829 was originally published in *Documents and Proceedings relating to the Formation and Progress of a Board in the City of New York, for the Emigration, Preservation, and Improvement of the Aborigines of America* (New York: Indian Board for the Emigration, Preservation, and Improvement of the Aborigines of America, 1829), p. 5.

46. Merk, Frederick, *Manifest Destiny and Mission in American History* (New York: Alfred A. Knopf Publisher, 1963).

47. Quoted in Lens, *op. cit.*, p. 100.

48. Actually, this transcontinental gallop represents a rather reserved script. As early as 1820, Luis de Onis, former Spanish governor of Florida, observed that, "The Americans...believe that their dominion is destined to extend, now to the Isthmus of Panama, and hereafter over all the regions of the New World...They consider themselves superior to the rest of mankind, and look upon their republic as the only establishment upon earth founded on a grand and solid basis, embellished by wisdom, and destined one day to become the sublime colossus of human power, and the wonder of the universe (quoted in Lens, *op. cit.*, pp. 94-95). It is a matter of record that William Henry Seward, Secretary of State under Lincoln and Johnson in the 1860s, advanced a serious plan to annex all of Canada west of Ontario, but was ultimately forced to content himself with acquiring Alaska Territory. See Van Alstyne, R. W., *The Rising American Empire* (London/New York: Oxford University Press, 1960).

49. A map delineating the "permanent" territories assigned these peoples after removal is contained in Forbes, Jack D., *Atlas of Native History* (Davis, CA: D-Q University Press, no date).

50. The federal government recognizes less than half (32) of these nations as still existing; see Morris, John W., Charles R. Goins, and Edward C. McReynolds, *Historical Atlas of Oklahoma* (Norman: University of Oklahoma Press, [third edition] 1986), Map 76.

51. According to *1980 Census of the Population, Supplementary Report* (Table I, *op. cit.*), Oklahoma's Indian population of 169,292 is second only to California's 198,275. The Osage Reservation evidences a population of 4,749 Indians, 12.1 percent of its 39,327 total inhabitants (*ibid.*, p. 22).

52. On the War with Mexico, see Garrison, George Pierce, *Westward Expansion, 1841-1850* (New York: Harper Publishers, 1937).

53. Svaldi, David, *Sand Creek and the Rhetoric of Extermination: A Case-Study in Indian-White Relations* (Washington, D.C.: University Press of America, 1989).

54. Much of this is covered in Andrist, Ralph K., *The Long Death: The Last Days of the Plains Indians* (New York: Collier Books, 1964). Also see Hutton, Paul Andrew, *Phil Sheridan and His Army* (Lincoln: University of Nebraska Press, 1985).

55. Bailey, L.R., *The Long Walk: A History of the Navajo Wars, 1846-68* (Pasadena, CA: Westernlore Publications, 1978).

56. This episode is covered adequately in Lazarus, Edward, *Black Hills, White Justice: The Sioux Nation versus the United States, 1775 to the Present* (New York: Harper Collins Publishers, 1991), pp. 71-95.

57. See Clark, Robert, ed., *The Killing of Chief Crazy Horse* (Lincoln: University of Nebraska Press, 1976), and the concluding chapter of Vestal, Stanley, *Sitting Bull: Champion of the Sioux* (Norman: University of Oklahoma Press, 1957).

58. The imprisonment program is described in some detail in the memoirs of the commandant of Marion Prison, later superintendent of the Carlisle Indian School. See Pratt, Richard Henry, *Battlefield and Classroom: Four Decades with the American Indian, 1867-1904* (New Haven, CT: Yale University Press, [reprint] 1964).

59. *Report on Indians Taxed and Indians Not Taxed, op. cit.*, pp. 637-38.

60. Lazarus, *op. cit.*, p. 29. It should be noted that, contrary to myth, scalping was a practice introduced to the Americas by Europeans, not native people. It was imported by the British—who had previously used it against the Irish—during the 17th century. See Canny, Nicholis P., "The Ideology of English Colonialism: From Ireland to America," *William and Mary Quarterly*, 3rd Series, XXX (1973): pp. 575-98.

61. Stiffarm, Lenore A., and Phil Lane, Jr., "The Demography of Native North America: A Question of American Indian Survival," in *The State of Native America: Genocide, Colonization and Resistance*, ed. M. Annette Jaimes (Boston, MA: South End Press, 1992), p. 35. It is instructive that the Texas state legislature framed its Indian policy as follows: "We recognize no title in the Indian tribes resident within the limits of the state to any portion of the soil thereof; and…we recognize no right of the Government of the United States to make any treaty of limits with the said Indian tribes without the consent of the Government of this state" (quoted in Washburn, *op. cit.*, p. 174). In other words, extermination was intended to be total.

62. Mooney, James M., "Population," in *Handbook of the Indians North of Mexico, Vol. 2*, bulletin no. 30, ed. Frederick W. Dodge (Washington, D.C.: Bureau of American Ethnology, Smithsonian Institution, 1910), pp. 286-87.

63. Cook, Sherburne F., *The Conflict Between the California Indian and White Civilization* (Berkeley: University of California Press, 1976), pp. 282-84.

64. Thornton, Russell, *American Indian Holocaust and Survival: A Population History Since 1492* (Norman: University of Oklahoma Press, 1987), p. 49.

65. Thornton (*ibid.*) estimates the aboriginal North American population to have been about 12.5 million, most of it within what is now the continental United States. Dobyns (*op. cit.*) estimates it as having been as high as 18.5 million. Kirkpatrick Sale, in his *The Conquest of Paradise: Christopher Columbus and the Columbian Legacy* (New York: Alfred A. Knopf, 1990), splits the difference, placing the figure at 15 million. Extreme attrition due to disease and colonial warfare had already occurred prior to the American War of Independence. Something on the order of two million survivors in 1776 therefore seems a reasonable estimate. Whatever the exact number in that year, it had been reduced to 237,196 according to U.S. census data for 1900. See U.S. Bureau of the Census, "Indian Population by

State, 1890-1930," Table 2, *Fifteenth Census of the United States, 1930: The Indian Population of the United States and Alaska* (Washington, D.C.: U.S. Government Printing Office, 1937), p. 3.

66. Cook, *op. cit.*, p. 284.

67. Berthrong, Donald J., *The Cheyenne and Arapaho Ordeal: Reservation and Agency Life in the Indian Territory, 1875-1907* (Norman: University of Oklahoma Press, 1976). Also see Sandoz, Mari, *Cheyenne Autumn* (New York: Avon Books, 1964).

68. Thrapp, Dan L., *The Conquest of Apacheria* (Norman: University of Oklahoma Press, 1967).

69. Beal, Merril, *I Will Fight No More Forever: Chief Joseph and the Nez Percé War* (Seattle: University of Washington Press, 1963).

70. Carley, Kenneth, *The Sioux Uprising of 1862* (St. Paul: Minnesota Historical Society, 1961).

71. Wilson, Edmund, *Apology to the Iroquois* (New York: Farrar, Strauss, and Cudahy Publishers, 1960).

72. As of 1980, a grand total of 582 members of these amalgamated peoples were reported as living on the Stockbridge Reservation. See *1980 Census of the Population, Supplementary Report*, Table I, *op. cit.*

73. The next major leap in this direction was passage of the Assimilative Crimes Act (30 *Stat.* 717) in 1898, applying state, territorial, and district criminal codes to "federal enclaves," such as Indian reservations. See generally, Clinton, Robert N., "Development of Criminal Jurisdiction on Reservations: A Journey Through a Jurisdictional Maze," *Arizona Law Review*, vol. 18, no. 3 (1976), pp. 503-83.

74. Overall, see McDonnell, Janet A., *The Dispossession of the American Indian, 1887-1934* (Bloomington/Indianapolis: Indiana University Press, 1991).

75. As is stated in the current procedures for enrollment provided by the Cherokee Nation of Oklahoma, "Many descendants of the Cherokee Indians can neither be certified nor qualify for tribal membership in the Cherokee Nation because their ancestors were not enrolled during the final enrollment [during allotment, 1899-1906]. Unfortunately, these ancestors did not meet the [federal] requirements for the final enrollment. The requirements at the time were…having a permanent residence within the Cherokee Nation (now the 14 northeastern counties of Oklahoma). If the ancestors had…settled in the states of Arkansas, Kansas, Missouri, or Texas, they lost their citizenship within the Cherokee Nation at that time."

76. Otis, D.S., *The Dawes Act and the Allotment of Indian Land* (Norman: University of Oklahoma Press, 1973).

77. Olson, James S., and Raymond Wilson, *Native Americans in the Twentieth Century* (Urbana: University of Illinois Press, 1984), pp. 82-83.

78. Bird, Kirk Kicking, and Karen Ducheneaux, *One Hundred Million Acres* (New York: Macmillan Publishers, 1973).

79. The powers of individual agents in this regard accrued from an amendment (26 *Stat.* 794) made in 1891. The language describing these powers comes from Deloria and Lytle, *op. cit.*, p. 10.

80. This is known as the "Heirship Problem," meaning that if a family head with four children began with a 160-acre parcel of marginal land in 1900, his/her heirs would each inherit 40 acres somewhere around 1920. If each of these heirs, in turn, had four children, then their heirs would inherit 10 acres, circa 1940. Following the

same formula, their heirs would have inherited two and a half acres each in 1960, and their heirs would have received about one-half acre each in 1980. In actuality, many families have been much larger during the 20th century—as is common among peoples recovering from genocide—and contemporary descendants of the original allottees often find themselves measuring their "holdings" in square inches. For a fuller discussion of the issue, and a description of the material circumstances otherwise confronting Indians during the early 20th century, see the opening chapters of Deloria, Vine, Jr., and Clifford M. Lytle, *The Nations Within: The Past and Future of American Indian Sovereignty (New York: Pantheon Books, 1984).*

81. Robbins, Rebecca L., *"Self-Determination and Subordination: The Past, Present and Future of American Indian Governance,"* in *The State of Native America, op. cit.*, p. 93. The quote from Leupp comes from his book, *The Indian and His Problem* (New York: Charles Scribner and Sons, Publishers, 1910), p. 93; that from Burke from a letter to William Williamson on September 16, 1921 (William Williamson Papers, Box 2, File—Indian Matters, Misc., I.D. Weeks Library, University of South Dakota).

82. Among other things, the decision meant that the United States had decided it could unilaterally absolve itself of any obligation or responsibility it had incurred under provision of any treaty with any indigenous nation while simultaneously considering the Indians to still be bound by *their* treaty commitments. See Estin, Ann Laquer, *"Lonewolf v. Hitchcock*: The Long Shadow," in *The Aggressions of Civilization: Federal Indian Policy Since the 1880s,* ed. Sandra L. Cadwallader and Vine Deloria, Jr. (Philadelphia, PA: Temple University Press, 1984), pp. 215-45. This was an utterly illegitimate posture under international custom and convention at the time, a matter amply reflected in contemporary international black letter law. See Sinclair, Sir Ian, *The Vienna Convention on the Law of Treaties* (Manchester: Manchester University Press, [second edition] 1984).

83. Much of this is covered—proudly—in Pratt, *op. cit.* Also see Fuchs, Estelle, and Robert J. Havighurst, *To Live on this Earth: American Indian Education* (Garden City, NY: Anchor Books, 1973).

84. Adams, Evelyn C., *American Indian Education: Government Schools and Economic Progress* (Morningside Heights, NY: King's Crown Press, 1946), pp. 55-56, 70.

85. The phrase used was picked up by the author in a 1979 conversation with Floyd Red Crow Westerman, a Sisseton Dakota who was sent to a boarding school at age six. For a broader statement of the same theme, see Deloria, Vine, Jr., "Education and Imperialism," *Integrateducation*, vol. XIX, nos. 1-2 (January 1982): pp. 58-63. For ample citation of the federal view, see Ogbu, J.U., "Cultural Discontinuities and Schooling," *Anthropology and Education Quarterly*, vol. 12, no. 4 (1982): pp. 1-10.

86. On adoption policies, including those pertaining to so-called "blind" adoptions (where children are prevented by law from ever learning their parents' or tribe's identities), see Walker, Tillie Blackbear, "American Indian Children: Foster Care and Adoptions," in *Conference on Educational and Occupational Needs of American Indian Women,* U.S. Office of Education, Office of Educational Research and Development, National Institute of Education (Washington, D.C.: U.S. Government Printing Office, 1980), pp. 185-210.

87. The entire program involving forced transfer of Indian children is contrary to Article II (d) of the United Nations 1948 Convention on Punishment and Preven-

tion of the Crime of Genocide. See Brownlie, Ian, *Basic Documents on Human Rights* (Oxford: Clarendon Press, 1982), p.32.

88. *American Indian Holocaust and Survival, op. cit.,* p. 227.

89. These estimates have been arrived at by deducting the reservation population totals from the overall census figures deployed in Prucha (*op. cit.*), and then subtracting the urban population totals used by Russell Thornton (see note 88, above).

90. The United States, as is well known, undertook the Spanish-American War in 1898 primarily to acquire overseas colonies, notably the Philippines and Cuba (for which Puerto Rico was substituted at the last moment). It also took the opportunity to usurp the government of Hawai'i, about which it had been expressing ambitions since 1867, and to obtain a piece of Samoa in 1899. This opened the door to its assuming "protectorate" responsibility over Guam and other German colonies after World War I, and many of the Micronesian possessions of Japan after World War II. See Pratt, Julius, *The Expansionists of 1898* (Baltimore, MD: Johns Hopkins University Press, 1936). Also see O'Connor, Richard, *Pacific Destiny: An Informal History of the U.S. in the Far East, 1776-1968* (Boston, MA: Little, Brown and Co., 1969).

91. Parlow, Anita, *Cry, Sacred Ground: Big Mountain, USA* (Washington, D.C.: Christic Institute, 1988), p. 30.

92. Olson and Wilson, *op. cit.,* p. 181.

93. For a good overview, see Miner, Craig H., *The Corporation and the Indian: Tribal Sovereignty and Industrial Civilization in Indian Territory, 1865-1907* (Columbia: University of Missouri Press, 1976).

94. This is brought out in thinly veiled fashion in official studies commissioned at the time. See, for example, U.S. House of Representatives, Committee of One Hundred, *The Indian Problem: Resolution of the Committee of One Hundred Appointed by the Secretary of Interior and Review of the Indian Problem* (Washington, D.C.: H. Doc. 149, Ser. 8392, 68th Cong., 1st Sess., 1925). Also see Merriam, Lewis, *et al., The Problem of Indian Administration* (Baltimore, MD: Johns Hopkins University Press, 1928).

95. This was standard colonialist practice during the same period. See Lindsey, Mark Frank, *The Acquisition and Government of Backward Territory in International Law* (London: Longmans, Green Publishers, 1926).

96. For what may be the first application of the term "internal colonies" to analysis of the situation of American Indians in the United States, see Thomas, Robert K., "Colonialism: Classic and Internal," *New University Thought*, vol. 4, no. 4 (winter 1966-67).

97. For the best account of how the IRA "package" was assembled, see the relevant chapters of *The Nations Within, op. cit.*

98. The classic example of this occurred at the Hopi reservation, where some 85 percent of all eligible voters actively boycotted the IRA referendum in 1936. Indian Commissioner John Collier then counted these abstentions as "aye" votes, making it appear as if the Hopis had been nearly unanimous in affirming reorganization rather than overwhelmingly rejecting it. See LaFarge, Oliver, *Running Narrative of the Organization of the Hopi Tribe of Indians,* unpublished manuscript in the LaFarge Collection, University of Texas at Austin. In general, the IRA referendum process was similar to—and served essentially the same purpose as—those more recently

orchestrated abroad by the State Department and CIA; see Herman, Edward S., and Frank Brodhead, *Demonstration Elections: U.S.-Staged Elections in the Dominican Republic, Vietnam, and El Salvador* (Boston, MA: South End Press, 1984).

99. Robbins, *op. cit.*, p. 95.

100. See generally, Churchill, Ward, and Winona LaDuke, "Native North America: The Political Economy of Radioactive Colonization," in this book, *op. cit.*, pp. 241-66.

101. Josephy, Alvin, "Murder of the Southwest," *Audubon Magazine* (September 1971): p. 42.

102. Johansen, Bruce, and Roberto Maestas, *Wasi'chu: The Continuing Indian Wars* (New York: Monthly Review Press, 1979), p. 162. The minimum rate was established by the Federal Coal Leasing Act of 1975, applicable everywhere in the United States except Indian reservations.

103. Olson and Wilson, *op. cit.*, p. 200.

104. The term "super-profits" is used in the manner defined by Barnet, Richard J., and Ronald E. Müller in their *Global Reach: The Power of the Multinational Corporations* (New York: Touchstone Books, 1974).

105. U.S. Department of Interior, Bureau of Indian Affairs, *Indian Service Population and Labor Force Estimates* (Washington, D.C.: U.S. Government Printing Office, 1989). The study shows one-third of the 635,000 reservation-based Indians surveyed had an annual income of less than $7,000.

106. U.S. Senate, Committee on Labor and Human Resources, *Guaranteed Job Opportunity Act: Hearing on S. 777* (Washington, D.C.: 100th Cong., 1st Sess., 23 March 1987), Appendix A.

107. The classic image of this is that of Emma Yazzie, an elderly and very traditional Diné who subsists on her flock of sheep, standing forlornly before a gigantic Peabody coal shovel that is digging up her scrubby grazing land on Black Mesa. The coal is to produce electricity for Phoenix and Las Vegas, but Yazzie has never had electricity (or running water) in her home. She gains nothing from the enterprise. To the contrary, her very way of life is being destroyed before her eyes. See Johansen and Maestas, *op. cit.*, p. 141.

108. The term "underdevelopment" is used in the sense defined by Frank, Andre Gunder, in his *Capitalism and Underdevelopment in Latin America* (New York: Monthly Review Press, 1967).

109. U.S. Bureau of the Census, *A Statistical Profile of the American Indian Population* (Washington, D.C.: U.S. Government Printing Office, 1984). Also see U.S. Department of Health and Human Services, *Chart Series Book* (Washington, D.C.: Public Health Service HE20.9409.988, 1988).

110. The terminology accrues from Galeano, Eduardo, *The Open Veins of Latin America: Five Centuries of the Pillage of a Continent* (New York: Monthly Review Press, 1973).

111. Thus far, the only people that has been able to turn this around has been the Northern Cheyenne, which won a 1976 lawsuit to have Class I environmental protection standards applied to their reservation, thereby halting construction of two coal-fired generating plants before they began. The BIA had already waived such protections on the Cheyennes' "behalf." See Johansen and Maestas, *op. cit.*, p. 174.

112. Weyler, Rex, *Blood of the Land: The U.S. Government and Corporate War Against the American Indian Movement* (New York: Everest House Publishers, 1982), pp. 154-55.

113. Barry, Tom, "Bury My Lungs at Red Rock," *The Progressive* (February 1979): pp. 197-99.

114. On tailings and associated problems, such as radon gas emissions, see Sorenson, J. B., *Radiation Issues: Government Decision Making and Uranium Expansion in Northern New Mexico* (Albuquerque, NM: San Juan Regional Study Group, Working Paper 14, 1978). On carcinogenic/mutogenic effects, see J. M. Samet, *et al.*, "Uranium Mining and Lung Cancer in Navajo Men," *New England Journal of Medicine,* no. 310 (1984): pp. 1481-84. Also see Tso, Harold, and Laura Mangum Shields, "Navajo Mining Operations: Early Hazards and Recent Interventions," *New Mexico Journal of Science,* vol. 20, no. 1 (June 1980).

115. Hoppe, Richard, "A stretch of desert along Route 66—the Grants Belt—is chief locale for U.S. uranium," *Engineering and Mining Journal* (November 1978). Also see Owens, Nancy J., "Can Tribes Control Energy Development?" in *American Indians and Energy Development,* ed. Joseph Jorgenson (Cambridge, MA: Anthropology Resource Center, 1978).

116. Irvin, Amelia, "Energy Development and the Effects of Mining on the Lakota Nation," *Journal of Ethnic Studies,* vol. 10, no. 2 (spring 1982).

117. Schumacher, Elouise, "440 billion gallons: Hanford wastes would fill 900 King Domes," *Seattle Times* (April 13, 1991).

118. Johansen and Maestas, *op. cit.,* p. 154. They are referring to Box, Thadis, *et al., Rehabilitation Potential for Western Coal Lands* (Cambridge, MA: Ballinger Publishing Co., 1974). The book is the published version of a study commissioned by the National Academy of Sciences and submitted to the Nixon administration in 1972.

119. Means, Russell, "Fighting Words on the Future of Mother Earth," *Mother Jones* (December 1980): p. 27.

120. Bringing about the destruction of an identifiable "human racial, ethnical, or racial group," as such, is and always has been the defining criterion of genocide. As the matter was framed by Raphael Lemkin, who coined the term: "Generally speaking, genocide does not necessarily mean the immediate destruction of a nation, *except when* accomplished by mass killing of all the members of a nation. It is intended rather to signify a coordinated plan of different actions aimed at destruction of the essential foundations of the life of national groups, with the aim of annihilating the groups themselves. The objective of such a plan would be disintegration of the political and social institutions, of culture, language, national feelings, religion, and the economic existence of national groups, and the destruction of personal security, liberty, health, dignity, and the lives of individuals belonging to such groups. Genocide is the destruction of the national group as an entity, and the actions involved are directed against individuals, not in their individual capacity but as members of the national group [emphasis added]"; see Lemkin, Raphael, *Axis Rule in Occupied Europe* (Concord, NH: Carnegie Endowment for International Peace/Rumford Press, 1944), p. 79. The view is reflected in the 1948 Convention on Punishment and Prevention of the Crime of Genocide; see Brownlie, *op. cit.*

121. Means, *op. cit.*

122. Robbins, *op. cit.*, p. 97.

123. The complete text of House Resolution 108 appears in Part II of Edward H. Spicer's *A Short History of the United States* (New York: Van Nostrum Publishers, 1968).

124. Officer, James E., "Termination as Federal Policy: An Overview," in *Indian Self-Rule: First-Hand Accounts of Indian-White Relations from Roosevelt to Reagan*, ed. Kenneth R. Philp (Salt Lake City, UT: Howe Brothers Publishers, 1986), p. 125.

125. Drinnon, Richard, *Keeper of Concentration Camps: Dillon S. Myer and American Racism* (Berkeley: University of California Press, 1987).

126. Butler, Raymond V., "The Bureau of Indian Affairs Activities Since 1945," *Annals of the American Academy of Political and Social Science*, no. 436 (1978): pp. 50-60. The last dissolution, that of the Oklahoma Ponca, was delayed in committee and was not consummated until 1966.

127. See generally, Peroff, Nicholas, *Menominee DRUMS: Tribal Termination and Restoration, 1954-1974* (Norman: University of Oklahoma Press, 1982).

128. LaFarge, Oliver, "Termination of Federal Supervision: Disintegration and the American Indian," *Annals of the American Academy of Political and Social Science*, no. 311 (May 1975): pp. 56-70.

129. See generally, Fixico, Donald L., *Termination and Relocation: Federal Indian Policy, 1945-1960* (Albuquerque: University of New Mexico Press, 1986).

130. O'Brien, Sharon, *American Indian Tribal Governments* (Norman: University of Oklahoma Press, 1989), p. 86.

131. U.S. Bureau of the Census, *General Social and Economic Characteristics: United States Summary* (Washington, D.C.: U.S. Government Printing Office, 1983), p. 92. Also see *American Indian Holocaust and Survival, op. cit.*, p. 227.

132. NCAI Briefing Paper, *op. cit.*

133. For use of the term "migration" to describe the effects of termination and relocation, see Gundlach, James H., Nelson P. Reid, and Alden E. Roberts, "Native American Migration and Relocation," *Pacific Sociological Review*, no. 21 (1978): pp. 117-27. On the "discarded and forgotten," see American Indian Policy Review Commission, Task Force Ten, *Report on Terminated and Nonfederally Recognized Tribes* (Washington, D.C.: U.S. Government Printing Office, 1976).

134. Alan L. Sokin, *The Urban American Indian* (Lexington, MA: Lexington Books, 1978).

135. The term was coined in the mid-1970s to describe the self-destructive behavior exhibited by the Khmer Rouge regime in Kampuchea (Cambodia) in response to genocidal policies earlier extended against that country by the United States. For analysis, see Chomsky, Noam, and Edward S. Herman, *After the Cataclysm: Postwar Indochina and the Reconstruction of Imperial Ideology* (Boston, MA: South End Press, 1979).

136. Tocqueville, Alexis de, *Democracy in America* (New York: Harper & Row Publishers, 1966), p. 312.

137. "Hitler's concept of concentration camps as well as the practicality of genocide owed much, so he claimed, to his studies of British and United States history. He admired the camps for Boer prisoners in South Africa and for the Indians in the wild West; and often praised to his inner circle the efficiency of America's extermination—by starvation and uneven combat—of the red savages who could not be tamed by captivity." Toland, John, *Adolf Hitler* (New York: Doubleday and Co., 1976), p. 802.

138. Rich, Norman, *Hitler's War Aims: Ideology, the Nazi State, and the Course of Expansion* (New York: W.W. Norton Publishers, 1973), p. 8. Rich is relying primarily on the secret, but nonetheless official policy position articulated by Hitler during a meeting on November 5, 1937 and recorded by his adjutant, Freidrich Hossbach. The "Hossbach Memorandum" is contained in *Trial of the Major War Criminals before the International Military Tribunal, Proceedings and Documents*, vol. 25 (Nuremberg: 1947-1949), pp. 402-6.

139. Smyth, John F. D., *A Tour of the United States of America* (London: privately published, 1784), p. 346.

140. Quoted in Horsman, Reginald, *Race and Manifest Destiny: The Origins of Racial Anglo-Saxonism* (Cambridge, MA: Harvard University Press, 1981), p. 198.

141. See the various quotes in Hutton, *op. cit.*

142. Fritz, Henry E., *The Movement for Indian Assimilation, 1860-1890* (Philadelphia, PA: University of Pennsylvania Press, 1963).

143. The classic articulation, of course, is Dixon, Joseph K., *The Vanishing Race* (1913; New York: recently reprinted by Bonanza Books). An excellent examination of the phenomenon may be found in Steiner, Stan, *The Vanishing White Man* (Norman: University of Oklahoma Press, 1976).

144. Parlow, *op. cit.* Also see Kammer, Jerry, *The Second Long Walk: The Navajo-Hopi Land Dispute* (Albuquerque: University of New Mexico Press, 1980).

145. Scudder, Thayer, *et al.*, *No Place to Go: Effects of Compulsory Relocation on Navajos* (Philadelphia, PA: Institute for the Study of Human Issues, 1982).

146. Thorpe, Dagmar, *Newe Segobia: The Western Shoshone People and Land* (Battle Mountain, NV: Western Shoshone Sacred Lands Association, 1981). Also see Morris, Glenn T., "The Battle for Newe Segobia: The Western Shoshone Land Rights Struggle," in *Critical Issues in Native North America, Vol. II*, ed. Ward Churchill (Copenhagen: IWGIA Document 68, 1991), pp. 86-98.

147. Barry, M. C., *The Alaska Pipeline: The Politics of Oil and Native Land Claims* (Bloomington/Indianapolis: Indiana University Press, 1975). Also see Berger, Thomas R., *Village Journey: The Report of the Alaska Native Review Commission* (New York: Hill and Wang Publishers, 1985).

148. The plan is known by the title of its sponsoring organization, the North American Water and Power Association (NAWAPA). It is covered in Reisner, Mark, *Cadillac Desert: The American West and Its Disappearing Water* (New York: Viking Press, 1986).

149. For analysis, see Anaya, S. James, "The Rights of Indigenous Peoples and International Law in Historical and Contemporary Perspective," in *American Indian Law: Cases and Materials*, Robert N. Clinton, Nell Jessup Newton, and Monroe E. Price (Charlottesville, VA: Michie Co., 1991), pp. 1257-69. Also see Morris, Glenn T., "International Law and Politics: Toward a Right to Self-Determination for Indigenous Peoples," in *The State of Native America, op. cit.*, pp. 55-86.

150. This includes a rather large array of covenants and conventions pertaining to everything from the binding effect of treaties to the Laws of War. It also includes Ronald Reagan's postulation, advanced in October 1985, that the International Court of Justice holds no authority other than in matters of trade. A detailed examination of United States posturing in this regard may be found in LeBlanc, Lawrence W., *The United States and the Genocide Convention* (Durham, NC: Duke University Press, 1991).

DEATH SQUADS IN THE UNITED STATES
Confessions of a Government Terrorist

The reality is a continuum which connects Indian flesh sizzling over Puritan fires and Vietnamese flesh roasting under American napalm. The reality is the compulsion of a sick society to rid itself of men like Nat Turner and Crazy Horse, George Jackson and Richard Oaks, whose defiance uncovers the hypocrisy of a declaration affirming everyone's right to liberty and life. The reality is an overwhelming greed which began with the theft of a continent and continues with the merciless looting of every country on the face of the earth which lacks the strength to defend itself.

— Richard Lundstrom

During the first half of the 1970s, the American Indian Movement (AIM) came to the forefront of a drive to realize the rights of treaty-guaranteed national sovereignty on behalf of North America's indigenous peoples. For the government and major corporate interests of the United States, this liberatory challenge represented a considerable threat, given on the one hand that Indians possess clear legal and moral rights to the full exercise of self-determination and, on the other hand, that their reserved land base contains substantial quantities of critical mineral resources. Upwards of half of all known "domestic" U.S. uranium reserves lie within the boundaries of present-day Indian reservations, as do as much as a quarter of the high-grade low-sulfur coal, a fifth of the oil and natural gas, and major deposits of copper and other metals.[1] Loss of internal colonial control over these items would confront U.S. elites with significant strategic and economic problems.

Predictably, the government set out to liquidate AIM's political effectiveness as a means of maintaining and reinforcing the federal system of administering Indian Country. For a number of reasons, the crux of the conflict came to be situated on the Pine Ridge Sioux Reservation, home of the Oglala Lakota people, in what is now the state of South Dakota. Throughout the mid-'70s, what amounted to low-intensity warfare was conducted against AIM in this remote locale by the FBI and a surrogate organization calling itself Guardians of the Oglala Nation (GOONs).[2] The Bureau and its various apologists—often "scholarly experts" like Athan Theoharis and Alan Dershowitz—have consistently denied not only that a *de facto* counterinsurgency effort was mounted on Pine Ridge, but also any direct relationship between the FBI and the GOONs. Those uttering claims to the contrary have been publicly dubbed "left wing McCarthyites," accused of engaging in "innuendo" and attributing "guilt by association."[3]

Writer Peter Matthiessen, one of the more comprehensive and careful analysts of the "AIM/GOON Wars," has also been the target of two frivolous but massive and prolonged lawsuits, designed to suppress his 1983 book on the topic, *In the Spirit of Crazy Horse*. Matthiessen's sins were allegedly a "defaming of the characters" of David Price, an agent heavily involved in the repression of AIM, and William "Wild Bill" Janklow, former attorney general and then governor of the State of South Dakota, who headed one of the many white vigilante groups operating in the Pine Ridge area during the mid-'70s. Both Price and Janklow, it appears, received substantial support from governmental and corporate quarters—as well as financing from such overtly right wing entities as the Heritage Foundation—in keeping the Matthiessen study off the shelves for nearly a decade.[4] As a consequence, it was not until the spring of 1991 that the American public was accorded an opportunity to read what this much celebrated author has to say about the events in question.

A major chink in the stone wall of official and quasiofficial "plausible deniability" has now appeared. This assumes the form of Duane Brewer, former second in command of the Bureau of Indian Affairs (BIA) police and eventual head of the Highway Safety Program on Pine Ridge. Along with his superior in the constabulary, Delmar Eastman, Brewer served by his own admission as a primary commander of the reservation GOON squads and participated directly in many of the organization's most virulent anti-AIM actions. In a previously undisclosed interview, undertaken by independent filmmakers Michel Dubois and Kevin Barry McKiernan in 1987 and televised in part through a 1990 PBS television documentary, Brewer does much to nail down exactly how the GOONs were utilized by the FBI within a wider campaign to destroy AIM and "Indian militancy" more generally.[5] His statements should go far in establishing that the federal government has resorted to employment of outright death squads within the borders as an integral aspect of its programs of domestic political and social repression.

The Pine Ridge Bloodbath

During the three-year period running from roughly mid-1973 through mid-1976, at least 69 members and supporters of AIM died violently on Pine Ridge (see accompanying list, "AIM Casualties on Pine Ridge, 1973-76" on pp. 256-260). Nearly 350 others suffered serious physical assaults, including gunshot wounds and stabbings, beatings administered with baseball bats and tire irons, having their cars rammed and run off the road at high speed, and their homes torched as they slept.[6] Researchers Bruce Johansen and Roberto Maestas have determined that the politically motivated death toll on Pine Ridge made the murder rate for the reservation 170 per 100,000 during the crucial period.[7]

> By comparison, Detroit, the reputed "murder capital of the United States," had a rate of 20.2 per 100,000 in 1974. The U.S. average rate was 9.7 per 100,000, with the average for large cities as follows: Chicago, 15.9; New York City, 16.3; Washington, D.C., 13.4; Los Angeles, 12.9; Seattle, 5.6; and Boston, 5.6. An estimated 20,000 persons were murdered in the United States in 1974. In a nation of 200 million persons, a murder rate comparable with that of Pine Ridge between 1973 and 1976 would have left 340,000 persons dead for political reasons in one year; 1.32 million in three. A similar rate for a city of 500,000 would have produced 850 political murders in a year; 2,550 in three. For a metropolis of 5 million, the figures would have been 8,500 in one year and 25,500 in three.[8]

As Johansen and Maestas go on to point out, their figures do not include the "typical" high rate of fatalities experienced on Pine Ridge and most other American Indian reservations. Rather, the "murder rate of 170 per 100,000—almost nine times that of Detroit—takes into account only deaths caused by the *physical* repression of Indian resistance."[9] Nowhere in North America has there been a comparable rate of homicide during the twentieth century. To find counterparts, one must turn to contexts of U.S.-sponsored political repression in the Third World.

> The political murder rate at Pine Ridge…was almost equivalent to that in Chile during the three years after a military coup supported by the United States deposed and killed President Salvador Allende…Based on Chile's population of 10 million, the estimated fifty thousand persons killed in the three years of political repression in Chile at about the same time (1973-1976) roughly paralleled the murder rate at Pine Ridge.[10]

Under provision of the Major Crimes Act (18 U.S.C.A. § 1153), murder on an Indian reservation is an offense falling under jurisdiction of "federal authorities." Since at least as early as 1953, this has specifically meant the FBI.[11] Not one of the murders of AIM people on Pine Ridge during the mid-'70s was ever solved by the Bureau, despite the fact that in a number of instances the assailants were identified by one or more eyewitnesses. In many cases, investigations were never opened. When queried with regard to this apparent inactivity on the part of his personnel, George O'Clock, Assistant Special Agent in Charge (ASAC) of the FBI's Rapid City Resident Agency (under which jurisdiction Pine Ridge falls) until mid-1975, pleaded "lack of man-power" as the reason.[12] At the very moment he spoke, O'Clock was overseeing the highest ratio of agents to citizens over a sustained period enjoyed by any resident agency in the history of the Bureau.[13] As he himself later put it, the normal complement of personnel for Rapid City was four agents, three investigators, plus the ASAC. During the anti-AIM campaign, however, things were different:

> Most of the time before the 1970s, there were just four agents assigned to this resident agency and we covered the western half of South Dakota…which included the Rosebud and Pine Ridge Indian Reservations. Then, from 1972-73 to the time of my retirement, the resident agency almost tripled in size insofar as agents and FBI personnel were concerned…[Actually, by the summer of 1975, the resident agency had more than quadrupled]; there were probably eighteen agents assigned there. [After that], there were many, many more, at different times, thirty to forty agents working….[14]

All told, O'Clock admits, between January of 1973 and the end of 1975, "there were at least 2,500 different Bureau personnel temporarily assigned to [his office]." A peak number of "probably 350" was reached during July of 1975, with an average of "about 200 to 250" maintained for the six months beginning on July 1 and ending on December 31, 1975. Far from there being a "lack," O'Clock now acknowledges there were in fact "*too many agents* in the area [emphasis added]" to be effective, or even to be kept track of by administrators. Consequently, by August of 1975, Norman Zigrossi, who succeeded O'Clock as Rapid City ASAC, was actively reducing a *100-agent surplus* in his roster.[15] In other words, the Rapid City office was consistently overstaffed throughout the crucial three-year period, and at times the entire western South Dakota region was absolutely saturated with FBI personnel. It is also readily apparent that these personnel engaged in a virtual orgy of investigative and other activities while posted to the Pine Ridge locale.

For instance, while professing to be too shorthanded to assign agents to look into the killing and maiming of AIM members and supporters, O'Clock managed to find ample resources to investigate *the victims*. Some 316,000 separate investigative file classifications were amassed by the Rapid City FBI office with regard to AIM activities during the 1973 siege of Wounded Knee alone.[16] This enormous expenditure of investigative energy made possible the filing of 562 federal charges against various AIM members during the second half of 1973.[17] The result, after more than two years of trials, was a paltry 15 convictions—far and away the lowest yield of guilty verdicts to investigative hours invested and charges filed in FBI history—all of them on such trivial matters as "interference with a postal inspector in performance of his lawful duty."[18]

Nonetheless, O'Clock's effort cannot be assessed as a failure. The method inherent to his endeavor was perhaps best explained in 1974 by Colonel Volney Warner, a counterinsurgency warfare specialist and military advisor to the FBI on Pine Ridge, when he observed that convictions weren't the point. By virtue of simply causing charges, however spurious, to be filed, Warner said, the Bureau was able to keep "many of AIM's most militant leaders and followers under indictment, in jail or [with] warrants out for their arrest." Concomitantly, the movement's financial resources were necessarily diverted to legal defense efforts. By pursuing such tactics, Warner argued, AIM could be effectively neutralized as a political force: "The government can win, even if no one goes to [prison]."[19] Meanwhile, what the U.S. Commission on Civil Rights described as "a reign of terror" on Pine

Ridge continued, unimpeded by interference from the FBI.[20] Indeed, all indications are that the Bureau not only encouraged, but actively aided and abetted it.

The GOONs and the FBI

A number of studies have concluded the GOONs were responsible for the bulk of the AIM fatalities on Pine Ridge. In those cases in which witnesses identified the murderers, the culprits were invariably known members of the reservation GOON squad. Yet, in most instances, no formal FBI investigation resulted.

On the afternoon of March 21, 1975, Edith Eagle Hawk, her four-month-old daughter, and three-year-old grandson were killed when their car was forced into a deep ditch alongside Highway 44, between Scenic (South Dakota) and Rapid City. Edith Eagle Hawk was a defense (alibi) witness for AIM member Jerry Bear Shield, who was at the time accused of killing a GOON, William Jack Steele, on March 9 (charges against Bear Shield were later dropped when it was revealed Steele had probably died at the hands of GOON associates). The driver of the car which struck the Eagle Hawk vehicle—Albert Coomes, a white on-reservation rancher who was allowed by the Wilsonites to serve as an active GOON—also lost control of his car, went into the ditch and was killed. Eugene Eagle Hawk, who was badly injured but survived the crash, identified a second occupant of the Coomes car as being Mark Clifford, a prominent GOON. BIA and FBI reports on the matter fail to make mention of Clifford (who had survived and escaped the scene).[21]

On other occasions, the victims themselves, or their associates, were investigated and sometimes charged—with attendant publicity to establish the "violence prone" characteristics of their organization—with having perpetrated the violence directed against them.

> On June 19, 1973, brothers (and AIM supporters) Clarence and Vernal Cross were sitting in their car by the side of the road near Pine Ridge [village] when they began receiving rifle fire. Clarence died of gunshot wounds. Vernal, severely injured [by a bullet through the throat] but alive, was charged by Delmar Eastman with the murder of his brother (charges were later dropped). Nine-year-old Mary Ann Little Bear, who was riding past the Cross car in a vehicle driven by her father at the time

of the shooting, was struck in the face by a stray round, suffering a wound which cost her an eye. Witnesses named three GOONs—Francis Randall, John Hussman and Woody Richards—as the gunmen involved [but no investigation resulted].[22]

The tally in these two incidents alone stands at five fatalities, three serious injuries, one blatantly false charge filed by the BIA police, and no subsequent FBI investigations. And, to be sure, there are many comparable incidents. The question, of course, is why such a pattern might exist. That the GOONs had a tangible relationship to the federal government has all along been clear, given that the group was formed in late 1972 through a BIA grant of $62,000 to then Pine Ridge Tribal President Dick Wilson for purposes of establishing a "Tribal Ranger Group."[23] From 1973 onward, funding of GOON payrolls seems to have accrued from the Wilson administration's misappropriation of block-granted federal highway improvement monies (the "Rangers" were officially expanded to include a "Highway Safety Program" for this purpose).[24] Most federal housing funds allocated to Pine Ridge during the two terms of Wilson's presidency also appear to have been devoted to rewarding members of the GOON squad for services rendered.[25] Many of Wilson's relatives[26] as well as perhaps one-third of the BIA police force on the reservation were quickly rostered as GOONs.[27]

The *quid pro quo* seems originally to have been that Wilson would receive quiet federal support in running Pine Ridge as a personal fiefdom in exchange for his cooperation in casting an appearance of legitimacy upon an illegal transfer of the Sheep Mountain Gunnery Range—approximately one-eighth of the total reservation area—from Indian to federal ownership. Although it was a matter of official secrecy at the time, the motivation for this federal maneuver concerned discovery of rich molybdenum and uranium deposits within the Gunnery Range; both are considered critical strategic minerals by the Pentagon, and access to them a matter of "National Security."[28] The GOONs were necessary to quell resistance among traditional grassroots Oglalas to any such transaction.[29] When AIM moved in at the request of the traditionals, the ante went up appreciably, and the GOONs shifted from intimidation tactics to outright death squad activities, thus pursuing not only their original objective but the broader federal goal of eliminating AIM as a viable political force as well.

On the face of it, the FBI's main complicity in the bloodbath which ensued was to conscientiously look the other way as the GOONs went about their grisly work. This would be bad enough. However, there has always been ample indication that the Bureau's role was much more substantial. For instance, when, during the siege of Wounded Knee, U.S. marshals on the scene attempted to dismantle a GOON roadblock (at which an FBI agent was continuously posted, according to Brewer)—the occupants of which Chief U.S. Marshal Wayne Colburn had decided were uncontrollable and a menace to his own men—head of the FBI Internal Security Section Richard G. Held flew to the site by helicopter to "straighten things out." Held, assigned to the reservation as a "consultant," informed the chief marshal that "the highest authority" had instructed that the GOON position would remain in place. Similarly, when several GOONs were arrested by Colburn's deputies after pointing weapons at both the chief marshal and U.S. Justice Department Solicitor General Kent Frizzell, the FBI again intervened, causing the men to be released prior to booking.[30]

More importantly, toward the end of the Wounded Knee siege—a period when Colburn was actively disarming the GOONs after it appeared possible that one of his men had been seriously wounded by a round fired by the Wilsonites—those who were relieved of the hunting rifles and shotguns which until then had comprised their typical weaponry suddenly began to sport fully automatic, government-issue M-16 assault rifles.[31] A much improved inventory of explosive devices and an abundance of ammunition also made appearances among the GOONs during this period. At about the same time, the Wilsonites experienced a marked upgrade in the quality of their communications gear, acquiring scanners and other electronic paraphernalia which allowed them to monitor federal police frequencies. To top it off, it began to appear as if the GOONs' operational intelligence had undergone considerable improvement during the 71 days of the siege.

It has been substantiated that the U.S. military provided no ordnance or other equipment directly to nonfederal agencies during the siege of Wounded Knee. It is also clear that the U.S. marshals, for reasons of their own, were genuinely attempting to reduce rather than enhance GOON weaponry while the siege was going on. In any event,

Colburn withdrew his personnel as rapidly as possible from Pine Ridge in the aftermath of Wounded Knee, leaving the FBI as the only federal force on the reservation until mid-1975. And, in the months following the siege—the period when the Wilsonites' activities became increasingly lethal—both the quantity and the quality of GOON firepower increased steadily. All things considered, it is widely believed among reservation residents—and several researchers have also concluded, by process of elimination, if nothing else—that the FBI not only equipped, but also provided field intelligence and other support to the death squads operating on Pine Ridge from 1973 through 1976.[32]

The Brewer Revelations

Although much which might have been covered is not addressed in the existing interview with Duane Brewer, what *is* included is often quite explicit. For instance, he readily confirms the oft-leveled accusation that in order to be employed on Pine Ridge during the Wilson era, especially in the Tribal Rangers or Highway Safety Program, one was virtually required to serve simultaneously as a GOON: if "you were a GOON and supported Dick Wilson and hated AIM, you had a pretty good chance of getting a job" underwritten with federal funds. "[W]e had people from all over," he says. "Some of them you never had to ask to do anything, you know, like for Dick, you know. They were ready to do anything."

> A lot of them liked Dick Wilson and his ideas. And they thought that was pretty nice, a GOON squad. Hell, you don't see that very often in this world. Of course, it is going on all over the nation now, and different presidents and leaders have their crew of people. And, you know, I guess that's all, that's politics. You have your certain followers. But, in them days, you had real dedicated people. They would hurt somebody for their leader if they had to. And if anybody tried to hurt him or anything, then [they] were too outnumbered to go messing around. A lot of dedication.

The GOONs were organized on a community-by-community basis, according to Brewer, into "crews" of about a dozen men apiece, each headed up by one or another of "ten to fifteen pretty hard core individuals" such as Chuck and Emile "Woody" Richards, and Wilson's eldest son, Manny (Richard Jr.).[33] Brewer's own crew—of which

BIA police SWAT team commander Marvin Stolt, Manny Wilson, and John Hussman served as operational lieutenants, and which at its high point in 1975 rostered at least 22 other individuals—functioned more-or-less exclusively on the western side of Pine Ridge. Chuck Richards' group covered the northeastern quadrant of the reservation, and Woody Richards' the southeastern area. Essentially *ad hoc* units were formed from time to time. Combined operations between standing units occurred in all areas, as needed.

The result of such organization was a relatively constant reservation-wide fireforce of "about 100 men," sometimes expanded to twice that number, throughout the critical period. The GOONs themselves were augmented, not only by the BIA police, but also by non-Indian vigilante groups such as the "Bennett County Citizens' Committee," "Charles Mix County Rangers," "Faith Chapter of the John Birch Society," and other Birch-oriented "ranchers' associations" in South Dakota, Wyoming, and Nebraska. At present, "maybe ten or so" of the hardest-core GOON squad members have buried much of their best weaponry, as well as ample stocks of ammunition and explosives, around the reservation. They stand ready, in Brewer's view, to resume their role as a nucleus of GOON leadership "in case that's ever needed again." They are motivated, he says, "by a lot of hatred."

Relationship of the GOONs to the FBI

With regard to how he and his underlings got along with the agents on Pine Ridge during the GOONs' formative period, Brewer's estimation is that "we had a pretty good working relationship in those days." Part of this emerged, he believes, because his own BIA police *cum* GOON unit served as a sort of regional roving patrol, dispensing a bareknuckled "law and order" against AIM on various reservations.

> During the time I was an officer, we traveled all over the country following the Movement. We went to the Treaty Convention up at Fort Yates. We spent a lot of time in Rosebud. We went to Fort Totten when they [AIM] took the jail over. It was always Pine Ridge's little crew that went. So, we kind of had a reputation...[U]sually when they [the FBI] send you off like that, they tell you, you know, you don't cut them any slack. So, you know, you bust a few heads. It don't really take, you don't take any shit...You haul 'em in. You show them authority because there

is no law and order...I got to travel quite a bit when I was an officer. I enjoyed all of it.[34]

The choice to use Brewer's unit as an inter-reservation fire brigade against AIM was not merely the result of their attitudes towards "radicalism" and the appropriateness of suppressing it through liberal applications of gratuitous violence, but also because of a conscious federal policy—based on recognition of those attitudes—of equipping them for this purpose.

> [After a while] we had all the weaponry. We had fifteen AR-15s. We had long-range projectile smoke, I mean gas guns. We had a [tear gas] fogger. We had everything. So, it was our squad that usually went. And you get there, and you hear people say, "The Pine Ridgers are here." So, of course, a number of times we went to places, some officers busted heads...We had some pretty cocky guys, I guess you might say. Tough guys, is what you'd say. They're fighters from around [Pine Ridge].

He affirms that "the FBI was with the GOONs" because "we was fighting in the same thing—we wasn't supporting AIM. And I imagine it's because we got a lot of jobs that, you know, like kicking the hell out of some of these different [AIM] people, giving them trouble." Asked whether this meant the FBI "looked the other way" when GOONs engaged in physical assaults upon AIM members, he replied somewhat disingenuously that "we never, ever done anything with them [agents] around, but they probably would have...So anything we could get away with, we would."[35]

> I had a good relationship with them [the FBI] because I helped them a lot...They probably thought I was a funny guy, you know. (laugh) Have all these weapons and stand out as much as we did in them days. And all the situations we was involved in. Yeah, we wasn't afraid [of being arrested]...I probably have maybe four or five FBI agents who are real good friends. They tried to get me into the FBI Academy, tried to help me out, to get me out of this place.

Intelligence with which to conduct his more extracurricular anti-AIM operations was no particular problem because "the agents would come to my house" and "give [us] all kinds of information and things...they were probably giving [the GOONs] a lot more than they were supposed to. Which is good, hell, every little bit helps." Basically, "we could get information from them" whenever it was needed. Queried as to whether this meant the FBI thought it was "okay to rough up AIM supporters," Brewer responded, "I imagine they did...I think they did...They never did investigate any of them incidents [of GOON violence], you know." At another point, in response to a similar question, he replied that when the FBI brought information to his house, it was because "they wanted to see us go out and educate" AIM members and supporters; "I got the feeling they was hoping that I'd kick the shit out of somebody. Or have a war."

General GOON Violence

Asked to explain the term "educate" in the context in which he was using it, and thus the sort of activities the FBI had at least tacitly endorsed, Brewer offered the concept of "butt kickin'. Good word. We would educate them, like I said, we would kick their butt. Then they ain't going to come around and bug you any more." He went on to explain that the intended result of an "educational butt kickin'" was for the victim to "know that any time they move any part of their body it hurts 'em, [and] it could have been worse. I've educated a few who will never forget me, you know, or have never forgotten."

> I think ["education" occurs] when you, you give them a severe beating and, like I said, you don't cut no slack. You beat their face, you beat their arms and legs, and work them over good. So, like I said, when they wake up the next day, every time they move they're going to think about you and decide whether they want to come back and mess with you again. Or just let you go. And, you know, you do it good enough and they're not going to be thinking about coming back for more of the pain. They're going to forget about it.

The Wilsonites' repertoire of "educational" techniques was often even more extreme. At one point, Brewer recounts how a GOON named Sonny Dion "beat this [AIM] guy up so bad and then he used a saw and was trying to saw this guy up." Other GOONs, apparently shocked at the extent to which Dion was "getting out of hand," intervened to prevent consummation of this macabre act. Brewer goes on to note that Dion was eventually "shipped out"—that is, he was charged by the BIA police and eventually sent to federal prison—not for his murderous assault upon the AIM member, but for turning his brutal attentions upon another GOON, Chauncey Folsom, shooting him six times in the back with a .22-caliber revolver (the victim lived).

For his part, Brewer points out, Folsom was a key player in a notorious event occurring on February 27, 1975, at the Pine Ridge airport. In this incident, some 15 carloads of GOONs headed by Dick Wilson himself surrounded an automobile occupied by Bernard Escamilla, an AIM member charged with several offenses during the Wounded Knee siege, his legal counsel, National Lawyers Guild attorney Roger Finzel, and two paralegal assistants, Eva Gordon and Kathi James.[36] Wilson ordered the GOONs to "stomp" their quarry. Thereupon, Brewer admits, he personally led the charge, smashing the car's windshield. Other GOONs, whom Brewer does not identify, sliced open the top of the car (it was a convertible), dragged Finzel and Escamilla out, and, according to a *Rapid City Journal* article published the following day, "stomped, kicked and pummeled [them] to the ground. [GOONs] took turns kicking and stomping, while one slashed Finzel's face with a knife, [also] cutting Eva Gordon's hand as she attempted to shield him." Folsom, who, as Brewer put it, "was a really huge guy," proceeded to "educate" Escamilla, a much smaller man, "beat him up real bad, and then just sort of dumped him in a ditch full of water. Things kind of got out of hand, I guess."

No federal charges were ever filed against Wilson or any of his GOONs in this matter, although Finzel and Gordon provided detailed and mutually supporting depositions, naming several of their assailants.[37] Instead, the FBI busied itself administering polygraph examinations to the victims (which they passed with flying colors). Wilson, meanwhile, had conducted a press conference in which he claimed to know nothing about the incident other than that the violence was supposed to have been caused by "Russell Means and a large group of followers, last seen heading east out of Pine Ridge" village.[38] When they were nonetheless indicted by a federal grand jury, Wilson and his men quickly pleaded guilty to a misdemeanor charge in tribal court (the judges of which Wilson himself had appointed) and were assessed $10 fines. Assistant U.S. Attorney Bill Clayton thereupon announced that no federal prosecutions would be initiated because any felony charges brought by his office would constitute "double jeopardy." When asked by interviewers whether the whole thing hadn't been whitewashed, as critics have long contended, Brewer replied: "Yeah, I guess maybe it was."[39]

At one point the former GOON leader denies having personally killed anyone: "No, I never did. I never did kill anybody. Like I said, I might have smoked them up pretty bad where they thought they were gonna die. But I never did really kill them." However, he also says, "I've come close, I think, you know. I've beat some people with clubs that I was worried wouldn't live," and "I worried *the few times that I did kill somebody* [emphasis added]." Further, he readily admits that the GOONs as a whole did regularly commit homicide: "Some, let's say different incidents."[40] Certain of these "incidents" concern the much-rumored murder of at least 13 individuals engaged in transporting supplies through GOON and federal lines during the 1973 siege of Wounded Knee.

> I don't know if they killed them on the spot. Because, like I said, there would be witnesses. More likely, they took them off by themselves, if they did this. Like I say, I don't know! (laugh)...They probably, they might have done it. I know that there was one group of guys [Woody Richards' crew] that had that roadblock that, uh, done a guy in pretty bad just beatin' him with a weapon...[T]hey ended up really pistol whippin' him and usin' weapons on him, you know?...More, I've never heard of them ever taking a guy to the hospital as bad as he was beat up...He was probably killed somewhere.[41]

A customary GOON squad practice was to conduct driveby shootings of the homes of movement people: "You know, if there was too many AIM members there, or something, maybe [the GOONs] would take a cruise by and shoot them up." Often, Brewer recalls "we would set it up" so that drivebys "would be blamed on AIM." During the course of his interview, he drove reporters through the Cherry Hill Housing Project, where "a lot of AIM people used to live," pointing out specific dwellings which had been shot up and/or firebombed by GOON patrols.

> I know it was done quite a bit. Any time [AIM] gathered up...[the GOONs hit] the AIM people. A lot of times we had a little war. Somebody would go by and they would open up. I guess the housing that was really the one that was shot up the most was probably Cherry Hills. There was a lot of 'em. That's where AIM, the majority of them lived there at one

time, the supporters of AIM. So it was shot up a lot. Them houses are a
real mess.

Nor was Cherry Hill the only such target: "I know [the GOONs]
firebombed a house in Crazy Horse [housing project] once because one
of the guys that lived there was an AIM supporter." Brewer also acknowledges that it was GOONs who, on March 3, 1973, firebombed the home
of journalist Aaron DeSersa and his wife, Betty, in order to "send a
message" that they should suspend publication of an anti-Wilson tabloid
based in the reservation village of Manderson. Betty DeSersa was badly
burned in the ensuing blaze. Among other targets of GOON firebombings were the home of elderly traditional Oglala Lakota Chief
Frank Fools Crow on March 5, 1975, and that of his assistant, Matthew
King, on March 3. The home of AIM member Severt Young Bear, near the
reservation hamlet of Porcupine, was shot up on at least six occasions
and firebombed twice in little more than a year.[42]

In another of many more noteworthy incidents, this one occurring
on November 17, 1975, BIA police officer/GOON Jesse Trueblood shot
up an "AIM house" belonging to Chester and Bernice Stone in Oglala,
another reservation village. He seriously wounded all five occupants
and permanently maimed two of them, an adult named Louis Tyon
and three-year-old Johnny Mousseau. Trueblood himself was found
dead in his patrol car shortly thereafter, shot in the back of the head
with his own service revolver. The FBI, incredibly, listed the cause of
death as "suicide." Brewer concurs that the federal finding was absurd—"Jesse had a disability which prevented him from lifting his
arms in such a way that he could've shot himself like that"—but says
he has "no idea" who did the killing. It is commonly accepted around
Oglala that Trueblood was murdered by a prominent GOON leader
(not Brewer), who availed himself of the opportunity presented by the
confusion attending the driveby to settle a romantic dispute with his
erstwhile colleague.

GOON Weaponry

Asked about the source of the increasingly sophisticated weaponry the GOONs came to possess, Brewer alludes repeatedly to the
idea that the FBI armed his group—both directly and through indirect

conduits—with items such as Thompson submachine guns and M-16s: "Some of it was given, like I told you, in a little [undecipherable] in Rapid City where they would give you some weapons and in another location where they would tell you to come up with this amount of money and we'll turn all this over to you...We had M-16s," he says, ".30 caliber carbines, a lot of...military stuff." Supplies of ammunition for such hardware were lavish: "There's sometimes that you, like at one time I probably had five bandoliers full of [.223 caliber rounds for an M-16 rifle]. And boxes and boxes of ammo for this, the 9 m.m. [a type of pistol preferred by Brewer]...It looked like it was probably police stuff, [and] it was always cheap when we got it."

"All this" included more than ammunition and automatic weapons. Brewer itemizes provision of "Plastic explosives, det[onation] cord, [and] fragmentation grenades," as well as dynamite and blasting caps, to the GOONs. He contends that certain of the less exotic—but nonetheless expensive—weapons used by the GOONs, such as .300 Weatherby rifles (ideal for sniping purposes), were provided at little or no charge by white vigilante groups. Some of the M-16s, he says, accrued from BIA police inventories provided by the federal government. Most of the rest of the hard-to-get gear came in clandestine fashion from FBI personnel and/or "black drug-gun dealers" in Rapid City motel rooms, usually at the local Holiday Inn.

> [Y]ou'd go to their room with this big suitcase and [they'd] show you a bunch of weapons, grenades, det cord, blasting caps, whatever, and give you some. "Here, take this." A couple guys I know of walked around with blasting, you know, blasting caps in their shirt pockets.

In those instances where the "black gun dealers" effected transfer of weapons and explosives, agents were in the motel, monitoring the activity.[43] When asked whether the agents were aware the GOONs were in possession of such illegal paraphernalia, Brewer responded, "Sure." As an illustration, he recounted an occasion when, with FBI agents in adjoining rooms, a GOON "playing" with a newly acquired weapon accidentally discharged it in the Holiday Inn, blowing a hole in the floor. No investigation was made, nor was any other action taken by the Bureau. Brewer also mentions repeatedly that agents visiting his home were routinely shown illegal weapons in his personal possession, and often informed of how he planned to use them. Such matters failed to evoke a negative response—never mind an arrest—from the agents. To the contrary, they customarily advised him to "be careful" as he went about his business.

At another point Brewer explains that as a reward for his engaging in a fist fight with AIM leader Russell Means, he was given "a .357 magnum, 6-inch barrel…[worth] three hundred and some bucks, brand new. Real nice. I carried that a long time."[44] He also states categorically that the FBI supplied the GOONs with special types of "armor piercing ammunition," which was "real expensive" and "restricted to law enforcement personnel," so the gunmen could hit their AIM targets even if "they were in a brick building or something." This led to a question concerning "the best way to hit a house," to which the GOON leader responded:

> Best way to hit it is probably just to, like I say, have your lookouts and when there is nobody around and it's nice and quiet, have your, like I said, your assault car with all the weapons in it. And do it from the road. Don't cruise up to the house because then you got return fire. Then you got a war. Most of the point of shooting up a house is just to prove that we didn't approve of [AIM] gathering, you know, and we want them to know that we're on our toes and watching them.

When asked why the Bureau might provide—or arrange provision of—so much costly ordnance to an irregular force like the GOONs, Brewer was unequivocal: "They just didn't want them [AIM] people to survive. I thought that maybe they was, I think they was hoping that we would just kill them all, you know?"

GOON Murders

The former "Head GOON" offers considerable perspective upon the FBI's "inability to cope" with the wave of violent deaths on Pine Ridge. Take, for example, one of the more mysterious homicides involved in the entire reign of terror on the reservation, that of Jeanette Bissonette—a not especially prominent activist—at about 1:00 a.m. on the morning of March 27, 1975. Careful observers have all along suspected the victim was mistakenly killed by a GOON sniper who confused her car with a similar one driven by traditionalist leader and AIM supporter Ellen Moves Camp. The FBI, for reasons it has never adequately explained, insisted the killing "must" have been done by "militants" and expended an appreciable quantity of investigative energy attempting to link Northwest AIM leader Leonard Peltier to the crime. However, Brewer frames the matter a bit differently:

> I know there was [innocent] people killed during that time, like that Bissonette lady down in, near Oglala. We didn't do that type of stuff [ordinarily]. That was, must have been, a freak accident. They must have mistaken her for somebody else. I, I think that's what happened. But, you know, the weapon we used to kill that woman was also a weapon [provided by the FBI].

He also extends an interesting interpretation of what the FBI described as the "justifiable homicide" of AIM supporter Pedro Bissonette (brother of Jeanette) at a police roadblock near Pine Ridge village on the night of October 17, 1973. Brewer suggests the killer, BIA police officer/GOON Joe Clifford, may have been not so much politically motivated as he was enraged by the fact that Bissonette had undergone a stormy marriage to his (Clifford's) sister: "They had a real fiery romance, I guess. And it didn't end well. So maybe there was enough hatred [on the part of] this officer to, enough to end the guy's life...Maybe [Clifford] was worried that [Bissonette] was coming back to raise hell with his sister or something." In either event, whether it was motivated politically or on the basis of a personal grudge, the killing plainly added up to murder rather than the "self-defense" explanation officially registered by the FBI, and confirmed by government contract coroner W.O. Brown.[45]

Concerning the murder of AIM supporter Byron DeSersa near the reservation hamlet of Wanblee on January 30, 1976, Brewer states that he did not participate directly, since the locale was outside his normal area of operations. On the other hand, he candidly acknowledges providing "some of the weapons" used by GOON leader Chuck Richards, Dick Wilson's younger son, Billy, and others in committing the crime. Still, he holds his silence about the implications of two FBI agents arriving on the scene shortly after the murder, being informed by witnesses as to the identity of the killers (who were still assembled close at hand), and then making no arrests. Similarly, he stands mute with regard to the significance of Delmar Eastman's subsequent dispatch of a BIA police unit, not to arrest DeSersa's murderers, but to remove them safely from Wanblee when it became apparent area residents might retaliate.[46]

On the matter of the execution-style slaying of AIM activist Anna Mae Aquash, whose body was found in a ravine near Wanblee on February 24, 1976, Brewer admits there is strong evidence pointing to BIA police investigator (and GOON affiliate) Paul Herman. But, as Brewer puts it, the FBI couldn't "tie him in" to the Aquash murder because the nature of her death failed to conform to Herman's peculiar mode of killing.

> [Herman] got sent off [to prison] shortly after that. He, uh, he killed a young girl, burnt her with cigarette butts, just done a whole bunch of things. Anna Mae Aquash, she wasn't done like that. She was shot...if this guy was a maniac and burnt his victims with a cigarette and done things, why didn't he do it to [Aquash]?...She wasn't you know, sexual[ly] tortured, none of it, none of that stuff. Just a clean death.

The problem with such reasoning is striking. Although government contract coroner W.O. Brown—whose conclusions in this connection Brewer apparently wished his interviewers to accept—failed to find evidence that Aquash had been tortured or sexually abused, he also "determined" that she had died of "exposure."[47] Independent pathologist Garry Peterson, retained by the victim's family to perform a second autopsy, concluded immediately that her death had been caused by a "lead slug consistent with being from a .32 or .38 caliber handgun...fired pointblank into the base of the brain." Peterson also observed that the victim appeared to have been "beaten" and that there was "evidence of sexual contact" shortly before she was murdered. This says much to Brewer's contention that the Aquash murder was "out of character" with Paul Herman's lethal style. By implication, it says even more about the FBI's continuing insistence—announced even before its conclusion in the Herman investigation was officially reached—that the victim was "probably" killed by her "AIM associates," ostensibly because she was "suspected of being a government informant."[48]

At present, the FBI's investigation of AIM's possible involvement in the murder of Anna Mae Pictou Aquash is officially ongoing, a circumstance which exempts the Bureau from legal requirements that it disclose relevant documents to researchers. Meanwhile, by its own admission, it never got around to interviewing coroner Brown as to how he arrived at his novel cause of death finding.[49] Nor has it bothered to question two of its agents, Tom Green and William Wood, as to why they decided it was necessary to sever the victim's hands and ship them to the FBI fingerprint lab for *post mortem* identification purposes. In the alternative, they might have instructed Dr. Brown to conduct a much more conventional cranial x-ray, for purposes of identification by dental chart comparison (but, of course, this would have instantly disclosed the bullet lodged in the victim's skull).[50] Finally, the Bureau's sleuths have failed to interrogate agent David Price, who, by several accounts, had threatened Aquash's life during a 1975 interrogation session.[51]

The Oglala Firefight

By the spring of 1975, the level of GOON violence on Pine Ridge was so pronounced—and the lack of FBI response so conspicuous—that local traditionals requested that AIM undertake a policy of armed self-defense in order that opposition to Wilson might continue. AIM responded by establishing defensive encampments on properties owned by traditionals at various points around the reservation. Substantial evidence derived from FBI internal documents suggests the Bureau seized upon this situation as affording the opportunity to provoke an incident spectacular enough to bring about public acceptance of another massive paramilitary invasion of Pine Ridge.[52] Deployment of literally hundreds of agents in an extremely aggressive capacity, it was thought, would prove sufficient to finally break the backs of AIM and its supporters, already weakened by the war of attrition waged against them during the two years since Wounded Knee.

In the event, a camp set up by the Northwest AIM Group on the Jumping Bull family property, near Oglala, was selected as the target at which the catalyzing confrontation would occur. Two agents, Ron Williams and Jack Coler, were sent there during the late morning of June 26, 1975, and opened fire on several of the Indians they encountered. Almost immediately, the lead elements of a large and already-assembled force of more than a hundred agents, BIA SWAT personnel, and GOONs attempted to force their way onto the property. From there, things seem to have gone somewhat awry from the Bureau

point of view. Many more AIM members were present than anticipated, and the government reinforcements beat a hasty retreat to the
cover of roadside ditches while Coler and Williams were cut off from
their expected support. In the extended firefight which followed, both
agents were killed, as was an AIM member named Joe Stuntz
Killsright. Despite the presence of perhaps 200 police personnel,
GOONs, and white vigilantes by midafternoon, the remaining AIM
members escaped.[53]

Despite this undoubtedly unanticipated outcome, the Oglala firefight served its intended purpose for the FBI. Public endorsement of
the sort of "crushing blow" desired by Bureau strategists was inherent
to the situation, especially after it had been "packaged" by Bureau
propagandists. Hence, before nightfall on June 26, counterintelligence
expert Richard G. Held—detached from his normal duties *before* the
firefight and standing by in Minneapolis, ready to assume command
of the Pine Ridge operation—was on site.[54] With him, he brought a
young counterintelligence protégé, Norman Zigrossi, his son, Richard
Wallace Held, head of the FBI's COINTELPRO (Counterintelligence
Program) Section in Los Angeles, and a number of other specialists in
"political work."[55] They "hit the ground running," to borrow a phrase
from the vernacular of their trade.

By the morning of June 27, SWAT teams imported from Chicago,
Minneapolis, Milwaukee, and Quantico, Virginia, were on the reservation, giving the Bureau a military-style presence—complete with armored personnel carriers, Bell "Huey" helicopters, and other Vietnam-
type equipage—of some 250 agents (as O'Clock mentioned above, this
number had swelled to 350 by mid-July). For the next several months,
this huge force conducted sweeps back and forth across Pine Ridge,
abruptly kicking in doors to perform warrantless searches, making
arbitrary arrests, and engaging in air assaults upon assorted "centers of
AIM resistance," all in the process of conducting what the FBI called its
"RESMURS (for Reservation Murders) Investigation."[56] Subjected to
these sorts of official tactics, the AIM leadership reversed its position,
quietly withdrawing from the reservation as an expedient to relieve the
pressure imposed upon their traditional allies.

The firefight ultimately served much broader purposes as well. "Under the volatile circumstances caused by the deaths of Agents Coler and Williams," the Senate Select Committee on Government Operations (the so-called "Church Committee"), which had already issued the first subpoenas for a scheduled probe into the sorts of activities encompassed by the FBI's anti-AIM campaign, *especially* those on Pine Ridge, agreed to an "indefinite postponement" of its hearings.[57] In actuality, this exploration of the Bureau's repressive behavior in what has been called its "post-COINTELPRO era" was simply and permanently shelved by the committee (or, in any event, we are still waiting for it to start, 21 years later). And, of course, a few days after the firefight, the U.S. Department of Interior felt the time was "appropriate" for Dick Wilson to finally sign the instrument transferring title over the Sheep Mountain Gunnery Range to the National Forest Service.[58]

The Bureau and its supporters have always contended that no government plan to provoke a confrontation existed. The presence of large numbers of GOONs and BIA police in close proximity to the remote location in which the firefight occurred was, they say, the sheerest of coincidences, a matter which proves nothing at all. AIM, FBI media liaison Tom Coll initially claimed, was "the group with the plan," having "lured" the agents into a "carefully prepared ambush" where they were "fired upon with automatic weapons" from a "sophisticated bunker complex," "riddled with fifteen to twenty bullets" apiece, "dragged from their cars" and "stripped" and—in one version—"scalped." Coll was even thoughtful enough to quote Williams' last words, having the dead agent plead for his life, begging his "cold-blooded executioners" to "please remember my wife and children before you do this."[59]

After FBI Director Clarence M. Kelley finally admitted that *none* of this was true, the Bureau switched to the story that it maintains to this day: Coler and Williams were merely attempting to serve a "routine warrant" on a 19-year-old AIM member named Jimmy Eagle and ended up being brutally murdered for their trouble.[60] Duane Brewer tells a rather different story.

The thing that we was to do was use CB radios, have people placed, positioned in different places, on hills and things. And we was going to have an assault vehicle go to about three houses that we figured they was at, and shoot them up...We would do the shooting, shoot the place up and make our run and go to Rapid City. Stay up over night, party around and then come back the next day, you know. Not be in the area when it happened. But, like I said, *we had three or four different plans* that we was going to use...[B]ut our intentions never were, was to go right down into that place. That was just one of the places that we was going to hit. We could have hit them from the road, you know [emphasis added].

A second variation of the planning was for Brewer's GOONs to shoot up some of the Jumping Bull houses, precipitating a return of fire from the few AIM members expected to be gathered there. A force of FBI agents and a BIA SWAT team would then use this as a pretext to arrest everyone on the property, "and we [the GOONs] could cover for them on the way back. *We had three different plans*, I guess. We sat down there at the creek I don't know how many times and went over that [emphasis added]." As it happened, however, Coler and Williams were sent in to get things rolling, but "we never really knew they had this, the Jumping Bull Hall, the Jumping Bull place with all these warriors down there. And that's when they killed them agents." Asked why he and his men hadn't responded to Williams' radioed pleas, once the firefight had begun in earnest, for someone to "get on the high ground" adjacent to the Jumping Bull property and provide covering fire while he and his partner withdrew, Brewer responded:

If we could have got ourselves into that position where we went to the top of that hill, they [AIM] would have had us before we got out of the, got to the highway, the way they were set up. That would have been a losing battle there.

In the end, little more than this need be said about the circumstances in which Northwest AIM leader Leonard Peltier was brought to trial in 1977 and convicted of two counts of first-degree murder in the deaths of Williams and Coler. This, after an all-white jury in Cedar Rapids, Iowa, had acquitted his codefendants, Bob Robideau and Darelle "Dino" Butler, both of whom openly acknowledged at the trial having shot at the agents, by reason of their having plainly acted in self-defense.[61] Tellingly, Judge Gerald Heaney, head of the three-member panel of the Eighth Circuit Court of Appeals which last reviewed

Peltier's case, appeared on national television in 1989 to admit he was "deeply troubled" during his own investigation of the matter. The reason for the judge's discomfort? In his own words, "It became increasingly apparent to me that the FBI was at least as much to blame for what happened as Peltier."[62] More lately, Heaney has joined Hawaii Senator Daniel Inouye and other members of Congress in signing a petition to George Bush requesting that Peltier be pardoned.[63]

Death Squads in the United States

At one point toward the end of his interview, Brewer was asked how he justified the sorts of things he'd been involved in as a GOON. Almost pensively, he acknowledged that, "Well, you really can't. There really isn't no justification for it…It's just what we done at the time, and there's no way you can go back and change what's already done." Exactly. And no number of evasions, withheld documents, denials, or other lies on the part of the FBI and its friends will make the truth of what the Bureau did to AIM and its supporters any less true. The Federal Bureau of Investigation played much the same role on Pine Ridge during the mid-'70s that the CIA has played *vis-à-vis* Roberto D'Aubisson's hit teams in El Salvador throughout the 1980s. The GOONs, for their part, fulfilled exactly the same requirements on the reservation that other death squads have played throughout Latin America over the past four decades and more. Structurally, the forms and functions assumed by all parties to such comparisons are essentially the same.[64]

The FBI's employment of outright death squads to accomplish the repression of AIM may be the the most extreme example of its kind in modern U.S. history. It is nonetheless hardly isolated or unique in principle. To the contrary, ample evidence exists that the Bureau has been experimenting with and perfecting this technique of domestic counterinsurgency for nearly thirty years. There can be little question at this point that the Ku Klux Klan, riddled with FBI *agents provocateurs* such as Gary Thomas Rowe and overlapped as it was with local police forces in the Deep South, was used by the FBI during the early 1960s against the civil rights movement in much the same fashion as the GOONs were later used against AIM.[65] The same circumstances are at issue with regard to the Klan, in alliance with other neonazis, murdering five members of the Communist Workers Party in Greensboro, North Carolina, during November 1979.[66]

Certainly, the special unit of State's Attorney's Police which assassinated Black Panther Party leaders Fred Hampton and Mark Clark in Chicago on December 4, 1969, was functioning as a death squad under the Bureau's at least nominal control.[67] Similarly, the Windy City was afflicted with a neonazi/police/FBI/military intelligence amalgamation known as the "Legion of Justice" during the first half of the 1970s.[68] No less striking is the combination, evident during the late 1960s and described at length by *provocateur* Louis Tackwood in *The Glass House Tapes*, of state and local police red squads with the Bureau's Los Angeles COINTELPRO Section and area vigilante groups, for purposes of physically destroying the "California Left." As Tackwood and other Bureau-sponsored infiltrators of dissident organizations have stated, often and categorically, assassination of "key activists" is a standard part of the tactical methodology utilized by America's political police.[69]

Bearing this out, there was the Secret Army Organization (SAO), developed under the aegis of the FBI in southern California during the early '70s; its express purpose, among other things, was to liquidate "radical leaders."[70] On another front, there was the death squad formed by the Portland, Maine, police (with apparent cooperation from the local FBI resident agency) during the same period as a means of "coming to grips" with the area's antiwar and prison rights movements. Then again, there is the example of the consortium in Puerto Rico—consisting of a special police unit tightly interlocked with the island's FBI field office, the CIA, U.S. military intelligence units, and right wing Cuban exile groups—which was responsible for scores of bombings and beatings over the years. Also attributable to this entity are, at the very least, the execution-style murders of labor leader Juan Caballero in the island's El Yunque rain forest in 1977, and of *independentista* activists Arnaldo Dario Rosado and Carlos Soto Arrivi near the mountain village of Cerro Maravilla on July 25, 1978.[71]

Comparable illustrations might be recited at length, but the pattern will by now be clear to anyone willing to face facts. And it should be coupled to the fact that not one FBI agent has ever served so much as a minute of jail time because of the conduct involved in these atrocities. These realities must serve to inform and temper the understandings of activists and scholars alike, the former in terms of their appreciation of what they are up against as they struggle to achieve positive social change in the United States, the latter in terms of the paradigms by which they attempt to shed light on the nature of power dynamics in America. In either case, it is plain enough that there is no longer any real excuse for continuation of the generalized self-delusion among American progressives that such things are "anomalous" within the context of the contemporary United States. True death squads are not only possible in the United States; they have been a relatively common phenomenon for some time. It is already well past the point where we should have gotten the government's message, and begun to conduct ourselves accordingly.

AIM Casualties on Pine Ridge, 1973-1976
with Jim Vander Wall

In our books, *Agents of Repression* (South End Press, 1988) and *The COINTELPRO Papers* (South End Press, 1990) Jim Vander Wall and I have used the figure 69 as the minimum number of AIM members and supporters murdered on the Pine Ridge Reservation from mid-1973 through mid-1976. This has provoked claims on the parts of various FBI apologists that we "exaggerate" the gravity of the situation. Our first response to such critics is that it ultimately matters little in terms of the implications at issue whether the number of AIM casualties was in the upper forties—as the Bureau itself has admitted—the upper sixties, as we contend. Our second response is the following itemized list of casualties, including the names of the victims, the dates and causes of their deaths (where known), and, so far as is possible, the status of FBI investigations (if any) into their murders. Our third response is that, as we've said all along, even this itemization is undoubtedly incomplete. We therefore request any individuals having knowledge of murders other than those listed—or who are aware of the names of any of the individuals killed while packing supplies into Wounded Knee—to contact us with this information.

04/17/73   *Frank Clearwater*—AIM member killed by heavy machine gun round at Wounded Knee. No investigation.

04/23/73   *Between 8 and 12 individuals* (names unknown) packing supplies into Wounded Knee were intercepted by GOONs and vigilantes. None were ever heard from again. Former Rosebud Tribal President Robert Burnette and U.S. Justice Department Solicitor General Kent Frizzell conducted unsuccessful search for a mass grave after the Wounded Knee siege. No further investigation.

04/27/73   *Buddy Lamont*—AIM member hit by M-16 fire at Wounded Knee. Bled to death while pinned down by fire. No investigation.

06/19/73   *Clarence Cross*—AIM supporter shot to death in ambush by GOONS. Although assailants were identified by eyewitnesses, brother Vernal Cross—wounded in ambush—was briefly charged with crime. No further investigation.

07/14/73   *Priscilla White Plume*—AIM supporter killed at Manderson by GOONS. No investigation.

07/30/73   *Julius Bad Heart Bull*—AIM supporter killed at Oglala by "person or persons unknown." No investigation.

09/23/73   *Philip Black Elk*—AIM supporter killed when his house exploded. No investigation.

09/22/73   *Melvin Spider*—AIM member killed at Porcupine, S.D. No investigation.

10/05/73   *Aloysius Long Soldier*—AIM member killed at Kyle, S.D. by GOONS. No investigation.

10/10/73   *Phillip Little Crow*—AIM supporter beaten to death by GOONs at Pine Ridge. No investigation.

10/17/73   *Pedro Bissonette*—Oglala Sioux Civil Rights Organization (OSCRO) organizer and AIM supporter assassinated by BIA Police/GOONs. Body removed from Pine Ridge jurisdiction prior to autopsy by government contract coroner. No further investigation.

11/20/73   *Allison Fast Horse*—AIM supporter shot to death near Pine Ridge by "unknown assailants." No investigation.

01/17/74   *Edward Means, Jr.*—AIM member found dead in Pine Ridge alley, beaten. No investigation.

02/18/74	*Edward Standing Soldier*—AIM member killed near Pine Ridge by "party or parties unknown." No investigation.
02/27/74	*Lorinda Red Paint*—AIM supporter killed at Oglala by "unknown assailants." No investigation.
04/19/74	*Roxeine Roark*—AIM supporter killed at Porcupine by "unknown assailants." Investigation opened, still "pending."
09/07/74	*Dennis LeCompte*—AIM member killed at Pine Ridge by GOONS. No investigation.
09/11/74	*Jackson Washington Cutt*—AIM member killed at Parmalee by unknown individuals." Investigation still "ongoing."
09/16/74	*Robert Reddy*—AIM member killed at Kyle by gunshot. No investigation.
11/16/74	*Delphine Crow Dog*—sister of AIM spiritual leader Leonard Crow Dog. Beaten by BIA police and left lying in a field. Died from "exposure." No investigation.
11/30/74	*Elaine Wagner*—AIM supporter killed at Pine Ridge by "person or persons unknown." No investigation.
12/25/74	*Floyd S. Binias*—AIM supporter killed at Pine Ridge by GOONS. No investigation.
12/28/74	*Yvette Lorraine Lone Hill*—AIM supporter killed at Kyle by "unknown party or parties." No investigation.
01/05/75	*Leon L. Swift Bird*—AIM member killed at Pine Ridge by GOONS. Investigation still "ongoing."
03/01/75	*Martin Montileaux*—killed in a Scenic, S.D. bar. AIM leader Richard Marshall later framed for his murder. Russell Means also charged and acquitted.
03/20/75	*Stacy Cottie*—shot to death in an ambush at Manderson. No investigation.
03/21/75	*Edith Eagle Hawk and her two children*—AIM supporter killed in automobile accident after being run off the road by a white vigilante, Albert Coomes. Coomes was also killed in the accident. GOON Mark Clifford identified as having also been in Coomes car, escaped. Investigation closed without questioning of Clifford.
03/27/75	*Jeanette Bissonette*—AIM supporter killed by sniper in Pine Ridge. Unsuccessful attempt to link AIM members to murder; no other investigation.

03/30/75	*Richard Eagle*—grandson of AIM supporter Gladys Bissonette killed while playing with loaded gun kept in the house as protection from GOON attacks.
04/04/75	*Hilda R. Good Buffalo*—AIM supporter stabbed to death at Pine Ridge by GOONS. No investigation.
04/04/75	*Jancita Eagle Deer*—AIM member beaten and run over with automobile. Last seen in the company of FBI *agent provocateur* Douglass Durham. No investigation.
05/20/75	*Ben Sitting Up*— AIM member killed at Wanblee by "unknown assailants." No investigation.
06/01/75	*Kenneth Little*—AIM supporter killed at Pine Ridge by GOONS. Investigation still "pending."
06/15/75	*Leah Spotted Elk*—AIM supporter killed at Pine Ridge by GOONS. No investigation.
06/26/75	*Joseph Stuntz Killsright*—AIM member killed by FBI sniper during Oglala firefight. No investigation.
07/12/75	*James Brings Yellow*—heart attack caused by FBI air assault on his home. No investigation.
07/25/75	*Andrew Paul Stewart*—nephew of AIM spiritual leader, Leonard Crow Dog, killed by GOONs on Pine Ridge. No investigation.
08/25/75	*Randy Hunter*—AIM supporter killed at Kyle by "party or parties unknown." Investigation still "ongoing. "
09/09/75	*Howard Blue Bird*—AIM supporter killed at Pine Ridge by GOONS. No investigation.
09/10/75	*Jim Little*—AIM supporter stomped to death by GOONs in Oglala. No investigation.
10/26/75	*Olivia Binias*—AIM supporter killed in Porcupine by "person or persons unknown." Investigation still "open."
10/26/75	*Janice Black Bear*—AIM supporter killed at Manderson by GOONS. No investigation.
10/27/75	*Michelle Tobacco*—AIM supporter killed at Pine Ridge by "unknown assailants." Investigation still "ongoing."
12/06/75	*Carl Plenty Arrows, Sr.* — AIM supporter killed at Pine Ridge by "unknown persons." No investigation.
12/06/75	*Frank LaPointe*—AIM supporter killed at Pine Ridge by GOONS. No investigation.
02/??/76	*Anna Mae Pictou Aquash*—AIM organizer assassinated on Pine Ridge. FBI involved in attempt to conceal cause of

death. Ongoing attempt to establish "AIM involvement" in murder. Key FBI personnel never deposed. Coroner never deposed. Actual date of death is unknown.

01/05/76   *Lydia Cut Grass*—AIM member killed at Wounded Knee by GOONS. No investigation.

01/30/76   *Byron DeSersa*—OSCRO organizer and AIM supporter assassinated by GOONs in Wanblee. Arrests by local authorities result in two GOONs—Dale Janis and Charlie Winters—serving two years of five year state sentences for "manslaughter." Charges dropped against two GOON leaders, Manny Wilson and Chuck Richards, on the basis of "self-defense" despite DeSersa having been unarmed when shot to death.

02/06/76   *Lena R. Slow Bear*—AIM supporter killed at Oglala by GOONS. No investigation.

03/01/76   *Hobart Horse*—AIM member beaten, shot and repeatedly run over with automobile at Sharp's Comers. No investigation.

03/26/76   *Cleveland Reddest*—AIM member killed at Kyle by "person or persons unknown." No investigation.

04/28/76   *Betty Jo Dubray*—AIM supporter beaten to death at Martin, S.D. No investigation.

05/06/76   *Marvin Two Two*—AIM supporter shot to death at Pine Ridge. No investigation.

05/09/76   *Julia Pretty Hips*—AIM supporter killed at Pine Ridge by "unknown assailants." No investigation.

05/24/76   *Sam Afraid of Bear*—AIM supporter shot to death at Pine Ridge. Investigation "ongoing."

06/04/76   *Kevin Hill*—AIM supporter killed at Oglala by "party or parties unknown." Investigation still "open."

07/03/76   *Betty Means*—AIM member killed at Pine Ridge by GOONS. No investigation.

07/31/76   *Sandra Wounded Foot*—AIM supporter killed at Sharp's Comers by "unknown assailants." No investigation.

Note: The authors would like to express appreciation to Candy Hamilton, Bruce Ellison and Ken Tilson for their various assistance in assembling this detailed chronology.

Notes

1. See U.S. Senate, Select Committee on Indian Affairs, *Indian Mineral Development* (Washington, D.C.: 97th Cong., 2d Sess., U.S. Government Printing Office, 1982).

2. As to the accuracy and appropriateness of the term "low intensity warfare" in this connection, see Kitson, Frank, *Low Intensity Operations: Subversion, Insurgency and Peace-Keeping* (Harrisburg, PA: Stackpole Books, 1971). It should be noted that the FBI, in its internal documents of the mid-'70s, referred to AIM not as "militants," "radicals," or "political extremists," but as "insurgents"; see, for example, the memorandum from SAC Portland to the Director, FBI, dated February 6, 1976, and reproduced at p. 264 of Churchill, Ward, and Jim Vander Wall, *The COINTEL-PRO Papers: Documents from the FBI's Secret Wars Against Dissent in the United States* (Boston, MA: South End Press, 1990). It should also be noted that a former operational commander of the FBI forces on Pine Ridge, Norman Zigrossi, in a 1990 interview with filmmaker Michael Apted, repeatedly described his agents' mission on the reservation during the critical period not as "investigation" or "law enforcement," but as "peace-keeping" (copy on file).

3. For a sample of the Bureau's official denials, see excerpts from an interview with an FBI Public Information Officer, contained in Lan Brookees Ritz' documentary film, *Annie Mae: A Brave Hearted Woman* (Los Angeles: Brown Bird Productions, 1979). Concerning the "experts," see Theoharis, Athan, "Building a File: The Case Against the FBI," *Washington Post* (October 30, 1988); and Dershowitz, Alan, "Can Leonard Peltier be the Andrei Sakharov of America?", *Denver Post* (October 21, 1984). An interesting example of a "progressive" commentator regurgitating essentially the same reactionary views will be found in Gordon, Diana, "Doing Edgar Proud," *The Nation* (November 13, 1989).

4. On the suits against Matthiessen and his publisher, Viking Press, see Churchill, Ward, "GOONs, G-Men, and AIM: At last the story will be told," *The Progressive* (April 1990).

5. The documentary, entitled *The Spirit of Crazy Horse*, was produced by Michel Dubois and Kevin McKiernan, and first aired on December 18, 1990. The author is in possession of a 125-page transcription of the Brewer interview from which the televised excerpts were drawn.

6. These are minimum figures, derived from reports collected by researcher Candy Hamilton, who resided on Pine Ridge throughout the period at issue as an unpaid paralegal volunteer for the Wounded Knee Legal Offense/Defense Committee (WKLDOC).

7. Johansen, Bruce, and Roberto Maestas, *Wasi'chu: The Continuing Indian Wars* (New York: Monthly Review Press, 1979), p. 83.

8. *Ibid.* The authors are relying on data from the *FBI Uniform Crime Report* (Washington, D.C.: U.S. Government Printing Office, 1975).

9. Johansen and Maestas, *op. cit.*, p. 84.

10. *Ibid.*

11. For a capsule history of FBI jurisdiction on Indian reservations, see American Indian Policy Review Commission, *Final Report, Task Force Nine: Law Consolidation, Revision and Codification* (Washington, D.C.: U.S. Government Printing Office, 1977), pp. 173-74. Also see U.S. Commission on Civil Rights, *Indian Tribes: A*

Continuing Quest for Survival (Washington, D.C.: U.S. Government Printing Office, 1981), p. 145.

12. This is incorporated into official findings: "[W]hen Indians complain about the lack of investigation and prosecution on reservation crime, they are usually told the Federal government does not have the resources to handle the work." See U.S. Department of Justice, *Report of the Task Force on Indian Matters* (Washington, D.C.: U.S. Government Printing Office, 1975), pp. 42-43.

13. *Ibid.* , pp. 42-43.

14. Interview of retired Rapid City ASAC George O'Clock by Michel DuBois and Kevin Barry McKiernan, 1987; transcript copy on file.

15. Zigrossi is the FBI official who explained to investigative journalist David Weir and Lowell Bergman in 1978 that, in his view, the proper function of the Bureau on Indian reservations is to serve as a "colonial police force." See Weir, David, and Lowell Bergman, "The Killing of Anna Mae Aquash," *Rolling Stone* (April 7, 1977): p. 5.

16. U.S. Senate, Committee on the Judiciary, Subcommittee on Internal Security, *Revolutionary Activities Within the United States: The American Indian Movement* (Washington, D.C.: U.S. Government Printing Office, 1975), p. 61.

17. *U.S. v. Consolidated Wounded Knee Cases*, CR. 73-5019, U.S. District Court for Nebraska, Lincoln, 1974.

18. U.S. House of Representatives, *Hearings Before the Subcommittee on Civil and Constitutional Rights, 97th Congress, 1st Session on FBI Authorization, March 19, 24, 25; April 2 and 8, 1981* (Washington, D.C.: U.S. Government Printing Office, 1981).

19. Quoted from audiotape in Churchill, Ward, and Jim Vander Wall, *Agents of Repression: The FBI's Secret Wars Against the Black Panther Party and the American Indian Movement* (Boston, MA: South End Press, 1988), p. 329. Warner appears to be borrowing from the thinking of British counterinsurgency expert (and consultant to the U.S. government) Robin Evelegh, who explains the operant concept rather well in his *Peace-Keeping in a Democratic Society: The Lessons of Northern Ireland* (London: C. Hurst and Company, 1978).

20. Witt, Shirley Hill, and William Muldrow, *Monitoring of Events Related to the Shootings of Two FBI Agents on the Pine Ridge Reservation* (Denver, CO: U.S. Commission on Human Rights, Rocky Mountain Regional Office, July 9, 1975).

21. Churchill and Vander Wall, *op. cit.*, pp. 186-87.

22. *Ibid.*, p. 185. This is hardly the only incident in which innocent bystanders were on the receiving end of GOON bullets. For instance, on February 7, 1974, a round fired by an unidentified GOON at AIM member Milo Goings in the reservation-adjacent hamlet of Whiteclay, Nebraska missed and struck nine-year-old Harold Weasel Bear in the face, blinding him in one eye. No FBI investigation was opened.

23. The amount is from Wilson's testimony during congressional hearings on Pine Ridge violence excerpted in Saul Landau's documentary film, *Voices From Wounded Knee* (Washington, D.C.: Institute for Policy Studies, 1974). Why a ranger unit was needed on Pine Ridge when the BIA police already had sufficient numbers has never been adequately explained by federal authorities. Wilson's version is that the GOONs were to serve as "an auxiliary police force...to handle people like Russell Means and other radicals."

24. A 1974 GAO audit determined that the Wilson administration kept virtually no books on its expenditures of federal funds and that there were clear implications of

financial malfeasance. See Brand, Johanna, *The Life and Death of Anna Mae Aquash* (Toronto: James Lorimar Publishers, 1978), p. 62. Also see Muldrow, William, *Report of Investigation: Oglala Sioux Tribe, General Election, 1974* (Denver: U.S. Commission on Civil Rights, Rocky Mountain Regional Office, October 1974), and Matthiessen, Peter, *In the Spirit of Crazy Horse* (New York: Viking Press, [second edition] 1992), p. 62.

25. It is estimated that at least $200,000 in tribal housing funds were expended in 1973 and '74 in acquiring house trailers utilized exclusively by members of the GOON squad and their families. See Brand, *op. cit.*

26. The per capita annual income on Pine Ridge during this period was a little over $1,000. Wilson assigned himself a pay increase from $5,500 to $15,500 per year, as well as a $30,000 annual "consultancy" with the tribe, within six months of taking office. His wife was hired as director of the Pine Ridge Head Start Program (which she shortly bankrupted) at $22,500 per year, his brother Jim as director of tribal planning (where he was able to identify and earmark funds for expenditure on the GOONs) at $25,000 per year plus a $15,000 consultancy, and his brother George as director of the tribal water works, where he seems to have functioned mainly as a GOON recruiter at $23,000 per year. Wilson's son Manny as well as several cousins and nephews were placed on more covert sorts of retainers, serving as GOON "soldiers" pure and simple. See editors, *Voices From Wounded Knee, 1973, Akwesasne Notes* (1974): p. 21; McCall, Cheryl, "Life on Pine Ridge Bleak," *Colorado Daily* (May 16, 1975); and *New York Times* (April 22, 1975).

27. The percentage of BIA police who actually moonlighted as GOONs in the classic fashion of the Latin American death squads is somewhat nebulous. Speculations have ranged from 25 to 50 percent.

28. The area, located in the northwestern quadrant of Pine Ridge, got its name when it was "borrowed" by the U.S. Army Air Corps in 1942 as a practice site for dive bombers and aerial gunners. By agreement, the government was to return the land to Oglala control at the end of World War II, but never did. Agitation among Oglala traditionals to recover the gunnery range had become pronounced by 1972, but unbeknownst to any of the Indians involved, a secret cooperative venture undertaken by NASA and the National Uranium Research and Evaluation Institute in 1970-71 had revealed through specialized satellite photography that the area contained a rich uranium deposit, intermingled with molybdenum; see Greis, J. P., *Status of Mineral Resource Information on the Pine Ridge Indian Reservation, S.D.* (Washington, D.C.: U.S. Department of Interior, BIA Report No. 12, 1976). The title transfer at issue was/is illegal under provision of the still-binding 1868 Fort Laramie Treaty, a stipulation requiring three-quarters express consent of all adult male Lakotas before any lawful land cession may take place.

29. The traditionals had formed the Oglala Sioux Civil Rights Organization (OSCRO), headed by Pedro Bissonette, in 1972 as a means to pursue recovery of the gunnery range, continue broader land claims under the 1868 treaty, and resolve heirship problems effecting reservation property owned by Pine Ridge residents, but administered "in trust" by the BIA. OSCRO naturally opposed the Wilson agenda and became the primary initial target of GOON terrorism. The traditionals then attempted to exercise their legal right of impeachment. The BIA responded by naming Wilson to head up his own impeachment proceedings and requested a 60-member Special Operations Group of SWAT-trained U.S. Marshals—com-

plete with flak vests and M-60 machine guns that they set up in sandbagged positions atop tribal buildings—to "maintain order" during the travesty. Immediately after continuing himself in office, Wilson proclaimed a reservation-wide ban on meetings of more than three people. It was at this point that AIM was called in to provide support and assistance.

30. The altercation at "The Residents' Roadblock" (as Wilson called it), Held's part in it, and the FBI's intervention to obtain the GOONs' release is described in *Voices From Wounded Knee, 1973*, op. cit., p. 123. Colburn's motive for attempting to dismantle the roadblock is explained in a 1989 interview of former Solicitor General Kent Frizzell by NPR reporter Scott Schlagle; Frizzell states that he was riding in Colburn's car on April 23, 1973 when they stopped at the GOON position. A Wilsonite, apparently incensed at the Justice Department's efforts to negotiate a cease-fire with AIM rather than unleashing the force necessary to kill the "militants" outright, proceeded to shove the muzzle of his weapon under Frizzell's chin and threatened to blow his head off. Colburn was forced to get out of the car and level his own weapon at the GOON, telling him to "go ahead and shoot Frizzell, and then I'm going to kill you," before the GOON backed off. Colburn then drove back to his command post in Pine Ridge village, assembled as many deputies as he could muster, and returned to the roadblock in a fury. In his own interview, Duane Brewer refers to a relative, BIA police officer/GOON Brian Brewer, leveling a weapon at Colburn himself during the subsequent confrontation.

31. The marshal, Lloyd Grimm, was apparently hit in the lower back by a round that permanently paralyzed him from the waist down while *facing* the AIM perimeter at Wounded Knee. The bullet that struck him was not federal issue. This combination of factors has caused considerable speculation that he may have been hit by a round fired by a GOON from a position behind the federal lines. Concerning M-16s in the possession of GOONs during the Wounded Knee siege, consider the following excerpt from federal radio monitoring of radio traffic on the night of April 23, 1973: *"Tribal Government [a euphemism for the GOONs] Roadblock to Tribal Roving Patrol*: How many M-16s you guys got? Where are the other guys? *Tribal Patrol to Tribal Roadblock*: We got eight M-16s and some men coming up on horseback…"

32. For researchers' conclusions, see Johansen and Maestas, *op. cit.*; Matthiessen, *op. cit.*; *Agents of Repression, op. cit.*; *The COINTELPRO Papers, op. cit.*; and Brand, *op. cit.* Also see Weyler, Rex, *Blood of the Land: The Governmental and Corporate War Against the American Indian Movement* (Philadelphia, PA: New Society Publishers, [second edition] 1992), and Messerschmidt, Jim, *The Trial of Leonard Peltier* (Boston, MA: South End Press, 1983).

33. Chuck Richards is the eldest son in a clan so grotesquely violent it is collectively referred to on Pine Ridge as the "Manson Family." Chuck, predictably, is known as "Charlie Manson." He was also Dick Wilson's son-in-law, before being sent to prison in 1978, presumably for holding a shotgun to the head of a tribal police officer during a post-GOON era altercation on the reservation. While incarcerated at the minimum security federal facility at Lompoc, California under an alias, he is believed to have been involved in an assassination plot against Northwest AIM leader Leonard Peltier, who had suddenly and unaccountably been transferred there directly from the "super-maximum" prison at Marion, Illinois. Richards'

younger brother Bennie, also a GOON, had by then become head of the BIA police on the Duck Valley Shoshoni Reservation, on the Nevada/Idaho border. He is suspected of involvement in the mass murder of AIM President John Trudell's entire family—wife Tina, daughters Ricarda Star (age five) and Sunshine Karma (age three), son Eli Changing Sun (age one), and mother-in-law Leah Hicks Manning—on the night of February 12, 1979.

34. Brewer's reference to a "Treaty Convention up at Fort Yates," on the Standing Rock Sioux Reservation, concerns the founding conference of the International Indian Treaty Council, AIM's diplomatic arm, in June 1974. "Pine Ridge's little crew" was also on hand at Standing Rock on June 8, 1975, when AIM leader Russell Means was shot in the back and nearly killed by BIA police.

35. In fact, FBI were "around," at least on some occasions. For example, on February 26, 1973, AIM leader Russell Means, accompanied by reservation residents Milo Goings and Pedro Bissonette, attempted to meet with Dick Wilson in a last ditch effort to avert the confrontation that became the siege of Wounded Knee only 24 hours later. For their trouble, they were assaulted in the parking lot of the tribal office building by five GOONs headed by Duane Brewer. At least two FBI agents were on hand as "observers." No further action was taken by the Bureau.

36. Finzel, Gordon and James were members of the Wounded Knee Legal Defense/Offense Committee (WKLD/OC), a National Lawyers Guild project initiated during the 1973 Wounded Knee siege to provide legal counsel to AIM members and supporters.

37. Aside from Dick Wilson, the victims identified GOONs Duane, Brian and Vincent Brewer, Chuck, Cliff, Bennie and Woody Richards, Mark and Greg Clifford, Lloyd and Toby Eagle Bull, Robert Ecoffey, Johnson Holy Rock, Bennett "Tuffy" Sierra, John Hussman, Glenn Little Bird, Marvin Stolt, Glenn Three Stars, James Wedell, Michael Weston, Dale Janis, Charlie Winters, Salty Twiss, Manny and Billy Wilson, Fred Two Bulls, and Francis Randall as being among their 50-odd attackers.

38. Quoted in the *Rapid City Journal* (February 28, 1975).

39. A further perspective has been offered in an interview by former WKLD/OC coordinator Ken Tilsen: "Somebody had to tell Dick Wilson how to go about beating the rap on this one. He wasn't smart enough to figure out the double jeopardy ploy all by himself. And you can bet that 'somebody' was in the U.S. Attorney's office or the FBI."

40. For instance, AIM supporter Phillip Little Crow was beaten to death as part of a GOON "educational seminar" on November 10, 1973; AIM supporter Jim Little was stomped to death by four GOONs on September 10, 1975; AIM member Hobart Horse was beaten, shot and run over repeatedly by a car on March 1, 1976. No one went to trial for any of these murders.

41. The late Robert Burnette, at the time tribal president of the Rosebud Sioux, has recounted how, immediately after the Wounded Knee siege ended, "[Solicitor General] Kent Frizzell...called me to request that I come to Wounded Knee with two FBI agents in an attempt to find eight graves that were around the perimeter. The activists who spoke of these graves believed they contained the bodies of Indians murdered by white ranchers or Wilson's men [or both]"; see Burnette, Robert, with John Koster, *The Road to Wounded Knee* (New York: Bantam Books,

1974), p. 248. The *Akwesasne Notes* book, *Voices From Wounded Knee, 1973* (*op. cit.*, p. 193) also contains an excerpt from the verbatim transcription of U.S. Marshal radio logs for the night in which it is reported that a GOON "roving patrol" had captured a group of 13 "hippies" attempting to backpack supplies into Wounded Knee. A BIA police unit dispatched by the marshals to take custody of the prisoners was fired upon by the GOONs and retreated. None of the prisoners were ever seen again. All told, the cumulative number of individuals believed by AIM to be missing as a result of their attempts to move in or out of Wounded Knee during the siege exceeds 40.

42. In late 1974, Young Bear requested that an AIM security unit be placed on his property in much the same fashion as the Northwest AIM group subsequently established its defensive encampment at the request of the Jumping Bull family, near Oglala. As a result, GOON violence directed at Young Bear's home "dropped off real fast," as he remembers it.

43. It is worth noting that there were no Afro-American gun dealers in Rapid City—or anywhere else in western South Dakota or adjoining areas of Wyoming and Nebraska—in those days, and still aren't. The individuals in question were therefore necessarily "imported" from some considerable distance in order to conduct their clandestine commerce. If the whole thing were a profit-making venture on their part, this might be understandable. But Brewer says repeatedly that they provided weapons and munitions to the GOONs either free of charge or at extremely low cost. So, the question of why a group of black men might undertake considerable effort and expense for no potential return in order to provide one group of Indians the means to slaughter another remains inexplicable on its face. This remains true unless one considers the probability that they were serving as go-betweens for someone else—say, a federal agency—and were compensated accordingly. The scenario fits well with the remainder of Brewer's commentary on arms transactions, and with the known means by which the Bureau armed the Secret Army Organization in southern California at about the same time. See Parenti, Michael, *Democracy for the Few* (New York: St. Martin's Press, 1982), p. 24.

44. This concerns the altercation outside the tribal office building in Pine Ridge village on February 26, 1973.

45. The cause of death listed in both the police report and coroner's report in the Pedro Bissonette slaying is also suspect. The time of the shooting reported by Clifford is 9:48 p.m., the time of the body's arrival by ambulance at the Pine Ridge hospital (a few minutes distance from the shooting scene) is 10:10, making it appear that the victim died more or less instantly from gunshot wounds. Several eyewitnesses who happened on the roadblock, however, contend that Bissonette was shot at approximately 9 p.m. This would mean the victim was left on the ground for nearly an hour before an ambulance was called, and likely bled to death. Such a possibility may explain why Delmar Eastman, acting on instructions from AUSA Bill Clayton, ordered the body secretly removed from the Pine Ridge morgue at 3 a.m. on the morning after the killing, and taken to Scottsbluff, Nebraska, where the autopsy was performed by Brown. See *Agents of Repression, op. cit.*, pp. 200-3, 206-11.

46. DeSersa was hit in the left thigh by a bullet fired from one of four carloads of GOONs pursuing his own vehicle in a high speed chase outside Wanblee. It severed the femoral artery and he bled to death in a ditch while the GOONs pursued his passengers through open fields. Charlie Winters, one of the assailants, was subsequently arrested for the crime by local police in nearby Martin, South Dakota. This led to a state (not federal) case in which not only Winters, but Chuck Richards, Billy Wilson, and Dale Janis were charged. Despite the fact that DeSersa and his companions had been unarmed, charges were dismissed against Richards and Wilson on the basis of their having acted in "self-defense." Winters and Janis were then allowed to plea bargain to second degree manslaughter and eventually served two years apiece. Neither the FBI nor the BIA police played any constructive role in obtaining even this minimal outcome.

47. Inexplicably, the FBI lab notes concerning Aquash (one of which is reproduced in *The COINTELPRO Papers, op. cit.,* p. 293) refer to the cause of death as neither "natural" nor "homicide," but as "possible manslaughter."

48. Indeed, the Bureau caused an article, headlined "FBI denies AIM implication that Aquash was informant," to appear in the March 11, 1976 edition of the *Rapid City Journal.* No one in AIM had implied that she was. Hence, the appearance is that the Bureau was deliberately attempting to create a public impression of its own. Bob Robideau, a member of the Northwest AIM Group, of which Aquash was also a part, states categorically that she was neither an informer nor suspected of being one. Rumors had been raised to that effect by FBI infiltrator/provocateur Douglass Durham nearly a year earlier. These had, according to Robideau, been "checked out" by AIM Security, and she had been immediately "cleared." Former AIM leaders John Trudell and Dennis Banks concur with Robideau's assessment of the situation. On Durham, see Giese, Paula, "Profile of an Informer," *Covert Action Information Bulletin,* no. 24 (summer 1985).

49. FBI representative James Frier was grilled by California Representative Don Edwards on this topic during appropriation hearings in 1980. Frier's responses were deemed "less than satisfactory" by this former FBI agent turned legislator. See U.S. House of Representatives, *Hearings Before the Subcommittee on Civil and Constitutional Rights of the Committee of the Judiciary: First Session on FBI Authorization, 1981* (Washington, D.C.: 97th Cong., 1st Sess., U.S. Government Printing Office, 1980), p. 666.

50. See analysis by Aquash's attorney, Bruce Ellison, and former AIM leader John Trudell in *Annie Mae: A Brave-Hearted Woman, op. cit.* For excerpts from an independent researcher's interview with Brown, see Brand, *op. cit.,* pp. 21-22.

51. Price was one of the agents who atypically gathered to view Aquash's "unidentified" body in situ. He then, even more atypically, accompanied the body more than 100 miles to the morgue at the Pine Ridge hospital, and professed to be unable to recognize the victim in either location. Morgue photos of the body, observed by the author (who never met her), are clearly identifiable as being of Anna Mae Aquash. As Congress subsequently put it: "SA Price had had personal contact with Ms. Aquash in the past and assisted in photographing the body at the PHS morgue on February 25, 1976...SA Price's previous contacts with Ms. Aquash occurred when he interviewed her in connection with an FBI investigation in the early spring of 1975 and again in September 1975...[On the latter occasion] she was

arrested…by agents of the FBI, one of whom was SA Price" (see *First Session on FBI Authorization, 1981, op. cit.,* p. 278). Concerning death threats, see McKiernan, Kevin, "Indian woman's death raises many troubling questions," *Minneapolis Tribune* (May 30, 1976), especially quotations from WKLD/OC researcher Candy Hamilton. Also see Churchill, Ward, "Who Killed Anna Mae?" *Z Magazine* (December 1988).

52. There is, for example, a report entitled "Law Enforcement on the Pine Ridge Indian Reservation," dated June 6, 1975, which calls for "massive military assault forces." A later memorandum, excerpted into a press release entitled "RESMURS Press Coverage Clarification" (July 8, 1975), calls for "automatic and semiautomatic weapons" deployment among the assault forces, as well as "heavy equipment such as armored personnel carriers."

53. These events are covered extremely well in Matthiessen, *op. cit.*

54. Concerning Held's prepositioning in Minneapolis, see June 27, 1975 memorandum, Gebhart to O'Connell, reproduced at p. 267 of *The COINTELPRO Papers, op. cit.*

55. Concerning Richard Wallace Held's involvement in the RESMURS operation from its first moments, and his eventual presence on Pine Ridge—both of which he and the Bureau have denied—see the documents reproduced at pp. 268-70 of *The COINTELPRO Papers, op. cit.*

56. One result of these tactics was the death of an elderly man named James Brings Yellow, who was startled into a fatal heart attack when a team of agents headed by J. Gary Adams suddenly kicked in his door on July 10, 1975. Air assaults included a raid on the property of AIM member Selo Black Crow, near Wanblee, on July 8 (50 agents involved), and another on the property of AIM spiritual leader Leonard Crow Dog on September 5, 1975 (100 agents involved).

57. The Senate Select Committee had issued a subpoena to FBI agent provocateur Douglass Durham, to begin hearings as of mid-July 1975. The proceedings were called off on July 3 by a letter from committee staff member Patrick Shae to Attorney General Edward S. Levi, stating in part: "[W]e will hold in abeyance any action…in view of the killing of the Agents at Pine Ridge Reservation, South Dakota."

58. The preliminary document was signed by Wilson on June 29, 1975. Another improved version was signed on January 2, 1976, shortly before Wilson left office. Congress then duly consecrated the arrangement as Public Law 90-468. When the legitimacy of this measure was subsequently challenged on the basis of treaty requirements, P.L. 90-468 was amended so that surface rights might revert to the Lakotas at any time they determined by referendum to recover them (thus neatly reversing the treaty stipulation), but leaving subsurface (i.e., mineral) rights under permanent federal ownership. See Huber, Jacqueline, *et al., The Gunnery Range Report* (Pine Ridge, SD: Oglala Sioux Tribe, Office of the President, 1981).

59. For analysis, see Weisman, Joel D., "About that 'Ambush' at Wounded Knee," *Columbia Journalism Review* (September-October 1975). Also see Churchill, Ward, "Renegades, Terrorists and Revolutionaries: The Government's Propaganda War Against the American Indian Movement," *Propaganda Review,* no. 4 (April 1989).

60. FBI Director Kelley "corrected misimpressions" at a press conference conducted at the Century Plaza Hotel in Los Angeles on July 1, 1975, an event timed

to coincide with the funerals of Williams and Coler. The major problems with the Bureau's replacement story are that the warrant allegedly being served on Jimmy Eagle is dated July 7, nearly two weeks *after* the firefight (and, for that matter, a week after Kelley's press conference), and is for the petty theft of a pair of used cowboy boots rather than "kidnapping and assault," as the Bureau originally informed the press. Even taken at face value, the scenario places the FBI in a posture of assigning *two* agents the weighty task of pursuing a teenaged member of AIM accused of stealing some old boots at a time when the Bureau was professing to be too shorthanded to investigate the murders (by that point) of about two-score AIM members. More, the Bureau's case was so weak against Eagle that he was eventually acquitted of any wrongdoing in "the cowboy boot caper."

61. The differences in evidentiary rulings extended by the judges presiding over the Peltier and Butler/Robideau cases account for the different outcomes of the two trials, and are analyzed quite well in Messerschmidt, *op. cit.* Suffice it here to note that the three-judge Eight Circuit Court panel that reviewed Peltier's first appeal found 23 reversible errors in the conduct of his trial, most of them associated with FBI misconduct. The court nonetheless allowed Peltier's conviction to stand. Interestingly, by the time the panel's opinion was rendered, its head, William Webster, had departed the bench to assume a new career. Webster had accepted a position as director of the FBI. For the Circuit Court's opinion, see *United States v. Leonard Peltier*, 858 F.2d 314, 335 (8th Cir. 1978), *cert denied*, 440 U.S. 945 (1979).

62. Judge Heaney made his remarks on the CBS news program *West 57th Street* in 1989. The reason for his consternation is apparent in the opinion rendered by the three-judge panel of the Eighth Circuit Court, headed by himself, which reviewed Peltier's second appeal. After first acknowledging that the original circumstantial ballistics case presented against the defendant was flawed beyond redemption, and could thus not really support the murder convictions, the panel went on to rebut prosecutorial arguments that Peltier was actually convicted of simply aiding and abetting in the alleged murders (recall that the Butler/Robideau jury had concluded for all intents and purposes that no murders had, in fact, occurred). The panel *still* allowed Peltier's conviction to stand—although they plainly could not say exactly what it is he was convicted of—because: "We recognize there is evidence in this record of improper conduct on the part of some FBI agents, but we are reluctant to impute even further improprieties to them." See United States Court of Appeals for the Eighth Circuit, "Appeal from the United States District Court for the District of North Dakota, *United States v. Peltier*," No. 95-5192 (*September 12, 1986), p. 16.*

63. A portion of the impetus behind this move may derive from the fact that the individual who actually shot Coler and Williams has now gone on record to this effect, explaining exactly what happened during the firefight, and why. See Matthiessen, Peter, "New Light on Peltier's Case: Who Really Killed the F.B.I. Men," *The Nation* (May 13, 1991).

64. There are a number of excellent readings mining this vein. Some of the best include Langguth, A. J., *Hidden Terrors: The Truth About U.S. Police Operations in Latin America* (New York: Pantheon Press, 1978); Lernoux, Penny, *Cry of the People: United States Involvement in the Rise of Fascism, Torture, and Murder and the Persecu-*

tion of the Catholic Church in Latin America (New York: Doubleday Publishers, 1980); and Herman, Edward S., *The Real Terror Network: Terrorism in Fact and Propaganda* (Boston, MA: South End Press, 1982).

65. For a partial (rather sanitized) record in this regard, see U.S. Senate, Select Committee to Study Government Operations with Respect to Intelligence Activities, *Final Report: Supplementary Detailed Staff Reports on Intelligence Activities and the Rights of Americans, Book III* (Washington, D.C.: 94th Cong., 2d Sess., U.S. Government Printing Office, 1976).

66. See Bermanzohm, Paul C. and Sally A., *The True Story of the Greensboro Massacre* (New York: César Chauce Publishers, 1980).

67. For the most comprehensive, accessible examination of the Hampton-Clark assassinations, see *Agents of Repression, op. cit.*, pp. 64-77, 397-404. For officially acknowledged (sanitized) context, see U.S. Senate, Select Committee to Study Government Operations with Respect to Intelligence Activities, *The FBI's Covert Program to Destroy the Black Panther Party* (Washington, D.C.: 94th Cong., 2d Sess., U.S. Government Printing Office, 1976).

68. See Jayko, Margaret, ed., *The FBI on Trial: The Victory of the Socialist Workers Party Suit Against Government Spying* (New York: Pathfinder Press, 1988). Also see editors, "The Red Squads Controversy," *The Nation* (July 11, 1981), and *Alliance to End Repression v. City of Chicago*, 742 F.2d (1984).

69. Tackwood, Louis E., and the Citizens Research and Investigation Committee, *The Glass House Tapes: The Story of an Agent Provocateur and the New Police-Intelligence Complex* (New York: Avon Books, 1973). Also see Durden-Smith, Jo, *Who Killed George Jackson? Fantasies, Paranoia and the Revolution* (New York: Alfred A. Knopf Publishers, 1976).

70. On the SAO, see Parenti, *op. cit.*, p. 24. Also see Zoccino, Nanda, "Ex-FBI Infiltrator Describes Terrorist Role," *Los Angeles Times* (January 26, 1976).

71. Suarez, Manuel, *Requiem on Cerro Maravilla: The Police Murders in Puerto Rico and the U.S. Government Coverup* (Maplewood, NJ: Waterfront Press, 1987). Also see Nelson, Anne, *Murder Under Two Flags: The U.S., Puerto Rico and the Cerro Maravilla Cover-Up* (New York: Ticknor and Fields Publishers, 1986).

WHITE STUDIES
The Intellectual Imperialism of U.S. Higher Education

Education should be adapted to the mentality, attitudes, occupation, and traditions of various peoples, conserving as far as possible all the sound and healthy elements in the fabric of their social life.

—David Abernathy, *The Dilemma of Popular Education*

Since schooling was brought to non-Europeans as a part of empire…it was integrated into the effort to bring indigenous peoples into imperial/colonial structures…After all, did not the European teacher and the school built on the European capitalist model transmit European values and norms and begin to transform traditional societies into "modern" ones?

—Martin Carnoy, *Education as Cultural Imperialism*

Over the past decade, the nature and adequacy of educational content have been matters for increasingly vociferous debate among everyone from academics to policymakers to lay preachers in the United States. The American educational system as a whole has been amply demonstrated to be locked firmly into a paradigm of Eurocentrism, not only in terms of its focus, but also in its discernible heritage, methodologies, and conceptual structure. Among people of non-European cultural derivation, the kind of "learning" inculcated through such a model is broadly seen as insulting, degrading, and functionally subordinative. More and more, these themes have found echoes among the more enlightened and progressive sectors of the dominant Euroamerican society itself. [1]

Such sentiments are born of an ever-widening cognition that, within any multicultural setting , this sort of monolithic pedagogical reliance upon a single cultural tradition constitutes a rather transparent form of intellectual domination, achievable only within the context of parallel forms of domination. This is meant in precisely the sense intended by David Landes when he observed, "It seems to me that one has to look at imperialism as a multifarious response to a common opportunity that consists simply as a disparity of power." [2]

In this connection, it is often pointed out that, while education in America has existed for some time, by law, as a "common opportunity," its shape has all along been defined exclusively via the "disparity of power" exercised by members of the ruling Euroamerican elite.[3]

Responses to this circumstance have, to date, concentrated primarily upon what might be best described as a "contributionist" approach to remedy. This is to say, they seek to bring about the inclusion of non-Europeans and/or non-European achievements in canonical subject matters, while leaving the methodological and conceptual parameters of the canon itself essentially intact.[4] The present essay represents an attempt to go a bit further, sketching out to some degree the preliminary requisites for challenging methods and concepts as well. It should be noted before proceeding that while my own grounding in American Indian Studies leads me to anchor my various alternatives in that particular perspective, the principles postulated should prove readily adaptable to other "minority" venues.

White Studies

As currently established, the university system in the United States offers little more than the presentation of "White Studies" to students, "general population," and minority alike.[5] The curriculum is virtually totalizing in its emphasis, not simply upon an imagined superiority of Western endeavors and accomplishments, but also upon the notion that the currents of European thinking comprise the only really "natural"—or at least truly useful—formation of knowledge/means of perceiving reality. In the vast bulk of curriculum content, Europe is not only the subject (in its conceptual mode, the very process of "learning to think"), but the object (subject matter) of investigation as well.

Consider a typical introductory level philosophy course. Students will in all probability explore the works of the ancient Greek philosophers,[6] the fundamentals of Cartesian logic and Spinoza, stop off for a visit with Thomas Hobbes, David Hume, and John Locke, cover a chapter or two of Kant's aesthetics, dabble a bit in Hegelian dialectics, and review Nietzsche's assorted rantings. A good leftist professor may add a dash of Marx's famous "inversion" of Hegel and, on a good day, his commentaries on the frailties of Feuerbach. In an exemplary class, things will end up in the 20th century with discussions of Schopenhauer, Heidegger and Husserl, Bertrand Russell and Alfred North Whitehead, perhaps an "adventurous" summarization of the existentialism of Sartre and Camus.

Advanced undergraduate courses typically delve into the same topics, with additive instruction in matters such as "Late Medieval Philosophy," "Monism," "Rousseau and Revolution," "The Morality of John Stuart Mill," "Einstein and the Generations of Science," "The Phenomenology of Merleau-Ponty," "Popper's Philosophy of Science," "Benjamin, Adorno and the Frankfurt School," "Meaning and Marcuse," "Structuralism/Post-Structuralism," even "The Critical Theory of Jürgen Habermas."[7] Graduate work usually consists of effecting a coherent synthesis of some combination of these elements.

Thus, from first-semester surveys through the Ph.D., philosophy majors—and non-majors fulfilling elective requirements, for that matter—are fed a consistent stream of data defining and presumably reproducing Western thought at its highest level of refinement, as well as inculcating insight into what is packaged as its historical evolution and line(s) of probable future development. Note that this is construed, for all practical intents and purposes, as being representative of philosophy *in toto* rather than of western European thought *per se*.

It seems reasonable to pose the question as to what consideration is typically accorded the non-European remainder of the human species in such a format. The answer is often that coursework does in fact exist, most usually in the form of upper-division undergraduate "broadening" curriculum: surveys of "Oriental Philosophy" are not unpopular,[8] "The Philosophy of Black Africa" exists as a catalogue entry at a number of institutions,[9] even "Native American Philosophical Traditions" (more casually titled "Black Elk Speaks," from time to time) makes its appearance here and there.[10] But nothing remotely approaching the depth and comprehensiveness with which Western thought is treated can be located in any quarter.

Clearly, the student who graduates, at whatever level, from a philosophy program constructed in this fashion—and all of them are—walks away with a concentrated knowledge of the European intellectual schema rather than any genuine appreciation of the philosophical attainments of humanity. Yet, equally clearly, a degree in "philosophy" implies, or at least should imply, the latter.

Nor is the phenomenon in any way restricted to the study of philosophy. One may search the catalogues of every college and university in the country, and undoubtedly the search will be in vain, for the department of history which accords the elaborate oral/pictorial "prehistories" of American Indians anything approximating the weight given to the semiliterate efforts at self-justification scrawled by early European colonists in this hemisphere.[11] Even the rich codigraphic records of cultures like the Mayas, Incas, and Mexicanos (Aztecs) are uniformly ignored by the "historical mainstream." Such matters are more properly the purview of anthropology than of history, or so it is said by those representing "responsible"scholarship in the United States.[12]

As a result, most intro courses on "American History" still begin for all practical intents and purposes in 1492, with only the most perfunctory acknowledgement that people existed in the Americas in precolumbian times. Predictably, any consideration accorded to precolumbian times typically revolves around anthropological rather than historical preoccupations, such as the point at which people were supposed to have first migrated across the Beringian Land Bridge to populate the hemisphere,[13] or whether native horticulturalists ever managed to discover fertilizer.[14] Another major classroom topic centers in the extent to which cannibalism may have prevailed among the proliferation of "nomadic Stone Age tribes" presumed to have wandered about America's endless reaches, perpetually hunting and gathering their way to the margin of raw subsistence.[15] Then again, there are the countless expositions on how few indigenous people there really were in North America prior to 1500,[16] and why genocide is an "inappropriate" term by which to explain why there were almost none by 1900.[17]

From there, many things begin to fall into place. Nowhere in modern American academe will one find the math course acknowledging, along with the importance of Archimedes and Pythagoras, the truly marvelous qualities of precolumbian mathematics: that which allowed the Mayas to invent the concept of zero, for example, and, absent computers, to work with multidigit prime numbers.[18] Nor is there mention of the Mexicano mathematics which allowed that culture to develop a calendrical system several decimal places more accurate than that commonly used today.[19] And again, the rich mathematical understandings which went into Mesoamerica's development of what may well have been the world's most advanced system of astronomy are typically ignored by mainstream mathematicians and astronomers alike.[20]

Similarly, departments of architecture and engineering do not teach that the Incas invented the suspension bridge, or that their 2,500-mile Royal Road—paved, leveled, graded, guttered, and complete with rest areas—was perhaps the world's first genuine superhighway, or that portions of it are still used for motorized transport in Peru.[21] No mention is made of the passive solar temperature control characteristics carefully designed by the Anasazi into the apartment complexes of their cities at Chaco Canyon, Mesa Verde, and elsewhere.[22] Nor are students drawn to examine the incorporation of thermal mass into Mandan and Hidatsa construction techniques,[23] the vast north Sonoran irrigation systems built by the Hohokam,[24] or the implications of the fact that, at the time of Cortez's arrival, Tenochtitlán (now Mexico City) accommodated a population of 350,000, a number making it one of the largest cities on earth, at least five times the size of London or Seville.[25]

In political science, readers are invited—no, defied—to locate the course acknowledging, as John Adams, Benjamin Franklin, and others among the U.S. "founding fathers" did, that the form of the American Republic and the framing of its constitution were heavily influenced by the preexisting model of the Haudenosaunee (Six Nations Iroquois Confederacy of present-day New York, Québec and Ontario).[26] Nor is mention made of the influence exerted by the workings of the "Iroquois League" in shaping the thinking of theorists such as Karl Marx and Friedrich Engels.[27] Even less discussion can be found on the comparably sophisticated political systems conceived and established by other indigenous peoples—the Creek Confederation, for example, or the Cherokees or Yaquis—long before the first European invader ever set foot on American soil.[28]

Where agriculture or the botanical sciences are concerned, one will not find the conventional department which wishes to "make anything special" of the fact that fully two-thirds of the vegetal foodstuffs now commonly consumed by all of humanity were under cultivation in the Americas, and nowhere else, in 1492.[29] Also unmentioned is the hybridization by Incan scientists of more than 3,000 varieties of potato,[30] or the vast herbal cornucopia discovered and deployed by native pharmacologists long before that.[31] In biology, pre-med, and medicine, nothing is said of the American Indian invention of surgical tubing and the syringe, or the fact that the Incas were successfully practicing brain surgery at a time when European physicians were still seeking to cure their patients by applying leeches to "draw off bad blood."[32]

To the contrary, from matters of governance, where the Greek and Roman democracies are habitually cited as being sole antecedents of "the American experiment,"[33] to agriculture, with its "Irish" potatoes, "Swiss" chocolate, "Italian" tomatoes, "French" vanilla, and "English" walnuts,[34] the accomplishments of American Indian cultures are quite simply expropriated and recast in the curriculum as if they had been European in origin.[35] Concomitantly, the native traditions which produced such things are themselves deculturated and negated, consigned to the status of being "people without history."[36]

Such grotesque distortion is, of course, fed to indigenous students right along with Euroamericans,[37] and by supposedly radical professors as readily as by more conservative ones.[38] Moreover, as was noted above, essentially the same set of circumstances prevails with regard to the traditions and attainments of all non-Western cultures.[39] Overall, the situation virtually demands to be viewed from a perspective best articulated by Albert Memmi:

> In order for the colonizer to be a complete master, it is not enough for him to be so in actual fact, but he must also believe in [the colonial system's] legitimacy. In order for that legitimacy to be complete, it is not enough for the colonized to be a slave; he must also accept his role. The bond between colonizer and colonized is thus destructive and creative. It destroys and recreates the two partners in colonization into colonizer and colonized. One is disfigured into an oppressor, a partial, unpatriotic and treacherous being, worrying only about his privileges and their

defense; the other into an oppressed creature, whose development is broken and who compromises by his defeat.[40]

In effect, the intellectual sophistry which goes into arguing the "radical" and "conservative" content options available within the prevailing monocultural paradigm, a paradigm which predictably corresponds to the culture of the colonizer, amounts to little more than a diversionary mechanism through which power relations are reinforced, the status quo maintained.[41] The monolithic White Studies configuration of U.S. higher education—a content heading which, unlike American Indian, African American, Asian American and Chicano Studies, has yet to find its way into a single college or university catalogue—thus serves to underpin the hegemony of white supremacism in its other, more literal manifestations: economic, political, military, and so on.[42]

Those of non-European background are integral to such a system. While consciousness of their own heritages is obliterated through falsehood and omission, they are indoctrinated to believe that legitimacy itself is something derived from European tradition, a tradition which can never be truly shared by non-Westerners, despite—or perhaps because of—their assimilation into Eurocentrism's doctrinal value structure. By and large, the "educated" American Indian or Black thereby becomes the aspect of "broken development" who "compromises [through the] defeat" of his or her people, aspiring only to serve the interests of the order he or she has been trained to see as his or her "natural" master.[43]

As Frantz Fanon and others have observed long-since, such psychological jujitsu can never be directly admitted, much less articulated, by its principal victims. Instead, they are compelled by illusions of sanity to deny their circumstance and the process which induced it. Their condition sublimated, they function as colonialism's covert hedge against the necessity of perpetual engagement in more overt and costly sorts of repression against its colonial subjects.[44] Put another way, the purpose of White Studies in this connection is to trick the colonized into materially supporting her/his colonization through the mechanisms of his/her own thought processes.[45]

There can be no reasonable or "value neutral" explanation for this situation. Those, regardless of race or ethnicity, who endeavor to apologize for or defend its prevalence in institutions of higher education on "scholarly" grounds do so without a shred of honesty or academic integrity.[46] Rather, whatever their intentions, they define themselves as accepting of the colonial order. In Memmi's terms, they accept the role of colonizer, which means "agreeing to be a…usurper. To be sure, a usurper claims his place and, if need be, will defend it with every means at his disposal…He endeavors to falsify history, he rewrites laws, he would extinguish memories—anything to succeed in transforming his usurpation into legitimacy."[47] They are, to borrow and slightly modify a term, "intellectual imperialists."[48]

An Indigenist Alternative

From the preceding observations as to what White Studies is, the extraordinary pervasiveness and corresponding secrecy of its practice, and the reasons underlying its existence, certain questions necessarily arise. For instance, the query might be posed as to whether a simple expansion of curriculum content to include material on non-Western contexts might be sufficient to redress matters. It follows that we should ask whether something beyond data or content is fundamentally at issue. Finally, there are structural considerations concerning how any genuinely corrective and liberatory curriculum or pedagogy might actually be inducted into academia. The first two questions dovetail rather nicely, and will be addressed in a single response. The third will be dealt with in the following section.

In response to the first question, the answer must be an unequivocal "no." Content is, of course, highly important, but, in and of itself, can never be sufficient to offset the cumulative effects of White Studies indoctrination. Non-Western content injected into the White Studies format can be—and, historically, has been—filtered through the lens of Eurocentric conceptualization, taking on meanings entirely alien to itself along the way.[49] The result is inevitably the reinforcement rather than the diminishment of colonialist hegemony. As Vine Deloria, Jr., has noted relative to just one aspect of this process:

> Therein lies the meaning of the white's fantasy about Indians—the problem of the Indian image. Underneath all the conflicting images of the Indian one fundamental truth emerges—the white man knows that he is an alien and he knows that North America is Indian—and he will never let go of the Indian image because he thinks that by some clever manipulation he can achieve an authenticity that cannot ever be his.[50]

Plainly, more is needed than the simple introduction of raw data for handling within the parameters of Eurocentric acceptability. The conceptual mode of intellectuality itself must be called into question. Perhaps a bit of "pictographic" communication will prove helpful in clarifying what is meant in this respect. The following schematic represents the manner in which two areas of inquiry, science and religion (spirituality), have been approached in the European tradition.

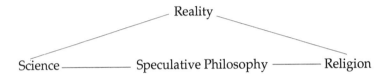

In this model, "knowledge" is divided into discrete content areas arranged in a linear structure. This division is permanent and culturally enforced; witness the Spanish Inquisition and "Scopes Monkey Trial" as but two historical illustrations.[51] In the cases of science and religion (as theology), the mutual opposition of their core assumptions has given rise to a third category, speculative philosophy, which is informed by both, and, in turn, informs them. Speculative philosophy, in this sense at least, serves to mediate and sometimes synthesize the linearly isolated components, science and religion, allowing them to communicate and "progress." Speculative philosophy is not, in itself, intended to apprehend reality, but rather to create an abstract reality in its place. Both religion and science, on the other hand, are, each according to its own internal dynamics, meant to effect a concrete understanding of and action upon "the real world."[52]

Such compartmentalization of knowledge is replicated in the departmentalization of the Eurocentric education itself. Sociology, theology, psychology, physiology, kinesiology, biology, cartography, anthropology, archaeology, geology, pharmacology, astronomy, agronomy, historiography, geography, demography—the whole vast proliferation of Western "ologies," "onomies," and "ographies"—are necessarily viewed as separate or at least separable areas of inquiry within the university. Indeed, the Western social structure both echoes and is echoed by the same sort of linear fragmentation, dividing itself into discrete organizational spheres: church, state, business, family, education, art, and so forth.[53] The structure involved readily lends itself to—perhaps demands—the sort of hierarchical ordering of things, both intellectually and physically, which is most clearly manifested in racism, militarism and colonial domination, class and gender oppression, and the systematic ravaging of the natural world.[54]

The obvious problems involved are greatly amplified when our schematic of the Eurocentric intellectual paradigm is contrasted to one of non-Western, in this case Native American, origin.

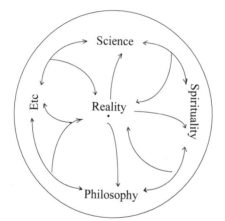

Within such a conceptual model, there is really no tangible delineation of compartmentalized "spheres of knowledge." All components or categories of intellectuality (by Eurocentric definition) tend to be mutually and perpetually informing. All tend to constantly concretize the human experience of reality (nature) while all are simultaneously and continuously informed by that reality. This is the "Hoop" or "Wheel" or "Circle" of Life—an organic rather than synthesizing or synthetic view, holding that all things are equally and indispensably interrelated—which forms the core of the native worldview.[55] Here, reality is not something "above" the human mind or being, but an integral aspect of the living/knowing process itself. The mode through which native thought devolves is thus inherently anti-hierarchical, incapable of manifesting the extreme forms of domination so pervasively evident in Eurocentric tradition.[56]

The crux of the White Studies problem, then, cannot be located amidst the mere omission or distortion of matters of fact, no matter how blatantly ignorant or culturally chauvinistic these omissions and distortions may be. Far more importantly, the system of Eurosupremacist domination depends for its continued maintenance and expansion, even its survival, upon the reproduction of its own intellectual paradigm—its approved way of thinking, seeing, understanding, and being—to the ultimate exclusion of all others. Consequently, White Studies simply cannot admit to the existence of viable conceptual structures other than its own.[57]

To introduce the facts of pre-colonial American Indian civilizations into the curriculum is to open the door to confronting the utterly different ways of knowing which caused such facts to be actualized in the first place.[58] It is thoroughly appreciated in ruling circles that any widespread and genuine understanding of such alternatives to the intrinsic oppressiveness of Eurocentrism could well unleash a liberatory dynamic among the oppressed resulting in the evaporation of Eurosupremacist hegemony and a corresponding collapse of the entire structure of domination and elite privilege which attends it.[59] The academic "battle lines" have therefore been drawn, not so much across the tactical terrain of fact and data as along the strategic high ground of Western versus non-Western conceptualization. It follows that if the latter is what proponents of the White Studies status quo find it most imperative to bar from academic inclusion, then it is precisely that area upon which those committed to liberatory education must place our greatest emphasis.

A Strategy to Win

Given the scope and depth of the formal problem outlined in the preceding section, the question of the means through which to address it takes on a crucial importance. If the objective in grappling with White Studies is to bring about conceptual—as opposed to merely contentual—inclusion of non-Western traditions in academia, then appropriate and effective methods must be employed. As was noted earlier, resort to inappropriate "remedies" leads only to cooptation and a reinforcement of White Studies as the prevailing educational norm.

One such false direction has concerned attempts to establish, essentially from scratch, whole new educational institutions, even systems, while leaving the institutional structure of the status quo very much intact.[60] Although sometimes evidencing a strong showing at the outset, these perpetually underfunded, understaffed, and unaccredited, "community-based"—often actually separatist—schools have almost universally ended up drifting and floundering before going out of existence altogether.[61] Alternately, more than a few have abandoned their original reason for being, accommodating themselves to the "standards" and other requirements of the mainstream system as an expedient for survival.[62] Either way, the outcome has been a considerable bolstering of the carefully nurtured public impression that "the system works" while alternatives don't.

A variation on this theme has been to establish separatist centers or programs, even whole departments, within existing colleges and universities. While this approach has alleviated to some extent (though not entirely) difficulties in securing funding, faculty, and accreditation, it has accomplished little if anything in terms of altering the delivery of White Studies instruction in the broader institutional context.[63] Instead, intentionally self-contained "Ethnic Studies" efforts have ended up "ghettoized"—that is, marginalized to the point of isolation and left talking only to themselves and the few majors they are able to attract—bitter, frustrated, and stalemated.[64] Worse, they serve to reinforce the perception, so desired by the status quo, that White Studies is valid and important while non-Western subject matters are invalid and irrelevant.

To effect the sort of transformation of institutional realities envisioned in this essay, it is necessary *not* to seek to create parallel structures as such, but instead to penetrate and subvert the existing structures themselves, both pedagogically and canonically. The strategy is one which was once described quite aptly by Rudi Dutschke, the German activist/theorist, as amounting to a "long march through the institutions."[65] In this view, Ethnic Studies entities, rather than constituting ends in themselves, serve as "enclaves" or "staging areas" from which forays into the mainstream arena can be launched with ever increasing frequency and vitality, and to which non-Western academic guerrillas can withdraw when needed to rest and regroup among themselves.[66]

As with any campaign of guerrilla warfare, however metaphorical, it is important to concentrate initially upon the opponent's point(s) of greatest vulnerability. Here, three prospects for action come immediately to mind, the basis for each of which already exists within most university settings in a form readily lending itself to utilization in undermining the rigid curricular compartmentalization and pedagogical constraints inherent in White Studies institutions. The key is to recognize and seize such tools, and then to apply them properly.

1) While tenure-track faculty must almost invariably be "credentialed"—i.e., hold the Ph.D. in a Western discipline, have a few publications in the "right" journals, etc.—to be hired into the academy, the same isn't necessarily true for guest professors, lecturers, and the like.[67] Every effort can and should be expended by the regular faculty—"cadre," if you will—of Ethnic Studies units to bring in guest instructors lacking in Western academic pedigree (the more conspicuously, the better), but who are in some way exemplary of non-Western intellectual traditions (especially oral forms). The initial purpose is to enhance cadre articulations with practical demonstrations of intellectual alternatives by consistently exposing students to "the real thing." Goals further on down the line should include incorporation of such individuals directly into the core faculty, and, eventually, challenging the current notion of academic credentialing in its entirety.[68]

2) There has been a good deal of interest over the past 20 years in what has come to be loosely termed "Interdisciplinary Studies." Insofar as there is a mainstream correspondent to the way in which American Indians and other non-Westerners conceive of and relate to the world, this is it. Ethnic Studies practitioners would do well to push hard in the Interdisciplinary Studies arena, expanding it whenever and wherever possible at the direct expense of customary Western disciplinary boundaries. The object, of course, is to steep students in

the knowledge that nothing can be understood other than in its relationship to everything else; that economics, for example, can never really make sense if arbitrarily divorced from history, politics, sociology, and geography. Eventually, the goal should be to dissolve the orthodox parameters of disciplines altogether, replacing them with something more akin to "areas of interest, inclination, and emphasis."[69]

3) For a variety of reasons, virtually all colleges and universities award tenure to certain faculty members in more than one discipline or department. Ethnic Studies cadres should insist that this be the case with them. Restricting their tenure and rostering exclusively to Ethnic Studies is not only a certain recipe for leaving them in a "last hired, first fired" situation during times of budget exigency, it is a standard institutional maneuver to preserve the sanctity of White Studies instruction elsewhere on campus. The fact is that an Ethnic Studies professor teaching American Indian or African American history is just as much an historian as a specialist in 19th-century British history; the Indian and the Black should therefore be rostered to and tenured in History, *as well as* in Ethnic Studies. This "foot in the door" is important, not only in terms of cadre longevity and the institutional dignity such appointments signify *vis-à-vis* Ethnic Studies, but it offers important advantages by way of allowing cadres to reach a greater breadth of students, participate in departmental policy formation and hiring decisions, claim additional resources, and so forth. On balance, success in this area can only enhance efforts in the two above.[70]

The objective is to begin to develop a critical mass, first in given spheres of campuses where opportunities present themselves—later throughout the academy as a whole—which is eventually capable of discrediting and supplanting the hegemony of White Studies. In this, the process can be accelerated, perhaps greatly, by identifying and allying with sectors of the professorate with whom a genuine affinity and commonality of interests may be said to exist at some level. These might include those from the environmental sciences who have achieved, or begun to achieve, a degree of serious ecological understanding.[71] It might include occasional mavericks from other fields, various applied anthropologists,[72] for instance, and certain of the better and more engaged literary and artistic deconstructionists,[73] as well as the anarchists like Murray Bookchin who pop up more or less randomly in a number of disciplines.[74]

By and large, however, it may well be that the largest reservoir of potential allies will be found among the relatively many faculty who profess to consider themselves, "philosophically" at least, to be marxian in their orientation. This is not said because marxists tend habitually to see themselves as being in opposition to the existing order (fascists express the same view of themselves, after all, and for equally valid reasons).[75] Nor is it because, where it has succeeded in overthrowing capitalism, marxism has amassed an especially sterling record where indigenous peoples are concerned.[76] In fact, it has been argued with some cogency that, in the latter connection, marxist practice has proven even more virulently Eurocentric than has capitalism in many cases.[77]

Nonetheless, one is drawn to conclude that there may still be a basis for constructive alliance, given Marx's positing of dialectics—a truly nonlinear and relational mode of analysis and understanding—as his central methodology. That he himself consistently violated his professed method,[78] and that subsequent generations of his adherents have proven themselves increasingly unable to distinguish between dialectics and such strictly linear propositions as cause/effect progressions,[79] does not inherently invalidate the whole of his project or its premises. If some significant proportion of today's self-proclaimed marxian intelligentsia can be convinced to actually learn and apply dialectical method, it stands to reason that they will finally think their way into a posture not unlike that elaborated herein (that they will in the process have transcended what has come be known as "marxism" is another story).[80]

Conclusion

This essay presents only the barest glimpse of its subject matter. It is plainly, its author hopes, not intended to be anything approximating an exhaustive or definitive exposition of its topics. To the contrary, it is meant only to act as, paraphrasing Marcuse, the Archimedean point upon which false consciousness may be breached en route to "a more comprehensive emancipation."[81] By this, we mean not only a generalized change in perspective which leads to the abolition of Eurocentrism's legacy of colonialist, racist, sexist, and classist domination, but the replacement of White Studies' Eurosupremacism with an educational context in which we can all, jointly and with true parity, "seek to expand our knowledge of the world" in full realization that,

> The signposts point to a reconciliation of the two approaches to experience. Western science must reintegrate human emotions and intuitions into its interpretation of phenomena; [non-Western] peoples must confront...the effects of [Western] technology...[We must] come to an integrated conception of how our species came to be, what it has accomplished, and where it can expect to go in the millennia ahead...[Then we will come to] understand as these traditionally opposing views seek a unity that the world of historical experience is far more mysterious and eventful than previously expected...Our next immediate task is the unification of human knowledge.[82]

There is, to be sure, much work to be done, both practically and cerebrally. The struggle will be long and difficult, frustrating many times to the point of sheer exasperation. It will require stamina and perseverance, a preparedness to incur risk, often a willingness to absorb the consequences of revolt, whether overt or covert. Many will be required to give up or forego aspects of a comfort zone academic existence, both mentally and materially.[83] But the pay-off may be found in freedom of the intellect, the pursuit of knowledge in a manner more proximate to truth, unfettered by the threats and constraints of narrow vested interest and imperial ideology. The reward, in effect, is participation in the process of human liberation, including our own. One can only assume that this is worth the fight.

Notes

1. For an overview of the evolution of the current conflict, see Shore, Ira, *Culture Wars: School and Society in the Conservative Restoration, 1969-1984* (Boston, MA: Routledge & Kegan Paul, 1986); for reactionary analysis, see Kimball, Roger, *Tenured Radicals: How Politics Has Corrupted Our Higher Education* (New York: Harper & Row, 1990).

2. Landes, David S., "The Nature of Economic Imperialism," *Journal of Economic History* 21 (December 1961), as quoted in *The Age of Imperialism,* Harry Magdoff (New York: Monthly Review Press, 1969), p. 13.

3. Jayne, Gerald, and Robbin Williams, ed., *A Common Destiny: Blacks and American Society* (Washington, D.C.: National Academy Press, 1989).

4. One solid summary of the contributionist trend will be found in Duster, Troy, *The Diversity Project: Final Report* (Berkeley: University of California Institute for Social Change, 1991); for complaints, see Alter, Robert, "The Revolt Against Tradition," *Partisan Review*, vol. 58, no. 2 (1991).

5. General population, or "G-Pop" as it is often put, is the standard institutional euphemism for white students.

6. A good case can be made that there is a great disjuncture between the Greek philosophers and the philosophies later arising in western Europe; see Bernal, Martin, *Black Athena: The Afro-Asiatic Roots of Ancient Greece, Vol. 1* (Princeton, NJ: Princeton University Press, 1987).

7. Marxian academics make another appearance here, insofar as they do tend to teach courses, or parts of courses, based in the thinking of non-Europeans. It should be noted, however, that those selected for exposition—Mao, Ho Chi Minh, Vo Nguyen Giap, Kim Il Sung, *et al.*—are uniformly those who have most thoroughly assimilated Western doctrines in displacement of their own intellectual traditions.

8. Probably the most stunning example of this I've ever encountered came when Will Durant casually attributed the thought of the East Indian philosopher Shankara to a "pre-plagiarism" (!!!) of Kant: "To Shankara the existence of God is no problem, for he defines God as existence, and identifies all real being with God. But the existence of a personal God, creator or redeemer, there may, he thinks, be some question; such a deity, says this pre-plagiarist of Kant, cannot be proved by reason, he can only be postulated as a practical necessity"; Durant, Will, *The History of Civilization, Vol. 1: Our Oriental Heritage* (New York: Simon & Schuster, 1954), p. 549. It should be remarked that Durant was not a reactionary of the stripe conventionally associated with white supremacism, but rather an intellectual of the marxian progressive variety. Yet, in this single book on the philosophical tradition of Asia, he makes no less than 10 references to Kant, all of them implying that the earlier philosophers of the East acted "precisely as if [they] were Immanual Kant" (p. 538), never that Kant might have predicated his own subsequent philosophical articulations in a reading of Asian texts. The point is raised to demonstrate the all but unbelievable lengths even the more dissident Western scholars have been prepared to go in reinforcing the mythos of Eurocentrism, and thus how such reinforcement transcends ideological divisions within the Eurocentric paradigm.

9. It should be noted, however, that the recent emergence of an "Afrocentric" philosophy and pedagogy, natural counterbalances to the persistence of Eurocentric orthodoxy, has met with fierce condemnation by defenders of the status quo; see Nicholson, David, "Afrocentrism and the Tribalization of America," *Washington Post National Weekly Edition* (October 8-14, 1990).

10. A big question, frequently mentioned, is whether American Indians ever acquired the epistemological sensibilities necessary for their thought to be correctly understood as having amounted to "philosophical inquiry." Given that epistemology simply means "investigation of the limits of human comprehension," one can only wonder what the gatekeepers of philosophy departments make of the American Indian conception, prevalent in myriad traditions, of there being a "Great Mystery" into which the human mind is incapable of penetrating;

see, e.g., Neihardt, John G., ed., *Black Elk Speaks* (New York: William Morrow Publisher, 1932), and Walker, J. R., *Lakota Belief and Ritual* (Lincoln: University of Nebraska Press, 1980). For an unconsciously comparable Western articulation, see Noam Chomsky's discussions of accessible and inaccessible knowledge in the chapters entitled "A Philosophy of Language?" and "Empiricism and Rationalism," in *Language and Responsibility: An Interview by Mitsou Ronat* (New York: Pantheon Books, 1977).

11. As illustration, see Washburn, Wilcomb E., "Distinguishing History for Moral Philosophy and Public Advocacy," in *The American Indian and the Problem of History,* ed. Calvin Martin (New York: Oxford University Press, 1987), pp. 91-97.

12. For a veritable case study of this mentality, see Axtell, James, *After Columbus: Essays in the Ethnohistory of Colonial North America* (New York: Oxford University Press, 1988).

13. For a solid critique of the Beringia Theory, see Goodman, Jeffrey, *American Genesis: The American Indian and the Origins of Modern Man* (New York: Summit Books, 1981); also see Ericson, Jonathan E., R. E. Taylor, and Rainier Berger, ed., *The Peopling of the New World* (Los Altos, CA: Ballena Press, 1982).

14. For an exhaustive enunciation of the "fertilizer dilemma," see Hurt, James C., *American Indian Agriculture* (Lawrence: University Press of Kansas, 1991).

15. An excellent analysis of this standard description of indigenous American realities may be found in Weatherford, Jack, *Indian Givers: How the Indians of the Americas Transformed the World* (New York: Crown, 1988). On cannibalism specifically, see Arens, W., *The Man-Eating Myth: Anthropology and Anthropophagy* (New York: Oxford University Press, 1979).

16. The manipulation of data undertaken by succeeding generations of Euroamerican historians and anthropologists in arriving at the official 20th century falsehood that there were "not more than one million Indians living north of the Rio Grande in 1492, including Greenland" is laid out very clearly by Jennings, Francis, *The Invasion of America: Indians, Colonialism and the Cant of Conquest* (Chapel Hill: University of North Carolina Press, 1975). For a far more honest estimate, deriving from the evidence rather than ideological preoccupations, see Dobyns, Henry F., *Their Number Become Thinned: Native American Population Dynamics in Eastern North America* (Knoxville: University of Tennessee Press, 1983); also see Thornton, Russell, *American Indian Holocaust and Survival: A Population History Since 1492* (Norman: University of Oklahoma Press, 1987). Dobyns places the actual number as high as 18.5 million; Thornton, more conservative, places it at 12.5 million.

17. During a keynote presentation at the annual meeting of the American History Association in 1992, James Axtell, one of the emergent "deans" of the field, actually argued that genocide was an "inaccurate and highly polemical descriptor" for what had happened. His reasoning? That he could find only five instances in the history of colonial North America in which genocides "indisputably" occurred. Leaving aside the obvious—that this in itself makes genocide an appropriate term by which to describe the obliteration of American Indians—a vastly more accurate chronicle of the process of extermination will be found in Stannard, David E., *American Holocaust: Columbus and the Conquest of the New World* (New York: Oxford University Press, 1992).

18. Morely, Syvanus G., and George W. Bainerd, *The Ancient Maya* (Stanford, CA: Stanford University Press, 1983); Carmack, Robert M., *Quichean Civilization* (Berkeley: University of California Press, 1973).

19. Aveni, Anthony, *Empires of Time: Calenders, Clocks and Cultures* (New York: Basic Books, 1989).

20. Mexicano astronomy is discussed in Durán, D., *Book of Gods and Rites and the Ancient Calendar* (Norman: University of Oklahoma Press, 1971); also see Radin, Paul, *The Sources and Authenticity of the History of Ancient Mexico* (Berkeley: University of California Publications in American Archeology and Ethnology, vol. 17, no. 1, 1920).

21. Von Hagen, Victor Wolfgang, *The Royal Road of the Inca* (London: Gordon and Cremonesi, 1976).

22. Lister, Robert H. and Florence C., *Chaco Canyon: Archeology and Archaeologists* (Albuquerque: University of New Mexico Press, 1981); also see Mays, Buddy, *Ancient Cities of the Southwest* (San Francisco, CA: Chronicle Books, 1962).

23. Nabokov, Peter, and Robert Easton, *American Indian Architecture* (New York: Oxford University Press, 1988); the "submerged" building principles developed by the Mandan and Hidatsa, ideal for the plains environment but long disparaged by the Euroamericans who displaced them, are now considered the "cutting edge" in some architectural circles. The Indians, of course, are not credited with having perfected such techniques more than a thousand years ago.

24. Haury, Emil W., *The Hohokam: Desert Farmers and Craftsmen* (Tucson: University of Arizona Press, 1976), pp. 120-51; the City of Phoenix and its suburbs still use portions of the several thousand miles of extraordinarily well-engineered Hohokam canals, constructed nearly a thousand years ago, to move their own water supplies around.

25. Cortez was effusive in his descriptions of Tenochtitlán as being, in terms of its design and architecture, "the most beautiful city on earth"; Díaz del Castillo, Bernal, *The Discovery and Conquest of Mexico, 1519-1810* (London: George Routledge & Sons, 1928), p. 268. On the size of Tenochtitlán, see Zantwijk, Rudolf A. M., *The Aztec Arrangement: The Social History of Pre-Spanish Mexico* (Norman: University of Oklahoma Press, 1985), p. 281; on the size of London in 1500, Stone, Lawrence, *The Family, Sex and Marriage in England, 1500-1800* (New York: Harper & Row, 1977), p. 147; for Seville, Elliott, J. H., *Imperial Spain, 1469-1716* (New York: St. Martin's Press, 1964), p. 177.

26. Grinde, Donald A., Jr., and Bruce E. Johansen, *Exemplar of Liberty: Native America and the Evolution of Democracy* (Los Angeles, CA: UCLA American Indian Studies Center, 1992).

27. Between December 1880 and March 1881, Marx read anthropologist Lewis Henry Morgan's 1871 book, *Ancient Society*, based in large part on his 1851 classic, *The League of the Hau-de-no-sau-nee or Iroquois*. Marx took at least 98 pages of dense notes during the reading, and, after his death, his collaborator, Friedrich Engels, expanded these into a short book entitled, *The Origin of the Family, Private Property and the State: In Light of the Researches of Lewis Henry Morgan*. The latter, minus its subtitle, appears in *Marx and Engels: Selected Works* (New York: International Publishers, 1968).

28. Weatherford, *op. cit.*

29. Crosby, Alfred W., Jr., *The Columbian Exchange: Biological and Cultural Consequences of 1492* (Westport, CT: Greenwood Press, 1972); Bryant, Carol A., Anita Courtney, Barbara A. Markesbery, and Kathleen M. DeWalt, *The Cultural Feast* (St. Paul, MN: West, 1985).

30. Salaman, Redcliffe N., *The History and Social Influence of the Potato* (Cambridge: Cambridge University Press, 1949).

31. Wissler, Clark, Wilton M. Krogman, and Walter Krickerberg, *Medicine Among the American Indians* (Ramona, CA: Acoma Press, 1939); Taylor, Norman, *Plant Drugs That Changed the World* (New York: Dodd, Meade, 1965).

32. Vogel, Virgil, *American Indian Medicine* (Norman: University of Oklahoma Press, 1970); Guzmán, Peredo, *Medical Practices in Ancient America* (Mexico City: Ediciones Euroamericana, 1985). On contemporaneous European medical practices, see McNeill, William H., *Plagues and Peoples* (Garden City, NJ: Anchor/Doubleday, 1976).

33. For good efforts at debunking such nonsense, see Arciniegas, Germán, *America in Europe: A History of the New World in Reverse* (New York: Harcourt Brace Jovanovich, 1986), and Brandon, William, *New Worlds for Old: Reports from the New World and Their Effect on Social Thought in Europe, 1500-1800* (Athens: Ohio University Press, 1986).

34. Sauer, Carl O., "The March of Agriculture Across the Western World," in his *Selected Essays, 1963-1975* (Berkeley, CA: Turtle Island Foundation, 1981); also see Weatherford, *op. cit.*

35. This is nothing new, or unique to the treatment of American Indians. Indeed, the West has comported itself in similar fashion *vis-à-vis* all non-Westerners since at least as early as the inception of "Europe"; see Wolf, Philippe, *The Awakening of Europe: The Growth of European Culture from the Ninth Century to the Twelfth* (London: Cox & Wyman, 1968).

36. For a much broader excursus on this phenomenon, see Wolf, Eric R., *Europe and the People Without History* (Berkeley: University of California Press, 1982).

37. For surveys of the effects, see Thompson, Thomas, ed., *The Schooling of Native America* (Washington, D.C.: American Association of Colleges for Teacher Education, 1978); Young, James R., ed., *Multicultural Education and the American Indian* (Los Angeles, CA: UCLA American Indian Studies Center, 1979), and Heath, Charlotte, and Susan Guyette, *Issues for the Future of American Indian Studies* (Los Angeles, CA: UCLA American Indian Studies Center, 1985).

38. Consider, e.g., the "Sixteen Thesis" advanced by the non-marxist intellectual Alvin Gouldner as alternatives through which to transform the educational status quo. It will be noted that the result, if Gouldner's pedagogical plan were implemented, would be tucked as neatly into the paradigm of Eurocentrism as the status quo itself. See Gouldner, Alvin W., *The Future of Intellectuals and the Rise of the New Class* (New York: Seabury Press, 1979). For marxian views falling in the same category, see Norton, Theodore Mills, and Bertell Ollman, ed., *Studies in Socialist Pedagogy* (New York: Monthly Review Press, 1978).

39. See generally, Said, Edward W., *Orientalism* (New York: Oxford University Press, 1987).

40. Memmi, Albert, *Colonizer and Colonized* (Boston, MA: Beacon Press, 1965), p. 89.

41. The procedure corresponds well in some ways with the kind of technique described by Herbert Marcuse as being applicable to broader social contexts in his

essay "Repressive Tolerance," in *A Critique of Pure Tolerance,* Robert Paul Wolff, Barrington Moore, Jr., and Herbert Marcuse (Boston, MA: Beacon Press, 1969).

42. The theme is handled well in Deloria, Vine, Jr., "Education and Imperialism," *Integrateducation,* vol. XIX, nos. 1-2 (January 1982). For structural analysis, see Arrighi, Giovanni, *The Geometry of Imperialism* (London: Verso, 1978).

43. Memmi develops these ideas further in his *Dominated Man* (Boston, MA: Beacon Press, 1969).

44. See especially, Fanon's *Wretched of the Earth* (New York: Grove Press, 1965) and *Black Skin/White Masks: The Experiences of a Black Man in a White World* (New York: Grove Press, 1967).

45. Probably the classic example of this, albeit in a somewhat different dimension, was the Gurkas, who forged a legendary reputation fighting on behalf of their British colonizers, usually against other colonized peoples; see McCrory, Patrick, *The Fierce Pawns* (Philadelphia, PA: J. B. Lippencott, 1966).

46. See, e.g., Bloom, Allan, *The Closing of the American Mind* (New York: Simon and Schuster, 1988); D'Sousa, Dinesh, *Illiberal Education: The Politics of Race and Sex on Campus* (New York: Free Press, 1991); Schlesinger, Arthur, Jr., *The Disuniting of America* (New York: W.W. Norton, 1992).

47. *Colonizer and Colonized, op. cit.,* pp. 52-53.

48. Carnoy, Martin, *Education as Cultural Imperialism* (New York: David McKay, 1974); also see Whitt, Laurie Anne, "Cultural Imperialism and the Marketing of Native America," forthcoming in *Historical Reflections* (1995).

49. A fascinating analysis of how this works, distorting the perspectives of perpetrator and victim alike, may be found in Blackburn, Richard James, *The Vampire of Reason: An Essay in the Philosophy of History* (London: Verso Press, 1990).

50. Deloria, Vine, Jr., "Forward: American Fantasy," in *The Pretend Indians: Images of Native Americans in the Movies,* ed. Gretchen M. Bataille and Charles L. P. Silet (Ames: Iowa State University Press, 1980), p. xvi.

51. On the Inquisition, see Perry, Mary Elizabeth, and Anne J. Cruz, ed., *Cultural Encounters: The Impact of the Inquisition in Spain and the New World* (Berkeley: University of California Press, 1991). On the context of the Scopes trial, see Gould, Stephan Jay, *The Mismeasure of Man* (New York: W.W. Norton, 1981).

52. For a sort of capstone rendering of this schema, see Popper, Karl, *Objective Knowledge: An Evolutionary Approach* (New York: Oxford University Press, 1975).

53. Useful analysis of this dialectic will be found in Reed, David, *Education for Building a People's Movement* (Boston, MA: South End Press, 1981).

54. For an interesting analysis of many of these cause/effect relations, see Mander, Jerry, *In the Absence of the Sacred: The Failure of Technology and the Survival of Indian Nations* (San Francisco, CA: Sierra Club Books, 1991). Also see McNeill, William H., ed., *Pursuit of Power: Technology, Armed Force and Society Since A.D. 1000* (Chicago, IL: University of Chicago Press, 1982).

55. For elaboration, see Deloria, Vine, Jr., *God Is Red* (New York: Grosset & Dunlap, 1973). Also see Mohawk, John, *A Basic Call to Consciousness* (Rooseveltown, NY: Akwesasne Notes, 1978).

56. A Westerner's solid apprehension of this point may be found in Diamond, Stanley, *In Search of the Primitive: A Critique of Civilization* (New Brunswick, NJ:

Transaction Books, 1974); also see Thomas, Keith, *Man and the Natural World: A History of Modern Sensibility* (New York: Pantheon Books, 1983).

57. The matter has been explored tangentially, from a number of angles. Some of the best, for purposes of this essay, include Asad, Tala, ed., *Anthropology and the Colonial Encounter* (New York: Humanities Press, 1973); Berkhofer, Robert, *The White Man's Indian: Images of the American Indian from Columbus to the Present* (New York: Alfred A. Knopf, 1978); Todorov, Tzvetan, *The Conquest of America: The Question of the Other* (New York: Harper & Row, 1984); and Young, Robert, *White Mythologies: Writing History and the West* (London: Routledge, 1990).

58. More broadly, the thrust of this negation has always pertained in the interactions between European/Euroamerican colonists and native cultures; see Drinnon, Richard, *Facing West: The Metaphysics of Indian Hating and Empire Building* (Minneapolis: University of Minnesota Press, 1980).

59. Aside from the paradigmatic shift, culturally-speaking, imbedded in this observation, it shares much with the insights into the function of higher education achieved by New Left theorists during the 1960s; see Davidson, Carl, *The New Student Radicals in the Multiversity and Other Writings on Student Syndicalism* (Chicago, IL: Charles Kerr, 1990).

60. In essence, this approach is the equivalent of Mao Tse-Tung's having declared the Chinese revolution victorious at the point it liberated and secured the Caves of Hunan.

61. One salient example is the system of "survival schools" started by AIM during the mid-'70s, only two of which still exist in any form; see Braudy, Susan, "We Will Remember Survival School: The Women and Children of the American Indian Movement," *Ms. Magazine*, no. 5 (July 1976).

62. For a case study of one initially separatist effort turned accommodationist, see Duchene, Maryls, "A Profile of American Indian Community Colleges"; more broadly, see Wilkenson, Gerald, "Educational Problems in the Indian Community: A Comment on Learning as Colonialism"; both essays will be found in *Integrateducation*, vol. XIX, nos. 1-2 (January-April 1982).

63. Churchill, Ward, and Norbert S. Hill, Jr., "Indian Education at the University Level: An Historical Survey," *Journal of Ethnic Studies*, vol. 7, no. 3 (1979).

64. Further elaboration of this theme will be found in Churchill, Ward, "White Studies or Isolation: An Alternative Model for American Indian Studies Programs," in *American Indian Issues in Higher Education*, ed. James R. Young (Los Angeles, CA: UCLA American Indian Studies Center, 1981).

65. So far as is known, Dutschke, head of the German SDS, first publicly issued a call for such a strategy during an address of a mass demonstration in Berlin during January 1968.

66. Tse-Tung, Mao, *On Protracted War* (Peking: Foreign Language Press, 1967); Guevara, Che, *Guerrilla Warfare* (New York: Vintage Books, 1961).

67. For an excellent and succinct examination of the implications of this point, see Herget, Jürgen, *And Sadly Teach: Teacher Education and Professionalization in American Culture* (Madison: University of Wisconsin Press, 1991).

68. The concept is elaborated much more fully and eloquently in Freire, Paulo, *Pedagogy of the Oppressed* (New York: Continuum Books, 1981).

69. Again, one can turn to Freire for development of the themes; see his *Education for Critical Consciousness* (New York: Continuum Books, 1982). For the results of a practical—and very successful—application of these principles in the United States, see *TRIBES 1989: Final Report and Evaluation* (Boulder: University of Colorado University Learning Center, August 1989).

70. For overall analysis, see Deloria, Vine, Jr., "Indian Studies—The Orphan of Academia," *Wicazo Sa Review,* vol. II, no. 2 (1986); also see Barriero, José, "The Dilemma of American Indian Education," *Indian Studies Quarterly,* vol. 1, no. 1 (1984).

71. As examples, Bill Devall and George Sessions; see their *Deep Ecology: Living as if Nature Mattered* (Salt Lake City, UT: Perigrine Smith Books, 1985). Also see Gorz, André, *Ecology as Politics* (Boston, MA: South End Press, 1981).

72. The matter is well-handled in Said, Edward W., "Representing the Colonized: Anthropology's Interlocutors," *Critical Inquiry,* no. 15 (1989).

73. See, for instance, Lippard, Lucy, *Mixed Blessings: New Art in Multicultural America* (New York: Pantheon, 1990).

74. Bookchin, Murray, *The Ecology of Freedom* (Palo Alto, CA: Cheshire Books, 1982); also see Chase, Steve, ed., *Defending the Earth: A Dialogue Between Murray Bookchin and Dave Foreman* (Boston, MA: South End Press, 1991).

75. Stern, Fritz, *The Politics of Cultural Despair: A Study in the Rise of Germanic Ideology* (Berkeley: University of California Press, 1961); also see Reich, Wilhelm, *The Mass Psychology of Fascism* (New York: Farrar, Strauss & Giroux, 1970).

76. See generally, Connor, Walker, *The National Question in Marxist-Leninist Theory and Strategy* (Princeton, NJ: Princeton University Press, 1984).

77. Means, Russell, "The Same Old Song," in *Marxism and Native Americans,* ed. Ward Churchill (Boston, MA: South End Press, 1983).

78. Churchill, Ward, and Elisabeth R. Lloyd, *Culture versus Economism: Essays on Marxism in the Multicultural Arena* (Denver: University of Colorado Center for the Study of Indigenous Law and Politics, 1990).

79. Albert, Michael, and Robin Hahnel, *Unorthodox Marxism* (Boston, MA: South End Press, 1978).

80. As illustration of one who made the transition, at least in substantial part, see Bahro, Rudolph, *From Red to Green* (London: Verso, 1984).

81. Marcuse, *op. cit.*

82. Deloria, Vine, Jr., *The Metaphysics of Modern Existence* (New York: Harper & Row, 1979), p. 213.

83. For insights, see Schrecker, Ellen, *No Ivory Tower: McCarthyism and the Universities* (New York: Oxford University Press, 1986).

LITERATURE AND THE COLONIZATION OF AMERICAN INDIANS

To retrench the traditional concept of Western history at this point would mean to invalidate the justifications for conquering the Western Hemisphere.

—Vine Deloria, Jr., *God Is Red*

During the late 1960s, American writers made inroads into advanced literary theory by announcing their intent to offer "the journal as novel/the novel as journal." Norman Mailer embarked overtly upon such a course of action with his *Armies of the Night* in 1967; Tom Wolfe published his *The Electric Kool-Aid Acid Test* the same year. Such early efforts were soon followed by a proliferation of journalist/novelist works including Kurt Vonnegut's *Slaughterhouse Five* and the great synthetic "gonzo" excursions of Hunter S. Thompson. According to popular wisdom of the day, a new literary genre had been born, a writing process defining the emergent contours of American letters.

One might be inclined to agree with the assessment that this intentionally eclectic stew of fact and fiction constitutes a representative image of what is characteristically American in American literature. One might, with equal certainty, dispute the notion that such a posture is new to the scene, particularly since the deliberate presentation of fictionalized material as fact has marked the nature of American writing almost since the first English-speaking colonist touched pen to paper. A symbiotic relationship has been established in America between truly fictional writing on the one hand and ostensibly factual material on the other. Perhaps it is true that this principle prevails in any literate culture. America, however, seems demonstrably to have gone beyond any discernible critical differentiation between fiction and non-fiction, a condition which has led to an acute blurring of the line between "truth" and "art."

In locating the roots of such a situation, it becomes necessary to examine the content of early archetypal works originating in the Atlantic coastal colonies. By doing so, it is possible to distinguish a common denominator in terms of subject matter between the various modes of writing (formal journals, reports, histories, and narrative accounts for the most part) then extant. This subject matter is the indigenous population of the region.

It next becomes necessary to determine concretely whether this early colonial preoccupation with "factually" fixing the realities of things Indian through fictive modes was a topical phenomenon or whether it has exhibited a longevity beyond its immediate context. An examination of 19th-century American writing, including the emergence of the novel and epic poetry in North America, serves this purpose, albeit in cursory fashion. Interestingly, as fictional literature evolves in America, it is relatively easy to point both to its concern with the pronouncements of earlier "nonfictive" material as well as to the beginning of an active withdrawal of information from the "factual" treatments of the day. As American fiction developed during the 19th century, it provided a return of information (if only "themes") to be pursued in non-fiction forums. Again, the American Indian emerges as the common denominator blending these two types of writing.

Whether such literary trends are merely aspects of historical Americana or whether they retain a contemporary force and vitality is a question. An examination of several recent works in American letters tends to reveal not only that the "Indian in American literature" genre is alive and well but also that it has undergone something of an arithmetic progression, assuming a position occupying simultaneously both fictional and non-fictional frames of reference. Works secretly composed of pure imagination and conjecture are presented as serious factual writing; works of acknowledged fictive content are presented as "authentic" accounting of the "true story." The journalist is and has always been novelist; the novelist has always pretended to journalistic "truth" in relation to the Native American, a condition which—in this sense at least—has served to define American literature itself.

We are not thus confronted with customary understandings of the status and function of literature. When fact and fiction fuse into an intentionally homogeneous whole, mythology becomes the norm. However, those who read, write, and publish American literature are unused to and quite unwilling to acknowledge their "truth" as myth; it is insisted upon in most quarters that that which is presented as fact *is* fact. Why this might be so constitutes a final question.

Viewed from the perspective of colonial analysis, I believe the enigmatic aspects of the handling of the American Indian in literature disappear. With literature perceived as a component part of a colonial system, within which Native America constituted and constitutes expropriated and subjugated peoples, the reworking of fact into convenient or expedient fantasies by the colonizer is a logical process rather than an inexplicable aberration. The merger of fact and fiction which was treated as such a rarefied accomplishment by Mailer, Wolfe, Thompson, *et al.* was already a time-honored practice in a colonial nation which has always insisted upon viewing itself as free of the colonial aspirations marking its European antecedents.

The Colonial Period

In May of 1607, three small ships sailed up the James River from Chesapeake Bay in search of a site for the first permanent English colony in North America. The prospective settlers chose a peninsula that had the clear disadvantage of being low and swampy. But it did provide a good anchorage, and the fact that it was a virtual island made it defensible against possible attacks by hostile Indians. By giving a high priority to physical security, the colonizers showed an awareness that this was not an empty land but one that was already occupied by another people who might well resist their incursion. Unlike earlier attempted settlements, Jamestown was not so much an outpost as a beachhead for the English invasion and conquest of what was to become the United States of America.

— George M. Frederickson,*White Supremacy*

American Indians seem to have provided the defining aspect of that portion of written expression which has come to be generically considered as "American literature." This has held true virtually since the first English set foot upon the soil of the North American continent.

As early as 1612, Captain John Smith was offering observations on native peoples to an eager audience in the "Mother Country":

> They [the Indians] are inconstant in everything, but what fear constraineth them to keep. Crafty, timorous, quick of apprehension and very ingenious, some are of disposition fearful, some bold, most cautious, all savage...they soon move to anger, and are so malicious that they seldom forget an injury: they seldom steal from one another, lest their conjurers reveal it, and so they be pursued and punished.[1]

Smith's commentary was followed in short order by that of Alexander Whitaker:

> Let the miserable condition of these naked slaves of the devil move you to compassion toward them. They acknowledge that there is a great God, but they know him not, wherefore they serve the devil for fear, after a most base manner...They live naked of body, as if the shame of their sin deserved no covering...They esteem it a virtue to lie, deceive, steal...if this be their life, what think you shall become of them after death, but to be partakers with the devil and his angels in hell for evermore?[2]

In 1632, Thomas Morton added to the growing list of English language publications originating in the Atlantic Seaboard colonies concerned with the indigenous population:

> Now since it is but foode and rayment that men that live needeth (though not all alike), why should not the Natives of New England be sayd to live richly, having no want of either: Cloakes are the badge of sinne, and the more variety of fashions is but the greater abuse of the Creature, the beasts of the forest there deserve to furnish them at any time when they please: fish and flesh they have in great abundance which they roast and boyle...The rarity of the air begot by the medicinal quality of the sweet herbes of the Country, always procures good stomaches to the inhabitants...According to humane reason guided onely by the light of nature, these people leade the more happy and freer life, being void of care, which torments the minds of so many Christians: they are not delighted in baubles, but in useful things.[3]

And, in 1654, Edward Johnson penned the following concerning the English colonists' 1637 extermination of the Pequot:

> The Lord in his mercy toward his poor churches having thus destroyed these bloody barbarous Indians, he returns his people safely to their vessels, where they take account of their prisoners. The squaws and some young youths they brought home with them, and finding the men guilty of the crimes they undertook the war for, they brought away only their heads.[4]

Each of the remarks cited here serves at least a twofold purpose:
first, each contributed decisively to establishing Native Americans
as a topic for English language writing originating in the Americas
(in fact, it becomes difficult to conceive a colonial writing not
preoccupied with things Indian); second, each established the
groundwork for a stereotype which assumed increasing promi-
nence in American literature.

Smith's writing played upon the persistent image of the Indian as a
sort of subhuman, animal-like creature who was a danger to hardy Anglo
frontiersmen. Whitaker reinforced an already pervasive European notion of the Indian as godless heathen subject to redemption through the
"civilizing" ministrations of Christian missionaries. Morton's often confused prattle went far in developing the "noble savage" mythology in
the Americas. Johnson mined the vein of a militaristic insistence that the
native was an incorrigible (even criminal) hindrance to European "progress" in North America, a miscreant barrier to be overcome only through
the most liberal applications of fire and cold steel.

With primary stereotyping trends isolated in letters, however, one
must also be aware of another important genre of the same period,
one which tends to cut across stereotypic lines and which might be
perceived as generating a most heatedly emotional and decidedly
anti-Indian popular response among readers: the so-called "narratives" of Indian captives. Perhaps the first manuscript of this school
was published in 1682 by Mrs. Mary Rowlandson. Samples of her
prose clearly meet the standards established above:

> Now away we must go with those barbarous creatures, with our bodies
> wounded and bleeding, and our hearts no less than our bodies...This
> was the dolefullest night that ever my eyes saw. Oh, the roaring and
> singing and dancing and yelling of those black creatures in the night,
> which made the place a lively resemblance of hell.[5]

Such narratives were copiously cited as "evidence" by such un-
abashed white supremacists as Increase Mather in his 1684 epic, *Essay
for the Recording of Illustrious Providences*. Not to be outdone, brother
Cotton joined in with his *Magnalia Christi Americana* of 1702:

> In fine, when the Children of the English Captives cried at any time, so
> that they were not presently quieted, the manner of the Indians was to
> dash out their brains against a tree...they took the small children, and

held 'em under Water till they had near Drowned them...And the Indians in their frolics would Whip and Beat the small children, until they set 'em into grievous Outcries, and then throw 'em to their amazed Mothers for them to quiet 'em as well as they could.[6]

This "accounting" was followed by others such as William Fleming's *Narrative of the sufferings and surprizing Deliverances of William and Elizabeth Fleming* in 1750 and the even more venomous (and very popular) *French and Indian Cruelty Exemplified, in the Life and Various Vicissitudes of Fortune*, of Peter Williamson in 1757:

From these few instances of savage cruelty, the deplorable situation of these defenceless inhabitants, and what they hourly suffered in that part of the globe, must strike the utmost horror to a human soul, and cause in every breast the utmost detestation, not only against the authors of such tragic scenes, but against those who through inattentions, or pusillanimous and erroneous principles, suffered these savages at first, unrepelled, or even unmolested, to commit such outrages and incredible depredations and murders.[7]

In themselves, each of the works produced by the writers covered in this section ostensibly has more to do with the non-fictional strains which have developed over the years in American literature than with the generic or popular term "literature." While the books and papers comprising historical archives are technically referred to (usually within scholarly circles) as "the literature," the generally understood and popularly held sense of the term refers quite specifically to material intentionally written and representative of fictive expression. The two modes are theoretically quite distinctive. Still, the allegedly non-fiction writing of the early English colonists noted above has had a large impact by creating the very conditions of stereotype and emotionalism from which later literary efforts sprang:

From the initial poorly-informed reports on the Red Man emerged the bigoted and ethnocentric literary attitudes of pious but land-hungry Puritans. Soon were to follow the commercial and greatly fictional captivity narratives, and then the turn of the century "histories" of the Indian wars (never the "White," or "Settlers" or "Colonists" wars)...Perhaps the most tragic thing is that this was only the beginning.[8]

The Literary Version of Manifest Destiny

Perhaps the first American work which might appropriately be termed a novel (which, along with short stories, novellas, plays, and poetry, constitutes true literature in the popular conception) concerning American Indians was Charles Brockden Brown's 1799 release, *Edgar Huntley*. It was followed, in reasonably short order for the time, by two chapters—"Traits of the Indian Character" and "Philip of Pokanoket"—devoted to the extermination of the Narragansets during what the colonists called "King Philip's War" in Washington Irving's *Sketch Book*, dating from 1819. The latter absorbs the "noble savage" stereotype associated with Thomas Morton's earlier work:

> Even in his last refuge of desperation and dispair a sullen grandure gathers round his [Philip's] memory. We picture him to ourselves seated among his careworn followers, brooding in silence over his blasted fortunes and acquiring a savage sublimity from the wilderness of his lurking place. Defeated but not dismayed, crushed to earth but not humiliated, he seemed to grow more haughty beneath disaster and experience a fierce satisfaction in draining the last dregs of bitterness.[9]

By 1823, James Fenimore Cooper was on the scene, and between then and 1841 his cumulative novels—including *The Pioneers, The Last of the Mohicans, The Deerslayer, The Prairie,* and *The Pathfinder*—had firmly established all four of the stereotypes denoted in Section I within the popular consciousness. Of course, Cooper had considerable help. During the same period, Chateaubriand's *Atala* appeared, as well as novels by William Gilmore Simms, including *The Yamassee* and *Guy Rovers*. Then, there were poems such as John Greenleaf Whittier's 1835 epic *Mogg Megone* and, by 1855, Henry W. Longfellow's *The Song of Hiawatha, To the Driving Cloud,* and *The Burial of Minnisink*. In a less pretentious vein, there was also during this general period the so-called "juvenile fiction" exemplified by Mayne Reid in *The Scalp Hunters* and *Desert Home*. The list is considerable.

The elements of this rapidly proliferating mass of creative output shared several features in common. For instance, none possessed the slightest concrete relationship to the actualities of native culture(s) they portrayed. Hence, each amounted to the imaginative invention of the authors, authors who by virtue of their medium were alien to the context (oral tradition) of which they presumed to write. It can be argued, and has,[10] that such prerogatives rest squarely within the realm of the fiction writer. While this may be true in an aesthetic sense, the practical application of the principle breaks down (for each of these works) on at least two levels:

- The justifying aesthetic rationale is itself an aspect of the European cultural context which generated the literate format at issue. Hence, utilizing aesthetic "freedom" as a justifying basis for the distortive literary manipulation of non-European cultural realities is merely a logically circular continuum. It may perhaps be reasonable that Europe is entitled (in the name of literature) to fabricate whole aspects of its own sociocultural existence. However, the unilaterally extended proposition that such entitlement reaches into crosscultural areas seems arrogant in the extreme, little more than a literary "Manifest Destiny."

- Regardless of the contradictions implied through application of purely European aesthetic values within a crosscultural context, it must be held in mind that none of the authors in question operated in this abstract sense (such turf being generally reserved for their defenders). In each case, a more or less fictionally intended novel or poetic development was derived from the equally European (Anglo) but ostensibly non-fictive works cited in the previous section. Consequently, each later literary figure could lay claim to the "authenticity" of a firm grounding in the "historical record." That such history utterly ignored the indigenous oral accountings of the people/events thus portrayed, and did so in favor of the thoroughly alien literate record, serves to illustrate the self-contained dynamic through which literature dismisses anything beyond its pale (including what is being written about). Again, the logic describes a perfect circle: product and proof are one and the same.

The advent of the treatment of American Indians within a formalized American literature does not imply a cessation or even necessarily a diminishing of the "non-fictional" writing from which the fictional material grew. Perhaps its most telling example rests within the introduction of "Indian Religions" to the readership(s) of popular magazines during the 19th century. For example, in an 1884 essay published in *Atlantic Monthly*, writer Charles Leland asserted that "...there is no proof of the existence among our [*sic*] Indians of a belief in a Great Spirit or in an infinite God before the coming of the whites."[11] William Wassell, in an article in *Harper's Monthly*, felt a factual sort of hope in the freeing of "pagan savages" from "the sorcery and jugglery of weasoned medicine-men" by Christian missionaries who convinced them of "simple teachings of the Bible."[12] In the same vein, Amanda Miller celebrated the documentation of such "civilizing" successes in an 1869 issue of *Overland Monthly*:

> The contrast between the assemblage of hideously painted savages, whose countenances were rendered still the more revolting by their efforts to intensify their passions of hatred and revenge in their incantations of demonaltry, and the placid and devoted [Christian Indian] congregation at Simcoe, was wonderful and delightful.[13]

By 1891, a serious scholar such as Alfred Riggs could only conclude, on the basis of such a "factual" record, that the Christian influence was leading the American Indian to "a quickened conscience, a strengthened will, the power of self-restraint...power to labor patiently, economy, thrift...a new spiritual impulse, and a new revelation...and the customs of...a social order."[14] And there were many other similar pieces in journals with titles such as *Popular Science Monthly*, *North American Review*, *Nation*, *American Quarterly*, *Century*, *Scribner's Magazine*, *New Englander and Yale Review*, *Forum*, and others.[15] The conclusions of Alexander Whitaker were not only continued, but also expanded upon.

It is relatively easy to perceive how, during the 19th century, any valid concept ever possessed by the English-speaking population of North America as to Native Americans being peoples in their own right, peoples with entirely legitimate belief systems, values, knowledge, and lifeways, had been lost in distortion popularly presented through literature and pseudo-science. The stereotypes had assumed a documented "authenticity" in the public consciousness. Such a process cannot be viewed as meaningless distortion. For stereotyped and stereotyper alike, it becomes dehumanization.[16] As Russell Means recently stated:

> [W]ho seems most expert at dehumanizing other people? And why? Soldiers who have seen a lot of combat learn to do this to the enemy before going back into combat. Murderers do it before going out to murder. Nazi SS guards did it to concentration camp inmates. Cops do

it. Corporation leaders do it to the workers they send into uranium mines and steel mills. Politicians do it to everyone in sight. And what the process has in common for each group doing the dehumanizing is that it makes it alright to kill and otherwise destroy other people. One of the Christian commandments says, "Thou shalt not kill," at least not humans, so the trick is to mentally convert the victims into non-humans. Then you can claim a violation of your own commandment as a virtue.[17]

Viewed in this way, treatment of the American Indian in the arena of American literature must be seen as part and parcel of the Anglo American conquest of the North American continent. How else could general Euroamerican attitudes have been massively conditioned to accept, in their behalf, a system or policy of non-stop expropriation and genocide of the native population throughout U.S. history. The dehumanizing aspects of the stereotyping of American Indians in American literature may be seen as an historical requirement of an imperial process. No other description of the conquest of America seems adequate.

From the Invasion of the Shock Troops to the Redefinition of Indigenous Culture

The claim to a national culture in the past does not only rehabilitate that nation and serve as a justification for the hope of a future national culture. In the sphere of socioaffective equilibrium it is responsible for an important change in the native. Perhaps we have not sufficiently demonstrated that colonialism is not simply content to impose its rule upon the present and future of a dominated country. Colonialism is not merely satisfied with holding a people in its grip and emptying the native's brain of all form and content. By a kind of perverse logic, it turns to the past of an oppressed people, and distorts, disfigures and destroys it.

—Frantz Fanon, *The Wretched of the Earth*

The representation, indeed misrepresentation is a more accurate word, of indigenous people began virtually with the advent of English colonization of the Western hemisphere. Within a relatively short period, styles of exposition emerged which identified primary modes of stereotype, modes which are continued in evolved formations today and which must rightfully be viewed as having their roots within the literature and culture of England itself. This latter seems true both on the basis of the sheer falsity of colonial pronouncements concerning the indigenous American population, which implies that the notions involved were imported rather than located upon arrival by the colonists, as well as on the identifiable prior existence of similar tendencies in "Mother England." Concerning this last:

> Whatever their practical intentions or purposes, the invaders did not confront the native peoples without certain preconceptions about their nature which help shape the way they pursued their goals. Conceptions of "savagery" that developed in the sixteenth and seventeenth centuries and became the common property of Western European culture constituted a distorting lens through which the early colonists assessed the potential and predicted the fate of the non-European peoples they encountered.[18]

The specific stereotypes of American Indians finally deployed in the New England colonies amount to elaboration and continuation of a stream of literary efforts already sanctioned by the Crown and its subjects. In practical terms, the established contours of this writing may be assessed as following a roughly "them vs. us" pathway:

> There were two crucial distinctions which allowed Europeans of the Renaissance and Reformation period to divide the human race into superior and inferior categories. One was between Christian and heathen and the other between "civil" and "savage."[19]

As we have seen, the primary stereotypes developed in the Americas did not vary from the established categories. Rather they represent merely the application of the prescribed generalities within a given context; that is, application to the indigenous populations within the territory of the New England Colonies.

It is hardly an overstatement that the initial wave of any colonial invasion has been comprised of both the "cutting edge" and "hard core" of empire. These are the shock troops, arrogant, indoctrinated with the ideology of conquest, prepared to undergo hardship and sacrifice in order to actualize the ideal of their own inherent superiority to all that they encounter. Small wonder then that such "pioneers" would be prepared to bear false witness against those inhabitants of alien lands who would dare to stand in the way. A twofold purpose is served thereby: first, in an immediate tactical sense, the overtly physical elimination and expropriation of indigenous peoples, which is the abrupt necessity of any preliminary colonization, is provided self-justification and even (in the hands of able propagandists) righteousness; second, a longer-term, strategic consideration applies in that a less brutally doctrinaire segment of the Mother Country population must ultimately be attracted to the task of settling that which the invaders have conquered.

The latter point cannot be emphasized too strongly. Mere conquest is never the course of empire. Colonial warriors tend to realize their limitations, their own mortality. The achievement of mission can only be attained through the productive utilization of captured ground, the inevitable role of farmers, miners, and merchants rather than soldiers. Hence, the literature of colonialism follows a course from the immediate self-glorifying accounts of first wave assault troops, such as John Smith and Alexander Whitaker, to the salesmanship of Thomas Morton, and on to the longer-term restructuring of the past to serve present and future needs, at which Edward Johnson proved so adept. Things are never quite so clear cut in practice as they might be posed in theory. Smith blurred his efforts at self-justification into sales pitches concerning colonial real estate. Morton's advertisements of terrain contain residues of self-justification. Johnson reveals both aspects of concern within his historiography. But the emphases hold, in the main.

It is at that point that a shift becomes evident. Immediate polemics fade into the background as tools of colonization. Now, historical recounting becomes feasible as an operant norm of literature, and the literary effort begins to proliferate within the colonial context. Understandably, this seems due to relaxation of initial tensions. The combat associated with the establishment of bridgeheads must end before significant writing can occur. In the Americas, this is evidenced through the work of the Mathers and others of the Puritan persuasion. Such material marks a shift from the need to establish that settlement was in fact both possible and justifiable, that the colonies were viable entities for occupation by farmers as well as assault troops, to emphasis upon the historical inevitability and moral correctness of colonial growth and perpetuation.

In inhabited areas, growth by one population segment is generally accommodated at the expense of another. And so it was in the

Americas. The Puritan ideologues set the tone for a more or less continuous expansion of the English-speaking colonies, precipitating perpetual warfare with and expropriation of the various tribes encountered in the process. Yet, at this late date, John Smith had long since passed and, along with him, the cutting edge. The task then was to deploy the means to provoke and sanctify systematic warfare on the part of the settlement population itself. In this, the so-called captive narratives of Mary Rowlandson, William Fleming, and others may be seen as having accrued a certain tactical utility.

At the onset of the 19th century, a new process had begun. Revolution had stripped England of its external colonies in the Americas, and consolidation of the American nation-state had begun. The emphasis in arts and letters became that of creating the "national heritage" of the emerging state, a source of patriotism and pride within which history (whether real or wholly fabricated) played no part. Hence, the preoccupation with "histories of the Americas" during this period, and the historical "groundings" provided to incipient American fiction. But, and there was never a way to avoid this, the course of the European presence in the hemisphere had always been intertwined with that of the original inhabitants to the most intimate degree. The construction of the U.S. national heritage in terms of history therefore necessarily entailed the reconstruction of American Indian history and reality to conform to the desired image.

An obvious route to achieve this end was to incorporate preceding literature by English speakers (who constituted the preponderant population of the new American state) into the national heritage as the factual/perceptual basis for both current and future literature. The rupture of English colonization in North America really marked no change in literary treatment accorded the American Indian. To the contrary, it marked both the continuation and intensification of practices initiated at the height of the colonial process. In both figurative and literal effect, the United States merely supplanted England as the new preeminent colonial power relative to Indians, with the alteration that where the colonies had been maintained as external to the British nation proper, they were ultimately to become internal to the territorial integrity of the United States.

In Fanon's terms, the colonist who had metaphorically stripped the native of his/her present through creation of a surrogate literary reality, defined to the convenience of the colonizer, was now turning the metaphoric/mythic siege guns fully to the past. In this way, the present for the native could be perpetually precluded through the maintenance of this seamlessly constituted surrogate reality as myth. Clearly too, any perpetual "present" must encompass the future as well as the moment. The indigenous reality, the "national culture" of Fanon's thesis, is thereby hopelessly trapped within the definitional power of the oppressor, drifting endlessly in lazy hermeneutic circles, stranded in a pastless/presentless/futureless vacuum. The national identity of the colonizer is created and maintained through the usurpation of the national identity of the colonized, a causal relationship.

The final conquest of its continental land mass by the United States absorbed the whole of the 19th century, a period which coincided with the formal creation of American literature. Region by region, tribe by tribe, indigenous cultures were overwhelmed and consigned to the reservation status marking the physical characteristics of U.S. internal colonialism. Throughout this era an overarching theme in American writing, from the embryonic work of Charles Brockden Brown and Washington Irving to the late-century tracts of Charles Leland and Alfred Riggs, was the Indian. Or, rather, a certain image of the Indian which complemented the need of the nation's Euroamerican population to supplant the original inhabitants of the land.

Replacing Troops and Guns with Self-Colonization

In the late 19th century, another shift occurs. Where initial English colonial writings seem primarily to be seriously concerned with the Christian/heathen dichotomy, 19th-century American literature gravitates more and more toward themes involving the civil versus savage juxtaposition. The trappings of quasi-missionary rhetoric are maintained in treatments such as that written by Amanda Miller, to be sure, but this is a blurring of distinctions of the same order as the overlapping of content evident between Smith, Whitaker, and Morton in an earlier period. By the late 1800s, the original imperatives of missionarism, obvious enough in Puritan literature, had given way to a posture whereby christianization simply marked a signification of the transition of the savage to civilized (non-obstructionist) status.

Another signification of the civilizing process was literacy itself. Therein, a primary tool of the formulation and justification of European colonialism was offered up as a focus for attainment to the colonized. As the articulation of Manifest Destiny doctrine underscored Euroamerica's assumed right to its concrete territorial ambitions, so too did articulation of aesthetic doctrine reserve unto the literate the right to interpret history and reality at will. In America, both theses were developed during the same period and progressed virtually in tandem. Both were designed to serve the population which invented them at the direct expense of others. But, while the most overt expressions of manifest destiny have become politically outmoded and have fallen into disrepute, the logic of literate aesthetic primacy has, if anything, become a dominant social norm.

The final absorption of the western United States into the national domain was accompanied by a constantly increasing public zeal to civilize the savage, or at least the popular conception of the savage. This latter is of considerable importance insofar as therein lies the primary function of literature within colonialism. The overwhelming preponderance of writing concerning the American Indian during the U.S. expansion was designed to create an image allowing conquest "for the Indians' own good," to effect "betterment" and "progress." The potential for a mass psychology of national guilt at its apparent policy of genocide and theft could be offset in no other conceivable fashion at that time. Further, the imposition of literacy and "education" can be perceived as the most effective means to inculcate in the Indians themselves a "correct" understanding (in future generations, at least) of the appropriateness of their physical and cultural demise. As has been noted in this connection:

> Since schooling was brought to non-Europeans as a part of empire...it was integrated into an effort to bring indigenous peoples into imperial/colonial structures...After all, did not the European teacher and the school built on the European capitalist model transmit European values and norms and begin to transform traditional societies into "modern" ones...[?][20]

At this juncture, a truly seamless model of colonialism makes its appearance: the training of the colonized to colonize themselves. In this sense, hegemony over truth and knowledge replaces troops and guns finally as the relevant tool of colonization. Literature, always an important property of the European colonial process, assumes an increasingly important centrality to maintenance of the system. As Albert Memmi has observed:

> In order for the colonizer to be a complete master, it is not enough for him to be so in actual fact, but he must also believe in its [the colonial system's] legitimacy. In order for that legitimacy to be complete, it is not enough for the colonized to be a slave, he must also accept his role. The bond between the colonizer and the colonized is thus destructive and creative. It destroys and recreates the two partners in colonization into the colonizer and the colonized. One is disfigured into the oppressor, a partial, unpatriotic and treacherous being, worrying about his privileges and their defense; the other into an oppressed creature, whose development is broken and who compromises by his defeat.[21]

Such a view goes far towards answering the obvious questions concerning why, nearly a century after the conclusion of the primary U.S. territorial expansion, American literature still treats the Indian within its own desired framework. Witness the works of Carlos Castaneda, Ruth Beebe Hill, and Cash Asher. In the same sense, it explains the nature of the support from publishers, a massive reading audience, and the academic community as a whole.

Removing the Last Vestiges of Literal and Figurative Threat

That which is cannot be admitted. That which will be must be converted by literate logic into that which cannot be. To this end, the publishers publish, the writers invent, the readers consume in as great a portion as may be provided, and the academics sanctify (over and over) the "last word" in true explanation as to where we've been, come from, and are going. None, or at least few, seem to act from outright malice; most are moved compulsively by internalized forces of fear (of retribution?), guilt, and greed.

How then to best deploy the sophistry of literature within such a context? Certainly not in the crude polemical fashion of the Mathers and the Smiths. Those days passed with the need for blatant military suppression of tribal autonomy. No, direct attack is obsolete. In the post-holocaust era there is no viable ability to justify Sand Creek, the Washita, and Wounded Knee. Rather, these are to be purged through a reconstitution of history as a series of tragic aberrations beginning and ending nowhere in time. The literal meaning of such events must at all costs be voided by sentiment and false nostalgia rather than treated as parts of an ongoing process. The literal is rendered tenuously figurative, and then dismissed altogether.

From there, reality can be reconstructed at will. Witness the contemporary obsession with establishing "authenticity." Ruth Beebe Hill requires the services of an aging Indian to verify her every word. Cash Asher requires another aging Indian to step forward and attest the truth of every word. Carlos Castaneda relies upon a truly massive and sustained support from both the publishing and professional academic communities to validate his efforts. Schneebaum, Waldo, Lamb, Storm, all within the past 15 years, received considerable support from "reputable" publishers and from some of the most prestigious scholarly establishments in the country.[22]

It is not that they are "ordered" to say specific things about the Indian, although the ancient stereotypes are maintained (albeit, in mutated form). Rather, it seems that the current goal of literature concerning American Indians is to create them, if not out of whole cloth, then from only the bare minimum of fact needed to give the resulting fiction the "ring of truth," to those Indians bound to colonialism as readily as to people of European heritage.

At the dawn of English colonization of the New World, Sir Walter Raleigh was able to write that the natives of Guyana, "have their eyes in their shoulders, and their mouths in the middle of their breasts." He was believed then by the English reading public, although his words assume proportions of absurdity today (as, one assumes, they must have to those in a position to know better at the time).

Things have come full circle on the literary front. Where, in the beginning, it was necessary to alter indigenous realities in order to assuage the invading colonial conscience, so it seems necessary today to alter these realities to assure the maintenance of empire. It seems to matter little what American Indians are converted into, as long as it is into other than what they are, have been, and might become. Consigned to a mythical realm, they constitute no threat to the established order either figuratively (as matters of guilt and conscience) or literally (in terms of concrete opposition). That which is mythic in nature cannot be, or has been murdered, expropriated, and colonized in the "real world." The potential problem is solved through intellectual sleight of hand, aesthetic gimmickry, and polemical discourse with specters. The objective is not art but absolution. As Vine Deloria, Jr. has observed in another context:

> [T]herein lies the meaning of the white's fantasy about Indians—the problem of the Indian image. Underneath all the conflicting images of the Indian one fundamental truth emerges—the white man knows that he is alien and he knows that North America is Indian—and he will never let go of the Indian image because he thinks that by some clever manipulation he can achieve an authenticity which can never be his.[23]

In this sense at least, literature in America is and always has been part and parcel of the colonial process. In this sense too, it has always been that American literature constituted a confused netherworld wherein fictionalized journals met journalized fiction in a jumble of verbiage requisite only to the masking of a disavowed and painful reality.

Notes

1. Smith, John, *A Map of Virginia, with a description of the Country, the Commodities, People, Government and Religion* (1621) as cited in *History in American Literature,* Reuben Post Halleck (New York, 1911), p. 18.
2. Whitaker, Alexander, *Good News from Virginia* as cited in *A History of American Literature, 1607-1765,* Moses Goit Tyler (Ithaca, 1949), pp. 41-43.
3. Morton, Thomas, *New English Canaan* (1632) as cited in *The Indian and the White Man*, ed. Wilcomb E. Washburn (New York, 1965), pp. 35-38.
4. Johnson, Edward, *Wonder-Working Providence of Zion's Savior in New England* (1654) as cited in Tyler, pp. 122-215.
5. Rowlandson, Mary, *The Sovereignty and Goodness of God Together With the Faithfulness of His Promise Displayed: Being a Narrative of the Captivity and Restoration of Mrs. Mary Rowlandson* (1682) as cited in "Significance of the Captivity Narrative," R. H. Pearce, *American Literature XIX* (March 1947): pp. 1-20.
6. Mather, Cotton, *Magnalia Christi Americana* (1702), *Ibid.*, pp. 3-4; *The Readers' Encyclopedia of American Literature*, ed. Max J. Herzog (New York: 1962). Also cites another work closely related to the Mather opus, but bearing the even more unlikely title of *The Redeemed Captive Returning to Zion or a faithful history of Remarkable Occurrences in the Captivity and Deliverance of Mr. John Williams (Minister of the Gospel in Deerfield) who in the Desolation which befell the Plantation by the*

incursion of the French and Indians, was by them carried away, with his family and his neighborhood into Canada (!!!) (1707).

7. Williamson, Peter, *French and Indian Cruelty Exemplified, in the Life and Various Vicissitudes of Fortune, of Peter Williamson* (1757) as cited in Pearce, pp. 7-8.

8. Beer, David F., "Anti-Indian Sentiment in Early Colonial Literature," *The Indian Historian*, vol. 2, no. 1, (spring 1969): p. 48.

9. Irving, Washington, *Sketch Book* (1819), as cited in "The Indian in American Literature" (1919), C. F. Ten Kate, *Smithsonian Annual Reports, 1921*, reprinted in *The American Indian Reader: Literature* (San Francisco, CA: American Indian Historical Society, 1973). Citation is from p. 189 of the latter volume.

10. See, as but one example, the subtle justification(s) advanced in Ten Kate.

11. Leland, Charles G., "The Edda Among the Algonquin Indians," *Atlantic Monthly*, LIV (August 1884): p. 223.

12. Wassell, William, "The Religion of the Sioux," *Harper's New Monthly Magazine*, LXXXIX (November 1894): p. 945.

13. Miller, Amanda, "To Simcoe," *Overland Monthly*, III (August 1869): p. 176.

14. Riggs, Alfred, "Some Difficulties of the Indian Problem," *New Englander and Yale Review*, LIV (April 1891): p. 329.

15. A sampling of the essays and articles intended here is: Powell, John Westley, "Mythologic Philosophy I," *Popular Science Monthly*, XV (October 1879); Tripple, Eugene J., "Primitive Indian Tribes," *North American Review*, CI (July 1865); Schwatka, Frederick, "The Sun-Dance of the Sioux," *Century*, XVII (March 1890); Walsh, Herbert, "The Meaning of the Dakota Outbreak," *Scribner's Magazine*, IX (April 1891); Bourke, John G., "The Indian Messiah," *Nation* (December 4, 1890); Price, Hiram, "The Government and the Indians," *Forum*, X (February 1891); Parkman, Francis, "Indian Superstitions," *North American Review*, CIII (July 1866). As noted in the text, the listing could be continued *ad nauseum*.

16. The sense of the definition of "dehumanization" intended here is as simple as that offered by *The Merriam-Webster Dictionary* (New York: 1974): "...the divestiture of human qualities or personality..." Surely this is an apt summation of the fate experienced by the native in the literature covered so far.

17. Means, Russell, "Fighting Words on the Future of Mother Earth," *Mother Jones* (November 1980): pp. 26-27.

18. Fredrickson, George M., *White Supremacy: A Comparative Study in American and South African History* (New York: Oxford University Press, 1981), p. 7.

19. *Ibid.*, pp. 7-8.

20. Carnoy, Martin, *Education as Cultural Imperialism* (New York: David McKay and Co., 1974), p. 16.

21. Memmi, Albert, *Colonizer and Colonized* (New York: Orion Press, 1965), p. 89.

22. Some of the specific material intended within this observation includes Asher, Cash, and Chief Red Fox, *The Memoirs of Chief Red Fox* (New York: Fawcett Books, 1972); Hill, Ruth Beebe, with Chunksa Yuha (Alonzo Blacksmith), *Hanta Yo: An American Saga* (New York: Doubleday, 1979); Storm, Hyemeyohsts, *Seven Arrows* (New York: Ballantine Books, 1972); Waldo, Anna Lee, *Sacajawea* (New York: Avon Books, 1978); Schneebaum, Tobias, *Keep the River on Your Right* (New York: Grove Press, 1970); as well as at least the first three books by Carlos Castaneda, the so-called "Castaneda Trilogy."

23. Deloria, Vine, Jr., "Foreword: American Fantasy," in *The Pretend Indians: Images of Native Americans in the Movies.* ed. Gretchen M. Bataille and Charles L. P. Silet (Ames: Iowa State University Press, 1980), p. xvi.

A LITTLE MATTER OF GENOCIDE
Colonialism and the Expropriation of Indigenous Spiritual Tradition in Academia

They came for our land, for what grew or could be grown on it, for the resources in it, and for our clean air and pure water. They stole these things from us, and in the taking they also stole our free ways and the best of our leaders, killed in battle or assassinated. And now, after all that, they've come for the very last of our possessions; now they want our pride, our history, our spiritual traditions. They want to rewrite and remake these things, to claim them for themselves. The lies and thefts just never end.

—Margo Thunderbird, 1988

The exploitation and appropriation of Native American spiritual tradition is nothing new. In many ways the process began the moment the first of Columbus' wayward seamen washed up on a Caribbean beach, returning home with wondrous tales of *los Dios*. And it has been functioning in increasingly concerted fashion, under rationales ranging from the crassly commercial to the purely academic, ever since. Over the past two decades, the ranks of those queuing up to cash in on the lucre and luster of "American Indian Religious Studies" have come to include a number of "New Age" luminaries reinforced by a significant portion of the university elite.

The classic example of this has been Carlos Castaneda (a.k.a.: Carlos Aranja), whose well-stewed borrowings from Timothy Leary, the Yogi Ramacharaka, and Barbara Meyerhoff were blended with a liberal dose of his own turgid fantasies, packaged as a "Yaqui way of knowledge," and resulted not only in a lengthy string of bestsellers but a Ph.D. in anthropology from UCLA. So lacking was/is the base of real knowledge concerning things Indian within academia that it took nearly a decade for Castaneda to be apprehended as "the greatest anthropological hoax since Piltdown Man," and one still encounters abundant instances of *The Teachings of Don Juan* and *Journey Through*

Ixtlan being utilized in courses and cited (apparently in all serious-ness) in ostensibly scholarly works as offering "insight" into Ameri-can Indian thought and spiritual practice.

Then there is "Dr. Jamake Highwater," an alleged Chero-kee/Blackfeet from either Montana or Canada (the story varies from time to time), born by his own accounts in several different years. In an earlier incarnation (*circa:* the late 1960s), this same individual appeared as "Jay Marks," a non-Indian modern dance promoter in the San Francisco area whose main literary claim-to-fame was in having penned an "authorized biography" of rock star Mick Jagger. Small wonder that the many later texts of "Dr. Highwater" on Native American spirituality and the nature of "the primal mind" bear more than passing resemblance to both the lore of Grecian mythos and the insights of hip-pop idiom *à la* magazines like *Rolling Stone*. Still, Highwater's material consistently finds itself required reading in undergraduate courses and referenced in supposedly scholarly fora. The man has also received more than one hefty grant to translate his literary ramblings into "educational" PBS film productions.

Then again, there was Ruth Beebe Hill, whose epic potboiler novel, *Hanta Yo*, set certain sales records during the late 1970s via the expedient of depicting the collectivist spirituality of the 19th-century Lakota as nothing so much as a living prefiguration of her friend Ayn Rand's grossly individualistic cryptofascism. In the face of near-uni-versal howls of outrage from the contemporary Lakota community, Hill resorted to "validating" her postulations by retaining the services of a single aging and impoverished Sioux man, Alonzo Blacksmith (a.k.a.: "Chunksa Yuha"), to attest to the book's "authenticity." Before dropping once again into a well-deserved obscurity, Blacksmith in-toned—allegedly in a "dialect" unknown to Siouxian linguistics—that what Hill had written was true because "I, Chunksa Yuha, say so, say so." This ludicrous performance was sufficient to allow a range of professors to argue that the controversy was really just "a matter of opinion" because *"all* Indians are not in agreement as to the inaccuracy of *Hanta Yo."* Such pronouncements virtually ensured that sales would remain brisk in supermarkets and college book stores, and that producer David Wolper would convert it into a TV mini-series entitled *Mystic Warrior* during the mid-'80s.

And, as if all this were not enough, we are currently treated to the spectacle of Lynn Andrews, an airhead "feminist" yuppie who once wrangled herself a weekend in the company of a pair of elderly Indian women of indistinct tribal origin. In her version of events, they had apparently been waiting their entire lives for just such an opportunity to unburden themselves of every innermost secret of their people's spiritual knowledge, immediately acquainted her with the previously unknown "facts" as to the presence of katchinas on the Arctic Circle and the power of "Jaguar Women," charged her with serving as their "messenger," and sent her forth to write a series of books so outlandish in their pretensions as to make Castaneda seem a model of propriety by comparison. Predictably, the Andrews books have begun to penetrate the "popular literature" curriculum of academe.

To round out the picture, beyond the roster of such heavy-hitters circle a host of also-rans extending from "Chief Red Fox" and "Nino Cochise" (real names and ethnicities unknown) to Hyemeyohsts Storm, David Seals, and scores of others, each of whom has made a significant recent contribution (for profit) to the misrepresentation and appropriation of indigenous spirituality, and most of whom have been tendered some measure of credibility by the "certified scholars" of American universities. One result is that at this juncture, scarcely an Indian in the United States has not been confronted by some hippie-like apparition wishing to teach crystal-healing methods to Navajo grandmothers, claiming to be a pipe-carrier reincarnated from a 17th-century Cheyenne warrior, and with an assumed "Indian name" such as "Beautiful Painted Arrow" or "Chief Piercing Eyes." Needless to say, this circumstance has in turn spawned a whole new clot of hucksters such as "Sun Bear" (Vincent LaDuke, a Chippewa) who—along with his non-Indian consort *cum* business manager, "Wabun" (Marlise James)—has been able to make himself rather wealthy over the past few years by forming (on the basis of suitable "membership fees") what he calls "the Bear Tribe," and the selling of ersatz sweat lodge and medicine wheel ceremonies to anyone who wants to play Indian for a day and can afford the price of admission.

As the Sioux scholar Vine Deloria, Jr., put it in 1982,

> The realities of Indian belief and existence have become so misunder-
> stood and distorted at this point that when a real Indian stands up and
> speaks the truth at any given moment, he or she is not only unlikely to
> be believed, but will probably be publicly contradicted and 'corrected'
> by the citation of some non-Indian and totally inaccurate 'expert.' More,
> young Indians in universities are now being trained to view themselves
> and their cultures in the terms prescribed by such experts *rather than* in
> the traditional terms of the tribal elders. The process automatically sets
> the members of Indian communities at odds with one another, while
> outsiders run around picking up the pieces for themselves. In this way,
> the experts are perfecting a system of self-validation in which all sem-
> blance of honesty and accuracy are lost. This is not only a travesty of
> scholarship, but it is absolutely devastating to Indian societies.

Pam Colorado, an Oneida academic working in Canada, goes further:

> The process is ultimately intended to supplant Indians, even in areas of
> their own customs and spirituality. In the end, non-Indians will have
> complete power to define what is and is not Indian, even for Indians. We
> are talking here about an absolute ideological/conceptual subordination
> of Indian people in addition to the total physical subordination they
> already experience. When this happens, the last vestiges of real Indian
> society and Indian rights will disappear. Non-Indians will then 'own'
> our heritage and ideas as thoroughly as they now claim to own our land
> and resources.

A Little Matter of Genocide

Those who engage in such activities usually claim to do so not for
the fame and fortune (real or potential) involved, but for loftier
motives. Many of Castaneda's defenders, for example, have argued
that despite the blatant misrepresentation of Yaqui culture in which
he has engaged, his books nonetheless articulate valid spiritual principles, the "higher truth value" of which simply transcends such
"petty criticism" as demanding at least minimal adherence to facts.
Similar themes have been sounded with regard to Highwater, Andrews, and others. Within academia proper, such thinking has led to
the emergence of a whole new pseudo-discipline termed "ethnomethodology" in which inconvenient realities can be simply disregarded and allegorical "truth" is habitually substituted for conventional data. Harold Garfinkle, a founder of ethnomethodology at

UCLA, has contended that such an approach represents "the pursuit of knowledge in its purest form."

At another level, the poet Gary Snyder, who has won literary awards for the penning of verse in which he pretends to see the world through the eyes of an American Indian "shaman," has framed things more clearly: "Spirituality is not something which can be 'owned' like a car or a house," says Snyder. "Spiritual knowledge belongs to all humanity equally. Given the state of the world today, we all have not only the right but the obligation to pursue all forms of spiritual insight, and at every possible level. In this sense, it seems to me that I have as much right to pursue and articulate the belief systems developed by Native Americans as they do, and arguments to the contrary strike me as absurd in the extreme."

Indeed, the expression of such proprietary interest in native spiritual tradition is hardly unique to Snyder. For instance, at a 1986 benefit concert staged to raise funds to support the efforts of traditional Navajos resisting forcible relocation from their homes around Big Mountain, Arizona, one non-Indian performer took the opportunity between each of her songs to "explain" one or another element of "Navajo religion" to the audience. Her presumption in this regard deeply offended several Navajos in attendance and, during an intermission, she was quietly told to refrain from any further such commentary. She thereupon returned to the stage and announced that her performance was over and that she was withdrawing her support of the Big Mountain struggle because the people of that area were "oppressing" her through denial of her "right" to serve as a self-appointed spokesperson for their spirituality. "I have," she said, "just as much right to spiritual freedom as they do."

Those who hold positions of this sort often go beyond assertion of their supposed rights to contend that the arguments of their opponents are altogether lacking in substance. "What does it hurt if a bunch of people want to believe they're the personification of Hiawatha?" asks the manager of a natural foods store in Boulder, Colorado. "I will admit that things can get pretty silly in these circles, but so what? People have a right to be silly if they want to. And it's not like the old days when Indians were being killed left and right. You could even say that the attention being paid to Indian religions these days is sort of flattering. Anyway, there's no harm to anybody, and it's good for the people who do it."

The traditional Indian perspective is diametrically opposed. As Barbara Owl, a White Earth Anishinabe, recently put it, "We have many particular things which we hold internal to our cultures. These things are spiritual in nature, and they are for *us*, not for anyone who happens to walk in off the street. They are *ours* and they are *not* for sale. Because of this, I suppose it's accurate to say that such matters are our 'secrets,' the things which bind us together in our identities as distinct peoples. It's not that we never make outsiders aware of our secrets, but *we*—not *they*—decide what, how much, and to what purpose this knowledge is to be put. That's absolutely essential to our cultural integrity, and thus to our survival as peoples. Now, *surely* we Indians are entitled to *that*. Everything else has been stripped from us already."

"I'll tell you something else," Owl continued. "A lot of things about our spiritual ways may be secret, but the core idea never has been. And you can sum up that idea in one word spelled R-E-S-P-E-C-T. Respect for and balance between all things, that's our most fundamental spiritual concept. Now, obviously, those who would violate the trust and confidence which is placed in them when we share some of our secrets, they don't have the slightest sense of the word. Even worse are those who take this information and misuse or abuse it for their own purposes, marketing it in some way or another, turning our spirituality into a commodity in books or movies or classes or 'ceremonials.' And it doesn't really matter whether they are Indians or non-Indians when they do such things; the non-Indians who do it are thieves, and the Indians who do it are sellouts and traitors."

Former American Indian Movement (AIM) leader Russell Means not only concurs with Owl's assessment, but adds a touch of terminological clarity to her argument. "What's at issue here is the same old question that Europeans have always posed with regard to American Indians, whether what's ours isn't somehow theirs. And, of course, they've always answered the question in the affirmative. When they wanted our land they just announced that they had a right to it and therefore owned it. When we resisted their taking of our land they claimed we were being unreasonable and committed physical genocide upon us in order to convince us to see things their way. Now, being spiritually bankrupt themselves, they want our spirituality as well. So they're making up rationalizations to explain why they're entitled to it."

"We are resisting this," Means goes on, "because spirituality is the basis of our culture; if it is stolen, our culture will be dissolved. If our culture is dissolved, Indian people *as such* will cease to exist. By definition, the causing of any culture to cease to exist is an act of genocide. That's a matter of international law; look it up in the *1948 Genocide Convention*. So, maybe this'll give you another way of looking at these culture vultures who are ripping off Indian tradition. It's not an amusing or trivial matter, and its not innocent or innocuous. And those who engage in this are not cute, groovy, hip, enlightened, or any of the rest of the things they want to project themselves as being. No, what they're about is cultural genocide. And genocide is genocide, regardless of how you want to 'qualify' it. So some of us are starting to react to these folks accordingly."

For those who would scoff at Means' concept of genocide, Mark Davis and Robert Zannis, Canadian researchers on the topic, offer the following observation:

> If people suddenly lose their 'prime symbol,' the basis of their culture, their lives lose meaning. They become disoriented, with no hope. A social disorganization often follows such a loss, they are often unable to insure their own survival...The loss and human suffering of those whose culture has been healthy and is suddenly attacked and disintegrated are incalculable.

Therefore, Davis and Zannis conclude, "One should not speak lightly of 'cultural genocide' as if it were a fanciful invention. The consequence in real life is far too grim to speak of cultural genocide as if it were a rhetorical device to beat the drums for 'human rights.' The cultural mode of group extermination is genocide, a crime. Nor should 'cultural genocide' be used in the game: 'Which is more horrible, to kill and torture; or remove [the prime cultural symbol which is] the will and reason to live?' *Both* are horrible."

Recreating Indians as Destroyers of the Ecology

The analysis advanced by Russell Means, Pam Colorado, and other American Indians is substantially borne out by developments during the second half of the 1980s, as the line separating appropriation of the forms of indigenous spiritual tradition from the outright expropriation of that tradition has evaporated. Over the past few years, a major intellectual enterprise among New Age adherents has been the "demystification" of precontact Native America. Although the variants of this effort vary widely, they take as a common objective the "reinterpretation" of one or more positive aspects and attainments of autonomous indigenous society, "proving" that they never existed. Inevitably, the conclusion is reached that whatever is under discussion was "actually" introduced to the hemisphere by European invaders at some point after 1500.

Hence, we find "radical ecologists" such as George Weurthner arguing in the pages of the supposedly progressive journal *Earth First!* that, far from having achieved spiritual traditions predicated in an understanding of natural harmony and balance, ancient American Indians were really the "first environmental pillagers." This flat reversal of even the most elementary meanings of Native tradition is then "explained" as Weurthner wanders through a consistently self-contradictory and wildly convoluted monologue in which he saddles North American indigenous societies with everything from the extinction of the wooly mammoth to desertification of the Sonora. That he deviates radically from logic, known fact, and even plain common sense while making his "case" does nothing to deter his stream of bald assertion.

Predictably, from this contrived springboard he is able to contend with superficial plausibility that the conceptualization now termed "ecology" did not—as is popularly imagined—spring from traditional Native American practice. Rather, in Weurthner's more "informed" view, it stems from the fertility of advanced brains such as his own. It follows that he feels compelled to demand that American Indians abandon the "myth and falsity" of their own belief structures in favor of the outlook he and his colleagues have expropriated from them.

In a more public vein, the thinly veiled racism of Weurthner's sort of theorizing has set the stage for the celebrated environmentalist author (and Earth First! guru) Edward Abbey to launch himself full-tilt into avowals of an imagined "superiority of northern European culture" worthy of Josef Goebbels and Alfred Rosenberg. Perhaps more pragmatically, it has simultaneously laid the basis for Earth First! political leader Dave Foreman to declare Indian peoples a "threat to the habitat" and urge both ecologists and New Agers to actively resist their land and water rights claims. All of this might be to some extent dismissable as the ravings of an irrelevant lunatic fringe were it not for the fact that, as usual, such ideas are finding their way into the realm of mainstream academia, where they are being sanctioned and codified as "knowledge, truth, and scholarship." The interlock and continuity between the expropriation of the physical resources of Native America on the one hand, and the expropriation of its spiritual/conceptual traditions on the other, could not be more clearly revealed.

Comes now Sam D. Gill, a non-Indian professor of Religious Studies at the University of Colorado/Boulder, and an alleged specialist in Native American spirituality. In all fairness, it should be noted that Gill has heretofore been known primarily not so much on the grounds of his theses on Indian religion as for his advocacy of a rather novel approach to teaching. In essence, this seems to be that the crucial qualification for achieving university-level faculty status is to admittedly know little or nothing of the subject matter one is supposed to teach. As he himself put it in an essay contained in *On Teaching*, a 1987 anthology of "teaching excellence":

> In my classes on Native American religions I found I could not adequately describe the roles of women in Native American cultures and religions...To begin to resolve my *ignorance* about Native American women and to pursue research...I finally offered a senior-level course on Native American women and religions...This course formally *initiated* my long-term research on Mother Earth [emphasis added].

One might have thought that filling a seat as a professor at a major institution of higher learning would imply not "ignorance," but rather the possession of some body of knowledge about or from which one is prepared to profess. Similarly, it might be thought that the offering of an advanced course in a particular content area might imply some sort of relationship to the *results* of research rather than the "initiation" of it. At the very least, one might expect that if a course needs to be taught for canonical reasons, and the instructor of record finds him/herself lacking in the knowledge required to teach it, he or she might retain the services of someone who *does* have the knowledge. Not so within the preferred pedagogy of Dr. Gill. Instead, he posits that "student questions and concerns" are most important in "shaping" what he does. In other words: "pitch your performance to the crowd."

In any event, it was in this interesting commentary on the application of Harold Garfinkle's principles of attaining "pure knowledge" that Gill announced he had "a book in the process of being published by the University of Chicago Press. It is entitled *Mother Earth: An American Story.*" He had thus assigned himself the task of articulating the "truth" of what is possibly the most central of all Native American spiritual concepts. Worse, he went on to remark that in order to "encourage my expeditious writing of the book, I committed myself to a presentation of it as a portion of a summer course entitled 'Native American Goddesses' to be offered the second five-week summer session. With that incentive I completed the writing by July 15 and was able to present the manuscript to this senior and graduate-level class. The manuscript was quickly revised based in part upon student responses and sent off to press." Again, Gill's students (the vast bulk of whom are non-Indian) inform the teacher (also a non-Indian) of what they want to hear, he responds by accommodating their desires, and the result becomes the stuff which passes as "proper understanding" of Indians in academe.

News of this incipient text induced a certain rumbling among Denver-area Indians, complete with letters of outrage from community leaders. The institutional response was that Gill, regardless of the merits of anything he may have said or written, was protected within the rubric of "academic freedom." Wallace Coffey, a Comanche who directs the Denver Indian center, summed up community feeling at the time by observing that while the university was no doubt correct in claiming Gill's activities should be covered by academic freedom guarantees, "It's funny that every time a non-Indian wants to say something about Indians, no matter how outlandish or inaccurate, they start to talk about academic freedom. But every time an Indian applies for a faculty job, all they can talk about are 'academic standards.' I guess I'll be forgiven for saying it seems to me somebody's talking out of both sides of their mouth here. And I don't mind saying that I think this situation has a lot to do with why so few Indians ever get to teach in the universities in this state."

Unsurprisingly, given the circumstances and overall context of its creation, when *Mother Earth* was eventually released it extended the thesis that its subject had never been a *bona fide* element of indigenous tradition at all. Instead, its author held that the whole idea had been inculcated among American Indians by early European colonists, and had been developed and perfected since the conquest. With deadly predictability, he went on to conclude that insofar as any special rights to North America accrue to a belief in Mother Earth, they must accrue to everyone—Native and Euroamerican alike—equally (one is left a bit unclear as to Gill's views on the proprietary interests of African and Asian Americans on the continent). Thus, *Mother Earth* is *An American* (rather than Native American) *Story*.

A Discussion with Sam Gill

Shortly after his book's release, I called Sam Gill on the phone. After a few moments of conversation, he asked whether I was upset by what he'd written. I replied that I was indeed quite upset and responded to his query as to why this might be with a long and somewhat disjointed discourse on the nature of cultural imperialism, the fact that he'd quoted material I'd ghost-written for others quite out of context, and my impression that he'd quite deliberately avoided including *any* American Indians directly in the research process by which he'd reached conclusions about them so profoundly antithetical to their own. "I think we had better meet in person," he said.

To his credit, Gill kept the appointment, arriving as scheduled at my office. In response to his request to go deeper into some of the issues I'd raised on the phone, I explained that I felt there was probably validity to the idea he'd articulated in *Mother Earth* that the interpretation and reinterpretation of the Mother Earth concept by succeeding generations of Euroamericans (such as Gill himself) had blocked any broad understanding of the original indigenous meaning of it. I also acknowledged that this additive phenomenon had, over the years, no doubt carried the popular notion of Mother Earth very far from any indigenous meaning. However, with that said, I stressed that nothing in either postulation precluded there having already been a well-developed indigenous Mother Earth concept operant in North America before contact. Further, I emphasized, he'd brought out nothing in his book which precluded an *ongoing* and autonomous Native American conceptualization of Mother Earth, divorced from popular (mis)understandings, exactly as traditionalist Indians presently claim.

"Well," he said, "this is interesting. I quite agree with you, and I think that's pretty much what I said in the book. Have you read it?" Taken by surprise, I reached across my desk for a copy and read an excerpt from page six:

> As I have come to know it, the story of Mother Earth is a distinctively American story. Mother Earth, as she has existed in North America, cannot be adequately understood and appreciated apart from the complex history of the encounter between Native Americans and Americans of European ancestry, nor apart from comprehending that *the scholarly enterprise that has sought to describe her has had a hand in bringing her into existence, a hand even in introducing her to Native American peoples* [emphasis added].

Without looking up, I skipped to page seven: "*Mother Earth has come into existence in America largely within the last one hundred years*...When her story is told, it becomes clear how all Americans, whatever their heritage, may proclaim Mother Earth to be the mother of us all [emphasis added]." And again, almost at random, from page 157: "Mother Earth is also mother to the Indians. This study has shown that *she has become so only recently,* and then not without influence from Americans [emphasis added]." With the third quote, I indicated I could go on but figured the point had been made. At this juncture Gill suggested that perhaps he'd not been as clear in the writing of the book as he'd intended. I countered that while I agreed the text suffered certain difficulties in exposition, these particular passages seemed quite clear, in line with his overall treatise as I understood it, and lacking only in possible alternative interpretations. "Oh well," he said with a small shrug, "I never intended this as a book on religion anyway. I wrote it as a study in American history. Are you planning to review it?"

When I replied that, yes, I was, and as widely as possible, he said, "Then I'd very much appreciate it if you'd treat it as an historical work, not in the framework of religious studies. Fair enough?" Surprised again, I agreed.

Gill's Historiography

There are a number of points of departure from which one might begin to assess Sam Gill's historical project, none of them as telling as the way in which he defines the object of his quest. On the very first page he declares that, "Mother Earth is not only a Native American *goddess* but a *goddess* of people the world over…[emphasis added]." Two things are striking here:

- First, Gill seems from the outset to simply disregard the obvious literal meanings of statements by three different American Indians—the 19th-century Wanapum leader Smohalla, contemporary Navajo politician Peterson Zah, and AIM leader Russell Means—which he quotes on the same page. In each of these diverse utterances, the speaker refers to the earth *herself* as being "the mother." All allegorical references to human anatomy—*e.g.*, the soil as "skin," rocks as "bones"—are clearly extended *from* this premise in an effort to allow the (non-Indian) listener to apprehend the concept at issue. *No* attempt is being made to utilize the earth as an allegory by which to explain some humanesque entity.

- Second, Gill immediately insists upon precisely this reversal of polarities, quoting Edward Taylor to the effect that, "among the native races of America the Earth Mother is one of the great *personages* of mythology [emphasis added]." He then reinforces this by quoting Ake Haltkrantz, a major topical Swedish scholar on American Indian religions: "The belief in a *goddess*, usually identified with Mother Earth, is found almost everywhere in North America [emphasis added]."

This is what is commonly referred to as "setting up a straw man." By thus "establishing" on the opening page that the Native American conception of Mother Earth assumes the Eurocentric form of a "goddess"—rather than the literal "earth deity" embodied in the articulated indigenous meaning—Gill has contrived a false context for his historical examination which allows him to reach *only* the conclusions he desires: *i.e.*, Mother Earth did not exist in Native North America prior to the European invasion. Therefore, *ipso facto*, it follows that Europeans had as much or more to do with the creation of the indigenous conceptualization of Mother Earth as did the Indians themselves.

The conclusions will be "true," of course, given how the author has framed the questions. But one could as easily decide that, insofar as the yin and yang principles of Taoism embody female and male principles, they too "must" signify a god and goddess. Self-evidently, no amount of "historical scrutiny" will reveal the existence in these traditions of a goddess named "Yin" or a god named "Yang" (albeit, it may be possible to locate both "personages" at the Nairopa Institute in Boulder). Notwithstanding the fact that such god and goddess entities never had a place in the Taoist lexicons themselves, are we not bound by Gillian "logic" to conclude that neither the yin nor the yang principle ever had a place in the structure of either Taoist spiritual concepts? And, if we do manage to reach this absurd conclusion, does it not follow that since the terms ying and yang are now employed within the vernaculars of these traditions, they must have originated in the interaction between East and West, the concepts themselves "introduced" to the Orient by the Occident? To the extent that we can accept the whole charade up to this point, won't it follow that we are now entitled to consider Buddhism to be as much a part of our own non-Buddhist heritage (read: "property") as it is for the Buddhist Vietnamese, or even the Zen monks? Such questions tend to answer themselves.

In many ways, then, examination of Gill's historiography need go no further than this. A project as flawed at its inception as his offers little hope of reaching productive outcomes, a matter rendered all the more acute when an author exhibits as marked a propensity to manipulate his data as does Gill, forcing it to conform to his predispositions regardless of the maiming and distortion which ensue. Examples of this last appear not only in the manner described with regard to the first page of *Mother Earth*, but in abundance—through the sins of both omission and commission—within the remainder of the book.

As concerns omission, one need only turn to a section entitled "The Triumph of Civilization over Savagism" (pages 30-39) to catch the drift. Here, we find Gill making much of the female Indian ("Mother Earth") iconography being produced in Europe and its North American colonies from roughly 1575 until 1765. It is not that he handles what he discusses with any particular inaccuracy. Rather, it's that he completely neglects to mention that there was a roughly equal proportion of male Indian iconography streaming from the same sources during the same period. Along the same line, and in the same section, he goes into the impact of Pocahontas (female Indian, "Mother Earth") mythology on the formation of Americana without even an aside to the existence of its Hiawatha (male Indian) corollary. The result of this sort of skewed presentation is to preclude the drawing of reasoned conclusions from the subject matter, and to block the book from serving as a useful contribution to the literature in any positive way at all.

In terms of commission, there is a small matter of Gill putting words (or meanings) into people's mouths. The clearest examples of this lie in Chapter 7 (pages 129-50), in which he sets out to "prove" that the adoption of a belief in Mother Earth has led contemporary American Indians away from their traditional tribal/cultural specificity and toward a homogeneous sort of "pan-Indianism" (this is a variation on the standard rationalization that Indian rights no longer exist as such because Indians in the traditional sense no longer exist). To illustrate this idea, he selects quotations from several individuals, including Grace (Spotted Eagle) Black Elk, Sun Bear, and Russell Means.

Grace Black Elk died recently and is therefore no longer able to clarify or debunk the meanings Gill assigns her words. However, in my own (extensive) experience with her, she was always *very* clear that, while she strongly and unswervingly supported the rights of all indigenous peoples to pursue their traditional spirituality, she herself followed *only* what she described as "Lakota way." Further, she was consistently firm in her desire not to see the Lakota way diluted or "contaminated" by the introduction of other traditions. Such a position is obviously rather far from the somewhat amorphous, intertribal spiritual amalgam Gill claims she represented.

Sun Bear, for his part, has also been quite clear, albeit in an entirely different way. Marketing aside, he has stated repeatedly and for the record that the eclectic spiritual porridge he serves up has "nothing to do with Indian religion," "pan" or otherwise. He has also openly acknowledged that his adherents are composed almost exclusively of non-Indians; he admits that he tends to steer well clear of Indians these days, because they would "beat me up or kill me" due to the deliberately misleading marketing strategies he employs. *This* is the emblem of an "emerging pan-Indianism"? As concerns Russell Means, Gill quotes repeatedly from a single speech delivered at the 1980 Black Hills Survival Gathering. While assigning a pan-Indianist meaning to the passages he elects to use, he carefully destroys the context in which the words were spoken. This includes categorical statements, toward the end of the speech, that Means does *not* consider or intend himself to be a "leader" in the pan-Indian sense, and that his thinking and actions are guided by a view of himself as "an Oglala Lakota patriot." Again, it is difficult to conceive a much clearer statement of tribally specific orientation and motivation—and rejection of pan-Indianism—than this.

Ultimately, the reviewer is left with the feeling that he should replay in paraphrase a scene from the film *Apocalypse Now.* Sam Gill (playing Col. Kurtz; Marlon Brando) asks: "Do you find my methods to be unsound?" The reviewer (playing Capt. Willard; Martin Sheen) replies: "Frankly, sir, I can't find any valid method at all."

A Question of "Revisionism"

The point has been made by Roger Echohawk, a Pawnee student at the University of Colorado, that even if Gill's historiography is lacking in certain important respects, there could still be a practical value and utility to his analysis of particular themes or sub-topics. The point is accurate enough on its face, if a bit strained, and is therefore worth pursuing at least to some extent. By way of example, we will concentrate on Gill's examination of the first of the major historical occurrences dealt with in *Mother Earth*—Tecumseh's "Mother Earth statement"—the negation of which is a linchpin to the author's arguments throughout the rest of the book.

After a brief but reasonably accurate depiction of Tecumseh's diplomatic and military confrontations with the United States (pages 8-13), Gill sets out to prove that the great Shawnee leader never actually made a particular statement—"The earth is my mother, and on her bosom I will repose"—during negotiations with William Henry Harrison in 1810. On pages 13-14, he notes that he has discovered a total of 27 references to this statement in the literature of the 19th century, the first of these in an article in the *National Recorder* on May 12, 1821, by an anonymous author. The next, he says on page 15, comes in a little-read history written by Moses Dawson, a former aide to Harrison and eyewitness to the negotiations, published in 1824. Then came Henry Rowe Schoolcraft's *Travels in the Central Portions of the Mississippi Valley* in 1825. After that, there were a steady stream of references, several by other eyewitnesses.

The obvious conclusion to be drawn from all this is that so many people refer to the Tecumseh statement for the simple reason that this is what the man said. The problem for Gill in this proposition, however, is that Tecumseh's having said it would seriously unhinge a portion of the thesis presented in *Mother Earth*. Hence, he faces the need to demonstrate that the verbiage attributed to the Indian actually came from another, non-Indian source, and that all succeeding published references merely parroted what had been said before. The logical source in this scenario would be Schoolcraft, given that he was far and away the most popular, accessible, and thus quotable of the writers in question. This is problematic insofar as both the 1821 and 1824 references were published prior to Schoolcraft's book. Gill "solves" this difficulty on page 15 by quietly "suggesting" that for unexplained reasons Schoolcraft—who is not at all known for a tendency to write anonymous tracts, and who was a "name" any editor would have gladly afforded a byline—authored the unattributed *Recorder* article in 1821, unaccountably fabricating the Tecumseh statement.

An implication of this thoroughly unsubstantiated "historical discovery," never brought out in *Mother Earth,* is that for some equally unexplained reason Dawson must next have opted to deliberately falsify *his* historical record of the negotiations by borrowing this fictional quotation from an obscure three-year-old article which even Gill describes as "filler" in the back pages of a magazine. After Schoolcraft's book, of course, he is much freer in writing off other eyewitness accounts as fabrications (at least with regard to the Tecumseh statement); this includes the account contained in Josiah Gregg's 1844 *Commerce of the Prairies* (covered on pages 21-22), and the accounts of Augustus Jones and Major Joseph M. McCormick, recorded by Lyman D. Draper of the State Historical Society of Wisconsin during the mid-1880s (covered on pages 23-24). All one need do is accept Gill's utterly unsubstantiated—and unlikely—initial speculations, and his subsequent chronology of systematic plagiarism works out splendidly.

Having thus dismissed standard history as nothing short of a sustained hoax involving everyone from participants to playwrights, Gill next sets out to "correct" the record. This he purports to accomplish by reference to a solitary eyewitness account, this time by a man named Felix Bouchie, published in the *Vincennes Commercial* on January 8, 1889 (covered on pages 25-27). Therein is found a recounting of an interchange between Tecumseh and Harrison which occurred on a bench (not on the ground), lasting every bit of five minutes during two full days of negotiations, and in which the Mother Earth statement (an utterance which would require less than five seconds) is not made. Bouchie does not state that Tecumseh did *not* make the Mother Earth statement; he is simply recounting something else, and does not bring it up.

Again, there are obvious conclusions to be drawn. For instance, it would seem likely—since there was ample time available—that both the bench episode *and* the Mother Earth episode might have occurred at different points, or even on different days during the negotiations. Bouchie does not claim to have been present during the entirety of the sessions, and his account could be responsibly viewed as a valuable *addition* to the record. Gill, however, will have none of this. Rather, he insists that Bouchie's version of events "must" have occurred *instead of* the other 27 more-or-less harmonious versions. This, he says, constitutes his final (crushing?) "proof" that the extremely well-documented Tecumseh statement is a fiction.

One senior American Indian scholar (who wishes to remain anonymous), upon reviewing Gill's Tecumseh material, dismissed him as "a lunatic, not worth the time and energy to argue with." In a less emotional and more constructive vein, an Indian historian (who also asked to be left unnamed), offered a more thoughtful insight:

> You know, what we're confronted with here is not uniquely—and maybe at this point not even primarily—an American Indian issue. What this calls to mind more than anything is the sort of "historical revisionism" practiced by people like Arthur Butz and Richard Harwood, guys who use all sorts of pseudo-scholarly sleights-of-hand to "prove" the Holocaust never happened. Their stuff won't hold up to even minimal scrutiny, but they keep right on going because they're ideologically motivated.

Precisely. And with that, there seems very little left to say concerning the possible value of Sam Gill's historical analyses.

The New Age Ideological Project aka The Same Old Song of Europe

And so the question naturally arises as to what sort of ideology might prompt an individual like Sam Gill to write a book lending itself to comparison with the sordid neonazi sentiments of an Arthur Butz. Certainly he would recoil in horror at the suggestion of such linkage at any level. Likely, the same can be said for any of his cohorts from Castaneda to Highwater, from Sun Bear's ersatz Indians to the ecology movement (with the possible exception of the Earth First! Foreman/Abbey/Weurthner group, which seems to have found its preferred niche under the term "fascist").

By and large, it also appears just as probable that all the above entities would express a vehement and heartfelt disavowal of the historical processes of physical genocide and expropriation visited upon Native Americans by the federal government. In their own minds, they are typically steadfast opponents of all such policies and the ideologies of violence which undergird them. At some level they are no doubt sincere in their oft and loudly repeated professions of being true "friends of the Indian." There can be no question but that they've convinced themselves that they are divorced completely from the ugly flow of American history, and it would be worse than dubious to suggest that they might be inclined to muster forth the 7th Cavalry to work their will.

Yet, demonstrably, as much as any missionary, soldier, or government bureaucrat who preceded them, those of the New Age have proven themselves willing to disregard the rights of American Indians to any modicum of cultural sanctity or psychological sanctuary. They too willfully and consistently disregard the protests and objections of their victims, speaking only of their own "right to know" and to victimize. They too have exhibited an ability to pursue courses of conduct bearing arguably genocidal implications, to shrug off the danger, and to argue only that genocide couldn't be genocide if they are the perpetrators of it. They too have persistently shown themselves willing to lie, distort, fabricate, cheat, and steal in order to accomplish their agenda. The salient queries may thus be reduced to "why?" and "what are they after?"

The answers, in a real sense, are as simple as the facts that they are here and that they fully plan to stay. While the New Age can hardly be rationally accused of performing the conquest of the Americas, and its adherents go to great lengths in expressing their dismay at the methods used therein, they have clearly inherited what their ancestors gained thereby, both in terms of resources and in terms of relative power. The New Agers, for all their protestations to the contrary, aren't about to give up any of either. Their task, then, is that of simultaneously hanging on to what has been stolen while separating themselves from the *way* in which it was stolen. It is a somewhat tricky psychological project of being able to "feel good about themselves" (that ultimate expression of the New Age) through "legitimizing" the maintenance of their own colonial privilege. The project is essentially ideological. As Martin Carnoy has explained it:

> The legitimation of the colonist's role requires the destruction of the colonized's sense of culture and history, so the colonized is removed [or excluded] from all social and cultural responsibility.

Albert Memmi adds:

> In order for the legitimacy to be complete, it is not enough for the colonized to be a slave [or thoroughly dispossessed and disenfranchised], he must also accept his role. The bond between colonizer and colonized is thus [both] destructive and creative.

Within the context of our immediate concern, these insights add up to the circumstance where Native Americans are marginalized or barred from participation in the generation of "knowledge" concerning their histories, cultures, and beliefs. The realities at issue are then systematically supplanted, negated, and reconstructed to suit the psychological needs of the current crop of colonizers, and the result reproduced as "truth" among both the oppressors and the oppressed. As early as 1973, Jamake Highwater was telling us that, "[truth] is not simply a matter of getting the facts wrong, but of developing a credible falsehood." In 1984, he went further:

> The final belief is to believe in a fiction, which you know to be a fiction. There being nothing else, the exquisite truth is to know that it is a fiction and that you believe in it willingly.

In its final manifestation, the mythology which is forged ("created") in this process *always* assumes the form of an "inclusive" doctrine, legitimizing the present colonial status quo. The invaders' "contributions," however invented they may be, inevitably "entitle" them to superior status; there may have been a problem once, but it's in the past, so forget it; we're all in this together now, so let's move forward (with me in the lead); I'm OK, you're OK (so long as you stay in your place and don't upset me with questions of or challenges to my privilege), and so on. We can now name the ideology which motivates the Sam Gills of America. It is called "New Age," but as Russell Means once remarked (in another connection), it represents only "the same old song of Europe." And, in the contemporary United States, its codification has rapidly become an academic growth industry.

Hence, the living fabric of Indian society is to be destroyed as its youth are "educated" to view their heritage in exactly the same way as those who seek to subsume it. This is no rupture with, but rather a continuation and perfection of the twin systems of colonization and genocide which have afflicted Native America for the past 400 years. From this vantage point, false as it is from start to finish, the scholarly disgrace which constitutes *Mother Earth* really *is* "an American story."

Sources

Adams, Hank, *Cannibal Green* (on Jamake Highwater) (Olympia, WA: Survival of American Indians, Inc., 1984).

Butz, Arthur D., *The Hoax of the Twentieth Century: The Case Against the Presumed Extermination of European Jewry* (Torrance, CA: Institute for Historical Review, 1977).

Carnoy, Martin, *Education as Cultural Imperialism* (New York: David McKay Company, Inc., 1974).

Churchill, Ward, "Ayn Rand and the Sioux—Tonto Revisited: Another Look at *Hanta Yo*," *Lakota Eyapaha*, vol. 4, no. 2, Oglala Sioux Community College (June 1980).

DeMille, Richard, *Castaneda's Journey* (Santa Barbara, CA: Capra Press, 1976).

DeMille, Richard, ed., *The Don Juan Papers: Further Castaneda Controversies* (Santa Barbara, CA: Ross-Erikson Publishers, 1980).

Gill, Sam, "The Continuity of Research and Classroom Teaching, or How to Have Your Cake and Eat It Too," in *On Teaching*, ed. Mary Ann Shea (Boulder, CO: Faculty Teaching Excellence Program, University of Colorado at Boulder, 1987).

Harwood, Richard, *Did Six Million Really Die?* (Richmond, Surrey, England: Historical Review Press, 1974).

Means, Russell, "The Same Old Song," in *Marxism and Native Americans*, ed. Ward Churchill (Boston, MA: South End Press, 1983).

Memmi, Albert, *Colonizer and Colonized* (Boston, MA: Beacon Press, 1965).

Red Fox, William, *The Memoirs of Chief Red Fox* (New York: Fawcett Books, 1972).

Seals, David, *The Pow Wow Highway* (Denver, CO: Sky Press, 1984).

Storm, Hyemeyohsts, *Seven Arrows* (New York: Ballantine Books, 1972).

"Sun Bear" and "Wabun," *The Medicine Wheel: Earth Astrology* (Englewood Cliffs, NJ: Prentice-Hall Publishers, 1980).

Weurthner, George, "An Ecological View of the Indian," *Earth First!*, vol. VII, no. VII (August 1987).

ANOTHER DRY WHITE SEASON
Jerry Mander's *In the Absence of the Sacred*

In many ways, the issue is still one of appropriation. The dominant culture, or its representatives, entitle themselves to intellectual assets of the dominated in exactly the same ways they've historically entitled themselves to possession of land, resources, and other material assets. The present interaction, intellectually speaking, is simply an extension or broadening of the same old colonial paradigm.

—Jimmie Durham, Alfred University, 1991

They just can't help it. I swear, they really can't. It's too deeply ingrained in the subconscious, a matter of subliminal presumption. No matter how well-intentioned or insightful, regardless of how critical of the dominant conceptual paradigm and "sensitive" to non-Western perspectives, the theoretical writing of Euroamerican men—and most white women as well—seems destined with a sort of sad inevitability to become yet another exercise in intellectual appropriation, a reinforcement of the very hegemony they purport to oppose. To expect otherwise, one supposes, would be to expect that a leopard will (or can) change its spots. This remains true despite the authors' most genuinely held desires that things be otherwise, not to mention their oft and fervently expressed assertions that, in their own cases at least, such wishes have already been fulfilled.

Take, as a prime example, Jerry Mander's book, *In the Absence of the Sacred: The Failure of Technology and the Survival of Indian Nations* (Sierra Club, 1992). There can be no question that the author's credentials as a proponent of fundamental and positive social change are impeccable. He is committed to reestablishing global ecological equilibrium and opposing the blatant anthropocentrism which, more than any other factor, signifies the Judeo-Christian ("Western" or European) tradition of "knowing." He is undoubtedly sincere in his contention, voiced throughout his treatise, that the only viable route forward is a wholesale abandonment of Eurosupremacist assumptions and a concomitant (re)assertion of what may be termed the "indigenous world view" on a planetary scale. He is articulate and effective—at times even eloquent—in elaborating his thesis. Yet, in many respects, the book embodies the worst of what he intends to oppose.

The book, Mander explains in the introduction, was originally conceived as two different projects: one about the technological fetishism of "mainstream culture," the other about contemporary indigenous societies. The first was "intended to raise questions about whether technological [Eurocentric] society has lived up to its advertising, and also to address some grave concerns about its future direction…The second book was to be a kind of continuation and update of Dee Brown's *Bury My Heart At Wounded Knee*" (p. 4).[1] While "planning to write these two books," however, "it became apparent to me that their subjects were inseparable. They belonged together as one book. There is no way to understand the situation of the Indians, Eskimos, Aborigines, island peoples, or other native societies without understanding the outside societies that act upon them. And there is no way to understand the outside societies without understanding their relationships to native peoples and to nature itself" (p. 6).

> All things considered, it may be the central assumption of technological society that there is virtue in overpowering nature and native peoples…Save for such nascent movements as bioregionalism and Green politics, which have at least questioned the assumptions…most people in Western society are in agreement about our common superiority. So it becomes okay to humiliate—to find insignificant and thus subject to sacrifice—any way of life or thinking that stands in the way of the "progress" we have invented, which is scarcely a century old. In fact, having assumed such superiority, it becomes more than acceptable for us to bulldoze nature and native societies. To do so actually becomes desirable, inevitable, and possibly "divine" (pp. 6-7).

Formulated as a unified project, Mander's undertaking was therefore, in his own recounting, recast not only as a critique of what he apprehends as an hallucinatory and extremely dangerous "technotopianism" forming a core tenet of Eurocentrism, but as a means of addressing several other substantive questions: "Can we expect the situation to improve or worsen in the future? And what of the [native] people who always told us that this way would not work, and continue to say so now? Finally, which is the more 'romantic' viewpoint: that technology will fix itself and lead us to paradise, or that the answer is something far simpler?" (p. 7). In the latter connection, he implies that indigenous alternatives to the current Eurodominant status quo will be presented for consideration by readers. They will form a basis upon which the reader may form reasonable opinions as to which of the numerous options makes most sense. Fair enough. Even commendable. But the issue is how this worthy promise was approached, packaged, and presented by its author.

A Glimpse of the Technotopian Future

In terms of his first emphasis, upon the Western preoccupation with *techne* and its likely consequences, Mander succeeds admirably. His *tour de force* wholeheartedly embraces and gives non-fictional form to Kurt Vonnegut's sentiment that, "Just because some of us can read and write and do a little math, that doesn't mean we deserve to conquer the Universe."[2] He presents not only a summary of the analysis contained in his earlier *Four Arguments for the Elimination of Television*, but equally compelling chapters on biotechnology, the increasingly regimented corporate-state structure of "modern" society, computers, extraterrestrial exploration/colonization, and nanotechnology.[3] Much useful corroborative information is arrayed with respect to nuclear technology, robotics, aerospace technology, and so on.

It is a devastating panorama overflowing with portraits of rampant technocratic insanity. To produce the cultural uniformity necessary for "maximally efficient product consumption," an increasingly somnambulistic humanity is permanently plugged by its alpha brain waves into electronic t.v. pulses.[4] Bacteriological/viral strains designed to target and eliminate specific human groups are unleashed as a vehicle of "species improvement" (a theme which raises the specter that the current world AIDS epidemic is an experiment of the U.S. military/intelligence community gone out of control). A quasi-human "master race" is genetically engineered and manufactured while "undesirable" racial/ethnic characteristics among the actual human population are suppressed through a variety of means. Entire new species of life, deemed "useful" by technocrats, are created while existing—or "useless"—species are eradicated at an ever greater rate.

As a way of offsetting negative effects such as ozone depletion which accompany any permanent spiral of production and consumption, the molecular alteration ("re-engineering") of virtually the entire ecosphere is undertaken.[5]

The premise of technotopianism is that the natural world can and "must" be extinguished in its entirety, replaced with a marketable—and therefore "better"—artificial or "surrogate" environment.[6] This Doomsday Scenario is powerfully reinforced by the leading advocates of unrestrained technocracy spelling out their visions of our collective future. For instance, Mander quotes the president of the R.J. Nabisco Corporation:

> [I am] looking forward to the day when Arabs and Americans, Latins and Scandinavians will be munching Ritz crackers as enthusiastically as they already drink Coke or brush their teeth with Colgate (p. 136).[6]

He then juxtaposes this with a quote from radical social critic Holly Sklar to the effect that the ultimate goal of transnational corporatism is creation of an utterly Eurocentric global monoculture as a basis for profit maximization and consequent underwriting of perpetual technological innovation:

> Corporations not only advertise products, they promote lifestyles rooted in consumption, patterned largely after the United States…[They] look forward to a postnational age in which [Western] social, economic, and political values are transformed into universal values…a world economy in which all national economies beat to the rhythm of transnational corporate capitalism…The Western way is the good way, national culture is inferior (p. 136).[7]

Mander demonstrates conclusively that the technologies at issue are not merely the stuff of *Star Trek* fantasies but are already under development. Some are well on the way to "real world" manifestation. Lengthy quotes from such celebrated exponents of technotopianism as Herman Kahn (p. 144) and the late Gerard O'Neill (p. 145) illustrate the intended uses of such "advances."[8] To cap his presentation, he uses a passage which might have been drawn straight from the script of *Terminator*, showcasing the enthusiastic projections of Hans Moravec, a leading and highly respected pioneer in the field of nanotechnics:

Moravec calmly explains how in the next thirty years we will by-pass the present limits upon artificial intelligence and robotic mobility, to the point where we will be able to "download" all the content of our brains—which are now unfortunately stuck in decaying biological entities—into computers housed within mobile robots, thereby gaining "us" immortality, via these machines. The machines will "evolve" by their own design and, when given the knowledge of all the great thinkers on the planet, without the limitations and fragility of their flesh, will generate ideas and actions that will far exceed human achievement: "Such machines could carry on our cultural evolution, including their own construction and rapid self-improvement, without us, and without the genes that built us. When that happens, our DNA will find itself out of a job, having lost the evolutionary race to a new kind of competition...The new genetic takeover will be complete. Our culture will be able to evolve independently of human biology and its limitations, instead passing directly from generation to generation of ever more capable intelligent machinery" (p. 183).[9]

The overall exposition on the perils of proliferating techno-order, advanced with impeccable logic and anchored by the use of quotations, is marred only by occasional and relatively minor inaccuracies, e.g., observations that "the American and British military...first put [computers] to serious use...as guidance systems for missiles during World War II" (p. 68), and that U.S. nuclear testing in the Marshall Islands occurred during the same war (p. 345). Relatedly, the author states that the U.S. used "machine guns" to slaughter native people "100 years ago," while completing its conquest of their homelands in "the lower forty-eight" states (p. 287). In actuality, neither the United States nor Great Britain possessed guided missiles during World War II, that dubious distinction being reserved to Germany, which developed no computers, in its creation of V-1 and V-2 weapons; World War II Allied computing capacity was devoted primarily to cryptography and nuclear physics.[10] Similarly, U.S. atomic weapons testing in the Marshalls did not begin until well after World War II, and true machine guns did not see application until World War I, fully a quarter-century after the 1890 Wounded Knee Massacre (the last episode of the so-called "Indian Wars" in North America).[11]

The Native Alternative?

The same sorts of problems with factual details appear when Mander takes up his second emphasis, the ongoing existence of land-based/nature-oriented indigenous cultures, which he posits as containing the best and perhaps only valid conceptual and practical alternatives to the ecocide and species suicide inherent to finalization of Western technocracy.[12] For instance, the noted Anishinabe (Chippewa) activist Dennis Banks becomes "a fugitive Sioux Indian leader" (p. 242). The author also displays an odd and irritating habit of referring to *all* indigenous societies as "Indian"—"the Indian tribes" of the Philippines, for example (p. 353)—despite the fact that *no* native peoples outside the Americas refer to themselves in this fashion.

Nonetheless, he provides a lengthy and largely accurate catalogue of the circumstances presently confronting native people in the U.S., and their resistance to them. Illustrations range from the dire effects of the 1973 Alaska Native Claims Settlement Act upon the circumpolar peoples of the Arctic North to the expropriation of Western Shoshone land in Nevada, the struggles of Native Hawaiians to regain control over some portion of their homeland, the forced relocation of more than 10,000 traditional Big Mountain Diné (Navajos), the usurpation of indigenous self-governance through the 1934 Indian Reorganization Act, and the more recent impact of the Supreme Court's "G-O Road Decision" voiding native rights to religious freedom.[13] This exposition on the United States is coupled to a survey of the situations—which he follows University of California geographer Bernard Nietschmann in terming "Fourth World Wars"—of native nations in Canada, Central and South America, the Pacific Basin, Africa, Asia, and, to some extent, Europe.[14]

Such information is, like the analysis of technotopianism, undeniably useful and important, and one wishes to like the book on this basis alone. Equally undeniably, however, most of the material has been covered elsewhere, earlier, and often better, by various American Indian writers and spokespersons. Some are mentioned, but few cited, in Mander's text. Moreover, the great bulk of what he offers with regard to native peoples is little more than a journalistic litany chronicling who's doing what to whom, where, and why. In this sense, it is a continuation of the author's substantiation of the negative effects of technocratic mentality rather than the promised explanation of indigenous thinking. In this respect, aside from a couple of examples concerning "management of animal populations," the book does not come close—to borrow one of the author's pet phrases—to "living up to its advertising."

The reason for this becomes readily apparent when one considers the list of contemporary native "leaders and philosophers" Mander compiles on page 383—"the late Phillip Lame Deer [*sic*: he means Phillip Deer], Black Elk, Louis Bad Wound, Bill Wahpepah, and Dan Bomberry...Jeanette Armstrong, John Mohawk, Winona LaDuke, Dagmar Thorpe, Chris Peters, Oren Lyons, Leslie Silko, Vine Deloria, George Erasmus, N. Scott Momaday, Leonard Peltier, Leon Shenandoah, Alfonso Ortiz, Thomas Banyacya, Marie-Helen Laraque, Wilma Mankiller, and Paula Gunn Allen, to name a small number on this continent alone"—as having important things to tell non-Indians. This decidedly partial itemization of thinking Native Americans must be seen in the context that only three of them are quoted or cited at any point in the entire book. This stands in stark contrast to the author's extensive quotations/citations of Euroamericans (including, as was seen above, those with whom he professes to have the most fundamental disagreements).

Nor do the quotes selected from those on Mander's "Indian list" measure up in terms of content to those chosen to represent the thinking of their non-Indian counterparts. Poliklah activist Chris Peters is restricted to only a rhetorical flourish on the inability of the earth to sustain much more technocultural advancement (pp. 386-7). Acclaimed Seneca social philosopher John Mohawk is afforded space to advance the weighty notion that one must "listen with the heart" if one is to understand indigenous wisdom (p. 113). Onondaga faithkeeper Oren Lyons is interviewed to establish that the traditional government of the Haudenosaunee (Six Nations Iroquois Confederacy) still functions in what it considers to be a sovereign manner (pp. 240-45). Lyons is supported by a quote from Yamasee historian Donald Grinde on the influence of the Haudenosaunee on formation of the democratic ideals expressed by the U.S. founding fathers (p. 234). Elsewhere, Mander makes much of a pamphlet entitled *A Basic Call to Consciousness*, the edited transcript of a presentation made by the Haudenosaunee elders at a United Nations conference in 1977 (pp. 191-3).[15] And that's *it* for articulations of contemporary indigenous intellectualism.

It's not that these are the only native voices present in the volume. To the contrary, the author seems to have been at pains to assemble an impressive array of quotations—most of them lifted from books like Thomas R. Berger's superb *Village Journey* and Julian Burger's *Report from the Frontier*—from grassroots people in the Alaskan north country and elsewhere.[16] But, unmistakably, each of these statements assumes the form of "testimony." They are included not as intellectual contributions, but as documentation for the author's survey of damage and pain inflicted by the techno-order upon indigenous land and lives. Even quotations from activists such as Opegtah Mataemoh, a Menominee also known as Ingrid Washinawatok, are arrayed only to have them complain that "America never listens to American Indians" (p. 224). This is a far different matter than allowing them to explain for themselves what it is America hasn't heard and still isn't hearing.

When it comes time to wax philosophical, and to thus lend *meaning* to things, Mander inevitably turns not to native sources or "informants," but to an all but exclusively white, mostly male, oppositional intelligentsia of which he is a part. He designates this group as consisting of Jeremy Rifkin, as well as "Ernest Callenbach, Lester Brown, Wendell Berry, Thomas Berry, Wes Jackson, Ann Ehrlich, Paul Ehrlich, David Brower, Hazel Henderson, Gary Coats, Erik Dammann, Leopold Kohr, Kirkpatrick Sale, Joanna Macy, Carolyn Merchant, Delores LaChapelle, Riane Eisler, Ivan Illich, Peter Berg, Richard Register, Hunter Lovins, Amory Lovins, Gary Snyder, Langdon Winner, Frances Moore Lappé, Fritjof Capra, Stephanie Mills, Vandana Shiva, Elizabeth Dobson Grey, Charlene Spretnak, Arne Naess, Susan Griffin, Starhawk [a Euroamerican], Bill Devall, George Sessions, E.F. Schumacher, Malcolm Margolin, and Chellis Glendining" (p. 383). He might have added that notorious anthropological hoaxter, Carlos Castaneda, whose ersatz renderings of "native" philosophy are embraced more warmly and at much greater length by Mander than anything genuinely Native American (pp. 207-8).[17] In effect, real indigenous speakers are utilized throughout *In the Absence of the Sacred* as mere props, orchestrated by and large to accompany Mander's own "broader," more "universal" themes.

Cultural Imperialism

Of 305 bibliographical entries at the end of the book, only seventeen—three of them newspaper articles, two of them interviews, one an internal report, and another a memorandum—are identifiably written by American Indians.[18] Several others, such as Joseph Jorgenson's *Native Americans and Energy Development*, are anthologies assembled by Euroamerican editors, but containing one or more contributions by native researchers.[19] The remainder, more than 280 titles, mostly books and more than a hundred of them *about* indigenous peoples to one extent or another, are almost exclusively Euroamerican enterprises. Such a glaring skew simply *cannot* be attributed to a dearth of relevant and appropriate Native American material. Not one of the more than a dozen books by the acclaimed Lakota intellectual Vine Deloria, Jr., is so much as mentioned, for example.[20] This near-total eclipse of indigenous theory and scholarship, other than that which has been thoroughly "interpreted" by selected non-Indians, exists only because Mander wanted it that way.

One underlying message of *In the Absence of the Sacred* is clear enough. The traditional "mind/body split" by which Western intellectualism has always seen itself in relation to non-Westerners has been preserved in Mander's work. The "proper" role of native peoples is essentially physical (we experience, feel, suffer, and testify). The "natural" role of whites, on the other hand, is primarily cerebral. They think, explain, and philosophize, putting a "correct spin" on all phenomena, whether material or conceptual. Non-Western knowledge is thereby "naturally" reduced to the status of being an element or component. Western elites—Mander and his carefully chosen coterie of "culturally transcendent" Euroamerican thinkers no less than any other—are free (even obligated) to absorb these elements as their own "intellectual property." They go on to synthesize new (and therefore inherently "superior") vernaculars of societal/ecological reality. Thus they assume a self-reserved position of theoretical leadership, an effective monopoly on decisionmaking authority.[21] For Mander's group, this would be especially true in the event of anything resembling what they call the "paradigm shift" actually occurring.

Put another way, perceiving that the main body of their own tradition may be discarded in the near future—as surely it must be, given the technological precipice it has created for itself—Mander and his colleagues are busily projecting themselves as *the* group intrinsically best qualified to take charge of the replacement. The means to this end devolve upon the intellectual appropriation and continued Eurocentric domination of non-Western traditions. In principle, the process is not appreciably different from that of previous eras of European cultural imperialism, as when the Crusaders gained eventual "Renaissance" and ascendancy for their culture by seizing, among other things, the Arabic concepts of zero, infinity, and the vaulted arch.[23] Hence, far from representing a *bona fide* attempt to negate the "white skin privilege" embedded in Eurocentrism's undergirding attitudes, the thrust exhibited by Mander and kindred writers amounts to a sophisticated attempt to preserve its fundaments in a rapidly changing and ostensibly non-Western environment.

The technique is as subtle as it is perverse. The author rightly rejects the circular reasoning used to justify Eurocentric orthodoxy's insistent technotopian scientism: "It is true that the evolution of Western science and its proliferating technologies have brought us to our current dismal pass. *Therefore* only an ever greater abundance and refinement of science and technology can save us." This establishes him as a thoroughly "dissident" theoretician, one who can thus be trusted by the most oppressed. Simultaneously, however, precisely because of his stature as a dissident, he can replicate and extend much the same "logic" for his own purposes: it is true that the hegemonic tradition of Western intellectualism (of which scientism is only a part) has brought the entire planet to the brink of oblivion. *Therefore* only a continuation of this same hegemony (in the form of Mander's friends and himself) can fix things. Confronted with such a formulation, the author would probably acknowledge a "paradox" of sorts. But, for non-Western peoples, the words of Peter Townshend ring much truer: "Meet the new boss, same as the old boss."[23]

A Hidden Agenda

Admittedly, all of this may appear overstated and tendentious. It could be argued that whatever Mander's oversights and omissions, they are more inadvertent or careless than deliberate and systematic. However flawed his final product, it is by no means malicious. Such a premise *might* be conceded, were it not for the obvious fashion in which Mander *chose*—there is simply no other word for it—to ignore certain dimensions of Native North America he purports to examine. That these include many of the most visible and important figures, organizations, and events associated with Fourth World resistance on this continent over the past quarter-century speaks volumes to the idea that he might merely have "missed" a few things.[24] That he can be said to have pursued a readily discernible, and emphatically anti-indigenist, political agenda in leaving them unmentioned implies even more. Unquestionably, he consciously sought to impose his own entirely alien notions of "legitimacy"—rather than those reflecting the integrity of native positions—upon struggles for indigenous rights. What he accomplished instead was a serious undermining of the integrity of his own positions, not only in relation to native peoples, but *vis-à-vis* technology as well.

The first hint of what is occurring comes when he fails, other than in a pair of passing references (pp. 307, 315), to remark upon the Black Hills Land Claim of the Lakota Nation. This is the longest—and certainly one of the hardest fought and best publicized—campaigns of its sort in North America.[25] Initially, an omission of such magnitude seems inexplicable in a narrative which ostensibly focuses on native/state conflicts, including many more obscure. An explanation starts to present itself, however, when the author repeats the performance during his world survey. Despite having touched upon such little known but geographically proximate indigenous liberation struggles as those of the Kurds in Iraq, Iran, Turkey, and Azerbaijan (p. 355), the Dinkas and other Black nations of the Sudan (p. 366), and the Eritreans, Somalis, Tigrayans, and Oromos in Ethiopia (pp. 366-7), he avoids mentioning a far more visible and "sensitive" corollary: the efforts of Palestinian Arabs to throw off the yoke of Israeli occupation in their Mideastern homeland.

These two glaring "oversights" are tied together by a third: the author's scrupulous refusal to make *any* reference to the American Indian Movement (AIM), probably *the* preeminent native resistance group in the U.S. since 1970. In order to address the Black Hills Land Claim in any depth, Mander would have *had* to have considered AIM, which has stood almost from its inception at the center of the battle for the Hills. In discussing AIM, it would have been necessary to have acknowledged the "Palestinian Question," at least insofar as AIM and the Palestine Liberation Organization (PLO) have long expressed a formal solidarity based in "united resistance to a common form of oppression."[26] Any one piece of the equation opens the door, so to speak, to each of the others. And, since it is the door to scrutiny of the Israeli state's posture concerning indigenous Arabs that Mander is most anxious to keep firmly closed, he has little alternative but to resort to a series of conspicuous silences, as if these several crucial topics were somehow irrelevant (or did not exist at all).

From here, the dominoes of ideologically necessitated deletion really begin to tumble. If the Black Hills case had to be ignored because of AIM's links to the PLO, then it was also necessary to evade mention of a number of other vital actions in which AIM was a key player: the 1972 Trail of Broken Treaties, 1973 Siege of Wounded Knee, 1978 Longest Walk, Black Hills International Survival Gatherings, and the four-year occupation of Yellow Thunder Camp, just to name a few of the most widely publicized.[27] By the same token, the author could ill afford to bring up important organizations which have emerged as spin-offs from AIM. The International Indian Treaty Council, for example—a group which in its early years (1974-84) did more than any other to open international fora to indigenous participation—is noted only once, in passing (p. 285).[28] Another major entity coming out of AIM, Women of All Red Nations—which led the way in exposing the federal policy of involuntary sterilization directed against native women and which has figured crucially in documenting governmental/corporate uranium contamination of reservations—is not mentioned at all.[29]

Still less was Mander willing to attribute many of the ideas and positions he fields in his book to the various AIM leaders who first voiced or popularized them. The most obvious example comes when the author casually dismisses marxism as an alternative to capitalism in its effects upon indigenous societies (pp. 7, 373) without so much as an oblique reference to the seminal and quite influential indigenist critique of marxism published by Russell Means—complete with a cover photo and introduction comparing its import to Martin Luther King's 1963 "I Have a Dream" speech—in the well-circulated pages of *Mother Jones* magazine.[30] Similarly, while he applauds the fact that some elements of the Euroamerican environmental movement like Earth First!, the Rainforest Action Network, "Friends of the Earth, Earth Island Institute and others have [finally] allied themselves to [some] Indian causes in recent months" (p. 387), the author is careful to leave unmentioned the well-known and decisive effect the speeches, writings, and recordings of former AIM National Chair John Trudell have had in achieving precisely this positive result.[31]

This itemization of willful omissions could be continued at great length. Such distortions can hardly be termed "accidental." Mander did not "miss" or "forget to include" such things as are covered in this section. He *decided* to suppress them, and to do so with complete and ruthless consistency. Nor is the reason he did so particularly mysterious. There is a term defining the political persuasion he brought to bear in his tailoring of information. It is called "zionism." In its most predominant form, it is the assertion by a thoroughly Europeanized segment of the Jewish people of a self-proclaimed "inherent right" to the land of others.[32] Integral to zionist doctrine, quite similar in many ways to the sense of "Manifest Destiny" espoused by 19th-century Euroamerica,[33] has always been the contention that criticism of its tenets or practice is by definition "anti-semitic," therefore "illegitimate," unworthy of exposure, and to be suppressed by any means available.[34] The author follows this prescription to the letter. He knew exactly what he was doing and why, at least in a substantial number of instances. His stifling of the native voice in favor of his own, and his ideological associates, was thus often conscious and intentional.

The Solution as Problem

What is perhaps most telling in Mander's insinuation of a zionist agenda is the implication that his support for and identification with the rights of indigenous peoples is, in the end, just as equivocal and conditional as any other Eurocentrist's. While he is quite prepared to denounce the subordination and dispossession of native peoples in contexts of which he disapproves (which is *almost* all of them), he is equally willing to endorse and defend identical policies in contexts of which he approves for "personal" reasons (e.g., Israeli treatment of Palestinians). Such qualified championing of indigenous self-determination reduces to a kind of vulgar opportunism, little different in principle from Ronald Reagan's loudly professed concern during the 1980s for the "national and human rights" of Sumu, Rama, and Miskito Indians in Sandinista Nicaragua, while openly denying the same rights to native peoples within the United States.

Moreover, Mander's tacit zionist alignment qualifies—and thus flatly contradicts—the degree of his adherence to his own core perspective; that technoculture's massive alteration of nature has gone catastrophically wrong, can only get worse, and must therefore be opposed on all fronts. A main "proof" always advanced by apologists for Israel on the "Jewish right to occupancy" in Palestine is that the Israelis, unlike the Palestinians they've displaced, have "made the barren desert bloom" via a hydrological reworking of virtually the entire country.[35] This is no different in substance from the proud claims of Arizona land developers, whose huge high-tech water diversion projects the author rightly decries as being suicidally destructive to the ecosphere. By standing mute concerning Israel's pronounced and accelerating transformation of its Mideastern habitat, he again demonstrates a willingness to accept such things, so long as they are undertaken by entities of which he otherwise approves.

Back in the '60s, the Students for a Democratic Society (SDS) employed a slogan which contended that "if you're not part of the solution, you're part of the problem." Things have advanced a long distance since then, as *In the Absence of the Sacred* readily demonstrates. In handling this desperately important subject matter the way he has, seeking covertly to extend Western intellectual dominance across overtly non-Western thought and action, Jerry Mander has done much to take a substantial portion of the solution to our current technocratic dilemma and convert it into an aspect of the problem itself. We—every one of us—had a right to expect far more, and far better, from this self-styled "alternative thinker." This book held the potential to yield a genuine breakthrough in popular consciousness regarding the possibility of a "Third Way" lying outside the capitalist/communist technological paradigm altogether. Instead, Mander has produced just another "dry white season," one more excursion into that all-pervasive will to dominate which emblemizes the Eurocentric mind. For this, we owe him no debt of gratitude.

Notes

1. Brown, Dee, *Bury My Heart at Wounded Knee: An Indian History of the American West* (New York: Henry Holt Publishers, 1970).

2. Vonnegut, Kurt, Jr., *Hocus Pocus* (New York: G.P. Putnam's Sons, 1990), p. 324.

3. See Mander, Jerry, *Four Arguments for the Elimination of Television* (New York: William Morrow/Quill Publishers, 1977).

4. In addition to his own earlier work on the effects of television, Mander relies heavily on three other sources in making his current arguments: Winn, Marie, *The Plug-In Drug* (New York: Viking Press, 1977); Winn, Marie, *Unplugging the Plug-In Drug* (New York: Viking/Penguin Publisher, 1987); and Emery, Fred and Merrelyn, *A Choice of Futures: To Enlighten or Inform?* (Canbarra: Center for Continuing Education, Australian National University, 1975).

5. Mander follows the articulations of Pillar, Charles, and Keith R. Yamamoto, in their *Gene Wars: Military Control Over the New Genetic Technologies* (New York: Beech Tree Books, 1988), while making his arguments in this connection.

6. Mander acknowledges borrowing heavily from the thought of French philosopher/techocritic Ellul, Jacques, especially the arguments advanced in his *Propaganda: The Formation of Men's Attitudes* (New York: Vintage/Random House Publishers, 1973); and *The Technological Society* (New York: Alfred A. Knopf Publishers, 1964).

7. Quoted from Sklar, Holly, ed., *Trilateralism: The Trilateral Commission and Elite Planning for World Management* (Boston, MA: South End Press, 1980).

8. *Ibid.*

9. See Kahn, Herman, *World Economic Development* (New York: William Morrow/McQuill Publishers, 1979); and O'Neal, Gerald K., *The High Frontier* (New York: Bantam Books, 1976).

10. Mander is referencing Moravec, Hans, *Mind Children: The Future of Robot and Human Intelligence* (Cambridge, MA: Harvard University Press, 1988), in this passage.

11. On German missile development during World War II, and the absence of British or American counterpart technology, see Young, Richard Anthony, *The Flying Bomb* (London: Ian Allan Publishers, 1978). On Allied use of computers in cryptography, see Kahn, David, *The Codebreakers* (New York: Alfred A. Knopf Publishers, 1967); on their use in nuclear physics, see Hewlett, Richard G., and Oscar E. Anderson, Jr., *The New World, 1939-1946, Vol. I: A History of the United States Atomic Energy Commission* (University Park, PA: Pennsylvania State University Press, 1962).

12. On nuclear testing in the Marshall Islands, see Cockburn, Alex, and James Ridgeway, "An Atoll, A Submarine and the U.S. Economy," in *Beyond Survival: New Directions for the Disarmament Movement*, ed. Michael Albert and David Dellinger (Boston, MA: South End Press, 1983), pp. 155-86. On the development and use of machine guns, see Hobart, F. W. A., *Pictoral History of the Machine Gun* (London: Ian Allan Publisher, 1971); the weapon used at Wounded Knee was a Hotchkiss Gun, a Gatling Gun-like precursor of actual machine guns.

13. It should be noted that Mander follows Cree author George Manual—without attribution—in describing indigenous peoples as "Fourth World nations"; see Manual, George, and Michael Posluns, *The Fourth World: An Indian Reality* (New York: The Free Press, 1974). The nonindustrial reality posed by the term is as contrasted to the industrial-capitalist "First World," industrial-socialist "Second World," and industrializing-nonaligned "Third World" once described by Mao Tse-Tung. Anishinabe activist Winona LaDuke has suggested that the Fourth World should actually be termed the "Host World," insofar as all of the other three are constructed squarely atop it.

14. As will be dealt with more thoroughly later, attribution to native—as opposed to Euroamerican—sources is not Mander's strong suit. Abundant citation with regard to each of these examples may be found in Churchill, Ward, *Struggle for the Land: Indigenous Resistance to Genocide, Ecocide and Expropriation in Contemporary North America* (Monroe, ME: Common Courage Press, 1992); Jaimes, M. Annette, ed., *The State of Native America: Genocide, Colonization and Resistance* (Boston, MA: South End Press, 1992); and Trask, Haunani-Kay, *From a Native Daughter: Colonialism and Sovereignty in Hawai'i* (Monroe, ME: Common Courage Press, 1993).

15. Nietschmann deploys the term in a deceptively-titled essay, "The Third World War," *Cultural Survival Quarterly*, vol. 11, no. 3 (fall 1987).

16. Editors (Mohawk, John), *A Basic Call to Consciousness* (Rooseveltown, NY: Akwesasne Notes, 1978).

17. Berger, Thomas R., *Village Journey: The Report of the Alaska Native Review Commission* (New York: Hill and Wang Publishers, 1985); Burger, Julian, *Report from the Frontier: The State of the World's Indigenous Peoples* (London: Zed Books, 1987).

18. Mander includes Castaneda's *The Teachings of Don Juan: A Yaqui Way of Knowledge* (Los Angeles: University of California Press, 1968) and *A Separate Reality: Further Conversations with Don Juan* (New York: Simon and Schuster, 1971) in his bibliography as "reputable" sources on indigenous thought. For a brief summary of the problems in this regard, see Churchill, Ward, "Carlos Castaneda: The

Greatest Hoax Since Piltdown Man," in *Fantasies of the Master Race: Literature, Cinema and the Colonization of American Indians*, ed. M. Annette Jaimes (Monroe, ME: Common Courage Press, 1991), pp. 43-64.

19. The following are those native-authored sources actually contained in Mander's bibliography. Books and pamphlets: *A Basic Call to Consciousness, op. cit.*; Armstrong, Jeanette, *Slash* (Penticton, B.C.: Theytus Books, 1985) and *The Native Creative Process* (Penticton, B.C.: Theytus Books, 1991); Davidson, Art, and the Association of Village Council Presidents, ed., *Does One Way of Life Have to Die So Another Can Live?* (Bethel, AL: Yupik Nation, 1974); editors, *Denedeh: A Dene Celebration* (Yellowknife, NWT: Dene Nation, 1984); Forbes, Jack D., *Tribes and Masses: Explorations in Red, White and Black* (Davis, CA: D-Q University Press, 1978); Grinde, Donald A., Jr., *The Iroquois and the Founding of the American Nation* (San Francisco, CA: American Indian Historical Society, 1977); Lame Deer, John Fire, and Richard Erdoes, *Lame Deer: Seeker of Visions* (New York: Simon and Schuster Publishers, 1972); Momaday, N. Scott, *A House Made of Dawn* (New York: Harper & Row Publishers, 1985); Ortiz, Roxanne Dunbar, *Roots of Resistance: Land Tenure in New Mexico, 1680-1980* (Los Angeles, CA: UCLA Chicano Studies Research Publications and American Indian Studies Center, 1980); Thorpe, Dagmar, *New Segobia: The Western Shoshone People and Land* (Lee, NV: Western Shoshoni Sacred Lands Association, 1982). Newspaper articles: Horn, Kahn-Tineta, "The Akwesasne War: Why Can't the Mohawks Settle It Themselves?", *Toronto Globe and Mail* (May 3, 1990); Laraque, M. Helene, "Unity Grows After 500 Years," *Native Press* (September 28, 1990) and "Toward the Next 500 Years," *Native Press* (October 12, 1990). Interviews: Grinde, Donald A., Jr. Memoranda and reports: Coulter, Robert T., and Steven Tullburg, *Report to the Kikmongwes* (Washington, D.C.: American Indian Law Resource Center, 1979); Peters, Chris, "Native Thinking and Social Transformation" (Berkeley, CA: Elmwood Institute, January 11, 1991).

20. Jorgenson, Joseph, ed., *American Indians and Energy Development* (Cambridge: Anthropology Resource Center, 1978).

21. The relevance of Deloria's work to Mander's project seems undeniable; see his *God Is Red* (New York: Delta Books, 1973) for a particularly clear example.

22. For further elaboration of this process, see Amin, Samir, *Eurocentrism* (New York: Monthly Review Press, 1989).

23. For details, see Atiya, Aziz S., *Crusade, Commerce and Culture* (New York: John Wiley and Sons, Publishers, 1962).

24. Lyric from "Won't Get Fooled Again," by songwriter/guitarist Peter Townsend, recorded on the album *Who's Next* (Los Angeles: MCA Records, 1971).

25. He just happens, as examples, to overlook any mention whatsoever of such rather conspicuous figures in the contemporary North American struggle for indigenous liberation as Jimmie Durham, Janet McCloud, Russell, Bill, Lorelei and Ted Means, Madonna Thunderhawk, John Trudell, and Phyllis Young.

26. The formal legislative and judicial aspects of the Black Hills Land Claim were initiated in 1921, nearly 25 years before its next closest competitor; see the special issue of *Wicazo Sa Review*, vol. IV, no. 1 (spring 1988) devoted to the topic.

27. This has been very well publicized. During the 1982 Israeli assault upon the city of Beirut, for instance, AIM leader Russell Means was widely quoted as stating

that "the Palestinians of North America offer sanctuary to the American Indians of the Middle East."

28. On these matters, see Matthiessen, Peter, *In the Spirit of Crazy Horse* (New York: Viking Press, 1983).

29. The IITC and its work are covered in Weyler, Rex, *Blood of the Land: The U.S. Government and Corporate War Against the American Indian Movement* (New York: Everest House Publishers, 1982).

30. On WARN, see Jaimes, M. Annette, and Theresa Halsey, "American Indian Women: At the Center of Indigenous Resistance in North America," in *The State of Native America, op. cit.*, pp. 311-44.

31. Means, Russell, "Fighting Words on the Future of Mother Earth," *Mother Jones* (January 1981); included under the title, "The Same Old Song," in *Marxism and Native Americans*, ed. Ward Churchill (Boston, MA: South End Press, 1983), pp. 19-34.

32. For instance, Trudell, John, *Living in Reality* (Minneapolis, MN: Society of People Struggling to be Free, 1982); Trudell's several recordings—*Tribal Voice (1982), JT/JED (1985), Heart Jump Bouquet (1986), But This Isn't El Salvador (1987),* and *AKA: Graffiti Man (1988, 1992)*—have also been mainstay indigenous articulations of the very themes Mander pursues.

33. See International Organization for the Elimination of All Forms of Racial Discrimination, *Zionism and Racism: Proceedings of an International Symposium* (New York: North American Publishers, 1979).

34. See Horsman, Reginald, *Racism and Manifest Destiny: The Origins of Racial Anglo-Saxonism* (Cambridge, MA: Harvard University Press, 1981).

35. This is covered very well in Chomsky, Noam, *The Fateful Triangle: Israel, Palestine and the United States* (Boston, MA: South End Press, 1983). Also see Said, Edward W., *The Question of Palestine* (New York: Vintage Books, [second edition] 1992).

36. See Robinson, Maxime, *Israel: A Colonial-Settler State* (New York: Monad Press, 1973). Another good reading in this regard is Zurayk, Elia T., *The Palestinians in Israel: A Study in Internal Colonialism* (London: Routledge and Kegan Paul Publishers, 1979).

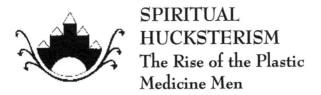

SPIRITUAL HUCKSTERISM
The Rise of the Plastic Medicine Men

Yes, I know of Sun Bear. He's a plastic medicine man.

—Matthew King, Oglala Lakota Elder, 1985

The past 20 years have seen the birth of a new growth industry in the United States. Known as "American Indian Spiritualism," this profitable enterprise apparently began with a number of literary hoaxes undertaken by non-Indians such as Carlos Castaneda, Jay Marks (a.k.a.: "Jamake Highwater," author of *The Primal Mind*, etc.), Ruth Beebe Hill (of *Hanta Yo* notoriety), and Lynn Andrews (*Medicine Woman, Jaguar Woman, Chrystal Woman, Spirit Woman*, etc.). A few Indians such as Alonzo Blacksmith (a.k.a.: "Chunksa Yuha," the "Indian authenticator" of *Hanta Yo*), "Chief Red Fox" (*Memoirs of Chief Red Fox*), and Hyemeyohsts Storm (*Seven Arrows*, etc.) also cashed in, writing bad distortions and outright lies about indigenous spirituality for consumption in the mass market.The authors grew rich peddling their trash, while real Indians starved to death, out of the sight and mind of America.

This situation has been long and bitterly attacked by legitimate Indian scholars, from Vine Deloria, Jr., to Bea Medicine, and by activists such as American Indian Movement (AIM) leader Russell Means, Survival of American Indians, Inc. (SAIL) director Hank Adams, and the late Gerald Wilkenson, head of the National Indian Youth Council (NIYC). Nonetheless, the list of phony books claiming alternately to "debunk" or to "expose the innermost meanings of" Indian spirituality continues to grow, as publishers recognize a sure-fire moneymaker when they see one. Most lately, ostensibly scholarly publishers like the University of Chicago Press have joined the parade, generating travesties such as University of Colorado Professor Sam Gill's *Mother Earth: An American Story*.

The insistence of mainstream America upon buying such non-sense has led Deloria to conclude that, "White people in this country are so alienated from their own lives and so hungry for some sort of real life that they'll grasp at any straw to save themselves. But high tech society has given them a taste for the 'quick fix.' They want their spirituality pre-packaged in such a way as to provide *instant* insight, the more sensational and preposterous the better. They'll pay big bucks to anybody dishonest enough to offer them spiritual salvation after reading the right book or sitting still for the right 15 minute session. And, of course, this opens them up to every kind of mercenary hustler imaginable. It's all very pathetic, really."

Oren Lyons, a traditional chief of the Onondaga Nation, concedes Deloria's point, but says the problem goes much deeper. "Non-Indians have become so used to all this hype on the part of imposters and liars that when a real Indian spiritual leader tries to offer them useful advice, he [or she] is rejected. He [or she] isn't 'Indian' enough for all these non-Indian experts on Indian religion. Now, this is not only degrading to Indian people; it's downright delusional behavior on the part of the instant experts who think they've got all the answers before they even hear the questions."

"The bottom line here," says Lyons, "is that we have more need for intercultural respect today than at any time in human history. And nothing blocks respect and communication faster and more effectively than delusions by one party about another. We've got real problems today, tremendous problems, problems which threaten the survival of the planet. Indians and non-Indians *must* confront these problems together, and this means we *must* have honest dialogue, but this dialogue is impossible so long as non-Indians remain deluded about things as basic as Indian spirituality."

Things would be bad enough if American Indian realities were being distorted only through books and movies. But, since 1970, there has also been a rapid increase in the number of individuals purporting to sell "Indian wisdom" in a more practical way. Following the example of people such as the "Yogi Ramacharaka" and "Maharaji Ji," who have built lucrative careers marketing bastardizations of East Asian mysticism, these new entrepreneurs have begun cleaning up on selling "Native American Ceremonies" for a fee.

As Janet McCloud, a longtime fishing rights activist and elder of the Nisqually Nation, puts it, "First they came to take our land and water, then our fish and game. Then they wanted our mineral resources and, to get them, they tried to take our governments. Now they want our religions as well. All of a sudden, we have a lot of unscrupulous idiots running around saying they're medicine people. And they'll sell you a sweat lodge ceremony for fifty bucks. It's not only wrong, it's obscene. Indians don't sell their spirituality to anybody, for any price. This is just another in a very long series of thefts from Indian people and, in some ways, this is the worst one yet."

McCloud is scornful of the many non-Indian individuals who have taken up such practices professionally. "These people run off to reservations acting all lost and hopeless, really pathetic. So, some elder is nice enough, considerate enough to be kind to them, and how do they repay this generosity? After fifteen minutes with a spiritual leader, they consider themselves 'certified' medicine people, and then run amok, 'spreading the word'—for a fee. Some of them even proclaim themselves to be 'official spiritual representatives' of various Indian peoples. I'm talking about people like Dyhani Ywahoo and Lynn Andrews. It's absolutely disgusting."

But her real disdain is for those Indians who have taken up the practice of marketing their heritage to the highest bidder. "We've also got Indians who are doing these things," McCloud continues. "We've got our Sun Bears and our Wallace Black Elks and others who'd sell their own mother if they thought it would turn a quick buck. What they're selling isn't theirs to sell, and they know it. They're thieves and sellouts, and they know that too. That's why you never see them around Indian people anymore. When we have our traditional meetings and gatherings, you never see the Sun Bears and those sorts showing up."

As Thomas Banyacya, a spiritual elder of the Hopi, explains, "these people have nothing to say on the matters they claim to be so expert about. To whites, they claim they're 'messengers,' but from whom? They are not the messengers of Indian people. I am a messenger, and I do not charge for my ceremonies."

Some of the more sophisticated marketeers, such as Sun Bear, have argued that the criticisms of McCloud and Banyacya are misguided. Sun Bear has claimed that the ceremonies and "wisdom" he peddles are not truly Indian, although they are still "based on" Indian traditions. Yet his promotional literature refers to "Native American Spiritual Wisdom," and offers ceremonies such as the sweat lodge for $50 per session, and "vision quests" at $150.

"Since when is the sweat not an Indian ceremony?" demands Russell Means, an outspoken critic of Sun Bear and his colleagues. "It's not 'based on' an Indian ceremony, it *is* an Indian ceremony. So is his so-called 'vision quest,' the pipe, his use of the pipe, sage, and all the rest of it. Sun Bear is a liar, and so are all the rest of them who are doing what he's doing. All of them know good and well that the only reason anybody is buying their product is because of this image of 'Indian-ness' they project. The most non-Indian thing about Sun Bear's ceremonies is that he's personally prostituted the whole thing by turning it into a money-making venture."

Sun Bear has also contended that criticism of his activities is ill-founded because he has arrived at a spiritual stew of several traditions—his medicine wheel is Shoshone, and his herbal and other healing remedies accrue from numerous peoples, while many of his other ceremonies are Lakota in origin—and because he's started his own "tribe," of which he's pronounced himself "medicine chief." Of course, membership in this odd new entity, composed almost exclusively of Euroamericans, comes with a hefty price tag attached. The idea has caught on among spiritual hucksters, as is witnessed by the formation of a similar fees-paid group in Florida, headed by a non-Indian calling himself "Chief Piercing Eyes."

"This is exactly the problem," says Nilak Butler, an Inuit activist working in San Francisco. "Sun Bear says he's not revealing some sort of secret Indian ways whenever there are Indians around to hear him. The rest of the time, he's the most 'Indian' guy around, to hear him tell it. Whenever he's doing his spiel, anyway. But, you see, if there were any truth to his rap, he wouldn't have to be running around starting 'new tribes' and naming himself head honcho and dues collector. He'd be a leader among his own people."

"The thing is," says Rick Williams, a Cheyenne/Lakota working at the University of Colorado, "Sun Bear isn't recognized as any sort of leader, spiritual or otherwise, among his own Chippewa people. He's not qualified. It takes a lifetime of apprenticeship to become the sort of spiritual leader Sun Bear claims to be, and he never went through any of that. He's just a guy who hasn't been home to the White Earth Reservation in 25 years, pretending to be something he's not, feeding his own ego and making his living misleading a lot of sincere, but very silly people. In a lot of ways he reminds you of a low-grade Jimmy Swaggart or Pat Robertson type of individual."

"And another thing," Williams continues, "Sun Bear hasn't started a new tribe. *Nobody* can just up and start a new tribe. What he's done is start a cult. And this cult he's started is playing with some very powerful things, like the pipe. That's not only stupid and malicious; it's *dangerous*."

The danger Williams refers to has to do with the very power which makes American Indian spirituality so appealing to non-Indians in the first place. According to the late Matthew King, an elder spiritual leader among the Oglala Lakota, "Each part of our religion has its power and its purpose. Each people has their own ways. You cannot mix these ways together, because each people's ways are balanced. Destroying balance is a disrespect and very dangerous. This is why it's forbidden.

"Many things are forbidden in our religion," King continued. "The forbidden things are acts of disrespect, things which unbalance power. These things must be learned, and the learning is very difficult. This is why there are very few real 'medicine men [or medicine women]' among us; only a few are chosen. For someone who has not learned how our balance is maintained to pretend to be a medicine man is very, very dangerous. It is a big disrespect to the powers and can cause great harm to whoever is doing it, to those he claims to be teaching, to nature, to everything. It is very bad."

For all the above reasons, the Circle of Elders of the Indigenous Nations of North America, the representative body of traditional indigenous leadership on this continent, requested that the American Indian Movement undertake to end the activities of those described as "plastic medicine men." The possibly sexist descriptor refers to individuals of both genders trading in the commercialization of indigenous spirituality. At its National Leadership Conference in 1984, AIM passed a resolution indicating that the will of the elders would be implemented. Specifically mentioned in the AIM resolution were "Sun Bear and the so-called Bear Tribe Medicine Society" and "Wallace Black Elk and [the late] Grace Spotted Eagle of Denver, Colorado," as well as others like Cyfus McDonald, Brooke Medicine Eagle (spelled "Ego" in the resolution), Osheana Fast Wolf, and a corporation dubbed "Vision Quest." Others, such as Dyhani Ywahoo, Rolling Thunder, and "Beautiful Painted Arrow" have been subsequently added to the list.

As Russell Means put it at the time, "These people have insisted upon making themselves pariahs within their own communities, and they will have to bear the consequences of that. As to white people who think it's cute, or neat or groovy or keen to hook up with plastic medicine men, to subsidize and promote them, and claim you and they have some fundamental 'right' to desecrate our spiritual traditions, I've got a piece of news for you. You have *no* such right. Our religions are *ours*. Period. We have very strong reasons for keeping certain things private, whether you understand them or not. And we have every human right to deny them to you, whether you like it or not.

"You can either respect our basic rights or not respect them," Means went on. "If you do, you're an ally and we're ready and willing to join hands with you on other issues. If you do not, you are at best a thief. More importantly, you are a thief of the sort who is willing to risk undermining our sense of the integrity of our cultures for your own perceived self-interest. That means you are complicit in a process of cultural genocide, or at least attempted cultural genocide, aimed at American Indian people. That makes you an enemy, to say the least. And believe me when I say we're prepared to deal with you as such."

Almost immediately, the Colorado AIM chapter undertook a confrontation with Sun Bear in the midst of a $500-per-head, weekend-long "spiritual retreat" being conducted near the mountain town of Granby. The action provoked the following endorsement from the normally more staid NIYC:

> The National Indian Youth Council fully supports your efforts to denounce, embarrass, disrupt, or otherwise run out of Colorado, the Medicine Wheel Gathering… For too long the Bear Tribe Medicine Society has been considered repugnant but harmless to Indian people. We believe they not only line their pockets but do great damage to all of us. Anything you can do to them will not be enough.

The Colorado AIM action, and the strength of indigenous support it received, resulted in a marked diminishment of Sun Bear's reliance upon the state as a source of revenue.

Since then, AIM has aligned itself solidly and consistently with indigenous traditionalism, criticizing Sun Bear and others of his ilk in public fashion, and occasionally physically disrupting their activities in locations as diverse as Denver and Atlanta. Those who wish to assist in this endeavor should do so by denouncing plastic medicine folk wherever they appear, organizing pro-active boycotts of their events, and demanding that local bookstores stop carrying titles, not only by Sun Bear and his non-Indian sidekick "Wabun," but by charlatans like Castaneda, Jamake Highwater, Lynn Andrews, and Hyemeyohsts Storm as well. Use your imagination as to how to get the job done in your area, but make it stick. You should also be aware that Sun Bear and others have increasingly aligned themselves with such non-Indian support groups as local police departments, calling upon them to protect him from "Indian interference" with his unauthorized sale of Indian spirituality.

Resolution of the 5th Annual Meeting of the Traditional Elders Circle
Northern Cheyenne Nation, Two Moons' Camp, Rosebud Creek, Montana Center, October 5, 1980

It has been brought to the attention of the Elders and their representatives in Council that various individuals are moving about this Great Turtle Island and across the great waters to foreign soil, purporting to be spiritual leaders. They carry pipes and other objects sacred to the Red Nations, the indigenous people of the western hemisphere.

These individuals are gathering non-Indian people as followers who believe they are receiving instructions of the original people. We the Elders and our representatives sitting in Council give warning to these non-Indian followers that it is our understanding this is not a proper process and the authority to carry these sacred objects is given by the people and the purpose and procedure are specific to the time and the needs of the people.

The medicine people are chosen by the medicine and long instruction and discipline are necessary before ceremonies and healing can be done. These procedures are always in the Native tongue; there are no exceptions and profit is not the motivation.

There are many Nations with many and varied procedures specifically for the welfare of their people. These processes and ceremonies are of the most Sacred Nature. The Council finds the open display of these ceremonies contrary to these Sacred instructions.

Therefore, be warned that these individuals are moving about playing upon the spiritual needs and ignorance of our non-Indian brothers and sisters. The value of these instructions and ceremonies is questionable, maybe meaningless, and hurtful to the individual carrying false messages. There are questions that should be asked of these individuals:

1) What Nation does the person represent?
2) What is their Clan and Society?
3) Who instructed them and where did they learn?
4) What is their home address?

If no information is forthcoming, you may inquire at the addresses listed below, and we will try to find out about them for you.

We concern ourselves only with those people who use spiritual ceremonies with non-Indian people for profit. There are many things to be shared with the Four Colors of humanity in our common destiny as one with our Mother the Earth. It is this sharing that must be considered with great care by the Elders and the medicine people who carry the Sacred Trusts, so that no harm may come to people through ignorance and misuse of these powerful forces.

Signed,

Tom Yellowtail
Wyola, MT

Larry Anderson
Navajo Nation
P.O. Box 342
Fort Defiance, AZ

Izadore Thom
Beech Star Route
Bellingham, WA

Thomas Banyacya
Hopi Independent Nation
Shungopavy Pueblo
Second Mesa via AZ

Phillip Deer (deceased)
Muskogee (Creek) Nation

Walter Denny
Chippewa-Cree Nation
Rocky Boy Route
Box Elder, MT

Austin Two Moons
Northern Cheyenne Nation
Rosebud Creek, MT

Tadadaho
Haudenosaunee
Onondaga Nation via
Nedrow, NY

Chief Fools Crow (deceased)
Lakota Nation (in tribute)

Frank Cardinal, Sr.
Chateh, P.O. Box 120
Assumption, Alberta
Canada

Peter O'Chiese
Entrance Terry Ranch
Entrance, Alberta
Canada

AIM Resolution
Sovereign Diné Nation,
Window Rock, AZ
May 11, 1984

Whereas the Spiritual wisdom which is shared by the Elders with the people has been passed to us through the Creation from time immemorial; and

Whereas the Spirituality of Indian Nations is inseparable from the people themselves; and

Whereas the attempted theft of Indian ceremonies is a direct attack on and theft from Indian people themselves; and

Whereas there has been a dramatic increase in the incidence of selling of Sacred ceremonies, such as the sweat lodge and the vision quest, and of Sacred articles, such as religious pipes, feathers, and stones; and

Whereas these practices have been and continue to be conducted by Indians and non-Indians alike, constituting not only insult and disrespect for the wisdom of the ancients, but also exposing ignorant non-Indians to potential harm and even death through the misuse of these ceremonies; and

Whereas the traditional Elders and Spiritual leaders have repeatedly warned against and condemned the commercialization of our ceremonies; and

Whereas such commercialization has increased dramatically in recent years, to wit:

- The representations of Cyfus McDonald, Osheana Fast Wolf, and Brooke Medicine Ego, all non-Indian women representing themselves as "Sacred Women," and who, in the case of Cyfus McDonald, have defrauded Indian people of Sacred articles;

- A non-Indian woman going by the name of "Quanda" representing herself as a "Healing Woman" and charging $20 for sweat lodges;

- Sun Bear and the so-called "Bear Tribe Medicine Society," who engage in the sale of Indian ceremonies and Sacred objects, operating out of the state of Washington, but traveling and speaking throughout the United States;

- Wallace Black Elk and Grace Spotted Eagle, Indian people operating in Denver, Colorado, charging up to $50 for so-called "Sweat Lodge Workshops";

- A group of non-Indians operating out of Boulder, Colorado, and throughout the Southwest, and audaciously calling itself "Vision Quest, Inc.," thereby stealing the name and attempting to steal the concept of one of our most Spiritual ceremonies;

Therefore, be it resolved that the Southwest AIM Leadership Conference reiterates the position articulated by our Elders at the First American Indian Tribunal held at D-Q University, September 1982, as follows:

Now, to those who are doing these things, we send our third warning. Our Elders ask, "Are you prepared to take the consequences of your actions? You will be outcasts from your people if you continue these practices"…Now, this is another one, our young people are getting restless. They are the ones who sought their Elders in the first place to teach them the Sacred ways. They have said they will take care of those who are abusing our Sacred ceremonies and Sacred objects in their own way. In this way they will take care of their Elders.

We Resolve to protect our Elders and our traditions, and we condemn those who seek to profit from Indian Spirituality. We put them on notice that our patience grows thin with them and they continue their disrespect at their own risk.

INDIANS "R" US?
Reflections on the "Men's Movement"

We are living at an important and fruitful moment, now, for it is clear to men that the images of adult manhood given by the popular culture are worn out; a man can no longer depend on them. By the time a man is thirty-five he knows that the images of the right man, the tough man, the true man he received in high school do not work in life. Such a man is open to new visions of what a man is supposed to be.

—Robert Bly, 1990

There are few things in this world I can conceive as being more instantly ludicrous than a prosperously middle-aged lump of pudgy Euroamerican verse-monger, an apparition looking uncannily like some weird cross between the Mall-O-Milk Marshmallow Man and Pillsbury's Doughboy, suited up in a grotesque mismatch combining pleated Scottish tweeds with a striped Brookes Brothers shirt and Southwest Indian print vest, peering myopically along his nose through coke-bottle steelrim specs while holding forth in stilted and somewhat nasal tonalities on the essential virtues of virility, of masculinity, of being or becoming a "warrior." The intrinsic absurdity of such a scene is, moreover, compounded by a factor of five when it is witnessed by an audience—all male, virtually all white, and on the whole obviously well-accustomed to enjoying a certain pleasant standard of material comfort—which sits as if spellbound, rapt in its attention to every nuance of the speaker, altogether fawning in its collective nods and murmurs of devout agreement with each detail of his discourse.

At first glance, the image might seem to be the most vicious sort of parody, a satire offered in the worst of taste, perhaps a hallucinatory fragment of a cartoon or skit offered by the likes of *National Lampoon* or *Saturday Night Live*. Certainly, in a reasonable universe we would be entitled (perhaps required) to assume that no group of allegedly functional adults would take such a farce seriously, never mind line up to pay money for the privilege of participating in it. Yet, as we know, or should by now, the universe we are forced to inhabit has been transformed long since—notably by the very group so prominent in its representation among those constituting our warrior/mystic/wordsmith's assemblage—into something in which reasonable behavior and comportment play only the smallest of parts. And so the whole travesty is advanced with the utmost seriousness, at least by its proponents and a growing body of adherents who subsidize and otherwise support them.

The founder and reigning Grand Pooh-Bah of that variant of the "New Age" usually referred to as the "Men's Movement" is Robert Bly, a rather owlish butterball of a minor poet who seems to have set out at fifty-something to finally garner unto himself some smidgen of the macho self-esteem his physique and life-of-letters had conspired to deny him up to that point.[1] Writerly even in this pursuit, however, Bly has contented himself mainly with devising a vague theory of "masculinism" designed or at least intended to counter prevailing feminist dogma concerning "The Patriarchy," rising interest in "multicultural" interpretations of how things work, and an accompanying sense among middle-to-upper-middle-class males that they are "loosing influence" in contemporary society.[2]

A strange brew consisting of roughly equal parts Arthurian, Norse, and Celtic legend, occasional adaptations of fairy tales by the brothers Grimm, a scattering of his own and assorted dead white males' verse and prose, a dash of environmentalism, and, for spice, bits and pieces of Judaic, Islamic, East Asian, and American Indian spiritualism, Bly's message of "male liberation" has been delivered via an unending series of increasingly well-paid podium performances beginning in the mid-'80s. Presented in a manner falling somewhere between mystic parable and pop psychology, Bly's lectures are frequently tedious, often pedantic, pathetically pretentious in both content and elocution. Still, they find a powerful emotional resonance among those attracted to the central themes announced in his interviews and advertising circulars, especially when his verbiage focuses upon the ideas of "reclaiming the primitive within us...attaining freedom through use of appropriate ritual...[and] the rights of all men to transcend cultural boundaries in redeeming their warrior souls."[3]

By 1990, the master had perfected his pitch to the point of committing it to print in a turgid but rapidly selling tome entitled *Iron John*.[4] He had also established something like a franchise system, training cadres in various localities to provide "male empowerment rituals" for a fee (a "Wild Man Weekend" goes for $250 a pop; individual ceremonies are usually pro-rated). Meanwhile, the rising popularity and consequent profit potential of Bly's endeavor had spawned a number of imitators—Patrick M. Arnold, Asa Baber, Tom Daly, Robert Moore, Douglas Gillette, R.J. Stewart, Kenneth Wetcher, Art Barker, F.W. McCaughtry, John Matthews, and Christopher Harding among them—literary and otherwise.[5] Three years later, the "Men's Movement" has become pervasive enough to be viewed as a tangible and growing social force rather than merely as a peculiar fringe group; active chapters are listed in 43 of the 50 major U.S. cities (plus four in Canada) in the movement's "selected" address list; 25 periodicals are listed in the same directory.[6]

An Interlude with Columbus in Colorado

The ability of a male to shout and be fierce does not imply domination, treating people as if they were objects, demanding land or empire, holding on to the Cold War—the whole model of machismo...The Wild Man here amounts to an invisible presence, the companionship of the ancestors and the great artists among the dead...The native Americans believe in that healthful male power.

—Robert Bly, 1990

At first glance, none of this may seem particularly threatening. Indeed, the sheer silliness inherent to Bly's routine at many levels is painfully obvious, a matter driven home to me one morning last spring when, out looking for some early sage, I came upon a group of young Euroamerican males cavorting about stark naked in a meadow near Lyons, Colorado. Several had wildflowers braided into their hair. Some were attempting a chant I failed to recognize. I noticed an early growth of poison oak near where I was standing, but determined it was probably best not to disrupt whatever rite was being conducted

with anything so mundane as a warning about the presence of dis-
comforting types of plant life. As discreetly as possible, I turned
around and headed the other way, both puzzled and somewhat
amused by what I'd witnessed.

A few days later, I encountered one of the participants, whom I
knew slightly, and who kept scratching at his left thigh. Seizing the
opportunity, I inquired as to what it was they'd been doing. He
responded that since he and the others had attended a workshop
conducted by Robert Bly earlier in the year, they'd become active in
the Men's Movement and "made a commitment to recover the Druidic
rituals which are part of our heritage" (the man, who is an anthropology student at the University of Colorado, is of Slavic descent, making
Druidism about as distant from his own cultural tradition as Sufism
or Zen Buddhism). Interest piqued, I asked where they'd learned the
ritual form involved and its meaning. He replied that, while they'd
attempted to research the matter, "it turns out there's not really a lot
known about exactly how the Druids conducted their rituals."

"It's mostly guesswork," he went on. "We're just kind of making
it up as we go along." When I asked why, if that were the case, they
described their ritual as being Druidic, he shrugged. "It just sort of
feels good, I guess," he said. "We're trying to get in touch with
something primal in ourselves."

Harmless? Maybe. But then again, maybe not. The Druids, after
all, have reputedly been dead and gone for millennia. They are thus
immune to whatever culturally destructive effects might attend such
blatant appropriation, trivialization, and deformation of their sacred
rites by non-Druidic feel-gooders. Before departing from the meadow,
however, I had noticed that a couple of the men gamboling about in
the grass were adorned with facepaint and feathers. So I queried my
respondent as to whether in the view of his group such things comprised a part of Druid ritual life.

"Well, no," he confessed. "A couple of the guys are really into
American Indian stuff. Actually, we all are. Wallace Black Elk is our
teacher.[7] We run sweats on the weekends, and most of us have been
on the hill [insider slang for the undertaking of a Vision Quest]. I
myself carry a Sacred Pipe and am studying herbal healing, Lakota

Way. Three of us went to the Sun Dance at Crow Dog's place last summer. We've made vows, and are planning to dance when we're ready."[8] Intermingled with these remarks, he extended glowing bits of commentary on his and the others' abiding interest in a diversity of cultural/spiritual elements ranging from Balinese mask-making to Andean flute music, from Japanese scent/time orientation to the deities of the Assyrians, Polynesian water gods, and the clitoral circumcision of Somali women.

I thought about protesting that spiritual traditions cannot be used as some sort of Whitman's Sampler of ceremonial form, mixed and matched—here a little Druid, there a touch of Nordic mythology followed by a regimen of Hindu vegetarianism, a mishmash of American Indian rituals somewhere else—at the whim of people who are part of none of them. I knew I should say that to play at ritual potluck is to debase all spiritual traditions, voiding their internal coherence and leaving nothing usably sacrosanct as a cultural anchor for the peoples who conceived and developed them, and who have consequently organized their societies around them. But, then, in consideration of who it was I was talking to, I abruptly ended the conversation instead. I doubted he would have understood what I was trying to explain to him. More importantly, I had the distinct impression he wouldn't have cared, even if he had. Such observations on my part would most likely have only set loose "the warrior in him," a flow of verbal diarrhea in which he asserted his and his peers' "inalienable right" to take anything they found of value in the intellectual property of others, converting it to whatever use suited their purposes at the moment. I was a bit tired, having just come from a meeting with a white environmental group where I'd attempted unsuccessfully to explain how their support of native land rights might bear some positive relationship to their announced ecological concerns, and felt it just wasn't my night to deal with the ghost of Christopher Columbus for a second time, head on.

That's an excuse, to be sure. Probably, I failed in my duty. Perhaps, regardless of the odds against success, I should have tried reasoning with him. More likely, I should've done what my ancestors should have done to Columbus himself when the "Great Discoverer" first brought his embryo of the Men's Movement to this hemisphere. But the amount of prison time assigned these days to that sort of appropriate response to aggression is daunting, to say the least. And I really do lack the wall space to properly display his tanned hide after skinning him alive. So I did nothing more than walk out of the coffee shop in which we'd been seated, leaving him to wonder what it was that had made me upset. Not that he's likely to have gotten the message. The result of my inaction is that, so far as I know, the man is still out there cruising the cerebral seas in search of "spiritual landscapes" to explore and pillage. Worse, he's still sending his booty back to his buddies in hopes of their casting some "new synthesis of paganism"—read, "advancement of civilization as we know it"— in which they will be able to continue their occupancy of a presumed position at the center of the universe.

Indians "R" Us

We must get out of ourselves, or, more accurately, the selves we have been conned into believing are "us." We must break out of the cage of artificial "self" in which we have been entrapped as "men" by today's society. We must get in touch with our true selves, recapturing the Wild Man, the animal, the primitive warrior being which exists in the core of every man. We must rediscover the meaning of maleness, the art of being male, the way of the warrior priest. In doing so, we free ourselves from the alienating tyranny of being what it is we're told we are, or what it is we should be. We free ourselves to redefine the meaning of "man," to be who and what we can be, and what it is we ultimately must be. I speak here, of course, of genuine liberation from society's false expectations and thus from the false selves these expectations have instilled in each and every one of us here in this room. Let the Wild Man loose, I say! Free our warrior spirit!

—Robert Bly, 1991

In retrospect, it seems entirely predictable that, amidst Robert Bly's welter of babble concerning the value of assorted strains of imagined primitivism and warrior spirit, a substantial segment of his following—and he himself in the workshops he offers on "practical ritual"—would end up gravitating most heavily toward things Indian. After all, Native Americans and our ceremonial life constitute living, ongoing entities. We are therefore far more accessible in terms of both time and space than the Druids or the old Norse Odinists. Further, our traditions offer the distinct advantage of seeming satisfyingly exotic to the average Euroamerican yuppie male, even while not forcing them to clank about in the suits of chain mail and heavy steel armor which would be required if they were to opt to act out their leader's hyperliterate Arthurian fantasies. I mean, really...Jousting, anyone? A warrior-type fella could get seriously hurt that way.[9]

A main sticking point, of course, rests precisely in the fact that the cultures indigenous to America *are* living, ongoing entities. Unlike the Druids or the ancient Greek man-cults who thronged around Hector and Achilles, Native American societies *can* and *do* suffer the socioculturally debilitating effects of spiritual trivialization and appropriation at the hands of the massively larger Euro-immigrant population which has come to dominate literally every other aspect of our existence. As Margo Thunderbird, an activist of the Shinnecock Nation, has put it: "They came for our land, for what grew or could be grown on it, for the resources in it, and for our clean air and pure water. They stole these things from us, and in the taking they also stole our free ways and the best of our leaders, killed in battle or assassinated. And now, after all that, they've come for the very last of our possessions; now they want our pride, our history, our spiritual traditions. They want to rewrite and remake these things, to claim them for themselves. The lies and thefts just never end."[10] Or, as the Oneida scholar Pam Colorado frames the matter:

> The process is ultimately intended to supplant Indians, even in areas of their own culture and spirituality. In the end, non-Indians will have complete power to define what is and what is not Indian, even for Indians. We are talking here about a complete ideological/conceptual subordination of Indian people in addition to the total physical subordination they already experience. When this happens, the last vestiges of real Indian society and Indian rights will disappear. Non-Indians will then claim to "own" our heritage and ideas as thoroughly as they now claim to own our land and resources.[11]

From this perspective, the American Indian Movement passed a resolution at its 1984 Southwest Leadership Conference condemning the *laissez-faire* use of native ceremonies and/or ceremonial objects by anyone not sanctioned by traditional indigenous spiritual leaders.[12]

The AIM position also echoed an earlier resolution taken by the Traditional Elders Circle in 1980, condemning even Indians who engage in "use of [our] spiritual ceremonies with non-Indian people for profit."[13] Another such condemnation had been issued during the First American Indian Tribunal at D-Q University in 1982.[14] As of this writing—June 1993—the Lakota Nation as a whole is preparing to enact a similar resolution denouncing non-Lakotas who presume to "adopt" their rituals, and censoring those Lakotas who have chosen to facilitate such cultural appropriation. Several other indigenous nations and national organizations have already taken comparable positions, or are preparing to (see "Alert Concerning the Abuse and Exploitation of American Indian Sacred Traditions").

This may seem an exaggerated and overly harsh response to what the Spokane/Coeur d'Alene writer Sherman Alexie has laughingly dismissed as being little more than a "Society for Confused White Men."[15] But the hard edges of Euroamerican hubris and assertion of proprietary interest in native assets which have always marked Indian/white relations are abundantly manifested in the organizational literature of the Men's Movement itself. Of even greater concern is the fact that the sort of appropriation evidenced in these periodicals is no longer restricted simply to claiming "ownership" of Indian ceremonies and spiritual objects, as in a passage in a recent issue of the *Men's Council Journal* explaining that "sweats, drumming, dancing, [and] four direction-calling [are] once-indigenous, now-ours rituals."[16] Rather, participants have increasingly assumed a stance of expropriating native identity altogether, as when, in the same journal, it is repeatedly asserted that "we...are all Lakota" and that members of the Men's Movement are now displacing actual Lakotas from their "previous" role as "warrior protectors" (of what is left unclear).[17]

The indigenous response to such presumption was perhaps best expressed by AIM leader Russell Means, himself an Oglala Lakota, when he recently stated that, "This is the ultimate degradation of our people, even worse than what's been done to us by Hollywood and the publishing industry, or the sports teams who portray us as mascots and pets. What these people are doing is like Adolf Eichmann claiming during his trial that, at heart, he was really a zionist, or members of the Aryan Nation in Idaho claiming to be 'True Jews.'"[18] Elsewhere, Means has observed that:

> What's at issue here is the same old question that Europeans have always posed with regard to American Indians, whether what's ours isn't somehow theirs. And, of course, they've always answered the question in the affirmative...We are resisting this because spirituality is the basis of our culture. If our culture is dissolved [via the expedients of spiritual appropriation/expropriation], Indian people as such will cease to exist. By definition, the causing of any culture to cease to exist is an act of genocide.[19]

Noted Hunkpapa Lakota author Vine Deloria, Jr., agrees in principle, finding that, as a result of the presumption of groups like the Men's Movement, as well as academic anthropology, "the realities of Indian belief and existence have become so misunderstood and distorted at this point that when a real Indian stands up and speaks the truth at any given moment, he or she is not only unlikely to be believed, but will probably be publicly contradicted and 'corrected' by the citation of some non-Indian and totally inaccurate 'expert.'"[20]

> Moreover, young Indians in [cities and] universities are now being trained to view themselves and their cultures in the terms prescribed by such experts *rather than* in the traditional terms of the tribal elders. The process automatically sets the members of Indian communities at odds with one another, while outsiders run around picking up the pieces for themselves. In this way [groups like the Men's Movement] are perfecting a system of self-validation in which all semblance of honesty and accuracy are lost. This is...absolutely devastating to Indian societies.[21]

Even Sherman Alexie, while choosing to treat the Men's Movement phenomenon with scorn and ridicule rather than open hostility, is compelled to acknowledge that there is a serious problem with the direction taken by Bly's disciples. "Peyote is not just an excuse to get high," Alexie points out. "A Vision Quest cannot be completed in a convention room rented for that purpose...[T]he sweat lodge is a church, not a free clinic or something...A warrior does not have to scream to release the animal that is supposed to reside inside every man. A warrior does not necessarily have an animal inside him at all. If there happens to be an animal, it can be a parakeet or a mouse just as easily as it can be a bear or a wolf. When a white man adopts an animal, he [seems inevitably to choose] the largest animal possible. Whether this is because of possible phallic connotations or a kind of spiritual steroid abuse is debatable, [but] I can imagine a friend of mine, John, who is white, telling me that his spirit animal is the Tyrannosaurus Rex."[22]

The men's movement seems designed to appropriate and mutate so many aspects of native traditions. I worry about the possibilities: men's movement chain stores specializing in portable sweat lodges; the "Indians 'R' Us" commodification of ritual and artifact; white men who continue to show up at powwows in full regalia and to dance.[23]

Plainly, despite sharp differences in their respective temperaments and resultant stylistic approaches to dealing with problems, Alexie and many other Indians share Russell Means' overall conclusion that the "culture vultures" of the Men's Movement are "not innocent or innocuous...cute, groovy, hip, enlightened or any of the rest of the things they want to project themselves as being. No, what they're about is cultural genocide. And genocide is genocide, no matter how you want to 'qualify' it. So some of us are starting to react to these folks accordingly."[24]

View from a Foreign Shore

Western man's connection to the Wild Man has been disturbed for centuries now, and a lot of fear has been built up [but] Wild Man is part of a company or a community in a man's psyche. The Wild Man lives in complicated interchanges with other interior beings. A whole community of beings is what is called a grown man...Moreover, when we develop the inner Wild Man, he keeps track of the wild animals inside us, and warns when they are liable to become extinct. The Wild One in you is the one which is willing to leave the busy life, and able to be called away.

—Robert Bly, 1990

In many ways, the salient questions which present themselves with regard to the Men's Movement center on motivation. Why, in this day and age, would any group of well-educated and self-proclaimedly sensitive men, the vast majority of whom may be expected to exhibit genuine outrage at my earlier comparison of them to Columbus, elect to engage in activities which can be plausibly categorized as culturally genocidal? Assuming initial ignorance in this regard, why do they choose to persist in these activities, often escalating their behavior after its implications have been explained by its victims repeatedly and in no uncertain terms? And, perhaps most of all, why would such extraordinarily privileged individuals as those who've flocked to Robert Bly—a group marked by nothing so much as the kind of ego-driven self-absorption required to insist upon its "right" to impose itself on a tiny minority, even to the point of culturally exterminating it—opt to do so in a manner which makes them appear not only repugnant, but also utterly ridiculous to anyone outside their ranks?

Sometimes it is necessary to step away from a given setting in order to better understand it. For me, the answers to these seemingly inexplicable questions were to a large extent clarified during a recent (unpaid) political speaking tour of Germany, during which I was repeatedly confronted by the spectacle of Indian "hobbyists," all of them men resplendently attired in quillwork and bangles, beaded moccasins, chokers, amulets, medicine bags, and so on.[25] Some of them sported feathers and buckskin shirts or jackets; a few wore their blond hair braided with rawhide in what they imagined to be high plains style (in reality, they looked much more like Vikings than Cheyennes or Shoshones). When queried, many professed having handcrafted much of their own regalia.[26] A number also made mention of having fashioned their own pipestone pipes, or of having been presented with one, usually after making a hefty monetary contribution, by one of a gaggle of Indian or pretended-Indian hucksters.[27]

Among those falling into this classification, belonging to what Christian Feest has branded the "Faculty of Medicine" currently plying a lucrative "Greater Europa Medicine Man Circuit,"[28] are Wallace Black Elk, "Brooke Medicine Eagle" (a bogus Cherokee; real name unknown), "John Redtail Freesoul" (a purported Cheyenne-Arapaho; real unknown), Archie Fire Lamedeer (Northern Cheyenne), "Dhyani Ywahoo" (supposedly a 27th-generation member of the nonexistent "Etowah" band of the Eastern Cherokees; real name unknown), "Eagle Walking Turtle" (Gary McClain, an alleged Choctaw), "Eagle Man" (Ed McGaa, Oglala Lakota), "Beautiful Painted Arrow" (a supposed Shoshone; real name unknown).[29] Although the success of such people "is completely independent of traditional knowledge, just so long as they can impress a public impressed by the books of Carlos Castaneda,"[30] most of the hobbyists I talked to noted they'd "received instruction" from one or more of these "Indian spiritual teachers" and had now adopted various deformed fragments of Native American ritual life as being both authentic and their own.

Everyone felt they been "trained" to run sweats. Most had been provided similar tutelage in conducting Medicine Wheel Ceremonies and Vision Quests. Several were pursuing what they thought were Navajo crystal-healing techniques, and/or herbal healing (where they figured to gather herbs not native to their habitat was left unaddressed). Two mentioned they'd participated in a "sun dance" conducted several years ago in the Black Forest by an unspecified "Lakota medicine man" (they displayed chest scars verifying that they had indeed done something of the sort), and said they were now considering launching their own version on an annual basis. Half a dozen more inquired as to whether I could provide them entrée to the Sun Dances conducted each summer on stateside reservations (of special interest are those of the "Sioux").[31] One poor soul, a Swiss national as it turned out, proudly observed that he'd somehow managed to survive living in an Alpine tipi for the past several years.[32] All of them maintained that at this point they actually consider themselves to *be* Indians, at least "in spirit."[33]

These "Indians of Europe," as Feest has termed them, were uniformly quite candid as to why they felt this way.[34] Bluntly put—and the majority were precisely this harsh in their own articulations—they absolutely *hate* the idea of being Europeans, especially Germans. Abundant mention was made of their collective revulsion to the European heritage of colonization and genocide, particularly the ravages of nazism. Some went deeper, addressing what they felt to be the intrinsically unacceptable character of European civilization's relationship to the natural order in its entirety. Their response, as a group, was to try and disassociate themselves from what it was/is they object to by announcing their personal identities in terms as diametrically opposed to it as they could conceive. "Becoming" American Indians in their own minds apparently fulfilled this deep-seated need in the most gratifying fashion.[35]

Yet, when I delved deeper, virtually all of them ultimately admitted they were little more than weekend warriors, or "cultural transvestites," to borrow another of Feest's descriptors.[36] They typically engage in their Indianist preoccupations only during their off hours while maintaining regular jobs—mainly quite responsible and well-paying positions, at that—squarely within the very system of Germanic business-as-usual they claimed so heatedly to have disavowed, root and branch. The most candid respondents were even willing to admit, when pushed, that were it not for the income accruing from their daily roles as "Good Germans," they'd not be able to afford their hobby of imagining themselves as being something else...or to pay the fees charged by imported Native American "spirit leaders" to validate this impression. Further, without exception, when I inquired as to what they might be doing to challenge and transform the fundamental nature of the German culture, society, and state they profess to detest so deeply, they observed that they had become "spiritual people" and are therefore "apolitical." Queries concerning whether they might be willing to engage in activities to physically defend the rights and territories of indigenous peoples in North America drew much the same reply.

The upshot of German hobbyism, then, is that, far from constituting the sort of radical divorce from a Germanic context its adherents assert, part-time impersonation of American Indians represents a means through which they can psychologically reconcile themselves to it. By pretending to be what they are not—and in fact can never be, because the objects of their fantasies have never existed in real life—the hobbyists are freed to be what they are (but deny), and to "feel good about themselves" in the process.[37] And, since this sophistry allows them to contend in all apparent seriousness that they are somehow entirely separate from the oppressive status quo upon which they depend, and which their "real world" occupations do so much to make possible, they thereby absolve themselves of any obligation whatsoever to materially confront it (and thence themselves). Voilà! "Wildmen" and "primitives" carrying out the most refined functions of the German corporate state; "warriors" relieved of the necessity of doing battle other than in the most metaphorical of senses, and then always (and only) in service to the very structures and traditions they claim—and may even have convinced themselves to *believe* at some level or another—their perverse posturing negates.[38]

The Dynamics of Denial

Contemporary business life allows competitive relationships only, in which the major emotions are anxiety, tension, loneliness, rivalry and fear...Zeus energy has been steadily disintegrating decade after decade in the United States. Popular culture has been determined to destroy respect for it, beginning with the "Maggie and Jiggs" and "Dagwood and Blondie" comics of the 1920s and 1930s, in which the man is always weak and foolish...The recovery of some form of [powerful rituals of male] initiation is essential to the culture. The United States has undergone an unmistakable decline since 1950, and I believe if we do not find [these kinds of male ritual] the decline will continue.

—Robert Bly, 1990

Obviously, the liberatory potential of all this for actual American Indians is considerably less than zero. Instead, hobbyism is a decidedly parasitical enterprise, devoted exclusively to the emotional edification of individuals integrally and instrumentally involved in perpetuating and perfecting the system of global domination from which the genocidal colonization of Native America stemmed and by which it is continued. Equally obvious, there is a strikingly close, if somewhat antecedent, correspondence between German hobbyism on the one hand, and the North American Men's Movement on the other. The class and ethnic compositions are virtually identical, as are the resulting social functions, internal dynamics, and external impacts.[39] So close is the match, not only demographically, but motivationally and behaviorally as well, that Robert Bly himself has scheduled a tour of Germany during the summer of 1993 to bring the Old World's Teutonic sector into his burgeoning fold.[40]

Perhaps the only significant difference between the Men's Movement at home and hobbyism abroad is just that: the hobbyists at least are "over there," but the Men's Movement is right here, where we live. Hobbyism in Germany may contribute to what both Adolf Hitler and George Bush called the "New World Order," and thus yield a negative but somewhat indirect effect upon native people in North America, but the Men's Movement is quite *directly* connected to the ever more efficient imposition of that order upon Indian lands and lives in the United States and Canada. The mining engineer who joins the Men's Movement and thereafter spends his weekends "communing with nature in the manner of an Indian" does so—in precisely the same fashion as his German colleagues—in order to exempt himself from either literal or emotional responsibility for the fact that, to be who he is and live at the standard he does, he will spend the rest of his week making wholesale destruction of the environment an operant reality. Not infrequently, the land being stripmined under his supervision belongs to the very Indians whose spiritual traditions he appropriates and reifies in the process of "finding inner peace" (i.e., empowering himself to do what he does).[41]

By the same token, the corporate lawyer, the Wall Street broker, and the commercial banker who accompany the engineer into a sweat lodge do so because, intellectually, they understand quite well that, without them, his vocation would be impossible. The same can be said for the government bureaucrat, the corporate executive, and the marketing consultant who keep Sacred Pipes on the walls of their respective offices. All of them are engaged, to a greater or lesser degree—although, if asked, most will adamantly reject the slightest hint that they are involved at all—in the systematic destruction of the residue of territory upon which prospects of native life itself are balanced. The charade by which they cloak themselves in the identity of their victims is their best and ultimately most compulsive hedge against the psychic consequences of acknowledging who and what they really are.[42]

Self-evidently, then, New Age-style rhetoric to the contrary notwithstanding, this pattern of emotional/psychological avoidance embedded in the ritual role-playing of Indians by a relatively privileged strata of Euroamerican men represents no alternative to the status quo. To the contrary, it has become a steadily more crucial ingredient in an emergent complex of psychosocial mechanisms allowing North American business-as-usual to sustain, stabilize, and reenergize itself. Put another way, had the Men's Movement not come into being compliments of Robert Bly and his clones, it would have been necessary—just as the nazis found it useful to do in their day—for North America's governmental-corporate elite to have created it on their own.[43] On second thought, it's not altogether clear they didn't.[44]

Alternatives

The ancient societies believed that a boy becomes a man only through ritual and effort—only through the "active intervention of the older men." It's becoming clear to us that manhood doesn't happen by itself; it doesn't just happen because we eat Wheaties. The active intervention of the older men means the older men welcome the younger man into the ancient, mythologized, instinctive male world.

—Robert Bly, 1990

With all this said, it still must be admitted that there is a scent of undeniably real human desperation—an all but obsessive desire to find some avenue of alternative cultural expression different from that sketched above—clinging to the Men's Movement and its New Age and hobbyist equivalents. The palpable anguish this entails allows for, or requires, a somewhat more sympathetic construction of the motives prodding a segment of the movement's membership, and an illative obligation on the part of anyone not themselves experiencing it to respond in a firm, but helpful, rather than antagonistic manner.

Perhaps more accurately, it should be said that the sense of despair at issue evidences itself not so much in the ranks of the Men's Movement and related phenomena themselves, but within the milieu from which these manifestations have arisen: white, mostly urban, affluent or affluently reared, well-schooled, young (or youngish) people of both genders who, in one or another dimension, are thoroughly dis-eased by the socioeconomic order into which they were born and their seemingly predestined roles within it.[45] Many of them openly seek, some through serious attempts at political resistance, a viable option with which they may not only alter their own individual fates, but also transform the overall systemic realities they correctly perceive as having generated these fates in the first place.[46] As a whole, they seem sincerely baffled by the prospect of having to define for themselves the central aspect of this alternative.

They cannot put a name to it, and so they perpetually spin their wheels, waging continuous theoretical and sometimes practical battles against each "hierarchical" and "patriarchal" fragment of the whole they oppose: capitalism and fascism, colonialism, neocolonialism and imperialism, racism and sexism, ageism, consumerism, the entire vast plethora of "isms" and "ologies" making up the "modern" (or "post-modern") society they inhabit.[47] Frustrated and stymied in their efforts to come up with a new or different conceptualization by which to guide their oppositional project, many of the most alienated—and therefore most committed to achieving fundamental social change—eventually opt for the intellectual/emotional reassurance of prepackaged "radical solutions." Typically, these assume the form of yet another battery of "isms" based in all the same core assumptions as the system being opposed. This is especially true of that galaxy of doctrinal tendencies falling within the general rubric of "marxism"— bernsteinian revisionism, council communism, marxism-leninism, stalinism, maoism, etc.—but it is an actuality pervading most variants of feminism, environmentalism, and anarchism/anti-authoritarianism as well.[48]

Others, burned out by an endless diet of increasingly sterile polemical chatter and symbolic political action, defect from the resistance altogether, deforming what German New Left theorist Rudi Dutschke[49] once advocated as "a long march through the institutions" into an outright embrace of the false and reactionary "security" found in statism and bureaucratic corporatism. This is a tendency exemplified in the United States by such '60s radical figures as Tom Hayden, Jerry Rubin, Eldridge Cleaver, David Horowitz, and Rennie Davis.[50] A mainstay occupation of this coterie has been academia, wherein they typically maintain an increasingly irrelevant and detached "critical" discourse, calculated mainly to negate whatever transformative value or utility might be lodged in the concrete oppositional political engagement they formerly pursued.[51]

Some members of each group—formula radicals and sellouts— end up glossing over the psychic void left by their default in arriving at a genuinely alternative vision, immersing themselves either in some formalized religion (Catholicism, for example, or, somewhat less frequently, denominations of Islam or Buddhism), or the polyglot "spiritualism" offered by the New Age/Men's Movement/Hobbyism syndrome.[52] This futile cycle is now in its third successive generation of repetition among European and Euroamerican activists since the so-called "new student movement" was born only 30 years ago. At one level or another, almost all of those currently involved, and quite a large proportion of those who once were, are figuratively screaming for a workable means of breaking the cycle, some way of foundationing themselves for a sustained and successful effort to effect societal change rather than the series of dead-ends they've encountered up till now. Yet a functional alternative exists, and has always existed.

The German Tour Revisited

This was brought home to me most dramatically during my earlier-mentioned speaking tour of Germany.[53] The question most frequently asked by those who turned out to hear me speak on the struggle for liberation in Native North America was, "What can we do to help?" Quite uniformly, the answer I provided to this query was that, strategically, the most important assistance the people in the audience could render American Indians would be to win their own struggle for liberation in Germany. In effect, I reiterated time after time, this would eliminate the German corporate state as a linchpin of the global politicoeconomic order in which the United States (along with its Canadian satellite) serves as the hub.

"You must understand," I stated each time the question arose, "that I really mean it when I say we are all related. Consequently, I see the mechanisms of our oppression as being equally interrelated. Given this perspective, I cannot help but see a victory for you as being simultaneously a victory for American Indians, and vice versa; that a weakening of your enemy here in Germany necessarily weakens ours there, in North America; that your liberation is inseparably linked to our own, and that you should see ours as advancing yours. Perhaps, then, the question should be reversed: what is it that we can best do to help *you* succeed?"

As an expression of solidarity, these sentiments were on every occasion roundly applauded. Invariably, however, they also produced a set of rejoinders intended to qualify the implications of what we'd said to the point of negation. The usual drift of these responses was that the German and American Indian situations and resulting struggles are entirely different, and thus not to be compared in the manner I'd attempted. This is true, those making this point argued, because Indians are colonized peoples while the Germans are colonizers. Indians, they went on, must therefore fight to free our occupied and underdeveloped land base(s), while the German opposition, effectively landless, struggles to rearrange social and economic relations within an advanced industrial society. Most importantly, they concluded, native people in America hold the advantage of possessing cultures separate and distinct from that which we oppose, while the German opposition, by contrast, must contend with the circumstance of being essentially "cultureless" and disoriented.[54]

After every presentation, I was forced to take strong exception to such notions. "As long-term participants in the national liberation struggle of American Indians," I said, "we have been forced into knowing the nature of colonialism very well. Along with you, we understand that the colonization we experience finds its origin in the matrix of European culture. But, apparently unlike you, we also understand that in order for Europe to do what it has done to us—in fact, for Europe to become "Europe" at all—it first had to do the same thing to all of you. In other words, to become a colonizing culture, Europe had first to colonize *itself*.[55] To the extent that this is true, I find it fair to say that if our struggle must be explicitly anticolonial in its form, content, and aspirations, yours must be even more so. You have, after all, been colonized far longer than we, and therefore much more completely. In fact, your colonization has by now been consolidated to such an extent that—with certain notable exceptions, like the Irish and Euskadi (Basque) nationalists—you no longer even see yourselves as having been colonized.[56] The result is that you've become self-colonizing, conditioned to be so self-identified with your own oppression that you've lost your ability to see it for what it is, much less to resist it in any coherent way.

"You seem to feel that you are either completely disconnected from your own heritage of having been conquered and colonized, or that you can and should disconnect yourselves from it as a means of destroying that which oppresses you. I believe, on the other hand, that your internalization of this self-hating outlook is exactly what your oppressors want most to see you do. Such a posture on your part simply perfects and completes the structure of your domination. It is inherently self-defeating because in denying yourselves the meaning of your own history and traditions, you leave yourselves with neither an established point-of-departure from which to launch your own struggle for liberation, nor any set of goals and objectives to guide that struggle other than abstractions. You are thereby left effectively anchorless and rudderless, adrift on a stormy sea. You have lost your maps and compass, so you have no idea where you are or where to turn for help. Worst of all, you sense that the ship on which you find yourselves trapped is rapidly sinking. I can imagine no more terrifying situation to be in, and, as relatives, we would like to throw you a life preserver.

"So here it is," I went on. "It takes the form of an insight offered by our elders: 'To understand where you are, you must know where you've been, and you must know where you are to understand where you are going.'[57] For Indians, you see, the past, present, and future are all equally important parts of the same indivisible whole. And I believe this is as true for you as it is for us. In other words, you must set yourselves to reclaiming your own indigenous past. You must come to know it in its own terms—the terms of its internal values and understandings, and the way these were applied to living in this world—not the terms imposed upon it by the order which set out to destroy it. You must learn to put your knowledge of this heritage to use as a lens through which you can clarify your present circumstance, to "know where you are," so to speak. And, from this, you can begin to chart the course of your struggle into the future. Put still another way, you, no less than we, must forge the conceptual tools that will allow you to carefully and consciously orient your struggle toward regaining what it is that has been taken from you, rather than presuming a unique ability to invent it all anew. You must begin with the decolonization of your own minds, with a restoration of your understanding of who you are, where you come from, what it is that has been done to you to take you to the place in which you now find yourselves. Then, and *only* then, it seems to us, will you be able to free yourselves from your present dilemma.

"*Look* at us, and really *hear* what we're saying," I demanded. "We are not unique in being indigenous people. *Everyone* is indigenous somewhere. *You* are indigenous here. You, no more than we, are landless; your land is occupied by an alien force, just like ours. You, just like us, have an overriding obligation to liberate your homeland. You, no less than we, have models in your own traditions upon which to base your alternatives to the social, political, and economic structures now imposed upon you. It is your responsibility to put yourselves in direct communication with these traditions, just as it is our responsibility to remain in contact with ours. We cannot fulfil this responsibility for you any more than you can fulfil ours for us.

"You say that the knowledge we speak of was taken from you too long ago, at the time of Charlemagne, more than a thousand years ago. Because of this, you say, the gulf of time separating then from now is too great; that what was taken then is now lost and gone. We know better. We know, and so do you, that right up into the 1700s your 'European' colonizers were still busily burning 'witches' at the stake. We know, and you know too, that these women were the leaders of your own indigenous cultures.[58] The span of time separating you from a still-flourishing practice of your native ways is thus not so great as you would have us—and yourselves—believe. It's been 200 years, no more. And we also know that there are still those among your people who retain the knowledge of your past, knowledge handed down from one generation to the next, century after century. We can give you directions to some of them if you like, but we think you know they are there.[59] You *can* begin to draw appropriate lessons and instruction from these faithkeepers, if you want to.

"Indians have said that 'for the world to live, Europe must die.'[60] We meant it when we said it, and we still do. But do not be confused. The statement was never intended to exclude you or consign you, as people, to oblivion.We believe the idea underlying that statement holds just as true for you as it does for anyone else. You *do* have a choice, because you are *not* who you've been convinced to believe you are. Or, at least not necessarily. You are not necessarily a part of the colonizing, predatory reality of 'Europe.' You are not even necessarily 'Germans,' with all that that implies. You are, or can be, who your ancestors were and who the faithkeepers of your cultures remain: Angles, Saxons, Huns, Goths, Visigoths. The choice is yours, but in order for it to have meaning you must meet the responsibilities which come with it."

Objections and Responses

Such reasoning provoked considerable consternation among listeners. "But," more than one exclaimed with unpretended horror, "*think* of who you're speaking to! These are very dangerous ideas you are advocating. You are in Germany, among people raised to see themselves as Germans, and yet, at least in part, you are telling us we should do exactly what the nazis did! We Germans, at least those of us who are consciously anti-fascist and anti-racist, renounce such excavations of our heritage precisely because of our country's own recent experiences with them. We *know* where Hitler's politics of "blood and soil" led not just us but also the world. We *know* the outcome of Himmler's reassertion of 'Germanic paganism.' Right now, we are being forced to confront a resurgence of nazism in this country. Surely you can't be arguing that we should *join* in the resurrection of all that."

"Of course not!" I retorted. "We, as American Indians, have at least as much reason to hate nazism as any people on earth. Not much of anything done by the nazis to people here had not already been done to us, for centuries, and some of the things the nazis did during their 12 years in power are *still* being done to us today. Much of what has been done to us in North America was done, and continues to be done, on the basis of philosophical rationalizations indistinguishable from those used by the nazis to justify their policies. If you want to look at it that way, you could say that anti-nazism is part of the absolute bedrock upon which our struggle is based. So, don't even *hint* that any part of our perspective is somehow 'pro-nazi.'

"I am aware that this is a highly emotional issue for you. But try and bear in mind that the world isn't one-dimensional. Everything is multidimensional, possessed of positive as well as negative polarities. It should be obvious that the nazis didn't represent or crystallize your indigenous traditions. Instead, they perverted your heritage for their own purposes, using your ancestral traditions against themselves in a fashion meant to supplant and destroy them. The European predator has always done this, whenever it was not simply trying to suppress the indigenous host upon which it feeds. Perhaps the nazis were the most overt, and in some ways the most successful, in doing this in recent times. And for that reason some of us view them as being a sort of culmination of all that is European. But, the point is, they very deliberately tapped the negative rather than the positive potential of what we are discussing.

"Now, polarities aside," I continued, "the magnitude of favorable response accorded by the mass of Germans to the themes taken up by the nazis during the 1930s illustrates perfectly the importance of the question we are raising.[61] There is unquestionably a tremendous yearning among all peoples, including your own—and you yourselves, for that matter—for a sense of connectedness to their roots. This yearning, although often sublimated, translates quite readily into transformative power whenever (and however) it is effectively addressed.[62] Hence, part of what we are arguing is that you must consciously establish the positive polarity of your heritage as a counter to the negative impulse created by the nazis. If you don't, it's likely we're going to witness German officials walking around in black death's-head uniforms all over again. The signs are there, you must admit.[63] And you must also admit there's a certain logic involved, since you yourselves seem bent upon abandoning the power of your indigenous traditions to nazism. Suffice it to say, we'd not give *our* traditions over to the uncontested use of nazis. Maybe you shouldn't either."

Such remarks usually engendered commentary about how the audience had "never viewed the matter in this light," followed by questions as to how a positive expression of German indigenism might be fostered. "Actually," we said, "it seems to us you're already doing this. It's all in how you look at things and how you go about explaining them to others. Try this: you have currently, as a collective response to perceived problems of centralization within the German Left, atomized into what you call *autonomen*. These we understand to be a panorama of autonomous affinity groups bound together in certain lines of thought and action by a definable range of issues and aspirations.[64] Correct? So, instead of trying to explain this development to yourselves and everyone else as some "new and revolutionary tendency)"—which it certainly is not—how about conceiving of it as an effort to recreate the kinds of social organization and political consensus marking your ancient 'tribal' cultures (adapted of course to the contemporary context)?

"Making such an effort to connect what you are doing to what was done quite successfully by your ancestors, and using that connection as a mode through which to prefigure what you wish to accomplish in the future, would serve to (re)contextualize your efforts in a way you've never before attempted. It would allow you to obtain a sense of your own cultural continuity which, at present, appears to be conspicuously absent from your struggle. It would allow you to experience the sense of empowerment which comes with reaching into your own history at the deepest level and altering outcomes you've quite correctly decided are unacceptable. This is as opposed to your trying to invent some entirely different history for yourselves. We predict a project of this sort, if approached carefully and with considerable flexibility from the outset, would revitalize your struggle in ways which will astound you.

"Here's another possibility: you are at the moment seriously engaged in efforts to redefine power relations between men and women, and in finding ways to actualize these redefined relationships. Instead of trying to reinvent the wheel in this respect, why not see it as an attempt to reconstitute in the modern setting the kind of gender balance that prevailed among your ancestors? Surely this makes as much sense as attempting to fabricate a whole new set of relations. And, quite possibly, it would enable you to explain your intentions in this regard to a whole range of people who are frankly skeptical right now, in a manner which would attract them rather than repelling them.

"Again: you are primarily an urban-based movement in which 'squatting' plays a very prominent role.[65] Why not frame this in terms of liberating your space in very much the same way we approach the liberation of our land? The particulars are very different, but the principle involved would seem to us to be quite similar. And it looks likely to me that thinking of squatting in this way would tend to lead you right back toward your traditional relationship to land/space. This seems even more probable when squatting is considered in combination with the experiments in collectivism and communalism which are its integral aspects. A lot of translation is required to make these connections, but that too is exactly the point. Translation between the concrete and the theoretical is *always* necessary in the formation of praxis. What I'm recommending is no different from any other approach in this respect. The question is whether these translations will serve to link political activity to reassertion of indigenous traditions, or to force an even further disjuncture in that regard. That's true in any setting, whether it's yours or ours. As we said, there are choices to be made.

"These are merely a few preliminary possibilities we've been able to observe during the short time we've been here," we concluded. "We're sure there are many others. What's important, however, is that we can and must all begin wherever we find ourselves. Start with what already exists in terms of resistance, link this resistance directly to your own native traditions, and build from there. The sequence is a bit different, but that's basically what we in the American Indian Movement have had to do. And we can testify that the process works. You end up with a truly organic and internally sustainable framework within which to engage in liberatory struggle. Plainly, this is something very different from Adolf Hitler's conducting of 'blood rituals' on the playing fields of Nuremberg,[66] or Heinrich Himmler's convening of some kind of 'Mystic Order of the SS' in a castle at Wewelsburg,[67] just as it's something very different from tripped-out hippies prancing about in the grass every spring pretending they're 'rediscovering' the literal ceremonial forms of the ancient Celts, or a bunch of yuppies spending their off-hours playing at being American Indians. All of these are facets of the negative polarity you so rightly reject. I am arguing, not that you should drop your rejection of the negative, but that you should pursue its positive alternative. Let's not confuse the two. And let's not throw the baby out with the bath water. Okay?"

Applications to North America

It is not necessary for crows to become eagles.

—Sitting Bull, 1888

Much of what has been said with regard to Germany can be transposed for application in North America, albeit there can be no suggestion that Euroamericans are in any way indigenous to this land (cutesy bumper stickers reading "Colorado Native" and displayed by blond suburbanites do nothing to change this). What is meant is that the imperative of reconnecting themselves to their own traditional roots pertains as much, and in some ways more, to this dislocated segment of the European population as it does to their cousins who have remained in the Old World. By extension, the same point can be made with regard to the descendants of those groups of European invaders who washed up on the beach in other quarters of the planet these past 500 hundred years: in various locales of South and Central America, for instance, and in Australia, New Zealand, South Africa, and much of Polynesia and Micronesia. In effect, the rule would apply wherever settler state colonialism has come into existence.[68]

Likely, it will be far more difficult for those caught up in Europe's far-flung diaspora to accomplish this than it may be for those still within the confines of their native geography. The latter plainly enjoy a much greater proximity to the sources of their indigenous traditions, while the former have undergone several generations of continuous indoctrination to see themselves as "new peoples" forging entirely new cultures.[69] The sheer impossibility of this last has inflicted upon those among the Eurodiaspora an additional dimension of identity confusion largely absent among even the most conspicuously deculturated elements of the subcontinent itself. Rather than serving as a deterrent, however, this circumstance should be understood as heightening the urgency assigned the reconstructive task facing

Euroamericans and others, elsewhere, who find themselves in similar situations.

By and large, the Germans have at least come to understand, and to accept, what nazism was and is. This has allowed the best among them to seek to distance themselves from it by undertaking whatever political action is required to destroy it once and for all.[70] Their posture in this respect provides them a necessary foundation for resumption of cultural/spiritual traditions among themselves which constitute a direct and fully internalized antidote to the nazi impulse. In effecting this reconnection to their own indigenous heritage, the German dissidents will at last be able to see nazism—that logical culmination of so much of the predatory synthesis which is "Europe"—as being, not something born of their own traditions, but as something as alien and antithetical to those traditions as it was/is to the traditions of any other people in the world. In this way, by reintegrating themselves with their indigenous selves, they simultaneously reintegrate themselves with the rest of humanity itself.

In North America, by contrast, no such cognition can be said to have taken hold, even among the most politically developed sectors of the Euroamerican population. Instead, denial remains the norm. Otherwise progressive whites still seek at all costs to evade even the most obvious correlations between their own history in the New World and that of the nazis in the Old. A favorite intellectual parlor game remains the debate over whether genocide is "really" an "appropriate" term to describe the physical eradication of some 98 percent of the continent's native population between 1500 and 1900.[71] "Concern" is usually expressed that comparisons between the U.S. government's assertion of its "Manifest Destiny" to expropriate through armed force about 97.5 percent of all native land, and the nazis' subsequent effort to implement what they called "lebensraum-politik"—the expropriation through conquest of territory belonging to the Poles, Slavs, and other "inferior" peoples only a generation later—might be "misleading" or "oversimplified."[72]

The logical contortions through which Euroamericans persist in putting themselves, in this process of avoiding reality, are sometimes truly amazing. A salient example is that of James Axtell, a white "revisionist" historian quite prone to announcing his "sympathies" with Indians, who has repeatedly gone on record arguing in the most vociferous fashion that it is both "unfair" and "contrary to sound historiography" to compare European invaders and settlers in the Americas to nazis. His reasoning? Because, he says, the former were, "after all, human beings. They were husbands, fathers, brothers, uncles, sons and lovers. And we must try to reach back in time to understand them as such."[73] Exactly what he thinks the nazis were, if not human beings fulfilling identical roles in their society, is left unstated. For that matter, Axtell fails to address how he ever arrived at the novel conclusion that either the nazis or European invaders and Euroamerican settlers in the New World consisted only of men.

A more sophisticated ploy consists of a ready concession on the part of white activists/theorists that what was done to America's indigenous peoples was "tragic," even while raising carefully loaded questions suggesting that things are working out "for the best" in any event.[74] "Didn't Indians fight wars with one another?" the question goes, implying that the native practice of engaging in rough inter-group skirmishing—a matter more akin to full-contact sports like football, hockey, and rugby than anything else—somehow equates to Europe's wars of conquest and annihilation, and that traditional indigenous societies therefore stand to gain as much from Euroamerican conceptions of pacifism as anyone else.[75] (You bet, boss. Left to our own devices, we'd undoubtedly have exterminated ourselves. Praise the lord that y'all came along to save us from ourselves.)

Marxian organizations like the Revolutionary Communist Party USA express deep concern that native people's economies might have been so unrefined that we were commonly forced to eat our own excrement to survive, a premise clearly implying that Euroamerica's industrial devastation of our homelands has ultimately worked to our advantage, ensuring our "material security" whether we're gracious enough to admit it or not.[76] (Thanks, boss. We were tired of eating shit anyway. Glad you came and taught us to farm.[77]) The "cutting edge" ecologists of Earth First! have conjured up queries as to whether Indians weren't "the continent's first environmental pillagers"—they claim we beat all the wooly mammoths to death with sticks, among other things—

meaning we were always sorely in need of Euroamerica's much more advanced views on preserving the natural order.[78]

White male anarchists fret over possible "authoritarian" aspects of our societies—"You had *leaders*, didn't you? That's hierarchy!"[79]— while their feminist sisters worry that our societies may have been "sexist" in their functioning.[80] (Oh no, boss. We too managed to think our way through to a position in which women did the heavy lifting and men bore the children. Besides, hadn't you heard? We were all "queer," in the old days, so your concerns about our being patriarchal have always been unwarranted.[81]) Even the animal rights movement chimes in from time to time, discomfited that we were traditionally so unkind to "non-human members of our sacred natural order" as to eat their flesh.[82] (Hey, no sweat, boss. We'll jump right on your no-meat bandwagon. But don't forget the sacred Cherokee Clan of the Carrot. You'll have to reciprocate our gesture of solidarity by not eating any more fruits and vegetables either. Or had you forgotten that plants are non-human members of the natural order as well? Have a nice fast, buckaroo.)

Not until such apologist and ultimately white supremacist attitudes begin to be dispelled within at least that sector of Euroamerican society which claims to represent an alternative to U.S./Canadian business-as-usual can there be hope of *any* genuinely positive social transformation in North America. And only in acknowledging the real rather than invented nature of their history, as the German opposition has done long-since, can they begin to come to grips with such things.[83] From there, they too will be able to position themselves— psychologically, intellectually, and eventually in practical terms—to step outside that history, not in a manner which continues it by presuming to appropriate the histories and cultural identities of its victims, but in ways allowing them to recapture its antecedent meanings and values. Restated, Euroamericans, like their European counterparts, will then be able to start reconnecting themselves to their indigenous traditions and identities in ways which instill pride rather than guilt, empowering themselves to join in the negation of the construct of "Europe" which has temporarily suppressed their cultures as well as ours.

At base, the same principle applies here that pertains "over there." As our delegation put it repeatedly to the Germans in our closing remarks, "The indigenous peoples of the Americas can, have, and will continue to join hands with the indigenous peoples of this land, just as we do with those of any other. We are reaching out to you by our very act of being here, and of saying what we are saying to you. We have faith in you, a faith that you will be able to rejoin the family of humanity as peoples interacting respectfully and harmoniously—on the basis of your own ancestral ways—with the traditions of all other peoples. We are at this time expressing a faith in you that you perhaps lack in yourselves. But, and make no mistake about this, we *cannot* and *will not* join hands with those who default on this responsibility, who instead insist upon wielding an imagined right to stand as part of Europe's synthetic and predatory tradition, the tradition of colonization, genocide, racism, and ecocide. The choice, as we've said over and over again, is yours to make. It cannot be made for you. You alone must make your choice and act on it, just as we have had to make and act upon ours."

In North America, it will be evident that affirmative choices along these lines have begun to emerge among self-proclaimed progressives, not when figures like Robert Bly are simply dismissed as being ridiculous kooks, or condoned as harmless irrelevancies,[84] but when they come to be treated by "their own" as signifying the kind of menace they actually entail. Only when white males themselves start to display the sort of profound outrage at the activities of groups like the Men's Movement as is manifested by its victims—when they rather than we begin to shut down the movement's meetings, burn its sweat lodges, impound and return the sacred objects it desecrates, and otherwise make its functioning impossible—will we be able to say with confidence that Euroamerica has finally accepted that Indians are Indians, not toys to be played with by whoever can afford the price of the game. Only then will we be able to say that the "Indians 'R' Us" brand of cultural appropriation and genocide has passed, or at least is passing, and that Euroamericans are finally coming to terms with who they've been and, much more importantly, with who and what it is they can become. Then, finally, these immigrants can at last be accepted among us upon our shores, fulfilling the speculation of the Dwamish leader Seattle in 1854: " We may be brothers after all." As he said then, "We shall see."[85]

Notes

1. Bly's political dimension began to take form with the publication of his interview "What Men Really Want" in *New Age* (May 1982). For an overview of his verse, see Bly, Robert, *Selected Poems* (New York: Harper & Row Publishers, 1986). Earlier collections include *Silence in the Snowy Fields* (Middletown, CT: Wesleyan University Press, 1962), *This Body Is Made from Camphor and Gopherwood* (New York: Harper & Row Publishers, 1977), *This Tree Will Be Here for a Thousand Years* (New York: Harper & Row Publishers, 1979), *News of the Universe* (San Francisco, CA: Sierra Club Books, 1981), *The Man in the Black Coat Turns* (New York: Doubleday Publishers, 1981), and *Loving a Woman in Two Worlds* (New York: Doubleday Publishers, 1985).

2. See Susie Day, "Male Liberation," *Z Magazine* (June 1993): pp. 10-12. The author cites a recent *Newsweek* poll indicating that some 48 percent of Euroamerican males believe they are being "victimized" by a "loss of influence" in U.S. society. She points out that, by this, they appear to mean that they've been rendered marginally less empowered to dominate everyone else than they were three decades ago. Their response is increasingly to overcome this perceived victimization by finding ways and means, often through cooptation of the liberatory methods developed by those they're accustomed to dominating, of reestablishing their "proper authority."

3. Statements by Robert Bly during a workshop session at the University of Colorado at Boulder, 1992.

4. Bly, Robert, *Iron John: A Book About Men* (Reading, MA: Addison-Wesley Publishing, 1990). The title is taken from the fairy tale "The Story of Iron John" by Jacob and Wilhelm Grimm, of which Bly provides his own translation from the German.

5. As examples, see Arnold, Patrick M., *Wildmen, Warriors and Kings: Masculine Spirituality and the Bible* (New York: Crossroad Publishers, 1991); Moore, Robert, and Douglas Gillette, *King, Warrior, Magician, Lover: Rediscovering the Archetypes of Masculine Nature* (New York: Harper & Row Publishers, 1990); Stewart, R. J., *Celebrating the Male Mysteries* (Bath, UK: Arcania Publications, 1991); and Wetcher, Kenneth, Art Barker, and F. W. McCaughtry, *Save the Males: Why Men Are Mistreated, Misdiagnosed, and Misunderstood* (Washington, D.C.: Pia Press, 1991). Anthologies include Matthews, John, *Choirs of the God: Revisioning Masculinity* (London: Harper Mandala Books, 1991), and Harding, Christopher *Wingspan: Inside the Men's Movement* (New York: St. Martin's Press, 1992). Or, in another medium, try Moore, Robert, *Rediscovering Men's Potentials,* set of four cassette tapes (Wilmette, IL: Chiron, 1988).

6. Consider, for example, *Shaman's Drum* (produced in Willis, CA), described as a "glossy quarterly 'journal of experiential shamanism,' native medicineways, transpersonal healing, ecstatic spirituality, and caretaking the earth. Includes regional calendars, resource directory, information on drums."

7. Wallace Black Elk, an Oglala Lakota, is a former apprentice to Sicangu (Brûlé) Lakota spiritual leader Leonard Crow Dog and was a member of the American Indian Movement during the period of the Wounded Knee siege (*circa* 1972-76). Subsequently, he became associated with the late "Sun Bear" (Vincent LaDuke), an Anishinabe who served as something of a prototype for plastic medicine men and discovered the profit potential of peddling ersatz Indian spirituality to New Agers. Despite the fact that he is *not*, as he claims, the grand-nephew of the Black Elk made famous by John Neihardt (*Black Elk Speaks* [Lincoln: University of Nebraska Press, 1963]) and Joseph Epes Brown (*The Sacred Pipe* [Norman: University of Oklahoma Press, 1953])—it's an entirely different family—"Grampa Wallace" has become a favorite icon of the Men's Movement. In fact, the movement has made him, at age 71, something of a best-selling author; see Black Elk, Wallace, and William S. Lyon, *Black Elk: The Sacred Ways of the Lakota* (San Francisco, CA: Harper Books, 1991).

8. The Sun Dance is the central ceremony of Lakota ritual life; the geographical reference is to "Crow Dog's Paradise," near Grass Mountain, on the Rosebud Reservation in South Dakota.

9. Another obvious alternative to "American Indianism" for the Men's Movement might be to turn toward certain warrior-oriented strains of Buddhism or even Shintoism. But then, Bly and the boys would be compelled to compete directly—both financially and theologically—with much more longstanding and refined institutions of spiritual appropriation, like the Naropa Institute. Enterprises preoccupied with the various denominations of Islam are similarly well-rooted in North America.

10. Statement made at the Socialist Scholars Conference, New York, 1988.

11. Letter to the author, November 14, 1985.

12. The AIM resolution specifically identified several native people—the Sun Bear, Wallace Black Elk, and the late Grace Spotted Eagle (Oglala Lakota) among them—as being primary offenders. Also named were non-Indians, including Cyfus McDonald, "Osheana Fast Wolf," and "Brooke Medicine Eagle" (spelled "Medicine Ego" in the document), and one non-Indian organization, Vision Quest, Inc. The complete text can be found in this volume in Death Squads in the United States), pp. 256-28.

13. The resolution was signed by Tom Yellowtail (Crow), Larry Anderson (Navajo), Izador Thom (Lummi), Thomas Banyacya (Hopi), Walter Denni (Chippewa-Cree), Austin Two Moons (Northern Cheyenne), Tadadaho (Haudenosaunee), Frank Fools Crow (Oglala Lakota), Frank Cardinal (Cree), and Peter O'Chiese (Anishinabe), all well-respected traditional spiritual leaders within their respective nations. For the complete text, see *ibid.*, pp. 223-25.

14. For the complete text, see *Oyate Wicaho*, vol. 2, no. 3 (November 1982).

15. Alexie, Sherman, "White Men Can't Drum: In Going Native for Its Totems, the Men's Movement Misses the Beat," *New York Times Magazine* (October 4, 1992). For a Men's Movement perspective on the importance of drumming, and the association of their usage (in their minds) with African and American Indian rituals, see Parks, George A., "The Voice of the Drum," in *Wingspan, op. cit.*, pp. 206-13.

16. Reitman, Paul, "*Clearcut*: Ritual Gone Wrong," *The Men's Council Journal*, no. 16 (February 1993): p. 17.

17. Shippee, Paul, "Among the Dog Eaters," *The Men's Council Journal*, no. 16 (February 1993): pp. 7-8.

18. Telephone conversation, June 7, 1993. Means' comparisons to Eichmann and the Aryan Nation are not merely hyperbolic. Adolf Eichmann, SS "Jewish liaison" and transportation coordinator for the Holocaust, actually asserted on numerous occasions that he felt himself to be a zionist; see Arendt, Hannah, *Eichmann in Jerusalem: A Report on the Banality of Evil* (New York: Viking Press, 1963), p. 40. On the "True Jew" dogma of "Identity Christianity," religious creed of the rabidly antisemitic Idaho-based Aryan Nations, see Zeskind, Leonard, *The Christian Identity Movement: A Theological Justification for Racist and Anti-Semitic Violence* (New York: Division of Church and Society of the National Council of Churches of Christ in the U.S.A., 1986).

19. Means' characterization of the process corresponds quite well with the observations of many experts on cultural genocide. Consider, for example, the statement made by Davis, Mark, and Robert Zannis in their book, *The Genocide Machine in Canada: The Pacification of the North* (Montréal: Black Rose Books, 1973), p. 137: "If people suddenly lose their 'prime symbol' [such as the sanctity of spiritual tradition], the basis of their culture, their lives lose meaning. They become disoriented, with no hope. A social disorganization often follows such a loss, they are often unable to ensure their own survival...The loss and human suffering of those whose culture has been healthy and is suddenly attacked and disintegrated is incalculable."

20. Statement made at the 1982 Western Social Science Association Conference; quoted in *Fantasies of the Master Race, op. cit.*, p. 190.

21. *Ibid.*, pp. 190-91.

22. "White Men Can't Drum," *op. cit.*

23. *Ibid.* The final example refers to an anecdote with which Alexie opens his article: "Last year on the local television news, I watched a short feature on a meeting of the Confused White Men chapter in Spokane, Wash. They were all wearing war bonnets and beating drums, more or less. A few of the drums looked as if they might have come from K-mart, and one or two of the men just beat their chests. 'It's not just the drum,' the leader of the group said, 'it's the idea of the drum.' I was amazed at the lack of rhythm and laughed, even though I knew I supported a stereotype. But it's true: White men can't drum. They fail to understand that a drum is more than a heartbeat. Sometimes it is the sound of thunder, and many times it just means some Indians want to dance."

24. Quoted in *Fantasies of the Master Race, op. cit.*, p. 194. It should be noted that Means' sentiments correspond perfectly with those expressed by Gerald Wilkenson, head of the politically much more conservative National Indian Youth Council, in a letter endorsing an action planned by Colorado AIM to halt the sale of ceremonies to non-Indians in that state by Sun Bear in 1983: "The National Indian Youth Council fully supports your efforts to denounce, embarrass, disrupt, or otherwise run out of Colorado, [Sun Bear's] Medicine Wheel Gathering...For too long the Bear Tribe Medicine Society has been considered repugnant but harmless to Indian people. We believe they not only line their pockets but do great damage to us all. Anything you can do to them will not be enough." Clearly, opposition to

the misuse and appropriation of spiritual traditions is a transcendently unifying factor in Indian Country.

25. For an excellent overview of the German hobbyist tradition from its inception in the early 20th century, see Honour, Hugh, *The New Golden Land: European Images of the Indian from the Discovery to the Present Time* (New York: Pantheon Books, 1975).

26. Interestingly, at least some hobbyist replica objects—all of them produced by men who would otherwise view such things as "women's work"—are of such high quality that they have been exhibited in a number of ethnographic museums throughout Europe.

27. This seems to be something of a tradition on "The Continent." As examples, "William Augustus Bowles, an American Tory dressed up as an Indian, managed to pass in the upper crust of London's society in 1791 as 'commander-in-chief of the Creek and Cherokee' nations...A person calling himself Big Chief White Horse Eagle, whose somewhat fictional autobiography was written by a German admirer (Schmidt-Pauli, 1931), found it profitable to travel Europe in the 1920s and 1930s, adopting unsuspecting museum directors and chairmen of anthropology departments into his tribe...None of them, however, could match the most flamboyant fake Indian to visit Europe...This party, named Capo Cervo Bianco (Chief White Elk), arrived in Italy during the 1920s, claiming to be on his way to the League of Nations to represent the Iroquois of upstate New York. He was received by Mussolini and for a time managed to live richly out of his believers' purses [until he was] exposed as an Italo-American by the name of Edgardo Laplant"; see Feest, Christian F., "Europe's Indians," in *The Invented Indian: Cultural Fictions & Government Policies,* ed. James A. Clifton (New Brunswick, NJ: Transaction Publishers, 1990), pp. 322-23. The reference is to Schmidt-Pauli, Edgar von, *We Indians: The Passion of a Great Race by Big Chief White Horse Eagle* (London: 1931).

28. "Europe's Indians," *op. cit.,* p. 323.

29. "Freesoul" claims to be the "sacred pipe carrier" of something called the "Redtail Hawk Medicine Society...established by Natan Lupan and James Blue Wolf...in 1974...fulfill[ing a] Hopi prophecy that new clans and societies shall emerge as part of a larger revival and purification of the Red Road"; see Freesoul, John Redtail, *Breath of the Invisible: The Way of the Pipe* (Wheaton, IL: Theosophical Publishing House, 1986), pp. 104-5. For a heavy dose of the sort of metaphysical gibberish passed off as "traditional Cherokee religion" by "Ywahoo" and her Sunray Meditation Foundation, see her *Voices of Our Ancestors* (Boston, MA: Shambala Press, 1987). For analysis of "Eagle Man" McGaa's bilge, see the essay concerning his *Mother Earth Spirituality* (San Francisco: Harper Books, 1990) in this volume.

30. "Europe's Indians," *op. cit.,* p. 323. For a detailed exposure of Carlos Castaneda as a fraud, see De Mille, Richard, *Castaneda's Journey: The Power and the Allegory* (Santa Barbara, CA: Capra Press, 1976). In his recent essay "Of Wild Men and Warriors," however, Men's Movement practitioner Christopher X. Burant posits *Tales of Power* by "C. M. Castaneda" as one of his major sources (*Wingspan, op. cit.,* p. 176).

31. The Sun Dance is both culturally- and geographically-specific, and thus totally misplaced in the Black Forest among Germans. By extension, of course, this makes the series of Sun Dances conducted by Leonard Crow Dog in the Big Mountain

area of the Navajo Nation, in Arizona, over the past few years equally misplaced and sacrilegious. A culturally-specific ceremony is no more a "Pan-Indian" phenomenon than it is transcultural in any other sense.

32. Tipis were never designed to serve as mountain dwellings, which is why no American Indian people has ever used them for that purpose.

33. For a classic and somewhat earlier example of this sort of adoption of an outright "Indian identity" by a German, see the book by Gutohrlein, Adolf, who called himself "Adolf Hungry Wolf," *The Good Medicine* (New York: Warner Paperback Library, 1973). Also see the volume he coauthored with his Blackfeet wife, Beverly, *Shadows of the Buffalo* (New York: William Morrow and Co., 1983).

34. "Europe's Indians," *op. cit.*, pp. 313-32. For a broader view on this and related matters, see the selections from several analysts assembled by Feest as *Indians and Europe: An Interdisciplinary Collection of Essays* (Aachen: Rader Verlig, 1987).

35. The roots of this perspective extend deep within the European consciousness, having been first articulated in clear form at least as early as the 1703 publication of a book by the Baron de Lahontan (d'Arce, Louis-Armand Lom) entitled *New Voyages to North-America* (Chicago, IL: A.C. McClurg & Co., 1905).

36. "Europe's Indians," *op. cit.*, p. 327.

37. Concerning the fantasy dimension of hobbyist projections about "Indianness," Dutch analyst Ton Lemaire probably put it best (in Feest's translation): "On closer look, these 'Indians' turn out to be a population inhabiting the European mind, not the American landscape, a fictional assemblage fabricated over the past five centuries to serve specific cultural and emotional needs of its inventors"; *De Indiaan In Ons Bewustzijn: De Ontmoeting van de Oude met de Nieuwe Wereld* (Baarn: Ambo S.V., 1986).

38. Implications attending use of the term "Wildman" in the European context, from which Robert Bly borrowed the concept, sheds a certain light on the U.S. Men's Movement's deployment of the term. From there, the real attitudes of both groups regarding American Indians stand partially revealed. See Colin, Susi, "The Wild Man and the Indian in Early 16th Century Illustration," in *Indians and Europe, op. cit.*, pp. 5-36.

39. Absent the appropriative fetishism regarding American Indian spiritual life marking the Men's Movement, there is a remarkable similarity between its composition and sentiments, and those of another group of "Indian lovers" whose activities spawned disastrous consequences for native people during the 19th century. See Prucha, Francis Paul, *Americanizing the American Indian: Writings of the "Friends of the Indian," 1800-1900* (Lincoln: University of Nebraska Press, 1973).

40. There was some talk among German activists, while I was in Germany during May 1993, of disrupting Bly's planned tour in July of that year.

41. For analysis of the extent and implications of such activities on U.S. and Canadian reservation lands, see Churchill, Ward, *Struggle for the Land: Indigenous Resistance to Genocide, Ecocide and Expropriation in Contemporary North America* (Monroe, ME: Common Courage Press, 1992).

42. This represents an interesting inversion of the psychosis, in which the oppressed seeks to assume the identity of the oppressor, analyzed by Fanon, Frantz, in his *Black Skin, White Masks: The Experiences of a Black Man in a White World* (New

York: Grove Press, 1967). Perhaps an in-depth study of the Men's Movement should be correspondingly entitled *White Skin, Red Masks*.

43. In terms of content, this comparison of nazi mysticism to that of the Men's Movement is not superficial. Aside from preoccupations with a fantastic vision of "Indianness"—Hitler's favorite author was Karl May, writer of a lengthy series of potboilers on the topic—nazi "spirituality" focused upon the mythos of the Holy Grail; see Goodrick-Clark, Nicholas, *The Occult Roots of Nazism: Secret Aryan Cults and Their Influence on Nazi Ideology* (New York: New York University Press, 1992). Bly and the bunch have mixed up very much the same stew; see Cornett, Robert, "Still Questing for the Holy Grail," in *Wingspan, op. cit.*, pp. 137-42. Indeed, the movement pushes Jung, Emma, and Marie-Louise von Franz's neo-nazi tract on the topic, *The Grail Legend* (London: Hodder and Stoughton Publisher, 1960), as "essential reading." Another movement mainstay is Matthews, John, *The Grail Quest for the Eternal* (New York: Crossroads Publishing, 1981).

44. The Central Intelligence Agency, to name one governmental entity with an established track record of fabricating "social movements" that are anything but what they appear, has undertaken far more whacked out projects in the past; see Marks, John, *The Search for the Manchurian Candidate: The CIA and Mind Control* (New York: W.W. Norton & Co., 1979).

45. This is hardly a recent phenomenon, having been widely remarked in the literature by the mid-1960s. The semantic construction "dis-ease" accrues from British psychiatrist Laing, R. D., *The Politics of Experience* (New York: Ballantine Books, 1967).

46. Tapping into the malaise afflicting precisely this social strata was the impetus behind the so-called "New Left" during the 1960s. For alternative approaches to organizing strategies in this sector, both of which failed, see Sale, Kirkpatrick, *SDS* (New York: Random House Publishers, 1973), and Hoffman, Abbie, *The Woodstock Nation* (New York: Vintage Books, 1969).

47. Occasionally, unsuccessful attempts are made to effect a synthesis addressing the whole. See, for example, Albert, Michael, Leslie Cagan, Noam Chomsky, Robin Hahnel, Mel King, Lydia Sargent, and Holly Sklar, *Liberating Theory* (Boston, MA: South End Press, 1986).

48. For indigenous critique of marxism as being part and parcel of Eurocentrism, see Churchill, Ward, ed., *Marxism and Native Americans* (Boston, MA: South End Press, 1983).

49. Rudi Dutschke was a crucially important leader of the German SDS (*Socialistischer Deutscher Studentenbund*) during the first major wave of student confrontation with state authority during the late 1960s. On March 11, 1968, he was shot in the head at close range by a would-be neo-nazi assassin. The wounds severely and permanently impaired Dutschke's physical abilities, and eventually, in 1980, resulted in his death. A seminal New Left theorist on anti-authoritarianism, the great bulk of his writing has, unfortunately, yet to be published in English translation. For one of the few exceptions, see his essay "On Anti-Authoritarianism," in *The New Left Reader*, ed. Carl Oglesby (New York: Grove Press, 1969), pp. 243-53.

50. As concerns American SDS (Students for a Democratic Society) founder Tom Hayden, he is now a very wealthy and increasingly liberal member of the Califor-

nia state legislature. Former SDS and YIPPIE! leader Jerry Rubin is now a stock consultant and operator of a singles club in Manhattan. Eldridge Cleaver, former Minister of Information of the Black Panther Party and a founder of the Black Liberation Army, now earns his living trumpeting right-wing propaganda, as does David Horowitz, former editor of the radical *Ramparts* magazine. Rennie Davis, former SDS organizer and leader of the Student Mobilization to End the War in Vietnam, became an insurance salesperson and real estate speculator. Hayden, Rubin, and Davis, defendants in the "Chicago 8" (Seditious) Conspiracy Trial, were considered at the time to be the "benchmark" Euroamerican radicals of their generation. The German SDS has surpassed all this: its first president, Helmut Schmidt, actually went on to become president of West Germany during the 1980s.

51. For a partial analysis of this phenomenon in the United States, see Jacoby, Russell, *The Last Intellectuals: American Culture in the Age of Academe* (New York: Basic Books, 1987).

52. Eldridge Cleaver, for instance, first became a "born again" Christian, and then converted to Mormonism. In 1971, Rennie Davis became a groupie of the then-adolescent guru, Maharaji Ji.

53. The trip was made with Bob Robideau, long-time AIM activist, codefendant of Leonard Peltier, and former national director of the Peltier Defense Committee.

54. The same recording is played in a seemingly endless loop in the United States. If I had a dollar for every white student or activist who has approached me over the past decade bemoaning the fact that he or she has "no culture," I'd need no other income next year. If American Indians as a whole received such payment, we could probably just buy back North America and be done with it (just kidding, folks).

55. I personally date the advent of Europe from the coronation of Charlemagne as Holy Roman Emperor in A.D. 800, and the subsequent systematic subordination of indigenous Teutonic peoples to central authority. In his book, *The Birth of Europe* (Philadelphia/New York: Evans-Lippencott Publishers, 1966), Lopez, Robert, treats this as a "prelude," and dates the advent about two centuries later. In some ways, an even better case can be made that "Europe," in any true sense, did not emerge until the mid-to-late 15th century, with the final Ottoman conquest of Byzantium (Constantinople), defeat of the Moors in Iberia, and the first Columbian voyage. In any event, the conquest and colonization of the disparate populations of the subcontinent must be viewed as an integral and requisite dimension of Europe's coming into being.

56. For interesting insights on the 800-year—and counting—Irish national liberation struggle against English colonization, see Baróid, Ciarán de, *Ballymurphy and the Irish War* (London: Pluto Press, 1990). On the Euskadi, see Guëll, Pedro Ibarra, *La evolución estratégica de ETA* (Donstia, 1987).

57. Although I doubt this is a "definitive" attribution, I first heard the matter put this way by the late Creek spiritual leader Philip Deer in 1982.

58. As Merchant, Carolyn, observes in her book, *The Death of Nature: Women, Ecology and the Scientific Revolution* (San Francisco, CA: Harper Publisher, 1980), pp. 134, 140: "Based on a fully articulated doctrine emerging at the end of the fifteenth century in the antifeminist tract *Malleus Maleficarum* (1486), or Hammer of the witches, by the German Dominicans Heinrich Institor and Jacob Sprenger, and in

a series of art works by Hans Baldung Grien and Albert Dürer, witch trials for the next two hundred years threatened the lives of women all over Europe, especially in the lands of the Holy Roman Empire...The view of nature associated with witchcraft was personal animism. The world of the witches was antihierarchical and everywhere infused with spirits. Every natural object, every animal, every tree contained a spirit..." Sound familiar? These women who were being burned alive were thus murdered precisely because they served as primary repositories of the European subcontinent's indigenous codes of knowledge and corresponding "pagan" ritual.

59. The Cherokee artist Jimmie Durham tells a story of related interest. In 1986, after delivering an invited lecture at Oxford, he was asked whether he'd like to visit a group "who are actually indigenous to these islands." Somewhat skeptically, he accepted the invitation and was driven to a nearby village where the inhabitants continued to perform rites utilizing a variety of objects, including a pair of reindeer antlers of a species extinct since the last Ice Age (roughly 15,000 years ago). It turns out the people were of direct lineal Pictic descent and still practiced their traditional ceremonies, handed down their traditional stories, and so forth. The British government, getting wind of this, subsequently impounded the antlers as being "too important for purposes of science" to be left in possession of the owners. The dispossessed Picts were then provided a plastic replica of their sacred item, "so as not to disturb their religious life."

60. From Means, Russell, "Fighting Words on the Future of Mother Earth," *Mother Jones* (February 1981).

61. See Reich, Wilhelm, *The Mass Psychology of Fascism* (New York: Farrar, Strauss & Giroux Publishers, 1970). Also see Mosse, George L., *Nazi Culture: Intellectual, Cultural and Social Life in the Third Reich* (New York: Schocken Books, 1966).

62. An excellent early study of these dynamics may be found in Raushning, Hermann, *The Revolution of Nihilism: A Warning to the West* (New York: Longmans, Green Publishers, 1939). More recently, see Stern, Fritz, *The Politics of Cultural Despair: A Study in the Rise of Germanic Ideology* (Berkeley: University of California Press, 1961), and Poos, Robert A., *National Socialism and the Religion of Nature* (London/Sydney: Croom Helm Publishers, 1986).

63. During the two weeks I was in the newly reunified Germany, five refugees—all people of color—were murdered by neo-nazi firebombings. Another 40 were injured in the same manner. The German legislature repealed Article 16 of the Constitution, an important anti-nazi clause guaranteeing political asylum to all legitimate applicants, and opening the door to mass deportation of non-whites. The legislature also severely restricted women's rights to abortions, while continuing its moves toward repeal of a constitutional prohibition against German troops operating anywhere beyond the national borders. Meanwhile, the government locked the Roma and Cinti Gypsies out of the former Neuengemme concentration camp where their ancestors had been locked in, en route to the extermination center at Auschwitz. This was/is part of an official effort to drive all gypsies out of Germany (again); 120 million Deutschmarks have been authorized for payment to Poland to convince it to accept an unlimited number of Roma deportees, while another 30 million each have been earmarked as payments to Romania and Macedonia for the same purpose (yet another such deal is being cut with Slovakia).

Overtly nazi-oriented organizations are calling for the reacquisition of Silesia and parts of Prussia—eastern territories lost to Poland at the end of World War II—and are striking responsive cords in some quarters.

64. The autonomen, which may be the defining characteristic of the German opposition movement today, are proliferate and essentially anarchistic in their perspective.

65. Our entire group was rather stunned by the sheer number of 'squats'—usually abandoned commercial or apartment buildings in which a large number of people can live comfortably—in Germany. Some, like the Haffenstrasse in Hamburg and Keiffenstrasse in Düsseldorf—each comprised of an entire block or more of buildings—have been occupied for more than a decade, and serve not only as residences, but as bases for political organizing and countercultural activities.

66. See Burden, Hamilton T., *The Nuremberg Party Rallies, 1923-39* (New York: Praeger Publishers, 1967).

67. On Wewelsburg castle, see Höhne, Heinz, *The Order of the Death's Head: The Story of Hitler's SS* (New York: Howard-McCann Publishers, 1969), pp. 151-53. For photographs, see the section entitled "Dark Rites of the Mystic Order," in *The SS*, editors (Alexandra, VA: Time-Life Books, 1988), pp. 38-49. The scenes of Wewelsburg should be compared to those described in Wyatt, Isabel, *From Round Table to Grail Castle* (Sussex, UK: Lanthorn Press, 1979), a work highly recommended by leaders of the U.S. Men's Movement today.

68. For analysis of the settler state phenomenon, see Sakai, J., *Settlers: The Mythology of the White Proletariat* (Chicago, IL: Morningstar Press, 1983). Also see Weitzer, Ronald, *Transforming Settler States: Communal Conflict and Internal Security in Northern Ireland and Zimbabwe* (Berkeley: University of California Press, 1992).

69. This bizarre concept cuts across all political lines in settler state settings. In the United States, to take what is probably the most pronounced example, reactionary ideologues have always advanced the thesis that American society comprises a racial/cultural "melting pot" that has produced a wholly new people, even while enforcing racial codes indicating the exact opposite. Their opposition, on the other hand, has consistently offered much the same spurious argument. Radical Chicanos, for instance, habitually assert that they represent "la Raza," a culturally-mixed "new race" developed in Mexico and composed of "equal parts Spanish and Indio blood." Setting aside the question of what, exactly, a "Spaniard" might be in genetic terms—the main "stock" would seem to be composed of Visigoths, who are "Germanic"—the contention is at best absurd. During the three centuries following the conquest of Mexico, approximately 200,000 immigrants arrived there from Iberia. Of these, about one-third were Moors, and another one-third were Jewish "conversos" (both groups were being systematically "exported" from Spain at the time, as an expedient to ridding Iberia of "racial contaminants"). This leaves fewer than 70,000 actual "Spaniards," by whatever biological definition, to be genetically balanced against nearly 140,000 "other" immigrants, and some 30 million Indians native to Mexico. Moreover, the settlers brought with them an estimated 250,000 black chattel slaves, virtually all of whom eventually intermarried. Now, how all this computes to leaving a "half-Spanish, half-Indio" Chicano population as an aftermath is anybody's guess. Objectively, the genetic heritage of

la Raza is far more African—black and Moorish—than European, and at least as much Jewish (semitic) as Spanish.

70. The worst among them, of course, understands the nature of nazism and therefore embraces it, while the "mainstream"—including the bulk of the government and state bureaucracy—accepts it as being their "destiny."

71. For a classic articulation of this pervasive theme, see Elliott, J. H., "The Rediscovery of America," *New York Review of Books* (June 24, 1993): "Stannard takes the easy way out by turning his book into a high-pitched catalogue of European crimes, diminishing in the process the message he wants to convey. In particular, his emotive vocabulary seems self-defeating. 'Holocaust,' 'genocide,' even 'racism,' carry with them powerful contemporary freight…'Genocide,' as used of the Nazi treatment of the Jews, implies not only mass extermination, but a clear intention on the part of a higher authority [and] it debases the word to write, as Stannard writes, of 'the genocidal encomienda system,' or to apply it to the extinction of a horrifyingly large proportion of the indigenous population through the spread of European diseases." Elliott is critiquing David E. Stannard's superb *American Holocaust: Columbus and the Conquest of the New World* (London/New York: Oxford University Press, 1992), in which official intentionality—including intentionality with regard to inculcation of disease as a means of extermination—is amply demonstrated.

72. Even Parella, Frank, whose graduate thesis *Lebensraum and Manifest Destiny: A Comparative Study in the Justification of Expansion* (Washington, D.C.: Georgetown University, 1950) was seminal in opening up such comparisons, ultimately resorted to feeble "philosophical distinctions" in order to separate the two processes in his concluding section.

73. James Axtell, presentation at the American Historical Association Annual Conference, Washington, D.C., December 1992. For full elaboration of such inane apologia, see this "preeminent American historian's" *Beyond 1492: Encounters in Colonial America* (London/New York: Oxford University Press, 1992).

74. See, for example, Robert Roybal's observation in his *1492 and All That: Political Manipulations of History* (Washington, D.C.: Ethics and Public Policy Center, 1992): "Whatever evils the Spanish introduced [to the "New World" of the Aztecs]—and they were many and varied—they at least cracked the age-old shell of a culture admirable in many ways but pervaded by repugnant atrocities and petrification." Leaving aside the matter of Aztec "atrocities"—which mostly add up to time-honored but dubious Euroamerican mythology—the idea of applying terms like "age-old" or "petrified" to this culture, barely 500 years old at the time of the Spanish conquest, speaks for itself. Roybal hadn't a clue what he was prattling on about.

75. For a good overview of traditional American Indian concepts and modes of warfare, see Holm, Tom, "Patriots and Pawns: State Use of American Indians in the Military and the Process of Nativization in the United States," in *The State of Native America, op. cit.*, pp. 345-70.

76. Revolutionary Communist Party USA, "Searching for the Second Harvest," in *Marxism and Native Americans, op. cit.*, pp. 35-58. It is illuminating to note that the RCP, which professes to be totally at odds with the perspectives held by the Euroamerican status quo, lifted its assertion that ancient Indians consumed a "second harvest" of their own excrement verbatim from a hypothesis recently

developed by a pair of the most "bourgeois" anthropologists imaginable, as summarized in that "citadel of establishment propaganda," the *New York Times* (August 12, 1980). A better illustration of the confluence of interest and outlook regarding native people in Euroamerica, between what the RCP habitually (and accurately) describes as "fascism," and the party itself, would be difficult to find.

77. In reality, about two-thirds of all vegetal foodstuffs commonly consumed by all of humanity today were under cultivation in the Americas—and nowhere else in the world—at the time the European invasion begin. Indians were thus the consumate farmers on the planet in 1492. Plainly, then, we taught Europe the art of diversified agriculture, not the other way around (as Eurocentric mythology insists). For further information, see Weatherford, Jack, *Indian Givers: How the Indians of the Americas Transformed the World* (New York: Crown Publishers, 1988).

78. For example: Weurthner, George, "An Ecological View of the Indian," *Earth First!*, vol. 7, no. 7 (August 1987). This rather idiotic argument is closely related to that of the quasi-official Smithsonian Institution, adopted en toto by the RCP, that native people traditionally engaged in such environmentally devastating practices as "jumpkilling" masses of bison—that is to say, driving entire herds off cliffs—in order to make use of a single animal ("Searching for the Second Harvest," *op. cit.*, p. 45).

79. In the magazine *Anarchy* (no. 37 [Summer 1993]: p. 74), for instance, editor Jason McQuinn patronizingly dismisses the idea that certain extreme anarchist arguments against social hierarchy are "anti-natural" (since nature itself functions in terms of multitudinous interactive hierarchies) as being "authoritarian" by a person "not overly concerned with freedom." In the process, he neatly (if unwittingly) replicates Eurocentrism's fundamental flaw, separating human—"*social* and *institutional*" (his emphasis)—undertakings from nature altogether. Yup. White boys certainly do have all the answers…to everything.

80. For a solid rejoinder to such "worries" on the part of Euroamerican feminists, see Stilman, Janet, ed., *Enough is Enough: Aboriginal Women Speak Out* (Toronto: Women's Press, 1987).

81. For a foremost articulation of the absurd notion that all or even most Indians were traditionally homosexual or at least bisexual—which has made its author a sudden celebrity among white radical feminists and recipient of the proceeds deriving from having a mini-bestseller on her hands as a result—see Allen, Paula Gunn, *The Sacred Hoop: Recovering the Feminine in Native American Traditions* (Boston, MA: Beacon Press, 1986), p. 256: "[L]esbianism and homosexuality were probably commonplace. Indeed, same-sex relationships may have been the norm for primary pair bonding…the primary personal unit tended to include members of one's own sex rather than members of the opposite sex." For a counterpart male proclamation, see Williams, Walter, *The Spirit and the Flesh: Sexual Diversity in American Indian Culture* (Boston, MA: Beacon Press, 1986). Both writers waltz right by the fact that if homosexuals were considered special, and therefore sacred, in traditional native societies—a matter upon which they each remark accurately and approvingly—then homosexuality could not by definition have been "commonplace" since that is a status diametrically opposed to that of being "special." Both Allen and Walters are simply playing to the fantasies of gay rights activists, using Indians as props in the customary manner of Euroamerica.

82. The language is taken from a note sent to me on June 7, 1993, by an airhead calling himself "Sky" Hiatt. It was enclosed along with a copy of Singer, Peter, *Animal Liberation* (New York: *New York Review of Books*, 1975). Actually, the Euroamerican "animal liberation" movement is no joking matter to native people, as white activists—most of whom have never lifted a finger in defense of indigenous rights of any sort, and some of whom have openly opposed them—have come close to destroying what remains of traditional Inuit and Indian subsistence economies in Alaska and Canada; see Mander, Jerry, *In the Absence of the Sacred: The Failure of Technology & the Survival of the Indian Nations* (San Francisco, CA: Sierra Club Books, 1991), pp. 287, 296, 387.

83. This premise is simply a cultural paraphrase of the standard psychotherapeutic tenet that a pathology cannot begin to be cured of it until s/he first genuinely acknowledges that he/she is afflicted with it.

84. This is, of course, already happening. Witness the observation of Lance Morrow in the August 19, 1991 issue of *Time* magazine, for example: "Bly may not be alive to certain absurdities in the men's movement…a silly, self-conscious attempt at manly authenticity, almost a satire of the hairy-chested…As a spiritual showman (shaman), Bly seeks to produce certain effects. He is good at them. He [therefore] could not begin to see the men's movement, and his place within it, as a depthless happening in the goofy circus of America."

85. Quoted in Armstrong, Virginia Irving, ed., *I Have Spoken: American History Through the Voices of the Indians* (Chicago, IL: The Swallow Press, 1971), p. 79.

FANTASIES OF THE MASTER RACE
Categories of Stereotyping American Indians in Film

Now those movie Indians wearing all those feathers can't come out as human beings. They're not expected to come out as human beings because I think the American people do not regard them as wholly human. We must remember that many, many American children believe that feathers grow out of Indian heads.

—Stephan Feraca, motion picture director, 1964

The handling of American Indians and American Indian subject matter within the context of commercial U.S. cinema is objectively racist on all levels, an observation that extends to television as well as those works produced for showing behind the box office. In this, it is linked closely to literature of both the fictional and ostensibly nonfictional varieties, upon which many if not most movie scripts are at least loosely based. In a very real sense, it is fair to observe that all modes of projecting concepts and images of the Indian before the contemporary U.S. public fit the same mold, and do so for the same fundamental "real world" reasons. In this paper, we will attempt to come to grips with both the method and the motivation for this, albeit within a given medium and by way of a somewhat restricted range of the tactics employed. The medium selected for this purpose is commercial film, the technique examined that of stereotypic projection. The matter divides itself somewhat automatically into three major categories of emphasis. These may be elucidated as follows.

The American Indian as a Creature of Another Time

We are all aware of the standard motion picture technique of portraying the Native American with galloping pony and flowing headdress. We have seen the tipi and the buffalo hunt, the attack on the wagon train and the ambush of the stagecoach until they are scenes so totally ingrained in the American consciousness as to be synonymous with the very concept of the American Indian (to non-Indian minds at any rate and, unfortunately, to many "Indian" minds as well). It is not the technical defects of the scenes depicted here—although often they are many—which present the basic problem. Rather, it is a salient fact that the historical era involved with the depiction spans a period scarcely exceeding 50 years' duration. Hence, the Indian has been restricted in the public mind, not only in terms of the people portrayed (the Plains nations), but also in terms of the time of their collective existence (roughly 1825-1880).

The essential idea of Native America instilled cinematically is that of a quite uniform aggregation of peoples (in dress, custom, and actions) who flourished with the arrival of whites upon their land and then vanished somewhat mysteriously, along with the bison and the open prairie. There is no before to this story, and there is no after. Such is the content of *They Died With Their Boots On, Boots and Saddles, Cheyenne Autumn, Tonka Wakan* and *Little Big Man,* to list but five examples from among hundreds. Of course, commercial film has—through a vastly reduced number of titles—slightly expanded the scope of the stereotype at hand. The existence of the peoples of the Northeast receive recognition in such epics as *Drums Along the Mohawk* and *The Deerslayer.* The peoples of the Southwest have been included to some extent in scattered fare such as *Broken Arrow, Fort Apache,* and *Tell'em Willie Boy Is Here.* The Southeastern nations even claim passing attention in efforts such as the Walt Disney *Davy Crockett* series and biographical features about the lives of such Euroamerican heroes as Andrew Jackson and Sam Houston.

The latter deviations from the Plains stereotype—which has assumed proportions of a valid archetype in the public consciousness—drive the timeline back some 75 years at most. A century-and-a-quarter selected for depiction is hardly less a focus on a particular time than is a 50-year span. Further, it should be noted that, costuming aside, literally all the geographical/cultural groups presented are portrayed in exactly the same manner, a matter we will consider in the following two sections. The point of the historical confines involved in this category is, however, that indigenous people are defined exclusively in terms of certain (conflict and demise) interactions with Euroamericans. There is no cinematic recognition whatsoever of a white-free and autonomous native past. Similarly, no attention is paid at all to the myriad indigenous nations not heavily and dramatically involved in the final period of Anglo-Indian warfare. U.S. audiences know no Aztec, Inca, or Anasazi parallel to *Cleopatra*, *The Robe*, or *Ben Hur*. Small wonder the public views the native as some briefly extant, mythic, and usually hostile apparition. As a consequence, the public perception of the historical existence of Native Americans is of beings who spent their time serving as little other than figurative pop-up targets for non-Indian guns.

Nor is there any abundance of films attempting to deal with contemporary Indian realities. In effect, the native ceased to exist at the onset of the reservation period of the Plains peoples. This is evidenced by the fact that the author could find only two films listed—biographies of Jim Thorpe and Ira Hayes, both starring Burt Lancaster—released prior to 1980 which featured the indigenous experience after 1880 in any meaningful way at all. As to current events, well... There's always the *Billy Jack* series: *Born Losers*, *Billy Jack*, *The Trial of Billy Jack* and *Billy Jack Goes to Washington* (the latter, thankfully, was shelved before release), utilizing the vehicle of an ex-Special Forces mixed-blood karate expert to exploit the grisly mystique of *Shaft* and *Superfly*-type superheroes (or anti-heroes, if you prefer). The result is a predictably shallow and idiotic parallel to the *Batman* television series.

The single (lackluster) attempt by Hollywood to equal for American Indians what *Sounder* and *Lady Sings the Blues* have achieved for African Americans was rapidly withdrawn from circulation as an "embarrassment." So steeped in celluloid myopia are filmdom's critics—so full, that is, of their own self-perpetuating stereotyping—that they panned *Journey Through Rosebud*'s characters as being "wooden Indians." This, despite these characterizations being ranked by most Native Americans viewing them as being the most accurate and convincing ever to come from the studios. Possibly, other films of the stature of *Journey Through Rosebud* have been made but not released, a matter which leaves the impact of the timewarp involving American Indians as great as if they'd never been done. A result is that the U.S. mainstream population finds itself under no particular moral or psychic obligation to confront the fact of Native America, as either an historical or topical reality.

Native Cultures Defined by Eurocentric Values

An Anishinabe (Chippewa) friend of mine once visited the Field Museum in Chicago. While examining the exhibits of American Indian artifacts located there, she came across an object which she immediately recognized as being her grandmother's root digger, an item the museum's anthropological "experts" had identified and labeled as a "Winnebago hide scraper." She called the mistake to the attention of the departmental director and was told that she, not the museum, was wrong. "If you knew anything at all about your heritage," he informed her, "you'd know that tool is a hide scraper." My friend, helpless to correct this obvious (to her) misinformation, went away. "They never listen to the people who really know these things," she said later. "And so they never understand what they think they know."

The above sad but true story is not unusual. It serves to illustrate a pattern in Euroamerican dealings with indigenous people which extends vastly beyond the mere identification of objects. In terms of commercial cinema and acting, the problem may be considered on the basis of "context" and "motivation." Put most simply, the question of context is one in which specific acts of certain American Indians are portrayed in scenes devoid of all cultural grounding and explanation. From whence is comprehension of the real nature of these acts to come? The viewing audience is composed overwhelmingly of non-Indians who obviously hold no automatic insight into native cultures and values, yet somehow they must affix meaning to the actions presented on the screen before them. Thus, the real acts of indigenous people—even when depicted more or less accurately—often appear irrational, cruel, unintelligent, or silly when displayed in film. Scenes such as those presented in the John Ford "classic," *Stagecoach*, are fine examples of this stereotyping approach.

Motivation is a more sophisticated, and consequently more dangerous, consideration. Here, a cultural context of sorts *is* provided, at least to some degree, but it is a context comprised exclusively of ideas, values, emotions, and other meanings assigned by Euroamerica to the native cultures portrayed. Insofar as indigenous American and Euro-derived worldviews are radically and demonstrably different in almost every way, such a projection can only serve to dramatically misrepresent the native cultures involved and, at best, render them nonsensical. Such misrepresentation serves two major stereotyping functions:

- Since the complex of dominant and comparatively monolithic cultural values and beliefs of Eurocentrism presently held by the bulk of the U.S. population are utilized to provide motivation for virtually all American Indians portrayed in commercial film, all native values and beliefs appear to be lumped together into a single homogeneous and consistent whole, regardless of actual variances and distinctions (see the next section for discussion of the result of this aspect).

- Given that the cultural values and beliefs extended as the contextual basis for motivation are misrepresentative of the actual cultural context of Native America—and are thus totally out of alignment with the actions portrayed—the behavior of American Indians is often made to appear more uniformly vicious, crude, primitive, and unintelligent than in cases where context and motivation are dispensed with altogether.

A primary device used by Hollywood to attach Euro values to native acts has been to script a white character to literally narrate the story-line. Films such as *Cheyenne Autumn*, *A Man Called Horse* (and its sequels), *Soldier Blue*, and *Little Big Man* serve to exemplify the point. Each purports to provide an "accurate and sympathetic treatment of the American Indian" (of yesteryear) while utterly crushing native identity under the heel of Euroamerican interpretation. To date, all claims to the contrary notwithstanding, there has not been an attempt at putting out a commercial film which deals with native reality through native eyes.

"Seen One Indian, Seen 'Em All"

This third category is, in some ways, a synthesis of the preceding two. It has, however, assumed an identity of its own which extends far beyond the scope of the others. Within this area lies the implied assumption that distinctions between cultural groupings of indigenous people are either nonexistent (ignorance) or irrelevant (arrogance). Given this attitude regarding the portrayal of Indians in film, it is inevitable that the native be reduced from reality to a strange amalgamation of dress, speech, custom, and belief. All vestiges of truth—and thereby of intercultural understanding—give way here before the onslaught of movieland's mythic creation.

The film *A Man Called Horse* may serve as the primary tool of explanation. This droll adventure, promoted as "the most authentic description of North American Indian life ever filmed," provides its audience with the depiction of a people whose language is Lakota, whose hairstyles range from Assiniboin through Nez Percé to Comanche, whose tipi design is Crow, and whose Sun Dance ceremony and the lodge in which it is held are both typically Mandan. They are referred to throughout the film as "Sioux," but to which group do they supposedly belong? Secungu (Brûlé)? Oglala? Santee? Sisseton? Yanktonai? Minneconjou? Hunkpapa? Those generically—and rather pejoratively—called "Sioux" were/are of three major geographic/cultural divisions: the Dakotas of the Minnesota woodlands, the Nakotas of the prairie region east of the Missouri River, and the Lakotas of the high plains proper. These groups were/are quite distinct from one another, and the distinctions *do* make a difference in terms of accuracy and "authenticity."

The source material utilized to create the cinematic imagery involved in *A Man Called Horse* was the large number of portraits of American Indians executed by George Catlin during the first half of the 19th century and now housed in the Smithsonian Institution. However, while Catlin was meticulous in attributing tribal and even band affiliations to the subjects of his paintings, the filmmakers were not. The result is a massive misrepresentation of the whole variety of real peoples, aspects of whose material cultures are incorporated, gratuitously, into that of the hybrid "Indians" who inhabit the movie. What occurs on screen is roughly parallel to a director having a Catholic priest wear a Rabbi's headgear and Protestant cleric's garb while conducting high mass before a Satanist pentagon, not to make some abstract theological/philosophical point, but simply because each of these disparate physical manifestations of spiritual culture is "visually interesting in its own right."

Nor does the dismemberment of reality in this "most realistic of westerns" end with visual catastrophe. The door to cultural reduction is merely opened by such devices. Both the rationale and spiritual ramifications of the Sun Dance are voided by the film's Eurocentric explanation of its form and function. Thus is the central and most profoundly sacred of all ceremonies for the Lakota converted into a macho exercise in "self-mutilation," a "primitive initiation rite" showing nothing so much as that the Indian male could "take it." It follows that all the film's Anglo lead, played by Richard Harris, must do is prove that he is "as tough as the Sioux" by eagerly seeking out his fair share of pain during a Sun Dance. He does this in order to be accepted as "one of them." Just bloody up your chest, and no further questions will be asked. How quaint.

This, of course, paves the way for the Harris character to become leader of the group. The Sioux, once they have been reduced to little more than a gaggle of prideful masochists, can be readily shown as not being possessed of the highest of collective intellects (surprise, surprise). Hence, it becomes necessary for the Anglo captive to save his savage captors from an even more ferocious group of primitives coming over the hill. He manages this somewhat spectacular feat by instructing his aboriginal colleagues in the finer points of using the long bow, a weapon in uninterrupted use by the people in question for several hundred generations, and out of use by the English for about 200 years at the time the events in the film supposedly occur. But no matter, the trivial details. The presumed inherent superiority of Eurocentric minds has once again been demonstrated for all the world to witness. All that was *necessary* to accomplish this was to replace a *bona fide* native culture with something else.

The technique deployed in *A Man Called Horse* is by no means novel or unique. Even the highly touted (in terms of making Indians "the good guys") *Billy Jack* series could never lock in any specific people it sought to portray. The Indians depicted remain a weird confluence of Navajos and various Pueblos, occasionally practicing what appear to be bastardizations of Cheyenne and Kiowa ceremonies. All the better to trot them around as props serving as proponents of every non-Indian fad from the benefits of macrobiotic cookery to those of *Haikido* karate.

It requires elementary logic to realize that when the cultural identity of a people is symbolically demolished, the achievements and very humanity of that people must also be disregarded. The people, as such, disappear, usually to the benefit—both material and psychic—of those performing the symbolic demolition. There are accurate and appropriate terms by which the phenomena at issue may be described. Dehumanization, obliteration or appropriation of identity, political subordination, and material colonization are all elements of a common process of imperialism. The meaning of Hollywood's stereotyping of American Indians can be truly apprehended only against this backdrop.

Conclusion

It should be relatively easy at this point to identify film stereotyping of American Indians as an accurate reflection of the actual conduct of the Euroamerican population *vis à vis* Native America in both historical and topical senses. North American indigenous peoples have been reduced in terms of cultural identity within the popular consciousness—through a combination of movie treatments, television programming and distortive literature—to a point where the general public perceives them as extinct for all practical intents and purposes. Given that they no longer exist, that which *was* theirs—whether that be land and the resources on and beneath it, or their heritage—can *now* be said, without pangs of guilt, to belong to those who displaced and ultimately supplanted them. Such is one function of cinematic stereotyping within North America's advanced colonial system.

Another is to quell potential remorse among the population at large with regard to how it was that things ever reached the present state. Genocide is, after all, an extremely ugly word. Far better that the contemporary mainstream believe their antecedents destroyed mindless and intrinsically warlike savages, devoid of true culture and humanity, rather than that they systematically exterminated whole societies of highly intelligent and accomplished human beings desiring nothing so much as to be left in peace. Far better it be accepted by their descendants that the Euroamerican invader engaged in slaughter only in self-defense, when confronted with hordes of irrationally bloodthirsty heathen beasts, rather than coldly and calculatedly committing mass murder, planning step by step the eradication of the newest-born infants. "Nits make lice," to quote U.S. Colonel John M. Chivington.

Filmdom's handling of "history" in this regard is, with only a few marginal exceptions, nothing more or less than an elaborate denial of an essentially uniform European/Euroamerican criminality on this continent over the past 350 years. Implicitly then, it is an unbridled justification and glorification of the conquest and subordination of Native America. As such, it is a vitally necessary ingredient in the maintenance and perfection of the Euro-empire which has been constructed here since the Pilgrims landed in 1620. Hollywood's performance on this score has been, overall, what one might have legitimately expected to see from the heirs to Leni Riefenstahl, had the Third Reich won its War in the East during the 1940s.

As the Oneida comedian Charlie Hill has observed, the portrayal of Indians in the cinema has been such that it has made the playing of "Cowboys and Indians" a favorite American childhood game. The object of the "sport" is for the "cowboys" to "kill" all the "Indians," just like in the movies (a bitter irony associated with this is that Indian as well as non-Indian children heatedly demand to be identified as cowboys, a not unnatural outcome under the circumstances, but one which speaks volumes to the damage done to the American Indian self-concept by tinsel town propaganda). The meaning of this, as Hill notes, can best be appreciated if one were to imagine that the children were instead engaging in a game called "Nazis and Jews."

That movieland's image of the Indian is completely false—and often shoddily so—is entirely to the point. Only a completely false creation could be used to explain in "positive terms" what has actually happened here in centuries past. Only a literal blocking of modern realities can be used to rationalize present circumstances. Only a concerted effort to debunk Hollywood's mythology can hope to alter the situation for the better. While it's true that the immortal words of

General Phil Sheridan—"The only good Indian is a dead Indian"—have continued to enjoy a certain appeal with the American body politic, and equally true that dead Indians are hardly in a position to call the liars to task, there are a few of us left out here who might just be up to the task.

LAWRENCE OF SOUTH DAKOTA

Dances With Wolves and the Maintenance of the American Empire

Well, here we go again. The ol' silver screen is alight once more with images of Indians swirling through the murky mists of time, replete with all the paint, ponies, and feathers demanded by the box office. True, we are not confronted in this instance with the likes of Chuck Conners playing *Geronimo*, Victor Mature standing in as *Chief Crazy Horse*, or Jeff Chandler cast in the role of *Broken Arrow*'s Cochise. Nor are we beset by the sort of wanton anti-Indianism which runs so rampant in John Ford's *Stagecoach*, *Fort Apache*, *She Wore a Yellow Ribbon,* and *Sergeant Rutledge.* Even the sort of "rebel without a cause" trivialization of Indian anger offered by Robert Blake in *Tell 'em Willie Boy Was Here*—or Lou Diamond Philips in *Young Guns* and *Young Guns II*—is not at hand. Yet, in some ways the latest "Indian movie," a cinematic extravaganza packaged under the title *Dances With Wolves* is just as bad.

This statement has nothing to do with the entirely predictable complaints raised by reviewers in the *New York Times*, *Washington Post,* and similar bastions of the status quo. Self-evidently, the movie's flaws do not—as such reviewers claim—rest in a "negative handling" of whites or "over-sentimentalizing" of Indians. Rather, although he tries harder than most, producer-director-star Kevin Costner holds closely to certain sympathetic stereotypes of Euroamerican behavior on the "frontier," at least insofar as he never quite explains how completely, systematically, and persistently the invaders violated every conceivable standard of human decency in the process of conquest. As to those media pundits who have sought to "debunk" the film's positive portrayal of native people, they may be seen quite simply as liars, deliberately and often wildly inaccurate on virtually every point they've raised. Theirs is the task of (re)asserting the reactionary core of racist mythology so important to conventional justifications for America's "winning of the West."

Contrary to the carping of such paleocritics, Costner did attain several noteworthy breakthroughs in his production. For instance, he invariably cast Indians to fill his script's Indian roles, a Hollywood first. And, to an extent surpassing anything else ever emerging from tinsel town—including the celebrated roles of Chief Dan George in *Little Big Man* and Will Sampson in *One Flew Over the Cuckoo's Nest*—these Indians were allowed to serve as more than mere props. Throughout the movie, they were called upon to demonstrate motive and emotion, thereby assuming the dimensions of real human beings. Further, the film is technically and geographically accurate, factors superbly captured in the cinematography of Photographic Director Dean Semler and his crew.

But let's not overstate the case. Costner's talents as a filmmaker have been remarked upon, *ad nauseam*, not only by the motion picture academy during the orgy of Oscars recently bestowed upon him and his colleagues, but by revenues grossed at the nation's theaters and by the misguided and fawning sort of gratitude expressed by some Indians at their cultures' having finally been cinematically accorded a semblance of the respect to which they have been entitled all along. The vaunted achievements of *Dances With Wolves* in this regard should, by rights, be commonplace. That they are not says all that needs saying in this regard.

In any event, the issue is not the manner in which the film's native characters and cultures are presented. The problems lie elsewhere, at the level of the context in which they are embedded. Stripped of its pretty pictures and progressive flourishes in directions like affirmative action hiring, *Dances With Wolves* is by no means a movie about Indians. Instead, it is at base an elaboration of movieland's Great White Hunter theme, albeit one with a decidedly different ("nicer" and, therefore, "better") personality than the usual example of the genre, and much more elegantly done. Above all, it follows the formula established by *Lawrence of Arabia*: Arabs and Arab culture handled in a superficially respectful manner, and framed by some of the most gorgeous landscape photography imaginable. So much the

better for sophisticated propagandists to render "realistic" the undeniably heroic stature of Lt. Lawrence, the film's central—and ultimately most Eurocentric—character.

In order to understand the implications of this structural linkage
between the two movies, it is important to remember that despite the
hoopla attending *Lawrence*'s calculated gestures to the Bedouins, the film
proved to be of absolutely no benefit to the peoples of the Middle East
(just ask the Palestinians and Lebanese). To the contrary, its major impact
was to put a "tragic" but far more humane face upon the nature of
Britain's imperial pretensions in the region, making colonization of the
Arabs seem more acceptable—or at least more inevitable—than might
otherwise have been the case. So too do we encounter this contrived
sense of sad inevitability in the closing scenes of *Dances With Wolves*, as
Lt. Dunbar and the female "captive" he has "recovered" ride off into the
proverbial sunset, leaving their Lakota "friends" to be slaughtered by
and subordinated to the United States. Fate closes upon Indian and Arab
alike, despite the best efforts of well-intentioned white men like the two
good lieutenants ("We're not *all* bad, y'know").

It's all in the past, so the story goes; regrettable, obviously, but
comfortably out of reach. Nothing to be done about it, really, at least
at this point. Best that everyone—Euroamericans, at any rate—pay a
bit of appropriately maudlin homage to "our heritage," feel better
about themselves for possessing such lofty sentiments, and get on
with business as usual. Meanwhile, native people are forced to live,
right now, today, in abject squalor under the heel of what is arguably
history's most seamlessly perfected system of internal colonization,
out of sight, out of mind, their rights and resources relentlessly consumed by the dominant society. That is, after all, the very business as
usual that a film like *Dances With Wolves* helps to perpetuate, by
diverting attention to its sensitive reinterpretations of yesteryear. So
much for Costner's loudly proclaimed desire to "help."

If Kevin Costner or anyone else in Hollywood held an honest
inclination to make a movie which would alter public perceptions of
Native America in some meaningful way, it would, first and foremost,
be set in the present day, not the mid-19th century. It would feature,
front and center, the real struggles of living native people to liberate

themselves from the oppression which has beset them in the contemporary era, not the adventures of some fictional non-Indian out to save the savage. It would engage directly with concrete issues like expropriation of water rights and minerals, involuntary sterilization, and FBI repression of Indian activists. It would not be made as another *Pow Wow Highway*-style entertainment venture, or one more trite excursion into spiritual philosophy and the martial arts *à la* the "Silly Jack" movies. Cinema focusing on sociopolitical and economic realities were developed with regard to Latin America in *Salvador*, *El Norte*, and *Under Fire*. Such efforts around Native American realities are woefully long overdue.

On second thought, maybe it wouldn't be such a good idea. Hollywood's record on Indian topics is such that, if it were to attempt to produce a script on, say, the events on Pine Ridge during the mid-'70s, it would probably end up being some twisted plot featuring an Indian FBI agent (undoubtedly a cross between Mike Hammer and Tonto) who jumps in to save his backwards reservation brethren from the evil plots of corrupt tribal officials working with sinister corporate executives, and maybe even a few of his own Bureau superiors. They'd probably cast a nice blond guy like Val Kilmer as the agent-hero, have it directed by someone like Michael Apted, and call it something really Indian-sounding, like *Thunderheart*. It stands to reason, after all: now that we're burdened with the legacy of *Lawrence of South Dakota*, we can all look forward to what will amount to *South Dakota Burning*. Next thing you know, they'll want to do a remake of *Last of the Mohicans*. Yup, the more things "change," the more they stay the same.

AND THEY DID IT LIKE DOGS IN THE DIRT...
An Indigenist Analysis of
Black Robe

As we learned from movies like *A Man Called Horse,* the more "accurate" and "authentic" a film is said to be, the more extravagant it is likely to be in at least some aspects of its misrepresentation of Indians...the more "even-handed" or even "sympathetic" a movie is supposed to be in its portrayal of Indians, the more demeaning it's likely to be in the end...the more "sophisticated" the treatment of Indians, the more dangerous it's likely to be.

—Vine Deloria, Jr., 1978

Perhaps the only honest way to begin a review of Bruce Beresford's new film, *Black Robe* (Alliance Communications, 1991), is to acknowledge that, as cinema, it is a truly magnificent achievement. Beginning with Brian Moore's adaptation of his own 1985 novel of the same title,[1] the Australian director of such earlier efforts as *Breaker Morant, The Fringe Dwellers, Driving Miss Daisy,* and *Mr. Johnson,* has forged yet another work of obvious beauty and artistic integrity, capturing a certain sense of his subject matter in ways which are not so much atmospheric as environmental in their nuance and intensity. In arriving at such an accomplishment, he has been assisted quite ably by cinematographer Peter James, whose camerawork in this instance genuinely earns the overworked accolade of being brilliant.[2] Tim Wellburn also excelled, attaining a nearly perfect editing balance of pace and continuity, carrying the viewer along through the movie's spare 100 minutes even while instilling the illusion that things are stretching out, incorporating a scope and dimension which, upon reflection, one finds to have been entirely absent.[3] The score, a superbly understated ensemble created by Georges Delerue, works with subtle efficiency to bind the whole package together.

Set in 1634 in that portion of Canada then known as "New France" (now Quebec), *Black Robe* purports to utilize the context of the period's Jesuit missionarism as a lens through which to explore the complexities of Indian/White interactions during the formative phase of European colonialism in North America. The film is expressly intended to convey a bedrock impression that what is depicted therein is "the way it *really* was," and no pain has been spared to obtain this result. As the producers put it, "Finding locations that looked remote enough for the film, as well as a river that was wide enough to double as the St. Lawrence, with no buildings or power lines in sight, was the job of Location Manager François Sylvester. [He] spent months flying up and down Quebec rivers until he found the perfect site on the banks of the Saguenay and Lac St. Jean."[4] Thereafter, cast and crew spent eleven weeks under rugged conditions in the Canadian north pursuing the desired effect.

> Rushes show the cast paddling canoes in icy water (Beresford fell in twice), dragging canoes on slippery, icy snow along the riverbanks, stumbling through the forest, trudging through the brush. This is neither glamorous or comfortable. The landscape...is a mix of wide valleys and mountains; ice has choked some of the rivers into narrow channels, and the light is steely grey...The look of the film [moves] from the amber of autumn to the grey/green of winter, with cold blues, and gradually moving into the contrast of black and white as the snow thickens. As Peter James sees it, the trees and rivers are as much characters as the people; they look brighter or bleaker, and they contribute to the mood.[5]

Similarly, Herbert Pinter's production design is authentic to the minutest detail: "Some people said to me, 'It's the 17th Century, so who's going to remember?', but that's not how I work. I'd say 99 per cent of what you see is accurate. We really did a lot of research. It's actually easier this way, because if you do your homework, you avoid silly mistakes."[6]

Pinter fashioned rectangular shovels out of birch bark, used shoulder bones of a moose for another digging implement, bound stone axes with spruce roots, knitted ropes of fibre, and used cedar bark (obtained free from a merchant in Vancouver, but costing $37,000 in transport) to build the outer walls of huts...In the Huron village scene at the end of the film, Pinter created a strikingly authentic little chapel, lit only by candles waxed onto stones that are wedged into the fork of stag antlers.[7]

The many extras used to represent the indigenous peoples involved are actually Indians, many of them Crees from villages located in the general area of the shoot. Native languages are spoken throughout the movie, and the corresponding subtitles deployed do no particular damage to the content of the dialogue. The construction of both the Mohawk and Huron villages used as sets—each of which took about six weeks to complete—is accurate right down to the cloying smoke persistently drifting about the interior of buildings, a standard means by which Indians traditionally repelled insects. The inside of a Mohawk longhouse is adorned with scores of real rabbit and goose carcasses strung from racks, many of them slowly dripping blood which begins to coagulate as a scene wears on.

The entire stew was completed with the deployment of an astutely selected combination of veteran and first-time actors. They are headed by Lothaire Bluteau, noted for his lead role in *Jesus of Montréal*, who plays Father LaForge, *Black Robe*'s fictionalized protagonist. Bluteau also appears to have served as something of a "team captain" among the cast. As critic Andrew Urban observed after visiting the location of the work-in-progress:

> Bluteau is...the most dedicated actor I have ever seen on a set. Whether he is called or not, he is there, absorbing, watching—and discussing details with Beresford, or James. He wants to know every frame, and has a possessive view of the film...He wants to know, and to agree with, all the major creative decisions. He wants it to be a film he endorses.[8]

Bluteau's devotion to his craft is ably complemented by that of the prolific August Shellenberg, who plays Chomina, a major Indian character. Several of the Indians who garnered support roles—Billy Two Rivers, Lawrence Bayne, Harrison Liu, and Tantoo Cardinal among them—are also longtime professionals who brought their well-refined and not insignificant talents to bear. These seasoned pros appear to have established a momentum which allowed several cinematic novices to transcend themselves in the quality of their performances. This is particularly true of Adan Young, an 18-year-old Canadian-born actor picked up during a casual audition in Australia to play Daniel (the main European character behind LaForge), and Sandrine Holt, a 17-year-old Eurasian from Toronto who was cast as Annuka, the Indian female lead. All told, the competence in acting displayed throughout the film lends an essential weight and substance to the sheer technical acumen embodied in its production.

"More than Just a Movie"

It should be noted that the production of *Black Robe* was made possible only by virtue of a formal treaty allowing for largescale cinematic collaboration between Canadian and Australian concerns. As Robert Lantos, whose Alliance Entertainment is the largest production and independent distribution house in Canada, put it, "We pursued, lobbied and pressured both governments to get it signed and we got good co-operation from Canada's Department of Communication."[9] This allowed the project to be underwritten with a budget of $12 million (U.S.), the highest ever—by a margin of more than twenty percent—for a "Canadian" undertaking.[10]

Given the sort of deadly seriousness with which the making of *Black Robe* was approached by all concerned, it was predictable that it would be treated as something more than just another movie by analysts. Indeed, from the outset, the mainstream media have rushed to accept at face value the pronouncements of Australian producer Sue Milliken, that the film is meant as an important tool for the understanding of "[Canada's] social history,"[11] and Lantos, that, because *Black Robe* was intended to be at least as much a work of history as of art, no attempt had been made to "tamper with its heart, its honesty."[12] Some papers have even gone so far as to enlist the services of professional historians to assess the picture on the basis of its historiography rather than its aesthetics.[13] Where this has not been the case, film critics themselves have postured as if they were suddenly possessed of an all-encompassing and scholarly historical competence.

Jay Scott of the *Toronto Globe and Mail*, for instance, immediately hailed *Black Robe* as an "honest, historically sound film," because it is handled with an appropriately "journalistic rather than moralistic...tone."[14] He then proceeded—while simply ignoring facts as obvious as that the Cree verbiage uttered throughout the flick was *not* the language spoken by *any* of the Indians to whom it is attributed—to offer his readers the sweeping assertion that the epic's "[sole] historical departure" is that "the actors playing the French characters...speak English."[15] Scott is joined in applauding the "evenhandedness" with which *Black Robe* unfolds by reviewers like Caryn James of the *New York Times*, who concludes that it "pulls off a nearly impossible trick, combining high drama with high ideas."[16] James, in turn, is reinforced by Vincent Canby, also of the *Times*, who observes that, more than anything, Beresford's work is marked by its "historical authenticity."[17] The *New Yorker*, in its "Current Cinema" section, sums up the view of the status quo by proclaiming the film to be "a triumph" of unbiased cinematic presentation of history.[18]

Nor have reviewers writing for such periodicals been especially shy about what has motivated their praise. James, for example, is unequivocal in her contention that *Black Robe* stands as a useful and necessary counterbalance against what she describes as a wave of "Columbus bashing"—by which she means the assignment of some degree of tangible responsibility to Europeans and Euroamericans for their conduct during the conquest and colonization of the Americas over the past five centuries—currently sweeping the continent. The primary strength of Beresford's exposition, she argues, is that it presents an interpretation of early European colonialist thinking and behavior that embodies "no evil intentions." While one is free to disagree with or regret it in retrospect, one is compelled to acknowledge that, because they were "sincere," the colonists "must be respected for [their] motives" in perpetrating genocide, both cultural and physical, against American Indians.[19] Left conspicuously unmentioned in such formulations, of course, is the proposition that with only a minor shift in the frame of reference, the same "logic" might be applied with equal validity to the nazis and their implementation of *lebensraumpolitik* during the 1940s.

Such use of *Black Robe* as a device in an establishmentarian drive to sanitize and rehabilitate the European heritage in America has been coupled directly to a similar effort to keep Indians "in their place" in the popular imagination. This has mainly assumed the form of juxtaposing Beresford's portrait of Native North America to that developed by Kevin Costner in *Dances With Wolves*, a movie which abandoned many of Euroamerica's most cherished falsehoods concerning how people lived their lives before the coming of the white man. *Washington Post* reporter Paul Valentine, to name one prominent example, took Costner to task in the most vituperative possible fashion for having presented what he called a "romantic view of Native Americans,"[20] which lacked, among other things, reference to the following invented "facts":

> It is well documented, for example that [Indians] stampeded herds of bison into death traps by igniting uncontrolled grass fires on the prairies...For many years afterward, animals could not find food in such burned over areas, and starvation would finish the destruction [of buffalo herds]...Nomadic hunters and gatherers moved from spot to spot seeking food, strewing refuse in their wake...Women [were used to haul] the clumsy two-stick travois used to transport a family's belongings on the nomadic seasonal treks...[Indians] practiced...cannibalism.[21]

"*Black Robe* is no over-decorated, pumped-up boy's adventure yarn like *Dances With Wolves*," as Canby put it.[22] The *New Yorker* comments admiringly on the "straightforward, unromanticized...anthropological detachment" with which Indians are portrayed by Beresford.[23] Scott goes even further, contending that the film is not so much a story about the onset of the European invasion as it is a true "exploration of North American aboriginal history" itself.[24] Having thus equipped his audience with the "inside scoop" on traditional Indian realities, Beresford can, as *Variety* put it, "lead us into unknown territory, and keep on pushing us further and further on, until, by the end, we find ourselves deep in the wilderness of the seventeenth century consciousness."[25] There, we find, not good guys or bad guys, not right or wrong, but rather "well-meaning but ultimately devastating" European invaders doing various things to a native population which, through its own imperfections and "mystical" obstinacy, participates fully in bringing its eventual fate upon itself.[26]

It's just "one of those things," over which nobody had any genuine control, a "tragedy," no more. No one actually *did* anything to anyone, at least not with any discernible sense of malice. No one is culpable, there is no one to blame. Even at the level of cultural presumption, it's six of one, half-a-dozen of the other. The entire process was as natural, inevitable, and as free of human responsibility, as glaciation. Or an earthquake. As James sums up, her own infatuation with *Black Robe* derives precisely from its accomplishment, through the most popular of all media, of the most desirable objective assigned to "responsible" historiography in contemporary North American society: Spin Control. In effect, Beresford successfully rationalizes the past in such a way as to let her, and everyone like her, off the hook: "[He] criticizes cultural imperialism," she says with evident satisfaction, "without creating villains."[27]

No Villains?

James' smug accolade is, to be sure, partly true. But it is at least equally false. What she really means is that *Black Robe* contains no *white* villains, and that this is what counts in her ever so "balanced" scheme of things. The handling of the indigenous victims of Europe's "cultural imperialism" is another matter entirely. The first whiff of this comes fairly early in the movie, when Father LaForge recalls a meeting in France with an earless and fingerless priest (based on a real missionary, Isaac Jogues), prior to his own departure for the New World. "The savages did this," the mutilated man points out, and the audience is left to let the horror of such atrocities settle into its collective subconscious. James explains the meaning of the scene as being motivational: "LaForge sees this as a compelling reason to bring his faith to a godless people."[28] Neither she nor Beresford allow so much as a hint that both clergymen are representatives of a church which had only just completed two centuries of inquisitions in which the refinement of torture had been carried to extraordinary lengths, and in which the pyres of burning heretics numbered in the tens of thousands.[29]

Even as the two men spoke, the Thirty Years' War was raging in its full fury, as Catholics and Protestants battled to the death over which side would dominate the spiritual, political, and economic life of the European Continent.[30] But nary a word is murmured on this score either. Nor is the fact that Jesuit missionaries were hardly acting on the basis of some pure religious fervor, no matter how misguided. Instead, as their own writings compiled in *The Jesuit Relations* and elsewhere make patently clear, they were consciously—one is tempted to say, cynically—using their faith as a medium through which to transform Indians, not just into ostensible Catholics, but also into surrogate troops deployed as fodder by the French Crown in its struggle with Great Britain for imperial hegemony in North America (the series of so-called "French and Indian Wars" commencing in 1689).[31]

In any event, the exchange between LaForge and his senior colleague serves as a prelude, a means of setting the psychic stage for the capture of the former, his interpreter (Daniel), and their party of Algonquin guides by "violent Iroquois" (Mohawks) while making their way along a 1,500-mile journey to the christianized Huron village of Ihonataria.[32] First, the captive men are forced to "run the gauntlet" between two lengthy lines of blood-crazed warriors who beat them severely with all manner of stone clubs. Then, a leering "Mohawk chieftain"—a young male—brutally slashes the throat of an Algonquin child, announcing that the adults, men and women alike, will be ritually tortured to death in the morning. To further make his point, he calmly saws off one of LaForge's fingers with a clamshell. The condemned are at this point left to spend their last night under guard in a longhouse stuffed with the Mohawks' larder of recently killed game, most of it steadily oozing blood. Under the circumstances, the firelit interior scenes which follow take on an aura of nothing so much as a sequence from *The Texas Chainsaw Massacre*. Only a sexual deception by Annuka allows the guard to be overpowered, and the survivors to escape their desperate plight.

Actually, Beresford softened portions of his characterization of the Mohawks in the interest of not driving away even moderately squeamish viewers. In Moore's original novel—a book the director and several of *Black Robe*'s producers found to be so "beautiful" that it simply *had* to be made into a movie—the body of the child is hacked up, boiled, and eaten while his family is forced to watch.[33] Even in its revised form, however, the matter is very far from representing the sort of "anthropological" accuracy, distance, and integrity attributed to it by most reviewers. It is, for starters, well-established in even the most arcane anthropological sources that Iroquois village life was controlled, not by young men, but by elder women—who fail to appear anywhere in the film—known as Clan Mothers. The latitude of the women's decision-making included the disposition of captives, a circumstance which led invariably to children being adopted and raised as Mohawks rather than gratuitously slaughtered. By and large, the same rule would have applied to a young woman such as Annuka; she would have been mated to a Mohawk man, perhaps an unkind fate in the estimation of some, but certainly a substantially different fate than being dismembered and burned alive.[34]

In a project as exhaustively researched as Beresford's, it is unlikely to the point of impossibility that "errors" of such magnitude were unintentional. Hence, it is difficult to conclude that the extent to which the Mohawks were misrepresented, and the nature of that misrepresentation, were anything other than a deliberate exercise in vilification. Such a view is amply reinforced by the employment of more subtle means to convey the impression that these are, indeed, the bad guys. For example, all scenes of the Mohawk village are framed against an overcast and threatening sky, the pervasive darkness evoking a strong sense of the sinister. By contrast, when LaForge finally reaches Ihonataria, despite the fact that it is now much later in the winter than when the Mohawk sequence occurs, the setting is bathed in sunlight. To suggest that these subliminal cues were just "accidents" on the part of a veteran director, who is known to do the most detailed storyboarding well in advance of his shoots, would be insulting.

Ultimately, the Mohawks are used as mere props in a broader theme which is developed throughout the film. Beresford's play of good and evil goes much deeper than a simplistic notion that one particular group of Indians was "bad." Rather, the Mohawks are deployed only as the most dramatic illustration of a more-or-less subterranean message holding that that which is most emphatically resistant to the imposition of European values and belief systems—or, put another way, that which is most decisively *Indian*—is by definition evil. This is manifested most clearly in a confrontation between LaForge and an overtly anti-Christian Montagnais spiritual leader. The latter is personified as "a shaman (a nasty-spirited dwarf),"[35] his face continuously painted a vibrant ochre, standing in shocking contrast to the somber dignity of LaForge's attire and physical stature. The dwarf (indigenous spirituality) is self-serving, malicious, and vindictive, an altogether repulsive entity; LaForge (Christianity), on the other hand, is sensitive and selfless to the extent of self-flagellation and acceptance of martyrdom. Within such a consciously contrived scheme, there can be no question as to which tradition is most likely to win the sympathy of viewers.[36]

Nor do the Algonquins who serve as LaForge's guides, collaborating with the white man but unsure as to whether they should embrace his religion, escape such categorization. To the extent that they remain uncommitted to conversion, clinging somewhat pathetically to the vestiges of these own beliefs, they too are cast as being imbued with crude and sometimes bestial impulses. In his novel, Moore made the point by lacing their speech with obscenities for which there are no native counterparts (e.g., "Now we will all eat our fucking faces full"), contrasting this to LaForge's austere pursuit of purity. Once again, Beresford cleans things up a bit, substituting a tendency of the Indians to fart loudly throughout the night, the noise and the stench keeping the delicate Father LaForge awake until he is forced to witness an even more disturbing phenomenon.

This last has to do with Annuka's proclivity, fair and unmarried maiden though she is, to copulate voraciously with whatever male she happens to find convenient when the urge strikes. More shocking, she obviously prefers to do it in the dirt, on all fours, in what is colloquially referred to as "dog style" (like a dog, get it?). Well, if perchance viewers were too startled by such carnality to fully appreciate its significance the first time around, the director includes a second iteration. And, for those who are really slow to catch on, a third. The only deviation from such canine behavior is to be found in yet a fourth sex scene, when Annuka, Pocahontas-like,[37] falls in love with Daniel, LaForge's young French interpreter. In the best civilizing fashion (albeit still in the dirt, as befits a sin of the flesh), he teaches her the meaning of "the missionary position," still morally—and in some places, legally—defined as the only "unperverted" sexual posture in the United States, Canada, and Beresford's Australian homeland.[38]

When all is said and done, the only Indians exempted from what is plainly meant to be seen as the disgusting quality of indigenous existence are the Hurons, at least those who have converted to Christianity. Unfortunately, LaForge arrives at last to tend this promising flock only to find them mostly dead or dying from an unnamed "fever," perhaps smallpox, introduced by his predecessor. What an "irony" that in their "salvation" lay their extinction. Truly, God works in mysterious ways. Nothing to be done about it but carry on. That's progress, all for the best. Even for the victims, who might otherwise have been consigned to an eternity of farting and fornicating and wandering around at the command of yellow dwarfs. It is well that we remember, as *Black Robe* attempts to ensure that we will, that however "mistaken, naïve," or even "wrongheaded" the invaders "may have been at times," they "did what they did for love [of humanity], nothing else, and that is nothing less than sheer nobility."[39]

Conclusion

Returning for a moment to the earlier-mentioned Holocaust metaphor, such a conclusion—which derives logically enough from Beresford's presentation—is quite comparable to a film's serving not only to rehabilitate but even to ennoble the nazi exterminationist impulse through a systematic defamation of the Jewish *untermenschen* ("subhumans") based in such "historical documentation" as *The Protocols of the Elders of Zion*.[40] This, of course, was precisely the objective of Josef Goebbels' propaganda ministry and its cooperating filmmakers in producing such works as *Die Rothschilds, Jud Süss* and *Der ewige Jude* (*The Eternal Jew*) during the halcyon days of the Third Reich.[41] For all its pictorial beauty and technical sophistication (or because of them), *Black Robe* is different mainly in quality, not in kind.[42]

If there is a distinction to be drawn between the nazis' antisemitic cinema and the handling of indigenous subject matters in contemporary North America, it is that the former were designed to psychologically prepare an entire populace to accept a genocide which was even then on the verge of occurring. The latter is pitched more to rationalizing and redeeming a process of conquest and genocide which has already transpired. *Black Robe* is thus the sort of "sensitive" and "mature" cinematic exposition we might have expected of the nazis, had they won their war. Their state, much like the United States and Canada (and Australia, New Zealand, and South Africa, for that matter), would have been faced with the consequent necessity of achieving a complete psychic reconciliation of the horrors of victory experienced by the "Germanic settlers" upon whom it depended for consolidation of the *lebensraum* gained through invasion and subsequent liquidation of native populations.[43]

In the context of the present Columbian Quincentennial, a symbolic period ripe with opportunity for wholesale reassessment of the evolution and current reality of Indian/immigrant relations in the Americas, and with the potential for some constructive redefinition of these relations, the form and function of films like *Black Robe* speak for themselves: "Nothing was really wrong with what has happened," they proclaim. "Therefore, nothing really needs altering in the outcomes of what has happened, nor in the continuing and constantly accelerating conduct of business as usual in this hemisphere. There is no guilt, no responsibility, nothing to atone for. Don't worry. Be happy. To the victors belong the spoils." *Sieg Heil....*

Notes

1. Moore's earlier screenwriting credits include the script for Alfred Hitchcock's *Torn Curtain*.
2. James' credits include *Driving Miss Daisy* and *Mr. Johnson*.
3. Wellburn's credits include *The Fringe Dwellers*.
4. Alliance Communications press release, March 1991, p. 10.
5. Urban, Andrew L., "Black Robe," *Cinema Papers* (March 1991): pp. 6-12, quote at pp. 10-11.
6. Printer's credits include *Breaker Morant*, *The Fringe Dwellers* and *Mr. Johnson*. The quote is taken from *ibid.*, p. 10.
7. *Ibid.*
8. *Ibid.*, p. 12.
9. "Black Robe: Anatomy of a Co-Production," *Moving Pictures International*, special supplement (September 5, 1991): p. viii.
10. *Ibid.* The Australian Film Finance Corporation committed 30 percent of the budget, Canada's Alliance Entertainment 20 percent. The balance was provided by Jake Eberts of the U.S.-based Allied Filmmakers.
11. Quoted in Urban, *op. cit.*, p. 10.
12. Alliance press release, *op. cit.*, p. 10.
13. See, for example, Bosco, Antoinette, "Remembering Heaven-Bent Men Wearing Black Robes," *The Litchfield County Times* (February 14, 1992). Bosco is a nun who has authored two ostensibly nonfiction books on the Jesuit missionaries depicted in *Black Robe*.

14. Scott, Jay, "A hideous piece of history wrapped in frosty, ebony shroud," *Toronto Globe and Mail* (September 5, 1991).

15. *Ibid.* In fact, Scott posits an inaccurate belief that Hurons and Montaignais actually spoke Cree: "the natives in *Black Robe* speak their own languages."

16. James, Caryn, "Jesuits vs. Indians, With No Villains," *New York Times* (November 17, 1991).

17. Canby, Vincent, "Saving the Huron Indians: A Disaster for Both Sides," *New York Times* (October 30, 1991). Canby also joins Scott and others in asserting that the movie's Indians "speak their own languages."

18. "True Believers," *New Yorker* (November 18, 1991): pp. 120-22, quote at p. 122.

19. James, *op. cit.*

20. Valentine, Paul, "Dancing With Myths," *Washington Post* (April 7, 1991). Tellingly, a search of the indices reveal that Valentine has never, despite there being literally thousands of examples to choose from, published a review criticizing a filmmaker for engaging in a *negative* misrepresentation of Indians. Nor has he published anything critical of Hollywood's overwhelming romanticization of Euroamerican soldiers and "pioneers" engaged in the "Winning of the West." His agitation about Costner's allegedly "unbalanced portrayal" thus speaks for itself.

21. *Ibid.* Most of this is simply bizarre. For instance, it is a well-known principle of range management that burning off prairie grass in the fall causes it to grow back in the spring more luxuriously than ever. In fact, new grass tends to be choked out by dead material after a few years. Hence, occasional burn-offs—caused naturally by lightning strikes—are essential to the health of the prairies and, to the extent that Indians practiced this method of hunting at all (which is dubious in itself), they would have been enhancing rather than destroying buffalo graze. So much for their casually starving herds into extinction. Similarly, insofar as no one has suggested that inorganic substances had been created in precontact North America, exactly what sort of "refuse" are Indian "nomads" supposed to have "strewn in their wake"? Again, there is no substantiation at all for the notion that the travois was designed to be hauled by women. To the contrary, all indications are that it was meant to be, and was in fact, hauled by the dogs kept by every native group for that purpose. Finally, while there is no authentication whatsoever of a single incident of indigenous cannibalism anywhere in the Americas, there are numerous documented cases in which Euroamericans adopted the practice. Witness, as but two illustrations drawn from the 19th century, the matter of Colorado's Alfred Packer, and of the notorious Donner Party.

22. Canby, *op. cit.*

23. "True Believers," *op. cit.*, p. 120.

24. Scott, *op. cit.*

25. "True Believers," *op. cit.*, p. 121.

26. "Toronto Fest: *Black Robe*," *Variety* (September 9, 1991): p. 65.

27. James, *op. cit.*

28. *Ibid.*

29. The author has had occasion to visit what is formally titled the Torture Museum, in Amsterdam, in which a number of the utensils developed for use in the French Catholic Inquisition are displayed. Included are such items as the rack, the wheel, the iron maiden, the iron mask, special tongs for tearing out tongues, instruments

used in drawing and quartering, and coarse-toothed saws created for dismembering living bodies. It is estimated that the Church caused such devices to be used on more than a quarter-million Europeans between 1400 and 1500. Suffice it to say that Native North America offered no remote counterpart to such ferocity, either quantitatively or technologically.

30. See Parker, Geoffrey, *The Thirty Years' War* (New York: Military Heritage Press, [second edition] 1978). For thorough (and classic) contextualization of this conflict in France, see Thompson, James Westfall, *The Wars of Religion in France* (Chicago, IL: Aldine Publishers, 1909).

31. See Twaites, Rubin G., ed., *The Jesuit Relations and Allied Documents,* 73 vols. (Cleveland, OH: Burrows Brothers Publishers, 1919). Also see Wrong, George M., *The Rise and Fall of New France,* 2 vols. (New York: Macmillan Publishers, 1928).

32. The description of the Iroquois as "violent" accrues from "Toronto Fest," *op. cit.* It is the *only* adjective used with reference to the Iroquois in this article, thus the author must have intended it to be definitive of their character.

33. Here we encounter the standard fable of Indian cannibalism once again. It is noteworthy that even a reputedly progressive publication like *In These Times* seems quite attached to this time-honored Eurocentric fantasy. At least it published a review by Pat Aufderheide ("Red and white blues in the *Black Robe,*" November 20-26, 1991) in which Beresford's film, minus cannibalism, is thoroughly trashed in favor of Nelson Periera dos Santos' *How Tasty Was My Little Frenchman*. Stated reason? Because "the European is dinner" for a group of South American Indians.

34. All this has been common academic knowledge since at least as early as the publication of Morgan, Lewis Henry, *The League of the Ho-De'-No-Sau-Nee, or Iroquois* (Rochester, NY: Sage & Brother, 1851).

35. "True Believers," *op. cit.,* p. 121.

36. This is a standard method of distorting native spirituality for non-Indian consumption. See Kleber, L. C., "Religion Among American Indians," *History Today,* no. 28 (1978).

37. The Pocahontas legend is, of course, one of the oldest and most hackneyed of the stereotypes foisted off on native women by Euroamerica. See Bernstein, Allison, "Outgrowing the Pocahontas Myth: Toward a New History of American Indian Women," *Minority Notes,* vol. 2, nos. 1-2 (spring-summer 1981).

38. The entire handling of indigenous sexuality in *Black Robe* is analogous to Ruth Beebe Hill's fetish with portraying Indians engaging in oral sex—also considered bestial and criminally perverse under Anglo-Saxon law—in her epic travesty, *Hanta Yo* (New York: Doubleday Publishers, 1979). For commentary, see Medicine, Beatrice, "Hanta Yo: A New Phenomenon," *The Indian Historian,* vol. 12, no. 2 (spring 1979).

39. Bosco, *op. cit.* Anyone inclined to buy into the good sister's interpretation of things should refer to the recent work of Osage/Cherokee theologian George Tinker. In a fine study entitled *Missionary Conquest: The Gospel and Native American Cultural Genocide* (Minneapolis, MN: Fortress Press, 1993), he details not only the actions of, but the express motivations and underlying assumptions guiding four exemplary Christian proselytizers among "the savages of North America," each of them representing a particular period over a 200-year timespan.

40. The protocols—attributing a vast and carefully thought-out "anti-goyim" conspiracy to "World Jewry"—were fabricated and distributed by the Czarist political police in Russia during the early 20th century as a means of whipping up anti-Jewish sentiments and consequent "solidarity" among the non-Jewish population. Subsequently, the utterly invented "historical document" was republished and disseminated by such antisemites as the nazis, and American industrialist Henry Ford, as a means of justifying programs directed against Jews in both Germany and the United States. It is currently in circulation again in the United States after having been reprinted by various neo-nazi organizations.

41. See Hull, David Stewart, *Film in the Third Reich: A Study of German Cinema, 1933-1945* (Berkeley: University of California Press, 1969), pp. 157-77. Also see Leiser, Irwin, *Nazi Cinema* (New York: Macmillan Publishers, 1974), pp. 73-94.

42. Even the quasi-official rhetoric attending release of the nazi films was similar to that which has accompanied *Black Robe*. According to the minutes of a Conference of Ministers at the Reich Propaganda Ministry conducted on April 26, 1940, Goebbels explained that the films should be reviewed in periodicals, such as *Völkisher Beobacher,* as if they were utterly authentic in their depictions of Jews: The "publicity campaign for *Jud Süss* and *Die Rothschilds* should [make clear that they portray] Jewry as it really is...If they seem antisemitic, this is not because they are aiming at any particular bias." The minutes are reproduced in full in Boelcke, Willi A., *Secret Conferences of Dr. Goebbels: The Nazi Propaganda War, 1939-1945* (New York: Dutton Publishers, 1970). As Leiser (*op. cit.,* p. 76) observes, Goebbels' instruction was motivated by a conviction—apparently shared by contemporary publicists in North America—that "propaganda only achieves its desired objective when it is taken not for propaganda but for truth. In a speech to the film industry on 15 February 1941, Goebbels stated that it was necessary to act on the principle that 'the intention [of a picture] should not be revealed to avoid irritating people,'" thus causing them to resist or even reject inculcating the desired "message."

43. For more on what the nazis had in mind in this regard, see Kamenetsky, Ihor, *Secret Nazi Plans for Eastern Europe: A Study of Lebensraum Policies* (New York: Bookman Associates, 1961). On preliminary implementation, see Dallin, Alexander, *German Rule in Russia, 1941-1944* (London: Macmillan Publishers, 1957).

LET'S SPREAD THE "FUN" AROUND
The Issue of Sports Team Names and Mascots

If people are genuinely interested in honoring Indians, try getting your government to live up to the more than 400 treaties it signed with our nations. Try respecting our religious freedom which has been repeatedly denied in federal courts. Try stopping the ongoing theft of Indian water and other natural resources. Try reversing your colonial process that relegates us to the most impoverished, polluted, and desperate conditions in this country...Try understanding that the mascot issue is only the tip of a very huge problem of continuing racism against American Indians. Then maybe your ["honors"] will mean something. Until then, it's just so much superficial, hypocritical puffery. People should remember that an honor isn't born when it parts the honorer's lips, it is born when it is accepted in the honoree's ear.

—Glenn T. Morris, Colorado AIM, 1992

During the past couple of seasons, there has been an increasing wave of controversy regarding the names of professional sports teams like the Atlanta "Braves," Cleveland "Indians," Washington "Redskins," and Kansas City "Chiefs." The issue extends to the names of college teams like Florida State University "Seminoles," University of Illinois "Fighting Illini," and so on, right on down to high school outfits like the Lamar (Colorado) "Savages." Also involved have been team adoptions of "mascots," replete with feathers, buckskins, beads, spears, and "warpaint" (some fans have opted to adorn themselves in the same fashion), and nifty little "pep" gestures like the "Indian Chant" and "Tomahawk Chop."

A substantial number of American Indians have protested that use of native names, images, and symbols as sports team mascots and the like is, by definition, a virulently racist practice. Given the historical relationship between Indians and non-Indians during what has been called the "Conquest of America," American Indian Movement leader (and American Indian Anti-Defamation Council founder) Russell Means has compared the practice to contemporary Germans naming their soccer teams the "Jews," "Hebrews," and "Yids," while adorning their uniforms with grotesque caricatures of Jewish faces taken from the nazis' antisemitic propaganda of the 1930s. Numerous demonstrations have occurred in conjunction with games—most notably during the November 15, 1992, match-up between the Chiefs and Redskins in Kansas City—by angry Indians and their supporters.

In response, a number of players—especially African Americans and other minority athletes—have been trotted out by professional team owners like Ted Turner, as well as university and public school officials, to announce that they mean not to insult, but instead to "honor," native people. They have been joined by the television networks and most major newspapers, all of which have editorialized that Indian discomfort with the situation is "no big deal," insisting that the whole thing is just "good, clean fun." The country needs more such fun, they've argued, and "a few disgruntled Native Americans" have no right to undermine the nation's enjoyment of its leisure time by complaining. This is especially the case, some have contended, "in hard times like these." It has even been contended that Indian outrage at being systematically degraded—rather than the degradation itself—creates "a serious barrier to the sort of intergroup communication so necessary in a multicultural society such as ours."

Okay, let's communicate. We may be frankly dubious that those advancing such positions really believe in their own rhetoric, but, just for the sake of argument, let's accept the premise that they are sincere. If what they are saying is true in any way at all, then isn't it time we spread such "inoffensiveness" and "good cheer" around among *all* groups so that *everybody* can participate *equally* in fostering the round of national laughs they call for? Sure it is—the country can't have too *much* fun or "intergroup involvement"—so the more, the merrier. Simple consistency demands that anyone who thinks the Tomahawk Chop is a swell pastime must be just as hearty in their endorsement of the following ideas—which by the "logic" used to defend the defamation of American Indians—should help us all *really* start yukking it up.

First, as a counterpart to the Redskins, we need an NFL team called "Niggers" to "honor" African America. Half-time festivities for fans might include a simulated stewing of the opposing coach in a large pot while players and cheerleaders dance around it, garbed in leopard skins and wearing fake bones in their noses. This concept obviously goes along with the kind of gaiety attending the Chop, but also the actions of the Kansas City Chiefs, whose team members—prominently including black team members—lately appeared on a poster looking "fierce" and "savage" by way of wearing Indian regalia. Just a bit of harmless "morale boosting," says the Chiefs' front office. You bet.

So that the newly formed Niggers sports club won't end up too out of sync while expressing the "spirit" and "identity" of African Americans in the above fashion, a baseball franchise—let's call this one the "Sambos"—should be formed. How about a basketball team called the "Spearchuckers?" A hockey team called the "Jungle Bunnies?" Maybe the "essence" of these teams could be depicted by images of tiny black faces adorned with huge pairs of lips. The players could appear on television every week or so gnawing on chicken legs and spitting watermelon seeds at one another. Catchy, eh? Well, there's "nothing to be upset about," according to those who love wearing "war bonnets" to the Super Bowl or having "Chief Illiniwik" dance around the sports arenas of Urbana, Illinois.

And why stop there? There are plenty of other groups to include. Hispanics? They can be "represented" by the Galveston "Greasers" and San Diego "Spics," at least until the Wisconsin "Wetbacks" and Baltimore "Beaners" get off the ground. Asian Americans? How about the "Slopes," "Dinks," "Gooks," and "Zipperheads"? Owners of the latter teams might get their logo ideas from editorial page cartoons printed in the nation's newspapers during World War II: slant-eyes, buck teeth, big glasses, but nothing racially insulting or derogatory, according to the editors and artists involved at the time. Indeed, this Second World War-vintage stuff can be seen as just another barrel of laughs, at least by what current editors say are their "local standards" concerning American Indians.

Let's see. Who's been left out? Teams like the Kansas City "Kikes," Hanover "Honkies," San Leandro "Shylocks," Daytona "Dagos," and Pittsburgh "Polacks" will fill a certain social void among white folk. Have a religious belief? Let's all go for the gusto and gear up the

Milwaukee "Mackerel Snappers" and Hollywood "Holy Rollers." The Fighting Irish of Notre Dame can be rechristened the "Drunken Irish" or "Papist Pigs." Issues of gender and sexual preference can be addressed through creation of teams like the St. Louis "Sluts," Boston "Bimbos," Detroit "Dykes," and the Fresno "Faggots." How about the Gainesville "Gimps" and Richmond "Retards," so the physically and mentally impaired won't be excluded from our fun and games?

Now, don't go getting "overly sensitive" out there. *None* of this is demeaning or insulting, at least not when it's being done to Indians. Just ask the folks who are doing it, or their apologists like Andy Rooney in the national media. They'll tell you—as in fact they *have* been telling you—that there's been no harm done, regardless of what their victims think, feel, or say. The situation is exactly the same as when those with precisely the same mentality used to insist that Step'n'Fetchit was okay, or Rochester on the Jack Benny Show, or Amos and Andy, Charlie Chan, the Frito Bandito, or any of the other cutesy symbols making up the lexicon of American racism. Have we communicated yet?

Let's get just a little bit real here. The notion of "fun" embodied in rituals like the Tomahawk Chop must be understood for what it is. There's not a single non-Indian example deployed above which can be considered socially acceptable in even the most marginal sense. The reasons are obvious enough. So why is it different where American Indians are concerned? One can only conclude that, in contrast to the other groups at issue, Indians are (falsely) perceived as being too few, and therefore too weak, to defend themselves effectively against racist and otherwise offensive behavior. The sensibilities of those who take pleasure in things like the Chop are thus akin to those of schoolyard bullies and those twisted individuals who like to torture cats. At another level, their perspectives have much in common with those manifested more literally—and therefore more honestly—by groups like the nazis, Aryan Nations, and Ku Klux Klan. Those who suggest this is "okay" should be treated accordingly by anyone who opposes nazism and comparable belief systems.

Fortunately, there are a few glimmers of hope that this may become the case. A few teams and their fans have gotten the message and have responded appropriately. One illustration is Stanford University, which opted to drop the name "Indians" with regard to its sports teams (and, contrary to the myth perpetrated by those who enjoy insulting Native Americans, Stanford has experienced *no* resulting drop-off in attendance at its games). Meanwhile, the local newspaper in Portland, Oregon, recently decided its long-standing editorial policy prohibiting use of racial epithets should include derogatory sports team names. The Redskins, for instance, are now simply referred to as being "the Washington team," and will continue to be described in this way until the franchise adopts an inoffensive moniker (newspaper sales in Portland have suffered no decline as a result).

Such examples are to be applauded and encouraged. They stand as figurative beacons in the night, proving beyond all doubt that it is quite possible to indulge in the pleasure of athletics without accepting blatant racism into the bargain. The extent to which they do not represent the norm of American attitudes and behavior is exactly the extent to which America remains afflicted with an ugly reality which is far different from the noble and enlightened "moral leadership" it professes to show the world. Clearly, the United States has a very long way to go before it measures up to such an image of itself.

IN THE MATTER OF JULIUS STREICHER
Applying Nuremberg Precedents in the United States

The Issue: American Indians as sports team mascots.
Response: No big deal.

—*Rocky Mountain News*, 1992 editorial statement

On October 16, 1946, a man named Julius Streicher mounted the gallows. Moments later he was dead, the sentence of an international tribunal comprised of representatives of the United States, France, Great Britain, and the Soviet Union having been imposed. Streicher's body was cremated, and—so horrendous were his crimes thought to have been—his ashes dumped into an unspecified German river so that "no one should ever know a particular place to go for reasons of mourning his memory."[1]

Julius Streicher was convicted at Nuremberg, Germany, of what were termed "Crimes Against Humanity."[2] The lead prosecutor in his case—Justice Robert Jackson of the United States Supreme Court—did not argue that the defendant had killed anyone, nor that he had committed any especially violent act. Nor was it contended that Streicher held any particularly important position in the German government during the period when the "Third Reich" exterminated 6,000,000 Jews, as well as several million Gypsies, Poles, Slavs, homosexuals, and other *untermenschen* ("subhumans").[3]

Indeed, the sole offense for which the accused was ordered put to death was having served as publisher/editor of a Bavarian tabloid entitled *Der Stürmer* during the early to mid-1930s, years before the nazi genocide actually began. In this capacity, he had penned a long series of virulently anti-semitic editorials and "news" stories, usually accompanied by cartoons and images graphically depicting Jews in an extraordinarily derogatory fashion.[4] This, the prosecution asserted, had done much to "dehumanize" the Jews in the mind of the German public. Such dehumanization had made it possible—or at least easier—for average Germans to later indulge in the outright liquidation of Jewish "vermin." The tribunal agreed, holding that Streicher was therefore complicit in genocide and deserved death by hanging.[5]

During the trial, Justice Jackson observed that, in implementing its sentences, the participating powers were morally and legally binding themselves to adhere forever after to the same standards of conduct being applied to Streicher and other nazi leaders. In the alternative, he said, the victorious allies would be committing "pure murder" at Nuremberg—no different in substance from that committed by those they presumed to judge—rather than establishing the "permanent benchmark of justice" which was intended.[6] U.S. Secretary of War Henry L. Stimson publicly concurred, asserting in the pages of *Foreign Affairs* that "a standard has been raised to which Americans, at least, must repair; for it is only as this standard is accepted, supported and enforced that we can move onward to a world of law and peace."[7]

Yet in the United States of Robert Jackson and Henry Stimson, the indigenous American Indian population had already been reduced, in a process that is ongoing to this day, from 12.5 to 15 million in the year 1500 to fewer than 250,000 by the beginning of the 20th century.[8] This was accomplished, according to both official and unofficial sources, "largely through the cruelty of [Euroamerican] settlers," and a sometimes informal but nonetheless clear and consistent governmental policy which made it an articulated goal to "exterminate these red vermin," or at least whole segments of them.[9]

Official bounties had been placed on the scalps of Indians—*any* Indians—in places as diverse as Georgia, Kentucky, Texas, the Dakotas, Oregon, and California. They remained in effect until resident Indian populations were decimated or disappeared. Entire peoples such as the Cherokee were reduced by half through a policy of forced removal from their homelands east of the Mississippi River to less preferable areas in the West. Others, such as the Navajo, while concentrated under military guard, suffered much the same fate. The United States Army and cooperating militias perpetrated wholesale massacres of native people at places like Fallen Timbers, Horseshoe Bend, Bear River, Sand Creek, the Washita River, the Marias River, Camp Robinson and Wounded Knee Creek.[10]

Through it all, hundreds of dime novels—each competing with the next to make Indians appear more grotesque, menacing and inhuman—were sold in the tens of millions of copies.[11] Plainly, the Euroamerican public was being conditioned to see Indians in such a way as to allow their eradication to continue. And continue it did until the "Manifest Destiny" of the United States—a direct precursor to what Adolf Hitler would subsequently call *lebensraumpolitik* ("the politics of living space")—was consummated.[12]

By 1900, the national project of "clearing" Native Americans from their land and replacing them with "superior" Anglo-American" settlers was complete. The indigenous population had been reduced by as much as 98 percent. Approximately 97.5 percent of their original territory had "passed" to the invaders.[13] The survivors were concentrated, out of sight and mind of the public, on scattered "reservations," all of them under the self-assigned "plenary" (full) power of the federal government.[14] There was, of course, no tribunal comparable to that at Nuremberg passing judgement on those who had created such circumstances in North America. No U.S. official or private citizen was ever imprisoned—never mind hanged—for implementing or propagandizing what had been done. Nor had the process of genocide against Indians been completed. Instead, it merely changed form.

Between the 1880s and the 1980s, more than half of all American Indian children were coercively transferred from their own families, communities and cultures to those of the conquering society. This was done through compulsory attendance at remote boarding schools, often hundreds of miles from their homes. Native children were kept for years and systematically "deculturated": indoctrinated to think and act in the manner of Euroamericans rather than as Indians.[15] It was also accomplished through a pervasive foster home and adoption program—including "blind" adoptions, where children would be permanently denied information about their origins—placing native youth in non-Indian homes.[16]

The express purpose of all this was to facilitate a U.S. governmental policy to bring about the "assimilation" (dissolution) of indigenous societies. In other words, Indian cultures *as such* were to be caused to disappear.[17] Such policy objectives are in direct violation of the second article of the United Nations 1948 Convention on Punishment and Prevention of the Crime of Genocide—an element of international law arising from the Nuremberg proceedings—under which the forced "transfer of the children" of a targeted "racial, ethnical, national or religious group" is explicitly prohibited as a genocidal activity.

Article II of the Genocide Convention also expressly prohibits involuntary sterilization as a means of "preventing births among" a targeted population. Yet, in 1976, it was conceded by the U.S. government that its "Indian Health Service" (IHS) then a subpart of the Bureau of Indian Affairs (BIA), was even then conducting a secret program of involuntary sterilization which had affected approximately 40 percent of all Indian women of childbearing age.[18] The program was allegedly discontinued, and the IHS was transferred to the Public Health Service, but *no one was punished*. Hence, business as usual has continued in the "health" sphere: in 1990, for example, it came out that the IHS was inoculating Inuit children in Alaska with Hepatitus-B vaccine. The vaccine had already been banned by the World Health Organization as having a demonstrated correlation with the HIV-Syndrome which is itself correlated to AIDS. As this is written, a "field test" of Hepatitus-A vaccine, also HIV-correlated, is being conducted on Indian reservations in the northern Plains region.[19]

The Genocide Convention makes it a Crime Against Humanity to create conditions leading to the destruction of an identifiable human group. Yet the BIA has utilized the government's plenary prerogatives to negotiate mineral leases "on behalf of" Indian peoples paying a fraction of standard royalty rates for their natural resources. The result has been "super profits" for a number of preferred U.S. corporations.[20] Meanwhile, Indians, whose reservations ironically turned out to be in some of the most mineral-rich areas of North America, a matter which makes us the nominally *wealthiest* segment of the continent's population, live in dire poverty.

By the government's own data in the mid-1980s, Indians received the lowest annual and lifetime per capita incomes of any aggregate population group in the United States. Concomitantly, we suffer the highest rate of infant mortality, death by exposure and malnutrition, plague disease, and the like. Under such circumstances, alcoholism and other escapist forms of substance abuse are endemic in the Indian community. This situation leads both to a general physical debilitation of the population and a catastrophic accident rate. Teen suicide among Indians is several times the national average. The average life expectancy of a reservation-based Native American man is barely 45 years; women can expect to live less than three years longer.[21] This, in a country where average life expectancy exceeds 70 years.

Such itemizations could be continued at great length, including matters like the radioactive contamination of large portions of contemporary Indian Country, the forced relocation of traditional Navajos to make way for massive coal stripping operations around Big Mountain (Arizona), and so on.[22] But the point should be made: Genocide, as defined in "black letter" international law, is a persistent fact of day-to-day life—and death—for North America's native peoples. Yet there has been (and is) only the barest flicker of public concern about, or even consciousness of, this reality. Serious expression of public outrage is absent. No one is punished and the process continues.

A salient reason for public acquiescence to the ongoing holocaust in Native North America has been a continuation of the dime novel legacy, often through more effective media. Since 1925, Hollywood has released more than 2,000 films, many of them rerun frequently on television, portraying Indians as strange, perverted, ridiculous, and often very dangerous *things of the past*.[23] We are habitually presented to mass audiences in one-dimensional manner, devoid of recognizable human motivations and emotions, thoroughly and systematically dehumanized. Temporally, we have been consigned to another dimension entirely, drifting as myths through the vast panorama of Americana.

Nor is this the extent of it. Everywhere, we are used as logos, as mascots, as jokes: "Big Chief" writing tablets, "Red Man" chewing tobacco, "Winnebago" campers, "Navajo" and "Cherokee" and "Pontiac" and "Cadillac" pickups and automobiles. There are the Cleveland "Indians," the Kansas City "Chiefs," the Atlanta "Braves" and the Washington "Redskins" professional sports teams—not to to mention those in thousands of colleges, high schools, and elementary

schools across the country—each with their own degrading caricatures and parodies of Indians and/or things Indian. Pop fiction
continues in the same vein. There is an apparently unending stream
of "New Age" manuals purporting to expose the "inner workings"
of indigenous spirituality in everything from psuedo-philosophi-
cal to do-it-yourself-kind styles. Blond yuppies from Beverly Hills
amble about the country purporting to be reincarnated 17th-cen-
tury Cheyenne "shamans" ready to perform previously secret ceremonies for a fee.

A concerted, sustained, and in some ways accelerating effort has
gone into making Indians unreal. It follows, therefore, that what has
happened, is happening, and will *continue* to happen to Indians unless
something is done to fundamentally alter the terms of our existence,
is also unreal. And the unreal, of course, is purely a matter of entertainment in Euroamerican society, *not* a cause for attention or concern.
As was established in the Streicher precedent at Nuremberg, the cause
and effect relationship between racist propaganda on the one hand
and genocidal policy implementation on the other is quite plain.

It is thus of obvious importance that the American public—plain,
average, everyday U.S. citizens—begin to *think* about the implications
of such things the next time they witness a swarm of face-painted and
war-bonneted buffoons doing the "tomahawk chop" at a baseball or
football game. It is necessary that they *think* about the implications of
the grade-school teacher adorning their child in turkey feathers to
commemorate Thanksgiving. *Think* about the significance of John
Wayne or Charleton Heston killing a dozen "savages" with a single
bullet the next time a western comes on TV. *Think* about why Land-o-
Lakes finds it appropriate to market its butter through use of a
stereotyped image of an "Indian Princess" on the wrapper. *Think*
about what it means when non-Indian academics profess—as they
often do—to "know more about Indians than Indians do themselves."
Think about the significance of charlatans like Carlos Castaneda,
Jamake Highwater, Mary Summer Rain, and Lynn Andrews churning
out "Indian" bestsellers, one after the other, while Indians typically
can't get into print.

Think about the *real* situation of American Indians. *Think* about Julius Streicher. Remember Justice Jackson's admonition. *Understand* that the treatment of Indians in American popular culture is *not* "cute" or "amusing" or some sort of "good, clean fun." Know that it causes real pain and real suffering to real people. *Know* that it threatens our very survival. And *know* that this is just as much a Crime Against Humanity as anything the nazis ever did. It is likely that the indigenous people of the United States will never demand that those guilty of such criminal activity be punished for their deeds. But the least we have the right to expect—indeed, to *demand* —is that such practices finally be brought to a halt.

Notes

1. Probably the best biography of Streicher available in English is Bytwerk, Randall L., *Julius Streicher: The man who persuaded a nation to hate Jews* (New York: Dorset Press, 1983). Also see Varga, William, *The Number One Nazi Jew Baiter* (New York: Carlton Press, 1981).

2. This was, at the time, a wholly new category of criminal behavior, the composition of which was devised mainly by legal theorists in the United States. For details on the evolution of the concept, see Smith, Bradley F., *The Road to Nuremberg* (New York: Basic Books, 1982). Also see Smith's *The American Road to Nuremberg: The Documentary Record, 1944-1945* (Stanford, CA: Hoover Institution Press, 1982).

3. Davidson, Eugene, *The Trial of the Germans: Nuremberg, 1945-1946* (New York: Macmillan Publishers, 1966), 39-58. Concerning gypsies, Poles, Slavs, etc., see Berenbaum, Michael, *A Mosaic of Victims: Non-Jews Persecuted and Murdered by the Nazis* (New York/London: New York University Press, 1990).

4. For specifics, see Office of United States Chief of Counsel for Prosecution of Axis Criminality, "Julius Streicher," *Nazi Conspiracy and Aggression, Vol. II* (Washington, D.C.: U.S. Government Printing Office, 1946), pp. 689-715.

5. See Kipphan, Klaus, "Julius Streicher: Propagandist of the Holocaust," in *Juniata Studies: Peace, Justice and Conflict*, ed. Ralph Church and Klaus Kipphan (Huntington, PA: Juniata College, 1976). Also see Mosse, George L., *Toward the Final Solution* (New York: Howard Fertig Publisher, 1978).

6. In his opening statement to the tribunal on November 21, 1945, for instance, Jackson observed that "while this law is first applied against German aggressors...if it is to serve any useful purpose it must condemn aggression by any other nations, including those which sit here now in judgement. We are able to do away with domestic tyranny and violence and aggression...only when we make all men answerable to the law"; Baird, Jay W., ed., *From Nuremberg to My Lai* (Lexington, MA: D.C. Heath and Co., 1972), p. 28. For further elaboration, see Jackson, Robert H., *The Nürnberg Case* (New York: Alfred A. Knopf Publishers, 1947).

7. Stimson, Henry L., "The Nuremberg Trial: Landmark in Law," *Foreign Affairs* (January 1947): pp. 179-89.

8. According to the U.S. Bureau of the Census, the actual count was 237,196; see "Table II: Indian Population by Divisions and States, 1890-1930," *Fifteenth Census of the United States, 1930: The Indian Population of the United States and Alaska* (Washington, D.C.: U.S. Government Printing Office, 1937), p. 3. On preinvasion population levels, see Stiffarm, Lenore A., and Phil Lane, Jr., "The Demography of Native North America: A Question of American Indian Survival," in *The State of Native America: Genocide, Colonization, and Resistance,* ed. M. Annette Jaimes (Boston, MA: South End Press, 1992), pp. 23-53.

9. The first quotation comes from Mooney, James M., "Population," in *Handbook of the Indians North of Mexico, Vol. 2,* bulletin no. 30, ed. Frederick W. Dodge (Washington, D.C.: Bureau of Ethnology, Smithsonian Institution, 1910), pp. 286-87. Concerning the second quotation, see Svaldi, David, *Sand Creek and the Rhetoric of Extermination: A Case Study in Indian-White Relations* (Lanham, MD: University Press of America, 1989).

10. For a comprehensive overview of such processes on a hemispheric as well as United States-specific basis, see Stannard, David E., *American Holocaust: Columbus and the Conquest of the New World* (London/New York: Oxford University Press, 1992). Also see Jaimes, M. Annette, "Sand Creek: The Morning After," in *The State of Native America, op. cit.,* pp. 1-12.

11. Berkhofer, Robert F., Jr., *The White Man's Indian: Images of the American Indian from Columbus to the Present* (New York: Vintage Books, 1978). Also see Curti, Merle, "Dime Novels and the American Tradition," *Yale Review,* no. XXVI (June 1937): pp. 761-78.

12. "Neither Spain nor Britain should be the models of German expansion, but the Nordics of North America, who had ruthlessly pushed aside an inferior race to win for themselves soil and territory for the future. To undertake this essential task, sometimes difficult, always cruel—this was Hitler's version of the White Man's Burden"; Rich, Norman, *Hitler's War Aims: Ideology, the Nazi State, and the Course of Expansion* (New York: W.W. Norton & Co., 1973), p. 8. For an early and detailed examination of the conceptual and practical relationship between nazi and United States expansionism, see Parella, Frank, *Lebensraum and Manifest Destiny,* MA thesis in Political Science (Washington, D.C.: Georgetown University, 1950).

13. After an exhaustive review of the record over a period of 30 years, the federal government's Indian Claims Commission officially estimated the original holdings of indigenous peoples within the United States to have been a little over two billion acres, of which approximately 50 million remain nominally under Indian control at present; Indian Claims Commission, *Final Report* (Washington, D.C.: U.S. Government Printing Office, 1978).

14. For analysis, see Harvey, Charles, "Constitutional Law: Congressional Plenary Power Over Indian Affairs—A Doctrine Rooted in Prejudice," *American Indian Law Review,* no. 10, 1982): pp. 117-50.

15. U.S. Senate, Committee on Labor and Public Welfare, *Indian Education: A National Tragedy—A National Challenge* (Washington, D.C.: 91st Cong., 1st Sess. [Report No. 95-501], U.S. Government Printing Office, 1969).

16. Blackbear, Tillie Walker, "American Indian Children: Foster Care and Adoptions," in U.S. Department of Education, Office of Educational Research and

Development, National Institute of Education, Conference on Educational and Occupational Needs of American Indian Women (Washington, D.C.: U.S. Government Printing Office, 1980), pp. 185-210.

17. The classic articulation of assimilation policy may be found in the words of Indian Commissioner Leupp, Francis E., in his *The Indian and His Problem* (New York, Charles Scribner's Sons, 1910; reprinted by Arno Press, New York, 1971), p. 93; in Leupp's view, it was a "mighty pulverizing engine for breaking up the tribal mass." For a detailed examination of the context of Leupp's sentiments, see Fritz, Henry E., *The Movement for Indian Assimilation, 1860-1890* (Philadelphia: University of Pennsylvania Press, 1963).

18. Dillingham, Brint, "Indian Women and IHS Sterilization Practices," *American Indian Journal*, vol. 3, no. 1 (1977), pp. 27-28.

19. Smith, Andrea, "The HIV-Correlation to Hepatitis-A and B Vaccines," *WARN Newsletter* (Chicago: Women of All Red Nations, summer 1992).

20. An excellent and succinct explanation of how this works may be found in Garrity, Michael, "The U.S. Colonial Empire is as Close as the Nearest Reservation," in *Trilateralism: The Trilateral Commission and Elite Planning for World Government*, ed. Holly Sklar (Boston, MA: South End Press, 1980), pp. 236-68.

21. U.S. Bureau of the Census, Population Division, *A Statistical Profile of American Indian Population* (Washington, D.C.: U.S. Government Printing Office, 1984); U.S. Department of Health and Human Services, *Chart Series Book* (Washington, D.C.: Public Health Service Report No. HE20.9409.988, 1988).

22. See the author's "Radioactive Colonization: Hidden Holocaust in Native North America," and "Genocide in Arizona? The 'Navajo-Hopi Land Dispute' in Perspective," and in this volume.

23. See Friar, Ralph and Natasha, *The Only Good Indian... The Hollywood Gospel* (New York: Drama Book Specialists, 1972). Also see Georgakas, Dan, "They Have Not Spoken: American Indians in Film," *Film Quarterly*, no. XXV (spring 1972): pp. 26-32, and Price, John A., "The Stereotyping of North American Indians in Motion Pictures," *Ethnohistory*, no. XX (spring 1973): pp. 153-71.

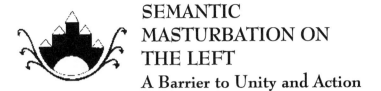

SEMANTIC MASTURBATION ON THE LEFT
A Barrier to Unity and Action

Essense resides in the code of the sign.

—Jean Baudrillard,
for a critique of the political and the economy of the sign

The galvanizing experience which led me to this article came, I suppose, in a trivial sort of way. I was giving a talk at University of Massachusetts/Amherst on FBI counterintelligence operations against the Black Liberation movement during the late '60s, specifically the Black Panther Party and the Student Nonviolent Coordinating Committee (SNCC), during the period of its call for Black Power. This is pretty grisly stuff, and I was hopeful my material would impress upon the assembled students a sense of the real magnitude of what the federal government had done to block positive social change for "minorities" in the United States. On this basis, I intended to guide discussion into the outcomes of this repression: everything from the emergence of the Black Liberation Army to the proliferation of homelessness during the '80s.

Toward the end of my presentation, a hand went up. Figuring things were already beginning to roll toward dialogue, I suspended my closing remarks to recognize the individual, who clearly had something important she wished to contribute. "You keep referring to us as 'Black'," she announced angrily. "This is insulting. We prefer to be called Afroamericans." Nonplussed by what I took to be an utter digression from the topic at hand, I responded somewhat flippantly: "Are you suggesting I've somehow misread history here, and that we're actually talking about something called the 'Afroamerican Panther Party'?"

I should have known better. "That's not the point!" she exclaimed. "What you're talking about happened 20 years ago. Things have evolved since then, and now we choose to be called Afroamericans, not Black. And the only politically correct thing for you to do, as a professed ally of our struggle, is to respect our wishes in the matter." Now *I* was growing angry. "You're right," I responded. "It's *not* the point. The point is this: you want to be called an Afroamerican. Fine. I'll call you anything you want. But understand that if I'm speaking with members of Kwame Turé's All-African Peoples Revolutionary Party, or folks who agree with them, then the preferred term is 'Africans.' Period. And if I'm talking to a group composed of the Republic of New Afrika, or any of its offshoots, 'New Afrikans' is going to be considered correct. Jesse Jackson and his followers seem to like the label 'African Americans' and, believe it or not, I still run into people who insist upon being called 'Negro.' So who exactly is this 'we' who wants to be called 'Afroamerican'? Certainly not the folks I've just mentioned. You'll have to forgive me for saying I think your notion of political correctitude is just a bit relative."

"And," I continued, "I think there's a larger point to be made here. The people we've been discussing tonight were always very clear that what they were about was *Black*. Along with Black Power and Black Liberation came something called Black *pride*. They didn't consider the term demeaning. To the contrary, they were harshly critical of those of us who—following the words of Malcolm X—clung to the term 'Afroamerican,' the very handle you insist upon. They corrected our language, much the way you're trying to, but in the opposite direction. And they fought, died, and went to prison for long periods because of the overtly *Black* consciousness they achieved. That was *their* evolution. I'm still in contact with a number of them, both in and out of prison. And *none* of them has ever said to me they've changed their minds, that 'Afroamerican' is more correct than 'Black.' Viewed from this perspective, I suggest your own position may represent not so much a further evolution, but a regression to something which came before. I'm not saying it's so, but it's definitely something you should think about. And, in any event, it's my opinion that your whole attitude on this shows a marked disrespect, not so much for me as for the people we've been talking about."

So much for the issues I'd spent the evening trying to raise. The student and several of her colleagues simply got up and walked out.

With the far more numerous group who remained, all concentration on the matter of counterintelligence was shattered; the substance of our subject had been subsumed in a shuffle of semantics. On the long plane ride back to Denver, I had ample time to reflect on the implications of the wordplay that had just transpired, and how endemic such things have become on the Left. This sort of terminological combat is, after all, hardly a phenomenon restricted to the Black/Afroamerican/African/New Afrikan/African American/Negro community.

American Indians too have become embroiled in controversy over whether they should be generically referred to by this customary description, or whether the newer term "Native American" doesn't somehow convey more "dignity." Others have opted for "first American" or "original American," while an even more "advanced" formulation may be found in the phrase "indigenous peoples of this hemisphere." Many of us, tiring of such idiot's fray, have resolved the matter by using several of these terms more or less interchangeably in our speech and writing. So long as no one resorts to such anthropological monstrosities as "Amerindian" or "aborigines"—or the marxian lexicon involving "primitives" and "preindustrials"—we tend to be rather semantically contented people. Still, there are those among us who have been conditioned to attach great importance to quibbling over such things.

Consider next the population derived from the former Spanish and Portuguese colonies in the Americas, south of those once claimed by France, England, and the Netherlands. Are they "Hispanics," as asserted by many groups, or "Latinos," as claimed by others? Or, to utilize a spelling and pronunciation currently in vogue among still others, should this be "Ladino"? Is one who comes from Puerto Rico a Puerto Rican, or a "Puertorriqueño"? Is it correct, as the Crusade for Justice and other organizations have long insisted, that the descendents of Mexican nationals who remained north of the Rio Grande after the Treaty of Guadalupe Hidalgo should be referred to as "Chicanos"? Or is it, as other groups contend, more correct to call them "Mexican Americans"? Again, is it true, as the *Movimiento de Liberacíon Nacional, Mexico* (MLNM) holds, that neither Chicanos nor Mexican Americans actually exist, and that the people in question are simply "Mexicans." Or is it "*Mexicanos*"?

To take another tack, is it appropriate to spell women "women," or must it be "womyn," or "wimmyn," or "wymmyn," or "wimmin"—all of which I've seen put in print by one or another feminist group—in order to be "politically correct" (p.c.)? And, if one of the latter should prevail, which *one* is to be used? In a related vein, must we, in order to be p.c., consciously capitalize the first letter in "women" and "Black" with equal deliberateness, decapitalize the same letter in "men" and "White"? How about decapitalizing the pronoun "I" while capitalizing the first letter in "we"?

Then there is the matter of "North American" political activists. For those who aren't conversant, this is the term lately ushered in to describe those who used to be called "White radicals" or "Euroamerican revolutionaries." Exactly how Caucasian politicos have managed to become exempted from the same sort of racial/cultural nomenclature applied to everyone else is a bit of a mystery. More, one wonders how they became, even in their own minds, more emblematic of North America than a Chicano, the descendent of a slave imported from Ghana, or—to take the most obvious point—a member of, say, the Iroquois confederacy. Do they have a set of honorary naturalization papers issued by the Haudenosaunee elders conveying some sort of original citizenship on Turtle Island, or what? If not, one is hard-pressed to discern the basis for this exceedingly odd term, applied as it is even to an Italian national currently imprisoned in the United States.

This takes us to another, perhaps even more perplexing, set of classifications presently seeing increasing use among progressives. These concern the categorization of those warehoused in U.S. prisons as "social prisoners," "political prisoners," and "Prisoners of War" (POWs). We might assume, by accepting the standard explanation of the code involved, that the first label pertains to persons imprisoned for acts devoid of conscious political content, while the second accrues to those doing time as a result of their politically motivated behavior. The status of POW is reserved for those caged because of their participation, as members of *bona fide* national liberation movements. So far, so good.

But does this really hold up? George Jackson, to name perhaps the most prominent example, went to prison for nothing more political than a $70 gas station stick up. By the above definitional schema, he should be classified as a social prisoner, pure and simple. But he is universally remembered as a political prisoner and a martyr in the "war for Black Liberation." This, of course, places him firmly within the ranks of POWs. The situation results exclusively from things that happened *after* he went to prison. Hence, there is need for at least one more term—perhaps "politicized social prisoner" would do—to make the labels work out, accounting for the fact that changes in consciousness and conduct occur among individuals inside as well as outside prison walls.

And there is more. In practice, POW status is applied only to people of color (another descriptive phrase that is bound to provoke howls of righteous outrage from somebody). This has to do with a United Nations definition of colonized entities, which are legally entitled to national liberation movements and which members of non-White armed formations in the United States argue (accurately) that they are, but which the UN refuses to acknowledge them as being. The upshot of this somewhat strained juridical contention is that Euroamerican revolutionaries—no matter how long or at what level of armed struggle they participate, or in how direct an alliance with non-White liberation movements—are inherently precluded (as members of "the oppressor nation") from POW classification. This holds true despite the fact that they confront the same opponent as their colonized counterparts, encounter the same risks, and lately have begun to incur much the same treatment when captured. Worse, in some ways, Euroamerican really should read "White," if it is to be understood accurately. A classic illustration of this concerns Joe Dougherty, a member of the Irish Republican Army (IRA)—a genuine national liberation movement if ever there was one—captured and incarcerated for several years in the United States, and finally extradicted back to Ireland. He has been referred to as a political prisoner rather than a POW as consistently as any Euroamerican.

There can be little doubt that matters of linguistic appropriateness and precision are of serious and legitimate concern. By the same token, however, it must be conceded that such preoccupations arrive at a point of diminishing return. After that, they degenerate rapidly into liabilities rather than benefits to comprehension. By now, it should be evident that much of what is mentioned in this article falls under the latter category; it is, by and large, inept, esoteric, and semantically silly, bearing no more relevance in the real world than the question of how many angels can dance on the head of a pin. Ultimately, it is a means to stultify and divide people rather than stimulate, and unite them.

Nonetheless, such "issues" of word choice have come to dominate dialogue in a significant and apparently growing segment of the Left. Speakers, writers, and organizers of all persuasions are drawn, with increasing vociferousness and persistence, into heated confrontations, not about what they've said, but about how they've said it. Decisions on whether to enter into alliances, or even to work with other parties, seem more and more contingent not upon the prospect of a common agenda, but upon mutual adherence to certain elements of a prescribed vernacular. Mounting quantities of progressive time, energy, and attention are squandered in perversions of Mao's principle of criticism/self-criticism—now variously called "process," "line sharpening," or even "struggle"—in which there occurs a virtually endless stream of talk about how to talk about "the issues." All of this happens at the direct expense of actually understanding the issues themselves, much less *doing* something about them.

It is impossible to escape the conclusion that the dynamic at hand adds up to a pronounced avoidance syndrome, a masturbatory ritual through which an opposition nearly paralyzed by its own deeply felt sense of impotence pretends to be engaged in something "meaningful." In the end, it reduces to tragic delusion at best, cynical game playing or intentional disruption at worst. With this said, it is only fair to observe that it's high time to get *off* this nonsense, and on with the real work of effecting positive social change.

FALSE PROMISES
An Indigenist Perspective on Marxist Theory and Practice

Sure, I'm a Marxist. But I've never been able to decide which one of them I like best: Groucho, Harpo, Chico, or Karl.

—American Indian Movement joke, circa 1975

H*au, Metakuyeayasi.* The greeting I have just given you is a Lakota phrase meaning, "Hello, my relatives." Now, I'm not a Lakota, and I'm not particularly fluent in the Lakota language, but I ask those of you who are to bear with me for a moment while I explore the meaning of the greeting because I think it is an important point of departure for our topic: the relationship, real and potential, which exists between the marxist tradition, on the one hand, and that of indigenous peoples—such as American Indians—on the other.

Dialectics

The operative words here are "relatives," "relationship," and, by minor extension, "relations." I have come to understand that when Lakota people use the word *Metakuyeayasi,* they are not simply referring to their mothers and fathers, grandparents, aunts and uncles, ancestors, nieces and nephews, children, grandchildren, cousins, future generations, and all the rest of humankind. These relatives are certainly included, but things don't stop there. Also involved is reference to the ground we stand on, the sky above us, the light from the sun and water in the oceans, lakes, rivers, and streams. The plants that populate our environment are included, as are the four-legged creatures around us, those who hop and crawl, the birds that fly, the fish that swim, the insects, the worms. Everything. These are all understood in the Lakota way as being relatives. What is conveyed in this Lakota concept is the notion of the universe as a relational whole, a single interactive organism in which all things, all beings are active and essential parts; the whole can never be understood without a knowledge of the function and meaning of each of the parts, while the parts cannot be understood other than in the context of the whole.

The formation of knowledge is, in such a construct, entirely dependent on the active maintenance of a fully symbiotic, relational—or, more appropriately, *inter*relational—approach to understanding. This fundamental appreciation of things, the predicate upon which a worldview is established, is, I would argue, common not only to the Lakota but to all American-Indian cultural systems. Further, it seems inherent to indigenous cultures the world over. At least I can say with certainty that I've looked in vain for a single concrete example to the contrary.

The ancient Greeks had a term, *dialitikus*, which was borrowed from an Egyptian concept, and which I'm told the civilization of the Nile had itself appropriated from the people of what is now called Ethiopia, describing such a way of viewing things. The Greeks held this to be a superior mode of thinking. In modern parlance, the word at issue has become "dialectics," popularized in this form by the German post-theological philosopher, G.W.F. Hegel. As has so often happened in the history of European intellectualism, Hegel's notable career spawned a bevy of philosophical groupies. Among the more illustrious, or at least more industrious, of these "Young Hegelians" was a doctoral student named Karl Marx.

Indeed, Marx was always clear in his student work—much of which can now be read in a volume titled *The Economic and Philosophic Manuscripts of 1844*—and forever after that it was the structure of "dialectical reasoning" he'd absorbed from Hegel that formed the foundation of his entire theoretical enterprise. He insisted to his dying day that this remained true despite his famous "inversion" of Hegel, that is, the reversal of Hegel's emphasis on such "mystical" categories as "the spirit" in favor of more "pragmatic" categories like "substance" and "material."

Let us be clear at this point. The dialectical theoretical methodology adopted by Marx stands—at least in principle—in as stark an oppositional contrast, and for all the same reasons, to the predominant and predominating tradition of linear and nonrelational European logic (exemplified by John Locke, David Hume, and Sir Isaac Newton) as do indigenous systems of knowledge. It follows from this that there should be a solid conceptual intersection between Marx, marxism, and indigenous peoples. Indeed, I myself have suggested such a possibility in a pair of 1982 essays, one published in the journal *Integrateducation,* and the other in an education reader produced by the American Indian Studies Center at UCLA.[1]

At an entirely abstract level, I remain convinced that this is in fact the case. There is, however, a quite substantial defect in such a thesis in any less rarefied sense. The most lucid articulation of the problem at hand was perhaps offered by Michael Albert and Robin Hahnel in their book, *Unorthodox Marxism:*

> [Marxist] dialecticians have never been able to indicate exactly how they see dialectical relations as different from any of the more complicated combinations of simple cause/effect relations such as co-causation, cumulative causation, or simultaneous determination of a many variable system where no variables are identified as dependent or independent in advance...for orthodox practitioners [of marxian dialectics] there is only the word and a lot of "hand waving" about its importance.[2]

A substantial case can be made that this confusion within marxism began with Marx himself. Having philosophically accepted and described a conceptual framework that allowed for a holistic and fully relational apprehension of the universe, Marx promptly abandoned it at the level of his applied intellectual practice. His impetus in this regard appears to have been his desire to see his theoretical endeavors used not simply as a tool of understanding, but as a pro-active agent for societal transformation, a matter bound up in his famous dictum that "the purpose of philosophy is not merely to understand the world, but to change it." Thus Marx, *a priori* and with no apparent questioning in the doing, proceeded to anchor the totality of his elaboration in the presumed primacy of a given relation—that sole entity that can be said to hold the capability of active and conscious pursuit of change, i.e., humanity—over any and all other relations. The marxian "dialectic" was thus unbalanced from the outset, skewed as a matter of *faith* in favor of humans. Such a disequilibrium is, of course, not dialectical at all. It *is,* however, quite specifically Eurocentric in its attributes, springing as it does from the late-Roman interpretation of the Judeo-Christian assertion of "man's" supposed responsibility to "exercise dominion over nature," a tradition which Marx (ironically) claimed oft and loudly to have "voided" in his rush to materialism.

All of this must be contrasted to the typical indigenous practice of dialectics, a worldview recognizing the human entity as being merely one relation among the myriad, each of which is *entirely* dependent on all others for its continued existence. Far from engendering some sense of "natural" human dominion over other relations, the indigenous view virtually requires a human behavior geared to keeping humanity *within* nature, maintaining relational balance and integrity (often called "harmony"), rather than attempting to harness and subordinate the universe. The crux of this distinction may be discovered in the Judeo-Christian assertion that "man was created in God's image," a notion which leads to the elevation of humans as a sort of surrogate deity, self-empowered to transform the universe at whim. Indigenous tradition, on the other hand, in keeping with its truly dialectical understandings, attributes the inherent ordering of things not to any given relation, but to another force often described as constituting a "Great Mystery," far beyond the realm of mere human comprehension.

We may take this differentiation to a somewhat more tangible level for purposes of clarity. The culmination of European tradition has been a homing-in on rationality, the innate characteristic of the human mind lending humanity the capacity to disrupt the order and composition of the universe. Rationality is held by those of the European persuasion—marxist and anti-marxist alike—to be the most important ("superior") relation of all; humans, being the only entity possessing it, are thus held *ipso facto* to be *the* superior beings of the universe. Manifestations of rationality, whether cerebral or physical, are therefore held to be the cardinal signifiers of virtue.

Within indigenous traditions, meanwhile, rationality is more often viewed as being something of a "curse," a facet of humanity that must be consistently leashed and controlled in order for it *not* to generate *precisely* this disruption. The dichotomy in outlooks could not be more pronounced. All of this is emphatically *not* to suggest that indigenous cultures are somehow "irrational" in their makeup (to borrow a pet epithet hurled against challengers by the Euro-supremacists of academia). Rather, it is to observe that, as consummate dialecticians, they have long since developed functional and functioning methods of keeping their own rationality meshed with the rest of the natural order. And this, in my view, is the most rational exercise of all.

Dialectical Materialism

In any event, having wholeheartedly accepted the European mainstream's anti-dialectical premise that the human relation is paramount beyond all others in what are termed "external relations," Marx inevitably set out to discover that which occupied the same preeminence among "internal relations" (that is, those relations comprising the nature of the human project itself). With perhaps equal inevitability, his inverted Hegelianism—which he dubbed "dialectical materialism"—led him to locate this in the need of humans to *consciously* transform one aspect of nature into another, a process he designated by the term "production." It is important to note in this regard that Marx focused on what is arguably the most rationalized, and therefore most unique, characteristic of human behavior, thus establishing a mutually reinforcing interlock between that relation which he advanced as being most important externally and that which he assigned the same position internally. So interwoven have these two relations become in the marxian mind that today we find marxists utilizing the terms "rationality" and "productivity" almost interchangeably, and with a virtually biblical circularity of reasoning. It goes like this: the ability to produce demonstrates human rationality, thereby distinguishing humans as superior to all other external relations, while rationality (left unchecked) leads unerringly to proliferating productivity, thereby establishing the latter as more important than any other among humans (internally). The record, of course, can be played in reverse with equally satisfying results.

From here, Marx was in a position to launch his general theory, laid out in the thousands of pages of his major published works—*Grundrisse, A Contribution to the Critique of Political Economy,* and the three volumes of *Capital*—in which he attempted to explain the full range of implications attendant to what he described as "the relations of production." Initially, he was preoccupied with applying his concepts temporally, a project he tagged as "historical materialism," in order to assess and articulate the nature of the development of society through time. In *Capital*, he theorized that the various relations of society—e.g., ways of holding land, kinship structures, systems of governance, spiritual beliefs, and so on—represented not a unified whole, but a complex of "contradictions" (in varying degrees) to the central, productive relation. All history, for Marx, become a stream of conflict within which these contradictions were increasingly "reconciled with" (subordinated to) production. As such reconciliation occurred over time, various transformations in socio-cultural relations correspondingly took place. Hence, Marx sketched history as a grand "progression," beginning with the "pre-history" of the "Stone Age" (the most "primitive" level of truly human existence) and "advancing" to the emergent capitalism of his own day. "Productive relations," in such a schema, determine all and everything.

One of Marx's theoretical heirs, the 20th century French structuralist marxist Louis Althusser, summed up historical materialism up quite succinctly when he defined production as being the "overdetermined contradiction of all human history," and observed that, from a marxian standpoint, society would not, in fact *could not*, exist as a unified whole until the process had worked its way through to culmination, a point at which all other social relations would stand properly reconciled to the "productive mission" of humanity. In a more critical vein, we might note another summation offered by Albert and Hahnel:

> [O]rthodox [marxism] doesn't stop at downgrading the importance of the creative aspect of human consciousness and the role it plays in historical development. According to the orthodox materialists, of all the different objective material conditions, those having to do with production are always the most critical. Production is the prerequisite to human existence. Productive activity is the basis for all other activity. Therefore, consciousness rests primarily on the nature of objective production relations. Cut to the bone, this is the essence of the orthodox materialist [marxist] argument.[3]

It is difficult to conceive of a more economistic or deterministic ideological construction than this. Indeed, the post-structuralist French philosopher Jean Baudrillard has pointed out in his book, *The Mirror of Production*, that Marx never so much offered a critique or alternative to the capitalist mode of political economy he claimed to oppose as he *completed* it, plugging its theoretical loopholes. This, in turn, has caused indigenous spokespersons such as Russell Means to view marxism not as a potential revolutionary transformation of world capitalism, but as a *continuation* of all of capitalism's worst vices "in a more efficient form."[4]

But, to move forward, there are a number of aspects of the marxian general theory—concepts such as surplus value, alienation, and domination among them—that might be important to explore at this juncture. Time is limited, however, and it seems to me the most fruitful avenue of pursuit lies in what Marx termed "the labor theory of value." By this, he meant that value can be assigned to anything *only* by virtue of the quantity and quality of human labor—i.e., productive, transformative effort—put into it. This idea carries with it several interesting sub-properties, most strikingly that the natural world holds no intrinsic value of its own. A mountain is worth nothing as a mountain; it only accrues value by being "developed" into its raw productive materials, such as ores or even gravel. It can hold a certain speculative value, and thus be bought and sold, but only with such developmental ends in view. Similarly, a forest holds value only in the sense that it can be converted into a product known as lumber; otherwise, it is merely an obstacle to valuable, productive use of land through agriculture or stockraising, etc. (an interesting commentary on the marxian view of the land itself). Again, other species hold value only in terms of their utility to productive processes (e.g., meat, fur, leather, various body oils, eggs, milk, transportation in some instances, even fertilizer); otherwise they may, indeed *must,* be preempted and supplanted by the more productive use of the habitat by humans.

This, no doubt, is an extreme formulation. There have been a number of "mediations" of this particular trajectory by 20th century marxian theorists. Still, at base, the difference they offer lies more in the degree of virulence with which they express the thesis than any essential break with it. All self-professing marxists, in order to be marxists at all, must share in the fundamental premise involved. And this goes for sophisticated phenomenological marxists such as Maurice Merleau-Ponty, existential marxists such as Jean-Paul Sartre, critical theorists such as Herbert Marcuse and Theodor Adorno, and

Jürgen Habermas, right along with "mechanistic vulgarians" of the leninist persuasion (a term I use to encompass all those who trace their theoretical foundations directly to Lenin: stalinists, maoists, castroites, althusserian structuralists, *et. al.*). To put a cap on this particular point, I would offer the observation that the labor theory of value is the underpinning of a perspective which is about as contrary to the indigenous worldview as it is possible to define.

It goes without saying that there are other implications in this connection, as concerns indigenous cultures and people. Marx's concept of value ties directly to his notion of history, wherein progress is defined in terms of the evolution of production. From this juxtaposition we may discern that agricultural society is viewed as an "advance" over hunting and gathering society, feudalism is an advance over simple agriculture, mercantilism is seen as an advance over feudalism, and capitalism over mercantilism. Marx's supposed "revolutionary" content comes from his projection that socialism will "inevitably" be the next advance over capitalism and that it, in turn, will give way to communism. Okay, the first key here is that each advance represents not only a quantitative/qualitative step "forward" in terms of productivity, but also a corresponding rearrangement of other social relations. Both of these factors are assigned a greater degree of *value* than their "predecessors." In other words, agricultural society is seen by marxists as being more valuable than hunting and gathering society, feudalism as more valuable than mere agriculture, and so on. The picture should be becoming clear.

Now, there is a second facet. Marx was very straightforward in acknowledging that the sole cultural model on which he was basing his theses on history and value was his own, that is to say European (or, more accurately, northwestern European) context. He even committed to paper several provisos stipulating that it would be inappropriate and misleading to attempt to apply the principles deriving from his examination of the dominant matrix in Europe to other, non-European contexts, each of which he (correctly) pointed out would have to be understood *in its own terms* before it could be properly understood *vis-à-vis* Europe. With this said, however, Marx promptly violated his own posited methodology in this regard, offering a number of non-

European examples—of which he admittedly knew little or nothing—as illustration of various points he wished to make in his elaboration on the historical development of Europe. Chinese society, to name a prominent example of this, was cast (really miscast) as "Oriental feudalism," thus supposedly shedding a certain light on this stage of European history. "Red Indians," about whom Marx knew even less than he did of the Chinese, became examples of "primitive society," illustrating what he wanted to say about Europe's stone age. In this fashion, Marx universalized what he claimed were the primary ingredients of Anglo-Saxon-Teutonic history, extending the *de facto* contention that *all* cultures are subject to the same essential dynamics and, therefore, follow essentially the same historical progression.

Insofar as all cultures were made to conform with the material correspondences of one or another moment in European history, and given that only Europe exhibited a "capitalist mode of production" and social organization—which Marx held to be the "highest form of social advancement" as of the point he was writing—it follows that all non-European cultures could be seen as objectively lagging behind Europe. We are presented here with a sort of "universal Euro yardstick" by which we can measure with considerable precision the relative ("dialectical") degree of retardation shown by each and every culture on the planet, *vis-à-vis* Europe. Simultaneously, we are able to assign, again with reasonable precision, a relatively ("dialectically") lesser value to each of these cultures as compared to that of Europe. We are dealing here with the internal relations of humanity, but in order to understand the import of such thinking we must bear in mind the fate assigned "inferior" (less valuable) *external* relations—mountains, trees, deer—within the marxian vision. In plainest terms, marxism holds as "an immutable law of history" that all non-European cultures must be subsumed in what is now called "Europeanization." It is their inevitable destiny, a matter to be accomplished in the name of progress and "for their own good." Again, we may detect echoes of the Jesuits within the "anti-spiritualist" marxian construct.

Those who would reject such an assessment should consider the matter more carefully. Do not such terms such as "pre-industrial" riddle the marxian vernacular whenever analysis of non-European ("primitive") culture is at hand? What possible purpose does the qualifier "pre" (as opposed to, say, "non") serve in this connection other than to argue that such societies are *in the process of becoming* capitalist? And is this not simply another way of stating that they are lagging behind those societies that have *already become* industrialized? Or, to take another example, to what end do marxists habitually refer to those societies that have "failed" (refused) to even enter a productive progression as being "ahistorical" or "outside of history"? Is this to suggest that such cultures have *no* history, or is it to say that they have the wrong *kind* of history, that only a certain (marxian) sense of history is true? And again: do marxists not hold that the socialist revolution will be the outcome of history for *all* humanity? Is there another sense in which we can understand the term *"world* revolution"? Did Marx himself not proclaim—and in no uncertain terms— that the attainment of the "capitalist stage of development" is an *absolute* prerequisite for the social transformation *he* meant when he spoke of the "socialist revolution"? I suggest that, given the only possible honest answers to these questions, there really are no other conclusions to be drawn from the corpus of marxist theory than those I am drawing here. The punchline is that marxism as a worldview is not only diametrically opposed to that held by indigenous peoples, it quite literally precludes their right to a continued existence as functioning socio-cultural entities. This, I submit, will remain true despite the fact that we may legitimately disagree on the nuance and detail of precisely how it happens to be true.

The National Question

Up to this point, our discussion has been restricted to the consideration of marxist theory. It is one thing to say that there are problems with a set of ideas, and that those ideas carry unacceptable implications *if* they were to be put into practice. The "proof," however, is *in* the practice, or "praxis" if you follow the marxian conception that theory and practice are a unified whole and must consequently be maintained in a dialectically reciprocal and interactive state at all times. Hence, it is quite another matter to assert that the negative implications of doctrine and ideology have in fact been actualized in "the real world" and are thereby subject to concrete examination. Yet marxism offers us exactly this method of substantiating our theoretical conclusions.

To be fair, when we move into this area, we are no longer concerned with the totality of marxism *per se*. Rather, we must focus on that stream which owes a special allegiance to the legacy of Lenin. The reason for this is that *all* "marxist" revolutions, beginning with the one in Russia, have been carried out under the mantle of Lenin's interpretation, expansion, and revision of Marx. This is true for the revolutionary processes in China, Cuba, North Korea, Algeria, Kampuchea (Cambodia), Laos, Albania, Mozambique, Angola, and Nicaragua. Arguably, it is also true for Zimbabwe (Rhodesia), and it is certainly true for those countries brought into a marxian orbit mainly by force: Latvia, Lithuania, Estonia, Poland, East Germany, Czechoslovakia, Hungary, Rumania, Bulgaria, Mongolia, Tibet, and Afghanistan. Yugoslavia represents a special case, but its differentiation seems largely due to capitalist influences, rather than that of other strains of marxism. One might go on to say that those self-proclaimed revolutionary marxist formations worldwide which seem likely to effect a seizure of state power at any point in the foreseeable future—e.g., those in Namibia and El Salvador—are *all* leninist in orientation. They certainly have disagreements among themselves, but this does not change the nature of their foundations. There have been *no* non-leninist marxian revolutions to date, nor does it seem likely there will be in the coming decades.

Be this as it may, there are again a number of aspects of marxist-leninist post-revolutionary practice that we might consider, e.g., the application of Lenin's concept of "the dictatorship of the proletariat," centralized state economic planning, the issue of forced labor, the imposition of rigid state parameters on political discourse of all types, and so forth. Each of these holds obvious and direct consequences for the populations involved, including whatever indigenous peoples happen to become encapsulated within one or another (sometimes more than one) revolutionary state. Time, however, remains short and so it is necessary that we limit our scope. In this, it seems appropriate that we follow the lead of Albert and Hahnel in "cutting to the bone."

We will therefore take up that aspect of marxist-leninist praxis which has led to indigenous peoples being encapsulated in revolutionary states at all. In the vernacular, this centers on what is called the "national question" (or "nationalities question").

The principle at issue here devolves from a concept which has come to be known as "the right to self-determination of all peoples," codified in international law by the United Nations during the '60s, but originally espoused by Marx and his colleague, Frederick Engels, during the London Conference of the First International in 1864.[5] In essence, the right to self-determination has come to mean that each people, identifiable as such (through the sharing of a common language and cultural understandings, system of governance and social regulation, and a definable territorality within which to maintain a viable economy) is *inherently* entitled to decide for itself whether or not and to what extent it wishes to merge itself culturally, politically, territorially, and economically with any other (usually larger) group. The right to self-determination thus accords to each identifiable people on the planet the prerogative of (re)-establishing and/or continuing themselves as culturally distinct, territorially and economically autonomous, and politically sovereign entities (as *nations*, in other words). Correspondingly, no nation has the right to preempt such rights on the part of another. For these reasons, the right of self-determination has been linked closely with the movement toward global decolonization, and the resultant body of international law that has emerged on this subject. All this, to be sure, is very much in line with the stated aspirations of American Indians and other indigenous peoples around the world.

But marxism's handling of the right to self-determination has not followed the general development of the concept. Having opened the door in this regard, Marx and Engels adopted what seems (superficially, at least) to be a very curious posture. They argued that self-determining rights pertained only to *some* peoples. For instance, they were quite strong in their assertions that the Irish, who were even then waging a serious struggle to rid themselves of British colonization, must be supported in this effort. Similarly, Marx came out unequivocally in favor of the right (even the obligation) of the Poles to break free from Russian colonialism. On the other hand, Engels argued vociferously that "questions as to the right of independent national existence of those small relics of peoples" such as the Highland Scots (Gaels), Welsh, Manxmen, Serbs, Croats, Ruthenes, Slovaks, and Czechs constitute "an absurdity."[6] Marx concurred, and proceeded to openly advocate the imposition of European colonialism on the "backward peoples" of Africa, Asia, and elsewhere.[7]

Such positioning may initially seem confusing, even contradictory. A closer examination, however, reveals consistency with Marx's broader and more philosophical pronouncements. The Irish and Poles had been, over the course of several centuries of English and Russo-German colonization, sufficiently "advanced" by the experience (i.e., reformed in the image of their conquerors) to be entitled to determine their own future in accordance with the "iron laws" of historical materialism. The other peoples in question, *especially* the tribal peoples of Africa and Asia (and one may assume American Indians were categorized along with these), were not seen as being comparably "developed." A continuing dose of colonization—subjugation by superior beings, from superior cultures—was thus prescribed to help them overcome their "problem."

A second level of consideration also entered Marx's and Engels' reasoning on these matters. This concerns the notion of "economies of scale." Marx held that the larger an "economic unit" became, the more rationalized and efficient it could be rendered. Conversely, smaller economic units were considered to be inefficient by virtue of being "irrationally" duplicative and redundant. The Irish and Poles were not only populous enough to be considered among Engels' "great peoples," but—viewed as economic units—large enough to justify support in their own right, at least during a transitional phase en route to the consolidation of "world communism." The other peoples in question were not only too backward, but too *small* to warrant support in their quests for freedom and independence; their *only* real destiny, from the marxist perspective, was therefore to be consigned to what Leon Trotsky would later call "the dustbin of history," totally and irrevocably subsumed within larger and more efficient economic units.

The national question thus emerged for marxists as a problem in determining precisely which peoples were entitled to enjoy even a transient national existence along the way to the "true internationalism" of world communism and which should have such rights foreclosed out of hand. This in itself became quite a controversial discussion when marxism faced the issue of adopting tactics with which to wage its own revolutionary struggles, rather than simply tendering or denying support to the struggles of others. At this point, things become truly cynical and mercenary. While marxism is, as we have seen, hostile to the nationalistic aspirations of "marginal" peoples, it was simultaneously perceived by many marxists that a certain advantage might accrue to marxian revolutionaries if they were to *pretend* to feel otherwise. The struggles of even the smallest and least developed nationalities might be counted on to sap the strength of the capitalist/colonialist status quo while marxist cadres went about the real business of overthrowing it; in certain instances, "national minorities" might even be counted on to absorb the brunt of the fighting, thus sparing marxism the unnecessary loss of highly trained personnel. After the revolution, it was reasoned, the marxists could simply employ their political acumen to consolidate state power in their own hands and revoke as "unrealistic" (even "counterrevolutionary") the claims to national integrity for which those of the minority nationalities had fought and died. It was also calculated that, once in power, marxism could accomplish the desired abrogation of independent national minority existence either rapidly or more gradually, depending on the dictates of "objective conditions." As Walker Connor has put it in his definitive study of the subject, "Grand strategy was...to take precedence over ideological purity and consistency" where the national question was concerned.[8]

It is not that all this was agreed on in anything resembling a harmonious or unanimous fashion by marxists. To the contrary, during the period leading up to the Russian Revolution, the national question was the topic of an extremely contentious debate within the Second International. On one side was Rosa Luxemburg and the bulk of all delegates, arguing a "purist" line that the right to self-determination does not exist in and of itself and should thus be renounced by marxism. On the other side was a rather smaller group clustered around Lenin. They insisted not only that marxism should view with favor *any* struggle against the status quo prior to the revolution, but that the International should extend any and all sorts of guarantees that might serve to stir national minorities into action. Toward this end, Lenin wrote that from the Bolshevik perspective all nations have an *absolute* right to self-determination, including the right to total secession and independence from any marxist revolutionary state. He also endorsed, as the party position on the national question, the formulation of Joseph Stalin that:

> The right to self-determination means that a nation can arrange its life according to its own will. It has the right to arrange its life on the basis of autonomy. It has the right to enter into federal relations with other nations. It has the right to complete secession. Nations are sovereign and all nations are equal.[9]

Of course, as Connor points out, "Lenin...made a distinction between the abstract right of self-determination, which is enjoyed by all nations, and the right to exercise that right, which evidently is not," at least where small or "marginal" populations are concerned.[10] Thus, shortly after the Bolshevik attainment of power came the pronouncement that, "The principle of self-determination must be subordinated to the principles of socialism."[11] The result, predictably, was that of the more than 300 distinct nationalities readily observable in what had been the czarist Russian empire, only 28—consisting almost entirely of substantial and relatively Europeanized population blocks such as the Ukranians, Armenians, Moldavians, Byelorussians, and citizens of the Baltic states—were accorded even the gesture of being designated as "republics," and this only after the matter of secession had been foreclosed. The supposed "right to enter into federal relations with other nations" was also immediately circumscribed to mean only with each other and with the central government which, of course, was seated in the former czarist citadel in Moscow. Those, such as the Ukranians, who persisted in pursuing a broader definition of self-determination were first branded as counterrevolutionary, and then radically undercut through liquidation of their sociocultural and political leadership during the stalinist purges of the '20s and '30s. There is simply no other way in which to describe the Soviet marxist process of state consolidation than the ruthlessly forcible incorporation of all the various peoples conquered by the czars into a single, seamless economic polity. As Marx once completed the capitalist model of political economy, so too did the Bolsheviks complete the unification of the Great Russian empire.

In China, the practical experience was much the same. During the so-called "Long March" of the mid-'30s, Mao Tse Tung's army of marxist insurgents traversed nearly the whole of the country. In the midst of this undertaking, they "successfully communicated the party's public position [favoring] self-determination to the minorities they encountered," virtually all of whom were well known to be yearning for freedom from the domination of the Han empire.[12] The marxists gained considerable, perhaps decisive support as a result of this tactic. But, to quote Connor:

> While thus engaged in parlaying its intermittent offers of national independence into necessary support for its cause, the party never fell prey to its own rhetoric but continued to differentiate between its propaganda and its more privately held commitment to maintaining the territorial integrity of the Chinese state.[13]

As had been the case in the USSR, the immediate wake of the Chinese revolution in 1949 saw marxist language suddenly shift, abandoning terms such as secession and self-determination altogether. Instead, the new Chinese constitution was written to decry "nationalism and national chauvinism," as "the peoples who, during the revolution, were promised the right of political independence were subsequently reincorporated by force and offered the diminished prospect of regional autonomy."[14] Only Outer Mongolia was accorded the status of existing even in the truncated Soviet sense of being a republic.

In Vietnam and Laos, leaving aside the lowland ethnic Nungs (Chinese), the only peoples holding the requisites of national identity apart from the Vietnamese and Lao themselves were the tribal mountain cultures—often referred to as "montagnards"—such as the Rhadé, Krak, Bru, Bahnar, and Hmong. Insofar as they were neither populous nor "advanced" enough to comprise promising marxian-style economic units, they were never so much as offered the "courtesy" of being lied to before the revolution; national self-determination for the mountain people was never mentioned in Ho Chi Minh's agenda. Consequently, the "yards" (as they were dubbed by U.S. military personnel) formed their own political independence organization called the *Front Unifé pour la Libération des Races Opprimées* (Unified Front for the Liberation of Oppressed Peoples) or FULRO during the early 1960s. The purpose of FULRO was and still is to resist *any* Vietnamese encroachment on montagnard national rights. Consequently, U.S. Special Forces troopers were able to utilize the FULRO consortium to good advantage as a highland mobile force interdicting the supply routes and attacking the staging areas of both National Liberation Front (NLF) main force units and units of the regular NVA (both of which were viewed by the mountain people as threats). Much to the surprise of U.S. military advisers, however, beginning in 1964 FULRO *also* started using its military equipment to fight the troops of the American-backed Saigon regime whenever *they* entered the mountains.

The message was plain enough. The montagnards rejected incorporation into *any* Vietnamese state, whether "capitalist" or "communist." In post-revolutionary Vietnam, FULRO has continued to exist and to conduct armed resistance against the imposition of Vietnamese hegemony. For its part, the Hanoi government refuses to acknowledge either the fact of the resistance or its basis. The rather better known example of the Hmong in Laos follows very much the same contours as the struggle in the south. Such a recounting could be continued at length, but the point should be made: in *no* marxist-leninist setting have the national rights of *any* small people been respected, most especially those of land-based, indigenous ("tribal") peoples. Their very right to exist as national entities has instead been denied *as such*. Always and everywhere, marxism-leninism has assigned itself a practical priority leading directly to the incorporation, subordination, and dissolution of these peoples *as such*. This is quite revealing when one considers that the term "genocide" (as opposed to "mass murder") was coined to express the reality of policies that lead not simply to the physical liquidation of groups of individuals targeted as belonging to an identified "ethnic, racial, religious, or national" entity, but to bring about the destruction of the entity itself, *as such*, through any means. Marxism-leninism, viewed in this way, is a quite consciously and specifically *genocidal* doctrine, at least where indigenous cultures are concerned.

There has been no relaxation or deviation in this circumstance during the 1980s. Most notably, during the present decade there has been the situation in Nicaragua where three Indian peoples—the Miskitos, Sumus, and Ramas—are resisting their forced incorporation into yet another revolutionary state, tacitly acknowledged by two of its principle leaders (Daniel Ortéga and Tomas Borgé Martinez) to be guided by marxist-leninist principles. The Indian nations in question have historically maintained a high degree of insularity and autonomy *vis-à-vis* Nicaragua's dominant (Latino) society, and they have also continued a viable economic life within their own territories on the Atlantic Coast. Their sole requirement of the Sandinista revolution has been that they be free to *continue* to do so, as an "autonomous zone"—by their own definition and on their own terms—within revolutionary Nicaragua. The response of the "progressive" government in Managua has been that this would be impossible because such self-determination on the part of Indians would constitute a "state within a state" (*precisely* the sort of circumstance supposedly guaranteed in leninist doctrine), and because "there are no more Indians, Creoles, or Ladinos...[w]e are *all* Nicaraguans now."[15] In other words, the Miskito, Sumu, and Rama are required by the revolution to cease to exist *as such*.

Conclusion

None of what has been said here should be taken as an apology or defense, direct or indirect, of U.S. (or other capitalist) state policies. American Indians, first and foremost, know what the United States has done and what it's about. We've experienced the meaning of the United States since long before there were marxists around to "explain" it to us. And we've continued to experience it in ways that leave little room for confusion on the matter. That's *why* we seek change. That's *why* we demand sovereignty and self-determination. That's *why* we cast about for allies and alternatives of the sort marxists have often *claimed* to be.

The purpose of our endeavor here this evening has thus been to examine the prospects for collaboration with marxism to the end that U.S. domination will be cast out of our lives once and for all. In doing so, we *must* ask—only fools would not—whether marxism offers an alternative vision to that which capitalism has imposed on us. And from the answers to this, we can discern whether marxists can really be the sort of allies that would, or even *could* actually guarantee us a positive change "come the revolution." In this regard, we need to *know* exactly what is meant when a marxist "friend" such as David Muga assures us, as he recently did, that the solutions to our present problems lie in the models offered by the USSR, China, and revolutionary Nicaragua.[16] The answers are rather painfully evident in what has I've discussed above. Marxism, in its present form at least, offers us far worse than nothing. With friends such as these, we will be truly doomed.

So it is. But must it be? I think not. An increasing number of thoughtful marxists have broken with at least the worst of marxian economism, determinism, and human chauvinism. I have noted salient examples such as Albert, Hahnel, and Baudrillard. The German Green Movement, involving a number of marxists or former marxists such as Rudi Dutschke and Rudolph Bahro, is an extremely hopeful phenomenon (although, it has thus far failed spectacularly to congeal in this country). All in all, there is sufficient basis to suggest that at least some elements of the marxian tradition are capable of transcending dogma to the extent that they may possess the potential to forge mutually fruitful alliances with American Indians and other indigenous peoples (although, at the point where this becomes true, one has reason to ask whether they may be rightly viewed as marxists any longer).

The key for us, it would seem to me, is to remain firm in the values and insights of our own traditions. We must hold true to the dialectical understanding embodied in the expression *Metakuyeayasi* and reject anything less as an unbalanced and imperfect view, even a mutilation of reality. We must continue to pursue our traditional vision of a humanity *within* rather than *upon* the natural order. We must continue to insist on, as an absolutely fundamental principle, the right of *all*

peoples—each and every one, no matter how small and "primitive"—
to freely select the fact and form of their ongoing national existence.
Concomitantly, we must reject *all* contentions by *any* state that it has
the right—for *any* reason—to subordinate or dissolve the inherent
rights of *any* other nation. And, perhaps most importantly of all, we
must choose our friends and allies accordingly. I submit that there's
nothing in this game plan that contradicts any aspect of what we've
come to describe as "the Indian way."

In conclusion, I must say that I believe such an agenda, which I
call "indigenist," can and will attract real friends, real allies, and offer
real alternatives to *both* marxism and capitalism. What will result, in
my view, is the emergence of a movement predicated on the principles
of what are termed "deep ecology," "soft-path technology," "anar-
chism" (or, probably more accurately, "minarchism"), and global
"balkanization." But we are now entering into the topic of a whole
different discussion.

Notes

1. See "White Studies or Isolation: An Alternative Model for American Indian
Studies Programs," *American Indian Issues in Higher Education*, American Indian
Studies Program, UCLA (1982), and "White Studies: The Intellectual Imperialism
of Contemporary U.S. Education," *Integrateducation*, vol. XIX, nos. 1-2 (1982).
2. Albert, Michael, and Robin Hahnel, *Unorthodox Marxism: An Essay on Capitalism,
Socialism and Revolution* (Boston, MA: South End Press, 1978), pp. 52-53.
3. *Ibid.*, p. 58.
4. Means, Russell, "The Same Old Song," in my *Marxism and Native Americans*
(Boston, MA: South End Press, 1983). The essay was originally presented as a
speech at the 1980 Black Hills International Survival Gathering (near Rapid City,
SD). It has been published in various forms, under various titles, in *Mother Jones,
Lakota Eyapaha,* and *Akwesasne Notes.*
5. See Stekloff, G., *History of the First International* (New York: Russell and Russell
Publishers, 1968).
6. Engels is quoted abundantly on the topic in *ibid.*
7. Alvinari, Shlomo, in his book *Karl Marx on Colonization and Modernization* (New
York: Doubleday Publishers, 1969), offers a truly remarkable selection of quotations from Marx on this subject.
8. Connor, Walker, *The National Question in Marxist-Leninist Theory and Strategy*
(Princeton, NJ: Princeton University Press, 1984), p. 14.
9. Stalin, J. V., *Marxism and the National Question: Selected Writings and Speeches* (New
York: International Publishers, 1942), p. 23.
10. Connor, *op. cit.*, p. 35.

11. Quoted in Clarkson, Jesse, *A History of Russia* (New York: Random House Publishers, 1961), p. 636.

12. Connor, *op. cit.*, p. 77.

13. *Ibid.*, p. 79.

14. *Ibid.*, p. 87.

15. Statements made to the author by Sandinista Interior Minister Tomas Borgé (Martinez) in Havana, Cuba, December 1984.

16. Muga, David A., "Native Americans and the Nationalities Question: Premises for a Marxist Approach to Ethnicity and Self-Determination," *Nature, Society, Thought*, vol. 1, no. 1 (1987).

Select Bibliography

The following books are among those utilized in preparing this essay. Those desiring to pursue the matters raised here should consider this bibliography as a preliminary reading list.

Adams, Nina S., and Alfred W. McCoy, ed., *Laos: War and Revolution* (New York: Harper & Row Publishers, 1970).

Albert, Michael, and Robin Hahnel, *Unorthodox Marxism: An Essay on Capitalism, Socialism and Revolution* (Boston, MA: South End Press, 1978).

Althusser, Louis, *For Marx* (New York: Vintage Books, 1970).

Alvinari, Shlomo, *Karl Marx on Colonization and Modernization* (New York: Doubleday Publishers, 1969).

Baudrillard, Jean, *The Mirror of Production* (St. Louis, MO: Telos Press, 1975).

Bloom, Solomon, *The World of Nations: National Implications in the Work of Karl Marx* (New York: Columbia University Press, 1941).

Churchill, Ward, ed., *Marxism and Native Americans* (Boston, MA: South End Press, 1983).

Clarkson, Jesse, *A History of Russia* (New York: Random House Publishers, 1961).

Connor, Walker, *The National Question in Marxist-Leninist Theory and Strategy* (Princeton, NJ: Princeton University Press, 1984).

Fedoseyev, P. N., *et. al.*, *Leninism and the National Question* (Moscow: Progress Publishers, 1977).

Hoang Van Chi, *From Colonialism to Communism* (New York: Praeger Publishers, 1964).

Ho Chi Minh, *On Revolution: Selected Writings, 1920-1966* (New York: New American Library, 1967).

Karnow, Stanley, *Mao and China: From Revolution to Revolution* (New York: Viking Press, 1972).

Lenin, V. I., and J. V. Stalin, *Selections from V. I. Lenin and J. V. Stalin on the National Question* (Calcutta: Calcutta House Publishers, 1970).

Luxemburg, Rosa, *The National Question* (New York: Monthly Review Press, 1976).

Marx, Karl, *A Contribution to the Critique of Political Economy* (New York: International Publishers, 1970).

Marx, Karl, *Capital,* Vols. I-III (New York: International Publishers, 1967).

Marx, Karl, *The Economic and Philosophic Manuscripts of 1844* (New York: International Publishers, 1964).

Marx, Karl, *Grundrisse* (New York: Vintage Books, 1973).

Marx, Karl, and Friedrich Engels, *Ireland and the Irish Question* (New York: International Publishers, 1972).

Mole, Robert L., *The Montagnards of South Vietnam: A Study of Nine Tribes* (Rutland, VT: Charles E. Tuttle Co., 1970).

Munck, Renaldo, *The Difficult Dialogue: Marxism and the National Question* (London: Zed Press, 1986).

Rocket, R.L., *Ethnic Nationalities in the Soviet Union* (New York: Praeger Publishers, 1981).

Seitz, Paul, *Men of Dignity: The Montagnards of South Vietnam* (Paris: Jacques Barthelemy, 1975).

Shaheen, S., *The Communist Theory of Self-Determination* (The Hague: W. Van Hoeve Publishers, 1956).

Stalin, J. V., *Marxism and the National Question: Selected Writings and Speeches* (New York: International Publishers, 1942).

Stekloff, G., *History of the First International* (New York: Russell and Russell Publishers, 1968).

Wilson, Dick, *The Long March: The Epic of Chinese Communist Survival* (New York: Viking Press, 1971).

NOBODY'S PET POODLE
Jimmie Durham: An Artist
for Native North America

I've known Jimmie Durham for more than twenty years. He's personally
never been anything but stone Indian the whole time, and I mean that
in the fullest possible way. He's never done anything but good for Indian
people. Anybody who wants to mess with Jimmie better be ready to talk
to me. And I mean *that* too.

—Russell Means, 1990

I have a vision—a recurrent hallucination, if you will—of an installation summing up the state of contemporary "American Indian
art." It is of a life-sized plastic Indian man, seated in a director's chair
and outfitted in the high Santa Fe style: abundant turquois, fur and
leather, genuine piñon-scented aftershave or cologne, fashionably
long but neatly razor-cut black hair, a blanket-vest over an open-
necked silk shirt, his medicine bag filled with cocaine, a $5,000 antique
concho belt and Gucci loafers. Sometimes he wears a Billy Jack hat.
Altogether, looks like something of a combination of Rudy Gorman
and Earl Biss, but thinner, sleeker, a bit firmer of jaw. In one hand, he
holds a collection of sable artist's brushes, in the other, a wad of 100
dollar bills. Tattooed in blue on his left buttock is the inscription
"Government Inspected, U.S. Department of Interior Certified Grade-
A Prime Meat." Suspended from a genuine platinum Charles Loloma
chain around his neck is a small laminated card reading "Federal
Certificate of Degree of Indian Blood."

In my mind, the plastic Indian is flanked by a pair of stuffed
poodles. Perhaps they are Afghan hounds. From chains around their
necks, both dogs also sport *their* pedigree papers. Arrayed behind this
triad is another, a row of rather shadowy and mysterious human
forms. They are standing, heads bowed, representing, each in turn,
certain other peoples, who have been officially defined in accordance
with eugenics codes during the present century. Around each of their
necks is a noose of the coarsest hemp rope from which hangs a small

spot-lit plaque. One bears a yellow Star-of-David symbol and reads "Jude." It was presented to the figure who wears it by the Ministry of Racial Purity of the Third Reich in 1936. The next, printed by South Africa's apartheid government in 1980 reads, with utter simplicity, "Colored." The third, more complex in design, offers its message in three languages. All translates as "Palestinian." It was issued in Israeli-occupied Gaza in 1991.

The plastic Indian in the foreground seems totally unaware of those standing behind him, whether human or canine. He may be conscious of them, but chooses to ignore their presence. He seems utterly resolute about focusing his attention elsewhere. After all, he has his money in hand and senses there is more to be had. Perhaps he will use some of it to buy another bracelet or some baskets from one of the old Pueblo women eking out a living down on the plaza. Or maybe the chump change will go for purchase of a bumper-sticker reading, "Indian and Proud." Who knows? Compensating for a sense of all-pervasive guilt—of downright psychological and spiritual *filthiness*—induced by selling out can be a very tricky business. And, make no mistake about it, the "Indian" in my installation knows, just like those he reflects in real life, deep down, where it counts most …he *knows* he's guilty. He *knows* he's sold his ass for a song. And he *knows* he's pandered his people, all of their heritage and whatever future they might have, for even less. Still, compulsively, he continues to wag his tail and lick the feet of whatever white patron comes before him.

Arithmetical Genocide

There is a basis to this idea which haunts me. It is called, in the sort of Orwellian turn of phrase so characteristic of colonizing bureaucracies, an "Act to Promote Development of Indian Arts and Crafts." Drafted by then-Representative (now Senator) Ben Nighthorse Campbell of Colorado in combination with Hawaii Senator Daniel Inouye's Select Committee on Indian Affairs, the law, Public Law 101-644 (104 Stat. 4662), was signed into effect by George Bush on November 29, 1990.[1] PL 101-644 makes it a crime punishable by up to $1 million in fines and up to *15 years* in federal prison for anyone not federally recognized as being a Native American to "offer to display for sale or to sell any good, with or without a Government trademark, which...suggests it is Indian produced." For galleries, museums, and other "private concerns," which might elect to market or display as "Indian arts and crafts" the work of any person not meeting the federal definition of "Indianness," a fine of up to $5 million is imposed.

The government "standard" involved—usually called "blood quantum" within the lexicon of "scientific" racism—is that a person can be an "American Indian artist" only if he or she is "certifiably" of "one-quarter or more degree of Indian blood by birth." Alternatively, the artist may be enrolled as a member of one or another of the federally sanctioned Indian "tribes" currently existing within the United States. These entities' membership rolls originated in the prevailing federal racial criteria of the late 19th century. The initial U.S. motive in quantifying the number of Indians by blood was to minimize the number of land parcels it would have to assign native people under provision of the 1887 Dawes Act, thereby freeing up about two-thirds of all reservation land for "homesteading" by non-Indians or conversion into U.S. park and forest land. Tribal rolls have typically been maintained in this reductionist fashion ever since, a matter which has served to keep federal expenditures in meeting the government's obligations—often deriving from treaty relationships with indigenous nations—at a very low level.

Obviously involved is a sort of "statistical extermination" whereby the government seeks not only to keep costs associated with its discharge of Indian Affairs at the lowest possible level, but, to eventually resolve its "Indian problem" altogether.[2] The thinking is simple. As historian Patricia Nelson Limerick frames it: "Set the blood quantum at one-quarter, hold to it as a rigid definition of Indians, let intermarriage proceed as it has for centuries, and eventually Indians will be defined out of existence."[3] Bearing out the validity of Limerick's observations is the fact that, in 1900, about half of all Indians in this country were "full-bloods." By 1990, the proportion had shrunk to about 20 percent, and is dropping steadily. Among certain populous peoples, such as the Chippewas of Minnesota and Wisconsin, only about 5 percent of all tribal members are full bloods. A third of all recognized Indians are at the quarter-blood cut-off point. Cherokee demographer Russell Thornton estimates that, given continued imposition of purely racial definitions, Native America as a whole will have disappeared by the year 2080.[4]

Probably the first consequence of the 1990 "Indian Arts and Crafts Act" was closure of the Cherokee National Museum in Muskogee, Oklahoma, a day after its passage. It seems that the late Willard Stone, whose large wood sculpture "The Trail of Tears"—incorporated into the Great Seal of the Cherokee Nation—serves as the museum's centerpiece display, failed to meet federal standards for being Indian. Stone, long considered the preeminent wood-carver in modern Cherokee history, was probably a full-blood or close to it. But he never deigned to register himself as such. The Cherokees always accepted him as Cherokee, treated him as an integral and important part of the community, and that was all that was necessary for Willard Stone. Cherokee leader Wilma Mankiller says the current tribal government will do whatever is necessary, given Stone's stature, to convey formal membership upon him posthumously.[5]

But what of the thousands of other, lesser known but still living, individuals who fall into the same category of circumstance?[6] What of the 200-odd native peoples—the Abenakis of Vermont, for example, or the Lumbees and Coatoan of North Carolina—who continue to exist, but who have always been denied federal recognition? What of groups such as the Juaneño of the San Diego area, who were once recognized by the government, but whose rolls were closed after they were unilaterally declared "extinct" as a matter of convenience by the Department of Interior during the 1970s?[7] These are questions of no small magnitude and import. All told, as Jack Forbes and others have pointed out, there are probably upwards of seven million persons in the United States today with a legitimate claim to being American Indian by descent, by culture, or both. The U.S. Bureau of the Census admits to only about 1.6 million.[8] What is at issue is arithmetical genocide, the diminishment and ultimate elimination of an entire human group by accounting procedures rather than outright physical liquidation.

The Identity Police

What is ugliest about the Indian Arts and Crafts Act is that is being passed off as something demanded by native people themselves. Indeed, its most vocal and vociferous advocates have been—by some definition or another—"Indians."[9] Specifically, the prime movers have been a rather small clique of low-talent and no-talent individuals in the Santa Fe area calling themselves the "Native American Artists Association," gathered around an alleged Chippewa and maudlin primitivist named David Bradley.[10] Mainly, they are devoted to production of what the Luiseño artist Fritz Schölder once called "Bambi painting,"[11] and, together, the NAAA—or "Bradley Group," as it is more often called—generates a truly amazing volume of prints and canvases depicting themes centered in virtually every sentimental Indian stereotype from the dime novel version of Hiawatha to Lynn Andrews' notion of spirit women. Mostly, their work is rendered with pictorial clumsiness, in the harmoniously cloying pastel tonalities so sought after by interior designers specializing in the décor of Southwest motel rooms and bank lobbies. They are, in a word, one step removed from those who stock "starving artists' sales" advertised in television commercials from coast to coast.[12]

The Bradley Group, of course, insists its goals are worthy enough: to prevent non-Indian artists, primarily Euroamericans, from "ripping-off native culture" by pretending to be Indians for commercial purposes. The facts, however, tell another story, suggesting strongly that the group's motive has always been about personal profit and that their targets have usually been other Indians. At least there is no record of their ever having found and exposed a bona fide white man masquerading as an Indian to sell his work. Instead, they have labored mightily and viciously to negate the genuine heritage of as many self-identified—and, often, community-recognized—Indian competitors as possible. Their objective was and is to restrict as closely as possible the definition of who might be viewed as an Indian artist, and therefore the definition of Indian art itself, to themselves and their various products. Anyone wishing, for whatever reason, to purchase a definably Indian art object will, so the theory goes, be compelled to buy it from them. The results of such a definitional scam stands to be quite lucrative for anyone on the inside track.

The saga began about 1980, when Bradley was unaccountably afforded an opportunity to show a few of his small Carlos Castanéda-oriented canvases in Santa Fe's prestigious Elaine Horowitch Gallery. His problem, as he saw it, was that his work was displayed in proximity to the far superior pieces of another Indian, Randy Lee White, a mixed-blood Lakota Sun Dancer who was at the time exploring the motifs developed by his people in 19th century ledger book drawings. White's work sold steadily and at increasingly high prices. Bradley's material, even priced at a discount, moved slowly when it moved at all. Bradley was, to say the least, envious of White and thus goaded, genuine inspiration seems to have struck him for what may be the first and only time in his life. If only Randy White could be forced out of the gallery, he reasoned, his own work would increase in sales, both in terms of volume and by way of "price per unit." Bradley quickly became a "political organizer," sparking a series of pickets and newspaper editorials, television interviews and meetings with the Santa Fe Chamber of Commerce. White, mortified that what had been a source of true pride and commitment on his part had become the point of such contention, stopped identifying as who he was (and is).[13] The Bradleys had scored their first victory.

Considerable irony, some of it delicious and some of it the reverse, may be found in the outcome of the "Bradley/White controversy." On the tasty side, Randy Lee White, relocated from New Mexico to Los Angeles, successfully continued his life and career, and is widely recognized as an important contemporary painter. For his part, David Bradley also left the Horowitch Gallery for a time, but for different reasons. His work continued to bomb—most serious collectors declining to acquire such hack painting, regardless of the "ethnic flavor" attached to it—even after he had managed to eliminate what he saw as his major competitor. Sometimes a kind of natural justice does prevail. Much less palatable is the loss to Native America of White's substantial painterly talent, a loss which is balanced against nothing at all. Actually, the exchange amounts to much worse than nothing when it is considered that the schmaltz Bradley applies to canvas is the ostensible replacement for White's work in signifying the quality of art Native America is capable of generating these days.

Meanwhile, the NAAA had already set out to "clean up Santa Fe" more generally, stopping in at local exhibitions to demand "proof" by way of federal documentation as to the genetic pedigrees of other Indians and threatening harassment in the event that "real" native work (their own) wasn't included in gallery inventories. Their position also evolved to hold that native people from south of the Río Grande—most of them with blood quanta discernibly higher than that of many members of the Bradley Group, but none of whom are endowed with federal credentials to that effect—shouldn't be classified as Indians. Even a full-blood and traditionally cultured Yaqui, Maya or Turahumara would be better categorized as "Hispanic," from the Bradley point of view. This novel interpretation of reality was followed by a heated questioning of the "authenticity" of Indians from Canada.[14]

This persistent and entirely self-serving narrowing of the criteria of Indianness conformed quite well with the earlier-mentioned needs of federal policymakers eager to dispense with governmental obligations to Indians once and for all. Consequently, the Bradleys were "noticed" by those inhabiting the corridors of power. Shortly, they were anointed as "expert consultants" on matters of native art and identity to Inouye's select committee, enjoying a degree of influence with their colonizers they doubtless never envisioned at the outset of their crusade to crush the competition.[15] Small wonder that PL 101-644 reads like a script the Bradleys themselves might have written. For all practical intents and purposes, they did. And, in the process, their people have been harmed, perhaps irreparably, as is always the case when important voices are stilled. The Bradley Group has acted, figuratively at least, in precisely the same fashion as the hang-around-the-fort Indians who helped assassinate Crazy Horse and Sitting Bull a century ago.

The Indigenous Alternative

It's not that there are no Indians who understand the nature and dynamics of the colonizing and genocidal processes to which we are subjected. Nor is it true that no Indians retain the courage and integrity necessary to stand up and resist against tremendous odds, regardless of personal cost or consequence. Numerous recent (and in some instances, current) examples spring readily to mind: Anna Mae Aquash, Leonard Peltier, Marie Leggo, Joe Stuntz Killsright, Tina Trudell, Buddy Lamont, Bob Robideau and Dino Butler, Janet McCloud, Pedro Bissonette, David So Happy, Eddie Hatcher, the elders at Big Mountain, Standing Deer, Byron DeSersa and many more. They, not the David Bradleys of the world, are the gut and sinew of that which has meaning in contemporary Indian life. These people, not some self-appointed identity police currying federal favor, represent the future of Native America. This is true, if indeed there is to be any native future at all.

The common denominator, aside from their intrinsic and undeniable Indianness, binding these individuals together is that each has been a member or supporter of the American Indian Movement over the past two decades. AIM, as is well known, has from its inception been constantly engaged, not only in the struggle for the survival of Native America, but in a struggle to attain its national liberation. So consistent is this pattern that members of the movement have come to be referred to in some circles as "the shock troops of Indian sovereignty in North America."[16] The effort has been grueling, its psychological and material costs in terms of personal comfort and often life itself extraordinarily high. AIM has changed substantially over the years, and has sustained a multitude of casualties, yet it has managed not merely to continue itself, but to grow in both size and strength. Today it exists in some form or another in virtually every native community on the North American continent.

Active participation in, or open support of, such a movement requires a certain outlook, a set of values and sensibilities which are deeply cynical with regard to the mores of the Eurocentric status quo, stubbornly combative yet able to find a certain irreverent humor in even the grimmest of circumstances, a quiet sense of spiritual grounding coupled to a willingness and ability to absorb considerable measures of pain and privation. Perseverance in a movement of this kind also demands an inclination to rethink the world as it is experienced, seeing it in terms of how it should be rather than as it is, an abiding sense of the rightness and wrongness of things and, perhaps most of all, an unshakable belief that the most fundamental sorts of justice can eventually be made to prevail. In sum, AIM—at least in its better moments—has truly embodied the indigenous alternative to U.S. business as usual, a living and viable American Indian worldview.[17]

Clearly, it is impossible to project the American Indian Movement as Bambi, to elaborate the essence of Wounded Knee, 1973, or the 1975 Oglala Firefight, in gentle contours or soft pastels. This can be done no more than a strip mine or slag heap can be transformed into the sort of tranquil landscape required for incorporation into Bambi art.[18] The movement has always been real, not red, at least not the red favored by buyers come to wax genteel in the glitz and glitter of the Santa Fe sunshine. One could as well reduce the horrors of Auschwitz or Babi Yar to a comfortable living room accent as to make AIM's sense of postcontact native reality, past or present, fit into such a mould. It follows that whatever AIM may be taken to be can be understood as an absolute antithesis of all and everything the NAAA stands for. It follows that the Bradleys stand as in diametrical opposition to all that remains really Indian in Native America today.

Jimmie Durham

A major difficulty has been that there has been no one to say what has needed saying in the mode of discourse the Bradleys have sought to claim as their own. Fragments of AIM conceptualization has emerged from time to time during the 1970s and '80s, mainly through the verse of Simon J. Ortiz and Wendy Rose, the songs of Floyd Westerman and the poetry, accompanied by traditional or rock music, of John Trudell. Elements of it have also been elucidated in the nonfiction books of writers such as Vine Deloria, Jr., the novels of Leslie Marmon Silko, and the stand-up comedic performances of Charlie Hill. But little of note has been done in the arenas of plastic or performance arts. In large part, this has been because those involved in AIM have been all but overwhelmed with the day-to-day demands of surviving as activists beset by some of the most virulent repression in U.S. history. To a lesser extent, it has been because, whenever time and opportunity presented themselves, AIM people concluded there were more important pursuits to claim their attention. This has been a substantial error in judgement on the part of the movement. It has given the Bradleys veritable command, however temporary, of a crucially important sphere of popular communications.

Since the late '70s, an exception to the rule has been Jimmie Durham, a mixed-blood Cherokee from western Arkansas. He came early to AIM and stayed with it as a member of organizational security and chief liaison to a nation-wide network of non-Indians called the Native American Support Committee during the worst governmental violence. From there, he went on to almost single-handedly create the International Indian Treaty Council, the movement's diplomatic arm and first indigenous group accepted as a Non-Governmental consultative organization by the United Nations. In 1977, he organized the first hemispheric delegation of native representatives to the Palace of Nations in Geneva, Switzerland. This led to formation of the UN Working Group on Indigenous Populations and the drafting, in 1992, of an element of international law entitled the "Universal Declaration of the Rights of Indigenous Peoples." Although IITC eventually collapsed as a functional entity, years after Durham's departure from its directorship in the early '80s, he had by then succeeded in using it as a vehicle on which to establish a crucial and ongoing and formal indigenous presence within the community of nations.[19]

Seeking a change of venue after his stint as IITC director, and plainly possessed of an inordinate ability to articulate meanings and motives in the most complex intercultural settings, Durham opted to redeploy his insights and experiences in the context of aesthetic rather than directly political expression. Still, his first preoccupation has remained that of expressing the sublime contradictions of "modern life" in ways that motivate his audience to become involved in progressive social change. From the outset of his artistic career, Durham has sought to strip away the intellectual veil obscuring the mechanics of the structure of social knowledge itself, compelling those with whom he interacted through his work to confront the inconsistency of even their most axiomatic "understandings" of social reality. The goal of this endeavor is, in the manner of semiotics and left deconstructionism, optimistically cerebral. What is intended is to induce a certain cognitive dissonance among participants with regard to sets of comfortably familiar assumptions about the meaning of things, societally speaking. Such dissonance generates a marked mental discomfort and compels participants, in order for psychic reconciliation to be attained, to engage in some degree of critical rethinking of their core values and beliefs. His method has been described as amounting to "a conscious and deliberate, but merciful and constructive exercise in psychological terrorism" designed to "produce a positive disordering of the existing social consensus."[20]

Towards this end, he has relied heavily upon a much-polished craft facility in combination with a biting satirical wit and acute sense of irony. He also demonstrates an uncanny knack for accentuating the tensions inherent between various aspects of his work and a complete disregard for what are normally considered to be "the rules of the game." His initial work was emphatically sculptural, and to a certain extent remains so, consisting mostly of the creation of objects, often painted, integrating traditional materials (bone, stones, hair and feathers, etc.) with aspects of modern contexts (such as steel, plastic, chrome and glass) in which they presently find themselves. Juxtaposition of these objects as a means of examining their relationality and dialectical unity quickly assumed an increasing importance. Such investigations soon came to be enhanced by incorporation of found objects, drawings or script, and photographs into the whole. Inevitably, this experimental coding of aggregations of objects led to their deployment in comprehensive mixed-media installations.[21]

Contextualization of the installations themselves—at least some of which have evolved to function as both literal and metaphorical environments—has dictated an ever more direct and active role for the artist himself in the presentation of his art. Such involvement often assumes the form of the artist's symbolically acting out, either theatrically or in more concrete ways, behavioral and/or attitudinal conceptions integral to a completion of a given work's intent. At other times, or simultaneously, the integration of art and artist requires an accompaniment to the physical display, some form of narrative elaboration, either written or verbal, sometimes both. It was this last dimension of his more general project that caused publication of a tightly orchestrated exposition of Durham's verse and prose vignettes in book form, as a 1983 volume entitled *Columbus Day*.[22] It has also prompted a decade-long series of essays and interviews published in journals such as *The Third Text* and *Artforum*.[23]

Throughout the 1980s, Durham was largely sustained by the warm reception accorded his work in settings relatively free of the dominating and rigidly maintained colonialist construction of what art by American Indians "is supposed to be" enforced in the United States. Ireland continues to serve as an admirable case in point. Meanwhile, there is some indication that the established "art world," both in New York and in the Southwest, went out of its way to ignore him. Suffice it to say that the form and content of what Durham has to offer—most especially his extension of the AIM sensibility into a wholly new and different communicative dimension—has hardly endeared him to the sources of order and authority, governmental or aesthetic, in North America. Hence, any broad appreciation on this continent of the substance and depth of Durham's efforts has been much slower in coming, a matter which did not really begin to change for the better until his prominent inclusion in critic Lucy Lippard's 1990 book, *Mixed Blessings*.[24]

An Artist for Native North America

The dawning awareness in the United States of what Jimmie Durham is about, and the increasingly favorable attention paid to what he does, has of course captured the notice of the Bradley Group. Undoubtedly, they are horrified at the situation, knowing as they must, and at the most primal of levels, that a single completed project of Durham's—let's take "Museum of the American Indian" as an example—will greatly outweigh in durability and importance the collective accumulation of kitsch and clichés they will likely produce in their lifetimes. They are not so void of intellect as to be unable to perceive the dimension of threat posed by his sheer existence, that his presence alone, by way of content and contrast, stands to negate the very shallowness and petty pretension they have embraced and sought to make synonymous with things Indian. Naturally enough, they have responded to this menace in the only way open to them, not by meeting Durham's conceptual and aesthetic challenges, but by making him a primary target of the insidious smear tactics at which they excel.

Predictably, the Bradleys' approach has been to assert that Jimmie Durham, all evidence to the contrary not withstanding, "isn't Indian" and is therefore "not credible or qualified to address Indian subject matters." Equally predictably, the only basis for these assertions is that he—like Willard Stone and countless others, the author of this essay included—has never officially enrolled at Cherokee. The accusers, since they already know the answer to be "yes," have carefully avoided questioning whether he would be enrollable, were he to decide for some reason to sign up. Less have they been willing to address the stated reason why Durham—as well as imprisoned AIM leader Leonard Peltier and many of the others most actively engaged in the struggle for Indian self-determination—have declined to participate in federally sponsored tribal enrollment procedures. As Peltier has put it:

> This is not our way. We never determined who our people were through numbers and lists. These are the rules of our colonizers, imposed for the benefit of our colonizers at our expense. They are meant to divide and weaken us. I will not comply with them.[25]

Durham himself has responded by applying the principle—so abundantly evident in both his art and in the indigenous traditions which inform it—of placing things in their proper perspective through the use of ridicule. Consider the sardonic "Artist's Disclaimer" with which he now accompanies his exhibitions:

> The U.S. Congress recently passed a law which states that American Indian artists and galleries which show their work must present government-authorized documentation of the artist's "Indian-ness." Personally, I do not much like Congress, and feel that they do not have American Indians' interests at heart. Nevertheless, to protect myself and the gallery from Congressional wrath, I hereby swear to the truth of the following statement: I am a full-blood contemporary artist, of the sub-group (or clan) called sculptors. I am not an American Indian, nor have I ever seen or sworn loyalty to India. I am not a Native "American," nor do I feel that "America" has any right to either name me or un-name me. I have previously stated that I should be considered a mixed-blood: that is, I claim to be a male but in fact only one of my parents was male.

In the end, there is a undeniable, if utterly unintended, dimension of appropriateness to the Bradleys' identification of this man as their primary adversary. It can be explained in a number of ways, but perhaps Marx's notion of "the negation of the negation" best serves our purposes here: Insofar as Durham and his work may be taken as signifying nothing so much as the negation of all the NAAA stands for, and because they in turn can only be construed as signifying an attempted final negation of all that is truly native in America, then Durham *must* be seen as representing affirmation of that which is most alive and promising for the future of Indian people in the United States. The Bradleys *have*, no matter how inadvertently, been entirely correct in their assessment of Jimmie Durham. He *is*, unquestionably, an artist of, by and for his people. By any reasonable assessment, his is the preeminent artistic voice of contemporary Native North America.

Notes

1. Ben "Nightmare" Campbell, who thinks he "might be" of three-eighths Northern Cheyenne blood quantum by birth, fashioned himself a lucrative career as an American Indian artist long before he sought tribal enrollment as part of a budding political career. Although Northern Cheyenne enrollment rules require positive proof of lineage, and Campbell by his own admission cannot provide it, these were apparently waived as part of a deal to make him the only "certified Indian in the U.S. Congress." The record of tribal enrollments is replete with comparable examples of individuals being gratuitously added to or subtracted from the rolls for reasons other than any sort of tangible Indianness. In any event, according to his own statutory criteria, Campbell made himself an appreciable fortune "ripping off Indian artists" before getting himself certified as "real."

2. Jaimes, M. Annette, "Federal Indian Identification Policy: A Usurpation of Indigenous Sovereignty in North America," in *Critical Issues in Native North America,* ed. Ward Churchill (Copenhagen: International Work Group on Indigenous Affairs, 1989), pp. 15-36. Also see Jaimes' much more extensive dissertation on the topic, *American Indian Identification-Eligibility Policy in Federal Indian Education Service Programs* (Ann Arbor, MI: University Microfilms International, Dissertation Information Service, [Order No. 9101887] 1990).

3. Limerick, Patricia Nelson, *The Legacy of Conquest: The Unbroken Past of the American West* (New York: W.W. Norton Co., 1987), p. 338.

4. Thornton, Russell, *American Indian Holocaust and Survival: A Population History Since 1492* (Norman: University of Oklahoma Press, 1987), pp. 174-82.

5. See Nichols, Lyn, "New Indian Art Regulations Shut Down Muskogee Museum," *San Francisco Examiner* (December 3, 1990).

6. Take, for example, the case of Jeanne Walker Rorex, a direct lineal descendant of Willard Stone, who was recently barred from participating in the American

Indian Heritage Exhibition at the Philbrook Museum in Tulsa (where she won awards during the 1980s). As even conservative—and usually anti-Indian—columnist James J. Kilpatrick has observed, although she is undeniably a Cherokee, "Ms. Rorex is not a tribal member. She probably could get herself certified, but as a matter of principle she has refused to petition the Cherokee council. Her point is that many true Indian artists cannot obtain certification under the act"; see Kirkpatrick's 1992 column "Government Playing the Indian Game," distributed in xerox form by the Thomas Jefferson Center, Charlottesville, VA.

7. For enumeration and analysis of these groups, see American Indian Policy Review Commission, Task Force Ten, *Report on Terminated and Nonfederally Recognized Tribes* (Washington, D.C.: U.S. Government Printing Office, 1976).

8. Forbes, Jack D., "Undercounting Native Americans: The 1980 Census and the Manipulation of Racial Identity in the United States," *Wicazo Sa Review*, vol. VI, no. 1 (spring 1990), pp. 2-26. More generally, see Gist, Noel P., and Anthony G. Dworkin, "The Blending of Races: Marginality and Identity" in *World Perspective* (New York: Wiley-Interscience Books, 1972).

9. A classic example of this is Suzan Shown Harjo, former director of the National Congress of American Indians and currently a vociferous advocate of enrollment in general, and the Arts and Crafts Act in particular. Interestingly, Harjo herself is a redhead who has come to rely rather heavily upon Lady Clairol to alter her appearance. Given that she was unable to engineer her own inclusion on the Southern Cheyenne roll until she was in her 40s—and well established politically—she herself would seem guilty of having spent much of her adult life engaged in the "fraud," to quote from one of her recent speeches, of "misrepresenting herself as an Indian for professional reasons." This is at least true under the standard of "Indianness" she is now so avid to impose on others. Moreover, she still identifies herself as being Muscogee as well as Cheyenne, yet remains unenrolled—and unenrollable—in the former "tribe." Consistency is plainly not one of the attributes of those comprising the identity police.

10. Bradley's is, in its way, a tragic and all-too-typical contemporary Indian story. A person of obviously mixed ancestry himself—he habitually wears sunglasses to hide his blue eyes—he was adopted by non-Indians at an early age and apparently was unaware of his own native identity until fairly late in life. Hence, contrary to insinuations made in his recent public utterances, he was neither raised on a Chippewa reservation in Minnesota nor in any sort of traditional manner. Throughout his adult life, he has, in fact, chosen to remain in Santa Fé, a great distance away from the people of whom he now claims to be a part. Profit aside, then, his present pose as a "super-Indian" seems motivated more than anything by a deep-seated psychological need to compensate for the degree of alienation and cultural disorientation inflicted upon him by the dominant society over the years; see his rambling, inaccurate and profoundly illogical attempt at self-justification distributed by NAAA as a mimeograph, "Columbus Quincentennial Newsletter Update," on the campus of the Institute of American Indian Arts (Santa Fé, NM) during the fall of 1992.

11. Schölder is quoted to this effect in the introduction to anonymous, *Schölder/Indians* (Flagstaff, AZ: Northland Press, 1972). Also see similar comments in the introduction to Adams, Clinton, *Fritz Schölder: Lithographs* (New York: New York

Graphic Society, 1975). For a study of alternatives in the sense that Schölder, at least, intended them—artists such as T. C. Cannon, Robert Penn, and Juane Quick-to-See Smith—see Ashton, Robert, Jr., and Jozefa Stuart, *Images of American Indian Art* (New York: Walker and Co., 1977).

12. For an in-depth examination of Bambi art, see Brody, J. J., *Indian Painters, White Patrons* (Albuquerque: University of New Mexico Press, 1971). Also see Highwater, Jamake (Jay Marks), *Many Smokes, Many Moons: A Chronology of American Indian History Through Indian Art* (Philadelphia, PA: J.B. Lippincott Publishers, 1978) and *The Sweetgrass Lives On: Fifty Contemporary American Indian Artists* (New York: Lippincott and Crowell Publishers, 1980).

13. This reconstruction comes from the recollections of participants, including Randy Lee White, with whom discussions occurred during his exhibitions at the McLaren-Markowitz Gallery (Boulder, CO) in 1985 and 1986, and at the Boulder Art Center in 1992.

14. The upshot of this in 1990 legislative terms is that a formal disclaimer must be posted in connection with exhibitions of Indian art from north or south of the U.S. borders. Art by Mexican Indians resident to the United States is—according to NAAA—only properly displayed under the label "Chicano" (witness the organization's 1991 attempts to impose this description upon Phoenix-area artist El Zarco Guerrero, who turned out to be enrolled in a southern California Mission Band).

15. Bradleyites were the only individuals queried on matters of "Indian arts and crafts" among the "over 1,000 interviews, by telephone and in person," of "federal employees, tribal members and others in the private sector who deal with Indian tribes," conducted by the Inouye Committee. For the count, see U.S. Senate, Select Committee on Indian Affairs, Special Committee on Investigations, *Federal Government's Relationship with American Indians* (Washington, D.C.: U.S. Government Printing Office, 1989), p. 3.

16. The description comes from a talk given by Janet McCloud during the 10th Annual Wounded Knee Memorial, Manderson, SD, March 1983.

17. For the best single overview of AIM and its implications, see Matthiessen, Peter, *In the Spirit of Crazy Horse* (New York: Viking Press, 1983).

18. The "real, not red" formulation accrues from Fritz Schölder's explanation of his own aspirations in approaching American Indian imagery. See Adams, *op. cit.*

19. Durham's international work is covered, to some extent, in Deloria, Vine, Jr., *Behind the Trail of Broken Treaties: An Indian Declaration of Independence* (Austin: University of Texas Press, [second edition] 1984).

20. See the videotaped 1990 interview with Durham by the author, available under the title *What Follows from the School of Fine Arts*, University of Colorado at Boulder.

21. A fine analysis of Durham's work may be found in Lippard, Lucy, "Jimmie Durham: Postmodernist 'Savage'," *Art in America* (February 1993): pp. 62-68. Also see Lippard's and other essays in the exhibition catalogue *Jimmie Durham: The Bishop's Moose and the Pinkerton Men* (New York: Exit Art, 1989).

22. Durham, Jimmie, *Columbus Day* (Minneapolis, MN: West End Press, 1983). Also see his *American Indian Culture: Traditionalism and Spiritualism in Revolutionary Struggle* (Chicago, IL: photocopied booklet, n.d.).

23. See, as examples, Durham, Jimmie, "Here at the Centre of the World," *The Third Text: Third World Perspectives on Contemporary Art and Culture*, no. 5 (winter

1988-89): pp. 21-32; Durham, Jimmie, and Jean Fisher, "The ground has been covered," *Art Forum* (summer 1989): pp. 99-105.

24. Lippard, Lucy, *Mixed Blessings: New Art in Multicultural America* (New York: Pantheon Books, 1990). Durham's work is discussed on pp. 48, 97, 183, 199, 204, 208-11.

25. Statement by Leonard Peltier to Paulette D'Auteuil at Leavenworth Federal Prison, June 1991. It should be noted that in 1988-89 David Bradley is reputed to have actively attempted to block Peltier's inclusion in Santa Fé art exhibits on the basis that the latter was a "Chicano" misrepresenting himself as a "real" Indian.

ANOTHER VISION OF AMERICA
Simon J. Ortiz's
From Sand Creek

Simon speaks in the tongue of time...

—Joy Harjo, 1989

The field of contemporary American Indian poetry is studded with luminous writers, among them Wendy Rose, Paula Gunn Allen, Adrian C. Louis, Joy Harjo, James Welch, Chrystos, Peter Blue Cloud, Maurice Kenny, Linda Hogan, Duane Niatum, Elizabeth Woody, Dian Million, Barney Bush, Carter Revard, Mary Tall Mountain, Pam Colorado, Roberta Hill Whiteman, Geary Hobson, Bill Oandasan, Leslie Marmon Silko, John Trudell, the list goes on and on. Without question, one of the very strongest voices to have emerged from this exceptionally strong showing over the past quarter-century has been that of Simon J. Ortiz, the Acoma poet.

Prior to his most recent effort, Ortiz has authored three collections of verse—*Going for the Rain* (1976), *A Good Journey* (1977), and *Fight Back: For the Sake of the Land, For the Sake of the People* (1980)—as well as a children's book entitled *The People Shall Continue* (1977). Aside from his compilations, his work has appeared over the years in numerous poetry journals and poetic anthologies in exclusively native venues, as well as those of mixed ethnicity. In whatever context, his writing has always stood out in an extraordinary fashion.

Known primarily for his longer epic narratives, Ortiz has also excelled at short impactive statements. In either format, he has always opted to serve in the time-honored capacity of tribal storyteller/historian (a common motivating factor in much modern Indian poetic endeavor) and to incorporate overt political analysis into his material. Often, he draws direct connections between the historical experiences of his own and other native peoples, on the one hand, and the current quandary in which most Indians find themselves, on the other. He has also been wont to draw clear parallels between the situation of Indians and the conditions suffered by other disenfranchised groups, including poor whites, in North America.

Ortiz's political message is straightforward enough: colonialism, the predicate to the emergence of European-style nation-states in this hemisphere, is not only alive and well today, its dynamic of domination has spread to societal proportions, becoming ever more prevalent, sublimated, and entrenched. In its most institutionalized form, colonialism, however unconsciously it may be received by those bent under its yoke, has become the normative expression of modern American life. It follows, according to Ortiz, that in order to be unburdened of colonialism—that is, to desublimate and decolonize—its victims must first be made aware of the true nature and dimension of their oppression. The best means to this end, he concludes, is to focus their attention on the commonalities of their circumstance as the most deeply oppressed and ignored of all social sectors: Native North Americans.

With the publication of *From Sand Creek* (Thunder's Mouth Press, 1981), Ortiz's first fully book-length poem, the author has accomplished two things aesthetically. First, he has transcended an earlier tension between his long and short narrative forms, revealing himself as an innovative and accomplished master of the epic. Second, in achieving this maturity, he has moved himself from his former status as a major talent among a welter of sometimes comparable indigenous writers to stand alone as the *poet laureate* of Native America. This description is not applied casually in any way at all; *From Sand Creek* is quite simply, and by a fair margin, the finest book of native verse ever produced.

From Sand Creek combines the various elements of its author's approach to poetic communication in a single continuous *tour de force* featuring a juxtaposition of biting prose passages on left-hand pages against bitterly brilliant segments of verse on the right. The emotive quality of the latter contrasts in eerily balanced harmony to the former, and the effect is devastating. At the outset, for instance, Ortiz employs a dry and matter-of-fact cadence to frame what will follow:

> November 29, 1864: On that cold dawn, about 600 Southern Cheyenne and Arapaho people, two-thirds of them women and children, were camped on a bend of Sand Creek in southeastern Colorado. The people

were at peace...The Reverend John Chivington and his Volunteers and Fort Lyons troops, numbering more than 700 heavily armed men, slaughtered 105 women and 28 men...By mid-1865, the Cheyenne and Arapaho had been driven out of Colorado Territory.

These facts have been recounted often enough, and come as no surprise to anyone acquainted with American history. To the contrary, their very redundancy has lead to a deadening of the reader to the intrinsic horror of their meaning; the information has long since lost whatever general impact it may once have possessed. Hence, on the facing page Ortiz graphically depicts, not what has just been said, but its inference, the very *essence* of it:

> This America
> has been a burden
> of steel and mad
> death

The lines, at first glance, might well have been penned by, say, Allen Ginsberg in a passage of "Howl." But here, through an intentional shifting of context away from symptoms such as the urban *zeitgeist* Ginsberg assailed in the '50s to the causes of such symptoms, Ortiz acquires a power and vision unattainable for even the best of the more topical poets. In a word, his analysis is fundamentally more *radical* (from the Greek *radix*, meaning to go to the root, or source of things). With this position firmly established, he immediately proceeds to expose the overarching theme of his book, the basis laid in understanding the carnage of the past for achieving an altogether different sort of future:

> but, look now,
> there are flowers
> and new grass
> and a spring wind
> rising
> from Sand Creek.

Elsewhere, Ortiz posits with great lucidity what he takes to be the social costs of a continuing failure to come to grips with the realities of Indian-White relations. On a left-hand page he notes that, "Repression works like a shadow, clouding memory and sometimes even to blind, and when it is on a national scale, it is just not good." Again, the reader might be prone to passing by the intensity of meaning imbedded in this sparse statement, were it not for the sudden jolt of implication Ortiz brings forth in the accompanying verse:

> In 1969
> XXXX Coloradoans
> were killed in Vietnam.
> In 1978
> XXX Coloradoans
> were killed on the highways.
>
> In 1864
> there were no Indians killed.
> Remember My Lai.
> In fifty years,
> nobody knew
> what happened.
>
> It wasn't only the Senators.
> Remember Sand Creek.

The facts are portrayed as being related, interconnected. Failure to absorb the significance of the massacre at Sand Creek, to deal with the outlooks and attitudes that caused it to happen and which made it emblematic of Euroamerica's "Winning of the West," have led consequentially to endless repetition. My Lai, that hideous symbol of the American "effort" in Southeast Asia, can *only* be understood through comprehension that it had happened before at Sand Creek. The reason of My Lai rests solidly in the forgetting of Sand Creek; the forgetting of My Lai leads inevitably to the bombing of a mental hospital in Grenada and the MOVE house in Philadelphia, a slit trench filled with 5,000 civilian corpses in Panama, the "Highway of Death" in Iraq, and even the gratuitous butchering of Branch Davidian children near Waco, Texas. Sand Creek, in the sense Simon Ortiz deploys the massacre, signifies the whole of an ongoing and very American process.

Had he ended his analysis at this point, the author's argument would have been primarily moral (albeit, correctly so). He is, however, much more far-reaching. As with any highly evolved system of colonization, the U.S. model long ago reached a point where the rank-and-file colonial victimizer began to become the victimized as well. Imperialism requires a continuously expanding pool of victims; it ultimately cares not a whit whether these be members of colonized nations, like the Cheyenne and Vietnamese, or constituents of the colonizing state itself. Thus Ortiz's reference to the number of citizens of Colorado—the entity built most literally upon the blood and bones of Sand Creek—who died in Vietnam and the highways a century later, casualties of the same consumptive process that had claimed so many native non-combatants that morning in 1864.

Ultimately, the reader is called on to engage not in some metaphorical and altruistic crusade to render abstract justice to the long dead, but to recognize and respond to a very personal and immediate jeopardy. The burned and mutilated remains shipped home in body bags from places like Khe Sahn and Plei Me were, after all, not Vietnamese or Cambodians. They were "the boy next door." The bodies will continue to come home, and increasingly so, Ortiz asserts, until those clinging to the perspectives that now sanctify America's purported right to imperial intervention—and that, sadly, is most of the population—are forced to cease in their presumption. The price of their arrogance is tremendously expensive, prohibitively so in the long run. The chickens, to paraphrase Malcolm X, will just keep coming home to roost.

This is a harsh lesson, tough enough to cast sensibilities of domination and repression in sharp relief. So too the haughty national chauvinism such a mentality engenders:

> no wonder
> they deny regret
> for the slaughter
> of their future.
>
> Denying eternity,
> it is no wonder
> they become so selflessly
> righteous.

While comprehensible, the attitude is nonetheless untenable. While facts, both historical and contemporary, can be intellectually equivocated or denied, the costs attendant to the facts continue to accrue unabated. Here, Ortiz offers a timeless observation on the warfare that is the core of colonialist reality, once the glossy veneer of the Manifest Destiny prevarication has been stripped away:

> They were amazed
> at so much blood.

> Spurting,
> Sparkling,
> splashing, bubbling, steady
> hot arching streams.
>
> Red
> and bright and vivid
> unto the grassed plains.
> Steaming.

In this passage, he could be referring equally to the agony of combat between the Cheyenne Dog Soldiers and the Colorado Volunteers during the summer of 1864, or between troopers of the 1st Air Cavalry Division and units of the People's Army of Vietnam in the Ia Drang Valley during the winter of 1965. Again, this very interchangeability of setting is precisely what Ortiz intended and he succeeds admirably. The same deftness of synonymy is then extended from Indian and Asian victims of Euroamerican "progress" to its White victims:

> Cold
> it is,
> the wind lurches
> blunt and sad.
>
> Below freezing in Colorado.
> Ghosts, Indian-like
> still driven
> towards Oklahoma.

From these White settlers, displaced and forcibly relocated ("Indian-like") by the pressures and imperatives surrounding the consolidation of American capital, Ortiz turns to his ultimate signifier of the experience shared by all who have been ground under the nailed boots of the United States: those maimed military veterans of all colors—the crippled residue of empire's cutting edge, used like toilet paper then cast aside—consigned to the dreary limbo-land reservations ("Indian-like," once again) of U.S. Veteran Administration hospitals where he himself was forced to spend an over-abundance of his life:

> O train and people and plains,
> look at me and the hospital
> where stricken men and broken boys
> are mortared and sealed

> into defensive walls. O look
> now.

In demonstrating finally and conclusively the commonality of pain and anguish wrought among colonial subjects, the author's insight is at last completely unveiled. He stares directly and unflinchingly into the depths of the pathos forming the duality of what has come to be known as "America": on the one hand, a lethal, screaming insanity which, like any cancer, destroys all it touches, including, eventually, itself; on the other, a wondrous physicality of earth, air, and water which gives, and has always given, promise of an infinitely different existence. His preoccupation with Indians and disabled veterans are, in this sense, merely the lens with which he illuminates the nature of the transformative consciousness required to realize the second potentiality.

Given that the implied, if never quite stated, objective of *From Sand Creek* is to provide an expressive vehicle upon which the sheer necessity of human liberation can be articulated and understood, it is fair to say Ortiz's project has been exceedingly ambitious. To the extent that the book attains this goal, it is equally fair to suggests it transcends its prose/poetic medium. This, of course, is the acid test as to whether a given body of verse is only very good, or if it can be legitimately said to have made the leap into the rarefied strata of poetry which is "great." *From Sand Creek* must, on balance, be accorded the latter distinction.

Even at that, however, the assessment seems insufficient. Such is the compelling quality of Ortiz's vision that we are all but helplessly drawn into a wholehearted pursuit of his essential dream:

> That dream
> shall have a name
> after all,
> and it will not be vengeful
> but wealthy with love
> and compassion
> and knowledge.
>
> And it will rise
> in this heart
> which is our America.

To Simon J. Ortiz we are obliged, collectively, to offer our sincerest thanks for having written *From Sand Creek*. And, because of the magnitude and nature of his achievement, we must at the same time enter a demand for more of the same. We are all so desperately in need of it.

I AM INDIGENIST
Notes on the Ideology
of the Fourth World

> The growth of ethnic consciousness and the consequent mobilization of
> Indian communities in the Western hemisphere since the early 1960s
> have been welcomed neither by government forces nor by opposition
> parties and revolutionary movements. The "Indian Question" has been
> an almost forbidden subject of debate throughout the entire political
> spectrum, although racism, discrimination and exploitation are roundly
> denounced on all sides.
>
> —Roxanne Dunbar Ortiz, *Indians of the Americas*

Very often in my writings and lectures, I have identified myself as
being "indigenist" in outlook. By this, I mean that I am one who
not only takes the rights of indigenous peoples as the highest priority
of my political life, but who draws on the traditions—the bodies of
knowledge and corresponding codes of value—evolved over many
thousands of years by native peoples the world over. This is the basis
on which I not only advance critiques of, but conceptualize alternatives to, the present social, political, economic, and philosophical
status quo. In turn, this gives shape not only to the sorts of goals and
objectives I pursue, but the kinds of strategy and tactics I advocate,
the variety of struggles I tend to support, the nature of the alliances
I'm inclined to enter into, and so on.

Let me say, before I go any further, that I am hardly unique or
alone in adopting this perspective. It is a complex of ideas, sentiments,
and understandings that motivates the whole of the American Indian
Movement, broadly defined, in North America. This is true whether
you call it AIM, Indians of All Tribes (as was done during the 1969
occupation of Alcatraz), the Warrior Society (as was the case with the
Mohawk rebellion at Oka in 1990), Women of All Red Nations, or
whatever.[1] It is the spirit of resistance which shapes the struggles of
traditional Indian people on the land, whether the struggle is down
at Big Mountain, in the Black Hills , up at James Bay, in the Nevada
desert, or out along the Columbia River in what is now called Wash-

ington State. [2] In the sense that I use the term, indigenism is also, I think, the outlook that guided our great leaders of the past: King Philip and Pontiac, Tecumseh and Creek Mary and Osceola, Black Hawk, Nancy Ward and Satanta, Lone Wolf and Red Cloud, Satank and Quannah Parker, Left Hand and Crazy Horse, Dull Knife and Chief Joseph, Sitting Bull, Roman Nose and Captain Jack, Louis Riel and Poundmaker and Geronimo, Cochise and Mangus, Victorio, Chief Seattle, and so on.[3]

In my view, those—Indian and non-Indian alike—who do not recognize these names and what they represent have no sense of the true history, the reality, of North America. They have no sense of where they've come from or where they are, and thus can have no genuine sense of who or what they are. By not looking at where they've come from, they cannot know where they're going, or where it is they should go. It follows that they cannot understand what it is they are to do, how to do it, or why. In their confusion, they identify with the wrong people, the wrong things, the wrong tradition. They therefore inevitably pursue the wrong goals and objectives, putting last things first and often forgetting the first things altogether, perpetuating the very structures of oppression and degradation they think they oppose. Obviously, if things are to be changed for the better in this world, then this particular problem must itself be changed as a matter of first priority.

In any event, all this is not to say that I think I'm one of the people I have named, or the host of others, equally worthy, who've gone unnamed. I have no "New Age" conception of myself as the reincarnation of someone who has come before. But it *is* to say that I take these ancestors as my inspiration, as the only historical examples of proper attitude and comportment on this continent, this place, this land on which I live and of which I am a part. I embrace them as my heritage, my role models, the standard by which I must measure myself. I try always to be worthy of the battles they fought, the sacrifices they made. For the record, I've always found myself wanting in this regard, but I subscribe to the notion that one is obligated to speak the truth, even if one cannot live up to or fully practice it. As Chief Dan George once put it, I "endeavor to persevere," and I suppose this is a circumstance that is shared more or less equally by everyone presently involved in what I refer to as "indigenism."

Others whose writings and speeches and actions may be familiar, and who fit the definition of indigenist—or "Fourth Worlder," as we are sometimes called—include Winona LaDuke and John Trudell, Simon Ortiz, Russell Means and Dennis Banks and Leonard Peltier, Glenn Morris and Leslie Silko, Jimmie Durham, John Mohawk and Chief Oren Lyons, Bob Robideau and Dino Butler, Vine Deloria, Ingrid Washinawatok, and Dagmar Thorpe. There are scholars and attorneys like Don Grinde, Pam Colorado, Sharon Venne, Tim Coulter, George Tinker, Bob Thomas, Jack Forbes, Rob Williams, and Hank Adams. There are poets like Wendy Rose, Adrian Louis, Dian Million, Chrystos, Elizabeth Woody, and Barney Bush. There are grassroots contemporary warriors, people like Roberto Cruz and Regina Brave, Bernard Ominayak, Art Montour and Buddy Lamont, Madonna Thunderhawk, Anna Mae Aquash, Kenny Kane and Joe Stuntz, Minnie Garrow and Bobby Garcia, Dallas Thundershield, Phyllis Young, Andrea Smith and Richard Oaks, Margo Thunderbird, Tina Trudell, and Roque Duenas. And, of course, there are the elders, those who have given, and continue to give, continuity and direction to indigenist expression. I'm referring to people like Chief Fools Crow and Matthew King, Henry Crow Dog and Grampa David So Happy, David Monongye and Janet McCloud and Thomas Banyacya, Roberta Blackgoat and Katherine Smith and Pauline Whitesinger, Marie Leggo and Phillip Deer and Ellen Moves Camp, Raymond Yowell, and Nellie Red Owl. [4]

Like the historical figures I mentioned earlier, these are names representing positions, struggles, and aspirations that should be well-known to every socially conscious person in North America. They embody the absolute antithesis of the order represented by the "Four Georges"—George Washington, George Custer, George Patton, and George Bush—emblemizing the sweep of "American" history as it is conventionally taught in that system of indoctrination the United States passes off as "education." They also stand as the negation of that long stream of "Vichy Indians" spawned and deemed "respectable" by the process of predation, colonialism, and genocide the Four Georges signify.[5]

The names I've named cannot be associated with the legacy of the "Hang Around the Fort" Indians, broken, disempowered, and intimidated by their conquerors, the sell-outs who undermined the integrity of their own cultures, appointed by the United States to sign away their peoples' homelands in exchange for trinkets, sugar, and alcohol. They are not the figurative descendants of those who participated in the assassination of men like Crazy Horse and Sitting Bull, and who filled the ranks of the colonial police to enforce an illegitimate and alien order against their own. They are not among those who have queued up to roster the regimes installed by the United States to administer Indian Country from the 1930s onward, the craven puppets who to this day cling to and promote the "lawful authority" of federal force as a means of protecting their positions of petty privilege, imagined prestige, and often their very identities as native people. No, indigenists and indigenism have nothing to do with the sorts of quisling impulses driving the Ross Swimmers, Dickie Wilsons, Webster Two Hawks, Peter McDonalds, and David Bradleys of this world.[6]

Instead, indigenism offers an antidote to all that, a vision of how things might be that is based on how things have been since time immemorial, and how things must be once again if the human species, and perhaps the planet itself, is to survive much longer. Predicated in a synthesis of the wisdom attained over thousands of years by indigenous, land-based peoples around the globe—the Fourth World or, as Winona LaDuke puts it, "The Host World on which the first, second, and third worlds all sit at the present time"—indigenism stands in diametrical opposition to the totality of what might be termed "Eurocentric business as usual."[6]

Indigenism

The manifestation of indigenism in North America has much in common with the articulation of what in Latin America is called *indigenismo*. One of the major proponents of this, the Mexican anthropologist/activist Guillermo Bonfil Batalla, has framed its precepts this way:

[I]n America there exists only one unitary Indian civilization. All the Indian peoples participate in this civilization. The diversity of cultures and languages is not an obstacle to affirmation of the unity of this civilization. It is a fact that all civilizations, including Western civilization, have these sorts of internal differences. But the level of unity—the civilization—is more profound than the level of of specificity (the cultures, the languages, the communities). The civilizing dimension transcends the concrete diversity. [8]

Differences between the diverse peoples (or ethnic groups) have been accentuated by the colonizers as part of the strategy of domination. There have been attempts by some to fragment the Indian peoples by establishing frontiers, deepening differences, and provoking rivalries. This strategy follows a principal objective: domination, to which end it is attempted ideologically to demonstrate that in America, Western civilization is confronted by a magnitude of atomized peoples, differing from one another (every day more and more languages are "discovered"). Thus, in consequence, such peoples are believed incapable of forging a future of their own. In contrast to this, indigenous thinking affirms the existence of one—a unique and different—Indian civilization, from which the cultures of diverse peoples extend as particular expressions. Thus the identification and solidarity among Indians. Their "Indianness" is not a simple tactic postulated, but rather the necessary expression of a historical unity, based in common civilization, which the colonizer has wanted to hide. Their Indianness, furthermore, is reinforced by the common experience of almost five centuries of Eurocentric domination. [9]

"The past is also unifying," Bonfil Batalla continues.

The achievements of the classic Mayas, for instance, can be reclaimed as part of the Quechua foundation [in present-day Guatemala], much the same as the French affirm their Greek past. And even beyond the remote past which is shared, and beyond the colonial experience that makes all Indians similar, Indian peoples also have a common historic project for the future. The legitimacy of that project rests precisely in the existence of an Indian civilization, within which framework it could be realized, once the 'chapter of colonialism ends.' One's own civilization signifies the right and the possibility to create one's own future, a different future, not Western." [10]

As has been noted elsewhere, the "new" indigenous movement Bonfil Batalla describes equates "colonialism/imperialism with the West; in opposing the West...[adherents] view themselves as anti-imperialist. Socialism, or Marxism, is viewed as just another Western manifestation." [11] A query is thus posed:

What, then, distinguishes Indian from Western civilization? Fundamentally, the difference can be summed up in terms of [humanity's] relationship with the natural world. For the West...the concept of nature is that of an enemy to be overcome, with man as boss on a cosmic scale. Man in the West believes he must dominate everything, including other [people around him] and other peoples. The converse is true in Indian civilization, where [humans are] part of an indivisible cosmos and fully aware of [their] harmonious relationship with the universal order of nature. [S]he neither dominates nor tries to dominate. On the contrary, she exists within nature as a moment of it...Traditionalism thus constitutes a potent weapon in the [indigenous] civilization's struggle for survival against colonial domination.[12]

Bonfil Batalla contends that the nature of the indigenist impulse is essentially socialist, insofar as socialism—or what Karl Marx described as "primitive communism"—was and remains the primary mode of indigenous social organization in the Americas.[13] Within this framework, he remarks that there are "six fundamental demands identified with the Indian movement," all of them associated with sociopolitical, cultural, and economic autonomy (or sovereignty), and self-determination:

First there is land. There are demands for occupied ancestral territories...demands for control of the use of the land and subsoil; and struggles against the invasion of...commercial interests. Defense of land held and recuperation of land lost are the central demands. Second, the demand for recognition of the ethnic and cultural specificity of the Indian is identified. All [indigenist] organizations reaffirm the right to be distinct in culture, language, and institutions, and to increase the value of their own technological, social, and ideological practices. Third is the demand for [parity] of political rights in relation to the state...Fourth, there is a call for the end of repression and violence, particularly that against the leaders, activists, and followers of the Indians' new political organizations. Fifth, Indians demand the end of family planning programs which have brought widespread sterilization of Indian women and men. Finally, tourism and folklore are rejected, and there is a demand for true Indian cultural expression to be respected. The commercialization of Indian music and dance are often mentioned...and there is a particular dislike for the exploitation of those that have sacred content and purpose for Indians. An end to the exploitation of Indian culture in general is [demanded].[14]

In North America, these *indigenista* demands have been adopted virtually intact, and have been conceived as encompassing basic needs of native peoples wherever they have been subsumed by the sweep of Western expansionism. This is the idea of the Fourth World, explained by Cree author George Manuel, founding president of the World Council of Indigenous Peoples:

> The 4th World is the name given to indigenous peoples descended from a country's aboriginal population and who today are completely or partly deprived of their own territory and its riches. The peoples of the 4th World have only limited influence or none at all in the nation state [in which they are now encapsulated]. The peoples to whom we refer are the Indians of North and South America, the Inuit (Eskimos), the Sami people [of northern Scandinavia], the Australian aborigines, as well as the various indigenous populations of Africa, Asia and Oceana.[15]

Manuel might well have included segments of the European population itself, as is evidenced by the ongoing struggles of the Irish, Welsh, Basques, and others to free themselves from the yoke of settler state oppression imposed on them as long as 800 years ago.[16] In such areas of Europe, as well as in "the Americas and [large portions of] Africa, the goal is not the creation of a state, but the expulsion of alien rule and the reconstruction of societies."[17] That such efforts are entirely serious is readily evidenced in the fact that, in a global survey conducted by University of California cultural geographer Bernard Neitschmann during 1985-87, it was discovered that of the more than 100 armed conflicts then underway, some 85 percent were being waged by indigenous peoples against the state or states that had laid claim to and occupied their territories.[18] As Theo Van Boven, former director of the United Nations Division (now Center) for Human Rights, put it in 1981: the circumstances precipitating armed struggle "may be seen with particular poignancy in relation to the indigenous peoples of the world, who have been described somewhat imaginatively—and perhaps not without justification—as representing the fourth world: the world on the margin, on the periphery."[19]

The Issue of Land in North America

What must be understood about the context of the Americas north of the Río Grande is that neither of the nation-states, the United States and Canada, that claim sovereignty over the territorality involved has any legitimate basis at all on which to anchor its absorption of huge portions of that territory. I'm going to restrict my remarks in this connection mostly to the United States, mainly because that's what I know best, but also because both the United States and Canada have evolved on the basis of the Anglo-Saxon common law tradition.[20] So, I think much of what can be said about the United States bears a certain utility in terms of understanding the situation in Canada. Certain of the principles, of course, also extend to the situation in Latin America, but there you have an evolution of nation-states based in the Spanish legal tradition, so a greater transposition in terms is required.[21] Let's just say that the shape of things down south was summarized eloquently enough by the Peruvian freedom fighter Hugo Blanco with his slogan, "Land or Death!"[22]

During the first 90-odd years of its existence, the United States entered into and ratified more than 370 separate treaties with the peoples indigenous to the area now known as the 48 contiguous states.[23] There are a number of important dimensions to this, but two aspects will do for our purposes here. First, by customary international law and provision of the U.S. Constitution itself, each treaty ratification represented a formal recognition by the federal government that the other parties to the treaties—the native peoples involved—were fully sovereign nations in their own right.[24] Second, the purpose of the treaties, from the point of view of the United States, was to serve as real estate documents through which it acquired legal title to specified portions of North American geography from the indigenous nations it was thereby acknowledging already owned it. From the viewpoint of the indigenous nations, of course, these treaties served other purposes: the securing of permanently guaranteed borders to what remained of their national territories, assurance of the continuation of their ongoing self-governance, trade and military alliances, and so forth. The treaty relationships were invariably reciprocal in nature: Indians ceded certain portions of their land to the United States, and the United States incurred certain obligations in exchange.[25]

Even at that, there were seldom any outright sales of land by Indian nations to the United States. Rather, the federal obligations incurred were usually couched in terms of perpetuity. The arrangements were set up by the Indians so that, as long as the United States honored its end of the bargains struck, it would have the right to occupy and use defined portions of Indian land. In this sense, the treaties more resemble rental or leasing instruments than actual deeds. And you know what happens under Anglo-Saxon common law when a tenant violates the provisions of a rental agreement. The point here is that the United States has long since defaulted on its responsibilities under every single treaty obligation it ever incurred with regard to Indians. There is really no dispute about this. In fact, there's even a Supreme Court opinion—the 1903 *Lonewolf* case—in which the good "justices" held that the United States enjoyed a "right" to disregard any treaty obligation to Indians it found inconvenient, but that the remaining treaty provisions continued to be binding on the Indians. This was, the high court said, because the United States was the stronger of the nations involved, and thus wielded "plenary" power—this simply means *full* power—over the affairs of the weaker indigenous nations. Therefore, the court felt itself free to unilaterally "interpret" each treaty as being a bill of sale rather than an rental agreement.[26]

Stripped of its fancy legal language, the Supreme Court's position was (and remains) astonishingly crude. There's an old adage that "possession is nine-tenths of the law." Well, in this case, the court went a bit further, arguing that possession was *all* of the law. Further, the highest court in the land went on record arguing bold-faced that, where Indian property rights are concerned, might, and might alone, makes right. The United States held the power to simply take Indian land, they said, and therefore it had the "right" to do so. If you think about it, that's precisely what the Nazis argued only 30 years later, and the United States had the unmitigated audacity to profess outrage and shock that Germany was so blatantly transgressing elementary standards of international law and the most basic requirements of human decency.[27] For that matter, this is all that Saddam Hussein was about when he took Kuwait—indeed, Iraq had a far stronger claim to rights over Kuwait than the United States has ever had with regard to Indian Country—with the result that George Bush began to babble about fighting a "just war" to "roll back naked aggression," "free occupied territory," and "reinstate a legitimate government." If he was in any way serious about that proposition, he'd have had to call air strikes in on himself instead of ordering the bombing of Baghdad.[28]

Be that as it may, there are a couple of other significant problems with the treaty constructions by which the United States allegedly assumed title over its land base. On the one hand, a number of the ratified treaties can be shown to be fraudulent or coerced, and thus invalid. The nature of the coercion is fairly well known, so let's just say that perhaps a third of the ratified treaties involved direct coercion and shift over to the matter of fraud. This assumes the form of everything from the deliberate misinterpretation of proposed treaty provisions to Indian representatives during negotiations to the Senate's alteration of treaty language after the fact and without the knowledge of the Indian signatories. On a number of occasions, the United States appointed its own preferred Indian "leaders" to represent nations in treaty negotiations.[29] In at least one instance—the 1861 Treaty of Fort Wise—U.S. negotiators appear to have forged the signatures of various Cheyenne and Arapaho leaders.[30] Additionally, there are about 400 treaties that were never ratified by the Senate, and were therefore never legally binding, but on which the United States now asserts its claims concerning lawful use and occupancy rights to, and jurisdiction over, appreciable portions of North America.[31]

When all is said and done, however, even these extremely dubious bases for United States title are insufficient to cover the gross territoriality at issue. The federal government itself tacitly admitted as much during the '70s, in the findings of the so-called Indian Claims Commission, an entity created to "quiet" title to all illegally taken Indian land within the lower 48 states.[32] What the commission did over the previous 35 years was in significant part to research the ostensible documentary basis for United States title to literally every square foot of its claimed territory. It found, among other things, that the United States had no legal basis whatsoever—no treaty, no agreement, not even an arbitrary act of congress—to fully one-third of the area within its boundaries.[33] At the same time, the data revealed that the reserved areas still nominally possessed by Indians had been reduced to about 2.5 percent of the same area.[34] What this means in plain English is that the United States cannot pretend to even a shred of legitimacy in its occupancy and control of upwards of 30 percent of its "home" territoriality. And, lest such matters be totally lost in the shuffle, I should note that it has even less legal basis for its claims to the land in Alaska and Hawai'i.[35] Beyond that, its "right" to assert dominion over Puerto Rico, the "U.S." Virgin Islands, "American" Samoa, Guam, and the Marshall Islands tends to speak for itself, don't you think?

Priority of Indian Land Recovery in the U.S.

Leaving aside questions concerning the validity of various treaties, the beginning point for any indigenist endeavor in the United States centers, logically enough, in efforts to restore direct Indian control over the huge portion of the continental United States that was plainly never ceded by native nations. On the bedrock of this foundation, a number of other problems integral to the present configuration of power and privilege in North American society can be resolved, not just for Indians, but for everyone else as well. It's probably impossible to solve, or even to begin meaningfully addressing, certain of these problems in any other way. But still, it is, as they say, "no easy sell" to convince anyone outside the more conscious sectors of the American Indian population itself of the truth of this very simple fact.

In part, uncomfortable as it may be to admit, this is because even the most progressive elements of the North American immigrant population share a perceived commonality of interest with the more reactionary segments. This takes the form of a mutual insistence on an imagined "right" to possess native property, merely because they are here, and because they desire it. The Great Fear within any settler state is that if indigenous land rights are ever openly acknowledged, and native people therefore begin to recover some significant portion of their land, the immigrants will correspondingly be dispossessed of that which they've come to consider "theirs"—most notably, individually held homes, small farms and ranches, and the like. Tellingly, every major Indian land recovery initiative in the United States during the second half of the 20th century—those in Maine, the Black Hills, the Oneida claims in New York State, and Western Shoshone are prime examples—has been met by a propaganda barrage from right-wing organizations ranging from the Ku Klux Klan to the John Birch Society to the Republican Party, warning individual non-Indian property holders of exactly this "peril."[36]

I'll debunk some of this nonsense in a moment, but first I want to take up the posture of self-proclaimed leftist radicals in the same connection. And I'll do so on the basis of principle, because justice is supposed to matter more to progressives than to right-wing hacks. Let me say that the pervasive and near-total silence of the Left in this connection has been quite illuminating. Non-Indian activists, with only a handful of exceptions, persistently plead that they can't really take a coherent position on the matter of Indian land rights because, "unfortunately," they're "not really conversant with the issues" (as if these were tremendously complex). Meanwhile, they do virtually nothing, generation after generation, to inform themselves on the topic of who actually owns the ground they're standing on. The record can be played only so many times before it wears out and becomes just another variation of "hear no evil, see no evil." At this point, it doesn't take Albert Einstein to figure out that the Left doesn't know much about such things because it's never *wanted* to know, or that this is so because it's always had its own plans for utilizing land it has no more right to than does the status quo it claims to oppose.

The usual technique for explaining this away has always been a sort of *pro forma* acknowledgment that Indian land rights are of course "really important stuff" (yawn), but that one "really doesn't have a lot of time" to get into it (I'll buy your book, though, and keep it on my shelf, even if I never read it). Reason? Well, one is just "overwhelmingly preoccupied" with working on "*other* important issues" (meaning, what they consider to be *more* important issues). Typically enumerated are sexism, racism, homophobia, class inequities, militarism, the environment, or some combination of these. It's a pretty good evasion, all in all. Certainly, there's no denying any of these issues their due; they *are* all important, obviously so. But more important than the question of land rights? There are some serious problems of primacy and priority imbedded in the orthodox script.

To frame things clearly in this regard, let's hypothesize for a moment that all of the various non-Indian movements concentrating on each of these issues were suddenly successful in accomplishing their objectives. Let's imagine that the United States as a whole were somehow transformed into an entity defined by the parity of its race, class, and gender relations, its embrace of unrestricted sexual preference, its rejection of militarism in all forms, and its abiding concern with environmental protection (I know, I know, this is a sheer impossibility, but that's my point). When all is said and done, the society resulting from this scenario is still, first and foremost, a colonialist society, an imperialist society in the most fundamental sense possible and with all that this implies. This is true because the scenario does nothing at all to address the fact that whatever is happening happens on someone else's land, not only without their consent, but through an adamant disregard for their rights to the land. Hence, all it means is that the immigrant or invading population has rearranged its affairs in such a way as to make itself more comfortable at the continuing expense of indigenous people. The colonial equation remains intact and may even be reinforced by a greater degree of participation and vested interest in maintenance of the colonial order among the settler population at large.[37]

The dynamic here is not very different from that evident in the American Revolution of the late 18th century, is it? And we all know very well where that led, don't we? Should we therefore begin to refer to socialist imperialism, feminist imperialism, gay and lesbian imperialism, environmentalist imperialism, African American, and la Raza imperialism? I would hope not.[38] I would hope this is all just a matter of confusion, of muddled priorities among people who really do mean well and who'd like to do better. If so, then all that is necessary to correct the situation is a basic rethinking of what must be done, and in what order. Here, I'd advance the straightforward premise that the land rights of "First Americans" should serve as a first priority for everyone seriously committed to accomplishing positive change in North America.

But before I suggest everyone jump up and adopt this priority, I suppose it's only fair that I interrogate the converse of the proposition: if making things like class inequity and sexism the preeminent focus of progressive action in North America inevitably perpetuates the internal colonial structure of the United States, does the reverse hold true? I'll state unequivocally that it does not. There is no indication whatsoever that a restoration of indigenous sovereignty in Indian Country would foster class stratification anywhere, least of all in Indian Country. In fact, all indications are that when left to their own devices, indigenous peoples have consistently organized their societies in the most class-free manners. Look to the example of the Haudenosaunee (Six Nations Iroquois Confederacy). Look to the Muscogee (Creek) Confederacy. Look to the confederations of the Yaqui and the Lakota, and those pursued and nearly perfected by Pontiac and Tecumseh. They represent the very essence of enlightened egalitarianism and democracy. Every imagined example to the contrary brought forth by even the most arcane anthropologist can be readily offset by a couple of dozen other illustrations along the lines of those I just mentioned.[39]

Would sexism be perpetuated? Ask one of the Haudenosaunee clan mothers, who continue to assert political leadership in their societies through the present day. Ask Wilma Mankiller, current head of the Cherokee nation, a people that traditionally led by what were called "Beloved Women." Ask a Lakota woman—or man, for that matter—about who it was that owned all real property in traditional society, and what that meant in terms of parity in gender relations. Ask a traditional Navajo grandmother about her social and political role among her people. Women in most traditional native societies not only enjoyed political, social, and economic parity with men, they often held a preponderance of power in one or more of these spheres.

Homophobia? Homosexuals of both genders were (and in many settings still are) deeply revered as special or extraordinary, and therefore spiritually significant, within most indigenous North American cultures. The extent to which these realities do not now pertain in native societies is exactly the extent to which Indians have been subordinated to the mores of the invading, dominating culture. Insofar as restoration of Indian land rights is tied directly to reconstitution of traditional indigenous social, political, and economic modes, you can see where this leads: the relations of sex and sexuality accord rather well with the aspirations of feminist and gay rights activism.[40]

How about a restoration of native land rights precipitating some sort of "environmental holocaust"? Let's get at least a little bit real here. If you're not addicted to the fabrications of Smithsonian anthropologists about how Indians lived,[41] or George Weurthner's Eurosupremacist Earth First! fantasies about how we beat all the wooly mammoths and mastodons and saber-toothed cats to death with sticks,[42] then this question isn't even on the board. I know it's become fashionable among *Washington Post* editorialists to make snide references to native people "strewing refuse in their wake" as they "wandered nomadically" about the "prehistoric" North American landscape.[43] What is that supposed to imply? That we, who were mostly "sedentary agriculturalists" in any event, were dropping plastic and aluminum cans as we went? Like I said, let's get real. Read the accounts of early European invaders about what they encountered: North America was invariably described as being a "pristine wilderness" at the point of European arrival, despite the fact that it had been occupied by 15 or 20 million people enjoying a remarkably high standard of living for nobody knows how long: 40,000 years? 50,000 years? longer?[44] Now contrast that reality to what's been done to this continent over the past couple of hundred years by the culture Weurthner, the Smithsonian, and the *Post* represent, and you tell *me* about environmental devastation.[45]

That leaves militarism and racism. Taking the last first, there really is no indication of racism in traditional Indian societies. To the contrary, the record reveals that Indians habitually intermarried between groups, and frequently adopted both children and adults from other groups. This occurred in pre-contact times between Indians, and the practice was broadened to include those of both African and European origin—and ultimately Asian origin as well—once contact occurred. Those who were naturalized by marriage or adoption were considered members of the group, pure and simple. This was always the Indian view.[46] The Europeans and subsequent Euroamerican settlers viewed things rather differently, however, and foisted off the notion that Indian identity should be determined primarily by "blood quantum," an outright eugenics code similar to those developed in places like Nazi Germany and apartheid South Africa. Now, *that's* a racist construction if there ever was one. Unfortunately, a lot of Indians have been conned into buying into this anti-Indian absurdity, and that's something to be overcome. But there's also solid indication that quite a number of native people continue to strongly resist such things as the quantum system.[47]

As to militarism, no one will deny that Indians fought wars among themselves both before and after the European invasion began. Probably half of all indigenous peoples in North America maintained permanent warrior societies. This could perhaps be reasonably construed as "militarism," but not, I think, with the sense the term conveys within the European/Euroamerican tradition. There were never, so far as anyone can demonstrate, wars of annihilation fought in this hemisphere prior to the Columbian arrival. None. In fact, it seems that it was a more or less firm principle of indigenous warfare *not* to kill, the object being to demonstrate personal bravery, something that could be done only against a *live* opponent. There's no honor to be had in killing another person, because a dead person can't hurt you. There's no risk. This is not to say that nobody ever died or was seriously injured in the fighting. They were, just as they are in full contact contemporary sports like football and boxing. Actually, these kinds of Euroamerican games are what I would take to be the closest modern parallels to traditional inter-Indian warfare. For Indians, it was a way of burning excess testosterone out of young males, and not much more. So, militarism in the way the term is used today is as alien to native tradition as smallpox and atomic bombs.[48]

Not only is it perfectly reasonable to assert that a restoration of Indian control over unceded lands within the United States would do nothing to perpetuate such problems as sexism and classism, but the reconstitution of indigenous societies this would entail stands to free the affected portions of North America from such maladies altogether. Moreover, it can be said that the process should have a tangible impact in terms of diminishing such oppressions elsewhere. The principle is this: sexism, racism, and all the rest arose here as a concomitant to the emergence and consolidation of the Eurocentric nation-state form of sociopolitical and economic organization. Everything the state does, everything it can do, is entirely contingent on its maintaining its internal cohesion, a cohesion signified above all by its pretended territorial integrity, its ongoing domination of Indian Country. Given this, it seems obvious that the literal dismemberment of the nation-state inherent to Indian land recovery correspondingly reduces the ability of the state to sustain the imposition of objectionable relations within itself. It follows that realization of indigenous land rights serves to undermine or destroy the ability of the status quo to continue imposing a racist, sexist, classist, homophobic, militaristic order on non-Indians.

A brief aside: Anyone with doubts as to whether it's possible to bring about the dismemberment from within of a superpower state in this day and age ought to sit down and have a long talk with a guy named Mikhail Gorbachev. It would be better yet if you could chew the fat with Leonid Brezhnev, a man who we can be sure would have replied in all sincerity—only a decade ago—that this was the most outlandish idea he'd ever heard. Well, look on a map today, and see if you can find the Union of Soviet Socialist Republics. It ain't there, my friends. Instead, you're seeing, and you're seeing it more and more, the reemergence of the very nations Leon Trotsky and his colleagues consigned to the "dustbin of history" clear back at the beginning of the century. These mega-states are not immutable. They can be taken apart. They can be destroyed. But first we have to decide that we can do it, and that we *will* do it.

So, all things considered, when indigenist movements like AIM advance slogans like "United States Out of North America," non-Indian radicals shouldn't react defensively. They should cheer. They should see what they might do to help. When they respond defensively to sentiments like those expressed by AIM, what they are ultimately defending is the very government, the very order they claim to oppose so resolutely. And if they manifest this contradiction often enough, consistently enough, pathologically enough, then we have no alternative but to take them at their word, that they really are at some deep level or another aligned—all protest to the contrary—with the mentality that endorses our permanent dispossession and disenfranchisement, our continuing oppression, and our ultimate genocidal obliteration as self-defining and self-determining peoples.

In other words, they make themselves part of the problem rather than becoming part of the solution.

The Thrust of Indian Land Restoration

There are certain implications to Indian control over Indian land that need to be clarified, beginning with a debunking of the "Great Fear," the reactionary myth that any substantive native land recovery would automatically lead to the mass dispossession and eviction of individual non-Indian home owners. Maybe in the process I can reassure a couple of radicals that it's okay to be on the right side of this issue, that they won't have to give something up in order to part company with George Bush on this. It's hard, frankly, to take this up without giggling because of some of the images it inspires. I mean, what *are* people worried about here? Do y'all really foresee Indians standing out on the piers of Boston and New York City, issuing sets of waterwings to long lines of non-Indians so they can all swim back to the Old World? Gimme a break.

Seriously, you can search high and low, and you'll never find an instance in which Indians have advocated that small property owners be pushed off the land in order to satisfy land claims. The thrust in every single case has been to recover land within national and state parks and forests, grasslands, military reservations, and the like. In a few instances, major corporate holdings have been targeted. A couple of times, as in the Black Hills, a sort of joint jurisdiction between Indians and the existing non-Indian government has been discussed with regard to an entire treaty area.[49] But even in the most hard-line of the indigenous positions concerning the Black Hills, that advanced by Russell Means in his TREATY Program, resumption of exclusively Lakota jurisdiction which demanded, there is no mention of dispossessing or evicting non-Indians.[50] Instead, other alternatives—which I'll take up later—were carefully spelled out.

But first, I'd like to share with you something the right-wing propagandists never mention when they're busy whipping up non-Indian sentiment against Indian rights. You'll recall I said that the quantity of unceded land within the continental United States makes up about one-third of the land mass. Let's just round this off to 30 percent, because there's the matter of the 2.5 percent of the overall land base still being set aside as Indian reservations. Now juxtapose that 30 percent to the approximately 35 percent of the same land mass the federal government presently holds in various kinds of trust status. Add the 10 or 12 percent of the land the 48 contiguous states hold in trust. You end up with a 30 percent Indian claim against a 45 to 47 percent *governmental* holding.[51] Never mind the percentage of the land held by major corporations. Conclusion? It is, and always has been, quite possible to accomplish the return of every square inch of unceded Indian Country in the United States without tossing a single non-Indian home owner off the land on which they live.

Critics—that's the amazingly charitable term employed by those who ultimately oppose the assertion of indigenous rights in any form and as a matter of principle—are always quick to point out that the problem with this arithmetic is that the boundaries of the government trust areas do not necessarily conform in all cases to the boundaries of unceded areas. That's true enough, although I'd just as quickly point out that more often than not they *do* correspond. This "problem" is nowhere near as big as it's made out to be. And there's nothing intrinsic to the boundary question that couldn't be negotiated, once non-Indian America acknowledges that Indians have an absolute moral and legal right to the quantity of territory that was never ceded. Boundaries can be adjusted, often in ways that can be beneficial to both sides of the negotiation.[52]

Let me give you an example. Along about 1980, a couple of Rutgers University professors, Frank and Deborah Popper, undertook a comprehensive study of land-use patterns and economy in the Great Plains region. What they discovered is that 110 counties—a quarter of all the counties in the entire Plains region, falling within the western portions of the states of North and South Dakota, Nebraska, Kansas, Oklahoma, and Texas, as well as eastern Montana, Wyoming, Colorado, and New Mexico—have been fiscally insolvent since the moment they were taken from native people a century or more ago. This is an area of about 140,000 square miles, inhabited by a widely dispersed non-Indian population of only around 400,000 attempting to maintain school districts, police and fire departments, road beds, and all the other basic accoutrements of "modern life" on the negligible incomes that can be eked out from cattle grazing and wheat farming on land which is patently unsuited for both enterprises. The Poppers found that, without considerable federal subsidy each and every year, none of these counties would ever have been viable. Nor, on the face of it, will any of them ever be. Put bluntly, the pretense of bringing Euroamerican "civilization" to the Plains represents nothing more than a massive economic burden on the rest of the United States.

What the Poppers proposed on the basis of these findings is that the government cut its perpetual losses, buying out the individual land holdings within the target counties, and convert them into open space wildlife sanctuaries known as the "Buffalo Commons." The whole area would in effect be turned back to the bison which were very nearly exterminated by Phil Sheridan's buffalo hunters back in the 19th century as a means of starving "recalcitrant" Indians into surrendering. The result would be, they argue, both environmentally and economically beneficial to the nation as a whole. It is instructive that their thinking has gained increasing credibility and support from Indians and non-Indians alike during the second half of the '80s. Another chuckle here: Indians have been trying to tell non-Indians that this would be the outcome of fencing in the Plains ever since 1850 or so, but some folks have a real hard time catching on. Anyway, it is entirely possible that we'll see some actual motion in this direction over the next few years.[53]

So, let's take the Poppers' idea to its next logical step. There are another hundred or so counties that have always been economically marginal adjoining the "perpetual red ink" counties they've identified. These don't represent an actual drain on the United States economy, but they don't contribute much either. They could be "written off" and included in the Buffalo Commons schema with no one feeling any ill effects whatsoever. Now add in adjacent areas like the national grasslands in Wyoming, the national forest and parklands in the Black Hills, extraneous military reservations like Ellsworth Air Force Base, and existing Indian reservations. What you end up with is a huge territory lying east of Denver, west of Lawrence, Kansas, and extending from the Canadian border to southern Texas, all of it "outside the loop" of United States business as usual.

The bulk of this area is unceded territory owned by the Lakota, Pawnee, Arikara, Hidatsa, Mandan, Crow, Shoshone, Assiniboine, Cheyenne, Arapaho, Kiowa, Comanche, Jicarilla, and Mescalero Apache nations. There would be little cost to the United States, and virtually no arbitrary dispossession or dislocation of non-Indians, if the entire Commons were restored to these peoples. Further, it would establish a concrete basis from which genuine expressions of indigenous self-determination could begin to reemerge on this continent, allowing the indigenous nations involved to begin the process of reconstituting themselves socially and politically, and to begin to recreate their traditional economies in ways that make contemporary sense. This would provide alternative socioeconomic models for possible adaptation by non-Indians, and alleviate a range of not inconsiderable costs to the public treasury incurred by keeping the Indians in question in a state of abject and permanent dependency.

All right, as critics will undoubtedly be quick to point out, an appreciable portion of the Buffalo Commons area I've sketched out—perhaps a million acres—lies outside the boundaries of unceded territory. That's the basis for the sorts of multilateral negotiations between the United States and indigenous nations I mentioned earlier. This land will need to be "charged off" in some fashion against unceded land elsewhere, and in such a way as to bring other native peoples into the mix. The Ponca, Omaha, and Osage, whose traditional territories fall within the area in question, come immediately to mind; but this would extend as well to all native peoples willing to exchange land claims somewhere else for actual acreage in this locale. The idea is to consolidate a distinct indigenous territorality while providing a definable land base to as many different Indian nations as possible in the process.

From there, the principle of the Buffalo Commons *cum* Indian Territory could be extended westward into areas that adjoin or are at least immediately proximate to the Commons area itself. The fact is that vast areas of the Great Basin and Sonoran Desert regions of the United States are even more sparsely populated and economically insolvent than the Plains. A great deal of the area is also held in federal trust. Hence, it is reasonable—in my view at least—to expand the Commons territory to include most of Utah and Nevada, northern Montana and Idaho, quite a lot of eastern Washington and Oregon, most of the rest of New Mexico, and the lion's share of Arizona. This would encompass the unceded lands of the Blackfoot and Gros Ventre, Salish, Kootenai, Nez Percé, Yakima, Western Shoshone, Goshutes and Utes, Paiutes, Navajo, Hopi and other Pueblos, Mescalero and Chiricahua Apache, Havasupi, Yavapai, and O'Odham. It would also set the stage for further exchange negotiations to consolidate this additional territory, which would serve to establish a land base for a number of other indigenous nations.

At this point, we've arrived at an area comprising roughly one third of the continental United States, a territory which—regardless of the internal political and geographical subdivisions effected by the array of native peoples within it—could be defined as a sort of "North American Union of Indigenous Nations." Such an entity would be in a position to assist other indigenous nations outside its borders, but still within the remaining territorial corpus of the United States, to resolve land claim issues accruing from fraudulent or coerced treaties of cession (another 15 or 20 percent of the present 48 states). It would also be in a position to facilitate an accommodation of the needs of untreatied peoples within the United States, the Abenaki of Vermont, for example, and the Native Hawaiians and Alaskans. Similarly, it would be able to help secure the self-determination of United States colonies like Puerto Rico. You can see the direction the dominoes begin to fall.

Nor does this end with the United States. Any sort of indigenous union of the kind I've described would be as eligible for admission as a fully participating member of the United Nations as, say, Croatia and the Ukraine have recently shown themselves to be. This would set a very important precedent, insofar as there's never been an American Indian entity of any sort accorded such political status on the world stage. The precedent could serve to pave the way for comparable recognition and attainments by other Native American nations, notably the confederation of Incan peoples of the Andean highlands and the Mayans of present-day Guatemala and southern Mexico (Indians are the majority population, decisively so, in both locales). And, from there, other indigenous nations, around the world. Again, you can see the direction the dominoes fall. If we're going to have a "New World Order," let's make it something just a bit different from what George Bush and his friends had in mind. Right?

Sharing the Land

There are several closely related matters that should be touched on before wrapping this up. One has to do with the idea of self-determination, what it is that is meant when indigenists demand this unrestricted right for native peoples. Most non-Indians, and even a lot of Indians, always seem confused by this and want to know whether it's not the same as complete separation from the United States, or Canada, or whatever the colonizing power may be. The answer is, "not necessarily." The unqualified acknowledgement of the right of the colonized to total separation ("secession") by the colonizer is the necessary point of departure for any exercise of self-determination. Decolonization means the colonized can then exercise the right in whole or in part, as they see fit, in accordance with their own customs and traditions and their own appreciation of their needs. They decide for themselves what degree of autonomy they wish to enjoy, and thus the nature of their political and economic relationships, not only with their former colonizers, but with all other nations as well.[54]

My own inclination, which is in some ways an emotional preference, tends to run toward complete sovereign independence, but that's not the point. I have no more right to impose my preferences on indigenous nations than do the colonizing powers; each indigenous nation will choose for itself the exact manner and extent to which it expresses its autonomy, its sovereignty. To be honest, I suspect very few would be inclined to adopt my sort of "go it alone" approach (and, actually, I must admit that part of my own insistence on it often has more to do with forcing concession of the right from those who seek to deny it than it does with putting it into practice). In the event, I expect you'd see the hammering out of a number of sets of international relations in the "free association" vein, a welter of variations of commonwealth and home rule governance.[55]

The intent here is not to visit some sort of retribution, real or symbolic, on the colonizing or former colonizing powers—no matter how much it may be deserved in an abstract sense. It is to arrive at new sets of relationships between peoples that effectively put an end to the era of international domination. The need is to gradually replace the existing world order with one that is predicated on collaboration and cooperation between nations. The only way to ever really accomplish that is to physically disassemble the gigantic state structures—structures that are literally predicated on systematic intergroup domination; they cannot in any sense exist without it—which evolved from the imperialist era. A concomitant of this disassembly is the inculcation of voluntary, consensual interdependence between formerly dominated and dominating nations, and a redefinition of the word "nation" itself to conform to its original meaning: bodies of people bound together by their bioregional and other natural cultural affinities.[56]

This last point is, it seems to me, crucially important. Partly, that's because of the persistent question of who it is who gets to remain in Indian Country once land restoration and consolidation has occurred. The answer, I think, is anyone who wants to, up to a point. By "anyone who wants to," I mean anyone who wishes to apply for formal citizenship within an indigenous nation, thereby accepting the idea that s/he is placing him or herself under unrestricted Indian jurisdiction and will thus be required to abide by native law.[57] Funny thing: I hear a lot of non-Indians asserting that they reject nearly every aspect of United States law, but the idea of placing themselves under anyone else's jurisdiction seems to leave them pretty queasy. I have no idea how many non-Indians might actually opt for citizenship in an Indian nation when push comes to shove, but I expect there will be some. And I suspect some Indians have been so indoctrinated by the dominant society that they'll elect to remain within it rather than availing themselves of their own citizenship. So there'll be a bit of a trade-off in this respect.

Now, there's the matter of the process working only "up to a point." That point is very real. It is defined not by political or racial considerations, but by the carrying capacity of the land. The population of indigenous nations everywhere has always been determined by the number of people who could be sustained in a given environment or bioregion without overpowering and thereby destroying that environment.[58] A very carefully calculated balance—one which was calibrated to the fact that in order to enjoy certain sorts of material comfort, the human population had to be kept at some level below saturation *per se*—was always maintained between the number of humans and the rest of the habitat. In order to accomplish this, Indians incorporated into the very core of their spiritual traditions the concept that all life forms and the earth itself possess rights equal to those enjoyed by humans.

Rephrased, this means it would be a violation of a foundation of traditional Indian law to supplant or eradicate another species, whether animal or plant, to make way for some greater number of humans, or to increase the level of material comfort available to those who already exist. Conversely, it is a fundamental requirement of traditional law that each human accept her or his primary responsibility, that of maintaining the balance and harmony of the natural order *as it is encountered*.[59] One is essentially free to do anything one wants in an Indian society so long as this cardinal rule is adhered to. The bottom line with regard to the maximum population limit of Indian Country as it has been sketched in this presentation is some very finite number. My best guess is that a couple of million people would be pushing things right through the roof. Whatever. Citizens can be admitted until that point has been reached, and no more. And the population cannot increase beyond that number over time, no matter at what rate. Carrying capacity is a fairly constant reality; it tends to change over thousands of years, when it changes at all.

Population and Environment

What I'm going to say next will probably startle a few people (as if what's been said already hasn't). I think this principle of population restraint is the single most important example Native North America can set for the rest of humanity. It is *the* example that is most crucial for others to emulate. Check it out. I just read that Japan, a small island nation which has so many people that they're literally tumbling into the sea, and which has exported about half again as many people as live on the home islands, is expressing "official concern" that its birth rate has declined very slightly over the last few years. The worry is that in 30 years there'll be fewer workers available to "produce" and to "consume" whatever it is that's produced.[60] Ever ask yourself what it is that's used in "producing" something? Or what it is that's being "consumed"? Yeah. You got it. Nature is being consumed, and with it the ingredients that allow ongoing human existence. It's true that nature can replenish some of what's consumed, but only at a certain rate. That rate has been vastly exceeded, and the excess is intensifying by the moment. An overburgeoning humanity is killing the natural world, and thus itself. It's no more complicated than that.[61]

Here we are in the midst of a rapidly worsening environmental crisis of truly global proportion, every last bit of it attributable to a wildly accelerating human consumption of the planetary habitat, and you have one of the world's major offenders expressing grave concern that the rate at which it is able to consume might actually drop a notch or two. *Think* about it. I suggest that this attitude signifies nothing so much as stark, raving madness. It is insane, suicidally, homicidally, and ecocidally insane. And, no, I'm not being rhetorical. I mean these terms in a clinically precise fashion. But I don't want to convey the misimpression that I'm singling out the Japanese. I only used them as an illustration of a far broader pathology called "industrialism"—or, lately, "post-industrialism." It is an indication of a sickness centered in an utterly obsessive drive to dominate and destroy the natural order (words like "production," "consumption," "development," and "progress" are mere code words masking this reality.[62]

It's not only the industrialized countries which are afflicted with this disease. One by-product of the past 500 years of European expansionism and the resulting hegemony of Eurocentric ideology is that this ideology has been drummed into the consciousness of *most* peoples to the point where it is now subconsciously internalized. Everywhere, you find people thinking it "natural" to view themselves as the incarnation of god on earth ("created in the image of God"), and thus duty-bound to "exercise dominion over nature" in order that they can "multiply, grow plentiful, and populate the land" in ever increasing "abundance."[63] The legacy of the forced labor of the *latifundia* and inculcation of Catholicism in Latin America is an overburdening population devoutly believing that "wealth" can be achieved (or is defined) by having ever *more* children.[64] The legacy of Mao's implementation of a "reverse technology" policy—the official encouragement of breakneck childbearing rates in an already overpopulated country, solely as a means to deploy massive labor power to offset capitalism's "technological advantage" in production—resulted in a tripling of China's population in only two generations.[65] And then there is India.

Make absolutely no mistake about it. The planet was never designed to accommodate five billion human beings, much less the *10* billion predicted to be here a mere 50 years hence.[66] If we are to be about turning power relations around between people, and between groups of people, we must also be about turning around the relationship between people and the rest of the natural order. If we don't, we'll die out as a species, just like any other species that irrevocably overshoots its habitat. The sheer number of humans on this planet needs to come down to about a quarter of what it is today, or maybe less, and the plain fact is that the bulk of these people are in the Third World.[67] So, I'll say this clearly: not only must the birth rate in the Third World come down, but the population levels of Asia, Latin America, and Africa *must be reduced* over the next few generations. The numbers must start to come down dramatically, beginning right now.

Of course, there's another dimension to the population issue, one that is in some ways even more important, and I want to get into it in a minute. But first I have to say something else. This is that I don't want a bunch of Third Worlders jumping up in my face screaming that I'm advocating "genocide." Get *off* that bullshit. It's genocide when some centralized state, or some colonizing power, imposes sterilization or abortion on target groups. It's not genocide at all when we recognize that we have a problem, and take the logical steps *ourselves* to solve them. Voluntary sterilization is not a part of genocide. Voluntary abortion is not a part of genocide. And, most importantly, educating ourselves and our respective peoples to bring our birth rates under control through conscious resort to birth control measures is not a part of genocide.[68] What it *is*, however, is part of taking responsibility for ourselves again, of taking responsibility for our destiny and our children's destiny. It's about rooting the ghost of the Vatican out of our collective psyches, and the ghost of Adam Smith, and the ghost of Karl Marx. It's about getting back in touch with our *own* ways, our *own* traditions, our *own* knowledge, and it's time we got out of our own way in this respect. We've got an awful lot to unlearn, and an awful lot to relearn, not much time in which we can afford the luxury of avoidance, and we need to get on with it.

The other aspect of population I wanted to take up is that there's another way of counting it. One way, the way I just did it, and the way its conventionally done, is to simply point to the number of bodies, or "people units." That's valid enough as far as it goes, so we can look at it and act on what we see, but it doesn't really go far enough. This brings up the second method, which is to count by the relative rate of resource consumption per body—the relative degree of environmental impact per individual—and to extrapolate that into people units. Using this method, which is actually more accurate in ecological terms, we arrive at conclusions that are a little different than the usual notion that the most overpopulated regions on earth are in the Third World. The average resident of the United States, for example, consumes about 30 times the resources of the average Ugandan or Laotian. Since a lot of poor folks reside in the United States, this translates into the average yuppie consuming about 70 times the resources of an average Third Worlder.[69] Every yuppie born counts as much as another 70 Chinese. Lay *that* one on the next Izod-clad geek who approaches you with a baby stroller and an outraged look, telling you to put your cigarette out, eh? Tell 'em you'll put it out when they snuff the kid, and not a moment before. Better yet, tell 'em they should snuff themselves, as well as the kid, and do the planet a *real* favor. Just "kidding" (heh-heh).[70]

Returning to the topic at hand, you have to multiply the United States population by a factor of 30—a noticeably higher ratio than either western Europe or Japan—to figure out how many Third Worlders it would take to have the same environmental impact. I make that to be 7.5

billion United States people units. I think I can thus safely say the most overpopulated portion of the globe is the United States. Either the consumption rates really have to be cut in this country, most especially in the more privileged social sectors, or the number of people must be drastically reduced, or both. I advocate both. How much? That's a bit subjective, but I'll tentatively accept the calculations of William Catton, a respected ecological demographer. He estimated that North America was thoroughly saturated with humans by 1840.[71] So we either need to get both population and consumption levels down to what they were in that year, or preferably a little earlier. Alternatively, we need to bring population down to an even lower level to sustain a correspondingly higher level of consumption.

Here's where I think the reconstitution of indigenous territorality and sovereignty in the West can be useful with regard to population. You see, land isn't just land; it's also the resources within the land, things like coal, oil, natural gas, uranium, and maybe most important, water. How does that bear on United States overpopulation? Simple. Much of the population expansion in this country over the past quarter-century has been into the southwestern desert region. How many people have they got living in the valley down there at Phoenix, a place which might be reasonably expected to support 500? Look at Los Angeles, which has 20 million people where there ought to be maybe a few thousand. How do they accomplish this? Well, for one thing, they've diverted the entire Colorado River from its natural purposes. They're syphoning off the Columbia River and piping it south. They've even got a project underway to divert the Yukon River all the way down from Alaska to support southwestern urban growth and to irrigate George Bush's proposed agribusiness penetration of northern Sonora and Chihuahua. Whole regions of our ecosphere are being destabilized in the process.

In the scenario I've described, the whole Colorado watershed will be in Indian Country, under Indian control. So will the source of the Columbia. And diversion of the Yukon would have to go right through Indian Country. Now, here's the deal. No more use of water to fill swimming pools and sprinkle golf courses in Phoenix and Los Angeles. No more watering Kentucky bluegrass lawns out on the yucca flats. No more drive-through car washes in Tucumcari. No more "Big Surf" amusement parks in the middle of the desert. Drinking water and such for the whole population, yes. But water for this other insanity? No way. I guarantee that'll stop the inflow of population cold. Hell, I'll guarantee it'll start a pretty substantial outflow. Most of these folks never wanted to live in the desert anyway. That's why they keep trying to make it look like Florida (another delicate environment which is buckling under the weight of population increases).[72]

And we can help move things along in other ways as well. Virtually all the electrical power for the southwestern urban sprawls comes from a combination of hydroelectric and coal-fired generation in the Four Corners area. This is smack dab in the middle of Indian Country, along with all the uranium with which a "friendly atom" alternative might be attempted, and most of the low sulfur coal. Goodbye to the neon glitter of Las Vegas and San Diego. Adios to air conditioners in every room. Sorry about your hundred mile expanses of formerly street-lit expressway. Basic needs will be met, and that's it. Which means we can also start saying goodbye to western rivers being backed up like so many sewage lagoons behind massive dams. The Glen Canyon and Hoover dams are coming down, boys and girls. And we can begin to experience things like a reduction in the acidity of southwestern rain water as facilities like the Four Corners Power Plant are cut back in generating time, and eventually eliminated altogether.

What I'm saying probably sounds extraordinarily cruel to a lot of people, particularly those imbued with the belief that they have a "God-given right" to play a round of golf on the well-watered green beneath the imported palm trees outside the air conditioned casino at the base of the Superstition Mountains. Tough. Those days can be ended without hesitation or apology. A much more legitimate concern rests in the fact that a lot of people who've drifted into the southwest have no place to go to. The places they came from are crammed. In many cases, that's why they left. To them, I say there's no need to panic; no one will abruptly pull the plug on you, or leave you to die of thirst. Nothing like that. But quantities of both water and power will be set at minimal levels. In order to have a surplus, you'll have to bring your number down to a certain level over a certain period. At that point, the levels will again be reduced, necessitating another population reduction. Things can be phased in over an extended period, several generations if need be.[73]

Probably, provision of key items such as western water and coal should be negotiated on the basis of reductions in population and consumption by the United States as a whole rather than simply the region served—much like the United States-controlled World Bank now dictates sweeping terms to Third World countries in exchange for relatively paltry investments, but for opposite reasons—in order to prevent population shifts being substituted for actual reductions.[74] Any such negotiated arrangement should also include an agreement to alter the United States distribution of food surpluses and the like, so as to ease the transition to lower population and correspondingly greater self-sufficiency in hard-pressed Third World areas.

While it is easy to raise objections over the particulars of the scenario sketched here, it's important to realize and act on the stark choice before us: on the one hand, we could manage a phased retreat from gluttonous, individualistically organized consumption. The only alternative is a catastrophic drop off the ecological cliff that we are now perched on. The objective inherent to every aspect of this process should be, and can be, to let everyone down as gently as possible from the long and intoxicating high that has beset so much of the human species in its hallucination that it, and it alone, is the only thing of value and importance in the universe. In doing so, and I believe *only* in doing so, can we fulfil our obligation to bequeath our grandchildren, and our grandchildren's grandchildren, a world which is fit (or even possible) to live in.[75]

I Am Indigenist

There are any number of other matters which by rights should be discussed, but they will of necessity have to await another occasion. What has been presented has been only the barest outline, a glimpse of what might be called an "indigenist vision." Hopefully, it provides enough shape and clarity to allow anyone who wishes to pursue the thinking further to fill in at least some of the gaps I've not had time to address, and to arrive at insights and conclusions of their own. Once the main tenets have been advanced, and I think to some extent that's been accomplished here, the perspective of indigenism is neither mystical nor mysterious.

In closing, I would like to turn again to the critics, the skeptics, those who will decry what has been said here as being "unrealistic" or even "crazy." On the former score, my reply is that so long as we define realism, or reality itself, in conventional terms, the terms imposed by the order of understanding in which we now live, we will be doomed to remain locked forever into the trajectory in which we presently find ourselves. We will never break free because any order, any structure, defines reality only in terms of itself. Consequently, allow me to echo the sentiments expressed in the French student revolt of 1968: "Be realistic, demand the impossible!"[76] If you read through a volume of American Indian oratory, and there are several available, you'll find that native people have been saying the same thing all along.[77]

As to my being crazy, I'd like to say, "Thanks for the compliment." Again, I follow my elders and my ancestors—and R.D. Laing, for that matter—in believing that when confronted with a society as obviously insane as this one, the only sane posture one can adopt is one that society would automatically designate as crazy.[78] I mean, it wasn't Indians who turned birthing into a religious fetish while butchering off a couple hundred million people with weapons of mass destruction and systematically starving another billion or so to death. Indians never had a Grand Inquisition, and we never came up with a plumbing plan to reroute the water flow on the entire continent. Nor did we ever produce "leaders" of the caliber of Ronald Reagan, Jean Kirkpatrick, and Ross Perot. Hell, we never even figured out that turning prison construction into a major growth industry was an indication of social progress and enlightenment. Maybe we were never so much crazy as we were congenitally retarded.

Whatever the reason, and you'll excuse me for suspecting it might be something other than craziness or retardation, I'm indescribably thankful that our cultures turned out to be so different, no matter how much abuse and sacrifice it's entailed. I'm proud to stand inside the heritage of native struggle. I'm proud to say that I'm an unreconstructable indigenist. For me, there's no other reasonable or realistic way to look at the world. And I invite anyone who shares that viewpoint to come aboard, regardless of your race, creed, or national origin. Maybe Chief Seattle said it best back in 1854:

> Tribe follows tribe, and nation follows nation, like the waves of the sea. Your time of decay may be distant, but it will surely come, for even the white man whose god walked with him and talked with him as friend with friend, cannot be exempt from the common destiny. We may be brothers after all. We will see.[79]

Notes

1. For what is probably the best available account of AIM, IAT, and WARN, see Matthiessen, Peter, *In the Spirit of Crazy Horse* (New York: Viking Press, [second edition] 1991). On Oka, see Hornung, Rick, *One Nation Under the Gun: Inside the Mohawk Civil War* (New York: Pantheon Books, 1991).

2. Most of these struggles are covered in Jaimes, M. Annette, ed. *The State of Native America: Genocide, Colonization, and Resistance* (Boston, MA: South End Press, 1992). On James Bay, see Richardson, Boyce, *Strangers Devour the Land* (Post Mills, VT: Chelsea Green Publishing, [second edition] 1991).

3. While it is hardly complete, a good point of departure for learning about many of the individuals named would be Josephy, Alvin, *The Patriot Chiefs* (New York: Viking Press, 1961).

4. The bulk of those mentioned, and a number of others as well, appear in Jaimes, *op. cit.*

5. The term "Vichy Indians" comes from Russell Means. See his "The Same Old Song" in *Marxism and Native Americans*, ed. Ward Churchill (Boston, MA: South End Press, [second edition] 1989), pp. 19-33.

6. Ross Swimmer is an alleged Cherokee and former Philips Petroleum executive who served as head of the United States Bureau of Indian Affairs under Ronald Reagan, and argued for suspension of federal obligations to Indians as a means of teaching native people "self-reliance." Dickie Wilson was head of the federal puppet government on Pine Ridge Reservation during the early 1970s, a capacity in which he formed an entity called the GOONs to physically assault and frequently kill members and supporters of AIM. Webster Two Hawks was head of the National Tribal Chairman's Association, funded by the Nixon administration. He used his federally-sponsored position to denounce Indian liberation struggles. Peter McDonald—often referred to as "McDollar" in Indian Country—utilized his position as head of the puppet government at Navajo to sell his people's interests to various mining corporations during the 1970s and '80s, greatly enriching himself in the process. David Bradley is a no-talent painter living in Santa Fe whose main claim to fame is having made a successful bid to have the federal government enforce "identification standards" against other Indian artists; he has subsequently set himself up as a self-anointed "Identity Police," a matter which, thankfully, leaves him little time to produce his typical graphic schlock. To hear them tell it, of course, each of these individuals acted in service to "Indian sovereignty."

7. See LaDuke's "Natural to Synthetic and Back Again," the preface to *Marxism and Native Americans, op. cit.*, pp. i-viii.

8. Batalla, Guillermo Bonfil, *Utopía y Revolución: El Pensamiento Político Contemporáneo de los Indios en América Latina* (Mexico: Editorial Nueva Imagen, S.A., 1981), p. 37; translation by Roxanne Dunbar Ortiz.

9. *Ibid.*, pp. 37-38.

10. *Ibid.* p. 38.

11. Ortiz, Roxanne Dunbar, *Indians of the Americas: Human Rights and Self-Determination* (London: Zed Press, 1984), p. 83.

12. *Ibid.* p. 84.

13. For an excellent overview on the implications of Marx's thinking in this regard, see the first couple of chapters in Connor, Walker, *The National Question in Marxist-Leninist Theory and Strategy* (Princeton, NJ: Princeton University Press, 1984).

14. Dunbar Ortiz, *op. cit.*, p. 85.

15. Manuel, George, and Michael Posluns, *The Fourth World: An Indian Reality* (New York: Free Press, 1974).

16. On the Irish and Welsh struggles see Hechter, Michael, *Internal Colonialism: The Celtic Fringe in British National Development, 1536-1966* (Berkeley: University of California Press, 1975). On the Basques, see Medhurst, Kenneth, *The Basques and Catalans* (London: Minority Rights Group Report No. 9, September 1977).

17. Dunbar Ortiz, *op. cit.*, p. 89.

18. Neitschmann, Bernard, "The Third World War," *Cultural Survival Quarterly*, vol. 11, no. 3 (1987).

19. Geneva Offices of the United Nations, Press Release, August 17, 1981 (HR/1080).

20. For an excellent analysis of this tradition from an indigenist perspective, see Williams, Robert A., Jr., *The American Indian in Western Legal Thought: The Discourses of Conquest* (London/New York: Oxford University Press, 1990).

21. On the Iberian legal tradition, see Scott, James Brown, *The Spanish Origin of International Law* (Oxford: Clarendon Press, 1934).

22. Blanco, Hugo, *Land or Death: The Peasant Struggle in Peru* (New York: Pathfinder Press, 1972). Blanco was a marxist, and thus sought to pervert indigenous issues through rigid class analysis—defining Indians as "peasants" rather than by nationality—but his identification of land as the central issue was/is nonetheless valid.

23. The complete texts of 371 of these ratified treaties will be found in Kappler, Charles J., comp., *American Indian Treaties, 1778-1883* (New York: Interland Publishers, 1973). The Lakota scholar Deloria, Vine, Jr., has also collected the texts of several more ratified treaties that do not appear in Kappler, but that will be published in a forthcoming collection.

24. The constitutional provision comes at Article I, Section 10. Codification of customary international law in this connection is explained in Sinclair, Sir Ian, *The Vienna Convention on the Law of Treaties* (Manchester: Manchester University Press, [second edition] 1984).

25. See generally, Deloria, Vine, Jr., and Clifford E. Lytle, *American Indians, American Justice* (Austin: University of Texas Press, 1983).

26. *Lonewolf v. Hitchcock*, 187 United States 553 (1903). For analysis, see Estin, Ann Laquer, "*Lonewolf v. Hitchcock*: The Long Shadow," in *The Aggressions of Civilization: Federal Indian Policy Since the 1880s*, ed. Sandra L. Cadwallader and Vine Deloria, Jr. (Philadelphia, PA: Temple University Press, 1984), pp. 215-45.

27. Probably the best exposition of the legal principles articulated by the United States as being violated by the nazis may be found in Smith, Bradley F., *The Road to Nuremberg* (New York: Basic Books, 1981).

28. A fuller articulation of this thesis may be found in the author's "On Gaining 'Moral High Ground': An Ode to George Bush and the 'New World Order'," in *Collateral Damage: The "New World Order" at Home and Abroad*, ed. Cynthia Peters (Boston, MA: South End Press, 1992), pp. 359-72.

29. For the origins of such practices, see Jones, Dorothy V., *License for Empire: Colonialism by Treaty in Early America* (Chicago, IL: University of Chicago Press, 1982). For a good survey of United States adaptations, see Worcester, Donald, ed., *Forked Tongues and Broken Treaties* (Caldwell, ID: Caxton Publishers, 1975).

30. The travesty at Fort Wise is adequately covered in Hoig, Stan, *The Sand Creek Massacre* (Norman: University of Oklahoma Press, 1961).

31. Deloria compilation, forthcoming.

32. On the purpose of the commission, see Rosenthal, Harvey D., "Indian Claims and the American Conscience: A Brief History of the Indian Claims Commission," in *Irredeemable America: The Indians' Estate and Land Tenure*, ed. Imre Sutton (Albuquerque: University of New Mexico Press, 1985), pp. 35-86. You have to read between the lines a bit.

33. See Barsh, Russel, "Indian Land Claims Policy in the United States," *North Dakota Law Review*, no. 58 (1982): pp. 1-82.

34. The percentage is arrived at by juxtaposing the approximately 50 million acres within the current reservation land base to the more than two *billion* acres of the lower 48. According to the Indian Claims Commission findings, Indians actually retain unfettered legal title to about 750 million acres of the continental United States.

35. Concerning Alaska, see Berry, M. C., *The Alaska Pipeline: The Politics of Oil and Native Land Claims* (Bloomington/Indianapolis: Indiana University Press, 1975). On Hawai'i, see the Haunani-Kay Trask, *From a Native Daughter: Colonialism and Sovereignty in Hawai'i* (Monroe, ME: Common Courage Press, 1993).

36. A good exposition on this phenomenon may be found in Brodeur, Paul, *Restitution: The Land Claims of the Mashpee, Passamaquoddy, and Penobscot Indians of New England* (Boston, MA: Northeastern University Press, 1985).

37. The problem is partially, but insightfully examined in Weitzer, Ronald, *Transforming Settler States: Communal Conflict and Internal Security in Zimbabwe and Northern Ireland* (Berkeley: University of California Press, 1992).

38. It is entirely possible to extend a logical analysis in this direction. See, for instance, Sakai, J., *Settlers: The Mythology of the White Proletariat* (Chicago, IL: Morningstar Press, 1983).

39. See O'Brien, Sharon, *American Indian Tribal Governments* (Norman: University of Oklahoma Press, 1989).

40. These matters are covered quite well in Silman, Janet, *Enough Is Enough: Aboriginal Women Speak Out* (Toronto: Women's Press, 1987).

41. The Smithsonian view of Indians has been adopted even by some of the more self-consciously "revolutionary" organizations in the United States. For a classic example, see Revolutionary Communist Party, USA, "Searching for the Second Harvest," in *Marxism and Native Americans, op. cit.*, pp. 35-58.

42. The thesis is, no kidding, that Indians were the first "environmental pillagers," and it took the invasion of enlightened Europeans like the author of the piece to save the American ecosphere from total destruction by its indigenous inhabitants; see Weurthner, George, "An Ecological View of the Indian," *Earth First!*, vol. 7, no. 7 (August 1987).

43. Valentine, Paul W., "Dances with Myths," *Arizona Republic* (April 7, 1991). Valentine is syndicated, but is on staff at the *Washington Post*.

44. A fine selection of such early colonialist impressions will be found in the first few chapters of Drinnon, Richard, *Facing West: The Metaphysics of Indian Hating and Empire Building* (New York: Schoken Books, 1980). On length of indigenous occupancy in the Americas, see Goodman, Jeffrey, *American Genesis* (New York: Summit Books, 1981). On precontact population, see Stiffarm, Lenore A., and Phil Lane, Jr., "The Demography of Native North America: A Question of American Indian Survival," in *The State of Native America, op. cit.*, pp. 23-53.

45. For a succinct, but reasonably comprehensive survey of actual precontact indigenous material and intellectual realities, see Weatherford, Jack, *Indian Givers: How the Indians of the Americas Transformed the World* (New York: Crown Publishers, 1988).

46. See Forbes, Jack D., *Black Africans and Native Americans: Race, Color and Caste in the Evolution of Red-Black Peoples* (London/New York: Oxford University Press, 1988).

47. On federal quantum policy, see Jaimes, M. Annette, "Federal Indian Identification Policy: A Usurpation of Indigenous Sovereignty in North America," in *The State of Native America, op. cit.*, pp. 123-38.

48. Probably the best examination of Indian warfare and "militaristic" tradition is Holm, Tom, "Patriots and Pawns: State Use of American Indians in the Military and the Process of Nativization in the United States," in *The State of Native America, op. cit.*, pp. 345-70.

49. Referred to here is the so-called "Bradley Bill" (S.1453), introduced before the senate by Bill Bradley in 1987. For analysis, see the special issue of *Wicazo Sa Review* (vol. XIV, no. 1 [spring 1988]) devoted to the topic.

50. Means, Russell, and Ward Churchill, *TREATY: The Campaign of Russell Means for the Presidency of the Oglala Sioux Tribe* (Porcupine, SD: TREATY Campaign, 1982).

51. Barsh, *op. cit.*

52. A number of examples may be found in Lindley, Mark Frank, *The Acquisition and Government of Backward Country in International Law: A Treatise on the Law and Practice Relating to Colonial Expansion* (London: Longmans, Green Publishers, 1926).

53. Probably the only accessible material to date on the Buffalo Commons idea is unfortunately a rather frothy little volume. See Matthews, Anne, *Where the Buffalo Roam: The Storm Over the Revolutionary Plan to Restore America's Great Plains* (New York: Grove Weidenfeld Publishers, 1992).

54. For one of the best elaborations of these principles, see Nanda, Zed, "Self-Determination in International Law: Validity of Claims to Secede," *Case Western Reserve Journal of International Law*, no. 13 (1981).

55. A prototype for this sort of arrangement exists between Greenland (populated mainly by Inuits) and Denmark. See Alfredsson, Gudmundur, "Greenland and the

Law of Political Decolonization," *German Yearbook on International Law*, no. 25 (1982).

56. Although my argument comes at it from a very different angle, the conclusion here is essentially the same as that reached by Falk, Richard, in his *The End of World Order: Essays in Normative International Relations* (New York/London: Holmes and Meier Publishers, 1983).

57. This is the basic idea set forth in *TREATY, op. cit.*

58. The concepts at issue here are brought out very well in Catton, William R., Jr., *Overshoot: The Ecological Basis of Revolutionary Change* (Urbana: University of Illinois Press, 1982).

59. For further elaboration, see Deloria, Vine, Jr., *God Is Red* (New York: Delta Books, 1973). The ideas have even caught on, at least as questions, among some Euroamerican legal practitioners; see Stone, Christopher D., *Should Trees Have Standing? Towards Legal Rights for Natural Objects* (Los Altos, CA: William Kaufman Publishers, 1972).

60. CNN *Dollars and Cents* reportage, May 27, 1992.

61. The idea is developed in detail in Rifkin, Jeremy, *Entropy: A New World View* (New York: Viking Press, 1980). It should be noted, however, that the world view in question is hardly new; indigenous peoples have held it all along.

62. One good summary of this, utilizing extensive native sources—albeit many of them go unattributed—is Mander, Jerry, *In the Absence of the Sacred: The Failure of Technology and the Survival of Indian Nations* (San Francisco, CA: Sierra Club Books, 1991).

63. If this sounds a bit scriptural, it's meant to. A number of us see a direct line of continuity from the core imperatives of Judeo-Christian theology, through the capitalist secularization of church doctrine and its alleged marxian antithesis, right on through to the burgeoning technotopianism of today. This is a major conceptual cornerstone of what indigenists view as Eurocentrism (a virulently anthropocentric outlook in its essence).

64. The information is there, but the conclusion avoided, in Frank, Andre Gunder, *Capitalism and Underdevelopment in Latin America* (New York: Monthly Review Press, 1967).

65. See Ch'en, Jerome, *Mao and the Chinese Revolution* (London/New York: Oxford University Press, 1967).

66. Ehrlich, Paul R., and Anne H. Ehrlich, *The Population Explosion* (New York: Simon and Schuster Publisher, 1990).

67. Extrapolating from the calculations of Catton in *Overshoot, op. cit.*

68. Sound arguments to this effect are advanced in Ehrlich, Paul R., and Anne H. Ehrlich, *Population/Resources/Environment* (San Francisco, CA: W.H. Freeman Publishers, 1970).

69. Ehrlich and Ehrlich, from their book *Healing the Earth*, quoted in CNN series *The Population Bomb*, May 1992.

70. Lest my remarks be taken out of context, the point isn't to get people to commit suicide or take the lives of others. Rather, I'm tired of sanctimonious environmental ravagers seizing on smoking as an issue despite its harm being virtually zero when stacked up against the impact the complainers make simply by living their daily lives in the manner that they do.

71. This would be about 50 million, or one-fifth of the present United States population; Catton, *op. cit.*, p. 53.

72. This is essentially the same argument, without ever quite arriving at the obvious conclusion, advanced by Reisner, Marc, in his *Cadillac Desert* (New York: Penguin Books, 1986). For a better, though less comprehensive job, see Guerrero, Marianna, "American Indian Water Rights: The Blood of Life in Native North America," in *The State of Native America, op. cit.*, pp. 189-216.

73. A good deal of the impact could also be offset by implementing the ideas contained in Todd, John, and George Tukel, *Reinhabiting Cities and Towns: Designing for Sustainability* (San Francisco: Planet Drum Foundation, 1981).

74. For purposes of comparison, see *Funding Ecological and Social Destruction: The World Bank and International Monetary Fund* (Washington, D.C.: Bank Information Center, 1990). By contrast, the concept described in the text might be dubbed "Struggling for Ecological and Social Preservation."

75. Many indigenous peoples take the position that all social policies should be entered into only after consideration of their likely implications, both environmentally and culturally, for descendants seven generations in the future. Consequently a number of seemingly good ideas for solving short-run problems are never entered into because no one can reasonably predict their longer term effects. See Morey, Sylvester M., ed., *Can the Red Man Help the White Man? A Denver Conference with Indian Elders* (New York: Myrin Institute Books, 1970).

76. Priaulx, Allan, and Sanford J. Ungar, *The Almost Revolution: France, 1968* (New York: Dell Books, 1969).

77. See, for example, Armstrong, Virginia Irving, ed., *I Have Spoken: American History Through the Voices of the Indians* (Chicago, IL: The Swallow Press, 1971).

78. Laing, R. D., *The Politics of Experience* (New York: Ballantine Books, 1967).

79. Armstrong, *op. cit.*, p. 79.

WORKS BY AUTHOR, 1980–1996

The following is a comprehensive itemization of the published essays of Ward Churchill since 1980. It should be noted that a number of pieces have been reprinted, in whole or in part, in small circulation periodicals both in North America and abroad without notification to either the author or original publisher. These, of course, are not included in the present bibliography.

Booklength Collections:

In *Since Predator Came: Notes on the Struggle for American Indian Liberation* (Littleton, CO: Aigis Publications, 1995):

1. "Remembering Bob Thomas"

2. "Deconstructing the Columbus Myth: Was the 'Great Discoverer' Spanish or Italian, Nazi or Jew?"

3. "Since Predator Came: A Survey of North America Since 1492"

4. "Genocide in the Americas: Landmarks in 'Latin' America Since 1492"

5. "Genocide: Toward a Functional Definition"

6. "The Earth is Our Mother: Struggles for American Indian Land and Liberation in the Contemporary United States"

7. "Like Sand in the Wind: The Making of an American Indian Diaspora"

8. "The Bloody Wake of Alcatraz: Political Repression of the American Indian Movement in the 1970s"

9. "White Studies: The Intellectual Imperialism of U.S. Higher Education"

10. "About That Bering Strait Land Bridge…Let's Turn the Footprints Around"

11. "On Gaining 'Moral High Ground': An Ode to George Bush and the 'New World Order'"

12. "False Promises: An Indigenist Perspective on Marxist Theory and Practice"

13. "Between a Rock and a Hard Place: Left-Wing Revolution, Right-Wing Reaction, and the Destruction of Indigenous Peoples" (with Glenn T. Morris)

14. "On Support of the Indian Resistance in Nicaragua: A Statement of Position and Principle"

15. "The Meaning of Chiapas: A North American Indigenist View"

16. "Generations of Resistance: American Indian Poetry and the Ghost Dance Spirit"

17. "From a Woman Warrior: Wendy Rose's *What Happened When the Hopi Hit New York*"

18. "Another View of America: Simon J. Ortiz's *From Sand Creek*"

In *Indians Are Us? Culture and Genocide in North America* (Monroe, ME: Common Courage Press, 1994):

1. "Bringing the Law Home: Application of the Genocide Convention in the United States"

2. "Let's Spread the 'Fun' Around: The Issue of Sports Team Names and Mascots"

3. "In the Matter of Julius Streicher: Applying Nuremberg Precedents in the United States"

4. "Nobody's Pet Poodle: Jimmie Durham, an Artist for Native North America"

5. "And They Did It Like Dogs in the Dirt: An American Indian Analysis of *Black Robe*"

6. "Another Dry White Season: Jerry Mander's *In the Absence of the Sacred*"

7. "'P' is for Plagiarism: A Closer Look at Jack Weatherford's *Indian Givers*"

8. "'Renegades, Terrorists and Revolutionaries': The Government's Propaganda War Against the American Indian Movement"

9. "The *Real* Revisionism: Notes on Stan Lyman's *Wounded Knee, 1973*"

10. "AIM Casualties on Pine Ridge, 1973-1976" (with Jim Vander Wall)

11. "Indians Are Us? Reflections on the 'Men's Movement'"

12. "Do It Yourself 'Indianism': The Case of Ed MaGaa's *Mother Earth Spirituality*"

13. "Naming Our Destiny: Toward a Language of American Indian Liberation"

In *Struggle for the Land: Indigenous Resistance to Genocide, Ecocide and Expropriation in Contemporary North America* (Monroe, ME: Common Courage Press, 1993):

1. "American Indian Lands: The Native Ethic Amid Resource Development"

2. "Perversions of Justice: Examining the Doctrine of U.S. Rights to Occupancy in North America"

3. "Struggle to Regain a Stolen Homeland: The Iroquois Land Claims in Upstate New York"

4. "The Black Hills Are Not for Sale: The Lakota Struggle for the 1868 Treaty Territory"

5. "Genocide in Arizona? The 'Navajo-Hopi Land Dispute' in Perspective"

6. "The Struggle for Newe Segobia: The Western Shoshone Battle for Their Homeland"

7. "Last Stand at Lubicon Lake: An Assertion of Indigenous Sovereignty in North America"

8. "Radioactive Colonization: A Hidden Holocaust in Native North America"

9. "The Water Plot: Hydrological Rape in Northern Canada"

10. "American Indian Self-Governance: Fact, Fantasy and Prospects for the Future"

11. "I Am Indigenist"

In *Fantasies of the Master Race: Literature, Cinema and the Colonization of American Indians* (Monroe, ME: Common Courage Press, 1992):

1. "Literature as a Weapon in the Colonization of the American Indian"

2. "Carlos Castañeda: The Greatest Hoax Since Piltdown Man"

3. "Ayn Rand and the Sioux: Tonto Revisited"

4. "*Creek Mary's Blood*: A Comparison to *Hanta Yo*"

5. "Revolution vs. Self-Determination: Roxanne Dunbar Ortiz's *Indians of the Americas*"

6. "It Did Happen Here: Sand Creek, Scholarship and the American Character"

7. "*That Day in Gordon*: Deformation of History and the American Novel"

8. "'Friends of the Indian': A Critical Appraisal of *Irredeemable America: The Indians' Estate and Land Claims*"

9. "*Interpreting the American Indian*: A Critique of Michael Castro's Apologia for Poetic Racism"

10. "*Beyond Ethnicity*: Werner Sollars' Deepest Avatar of Racism"

11. "The New Racism: A Critique of James A. Clifton's *The Invented Indian*"

12. "A Little Matter of Genocide: Sam Gill's *Mother Earth*, Colonialism and the Expropriation of Indigenous Spiritual Tradition in Academia"

13. "Spiritual Hucksterism: The Rise of the Plastic Medicine Men"

14. "Fantasies of the Master Race: Categories of Stereotyping of American Indians in Film"

15. "Lawrence of South Dakota: *Dances With Wolves* and the Maintenance of American Empire"

16. "Hi, Ho Hillerman...(Away): Unmasking the Role of Detective Fiction in Indian Country"

Included in Anthologies:

"A Survey of Tendencies in American Indian Higher Education Programs," in *Multicultural Education and the American Indian*, ed. James R. Young (Los Angeles: UCLA American Indian Studies Program, 1980).

"Examination of Stereotyping: An Analytical Survey of Twentieth Century Indian Entertainers" (coauthored with Mary Ann and Norbert S. Hill, Jr.), in

The Pretend Indians: Images of the Native American in Film, ed. Gretchen Bataille and Charles S. P. Silet (Ames: University of Iowa Press, 1980).

"Native American Substance Abuse: A Familial Solution?" (coauthored with Dora-Lee Larson), in *Selected Readings in Multicultural Prevention Issues* (Washington, D.C.: National Institute on Drug Abuse/Center for Multicultural Awareness, U.S. Department of Health and Human Services, 1980).

"White Studies or Isolation: An Alternative Model for American Indian Studies Programs," in *American Indian Issues in Higher Education*, ed. James R. Young (Los Angeles, CA: UCLA American Indian Studies Program, 1982).

"The Same Old Song in Sad Refrain: The Revolutionary Communist Party's Attack on Russell Means" (coauthored with Dora-Lee Larson), in *Marxism and Native Americans*, ed. Ward Churchill (Boston, MA: South End Press, 1983).

"Marxism and the Native American: Where Do We Go from Here?," in *Marxism and Native Americans*, ed. Ward Churchill (Boston, MA: South End Press, 1983).

"The New Genocide: A Hidden Holocaust in Native American Environments," in *Research in Inequality and Social Conflict*, ed. Michael Dobkowski and Isador Walliman (Greenwich, CT: JAI Press, 1989).

"The 1868 Fort Laramie Treaty Claim: The Black Hills Are Not for Sale," in *Critical Issues in Native North America, Vol. I*, ed. Ward Churchill (Copenhagen: IWGIA Doc. No. 62, 1989).

"Last Stand on Lubicon Lake," in *Critical Issues in Native North America, Vol. I*, ed. Ward Churchill (Copenhagen: IWGIA Doc. No. 62, 1989).

"Native America: The Political Economy of Radioactive Colonization" (coauthored with Winona LaDuke), in *Critical Issues in Native North America, Vol. II*, ed. Ward Churchill (Copenhagen: IWGIA Doc. 63, 1991).

"A Man Who Struggles for Liberation: An Interview with Geronimo Pratt," in *Cages of Steel: The Politics of Imprisonment in the United States*, ed. Ward Churchill and Jim Vander Wall (Washington, D.C.: Maisonneuve Press, 1992).

"The Wages of COINTELPRO: The Case of Mumia Abu-Jamal," in *Cages of Steel: The Politics of Imprisonment in the United States*, ed. Ward Churchill and Jim Vander Wall (Washington, D.C.: Maisonneuve Press, 1992).

"A Question of Sovereignty: The International Implications of Treaty Relationships Between the United States and Various American Indian Nations," in *Native Americans and Public Policy*, ed. Fremont Lyden and Lyman H. Letgers (Pittsburgh, PA: University of Pittsburgh Press, 1992).

"The 'Trial' of Leonard Peltier," in *1492-1992: Commemorating 500 Years of Indigenous Resistance*, ed. Donna Nicolino (Santa Cruz, CA: Resource Center for Nonviolence, 1992).

"The Battle for Newe Segobia," in *1492-1992: Commemorating 500 Years of Native Resistance*, ed. Donna Nicolino (Santa Cruz, CA: Resource Center for Nonviolence, 1992).

"Official Terrorism on the Pine Ridge Reservation, 1972-1976," in *Violent Persuasions: The Politics and Imagery of Terrorism*, ed. David J. Brown and Robert Merrill (Seattle, WA: Bay Shore Press, 1993).

"Crimes Against Humanity," in *Between Worlds: A Reader, Rhetoric and Handbook*, ed. Susan Bachman and Melinda Barth (New York: HarperCollins College Publishers, 1994).

"The Indian Chant," in *Encountering Cultures*, ed. Richard Holeton (Stanford, CA: Blair Press, 1995).

"A North American Indigenist View," in *First World, Ha-Ha-Ha! The Zapatista Challenge*, ed. Elaine Katzenberger (San Francisco, CA: City Lights Books, 1995).

"Genocide and Ecocide: An Intimate Relationship," in *Listening to the Land: Nature, Culture and Eros*, ed. Derrick Jensen (San Francisco, CA: Sierra Club Books, 1995).

Untitled excerpt from *The COINTELPRO Papers* in *Race For Justice: Mumia Abu-Jamal's Fight Against the Death Penalty*, Leonard Weinglass (Monroe, ME: Common Courage Press, 1995).

"Perversions of Justice: A Native American Examination of the Doctrine of U.S. Rights to Occupancy in North America," in *Social and Political Philosophy: Classical Western Texts in Feminist and Multicultural Perspectives*, ed. James P. Sterba (Belmont, CA: Wadsworth Publishers, 1995).

"COINTELPRO," in *USA on Trial: The International Tribunal on Indigenous Peoples and Oppressed Nations in the United States*, ed. Alejandro Luis Molina (Chicago, IL: Editorial El Coquí, 1996).

Forewords, Prefaces, and Introductions:

"Beyond the Myth" (coauthored with Jim Vander Wall), introduction to *Agents of Repression: The FBI's Secret Wars Against the Black Panther Party and the American Indian Movement*, Ward Churchill and Jim Vander Wall (Boston, MA: South End Press, 1988).

"Critical Issues in Native North America," introduction to *Critical Issues in Native North America*, ed. Ward Churchill (Copenhagen: IWGIA Document No. 62, 1989).

"The COINTELPRO Papers: A Glimpse Into the Files of America's Political Police" (coauthored with Jim Vander Wall), introduction to *COINTELPRO Papers: Documents from the FBI's Secret Wars Against Domestic Dissent*, Ward Churchill and Jim Vander Wall (Boston, MA: South End Press, 1990).

"Further Critical Issues in Native North America," introduction to *Critical Issues in Native North America, Vol. II*, ed. Ward Churchill (Copenhagen: IWGIA Document No. 68, 1991).

"Preface: The Open Veins of Native North America," in *Fantasies of the Master Race: Literature, Cinema and the Colonization of American Indians*, Ward Churchill (Monroe, ME: Common Courage Press, 1992).

"The Third World at Home: Political Prisons and Prisoners in the United States," in *Cages of Steel: The Politics of Imprisonment in the United States*, ed. Ward Churchill and Jim Vander Wall (Washington, D.C.: Maisonneuve Press, 1992).

"Introduction," in *Lessons From Native America: Knowing Who You Are,* Russell Means (Westfield, NJ: Open Pamphlet Series, 1994).

"Foreword: Lifting the Shroud of Secrecy," in *FBI Secrets,* M. Wesley Swearingen (Boston, MA: South End Press, 1995).

Encyclopedia Entries:

"American Indian Movement," "Red Power," and "Wounded Knee II," in *Native America in the Twentieth Century: An Encyclopedia,* ed. Mary Davis (New York: Garland Publishers, 1994).

"Ben Nighthorse Campbell," "Russell Means," "American Indian Movement," "International Indian Treaty Council," and "Indian Claims Commission," in *Ready Reference: American Indians,* ed. James McGill (Pasadena, CA: Salem Press, 1995).

"Radicals and Radicalism, 1900-Present," in *Encyclopedia of the American Indian,* ed. Fred Hoxie (New York: Houghton-Mifflin Publishers, 1996).

Scholarly Essays:

"Media Stereotyping and the Native Response: An Historical Overview" (coauthored with Mary Ann and Norbert S. Hill, Jr.), *The Indian Historian,* vol. 11, no. 4 (1978-79).

"An Historical Survey of Tendencies in American Indian Education: Higher Education" (coauthored with Norbert S. Hill, Jr.), *The Indian Historian,* vol. 12, no. 1 (1979).

"An Historical Survey of Twentieth Century Native American Athletes" (coauthored with Norbert S. Hill, Jr., and Mary Jo Barlow), *The Indian Historian,* vol. 12, no. 4 (1979-80).

"U.S. Mercenaries in Southern Africa: Facts and Context," *Africa Today,* vol. 27, no. 2 (1980).

"American Indian Art and Artists: In Search of a Definition," *Minority Notes,* vol. 1, no. 1 (1981).

"Categories of Film Stereotyping of Native Americans," *Minority Notes,* vol. 1, no. 2 (1981).

"Toward an Immanent Critique of Marxism: Notes on the Dichotomy of Cultural Consciousness," *Minority Notes,* vol. 2, nos. 1-2 (1982).

"Toward an Immanent Critique of Marxism: A Proposition to Marxists," *Minority Notes,* vol. 2, nos. 3-4 (1982).

"Literature in the Colonization of American Indians: An Historical Study," *The Journal of Ethnic Studies,* vol. 10, no. 3 (1982).

"The Extralegal Implications of Yellow Thunder *Tiospaye*: Misadventure or Watershed Action?" *Policy Perspectives,* vol. 2, no. 2 (1982).

"Implications of Treaty Relationships Between the United States of America and Various American Indian Nations," *Talking Leaf,* vol. 48, no. 10 (1983).

"The Situation of Indigenous Populations in the United States: A Contemporary Perspective," *Akwesasne Notes,* vol. 17, no. 1 (1985).

"JUA/Big Mountain: Examination and Analysis of U.S. Policy Within the Navajo-Hopi Joint Use Area Under Provisions of International Law," *Akwesasne Notes*, vol. 17, nos. 3-4 (1985).

"Pacifism as Pathology: Notes on an American Psuedo-Praxis (Parts I & II)," *Issues in Radical Therapy*, vol. 12, nos. 1-2 (1986).

"American Indian Lands: The Native Ethic and Resource Development," *Environment*, vol. 28, no. 6 (1986).

"Genocide: Toward a Functional Definition," *Alternatives: Social Transformation and Human Governance*, vol. 11, no. 3 (1986).

"Behind the Rhetoric: 'English Only' as Counterinsurgency Warfare," *Issues in Radical Therapy*, vol. 13, nos. 1-2 (1988).

"The Black Hills Are Not for Sale: The Lakota Struggle for the 1868 Fort Laramie Treaty Territory," *Journal of Ethnic Studies*, vol. 18, no. 1 (1990).

"In the Spirit of Crazy Horse: The Quasi-Official Censorship of Peter Matthiessen," *Index on Censorship*, vol. 19, no. 1 (1990).

"Death Squads in America: Confessions of a Government Terrorist," *Yale Journal of Law and Liberation*, no. 3 (1992).

"Since Predator Came: Native North America Since 1492," *Covert Action Information Bulletin*, no. 40 (1992).

"I Am Indigenist: Notes on the Ideology of the Fourth World," *Z Papers*, vol. 1, no. 3 (1992).

"Naming Our Destiny: Towards a Language of American Indian Liberation, *Global Justice*, vol. 3, nos. 2-3 (1992).

"The FBI Targets Judi Bari: A Case Study in Domestic Counterinsurgency," *Covert Action Quarterly*, no. 47 (1993-94).

"The Bloody Wake of Alcatraz: Political Repression of the American Indian Movement During the 1970s," *American Indian Culture and Research Journal*, vol. 18, no. 4 (1995).

"Perversions of Justice: Examining U.S. Rights to Occupancy in North America," *Historical Reflections*, vol. 21, no. 2 (1995).

Review Essays:

"Implications of Publishing *The Roots of Resistance:* On the Work of Roxanne Dunbar Ortiz," *Journal of Ethnic Studies*, vol. 9, no. 3 (1981).

"A Survey of Literature of the Vietnam War," *Issues in Radical Therapy*, vol. 10, no. 2 (1982).

"Review Essay: *The Trial of Leonard Peltier* by Jim Messerschmidt," *Talking Leaf*, vol. 48, no. 6 (1983).

"Retaining the Hoop: Leonard Peltier and the Contemporary American Indian Resistance in the United States," *Issues in Radical Therapy*, vol. 10, no. 4 (1983).

"The Historical Novel and *Creek Mary's Blood*," *Journal of Ethnic Studies*, vol. 12, no. 3 (1984).

"Roxanne Dunbar Ortiz's *Indians of the Americas*: A Travesty in Four Acts," *Akwesasne Notes*, vol. 17, no. 1 (1985).

"*Interpreting the American Indian*? A Critique of Michael Castro's Apologia," *Wicazo Sa Review*, vol. 1, no. 2 (1985).

"The Cry of the Wounded WASP: Werner Sollars' Deepest Avatar of Racism," *New Scholar*, vol. 10, nos. 1-2 (1986).

"A Critical Review of Raymond H. Abbott's *That Day in Gordon*," *Akwesasne Notes*, vol. 19, no. 1 (1987).

"Friends of the Indian? A Critical Assessment of Imre Sutton's *Irredeemable America: The Indians' Estate and Land Claims*," *Issues in Radical Therapy*, vol. 13, nos. 3-4 (1988).

"Sam Gill's *Mother Earth*: Colonialism, Genocide and the Expropriation of Indigenous Spiritual Tradition in Contemporary Academia," *American Indian Culture and Research Journal*, vol. 12, no. 3 (1988).

"To Serve and Protect? The Social Context of Michael Dewar's *Weapons and Equipment of Counter-Terrorism*," *New Studies on the Left*, vol. 14, nos. 1-2 (1989).

"The Literature of Sand Creek: A Critical Appraisal of David Svaldi's *Sand Creek and the Rhetoric of Extermination* and Duane Schultz' *Month of the Freezing Moon*," *American Indian Culture and Research Journal*, vol. 15, no. 1 (1991).

"The New Racism: A Critique of James E. Clifton's *The Invented Indian*," *Wicazo Sa Review*, vol. 7, no. 1 (1991).

Book Reviews:

"A Critique of Roxanne Dunbar Ortiz and Larry Emerson, ed., *Economic Development in American Indian Reservations*," *Journal of Ethnic Studies*, vol. 7, no. 4 (1980).

"Ayn Rand and the Sioux – Tonto Revisited: Another Look at *Hanta Yo*," *Lakota Eyapaha*, vol. 4, no. 2 (1980).

"A Review of Roxanne Dunbar Ortiz, *The Great Sioux Nation*," *American Indian Culture and Research Journal*, vol. 3, no. 3 (1980).

"A Critique of Noam Chomsky and Edward S. Herman,*The Political Economy of Human Rights*," *Minority Notes*, vol. 1, nos. 3-4 (1981).

"A Critique of Vine Deloria, Jr., *The Metaphysics of Modern Existence*," *American Indian Culture and Research Journal*, vol. 5, no. 3 (1981).

"Albert's and Hahnel's *Unorthodox Marxism*: A Step Away From Dogma," *Issues in Radical Therapy*, vol. 10, no. 1 (1982).

"*The French New Left*: An Unbalanced Portrayal," *Issues in Radical Therapy*, vol. 10, no. 3 (1982).

"A Corporate War Against the Indians? A Review of Rex Weyler's *Blood of the Land*," *Talking Leaf*, vol. 48, no. 7 (1983).

"A Review of Paula Gunn Allen's *Shadow Country*," *Talking Leaf*, vol. 48, no. 7 (1983).

"A Review of Barbara Burnaby, *The Role of Language in Education of American Indian Children*," *American Indian Culture and Research Journal*, vol. 7, no. 1 (1983).

"The Rehabilitation of *Ohiyesa:* Charles Eastman as Part of the AIM Heritage," *Western American Literature*, vol. 19, no. 3 (1983).

"Columbus Day Isn't Something Many Indians Want to Celebrate: A Review of Jimmie Durham, *Columbus Day*," *Colorado Daily* (October 10, 1983).

"A Review of Wendy Rose, *What Happened When the Hopi Hit New York*," *Akwesasne Notes*, vol. 16, no. 1 (1984).

"A Review of Rex Weyler's *Blood of the Land: The Government and Corporate War Against the American Indian Movement*," *American Indian Culture and Research Journal*, vol. 8, no. 1 (1984).

"Simon J. Ortiz's *From Sand Creek:* A Critical Review," *American Indian Culture and Research Journal*, vol. 8, no. 2 (1984).

"The Rehabilitation of Coyote: Peter Blue Cloud's *Elderberry Flute Song, Contact II*," no. 31 (1984).

"A Review of *Columbus Day* by Jimmie Durham," *American Indian Culture and Research Journal*, vol. 8, no. 1 (1985).

"A Review of Maurice Kenny's *Black Robe: Isaac Joques*," *American Indian Culture and Research Journal*, vol. 9, no. 3 (1985).

"Contra Terror: Book Catalogues Crimes, Perpetrators but Fails to Provide Links," *Colorado Daily* (December 13-14, 1985).

"*That Day in Gordon* by Raymond H. Abbott: A Critical Appraisal," *Western American Literature*, vol. 22, no. 1 (1987).

"A Critical Review of June Jordan's *On Call: Political Essays*," *Journal of Ethnic Studies*, vol. 15, no. 4 (1987).

"An Appreciation of Louis Littlecoon Oliver's *Chasers of the Sun*," *American Indian Culture and Research Journal*, vol. 15, no. 1 (1991).

"Rethinking Political Economy: Michael Albert's and Robin Hahnel's *Looking Forward* and *The Political Economy of Participatory Economics*," *Zeta* (July 1991).

"The *Real* Revisionism: A Critique of Stanley K. Lyman's *Wounded Knee, 1973*," *American Indian Quarterly*, vol. 16, no. 3 (1992).

"Just Like Tom Thumb's Blues: Gerald Vizenor's *Manifest Manners: Post-Indian Warriors of Survivance*," *American Indian Culture and Research Journal*, vol. 18, no. 3 (1994).

Film Reviews:

"Lawrence of South Dakota: The Myth of 'The Great White Hunter' in Kevin Costner's *Dances With Wolves*," *Spirit of Crazy Horse* (May/June 1991).

"And They Did It Like Dogs in the Dirt: A Review of *Black Robe*," *Z Magazine* (October 1992).

Journalism and Popular Essays:

"Investments in South Africa and the 'Big Lie,'" *Chronicle of Higher Education* (May 5, 1980).

"A Case Specific of the Historical Stereotyping of Native Americans in Print Advertising," *Minority Notes*, vol. 1, nos. 3-4 (1981).

"The Black Hills Are Not for Sale: Yellow Thunder *Tiospaye*, A Testament to Lakota Sovereignty," *Indian Times*, vol. 1, no. 4 (1981).

"Yellow Thunder Camp: Building a New Community," in *Yellow Thunder Camp: The Fourth Season* (summer 1982).

"An Anti-Colonialist Perspective on Native American Substance Abuse" (coauthored with Dora-Lee Larson), *Talking Leaf*, vol. 48, no. 8 (1983).

"Israeli Aggression in the Middle East" (coauthored with Russell Means), *Rebel* (February 1984).

"*Soldier of Fortune's* Robert K. Brown," *Covert Action Information Bulletin*, no. 22 (1984).

"The Navajo: No Home on the Range," *The Other Side*, vol. 21, no. 1 (1985).

"Genocide: Beyond the Holocaust," *Colorado Daily* (April 18-20, 1985).

"The Covert War Against American Indians," *CovertAction/Information Bulletin*, no. 24 (1985).

"The Strange Case of 'Wild Bill' Janklow," *Covert Action Information Bulletin*, no. 24 (1985).

"The FBI on Pine Ridge, 1973-76," *Covert Action Information Bulletin*, no. 24 (1985).

"Boulder Sends More to Central America than a Bunch of Peaceniks," *Colorado Daily* (August 11, 1985).

"On Screen: Super-Patriots Deluge Market With Off-Beat POW Flicks," *Audience* (August 22-28, 1985).

"The Commercialization of American Indian Spirituality," *Camp Crier* (October 1985).

"Letter from Big Mountain," *Dollars and Sense* (December 1985).

"Debacle in Santa Fe: The IX Inter-American Indian Congress," *Camp Crier* (December 1985).

"Indians Win and Lose in South Dakota Land Cases," *Camp Crier* (January 1986).

"An American Tragedy: The 'Navajo-Hopi' Land Dispute," *Colorado Daily* (February 19, 1986).

"Montana Court Asserts State Control Over Indian Water Rights," *Camp Crier* (March 1986).

"Eben Emael Revisited," *Nerve*, vol. 1, no. 1 (1987).

"The FBI Takes AIM: The FBI's Secret War Against the American Indian Movement" (coauthored with Jim Vander Wall), *The Other Side*, vol. 23, no. 5 (1987).

"Strange War on the Lakota: The Case for a Congressional Investigation into FBI Activity on Pine Ridge Reservation, 1972-76" (coauthored with Jim Vander Wall), *Rolling Stock*, no. 14 (1987).

"Due Process be Damned: The Case of the Portland Four," *Zeta* (January 1988).

"Leonard Peltier: The Struggle Continues," *Zeta* (April 1988).

"The Dilemma of American Indian Art," *Muse: Colorado's Journal of the Arts*, no. 53 (1988).

"Genocide," *Issues in Radical Therapy*, vol. 13, nos. 1-2 (1988).

"The Dawes Act," *Issues in Radical Therapy*, vol. 13, nos. 1-2 (1988).

"The Seamy Side of English Only," *Zeta* (July/August 1988).

"A Little Matter of Genocide: Native American Spirituality and New Age Hucksterism," *Bloomsbury Review*, vol. 8, no. 5 (1988).

"American Indian Studies: A Positive Alternative," *Bloomsbury Review*, vol. 8, no. 5 (1988).

"A Trail of Cherokee Tears," *The Guardian* (November 2, 1988).

"Thanksgiving: A Day of Mourning?" *The Guardian* (November 22, 1988).

"The Indian Way," *Issues in Radical Therapy*, vol. 13, nos. 3-4 (1988).

"Sand Creek: An Example of U.S. Genocide," *The Guardian* (December 7, 1988).

"Who Killed Anna Mae?" *Zeta* (December 1988).

"Unmasking the Custer Myth," *The Guardian* (December 21, 1988).

"COINTELPRO as a Family Business: The Strange Case of the FBI's Two Richard Helds," *Zeta* (March 1989).

"COINTELPRO Against the Black Panthers: The Case of Geronimo Pratt" (coauthored with Jim Vander Wall), *Covert Action Information Bulletin*, no. 31 (1989).

"Last Stand at Lubicon Lake," *Zeta* (September 1989).

"Semantic Masturbation on the Left," *Zeta* (November 1989).

"Equal Justice Before the Law?" *Colorado Daily* (April 6, 1990).

"The Third World at Home: Political Prisoners in the United States," *Z Magazine* (May 1990).

"Welcome to the Wonderful State of Red," *Z Magazine* (September 1990).

"A GOON's Tale," *Leonard Peltier Defense Newsletter* (March 1991).

"Hydrological Rape in Northern Canada," *Z Magazine* (April 1991).

"Death Squads in South Dakota: Confessions of a Government Terrorist," *Zeta* (May 1991).

"Leonard Peltier, Political Prisoner: A Case History of the Land Rip-Offs," *Red Road* (June 1991).

"Colonialism, Genocide and the Expropriation of Indigenous Spiritual Tradition in Contemporary Academia," *Border/Lines*, no. 23 (winter 1991-92).

"Nobody's Pet Poodle," *Z Magazine* (February 1992).

"A History of the Struggle at Wounded Knee," *Spirit of Crazy Horse* (February-March 1992).

"Indigenous Knowledge Not for Sale," *Twin Light Trail*, no. 3 (1992).

"Colonialism, Genocide and the Expropriation of Indigenous Spiritual Tradition," *First Nations Confederacy of Cultural Education Centers Newsletter* (spring 1995).

"The Meaning of Chiapas: A North American Indigenist View," *Dark Night field Notes*, nos. 3-4 (1995).

"The Judi Bari Bombing: How the FBI Targeted Earth First!" *Open Eye*, no. 3 (1995).

"Fascism, the FBI and Native Americans" (interview by David Barsamian), *Z Magazine* (December 1995).

INDEX

A

Abbey, Edward: 322, 333
Aberle, David: 123
Abernathy, David: 271
Aboriginies: *see* Indigenous peoples
Abourezk, Senator James: 141
Abenaki: *see* Indigenous peoples
Acoma Indians: *see* Indigenous peoples
Adams, Hank: 511
Adams, John: 39, 275
Adorno, Theodor: 273, 467
Afghanistan: 471
Afraid of Bear, Sam: 260
Africa: 181
    native nations in: 342, 515, 535
Agents of Repression: 256
Akwesasne Notes: 161, 163
Alabama: 198, 222
    massacre of Red Sticks at Tallapoosa River in: 222
Alabama Indians: *see* Indigenous peoples
Alaska: 217, 222
    Indian Health Service in, 448, 519, 537
Alaska Native Claims Settlement Act: 28, 55, 217, 342
Albania: 471
Albert, Michael: 463, 466, 471, 478
Albuquerque: *see* New Mexico
Alexie, Sherman: 374, 375
Alfred University: 1, 337
Algeria: 14, 471
Algonquin: *see* Indigenous peoples
All-African Peoples Revolutionary Party (A-APRP): 456
Allegheny Reservation: *see* American Indian reservations
Allende, President Salvatore: 234
Alliance Communications: 4
Alliance Entertainment: 426

Althusser, Louis: Althusserian structuralism: 466, 468
Amazon Basin: 184
American History Review: 12
American Indian Anti-Defamation Council: 439
American Indian Heritage Exhibition: 497
American Indian Movement (AIM): ii, 27, 29, AIM security: 267; survival schools of: 320, 348-9, 353, 439, 490-2; and Wounded Knee seige: 65, 76, 235, 239, 265-9, 348, 491; at Big Mountain: 128-30; Colorado AIM: 360-1, 364, 373-5, 397-9, 403, 439, 490-2; creation of International Treaty Council (IITC): 77; Jumping Bull Compound: 250, 253, 266; Longest Walk of: 131, 144; Northwest AIM Group: 250, 264, 266, 525, 541; Oglala Firefight of: 250-4, 259, 491; Resmurs investigation and: 25, 29, 268; Treaty Convention at Fort Yates: 265; Wounded Knee leadership trials of: 29, 51, 53; Yellow Thunder Camp of: 77-8
American Indian Religious Freedom Act (AIRFA): 78
American Indian Religious Studies: 315
American Indian reservations:
Allegheny Reservation: 60; Caughnawaga (Kahnawake) Mohawk Reserve (Canada): 63; Cattaraugus Reservation: 60; Cheyenne River Lakota Reservation: 73, 160; Cochiti Pueblo: 166; Fort Berthold Reservation: 160; Fort Totten: 240; Great Sioux Reservation: 69, 72, 73, 79, 150; Hard Rock Valley: 142; Hopi Reserva-